# Ekajati

AH BHYO
You wear a white cloud as raiment.
In your right hand is the red heart of the transgressor
    of samaya.
From your left hand you emanate in all directions
A hundred iron wolves as aides.
The single eye of dharmakaya manifests on your forehead.
Your single fang pierces the heart of Mara.
Your single breast nurtures supreme practitioners as
    your children.
You are naked but for a tiger skin round your waist.
When the practitioner is tormented by sloth
Be an arrow of awareness.
When the practitioner has lost the way
Be a torch of meditation.
When the practitioner is confused by doubt
Sound the great trumpet of confidence.
When the practitioner is attacked by enemies
Be the wrathful, wild protector.
Protect the teachings of Buddha.
Cause the domain of the three jewels to prosper.
Nurture the three sanghas as your children.

Those who profess the tantras to all,
Those who display arrogance as dharma,
Those who have perverted views:
By the miracles of the wrathful mamo,
Fiercely seize their hearts with venomous anguish;
Kill them and lead them to dharmadhatu.

*This was written by Chökyi Gyatso, the eleventh Trungpa.*
*Translated by the Nalanda Translation Committee.*

*Ekajati (Skt.: "One single lock of hair") is a fierce protector of the higher tantric teach-ings. She protects the tantric practitioner and destroys those who pervert the dharma. Above her head is Samantabhadra, the primordial buddha. On the facing page is an excerpt from a chant to the protector Ekajati composed by Chögyam Trungpa Rinpoche.*

# The Profound Treasury of the Ocean of Dharma

VOLUME ONE
*The Path of Individual Liberation*

VOLUME TWO
*The Bodhisattva Path of Wisdom and Compassion*

VOLUME THREE
*The Tantric Path of Indestructible Wakefulness*

Published in association with Vajradhatu Publications, a division of
Shambhala Media. www.shambhalamedia.org.

VOLUME THREE

THE PROFOUND TREASURY
OF THE OCEAN OF DHARMA

# The Tantric Path of Indestructible Wakefulness

## CHÖGYAM TRUNGPA

COMPILED AND EDITED BY

*Judith L. Lief*

SHAMBHALA • BOULDER • 2013

Shambhala Publications, Inc.
4720 Walnut Street
Boulder, Colorado 80301
www.shambhala.com

9  8  7  6  5  4  3

Printed in the United States of America

∞ This edition is printed on acid-free paper that meets the
American National Standards Institute z39.48 Standard.
♻ Shambhala makes every attempt to print on recycled paper.
For more information please visit www.shambhala.com.

Distributed in the United States by Penguin Random House LLC
and in Canada by Random House of Canada Ltd

Designed by Dede Cummings Designs

LIBRARY OF CONGRESS CATALOGING-IN-PUBLICATION DATA

Trungpa, Chögyam, 1939–1987.
The profound treasury of the ocean of dharma / Chögyam Trungpa;
compiled and edited by Judith L. Lief.—First Edition.
pages cm
Compilation of Chögyam Trungpa Rinpoche's
Vajradhatu Seminary teachings in three volumes.
Includes index.
ISBN 978-1-59030-708-3 (hardcover: alk. paper; set)—
ISBN 978-1-59030-802-8 (hardcover: alk. paper; vol. 1)—
ISBN 978-1-59030-803-5 (hardcover: alk. paper; vol. 2)—
ISBN 978-1-59030-804-2 (hardcover: alk. paper; vol. 3)
1. Buddhism—Doctrines. I. Lief, Judith L., editor of compilation. II. Title.
BQ4165.T75 2013
294.3'4—dc23
2012022795

# CONTENTS

CONTENTS

# CONTENTS

CONTENTS

# EDITOR'S INTRODUCTION

THE THIRD volume of *The Profound Treasury of the Ocean of Dharma* is a compilation of teachings on the view and practice of vajrayana. These teachings were primarily drawn from talks presented by the Vidyadhara Chögyam Trungpa Rinpoche at his Vajradhatu Seminary programs from 1973 to 1986.* However, in compiling these volumes, I realized that Trungpa Rinpoche assumed that students had a certain amount of background knowledge, which he did not repeat in the seminary teachings themselves, so I occasionally included material from additional sources to compensate for what might be missing

In terms of the three progressive stages (Skt.: *yanas*) of the Tibetan Buddhist path—hinayana, mahayana, and vajrayana—the vajrayana teachings, or tantra, are considered to be supreme. In his lifetime, the Vidyadhara closely guarded these advanced teachings, sharing them only with students who already had a good foundation, both in terms of their intellectual understanding of Buddhist teachings and their experience of meditation practice. At the same time, the Vidyadhara made clear to his publisher Samuel Bercholz and to his editors that in the future he wanted his seminary teachings on the three stages of the path compiled into three volumes that would be publicly available as a resource for scholars and practitioners. And now, twenty-five years after his death, this project has

---

* Chögyam Trungpa was referred to by many different titles. He could simply be called "Rinpoche" (Tib.: precious one). In 1974, the Sixteenth Gyalwa Karmapa gave him the title Dorje Dzinpa (Tib.: vajra holder). Trungpa Rinpoche was also referred to as the Vajracharya, or "vajra master." In later years, this was changed to the Vidyadhara (Skt.: knowledge holder) under the advice of the Venerable Tenga Rinpoche.

finally come to completion. So it is with great excitement and some trepidation that we now offer these teachings to the broader world.

The decision to publish the vajrayana seminary teachings was a weighty one, even though we knew that was the Vidyadhara's intention. Previously, transcripts of the vajrayana seminary talks were restricted to senior students who had heard them directly, and even the transcripts of the hinayana and mahayana portions of the seminary were not generally available to anyone who had not attended at least one seminary program. In order to be accepted to attend a seminary, students were required to have completed several years of preparation, comprised of both intellectual study of the Buddhist tradition and meditation practice. And during the seminary, before being introduced to the vajrayana teachings, students needed to progress through the hinayana and mahayana practice periods and the study sessions, which took one month each. Only after students were soaked in these two yanas could they begin to study the vajrayana path. Finally, having completed their seminary training, students could then request to be formally accepted into the vajrayana by the Vidyadhara, and empowered to begin the vajrayana preliminary practices, or *ngöndro*.

## VAJRADHATU SEMINARIES

Vajradhatu Seminary training exemplified Trungpa Rinpoche's emphasis on the value of understanding the fundamentals of the Buddhist tradition before embarking on more advanced teachings. The Vidyadhara put a lot of thought into how to structure the seminary experience, and particularly into how to shape the seminaries into a proper environment for transmitting the vajrayana. In a conversation with the translator Larry Mermelstein, the Vidyadhara remarked, "The seminary is my most important achievement." Larry asked if this was because of the way the seminary combined *shedra* and *drubdra,* or study and practice, along with the work of daily life, and the Vidyadhara replied, "Exactly. In Tibet, we never put them all together. They were always separate." Larry asked, "So what made you think of putting them together?" The Vidyadhara replied, "My teacher, Khenpo Gangshar Wangpo, put them together for me. I lived with my khenpo and he put them all together."

The seminary schedule, which alternated weeks of intensive meditation practice with weeks of intellectual study, and included the intimate

*1975 Seminary: Trungpa Rinpoche wearing a cowboy hat and armed with a pea shooter.*

connection Trungpa Rinpoche had with each of his students, created a powerful and protective container for his presentation of the vajrayana teachings. Throughout his seminaries, scholarly learning was joined with direct meditative experience in a creative fusion of the intellect and intuitive understanding. In the seminary environment, lectures by the Vidyadhara, group discussions, practice periods, kitchen and cleaning duties, and informal encounters all had a quality of direct dharma transmission.

Trungpa Rinpoche taught thirteen seminaries in all, and each year he added new teachings, building on both his previous seminary presentations and on the teachings that students were expected to study prior to attending the three-month program. While at seminary, students went on to study not only what was being presented in the seminary they were attending, but the teachings of all the previous seminaries as well. In describing this process, the Vidyadhara said that he intended to extend the teachings of the previous seminaries year by year so that eventually the whole collection would become a powerful bank of dharma. Trungpa Rinpoche encouraged his students to study the previous years' transcripts, making the point that "If you can study them clearly and properly, we will not even have to mention those basic principles again." (*1975 Seminary Transcripts, Talk 22*)*

Although different topics were introduced at each seminary, the basic structure of all the seminaries remained the same: a progression through the three yanas. In describing this approach, Trungpa Rinpoche said, "Each year that we have a new seminary, we can build from a different perspective of the three-yana principle. This has certainly inspired me, and I think that the students will also find it very stimulating." (*1974 Seminary Transcripts, Talk 22*) The Vidyadhara encouraged his students to work with the three yanas as a unified whole, a single coherent path. He never seemed to tire of reminding his students in one way or another not to forget the hinayana, not to bypass the mahayana, and not to pick and choose tidbits of dharma, but rather to always approach the three yanas as a whole.

---

* When Trungpa Rinpoche made this statement, there had only been two previous seminaries, in 1973 and 1974. As time went on, the number of previous seminary transcripts continued to grow at a rate of two volumes per year, which meant that in later seminaries the review of previous seminary teachings became more and more daunting.

## THE 1973 SEMINARY

At the first Vajradhatu Seminary, held in 1973 at Jackson Hole, Wyoming, Trungpa Rinpoche made the decision to open his vajrayana teachings to his Western students. He considered this a step of great significance that he was not undertaking lightly, and he expressed great delight in finally being able to present these teachings. In speaking of this decision, the Vidyadhara said, "I've been waiting to discuss this topic for a long time, in fact practically since I've been in this country. I am tickled by the idea of presenting a complete understanding, as far as my communication style and your communicational openness go, and there's no guarantee of course. In any case, it is a very mirage-like situation, and our dreams are extraordinarily powerful, which might dilute somewhat the essence of the vajra teaching." *(1973 Seminary Transcripts, Talk 20)*

During the 1973 seminary, the Vidyadhara stressed the power of the vajrayana, the danger of misinterpreting its teachings, and the importance of secrecy. When this first group of vajrayana students had completed their seminary training and were about to leave, he told them, "I hope you will be able to relate what you have studied and learned to others, but there is an exception: I would like to keep the tantric things that we discussed private. . . . As you know, there are no terribly embarrassing things contained in it. It is just the same old Buddhist stuff in many ways. But somehow the whole basic thing creates a lot of power, and it contains an enormous amount of magic and energy. We should be very careful." *(1973 Seminary Transcripts, Talk 27)*

### SECRET TEACHINGS

In the vajrayana, there is a tradition of secrecy. In the West, we tend to think of secrecy as something negative, indicating that someone has something to hide. We may view secrecy as a technique of obfuscation, or as a way of separating an elite in-group that possesses special knowledge. But in the context of vajrayana, secrecy has none of those implications.

### *Establishing a Proper Foundation*

According to Trungpa Rinpoche, in the vajrayana the need for secrecy is not based on having anything to hide. Instead, the point is that without first establishing a proper foundation and without proper guidance, a person encountering the vajrayana teachings could find them misleading and even harmful.

The vajrayana teachings, like all Buddhist teachings, are an expression of wisdom and compassion. However, these powerful teachings could be corrupted into further fuel for ego and its thirst for power. To prevent such possibilities, the Vidyadhara said that a degree of caution and secrecy made sense.

## Self-Secrecy

As an extension of this notion of secrecy, Trungpa Rinpoche also introduced the concept of self-secrecy, which is the idea that the vajrayana has inherent mechanisms that protect it from being corrupted and that avoid misleading students who are not ready for it. The idea of self-secrecy is that although many traditional tantric texts and many books on various aspects of the vajrayana are freely available, one needs direct instruction from an accomplished master in order to really understand them. The tantric guru holds the key to unlock the treasury of the vajrayana teachings.

## Protecting the Purity of the Transmission

The Vidyadhara also talked about the role of secrecy in protecting the purity of a student's transmission experience. He said that secrecy is valuable because it allows vajrayana transmission to work its power without being impeded by a student's concepts and preconceptions. That is, a student's reliance on conceptual understanding could weaken the ability of the transmission to shock that student into a more immediate and profound realization. Trungpa Rinpoche pointed out, "Sometimes the notion of secrecy is very helpful. If things have been kept secret from people, then when they do begin to receive the teachings, luckily they have not had any kind of warning. They do not have any preconceptions because they have not come across any literature or experiences of that nature. Then transmission can be direct and sudden, without preconceptions. It is like sneezing: the only warning you get is a few seconds before you sneeze. That is an important point. If people have heard too much already, they won't be shocked. That would be too bad." *(1983 Seminary Transcripts, Talk 13)*

## THE DECISION TO OPEN
## THE TEACHINGS TO WESTERNERS

Given the Vidyadhara's respect for the tradition of secrecy, opening the vajrayana oral teachings to Western students was a powerful statement for him. From our current vantage point, it may seem odd that Trungpa Rinpoche was so adamant about the special quality of these teachings. After all, even in the early seventies, more and more books on Tibetan Buddhism were being translated and published, a number of teachers were traveling widely in order to perform blessings and ceremonies, and the highest vajrayana teachings were becoming freely available to the public. But Trungpa Rinpoche was deeply concerned about the power of spiritual materialism. He was unhappy to see the vajrayana teachings being peddled as though they were milk in a market place. The Vidyadhara had no interest in feeding the Western fascination with the exotic East, Tibetan cultural trappings, or religiosity. So he took a conservative approach, and he placed high demands on his students. He was determined to present the dharma in a proper setting, with careful consideration and preparation every step of the way.

Trungpa Rinpoche was also well aware of the many traditional Tibetan Buddhist guidelines on when to present the vajrayana teachings and to whom they can be taught, which may be why he took such precautions. Referring to the idea of *samaya,* or the vow to protect the integrity of the teachings, he said, "According to one of the samaya vows, teaching vajrayana to those who are not ready for it is a violation; and according to another samaya, holding back from teaching vajrayana to those who *are* ready for it is also a violation. At this point I have decided to go along with the second of those vows. I have received so much encouragement from our lineage and from my teacher, and I have followed my personal intuition about the readiness of my students." *(1981 Seminary Transcripts, Talk 21)*

Once Trungpa Rinpoche made the decision to go ahead with the vajrayana teachings, he did not hold back. He allowed his students to determine if they could handle what he was presenting, saying, "The only problem in presenting the vajrayana teachings could be that when I spell out the whole thing—can you hear it? It is up to you. As far as I am concerned, there is no holding back. . . . So as far as my presentation is concerned, there is no censorship. The only censorship that could take place is in your own mind. It is like Montezuma's revenge: if you can't handle Mexican food, you get diarrhea. *(1981 Seminary Transcripts, Talk 21)*

## VAJRAYANA TRANSMISSION
## AND PRE-TRANSMISSION TEACHINGS

For students of the Vidyadhara, in order to become a tantric student, one first had to complete a Vajradhatu seminary, make a commitment to the vajrayana path, and request to be accepted as a student. If accepted, the Vidyadhara would then give the student vajrayana transmission, and authorize them to begin the ngöndro. Finally, after receiving vajrayana transmission and completing the ngöndro, a practice that could take several years, a student could request to take part in an empowerment ceremony, or *abhisheka,* and be formally entered into the vajra mandala, the circle of vajrayana practitioners.

The Vidyadhara placed great emphasis on the study of the collected seminary teachings not only as the foundation for beginning the ngöndro, but as a support for deepening one's understanding as one progressed along the path. Since the seminary teachings were given prior to receiving transmission and beginning vajrayana preliminary practices, they could be considered to be pre-transmission teachings. They are just a beginning. The Vidyadhara compared listening to these vajrayana teachings to hearing about the existence of a fish: "It is as if you had just heard that such a thing as a fish existed. You still have to talk to the fisherman, and the fisherman has to catch the fish. And not only that, but then you have to cook the fish and eat it. So far, you have just heard that such a thing as a fish exists." *(1983 Seminary Transcripts, Talk 14)* Trungpa Rinpoche made it clear that in his seminary teaching he was simply introducing the theory of tantra; these teachings were a vanguard to actually launching into the vajrayana. In his teachings altogether, Trungpa Rinpoche stressed that before making a commitment to pursue spiritual training in any tradition, it was important to first study the teachings of that tradition in order to have some idea what such a commitment actually involved.

The first few seminaries laid the groundwork for vajrayana transmission, but they did not actually empower students to enter into vajrayana practice and training. But several months after the end of the first Vajradhatu Seminary in 1973, the Vidyadhara empowered his first batch of students so they could begin the vajrayana preliminary practices. In later seminaries, Trungpa Rinpoche offered vajrayana transmission at the very end of each seminary. In order to qualify, students were expected to have completed their seminary training and to have taken both the hinayana refuge vow and the mahayana bodhisattva vow. After completing the vajrayana portion of a seminary, some students chose not to request transmission, or felt they were not yet ready for such a step. Other students were not accepted for transmission, or were encouraged to focus more on the hinayana or mahayana, or were told to wait.

## THE IMPORTANCE OF HINAYANA
## AND SHAMATHA-VIPASHYANA PRACTICE

The Vidyadhara repeatedly stressed the critical importance of the hinayana path and the ongoing cultivation of mindfulness and awareness as the essential underpinning of vajrayana practice and understanding. Throughout his teachings, he kept coming back to the need for grounding in *shamatha* (mindfulness) and *vipashyana* (awareness). By alternating weeks of intensive shamatha-vipashyana with weeks of study, Trungpa Rinpoche's seminary training gave his students a feel for the dynamic way in which meditation could inform study, as well as how study could enrich meditation. The practice atmosphere created by the days of group meditation created the kind of container that made it possible for students to hear the dharma in a deeper, more personal and heartfelt way. The power of such an atmosphere made it possible for a meeting of minds to occur between the teacher and his students.

## THE NEED FOR MAHAYANA BENEVOLENCE
## AND THE PRACTICE OF TONGLEN

Trungpa Rinpoche also emphasized that in order to enter the vajrayana properly, it was essential to understand the mahayana teachings of openness, benevolence, and compassion, and to engage in mind-training practices such as *tonglen,* or sending and taking. He stressed the importance of progressing from an attitude of self-help to the mahayana attitude of helping others, or at least opening to others, as essential preparation for the vajrayana. According to the Vidyadhara, by combining hinayana and mahayana training, students could create something for others and for themselves at the same time. He remarked that by training in this way, "You can build a solid foundation for tantra. It is like building a house out of rock: you get a lot of exercise and good health, but the house is built for somebody else rather than for you. Of course, you might occasionally walk into the house once it is built, but it is not yours. It is for all the people and is as limitless as the sky. We are going in that direction." *(1974 Seminary Transcripts, Talk 27)*

## THE NEED FOR GUIDANCE

The dharmic path is laid out in the three volumes of *The Profound Treasury* in terms of a progression through the hinayana, mahayana, and vajrayana, but it is in fact one continuous journey. How one approaches this journey is unique for each individual. It is personal, it is intimate, and as the Vidyadhara said, "It is up to you, sweetheart!" Some people prefer the straightforwardness and simplicity of the hinayana path; some are attracted by the benevolence and wisdom of the mahayana; others are drawn to the profundity and power of the vajrayana. But at whatever level you aspire to practice the teachings, working with an experienced guide is invaluable.

Working with a guide is particularly important in the vajrayana. There are many books on Buddhist tantra, more than any one person could ever read, but at heart the vajrayana is an oral tradition that is passed on directly from teacher to student. It is through that kind of interpersonal connection that the subtlety of these teachings can be imparted. As a traditional chant says, "The guru opens the gate to the treasury of oral instructions." It is fortunate that so many great teachings are available, and it is fine to leap into the dharma and begin to practice, but if you are inspired and want to go further, it is essential to work with an experienced guide, someone who can manifest what these teachings are all about and show you how to proceed.

*Trungpa Rinpoche teaching from a Tibetan throne, holding a Japanese fan, and wearing a Western suit.*

## THE STRUCTURE OF VOLUME THREE

Below is a brief overview of the structure of this volume, starting with the transition from the mahayana into the vajrayana, continuing with a discussion of different aspects of the vajrayana view, and culminating in a description of the vajrayana path from beginning to end.

### Approaching the Vajrayana

This volume begins with a discussion of the transition from the mahayana to the vajrayana path, and the implications of entering into the tantric path. In this section and throughout the three volumes, over and over, Trungpa Rinpoche stresses the necessity of the hinayana and the mahayana, and the importance of seeing the three yanas as one continuous journey. In particular, he stresses the power of shamatha and vipashyana. Trungpa Rinpoche then looks at different aspects of the vajrayana, both through traditional Tibetan Buddhist lenses and through the lens of Shambhala vision and the symbol of the Great Eastern Sun.* He introduces the concepts of basic goodness and the creation of enlightened society, and he also presents definitions of the tantric path and basic characteristics of the vajrayana approach.

## The Teacher-Student Relationship

Here the notion of the tantric teacher or vajra master is introduced. Trungpa Rinpoche elucidates the role of the vajra master, and the central role that the guru-student relationship plays on the vajrayana path. He also introduces the concept of sacred outlook, and the idea of the three roots: guru, *yidam,* and protector. Throughout this section, Trungpa Rinpoche makes it clear that in order to progress on the vajrayana path, one needs to work with an experienced teacher and cultivate devotion and trust. He shows how vajrayana practice transforms one's conventional view of the world into sacred outlook, which is characterized by expansiveness and freedom, gentleness and warmth, and has no struggle or aggression. He then traces the development of sacred outlook back to the mahayana and the practice of lojong, to the absence of grasping and fixation, and to the power of devotion. He also discusses the development of vajra body, vajra speech, and vajra mind.

## The Tülku Principle and the Trungpa Tülkus

In this section, Trungpa Rinpoche continues the discussion of the vajra master by introducing the tülku principle in general, and the history of his own lineage of Trungpa tulküs in particular.

---

* Trungpa Rinpoche developed a stream of teachings called Shambhala teachings, which provide a more secular approach to awakening wisdom and compassion, with an emphasis on spiritual warriorship and the creation of enlightened society. The imagery and terminology of the Shambhala path is distinctive and complementary to that of vajrayana Buddhism.

## Essential Teachings

Before proceeding to a discussion of the tantric yanas, the Vidyadhara introduces further key concepts of the vajrayana. He discusses in some detail the intricacies of space and insight, or *ying* and *rikpa,* and of the three *kayas,* or three bodies of enlightenment, in relationship to the eight kinds of consciousness. He then switches his focus to the energies and emotions that arise in space, and how to cut through these on the spot and rest in luminous emptiness.

## Complete Commitment

The level of commitment expected for both vajrayana practitioners and teachers is spelled out in this section quite strongly. There is a detailed discussion of the samaya vow as both a protective principle and as a discipline to follow. Trungpa Rinpoche emphasizes the power of the samaya vow and the inseparability of student, guru, and yidam, and warns of the dangers and consequences of corrupting the tantric teachings.

## The Mandala Principle

The mandala principle plays a key role in vajrayana practice and iconography. Here Trungpa Rinpoche elucidates the mandala principle, as well as the teachings of outer, inner, and secret mandalas. He also presents an overview of the mandala of the five buddha-families, which plays a central role in tantric iconography and in the tantric understanding of reality altogether.

## Preliminary Practices

Before formally embarking on the vajrayana path, a student must first complete a series of preliminary practices, which are called ngöndro. In this section, Trungpa Rinpoche explains the four general and four special preliminaries as ways of freeing oneself from conceptuality and sinking roots in nonconceptual wisdom. He discusses the practice of devotion or guru yoga as a path of blessings, perceptual breakthrough, and nonthought.

## Empowerment

Once a student has made a relationship with a vajra master, cultivated devotion, and prepared the ground by practicing the vajrayana preliminaries, that student may request to be accepted into the vajra world, or vajra mandala. In this section, Trungpa Rinpoche discusses the nature of vajrayana transmission, and explains the symbolism and components of a traditional empowerment ceremony or abhisheka. He talks about the abhisheka process in terms of establishing a powerful samaya bond between the vajra master and the student. He points out that the student's commitment to the vajra master and to the tantric teachings is mirrored by the vajra master's relentless and compassionate commitment to their students.

## Vajrayana Practice

Tantric practice takes many forms, but it can be simplified into two essential components: visualization practice and formless practice, also called the creation and completion stages. Here Trungpa Rinpoche discusses vajrayana liturgies, or *sadhanas,* and the nature of both visualization and formless practice. Since vajrayana visualizations involve deities of all kinds, Trungpa Rinpoche makes a point of distinguishing the tantric view of deities from the theistic approach, and stresses the importance of a nontheistic view.

## The Tantric Journey: Lower Tantra

According to the Nyingma tradition, the Tibetan Buddhist path can be looked at in terms of nine yanas or vehicles. Of these nine yanas, two are within the hinayana (*shravakayana* and *pratyekabuddhayana*); one is within the mahayana (mahayana or *bodhisattvayana*); and six are within the vajrayana (*kriyayogayana, upayogayana, yogayana, mahayogayana, anuyogayana,* and *atiyogayana*). In this section, the Vidyadhara discusses the first three tantric yanas (kriyayoga, upayoga, and yogayana), which are referred to as lower tantra.

## The Tantric Journey: Mahamudra

Weaving together the approaches of the Nyingma and Kagyü traditions, Trungpa Rinpoche presents the *mahamudra* or *anuttarayoga* teachings of the Kagyü tradition within the context of his presentation of the six tantric yanas. He discusses anuttarayoga both as the highest attainment of the mahamudra tradition and as a kind of bridge between the three lower and three higher tantric yanas. In this section, the Vidyadhara presents the view and practice of mahamudra, and he provides a commentary on "The Song of Lodrö Thaye," a pithy and profound realization song by Jamgön Kongtrül the Great that encapsulates the essence of ground mahamudra, path mahamudra, and fruition mahamudra.

## The Tantric Journey: Higher Tantra

The three higher tantric yanas (mahayogayana, anuyogayana, and atiyoga-yana) are referred to in Tibetan as *dzokchen*. Trungpa Rinpoche refers to these teachings as *maha ati,* a term that can refer to the ninth yana (atiyoga) or to higher tantra as a whole. Maha ati is presented as the culmination of the entire Buddhist path, and the Vidyadhara points out that although the maha ati teachings may seem complex, overpowering, or unreachable, they are in fact profoundly simple, absolutely pure, and completely immediate.

There is an oral quality and directness to the teachings in this volume. Trungpa Rinpoche not only describes the worldview and practices that make the tantric path so remarkable, but does so in a way that makes them accessible and relevant to modern students.

### HISTORY AND ASPIRATIONS

### History

It is exciting finally to be completing the work of preparing these three volumes. Those who are familiar with the Vajradhatu Seminary transcripts will recognize that these volumes are a rearrangement of a series of oral teachings presented to unique groups of people over a series of years. Each seminary had a unique flavor and tone, reflecting the changing cultural times and makeup of the students, and each talk the Vidyadhara gave was followed by a lively and often extensive question and answer period. Furthermore, the topics covered in Trungpa Rinpoche's main talks were in a kind of dialogue with the array of classes being taught in a particular seminary by his senior students. The original transcripts captured much of the spirit of the individual seminaries and serve as a dynamic and evocative record of those historic events.

I feel so fortunate to have been able to attend the 1973 Vajradhatu Seminary in Jackson Hole, Wyoming, as well as portions of several other seminaries. It was a privilege to have worked with the Vidyadhara at the 1978, 1979, and 1980 seminaries. These experiences were personally transformative and I shall never forget them. My aspiration is that *The Profound Treasury of the Ocean of Dharma* conveys some of that same excitement, tenderness, and power.

In compiling these teachings, my goal was to gather this material in a way that was true to the original content, as well as to make it readable and accessible to a broader audience. The idea was to convert the rich mixture found in the original transcripts from a chronological and historical record into a more topical approach. In editing these teachings, I aspired to transform the material into one coherent topical narrative without losing the freshness of the spoken word and the quality of direct oral instruction. I did my best to do so and I ask for your forgiveness for any errors or distortions.

In our initial attempt to categorize these teachings in the 1970s, Sarah Coleman and I literally took scissors and cut up the transcripts into piles of cuttings, which we put in different boxes. Later, I arrayed my office walls with charts of over two hundred and fifty seminary talks, color-coded to keep track of the main topics and of where particular topics were covered from year to year. Putting all of these puzzle pieces together was quite a struggle at times. Particularly in the vajrayana volume, the interconnectedness of the various topics was so exquisitely complete that it was difficult to begin with any one topic without at the same time discussing all the rest.

Although in a compilation such as this, it has not been possible to include everything found in the original transcripts, I have tried to be as inclusive as possible. Topics that arose in dialogue have been incorporated into the main body of the text.

In this volume, at the risk of being somewhat repetitive, I chose to include many of the recurring admonitions Trungpa Rinpoche gave again and again, in a variety of ways, about the ongoing importance of meditation practice. He never tired and in fact was relentless about driving home the importance of both mindfulness and awareness, or shamatha and vipashyana. He made it clear that the seeming complexities of the vajrayana rested on that simple yet profound foundation.

## NOTES ON FOREIGN TERMS AND DEFINITIONS

Tibetan, Sanskrit, and other foreign words and phrases are italicized on first appearance in these volumes. Tibetan terms are spelled phonetically in the body of the text. The glossary contains definitions of all terms, as well as transliterations of Tibetan terms. A special thank you to the Nalanda Translation Committee and to Ellen Kearney for preparing and editing the extensive glossary. Please see the credits page for a list of further acknowledgments.

## *Aspiration*

It is my hope that *The Profound Treasury of the Ocean of Dharma* will be a resource and inspiration for both practitioners and scholars, for both teachers and students, and that the Vidyadhara's seminary teachings continue to benefit many beings now and in the future. As a humble, undisciplined student, I am grateful to have had a small role in offering these teachings to the broader world.

## DEDICATION

*May the sharp knife of the vajra teachings*
*Cut though conventionality and cowardice.*
*And may this world of apparent confusion*
*Be seen as it is: the sacred playground of*
*luminosity and emptiness.*

# PRONUNCIATION OF
# SANSKRIT AND TIBETAN

## SANSKRIT

Sanskrit words may seem intimidating at first sight because they are so long. However, once they are broken into syllables, they are easy to pronounce. Sanskrit follows very regular rules and contains no "silent letters" such as those in English.

### Vowels

In general, vowels are pronounced as in Italian or Spanish. Sanskrit makes a distinction between long and short vowels in the case of *a, i,* and *u*. However, in this text they are not represented differently. Therefore, it is acceptable always to pronounce them as if they were long:

*a* as in c*a*r.
*i* as in f*ee*t.
*u* as in l*oo*t.

The following vowels are always considered long in Sanskrit:

*e* as in d*ay*
*ai* as in p*ie*
*o* as in g*o*
*au* as in h*ow*

## Consonants

Most consonants are pronounced as in English. The aspirated consonants (*kh, gh, ch, jh, th, dh, th, dh, ph, bh*) are pronounced as the consonant plus a noticeable aspiration of breath. In particular, note that the consonants *th* and *ph* are not pronounced as in the words *th*ing and *ph*oto, but as in po*th*ole and she*ph*erd. The letter *g* is always pronounced hard as in *g*o, never as in gem. The letter *h* is pronounced as a breathing sound at the end of a word.

## Accent

In classical Sanskrit, each syllable received approximately the same emphasis; vowels were lengthened rather than stressed. Although today we tend to stress syllables, it should not be so emphatic as in English. Accent is placed on the next-to-last syllable when this contains a long vowel or ends with more than one consonant (not including *h*). Otherwise, it is placed on the last previous syllable that contains a long vowel or ends in more than one consonant. If none exists, the stress is placed on the first syllable.

### TIBETAN

In this text, Tibetan words have been spelled to reflect pronunciation as accurately as possible. As in Sanskrit, the consonants *th* and *ph* are not pronounced as in the words *th*ing and *ph*oto, but as in po*th*ole and she*ph*-herd. The letters *ü* and *ö* are pronounced approximately as in the German words *über* and *möglich*, or as in the French words *connu* and *oeuvre*.

Note that the letter *e* is always pronounced at the end of a word. In some cases, words ending in *e* have been spelled with a hyphen in order to prevent mispronunciation: shi-ne, Ri-me.

*Part One*

# APPROACHING THE VAJRAYANA

# Introduction

*In the vajrayana, we learn how to respect our world. We realize that this particular world we live in is not an evil world, but a sacred world. It is filled with sacredness altogether. We learn to develop "sacred outlook."*

## PRESENTING THE VAJRAYANA

In this volume, we are just introducing the theory of vajrayana. In the vajrayana, or tantra, theoretical or intellectual understanding should act as a vanguard before you do anything. If you are thinking of launching into such elaborate and powerful teachings, it is necessary to know where you are going and what you are going to do as far as the practice is concerned. If you want to receive good hospitality when you are visiting friends, you send a letter to your friends before you arrive so your hosts can have a chance to say yes or no. You give them some kind of warning. It is necessary to approach the vajrayana in the same way.

It is important that you know what you are getting and what you are getting into. You have the right to know what you are doing, or some part of it, at least. If somebody is going to take you to the North Pole, you should have some idea of what the North Pole is all about. Maybe you will not know in great detail, but at least you will know that it is cold, it is in the north, food is difficult to get, you need special clothes, and so on. Likewise, by entering the vajrayana with good directions, nobody will be tricked into being enlightened, but there will be personal motivation.

At this point, you may not yet be practicing vajrayana, but you are learning something about it and about its preciousness. But first, a word of warning: in this discussion of the vajrayana, please do not expect great words of wisdom to come from me. You might be disappointed when I say very ordinary things about it. But I am telling you something personal, something I have experienced myself. Whether it is up to your expectations or not is up to you. I am just retelling what I myself have experienced.

You might feel that the approach of vajrayana is a complete hype or a complete exaggeration, or else you might feel that it is the real thing. Because of that sharp boundary, there is a need for fundamental trust. You could experience either trust or distrust when such truth is told. You might have doubts, but distrust and doubt are not the same: distrust means condemning the whole thing, whereas doubt is knowing that there are possibilities. Doubt is knowing that something is happening, but not knowing exactly what is going on. It provides you with the possibility of questioning yourself as to whether you have the faculties and capability to understand the vajrayana.

Before I began to present these teachings,* I first thought about what I was going to tell my students. Then I actually had a five-minute cry, because I missed my teacher, Jamgön Kongtrül of Shechen,† so much. Then I began to realize that there was no point in living in the past. I realized that trust and distrust are right here with me. I also thought of His Holiness the sixteenth Karmapa. I thought of what he would like to hear me say, how he would like to hear me expounding the dharma to the billions of people in the world, and some kind of natural confirmation began to take place. I realized I should not be too methodical or scholarly in expounding the vajrayana, but that I should speak from my heart. That was the message, or the conclusion, however you would like to take it.

So we are talking about something that is real, something that I have experienced personally. I feel that I do not have to con anyone or try to make a particularly excellent presentation, but I can simply launch into this particular vehicle, which is called the vajrayana. And I am still thankful to my teacher. So we might say this teaching is straight from the horse's mouth. I am sharing what I have experienced, what I have believed in, what I have felt, and how I have grown up.

---

* Chögyam Trungpa Rinpoche began his formal presentation of the vajrayana teachings at the first Vajradhatu Seminary, held in Jackson Hole, Wyoming, in 1973.

† Jamgön Kongtrül of Shechen (1901–1960) should not be confused with Jamgön Kongtrül Lodrö Thaye, aka Jamgön Kongtrül the Great (1813–1899).

*Photo taken by Trungpa Rinpoche of Jamgön Kongtrül of Shechen (1901–1960), his root guru.*

It is impossible to present vajrayana in its fullest sense. If there is enough general confusion, hinayana can be presented; and if there is enough confusion about benevolence, love, and religiosity, mahayana can be presented; but nobody would be crazy enough to present or to listen to vajrayana anywhere on this earth. Nonetheless, at this point, society has gone crazy, confusions dawn everywhere, and spiritual disciplines have gotten corrupted; and because of that, somehow or other, it is possible to present the vajrayana. In this land of North America, this beautiful land, it has become possible to present the vajrayana. That possibility has come about because of the ancestors of my tradition.

## ESTABLISHING A STRONG FOUNDATION

In order become decent vajrayana people, we need to establish a strong foundation through hinayana discipline and mahayana benevolence.

### Hinayana Discipline

The foundation of the path is hinayana discipline. You begin with *shamatha,* or mindfulness, and *vipashyana,* or awareness practice; and out of that, you learn how to synchronize your mind and body. The point of hinayana discipline is to make sure that you are not hurting yourself or others. It is based on recognizing your own confusion and suffering and wanting to end it. The hinayana discipline of shamatha actually tames individuals; it creates an environment of discipline.

### Mahayana Benevolence

With that foundation, you can take the bodhisattva vow and enter the mahayana. In the mahayana, you recognize others' suffering and want to end it. On the bodhisattva path you are somewhat shifting gears: you are shifting from self-help to helping others, or at least opening to others. Your attitude begins to change, and you develop an understanding of the mahayana principle of exchanging oneself with others. *Lojong,* or "mind-training," and the practice of *tonglen,* or "sending and taking," begin to become very powerful. With the inspiration of mind training, you realize that you can exchange yourself for others, that you can send out pleasure

6

*Rangjung Rikpe Dorje (1924–1982), the sixteenth Gyalwa Karmapa.*

and take in pain. That is definitely a very moving experience, and you can actually do it.

## Becoming Decent Vajrayana People

Because you have the capability of doing such a thing, that automatically allows you to develop twofold *bodhichitta,* or awakened heart, which consists of both absolute and relative bodhichitta. You can develop the gentle, compassionate, and soft mind of relative bodhichitta, and with ultimate bodhichitta, you can learn how to rest your mind in the basic goodness of *alaya,* the fundamental ground. You can develop *bodhi,* or wakefulness, which is the lessening of ego fixation and grasping.

The more we learn to let go of our own pleasure and take in our own pain, as well as the pain of the rest of the world, the more we are becoming very decent human beings. All of that is what enables us to become decent vajrayana people. In fact, we are becoming such decent human beings that we are candidates for enlightenment. We are becoming would-be buddhas.

By exchanging ourselves for others, we are taking an extraordinary step. We are developing the most extraordinary understanding ever comprehended in the history of humankind, the entire history of the universe. Learning how to let go of our pleasure and receive other people's pain is such a noble gesture. It allows us to become soft people, genuine people, extraordinarily good people. And with that merit, we begin to become worthy of receiving the vajrayana teachings.

If we are unable to hear the higher teachings of the vajrayana, the problem is that we have become deaf and dumb. We have no way of stepping out of our discursive thoughts, no way of stepping out of our ego fixation and grasping, because we are so caught up in that particular preoccupation. As far as we are concerned, we are the only center of the universe. That preoccupation with ourselves is problematic. We could go so far as to say that we have the potential of becoming egomaniacs.

But once we begin to understand, thoroughly and fully, the value of lojong training, we realize all that we have studied and learned, and we see how brave we have become. It is startling and precious and real. Because of that bravery, when conflicting emotions, or *kleshas,* such as passion, aggression, ignorance, and all kinds of discursive thoughts arise, we regard them as mere ripples on the pond. The pond itself is not disturbed; it remains clear and pure. We can realize this because we have understood our intrinsic *tathagatagarbha,* or buddha nature. It is because we have planted bodhichitta in ourselves that we are able to act in that way.

With the benevolence of the bodhisattva, we can give to others and build a strong foundation for ourselves at the same time. We can build a solid foundation for tantra. It is like building a house out of rocks: you get a lot of exercise and good health, but the house is built for somebody else rather than for you. Of course, you might occasionally walk into the house once it is built, but it is not yours. It is for all people, and it is as limitless as the sky. We are going in that direction.

In the vajrayana, we learn how to respect our world. We realize that this particular world we live in is not an evil world, but a sacred world. It is filled with sacredness altogether. We learn to develop sacred outlook. As we develop still further, we receive transmission. And from that, we develop a sense of how we could actually perceive phenomena without trying to perceive. We realize how we could appreciate phenomena instantly, without a struggle.

The vajrayana journey is short and concentrated, but this does not mean that we bypass the hinayana and mahayana. We never really abandon the previous *yanas,* but we constantly go back and forth. We keep trying to understand ourselves by realizing the gentleness of shamatha, the wakefulness of vipashyana, the reasonableness of lojong, and the greater warriorship of the bodhisattva path. Beyond that, we have to be willing to surrender ourselves into the state of intoxication of vajrayana. But we cannot make ourselves intoxicated; it will only happen spontaneously. So working with the basic approaches of the three yanas takes place spontaneously and always.

## THE GORILLA

Without taming yourself, you cannot train yourself. You are somewhat wild and untamable, so we have to catch you and put you in a zoo, like a wild gorilla. Traditionally, this particular zoo is known as monasticism. Actually we do not catch this gorilla, but it walks into our trap. And once it is caught, we have to do something with it, and the best thing to do is to educate and civilize that gorilla. Shamatha actually tames that gorilla; it creates an environment of discipline. Captivity in that particular discipline ensures that the gorilla no longer has crude animal instincts; it makes the gorilla more human.

From that ground, this gorilla can develop a more civilized nature. Its mentality has to change so that it relates much more with others. So we take this gorilla out for walks or hiking in the mountains. In that way, the gorilla develops more awareness of others and a quality of gentleness. We may take the gorilla into gorilla camps or show it baby gorillas in order to teach it how to relate with other gorillas. We also may show it bananas, oranges, and apples, so that the gorilla begins to learn how to eat with others without fighting. We are basically teaching this gorilla how to develop good table manners, so that it could become gentle, hospitable, and kind.

As we go on, we take the gorilla on a further journey, based on the training that it has already received. With this journey, its gorilla nature could begin to come out. So far we have been almost humanizing the gorilla. However, if the gorilla becomes highly humanized, we are in trouble: we are simply producing another anthropomorphic existence. So instead of that, we take the gorilla back into the jungle. We finally let it loose to reassume its own habitual patterns and style of relating with the phenomenal world. After its extensive training, the gorilla is finally liberated. The gorilla begins to teach the dharma and to manifest dharmic qualities to the world of gorillas and monkeys. That is the end of the story. However, after the gorilla has been freed into the world, it might slip back to untamed gorillahood. That is why the vajrayana is very tricky, and why it is special. The vajrayana tells you how to be yourself, but at the same time, it tells you how not to be yourself.

## THE THREE-YANA JOURNEY

By studying and practicing the three yanas, you are not graduating from hinayana to vajrayana, but you are doing the same thing all along. Studying vajrayana might be like becoming a professor and receiving a PhD; but professors still need to know how to spell words on the sixth-grade level. Therefore, it is necessary to reflect back on the hinayana. You need to keep going back to square one.

In the vajrayana, you want to liberate all and everything, yourself and others together. But in order to be ready for the vajrayana, you first need to become an excellent practitioner. You need to have an understanding of the journey, of the fruition as well as the ground. Vajrayana practice is like adding salt and pepper to your food—but first you have to cook the food and bring it to the table.

If we use the analogy of a mirror, in the hinayana stage you are working to free the mirror of dust, in the mahayana you are working to keep more dust from landing on the mirror, and at the vajrayana level you look directly into the mirror. You see that it is alpha pure, primordially pure, not pure as opposed to dirty. You see that it is basic goodness. Basic goodness does not mean that you are bad, and you finally find something good, but it is a natural quality of being. That naturalness means that you have nothing to dilute or to delete. You just remain as what you are. So the three yanas work together. If you are involved with the vajrayana, you should not only do vajrayana practice, but you should extend your vision to include hinayana and mahayana disciplines as well.

The three-yana journey is like plowing a field, sowing seeds, letting the crop grow, and finally harvesting it. In the harvest, the crop gets pulled out of the ground. Whether you are fruit or grain—or for that matter, flowers or berries—you have been too imbedded in the ground. If we let you stay that way, when winter comes you will fall apart. So you have to be cut out of the ground. In that way, everybody can eat the crops; they can make use of you.

This process is not regarded as sabotage or as killing. Nonetheless, we have to cut you from the earth and make you space-bound. It is like harvesting wonderful peaches and oranges and making marmalade, jam, and pies. So in the spring, you blossom, then you have a fantastic summer, and finally you have a good autumn. After that, it is time for you to gather your seeds and keep them carefully. In that way, future generations could continue the process by sowing the seeds we have collected from this particular farm. And if the altitude and the land that you are living on are too harsh, you have to save the seeds so you can sow them later. That is one analogy of the three-yana principle.

## A Golden Roof

In another analogy, the three yanas are said to be like building a house. The hinayana is the starting point or the foundation. In the mahayana, having discovered our enlightened potential, we can experience the reality of buddha nature, which is like erecting the walls of our house. Finally, having established the foundation and put up the walls, we are concerned with how we can finally make our house livable, with a ceiling inside and a roof on top. We need to have a roof, and with the vajrayana we are building that roof and ceiling out of gold.

So, having already built our house, the vajrayana stands out as a golden roof. The vajrayana is referred to as the "golden roof" because it is the final procedure through which we can become accomplished. It is not particularly regarded as the fruition, but it is, in a sense, the beginning of the fruition.

Fundamentally, we start with *vajra* mind, our inherent intelligence, and that keeps growing constantly in our environment through our training. So in the three-yana journey we begin by establishing a basic footing; from there, we evolve further, which is like putting the walls on the structure; and finally that development needs a finishing touch, which is like putting on the roof. With a roof, when the rain falls, our house does not get ruined, and when the sun shines too much, we are kept cool.

When this building is complete, it can connect with the natural environment around us. It is an ideal structure or state of existence to be involved in. Altogether, this state of existence is based on the idea of discriminating-awareness wisdom, not on a conceptualized notion of what should be happening. It is like knowing that at a certain stage in the change of seasons, we are going to open our windows and let the fresh air come in, and at another point, we have to exclude that possibility. But we need to get away from air-conditioning. If we want to take part in the reality of nature, we need to shut off the air-conditioning and just maintain ourselves.

## PROTECTING THE MIND

Maintaining our existence in this way is a form of protecting the mind. It is a way we can ensure that our mind does not create any unusual leakage. But we are not particularly holding ourselves back, in case there is a problem; we are simply maintaining ourselves intact, as it were. We are maintaining our existence in the teachings.

In talking about protecting the mind, we do not mean cognitive mind. The cognitive mind picks and chooses; it pushes away certain things that you do not like, and it keeps certain things that you do like. But if you cease to do that, then you really have your own mind back. So this is more like *having* mind rather than *protecting* mind, because mind is not regarded as an obstacle. You are not warding off any problems or dangers, but you are just maintaining your mind.

If your mind has been protected, when you speak you are not misunderstood. Mind consists of wise, confused, or neutral discursive thoughts. It includes anything that moves, flips, interprets, or goes into a deeper world. Mind appreciates and has tremendous understanding; it has passion. It also has incredible aggression; it can destroy you and others in great depth, boundlessly. Mind also has incredible generosity, which allows it to let go and appreciate nonduality and emptiness. That is the description of mind, and the vajrayana teachings protect all of those faculties and possibilities, so that you could use them all.

The idea is that your intelligence should be preserved within your own capability, rather than babbling around or just schmoozing. This has two qualities: one is not letting go too much, but holding yourself together as much as you can; the other is that as you try to maintain your existence as a perfect human being, you should also be kind to others. If you are able to maintain yourself as what you are, that also allows a lot of compassion and kindness in relating with others. So maintaining yourself at the same time as you are letting go is something that happens very naturally within you. It is not some kind of schizophrenia.

Studying the vajrayana is an important aspect of your development, but it does not mean that you have gone beyond the earlier yanas. However, although you are starting from the beginning with the hinayana, you should not view yourself as incapable of receiving the fullest understanding of the teachings. You could maintain your existence, and at the same time, maintain that particular endeavor. So we are talking about two things at once: how to be yourself and how not to be yourself. Learning how to be yourself and simultaneously how not to be yourself seems to be asking quite a lot. It may sound like a joke. It is letting go and not letting go at the same time, which is quite exciting.

## Shila, Samadhi, and Prajna

Throughout these three volumes, we have been working with three basic themes: discipline, meditation, and knowledge; or *shila, samadhi,* and *prajna.*

## Shila

In terms of discipline, I myself worked very hard for your sake. I got beaten, I got pinched, and I got punished many times. Usually, at least three punishments took place every day from the age of seven until the age of eleven. Every day there were big scenes about how to behave and how to sit. If I was slouching, I would get pinched; if I was mumbling, I would get pinched; if I was making conversation other than functional talking, I would get pinched. But I feel good about my education. I do not feel resentful about any of it. I would not mind reducing myself to a child and starting all over again. In fact, I would be quite delighted to start all over, and I appreciate the environment that my teacher and my tutors created. It was quite magnificent and remarkable.

We have been trying to shield off life for so long, for centuries, and we have been trying to be so polite. Pain is ugly and gross, and we keep trying to avoid it, which is somewhat of a problem. The interesting thing about real discipline is that you are actually willing to face facts properly, on the spot. You are even willing to face your own gross state of mind. You have to face facts rather than seeing the world through rose-tinted glasses. Discipline has to become the naked discipline of reality. With true discipline, there is no such thing as getting outside of the dharmic environment, even if you are scrubbing the floor in a factory. No matter what you may be doing, you are not particularly excluded.

## Samadhi

Samadhi is quite simple: it is meditation or sitting practice. Wherever you are, even if you are commuting on a train or traveling in an airplane—whatever you are doing—meditation practice is always the key point.

## Prajna

If you would like discipline and meditation to take place properly, you have to have intelligence. If you would like to have a house, you cannot just build a box, but you need to have bathrooms and electricity. And in order to have bathrooms and electricity, you need to have plumbing and electrical systems. And if you want to drill a hole, you cannot just drill in the middle of the room, because you might hurt your plumbing or electrical systems. You don't just dictate situations in that way.

Practicing dharma is not difficult; it comes naturally. It is free from hassle, and it brings a lot of health. As you practice more and more, you find that practice begins to grow inside your bones, in the marrow. Practice becomes natural. It is just like a horse that is used to being ridden: that horse begins to like the rider rather than feeling resentful. That is why we sometimes call practice "riding the mind." In your job situation, basic survival might be important to you; but at the same time, survival is based on a state of mind. When mind is healthier, then synchronizing body and mind becomes natural. Therefore, you have no problem and no obstacles. You have good health.

## THE UNBROKEN
## VAJRAYANA LINEAGE

The vajrayana tradition is very old. Some scholars or so-called Buddhologists claim that the vajrayana is not that old, that it was invented by later practitioners of Buddhism. Such scholars say that historically, when teachers could not present the true *buddhadharma*, or when the Buddhist teachings had become too flat, they invented vajrayana. But that is an erroneous statement. Other scholars say that vajrayana was presented to people who could not keep their monastic vows, but that is also an erroneous statement. Actually, the vajrayana is an unbroken lineage. It is a tradition that has been passed on from generation to generation, from the Buddha himself up to the present moment. It is an unbroken tradition, an unbroken lineage. And we will carry on this lineage and tradition for a long time.

The Buddha taught the mahayana later in his life, and he taught the vajrayana teachings toward the end of his life. When he introduced the mahayana, it is said that he asked some of his hinayana disciples to leave, so he could gather the students who were more perceptive and would be more receptive to the mahayana. It is said that he did a similar thing in introducing vajrayana to his mahayana students.

## THE LEGEND OF THE
## FIRST VAJRAYANA TEACHINGS

The Buddha connected with many of his vajrayana students when he was invited to teach by various Indian kings, including the first king of Shambhala, Dawa Sangpo, or Suchandra in Sanskrit.* Each of these kings said to him, "I cannot give up my kingdom to become a monk and abandon my world. Are there any instructions you could give me so that I could maintain my kingdom and, at the same time, practice your teachings?"

The Buddha said, "Very well." He then asked his disciples to leave, and he began to teach vajrayana. It is said that King Dawa Sangpo received a vajrayana teaching and practice known as the Kalachakra Tantra from the Buddha,† and similarly, that the Buddha taught the vajrayana to many other kings, and he did not ask any of them to give up their kingdoms. The Buddha was not purely trying to be diplomatic; he simply felt that such kings would benefit by the presentation of vajrayana. Because of that, the vajrayana began to flourish throughout the world.

More specifically, according to what has been recorded in the history of vajrayana, the Buddha's vajrayana teachings are said to be connected with the last one to three years of his life. At that time, the Buddha predicted that at the end of five hundred years, when his teachings would begin to wane in the world, the vajrayana would flourish.

Although Lord Buddha taught the vajrayana to kings, who could not practice the way of monks, Lord Buddha himself renounced his own title as crown prince and became a superking, beyond the ordinary understanding of a *chakravartin*.‡ In order to be the Buddha of this particular *kalpa*, or age, Gautama Buddha renounced the world of desire and entered into the dharma, which can be said to mean "freedom from desire."

---

* The kingdom of *Shambhala* is a mythical kingdom said to be hidden in Asia, and considered to be an embodiment of human goodness and enlightenment. Chögyam Trungpa Rinpoche used the Sanskrit term *Shambhala* for a stream of his teachings and practices based on the discovery and proclamation of basic goodness and the creation of enlightened society.

† The *Kalachakra Tantra*, or "wheel of time" tantric practice, is especially associated with the Shambhala kingdom and with King Suchandra, or (Tib.) Dawa Sangpo.

‡ The term *chakravartin* (Skt.: "wheel-turning ruler") refers to a world ruler.

# The Introduction
## of Vajrayana into Tibet

The original host of the Buddhist tradition in Tibet is said to have been King Songtsen Gampo (605–649 CE).* *Song* means "just," *tsen* means "powerful," and *gampo,* as in the name "Gampopa," means "profound"; so *songtsen gampo* means "just, powerful, profound." Later, King Trisong Detsen (755–797 CE) also played a prominent role. He hosted a famous debate between the Indian teacher Kamalashila and the Chinese Ch'an master Hashang Mahayana that contrasted the gradual path of the Tibetan approach with the sudden zap approach of Ch'an.[†]

Trisong Detsen also invited great Indian masters to teach in Tibet, such as Padmasambhava, the "Lotus Born," and Shantarakshita, the Indian Buddhist monk and a great saint. At the request of Padmasambhava, Shantarakshita decided to take the very simple action of ordaining seven boys into Buddhist monasticism. So the Tibetan vajrayana teachings started with Indian help, from the ordaining of a few little Tibetan boys.[‡] At that point, the dawning of the vajrayana, like the sun rising in the East, actually transpired. So in this story we are mingling three cultures together: Chinese, Indian, and Tibetan. The primordial quality of that presentation of Buddhism in Tibet was extremely powerful. Tantra was able to be presented on the basis of Tibetan pride, Tibetan-ness, and the good people there.

## Respect for the Lineage

What we are discussing here is not anything of an extraordinary nature, but just a kind of twist that exists in realizing the phenomenal world in its own light and its own perspective. By entering the vajrayana, we are actually getting ourselves into the enlightened side of this particular world.

---

* *King Songtsen Gampo* is credited with being the first ruler to bring Buddhism to Tibet. During his reign he built many temples and promoted translations of Buddhist literature into Tibetan.

† For Trungpa Rinpoche's description of this debate, conducted in highly colorful and symbolic form, see appendix 1, "Kamalashila and the Great Debate."

‡ The establishment of Tibet's first monastery, Samye, is said to have taken place in circa 787 CE.

We are hearing more about the truth of the teachings of Lord Buddha, who should be greatly admired and respected.

The same respect is due the lineage holders; they worked so hard for us, to the extent of sacrificing their comfort and their lives. We should realize that it took them immense time, space, and dedication to present the vajrayana teachings. As a spokesperson for the lineage, I would like you to realize how much pain, problems, discomfort, and outright obstacles have been a part of presenting vajrayana in this world. I would like you to think of all those people and all that they have done for your benefit. Considering how few people work for a greater vision, it is a very moving feeling to realize how many have actually worked with genuine compassion.

In his last words to me, my guru Jamgön Kongtrül of Shechen said, "I am getting old and I don't think I can handle the political changes taking place in Tibet, so I leave it up to you people to handle these situations." It was very sad that such a dignified person, such a great warrior, so powerful, energetic, and insightful, had come to that. It was heartbreaking, in a sense. One wonders what portion of his intention was directed toward filling me with sadness for the lack of a contemplative tradition in Buddhism, and what portion was because he wanted me to carry on as his heir, his offshoot. I think it was some of both. It was very sad and happy at the same time. I could weep, cry, or burst into tears, or I could dance and explore. And that seems to be the feeling of the vajrayana, actually: it is both of these at once.

# The Dawning of the Great Eastern Sun

*In talking about the Great Eastern kingdom, or vajrayana, we mean a human dawn: a dawn of humanity in which vajrayana can be presented, and in which vajrayana could happen in our existence. In the dawn of vajrayana, we are learning how to rise, rather than how to die. And at this point, the dawn of vajrayana has already happened.*

## THE GREAT EAST AND THE
## SETTING SUN OF THE WEST

My ancestors, persons of Tibetan blood, possessed the Oriental gut, which is the great sun of the East, or the Great East. If there were no such thing as the Great East, the vajrayana could not be presented. In the image of the Great East, if you do not have the East, you cannot have the sun shining out of the East. In this case, the East is mahayana, and the sun shining out of the East is vajrayana. The vision is mahayana, and executing the vision is vajrayana—always. In fact, there is no vision in the vajrayana, because you do not need it. Vision is a futuristic experience, whereas execution is the present situation, so you only need execution. And if you do not execute properly, you cut your finger, which is bad vision.

There is such a thing as the Great West as well, but that Great West has become the symbol of the setting sun, the destroying of light. Century after century, that great setting sun, as opposed to the great rising sun, has created conditions that block any possibilities of presenting enlightenment. The great setting sun of the West has provided us with beautiful, comfortable conditions for living our life, like central heating, air-conditioning, taxicabs, and numerous other conveniences. But that setting-sun approach has provided us purely with a comfortable way to die.

In the West, there are old-age homes, funeral homes, all sorts of shots in your arm, dope to puff up, and LSD to take so that we can realize how to make the sun set, meaning the sun of human dignity, the sun of human power. All those things we have in the Great West—including warfare, economic development, philosophy, psychology, and economic plans as well—have been about learning how to die rather than learning how to rise. So unfortunately, I have to say that the possibility of vajrayana involves the idea of the Great East as distinguished from the wretched West. Hopefully, you will not take this as a personal insult, but the West, at this point, is equivalent to the setting sun. It is equivalent to anti-enlightenment, and it is very wretched. There is too much poverty mentality.

The business and investment of people in the West is based more on pleasure, while people in the East base their activity more on responsibility, because of the very fact that they do not have that much pleasure. However, the idea of the Great East is not simply a question of Eastern people versus Western people. We are talking about mind, about conquering mind. It is a matter of where the mind rests, and whether you are interested in pleasure or responsibility.

In talking about the Great Eastern kingdom, or vajrayana, we mean a human dawn: a dawn of humanity in which vajrayana can be presented, and in which vajrayana could happen in our existence. In the dawn of vajrayana, we are learning how to rise, rather than how to die. And at this point, the dawn of vajrayana has already happened. This was planned a long time ago in the East; it was provided by the Central Eastern kingdom of Shambhala and by the first Buddhist emperor, Ashoka Maharaja. Ashoka was one of the first rulers in human history to provide hospitals where the sick could be brought and treated, and who also provided animal hospitals. That is Great Eastern thinking. And the Great East is here.

## THREE QUALITIES OF THE GREAT EAST

The Great East, or *Tai Tung* in Chinese, has three qualities: it is primordial, eternal, and self-existent.

The Great Eastern Sun. A calligraphy by ChögyamTrungpa Rinpoche.
The original calligraphy reads: Shar Chen Nyima, by Dorje Dradül ("Indestructible Warrior").

## Primordial

The first quality is the primordial quality, or *döma* in Tibetan. *Dö* means "original," and *ma* can mean "mother"; so *döma* means the "original mother," "original existence," or "primordial." It is general sanity. The present cannot be manipulated, and the past also cannot be manipulated, so you live longer because you are not hampered by manipulation.

## Eternal

The second quality is *takpa*, which means "eternal." Eternity can exist independent of manipulation.

## Self-Existent

The third quality is *lhündrup*, which means "self-existence," or "spontaneously present." It could also be described as simplicity. Lhündrup means that in the vajrayana, the basic nature is continuous, and at the same time, self-existent.

The vajrayana discipline can also be presented in terms of these three qualities. You could view the three characteristics as the transformation of the three marks of samsaric existence: suffering, change, and egolessness. Suffering is transformed into döma, primordial existence or bliss. Change becomes takpa, the continuous freshness of eternal existence. And egolessness becomes lhündrup, unborn self-existing being.

## The Dawning of Sanity

Although referred to as the Great East, these vajrayana principles are not particularly the possession of the Orientals, which would be absurd. They represent the intelligence and awareness of the rising sun of the Orient. You are giving up your connection to the West, which is the setting sun, and picking up on the possibility of Orientalness. That is Great East or rising sun. This dawning is also referred to as the dawn of Vajrasattva. It is as though light is coming from the East, and you have a glimpse of the possibility of awakening. So dawn means to awaken, and Vajrasattva, or "vajra being," is what you are awakening to. In terms of Great East, Vajra-sattva is *tai,* or "Great," and awakening to it is *tung,* or "East."

When we talk about the rising sun, we mean an eternally sane attitude, an experience in which the vajrayana is happening. The rising sun only comes from there being no setting sun. The setting sun is related with theism, and the rising sun with nontheism. The rising sun is saner because it is giving birth; the setting sun is dwelling on depression. An Occidental kingdom would not have the sun rising everywhere, whereas an Oriental kingdom would have sunshine throughout. Because the Oriental approach to reality is based on the nontheistic approach of *shunyata,* or emptiness, nobody has any basis at all. Everything is simple, so there is fullness all the time. That combination of simplicity and fullness is the ultimate culture: loneliness.* It is where vajrayana comes in.

## BUDDHAHOOD

Since the immense power and heroism of the Great East of the vajrayana is beginning to dawn on us, it is necessary to realize how that can be conducted and worked with properly. The possibility of doing so only comes from the realization of basic nontheistic Buddhism. At this point, a person's realization of the truth of twofold egolessness, or the egoless-ness of self and the egolessness of phenomena, goes beyond that of the highest levels of the bodhisattva path. It goes beyond the experience of indestructible meditation, or vajrasamadhi. You begin to realize that so-called tathagatagarbha, or buddha nature, is futile. It is futile because your experience is no longer *garbha,* which means "essence" or "nature." At this point, it is no longer just buddha *nature* that you have within you, but fully developed buddha*hood,* completely and utterly.

So in the vajrayana, instead of regarding practices such as benevolence and so forth in the context of an embryonic state from which you could reawaken your buddha nature, you realize that your buddha nature is present already; it is fully awakened right now. Therefore, the mahayana is known as the yana of seed, and the vajrayana is known as the yana of fruition. The idea is that if you do not understand the mahayana, it will

---

* Although *loneliness* is commonly viewed as a negative quality, Trungpa Rinpoche con-sistently points out the positive role of loneliness on the vajrayana path.

be very difficult for you to get into the vajrayana. If you do not realize the seed, you cannot have an understanding of the fruit.

In the vajrayana, the ground is more emphasized, but in order to realize the ground, you have to go through the disciplines—and when the ground is realized, that is attainment. So the ground is the fruition. Understanding the ground as the fruition means that there is fruit already. The ground is already cleared, and there is an apple dropping on your head; it is already happening.

A complete understanding of mahayana is not a complete understanding of vajrayana, but it gets us halfway through. Taking the bodhisattva vow is based on having immense devotion to the seed and the possibilities of the seed; it is the garbha principle. You are relating to the garbha, or essence, of everything. But the idea of tathagatagarbha is still very much a poverty approach. Shantideva, the eighth-century Indian Buddhist scholar, talks about how great it is that, although we may be wretched and terrible, we still have this little essence.* But in the vajrayana, your poverty is your wealth, and neurosis is sanity. That is not quite so simple to deduce, but it is true.

In the mahayana, you are looking into yourself, looking for that essence or seed, but in the vajrayana you are looking out, because you already have the fruition. You are not trying to look for some essence; you are looking for the real thing. It is like thinking you already have a fully grown-up child in your womb. At this point, your birth has already taken place, and you are already fully grown, so why talk about yourself as a fetus? You are not a fetus; you are a real person.

## Creating an Enlightened Society

We are trying to create a Buddhist world, an enlightened society, and one of the principal ways of doing that is for each one of us to become sane. In order to become sane, you have to become disciplined; and in order to become disciplined, you have to develop a sense of loyalty. In this case, loyalty is not at the boss-and-worker level, but it is an appreciation of

---

* In his text the *Bodhicharyavatara,* or *The Way of the Bodhisattva,* Shantideva refers to this essence as *bodhichitta,* which in this context Trungpa Rinpoche is equating with tathagatagarbha. See Shantideva, *The Way of the Bodhisattva,* trans. Padmakara Translation Group (Boston: Shambhala Publications, 1997).

what you are involved in. Loyalty applies to all the yanas: the hinayana, the mahayana, and needless to say, the vajrayana.

There are two levels of loyalty: setting-sun loyalty and Great Eastern Sun loyalty. The setting-sun version of loyalty is based on fear. You are afraid that if you do not do your job, you might be fired and lose your sandwich and your roof. But you think that if you become a good, loyal person, then you will have more than a sandwich and a roof. You might have a palace and eat gourmet food, and you might be able to take some time off. You might be able to go to a beach and lie in the dirt. That is what we call a vacation, although you never know what the vacation is a vacation from, exactly. That's it—full stop. There is nothing more than that. So setting-sun loyalty is a functional sort of loyalty. Obviously, you try to be happy, but that is just thrown in. And at some point, you are going to drop dead, and that's it—poof!

You might also apply this setting-sun approach to your children and your grandchildren. You hope your children could all go through the same process. You want them to get a good education so that they could get a good job. Hopefully, they could be disciplined, so that they do not get fired, and if they are successful enough, they too might have a chance to go to the beach and lie in the dirt. Your grandchildren and your great-grandchildren could do absolutely the same thing. Maybe they could go to the moon eventually, and lie in the dirt on the moon. They could eat lots of food, drink lots of booze, and consume lots of Alka-Seltzer.

The other side of the coin, heads rather than tails, is Great Eastern Sun loyalty, which is more fundamental. Great Eastern Sun loyalty is a question of what you are, rather than what you are doing. Someone might ask, "What are you doing?" But when someone asks, "Who are you?" or "What are you?" it is a more fundamental question. What you are is what you are, and what you are not is what you are not. By testing your setting-sun approach and the territoriality of your ego, you have a chance to look at those situations and find out who and what you are.

The Buddhist path is good, extraordinarily good. When I am on the streets and I see somebody walking along, I can always tell if that person is a practitioner from their walk and the way they hold their head and shoulders. Sometimes other people walk that way, too. We could say that such people have enlightened genes in them in a much more powerful way than simply as an undercurrent.

You could be cheerful, raise your head and your shoulders, and look straight ahead. You could be disciplined and compact at the hinayana level; you could be disciplined, gentle, and loving at the mahayana level; and at the vajrayana level, you could just be there.

Once you have understood, once you have studied and practiced, you might actually have to do something. Together we might need to wake up the whole world from its sleep, and create an enlightened society in accordance with Great Eastern Sun vision. So we should appreciate one another. We should appreciate that we are going to create a wakeful world.

## 2

# The Transition to Vajrayana

*The vajrayana is indestructible for the very fact that just like all the rivers go to the ocean, and you cannot drain the ocean, all dharmas go into the vajrayana. It is the truth of all truth. When you tell the ultimate truth, and even without telling the truth, that truth is so true that there is no reference point of falsity. It is real truth, like the ocean.*

THE VAJRAYANA path can actually present to you the realization of buddhahood. According to the vajrayana, you are already buddha, and you have to understand that and realize it. In the mahayana, you have inklings of buddha nature, inklings of being enlightened; but in the vajrayana, you are already buddha. That seems to be the difference between the two approaches. But if you have not understood the hinayana and the mahayana, you cannot understand the vajrayana. You will either trip out on your own expectations, or you will become completely confused, and consequently desecrate the dharma altogether. So in discussing the vajrayana, it is important to see its link with the mahayana.

The vajrayana is an extension of the mahayana, so before going on, it is essential that you are adequately prepared. Tantric texts say that first you should become accomplished on the hinayana level by realizing the truth of suffering; having realized that, you should begin to understand innate buddha nature; and at that point, you will be qualified to listen to the teachings of the ultimate result in the vajrayana.

In the mahayana, you develop a sympathetic attitude toward others and you are willing to work with them; you learn to overcome selfishness.

As well as learning how to treat others better, you also learn how to treat yourself better. You establish a relationship with a spiritual friend, and you develop prajna and compassion. It has been said that once you attain prajna and compassion, you will have no problem understanding your basic nature, or alaya. Through prajna, you begin to realize that your mind is luminous and free from ego. Therefore, you are able to work with your kleshas. With all that as your basis, you begin to be softened enough to receive the vajrayana teachings. On the ground of hinayana and mahayana, you are ready to hear the vajrayana.

## FULLNESS AND MAGIC

Mahayana is concerned with emptiness, or shunyata, with experience without a reference point. But according to the vajrayana, that nonreference point has to be workable. That nonreference point has to be an energizing situation, rather than energy being purely dependent on compassion. And if compassion arises, that compassion also has to be magical. From those conclusions, the word *siddhi* came to be. *Siddhi* means "complete achievement." It refers to power over your state of mind, as well as the power to order the phenomenal world in the way that you would like to see it, within the good intention of nonduality, of course.

So tantra exists from the viewpoint that shunyata has fullness or a magical quality; otherwise, it could not be empty. That fullness has never been explored completely in the lower yanas, but in the vajrayana we are surveying the contents of that fullness and asking what it means to us. Therefore, in order to fulfill sanity properly, it is necessary to get into vajrayana. Without vajrayana, there is no way to understand the fullness of enlightenment.

The closest the basic yanas have come to such fullness is the idea of compassion and the idea of exchanging yourself for others. In the mahayana, you are working with both sentient beings and enlightened beings equally, but according to the vajrayana, that is not quite enough. According to the vajrayana, in the samsaric world, sanity or enlightenment has the upper hand. In order to encounter such a chauvinistic view of enlightenment, it is absolutely necessary to study vajrayana. Otherwise, you will still be involved with the level of idiot democracy.

## GREAT EQUILIBRIUM

In the vajrayana, there is an emphasis on *upaya,* or skillful means. In fact, one of the definitions of *vajrayana* is that it is composed of teachings based on a particular state of mind or mental approach, in which shunyata and prajna are put together and are regarded as upaya. So the combination of the emptiness nature of the phenomenal world and clear seeing is regarded as great compassion, which is considered to be a skillful means.

One of the differences between the vajrayana and the mahayana is that the vajrayana teachings understand that even the relative truth is workable and insightful. On the level of relative truth, or the *kündzop* level, all dharmas are seen as equally important and in equilibrium. Kündzop is not regarded as a pick-and-choose situation; rather, everything taking place there is regarded as the real world. By equilibrium, we mean comprehensive evenness. If there is black, that is not particularly great, nor is white particularly great, nor yellow, nor green. Everything is seen as equal. In terms of the sense perceptions, what you are perceiving is never regarded as being on a higher level or a lower level. Everything is on just the basic phenomenal level that takes place constantly.

The nature of vajrayana is to see that quality of evenness. It is to relate much more with the phenomenal world, and with the absolute truth, or *töndam,* as a by-product of that. In the mahayana, we have a problem, in that the absolute truth is regarded as higher, much more chic. So we tend to cultivate that level more, and see the regular physical world as just completely ordinary. But at the vajrayana stage, that approach becomes a problem. In the vajrayana, we develop an understanding of the ordinary world and how it actually happens. We know how a sunny-side-up egg is cooked, how our tires go *psssss,* how we can be insulted at a cocktail party, how we could go bankrupt, how there can be somebody who hates us all our life.

## VAJRAYANA DELTA

The vajrayana is like a river delta: the place where the river meets the ocean is where the vajrayana actually occurs. In order to realize that, you have to appreciate the little brooks that rush from the mountains thousands of miles away. You have to appreciate how much hard work these brooks have done in order to get to the ocean. Hinayana discipline is like the little brooks that flow into the ocean; without the hinayana, there would be no continuity. Hinayana is the source of vajrayana: it is the source of mantra, of visualizing deities, of relating with the vajra master, of everything.

The vajrayana is indestructible for the very fact that just like all the rivers go to the ocean, and you cannot drain the ocean, all dharmas go into the vajrayana. It is the truth of all truth. When you tell the ultimate truth, and even without telling the truth, that truth is so true that there is no reference point of falsity. It is real truth, like the ocean. You cannot even think of lying; it does not make sense. It is true true, too true, real true. Truth is finally spelled out on the ultimate level.

The truth is big truth, very big. It is big like the sky. It is true. Fire burns—true. There is one truth, even on the relative level; it is just reflected in different ways. It is like the story of the ten blind men and the elephant. One blind man says the elephant is like a tree trunk, one says it is like a leaf, and so on, but really it is just one elephant. Likewise, truth is not relative truth, but it is *one* truth, which includes different discoveries.

We may come to tantra with doubt about whether there is a real connection between our projection and reality. That doubt may go all the way back to our understanding of the four noble truths: the truths of suffering, the origin of suffering, the cessation of suffering, and the path of liberation. But the more doubt there is, the better. When you have no doubt, that is the truth; and when you have doubt, that is also the truth. So doubt is very fertile ground.

Fundamentally, there is only one truth, although its expressions could be different. You might say that the sun is shiny and bright; you might say it is hot; you might say it dispels darkness. You could talk about the different attributes of the sun, but you are still talking about one particular sun. Sometimes you become too clever and try to get around the relative aspect of truth. But if you dig a hole under a tree, you always find the same root, no matter how many holes you might dig.

The truth is very interesting. It is painful. You could even call it dictatorial, because when you are hurt, you are hurt, and when you feel relaxed, you are relaxed. You cannot manipulate the truth. You cannot hold an election on your truth. You cannot change your truth. It is one truth; it is always one truth. According to vajrayana, it is one single syllable. It is just one word, one syllable. So truth could be quite painful, or it could be delightful.

People are afraid of the truth, so they come up with all sorts of techniques and tricks instead. And people try to find the truth in many different ways. This is the twenty-first century, and it has been many years since the earth was created. We no longer hunt for our food and live in caves, but instead we buy our food. We are no longer savages, but instead we have tailored suits and hairdos, and we have even learned how to wear glasses, if we cannot see far enough or near enough. Society has changed, and it has become more sophisticated; nonetheless, we are still doing the same thing. We are still always trying to find the truth in indirect ways, rather than directly. We have been trying to avoid the direct truth for a long time.

I am not particularly scolding anybody, but it is ironic how we have been able to cheat ourselves in spite of our sophistication. In fact, the more sophisticated we are, the more we come up with philosophies to avoid the truth and substitute something else. That is known as spiritual materialism.

Traditions based on spiritual materialism may be like lakes, or even like the Great Lakes, but they do not reach the ocean. The reason for this is because they do not see that the mind is at once fundamentally luminous and egoless. Vajrayana experience is luminous and bright, because you relate with the phenomenal world without cheating or giving anything up. It is luminous because you have a genuine sympathy and passion for helping others, even beyond the mahayana level. You also begin to have an element of craziness at the highest level of wisdom. You do not believe in the usual conventions that have developed throughout history, and you are willing to go beyond historical or sociological conventionality.

Because you feel free, your teaching techniques and your practice techniques are not stagnant or imprisoned. But being free from social norms does not make you crazy. Instead, you become reasonable, daring, and bright. Here, reasonable means that you are free from social norms; daring means that you are free from concepts; and bright means that you become a source of inspiration to others. With those three qualities, you can actually defeat the habitual patterns of samsara, and at the same time you can proclaim yourself elegantly and beautifully.

## SHOCK AND DANGER

The discovery that greater elegance and beauty is possible will shock a lot of people. Beyond that, they will realize that the vajrayana way of relating with pleasure is also greater, something nobody ever thought of in such a way before. Obviously, there are new ski slopes, new dishes, and new fashions every season. One year everybody has a thin tie, and the next year everybody has a thick tie; one year there are short skirts, and the next year there are long skirts. People want to alternate everything all the time, but they actually keep doing the same things. However, they would be shocked to discover that a different value can be put on society and experience altogether. When a fresh, new, beautiful mind comes into their world, that world is completely transformed. This is the definition of enlightened society. Enlightened society is not based on a gimmick; it is based on the beyond-mind concept of vajrayana. So if you ask why there is vajrayana, it is because it is necessary—always.

When you learn about the elements of the vajrayana path, it seems to be very easy. You think that you can tune in very fast, right away, right off the street. It is possible that if you started right off the sidewalk, you could be zapped in your ordinary mind, in some way. But it is also possible that if you do not know how to relate with the ocean, you could be pulled under the water. We do not want to take that kind of chance with anybody. The path and the work that has been done by our ancestors is very important, and we have to respect that. The ocean is very dangerous.

If you watch parachutists jumping so nicely, pulling their cords, opening their chutes, and landing gracefully, it looks very easy, very nice and pleasurable. But if you try to do it yourself and you don't pull the cord, you go straight down. Likewise, if you watch a master calligrapher doing brushstrokes, it looks very simple. The brush and the ink go along with the paper so nicely. But if you try to do it yourself, you find that you come out with a black hand, and the ink will not come off even if you use soap.

The vajrayana is that same kind of situation. It could be dangerous for you, because you might end up doing everything the wrong way. If someone said that you should develop egolessness, and you developed your ego instead, you could become an egomaniac. If you were told to express your emotions and develop compassion, and you misunderstood that instruction, you might think that expressing your hatred was the same as expressing your love; so you might decide to massacre a few people. If you heard that at the advanced level of vajrayana there is no need to meditate, you might take that literally and just hang around with no awareness and mindfulness.

Those kinds of misunderstandings could be very dangerous, so it is important to relate what you learn about the vajrayana path to the hinayana and mahayana. In order not to abuse the teachings or to view the vajrayana as a kind of Disneyland, it is necessary to continue the disciplines of the hinayana and mahayana. A Tibetan proverb says that if a fox tries to swim, his tail will get wet and he will lose his arrogance. He will end up with a big spongy bundle hanging behind him that he cannot even curl.

## STUDYING THE VAJRAYANA

Studying the vajrayana is not like studying in an ordinary education system where everything is presented on a silver platter. In this form of education, you are presented with choices and with trials and tribulations. As you pick up little things about the hinayana and mahayana, you might feel compelled to look into the vajrayana at the same time. And by being involved with all three perspectives, all three yanas, you might develop greater vision. But it also might make no sense to you at all, especially if you do not have a proper sitting practice or proper commitment. That could be a big problem. So I would like to invite you to study the vajrayana with genuine participation and openness.

At the same time, you should be cautious of people trying to teach you tantra, and you should look very critically at what they are doing. You should see if what a teacher is doing seems to be good, real, and legitimate. You should see if their teaching is according to the books, and has a quality of wisdom and insightfulness. If you get involved with some form of Buddhist tantric trip, it could be very dangerous.

When you study the vajrayana, self-deception is always possible. If you are learning about vajrayana purely by reading books, you have a problem, because you are not synchronizing your learning with your practice.

But as long as you are on guard, and as long as you practice as well as study, you have safeguards. So you have to synchronize your learning with your sitting meditation practice, or shamatha-vipashyana. Even if you are a vajrayana student or a would-be vajrayana student, it is still necessary to do that. Then you will be able to understand.

## WAYS TO ENTER

In a sense, entering the vajrayana is choiceless, but at the same time, there is a choice. As far as your own basic attitude is concerned, there is a choice as to what extent you will give up your clinging. If you do not enter the hinayana path of accumulation, then you can avoid getting into the vajrayana, but once you begin the path of accumulation and go on to the path of unification and so forth, you have no choice.* So even beginning to get into the hinayana seems to be equivalent to entering the vajrayana.

To clarify the whole thing, the various bodhisattva experiences are not intended to be the marks or signs that you are ready to enter into the vajrayana. You might be on the level of the first path, the path of accumulation, and still enter the vajrayana. In order to move from the mahayana to the vajrayana, you do not need to have fully realized the ten mahayana bhumis, although you do need to have had a glimpse of them and of the enlightenment of the eleventh bhumi.

In the same way, in order to move from the hinayana to the mahayana, you do not need to have fully realized awareness or mindfulness, but you do need to have had a glimpse of it. So we are not particularly discussing a person of the eleventh bhumi being a vajrayana practitioner, although they could be. We are talking about a person on the path of accumulation being a vajrayana practitioner at the same time. You may not be able to pull millions of buddhas out of your skin or become a universal monarch, but those are superficial credentials. In fact, even when you are still at the level of the first path, you could develop the same understanding and

---

* The *path of accumulation* and the *path of unification* are the first two of the five paths. For more on the five paths and the bodhisattva levels, or bhumis, see volume 1 of the *Profound Treasury*, chapter 60, "The Five Paths," and see volume 2, chapter 44, "The Paths and Bhumis."

meditative experience as a person at the eleventh bhumi level, and you could enter into the vajrayana.

When people enter the vajrayana, some are more attracted to one tantric yana, while others are more attracted to another yana. But the attraction is not quite the point; it is the practitioner's innate nature that is important. For instance, somebody could be highly attracted to *kriyayoga*, but actually be an *atiyoga* candidate, or vice versa.*

## NOT WASTING TIME

The vajrayana is based on very strict discipline. You cannot waste too much time. Otherwise, it might be like the story of the Tibetan spiritual leader and scholar Sakya Pandita (1182–1252 CE) and the Chinese emperor Goden Khan. When the Sakya Pandita went to China as the Imperial Spiritual Instructor, the emperor said, "I have to check on you for three years to see whether you are a suitable guru." At the end of three years he said, "I think you are a suitable guru. I would like to receive instruction from you." But the Sakya Pandita replied, "I now have to check on *you* for three years." And at the end of the three years, the Emperor died. The point is: don't waste time.†

## PICKING UP MESSAGES

In the vajrayana, you pick up messages at a much higher level of sensitivity. The clarity becomes very powerful and obvious, and a real flash occurs. You receive guidelines about how to handle your life from the point of view of symbolism and the self-existing messages of your lifestyle. You get feelings, for example, that indicate what the energy of the day will be. If you are in tune with reality, you receive constant, spontaneous guidance. Enormous powers of mental clarity can be developed even without attaining complete, full enlightenment. The question is how much you

---

* *Kriyayoga* and *atiyoga* are two of the six tantric yanas: kriyayoga, upayoga, yogayana, mahayoga, anuyoga, and atiyoga. For a discussion of these yanas, see part 10, "The Tantric Journey: Lower Tantra," and part 12, "The Tantric Journey: Higher Tantra."

† Other accounts relate that, after the testing period, Sakya Pandita did in fact end up giving teachings to Goden Khan.

are able to relate with your passions, and how much you are able to develop precision and clarity. The whole thing is completely workable.

## Fear of Tantra and Cosmic Alienation

In entering the vajrayana, a certain amount of fear is good. If you are overly eager and enthusiastic about the whole thing, you might make mistakes. But if you are fearful and you feel that you are not ready for the vajrayana, it is a very good sign. That is precisely why you are ready for the vajrayana. Because there is no pride, no sense of looking for another drama, the whole thing becomes very powerful and workable.

If you are at the level of entering the vajrayana, you do not know where you are going or whether you are going or coming. You have already gone through the shunyata experience, but now you are getting into something very foreign to shunyata experience, which is slightly crazy and scary. You are getting into something that does not really exist either in the shunyata experience of the bodhisattva or in the hinayana. You feel that you have been alienated from your familiar world, from your beliefs, from your practice, and from everything in your life. You have been alienated from a lot of things, but at the same time you find a quality of trust, and a hook or foothold into the bigger world.

You find that you are relating with something or other, but you do not know exactly what you are doing. Therefore, you begin to explore and to find out what it is all about. You do not want to go all the way back, and you do not want to go forward all that much either. You would like to have a convenient journey, one that takes place properly, and you find the various methods and means of vajrayana empowerments to be very concrete and helpful. In an empowerment ceremony you are told that now you are "Tathagata So-and-So," and therefore you are going to practice this way or that way. It is efficacious and very rewarding.

At the same time, the whole approach is somewhat outlandish. This has nothing to do with the particular culture of countries such as Tibet or India or wherever. It is a cosmic alienation that takes place. The logic of the vajrayana is not the usual logic that we use, so there is a feeling of being slightly haunted and fundamentally uncomfortable. It is quite right to develop a person in that way. Within that huge space of lostness and that feeling of hauntedness—big lost space—the various empowerments that take place are by no means overcrowded and busybody. They are a gift.

Fear of tantra arises because it is so unreasonable, particularly Buddhist tantra. For example, Buddhist tantra does not care at all about the ground it inherited from Hinduism. In fact, Buddhist tantric iconography shows wrathful deities stamping on the Hindu gods, saying, "Shiva is under my right foot, and Parvati is under my left foot, and I am stamping on all of your egos!" So the vajrayana is very unreasonable, and it is not hospitable. No gratitude is involved. As another example, Padmasambhava in his wrathful embodiment created earthquakes and landslides that shook the country landscapes of Tibet and changed them all around. Even the invitations presented to him by the local deities were rejected, and those deities were cut down immediately, one by one.

So Buddhist tantra is very strange and unreasonable, and the pride involved with it is tremendous—it is called vajra pride. Such pride could also be called crazy wisdom. In Tibetan, crazy wisdom is *yeshe chölwa: yeshe* means "wisdom," and *chölwa* means "gone wild." A description for crazy wisdom that is found in the scriptures states: "He subdues whoever needs to be subdued and destroys whoever needs to be destroyed." Crazy wisdom is just the action of truth. Unlike ordinary craziness, it is both ruthless and accurate. It is fantastic.

Fear of tantra is not just about your own personal existence, but you are also reflecting the fear that arises from national pride or national ego. Vajra pride does not accept that; you no longer let that kind of national ego come into your system. So vajra pride is a kind of vajra penicillin. At the same time, in both Hindu and Buddhist tantra, there is a danger that the quality of pride could become a problem. Tantra is proud of itself, and tantric teachers are also proud of themselves; and since the tantric teachings are self-contained, the teachers as well as the students may feel that they do not need any help from anything outside, none whatsoever. But by acting in that way, they screw themselves up, unless they first go through the hinayana and mahayana as preliminary training.

One of the weaknesses of tantra is that it has no inbuilt mechanism to help you rebound from going too far, nothing that acts as a moderating principle. The bodhisattva path is fantastic in that regard; there are constant self-corrective mechanisms. And in tantra, once you reach the advanced level of *mahamudra,* you can correct the situation by reading it accurately.* But as far as a tantric beginner is concerned, there is no corrective mechanism at all. By the time you discover that you have gone off, it is too late; you have already psychologically exploded. So either you are on the path or you are not. If you are on the path, then you can go on beyond that starting point. You have something definite to work on. But at the beginner's level of vajrayana, the only way to stay on the path is through good training in the previous yanas.

One way of looking at this is to use the old Zen proverb about the path to enlightenment: "First you see the mountain, then you don't see the mountain, then you see the mountain." In hinayana, you see the mountain; in mahayana, the mountain of suffering is dissolved into emptiness; and in tantra, you begin to see the mountain again. You are almost involved in a reacquaintance with, or re-creation of, the world. But you have to go slowly and ritually, so that this time you are conscious of what is happening. And to do this properly, you need to have had training in the hinayana and mahayana.

## THE DANGER OF TEACHING VAJRAYANA

The vajrayana is said to be both difficult to understand and difficult to teach. It is also said to be dangerous to teach. Those of us who are teachers, or vajra masters, have been told by the grandparents and the great-grandparents of the lineage not to proclaim vajrayana to those who are not ready. We were told that if we did so, we would suffer from proclaiming such secrets. It has even been said that we should not proclaim the vajrayana to anybody at all, because we would be wasting our time and people would not understand such teachings, so it would be better to do something else. Practices like sending and taking, or helping old people to cross the street might be better than proclaiming the vajrayana. Nonetheless, with permission from my root guru,† the lineage, and the protectors of the teachings, we will proceed with our discussion of the dharma.

---

* *Mahamudra* means "great symbol," and refers to the highest realization of the New Translation School. For a discussion of mahamudra, see part II, "The Tantric Journey: Mahamudra."

† The *root guru* refers to a student's primary teacher, and in particular, the teacher who enters that student into the vajrayana teachings. Trungpa Rinpoche's root guru was Jamgön Kongtrül of Shechen.

38

## Two Continuations

There are two styles of tantric tradition: spring continuation and autumn continuation. In spring continuation, you take the ground as the path, and in autumn continuation, you take the fruition as the path. But whether your tradition is that of ground or fruition, there is still the path. In either case, students have to work hard, so in that sense the path is always the same.

### Taking the Ground as the Path

Spring continuation means using the ground as the path. In Tibetan, this is called *shi lamdu chepa*. *Shi* is "base" or "basic ground," *lam* is "path," *du* is "as," and *chepa* means "doing it"; so *shi lamdu chepa* is "taking the ground as the path." Here the ground or first inspiration is made into the path. This approach is connected with what is known as lower tantra.*

In the springtime, the journey is one of sowing the seed, and the sprouting of the seed into greenery. Like a seed, you have great potential; therefore, you can journey in the vajrayana. So in spring continuation, the way you are is the ground, which can be used as the path.

### Taking the Fruition as the Path

Autumn continuation means using the fruition as path. In Tibetan this is *drebu lamdu chepa*. *Drebu* means "fruition," and again *lamdu chepa* means "taking as the path"; so *drebu lamdu chepa* means "taking the fruition as the path."

In the autumn, when you have gathered your harvest and stored your seeds and grains, you appreciate what you have harvested. Therefore, you can relate with sowing further seeds. You are inspired because you know that seeds can be grown, nice flowers can bloom, and you can produce more flowers next year.

Vajrayana teaching techniques are not particularly sneaky or magical.

---

* *Lower tantra* refers to the first three tantric yanas (kriyayoga, upayoga, and yogayana). *Higher tantra* refers to the second three tantric yanas (mahayoga, anuyoga, and atiyoga), and more generally to the *maha ati* or dzokchen teachings.

They simply make use of those two possibilities. Some teachers have a ground quality, as if they had grown out of the ground; other teachers are accomplished already, so their achievement is their path. You can find those two approaches to teaching in any kind of education system, even with ordinary subjects like mathematics or science. Some teachers teach from the point of view of what they *were*, and some teach from the point of view of what they *are*. As far as students are concerned, some people are inspired by the first approach, and other people are inspired by the second. It is very simple and straightforward.

In any case, even when we talk about taking the fruition, or autumn, as the path, you still have to go through the winter and the whole cycle all over again. One of the important points in vajrayana is that you have to learn to backtrack all the way to good old hinayana and fantastic mahayana. The precision of hinayana is absolutely necessary; otherwise, when you do vajrayana practice, you will have difficulty doing your mudras and mantras and visualizations. You will have difficulty quieting your mind, and you will be lost in the middle of nowhere. You might even think that you are in the middle of the New Jersey Turnpike.

The substance of the vajrayana comes only from the best of hinayana and the best of mahayana. When you begin to practice sending and taking, or tonglen, and you exchange yourselves for others, only then are you no longer soaked in setting-sun vision. Only then can you generate greater warriorship.

In turn, once you have finished your vajrayana preliminary practices, you could actually associate yourselves with the vajrayana path, and with whatever appears or is given in our discipline and tradition. Vajrayana preliminary practices require exertion, stillness of mind, thoroughness, and selflessness, so before beginning them, further training in the previous yanas makes sense. Because of that training, you can handle and experience properly the best of the vajrayana.*

---

\* Traditionally, before being formally empowered in the vajrayana path, students must complete a series of *preliminary practices,* called *ngöndro.* The four main preliminaries include 100,000 recitations of the refuge vow, 100,000 prostrations, 100,000 recitations of the Vajrasattva mantra, and 100,000 mandala offerings. For a discussion of ngöndro and these practices, see part 7, "Preliminary Practices."

## A Natural Ripening Process

In terms of beginning at the beginning, we find that we are born in the middle of winter when everything is frozen. The world outside is white with snow, and it is too cold to go outside. But when we begin on the spiritual path, we discover that winter has an end; we begin to discover spring. Everything is thawing, there is softness, and we see the green shoots of grasses and plants. The spring is a time for planting. So we begin to cultivate our field, to spread manure, and to sow seeds.

As our journey continues, we have summer. In this case it is a long summer, and it includes Indian summer. We have a long journey, a very long journey, a completely long journey. We do our practice again and again. We sit and meditate again and again and again. We sit, we practice, we sit, we practice. We continue to confront our emotions and everything else. It is a long summer.

Then something begins to break; some kind of opening happens. Autumn is coming. The leaves begin to change color, and there is a change of attitude. A change of season is in the air. That change could be seen as a warning of winter or as a threat, but it also could be seen as a celebration that the seeds we have sown have finally born their results.

The idea of the four-seasons metaphor is that a natural journey takes place. On that journey, you begin at the beginning, get used to practice and discipline, ripen, and finally see results. And you make that journey through the seasons again and again. For several years, you go through the seasons, and finally you realize that a journey has taken place. You see that you are not the same person you were originally, not the same Joe Schmidt. Your appearance and your existence altogether have begun to change and become softer.

The vajrayana path is designed to confirm your change or development as naturally as possible. It is a natural process, and at the same time it is good. Your intentions are good and gentle, because by that time you have already become a child of illusion.* You are already a thoroughly

---

* "In postmeditation, be a child of illusion" is one of the fifty-nine mind-training slogans attributed to Atisha. See volume 2 of the *Profound Treasury*, part 7, "Mind Training and Slogan Practice."

trained, or *shinjanged* person,* and you are already a tonglen-ed person. Therefore, you are capable of practicing vajrayana fully and thoroughly. That kind of training is important. Otherwise, if you were just an infant, and you were given tantric ritual instruments to play with such as a *ghanta, dorje,* or *damaru* (bell, scepter, or hand drum), you could get lead poisoning from chewing on your dorje, or puncture your damaru by trying to find out how strong it was. So the point is that when you become a vajrayanist, you should already be a fully grown hinayanist as well as a mahayanist.

Although at this level the vajrayana could be called a journey, it does not go anywhere and it does not come from anywhere. So the vajrayana is a vehicle that seems to have neither beginning nor end. You can neither reverse it nor proceed further along. The vajrayana is self-existent, by its own nature. Therefore, the vajrayana path could be said to be a nonjourney.

If something takes place as a journey, you can catch it. You can see whether it is going right or left, forward or backward, and you can always catch it either way. It is like catching flies. The best way to catch a fly is to know which way its head is facing; then you can interrupt the fly in its journey. But in the case of vajrayana, it is natural existence that does not come from anywhere and does not go anywhere. That is the highest form of journey: journey without journeying.

---

* *Shinjang* refers to the suppleness and thoroughly processed quality that results from shamatha practice. See volume 1 of the *Profound Treasury,* part 3, "Meditation/Samadhi."

## 3

# *Entering the Diamond Path on a Solid Foundation*

*The vajrayana, or diamond vehicle, is powerful because it is derived from the tranquillity and readiness of the hinayana and the purity and soft heart of the mahayana. When students have developed those qualities, the vajrayana becomes ready to launch its diamond ship into the oceans of those who are ready for it.*

## THE POSSIBILITY OF FEARLESSNESS

The precision of hinayana and the larger-mindedness of mahayana enable you to become fearless. Even though you still might be fearful, there is at least the potential or possibility of fearlessness. Fearlessness is based on making a commitment that from now onward until the attainment of enlightenment, you will continue working with yourself. It is based on developing *maitri*, or loving-kindness, thoroughly and fully. By doing so, you begin to feel that as a student of vajrayana, you have actual ground. There is something that you can hang on to, which is that you have already made friends with yourself. The vajrayana point of view enables you to maintain that basic trust or basic ground.

## HEIGHTENED NEUROSIS

Having developed that ground of maitri in yourself, you begin to find that nevertheless there are all kinds of neuroses. There are possible neuroses and actual neuroses. You might actually have to face hundreds of thousands or even millions of those neuroses. And in studying the vajrayana, you begin to find that your neuroses are heightened. Because you have developed openness and clarity, in the vajrayana even a little neurosis, such as having resistance to putting your mail in the mailbox, becomes tremendously heightened, dozens of times more heightened. At this point, we do not particularly want to borrow Freudian or Jungian ideas of neurosis. We are talking about a simple neurotic connection or attitude to ourselves..

## Three Levels of Neurosis

This neurotic attitude to ourselves breaks down into three levels: body, speech, and mind.

BODY NEUROSIS. First we have body. In the vajrayana, our attitude toward our body is important and becomes unusually clear. Our body is that which receives impressions. It reacts to hot and cold weather, relates to pleasure and pain, hunger and fullness, and all sorts of situations. But in the case of body neurosis, our body is something that we would like to hold on to, to keep back as our private property, our personal project.

SPEECH NEUROSIS. Next we have speech, which is related with our communication with the world. Speech neurosis includes any expressions coming from the subconscious-gossip level, such as expressions of hate or love, whether frivolous or meaningful.

MIND NEUROSIS. Then we have mind. Here, mind is basic mind, the mind with which we actually begin to make connections with our life. This mind seems to be comprised of both body and speech. In mind neurosis, our body neurosis and our speech neurosis team up, so we begin to develop passion, aggression, and ignorance throughout our life.

Basically speaking, all three neuroses are unreasonable from the point of view of vajrayana. But if you look at them from another point of view, they are all extraordinarily reasonable. They are all studies in cause and effect, in how you feel good, how you feel bad, how you feel you are hassled by the world, how you feel empty or lonely, how you feel needs of all kinds. In the vajrayana, you actually use all of these original, basic, fermented piles of shit as your working basis. You have had body, speech, and mind neuroses taking place all along, but they become much more vivid and real in the vajrayana, due to the very fact that you begin to work with them quite precisely.

## WORKING WITH NEUROSES

In entering the vajrayana, your neuroses actually become heightened. Because you are face-to-face with the real world, you begin to feel hurt. You are scorched by so much brilliant sunshine. Because of its closeness, you are bound to panic more. It is very immediate. When you work with neuroses, you clean them up. It is like using toilet tissue to wipe your bottom. You do not just say, "I don't want to work with my shit. I don't want to use my toilet tissue." You do not just go off like that; otherwise, you end up with a dirty bottom. So you just keep working with your neuroses as they come up.

If you try to get to the end of those neuroses, they never end. That never happens. Why would you want to end your neuroses, anyway? There needs to be some kind of bravery. But at the same time, we are trying to get rid of our neuroses. We are trying to get rid of them and create a vajra world, and we cannot be too sophisticated about that. You have to take that sort of hinayana and mahayana stand. You cannot just say, "I couldn't care less. I am going to change my shit into food." We are not talking about recycling here, but about the immediateness of the whole thing.

In the vajrayana, we are not very hip. We are talking about very basic things. If the tantric texts tell us to eat meat and drink liquor, what can we say about that, except to take it literally, on the spot. We eat meat, drink liquor, and expand our mind victoriously, and that brings us a tremendous sense of humor. We eat, drink, and make merry, but not in the Sunset Strip style or the California approach of naked bodies on the beach lying in the dirt. We are talking about some kind of celebration in eating meat and drinking liquor. It is very simple. This may seem to be somewhat crude and forceful, but it works. It is mysterious, but there is some kind of delight in the whole thing. We might add one more thing to the list: eat meat, drink liquor, and make love.

This process of working with neurosis begins with the idea of mindfulness-awareness in hinayana, and continues with the dedication and gentleness of mahayana. It is the development of hinayana and

45

mahayana that actually enables us to make our body, speech, and mind neuroses so vivid. We cannot just jump into the vajrayana right away without them; it is impossible to do so. First, the doctor finds symptoms of disease in you; then you go to the hospital and get operated on; and finally there is the transplantation of the various organs you need, which is what happens in the vajrayana.

We are so stubborn. Sometimes we glorify our body neurosis; sometimes we glorify our speech neurosis; and sometimes we also glorify our mind neurosis. We use animalistic language, intellectual language, or intuitive language. We try every possible way to get out of our particular neurosis, but not necessarily in the vajrayana style. We are always trying to fight. We declare our neuroses as if we were the kings and queens of the universe. We would like to hoist our flag of neurosis all along. Whether we speak the language of communism, women's liberation, men's liberation, psychosomatic liberation, parent's liberation, children's liberation, or whatever liberation, we always try to declare ourselves as if we were the world's greatest, most glorious, most powerful, most neurotic kings and queens.

This leads to two possibilities: either we recognize all such declarations as neurosis and immediately get into the vajrayana, or we remain stuck with our neurotic stuff all along, swimming in our own shit, piss, and blood. The vajrayana teaching instructs us to get out of, or resign from, that situation. It tells us that we should no longer declare our body, speech, and mind neuroses.

The interesting point here is that at the hinayana and mahayana levels, you are still able to hoist your flag of neurosis. I have met quite a number of students who are actually thriving on their neuroses. They feel great that they can hoist their flag of body, speech, and mind neurosis in the name of the hinayana or mahayana dharma. It might even be possible to find students who hoist their flag of neurosis in the name of the vajrayana. But thanks to the Great Eastern Sun, that has not yet happened, thank heavens.

At the same time, however, there is a kind of pride in the vajrayana. That kind of proclamation or declaration is the working basis of the vajrayana. It is why we call it the path in which the fruition is the journey. In the vajrayana, we do not talk about *developing* buddha nature, but we say that buddha nature is right here, on the spot, right now. We say that your potential is your fruition, that you are a fully realized being right here, on this very spot.

To discover the ground of vajrayana, you actually have to heighten your body, speech, and mind neuroses. You have to experience the fullness of those neuroses, in terms of their enlightened possibilities and their energetic aspect. Combining these different elements, bringing them together by means of discipline, is called *dompa,* which means "bondage" or "binding together." In dompa, skillful means and knowledge, or upaya and prajna, are bound together. That kind of bondage brings you into a one-level situation.

This message—that your emotions, or your body, speech, and mind neuroses, can be worked with by means of upaya and prajna—brings you into tantra. Basically, what we are saying is that in the vajrayana, you have a washcloth with which you wash your face and your body. You put soap on the washcloth and rub yourself all over. When the washcloth has collected enough soap and dirt from your body, you wring it out so the dirty water can be drained into the bath. That is the basic idea of tantra: neurosis can be taken off. Body, speech, and mind neurosis can be taken off by means of tantric-style upaya and prajna. Your washcloth can be twisted so that at the end you have tantra, which means continuity.

What is continuing is that you are constantly going through the process of washing and cleaning up body neurosis, speech neurosis, and mind neurosis. You are washing continuously; you are trying to push them out. You might ask, "Isn't that a drastic measure?" You are quite right. It is a drastic measure, due to the very fact that the bather has to stay in the bathtub or shower throughout the whole process. But after you have taken the shower, what is left is confidence. It is absolutely everything put together, which is much more delightful, fantastic, and quite haughty. However, if you try to run out halfway through, you come out half-dirty. You might catch something much more severe than pneumonia. You will be devastated, and you will have no way out.

## AN AWAKENING OF INSIGHT

The next point is that vajrayana provides an awakening of insight. We awaken our intrinsic insight, which is not particularly buddha nature or enlightened genes or bodhichitta—it is much more than that. We begin to experience what is known as freedom from fixation on our practice, and freedom from grasping onto our practice. In the lower yanas, practice is regarded as the only hope, but in the vajrayana, practice is not regarded that way. In fact, it is sometimes regarded as an obstacle. So fixation on practice and regarding practice as the only saving grace is freed. Therefore, there is the possibility of *vidya,* or "knowledge." Vajrayana knowledge is knowledge that does not cling to or fixate on any kind of personal desire or ego-centeredness, on anything that would allow you to recover your egoism. That is the definition of vidya, in this case.

This is a very simple skeleton of the whole vajrayana approach. The idea is that trying to understand your body, speech, and mind neurosis does not seem to work. Thinking about how you do not want to hear any vajrayana and how you wish that you did not have to also does not seem to work. Thinking about how Buddhism is good for your system, good for your jogging, or good for your evolutionary setting-sun schemes does not seem to work. If that is what you think, maybe you should stop right now.

## THE VIEW OF REALITY IN THE THREE YANAS

The vajrayana teaching is beyond words. It is exceptional, extraordinary. But such a thing can only come about by having properly understood the individual enlightenment of hinayana, and dedicated yourself to others by means of mahayana. Only then will you be able to hear and practice the vajrayana properly. We cannot forget what we have already discussed in the previous yanas.

We could look at the three yanas as three different ways of seeing reality, or as three different approaches to enlightenment. In the hinayana, we see reality in a factual, ordinary, but extremely wise way: as cause and effect, the manifestation of pain, the origin of pain, and so forth. In the hinayana we look at the way things function in terms of interdependent origination, or the twelve *nidanas,* and trace things back to the origin of reality, of matter and mind.\*

---

\* A reference to the unraveling of the interdependent karmic chain reaction. For more on the cycle of the *twelve nidanas,* see volume 1 of the *Profound Treasury,* chapter 9, "The Painful Reality of Samsara."

In the mahayana, we see the world in terms of the logic of the path. Although we experience the ordinary world in its true four-noble-truth nature, we see that even that is empty. According to the mahayana, reality is nonexistent, so there is a great emphasis on absolute truth, which is regarded as the highest truth. However, the picture of absolute truth in the various mahayana schools is somewhat cloudy and confused. Although they each have a different approach to the truth, and they might have seen just a fraction of the truth, nevertheless there is a sense of coming to a true understanding of absolute reality.

The bodhisattva comes to this understanding by means of studying sutra literature on the nature of reality and emptiness, in which the energy of reality is described in terms of compassion. This allows bodhisattvas to work with the experience of both emptiness and compassion, or shunyata and *karuna,* and by doing so they discover the perfect skillful means for dealing with reality. So the mahayana is about much more than just seeing critically; it includes the experience of openness, warmth, and compassion.

In the vajrayana, we are finally coming back or returning to the world. This is important and necessary. The vajrayana perspective is not one of entirely dwelling on the absolute truth or the absoluteness of reality, but it is based on paying more attention to the relative truth. According to the vajrayana, in order to understand the complete meaning of the whole thing—the *dharmadhatu,* or whatever you would like to call it—we have to understand and respect every aspect of truth.

The hinayana view of relative truth is too critical. So the saving grace for not being stuck with the hinayana focus on relative truth is the mahayana's transcendental truth. But having transcended the hinayana view of relative truth, we have never looked back toward the relative truth thoroughly and properly. Although we respected and studied reality in the mahayana, we missed something by rejecting relative truth halfway through. So tantra re-views the relative truth.

The vajrayana, or diamond vehicle, is powerful because it is derived from the tranquillity and readiness of the hinayana, and the purity and soft heart of the mahayana. When students have developed those qualities, the vajrayana becomes ready to launch its diamond ship into the oceans of those who are ready for it. At that point, students are prepared to practice the reality of the truth of Buddha's teaching.

## Revisiting Relative Truth, or Kündzop

The Tibetan term for relative truth is *kündzop,* and the term for absolute truth is *töndam. Tön* means "meaning" or "sense," and *dam* means "superior"; so *töndam* means "higher meaning" or "higher understanding." In terms of kündzop, *dzop* means "outfit," and *kün* means "all"; so *kündzop* means the "outfit of everything." It is similar to dressing up for Halloween: kündzop means that everything, the whole phenomenal world, is dressed up in your particular version.

But although kündzop is usually referred to as "relative truth," that may not be the most appropriate translation. "Relative" implies that relative truth is not self-sufficient, that it is dependent on something else that makes it relative. But in the vajrayana, we view kündzop as another form of absolute truth. We could almost say that kündzop is "primary truth" or "first truth." That is, with the experience of kündzop, the practitioner sees the phenomenal world from a certain distinct point of view, but the relativity of that point of view is not important. Kündzop is simply your outlook or your first glimpse of phenomena.

In the vajrayana, there is more of an emphasis on interest than on profound wisdom. On the mahayana level, profound wisdom is regarded as the working base, but here the working basis is simply interest. In tantra, the experience of interest is raised up almost to the level of sybaritic pleasure. You take a real interest in reality, and there is trust in what you see, what you hear, and what you do. That simple interest becomes highly significant. All kinds of tantric disciplines go along with this emphasis on relative or primary truth. The relative truth is emphasized, not in order to understand the absolute or ultimate, but to understand the relativity as the ultimate. It is to understand the relativity as the full truth, the complete truth, the primary truth, or kündzop.

## Brilliance and Sacredness

Vajrayana teaches that our existence as Joe Schmidt is no longer Joe Schmidt. According to the vajrayana, it is not that we have to transcend ego, but that ego does not exist. We know that ego does not exist because we realize what is known as vajra nature. Vajra nature is basically good. It is warm and living. So in the vajrayana, we are not studying or practicing a myth or a concept, but we are studying and practicing reality as it is, direct and obvious.

In vajrayana Buddhism, the quality of light or brilliance and the quality of sacredness are brought together. That sense of sacredness comes about from the continuity of tantra. When our body, speech, and mind are synchronized, we are fully here. Because we are fully here, we cannot help experiencing natural warmth, natural isness, and natural brilliance. Our experience of life is like gold, diamonds, and beautiful perfume put together. Light and warmth are connected with the idea of being true to yourself. If you are true to yourself—if you are here, with your body, speech, and mind joined together—that kind of reality begins to dawn on you.

Some traditions say that these kinds of experiences will happen to you after you die. They say that if you are a good boy or a good girl, when you go to heaven you will find such things. But in Buddhism, we say that you can find them right here, before you go to heaven, if there is such a thing as heaven at all. That richness, regal quality, and profundity, that beautiful fragrance, good feeling, and basic well-being, can occur by understanding vajrayana properly and fully.

Such experiences are transmitted from teacher to disciple by means of the teacher's skillfulness, precision, and accuracy. The teacher actually speaks the true dharma on the spot to those who are worthy of it and to those who are ready for it. I am afraid that I have to repeat this again and again and again: the teacher teaches the vajrayana to those who have been tamed and pacified by means of hinayana, and those who have become generous to themselves and others by means of mahayana.

According to the Buddha, the definition of *dharma* is "passionlessness." Passion refers to anxiety and anger of all kinds, and passionlessness means that when there is no anxiety and no anger, you become more clear-headed. You become clear and precisely on the dot. You become a good practitioner, a good listener, and a good student; and at the same time, you also find out whether your teacher is suitable for you or not.

## TAMING ONESELF

The fact that you are encountering these teachings means that you are karmically connected with the teachings of the Buddha. Your birth in a particular time and place has coincided with this presentation of the vajrayana, which is a wonderful coincidence. Therefore, you should place even greater importance on bringing yourself up as a person who pays attention to individual salvation and to taming yourself through shamatha and vipashyana. That is very important. By entering into the vajrayana, you are not departing from that approach and going to something more slick or sophisticated. In fact, you are going back. By understanding the vajrayana, you can begin to understand more about the basics of Buddhism. That is why we study the vajrayana. We appreciate that we have to build a solid foundation in order to have a golden roof.

## Discovering a Gigantic World of Awareness

In the vajrayana, along with faith and devotion, we find that relative bodhichitta manifests everywhere, and we also discover that absolute bodhichitta manifests everywhere. Basically, relative bodhichitta is benevolent compassion that is projected out in all directions, without exception. This kind of compassionate benevolence brings with it a notion of wakefulness, which is the product of vipashyana experience.

In vipashyana, awareness begins to be reflected throughout your life, throughout your day. You realize that the process of awareness is not based on your individual struggle or effort; rather, objects of awareness come to you and you acknowledge them. There is a gigantic world of awareness and mindfulness beginning to happen everywhere around you. That gigantic world continues whether you are sitting on the toilet, eating a meal, taking a shower, walking, driving, talking to people, doing business deals, or studying. So in whatever you do, an element of vipashyana, or awareness, is always taking place. That is a very important point for your understanding of the vajrayana.

## Natural Gentleness and Warmth

When you begin to develop a thorough and complete awareness of everything around you, wherever you are, that awareness is not purely mechanical; it also contains softness and warmth. It is as if the temperature around you rises slightly, so the whole area is always warm and pliable. Instead of eating cold food off a cold plate, you eat warm food off a warm plate. That kind of natural hospitality arises whenever a person has fully accomplished basic awareness practice. There is invitation everywhere, completely, so you begin to feel a quality of warmth and hospitality.

That hospitality and warmth automatically invites compassion and gentleness. Because of that warmth, you begin to trust situations more than you usually do. All of this is purely a product of your own mindfulness and awareness; it stems from your shamatha-vipashyana experience. As a practitioner, you begin to feel that, on the whole, the world is not filled with hostility. You see that in spite of its problems, the world is filled with possibilities of being genuine and opening up. So when we talk about devotion, we do not mean devotion to the teacher as someone who is on your side, as opposed to the rest of the world, which is attacking you: we mean a complete absence of warfare.

Because of that warmth, situations become pliable. You can sink your teeth into things without any problem or fear of the phenomenal world at all. Because such gentleness has developed in yourself, you begin to do a double take on the world: you begin to realize that there is warmth and gentleness in the phenomenal world as well as in yourself. You begin to realize that there is something very sacred about it.

## COMPLETE INVOLVEMENT

As we continue on our path, we commit ourselves to the vajrayana. We want to transform not only our state of thinking, our emotions, and our behavior patterns alone, but we want to change our entire existence altogether. We want to involve our body, speech, and mind completely in the approach to reality known as buddhadharma, the enlightened way of dealing with reality properly. Since we have come this far, we want to go further by committing our behavior patterns, our communication patterns, and our style of thinking.

The vajrayana will not give you a quick and sudden antidote of any kind; there has to be a base for it. Likewise, you might want to find a quick way to cure your sickness by getting a pill from a physician. But first, you have to be in the town where the physician lives; then you have to make an appointment with the physician; and having scheduled an appointment, you have to talk to the physician—and after all that, the physician might finally give you that good pill. In this analogy, being in that physician's country or town is like the hinayana; calling the physician and meeting with them is like the mahayana; and the physician finally giving you the pill is like the vajrayana. You cannot get a pill just by dialing the telephone; it is a three-stage process.

It may seem as if the vajrayana is doing the same things as the earlier yanas all over again, but in the vajrayana we are dealing much further with the negative and neurotic world. In the hinayana, the approach is to withdraw from the passion-and-aggression provoking world, and in the mahayana, it is to exchange self for other with tonglen practice. But in the vajrayana, we talk about vajra nature as an expression of being willing to relate more with the phenomenal world. Vajra nature is less a question of how high the state of existence is, and more about the workability of others. In the vajrayana, we are more than bodhisattvas; we work harder. We are willing to work with people's confusion more and more, further and further. So it is a much-expanded notion of the bodhisattva ideal.

Some people think the vajrayana approach is one in which you suddenly have an outburst of craziness, and manifest as a funny yogi or go naked in the middle of a big city. But that is complete nonsense. You may like that idea because there is not very much happening and the world is very dull. It is somewhat of a police state, and there are regulations and restrictions for everything. But you cannot expect any new entertainment to come out of your study of the vajrayana. You have to continue working from within.

4

# Uncovering Indestructible
# Goodness and Wakefulness

*In the vajrayana, your state of being is transformed into the highest level of shamatha mindfulness and meticulousness and the greatest vipashyana awareness put together. Your loving care for yourself and the greatest caring for others are put together, which allows you to perceive a greater world altogether.*

I N T H E vajrayana, you make a certain discovery—the discovery of buddha nature—and once you discover such a thing, you find that there are a great many possibilities, particularly in following the path. Buddha nature is twofold: one part is tenderness, and the other part is wisdom. Here, wisdom is discriminating-awareness wisdom, wisdom that can see situations very clearly and thoroughly. We could say that such higher awareness is the ultimate bodhichitta principle.

Traditionally, buddha nature is known as *sugatagarbha* in Sanskrit, or *dewar shek-pe nyingpo* in Tibetan, which means "gone beyond with bliss." Sugatagarbha, or actually the realization of sugatagarbha, is the starting point. You have a little glimpse of an experience that is very bright and luminous, and as you continue on the path, you begin to prolong or sustain that flash. You begin to realize that you are not so bad after all, but you have potential and you deserve some realization. So you begin to cheer up and smile.

## Vajra Nature

Out of the momentary experience of sugatagarbha, you also begin to develop what is known as vajra nature, or *dorje kham* in Tibetan. *Dorje,* or *vajra* in Sanskrit, means "indestructible" or "adamantine," and *kham* means a "realm" or a "state of being"; so *dorje kham* means "indestructible being" or "vajra nature." Vajra nature is a somewhat path-oriented concept, but at the same time it is a glimpse of your capability.

Vajra has many meanings. Vajra can refer to overcoming obstacles; and having overcome obstacles, it allows you to receive a glimpse of something indestructible and pure. Vajra can also mean awake and precise. Colloquially, it means not barking up the wrong tree. Precision, purity, luminosity, and clarity bring us to the realization of vajra-ness. When you take a photograph, if you do not focus properly on the object that you want to photograph, that photograph is non-vajra. Taking a vajra-like photograph is based on seeing the sharp corners and precise outlines. Vajra is as precise as a razor's edge.

## Workability

Out of vajra nature, the notion of workability, or *lesu rungwa,* develops. *Le* means "action," *su* means "for," and *rungwa* means "possible," "suitable," or "appropriate"; so *lesu rungwa* means "action that is possible." The total feeling is that there are possibilities. We could say that lesu rungwa is the proper way of working with meditation and postmeditation experiences. The point of lesu rungwa is that whatever we experience could become worthwhile and workable. This leads us to the idea of Samantabhadra.

## Complete Goodness / Samantabhadra

*Samantabhadra* is a Sanskrit term; in Tibetan it is *küntu sangpo. Küntu* means "completely," and *sangpo* means "good"; so *küntu sangpo* means "completely good." "Basic goodness" might be a rough translation of that particular state of being. Samantabhadra is connected with the ideas of sugatagarbha and vajra nature.

The state of being of küntu sangpo is inside of us and outside of us at the same time. When we look up at the sky, we find goodness, precision, cheerfulness, and purity existing there. When we look up at our

*The primordial Buddha, Samantabhadra, in union with Samantabhadri.*

ceiling, we could say the same thing; when we look at our rugs, we could say the same thing; when we look at the back of the person in front of us, we could say the same thing. When we eat food, when we drink, when we take a shower, when we rest, when we fall asleep, we could say there is basic goodness there. These are all expressions of küntu sangpo, or Samantabhadra.

## Five Types of Samantabhadra

There are five types of Samantabhadra: all-good path, all-good ornamentation, all-good teacher, all-good insight, and all-good realization.

ALL-GOOD PATH. The first type of Samantabhadra is *lam küntu sangpo*, which means the "path is all good." *Lam* means "path," and *küntu sangpo*, as before, means "completely good" or "all good"; so *lam küntu sangpo* means "all-good path." It refers to postmeditation experiences.

ALL-GOOD ORNAMENTATION. The second type of Samantabhadra is *gyen küntu sangpo*, which means "all-good ornamentation." *Gyen* means "ornamentation"; so *gyen küntu sangpo* means "all-good ornamentation."

There are lots of attributes or ornamentations connected with the possibility of attaining the küntu sangpo state, or the küntu sangpo environment. But the basic attribute is that no matter what occurs in apparent phenomena, we begin to experience that there are not really any obstacles; we begin to regard everything as a further step on the path.

ALL-GOOD TEACHER. The third type of Samantabhadra is *tönpa küntu sangpo*. *Tönpa* means "teacher" or the "shower of the path"; so *tönpa küntu sangpo* means "all-good teacher." This type of Samantabhadra provides us with such clarity and precision that the phenomenal world itself becomes a teacher to us. The more we fall down into our mud, confusion, and pollution, the more the phenomenal world becomes our teacher.

ALL-GOOD INSIGHT. The fourth type of Samantabhadra is called *rikpa küntu sangpo*. *Rikpa* means "insight"; so *rikpa küntu sangpo* means "all-good insight." With all-good insight, you are seeing things as they are, without any cloudiness or problem.

ALL-GOOD REALIZATION. The fifth type of Samantabhadra is *tokpa küntu sangpo*. *Tokpa* is "realization"; so *tokpa küntu sangpo* means "all-good realization." Tokpa küntu sangpo means not having any hesitation about situations. Even when you are confused, there is no hesitation about working with that confusion. If your automobile breaks down on the highway, instead of calling the mechanics to fix your car, you do it yourself. You fix your car and then drive it home. You realize that you are self-sufficient. You begin to perceive that your day-to-day life situations are not all that distant from the reality of Samantabhadra, which is all good.

## LETTING GO

Vajra nature and Samantabhadra come about naturally. They may come about by seeing the vajra master, but it is mainly a question of letting go. It depends on how much you preserve yourself as a samsaric person as opposed to how much you let go, so that you can face toward enlightenment. Letting go is relaxation, but it is a painful process as well. It is the tearing apart of the biggest part of yourself, which is the holding on to your ego. It is the tearing apart of your heart, tongue, and eyes, but at the same time it is pleasant. It is not a bad operation because nobody is at home, and there is no home; you are floating in space. That is why you can actually get into such a situation, why you can actually jump in. Nobody is there to jump in, but at the same time, there is a reference point. Ultimately, there is nobody, but we still seem to have somebody there.*

## DIAMOND WAKEFULNESS

Wakefulness is very important in vajrayana. Vajrayana wakefulness is indestructible, strong, and powerful, like the vajra scepter of Indra.†
It is indestructible, like a diamond. It cannot be defeated, fractured, or

---

* *Samantabhadra* and *Samantabhadri* depicted in inseparable union are the masculine and feminine embodiments of primordial buddhahood and the principle of fundamental goodness.

† Indra's *vajra scepter* is described as a magical and invincible weapon that, having destroyed the enemy, returns to Indra's hand like a boomerang.

destroyed. In the vajrayana, your state of being is transformed into the highest level of shamatha mindfulness and meticulousness and the greatest vipashyana awareness put together. Your loving care for yourself and the greatest caring for others are put together, which allows you to perceive a greater world altogether.

Vajrayana is not an ego trip. You have to give up a lot in order to become a vajra-like person. In order to become hardened like a diamond, you need to develop mindfulness, awareness, softness, and gentleness. This process is very much like the case history of a diamond itself. Originally a diamond is soft, but then it is compressed in the earth by environmental pressure. Vajrayana practice is like that sheer environmental pressure. Because vajra sanity is needed so badly, and because it is so rare, there is a need for that kind of pressure. We need to be compressed into diamond. In that way, as a vajrayana student, you cannot help but become diamond yourself. You could call yourself a diamond person.

Here, diamond means that you cannot be hampered or influenced by any form of klesha. You are completely free from kleshas because of your intense devotion to your vajra master and your intense practice throughout the three-yana journey. You have good personal manners as a result of hinayana, and you have good social manners as a result of mahayana, so you are fundamentally trustworthy. That two-yana journey is what makes vajrayana possible.

In order to be like a diamond, you have to understand indivisibility and egolessness. You have to understand that you cannot always have little kindnesses pumped in here and there, like intravenous feedings. Once you are a diamond, little things cannot be pumped into you; you are either there or not. You are strong and invincible, and because you are self-contained, you are ready to work for others. A diamond also has maitri and a great sense of humor. That quality of maitri and of humor shines right through. If you look at a diamond early in the morning, it shines, and if you look at it in the middle of the night, it still shines. A diamond is always glowing and glittering.

You may be uncertain whether you want to be a diamond, but if you look at hinayana discipline, you see that it already has that diamond-like quality. In the hinayana, you are trying to work with specks of dust and to overcome any dirt. Everything is crystal clear, pure, precise, and on the spot. Because of that diamond-like quality, the hinayana would be the best ground from which to hear the vajrayana. But the hinayana is coming up from below, which would be slightly difficult to maintain. The vajrayana is like a diamond ceiling coming down from above, or like a diamond umbrella, so there is a quality of confidence in vajrayana realization. With the vajrayana, you have a diamond umbrella shining in all directions, crystal clear, powerful, and strong.

To study the vajrayana, your mind has to be clear and precise. You have to be extremely disciplined. The further you go in the discipline, the further you understand. When you are less involved in the discipline, you tend to dream about the colorfulness of vajrayana and become clouded over, misty, and more confused. So if you want to hear the vajrayana properly and fully, a good suggestion is to go back to square one, to when you first encountered the dharma. You might discover greater things in that way. You should maintain your hinayana style of practice as if you were a newcomer, which in a sense you are; you are a newcomer to the vajra world. If you think you can bypass that kind of hinayana training, it will not work, and it will violate the mahayana as well. If you have managed to avoid the hinayana and mahayana, then you will not have the vajrayana either.

## SIDDHAS: VARIETIES OF TANTRIC LIFESTYLES

In the vajrayana, there are endless possibilities in terms of livelihood and lifestyle. For example, according to tradition, there were eighty-four *mahasiddhas,* who all had different occupations.* Some siddhas were drunkards who spent their life drinking; some were sleepers who spent their entire life sleeping; some were craftspeople who produced art; some were kings who ruled countries; some were pandits who taught in the universities; and some were robbers who stole things. But they all still practiced advanced tantric teachings, or mahamudra.†

---

* *Siddhas* are practitioners who have attained great spiritual power, or siddhi. Ordinary siddhis refer to various miraculous capabilities, and supreme siddhi is enlightenment. *Mahasiddhas,* or "great siddhas," have attained especially great powers. For more on the eighty-four mahasiddhas, see Abhayadatta, *Buddha's Lions: The Lives of the Eighty-Four Siddhas,* trans. James B. Robinson (Berkeley, Calif.: Dharma Publishing, 1979).

† For a discussion of *mahamudra* ("great symbol"), see part II, "The Tantric Journey: Mahamudra."

In tantra, there is a quality of intelligence that lets you relate with the phenomenal world directly and simply. You engage in Buddhist practice in order to work with your mental fixations. Like the siddhas, you can actually use whatever lifestyle you have as a practice and discipline. You do not just work in the factory for the hell of it; you do it because of your commitment to tantric practice. You do it fully and with dignity, so you become a good worker. Whatever you do, because your tantric involvement has brought you into that particular situation, and because you feel that it is your practice, you learn enormously from it. You are committed to it. So everything is a commitment; the whole thing is your practice. Otherwise, how would your actions be different from the ordinary aggression and passion that takes place all over the universe?

Once people are more realized, they tend to retire from the world. However, there is a need for familiarity with samsara, and according to the samsaric world you have to relate with a trade or profession. Siddhas did not necessarily want to be henchmen or pimps or whatever, but they were encouraged to do so as their practice. They did not particularly enjoy doing such work all that much. It was more of a pain in the neck than pleasurable. All the siddhas were willing to give up their jobs after a while, but the masters said, "Oh no, you're not going to do that. You go back to weaving, and you go back to making arrows. You go back to hunting, and you go back to fishing." So even people who were already realized continued to use those lifestyles rather than retiring from the world.

For tantric students, whether you are a good calligrapher or a good draftsperson, you are actually connecting with the world. And at that instant, there is some link to what you might eventually be, in terms of attaining spiritual power, or siddhi. That connection has to be made constantly. Whatever lifestyle you choose—if you decide to become a prostitute, a businessperson, or a thief—you cannot say later that you will not do it anymore. You have to stick with it for a long, long time. You need to have the strength and perseverance to do it properly, in an enlightened way, so that you can help people rather than harming them. That is a very big obligation, an enormous obligation, and it is not easy.

The siddhas of the past lived in the world in an ordinary way. They had jobs and they maintained their businesses, but they still found time to engage in vajrayana practice as well. Following that lifestyle is not so different from what we might do at this point. In the modern world, we could do more or less the same thing, alternating tantric practice and daily life. That may sound fun, but before you really get into it, it is a great deal of hassle. It is a pain. But the fact that you have physical or psychological pain is a sign of stimulation or circulation, a sign that your metabolism is functioning properly.

The inspiration in tantra comes from a vaster sense of things, larger or smaller. Small means large, if it is minute enough; and large means small, if it is large enough. You might ask what is the point, but there is no point and there are no expectations. You are not trying to make a profit, and it is not like the stock market. Instead, things begin to open and close simultaneously. They get wide and big and spacious, and they get minute and tiny constantly. That kind of pulsation goes on all the time in your life. As long as you do not label it as depression or excitement, when you have a minute experience, it is the largest vision that you could ever get, and when you have the largest experience you could ever have, it is micro-cosmic. So you cannot miss the boat; the boat is always there.

# 5

# The Multifaceted Diamond Path

*Altogether the vajrayana brings concentrated possibilities of wisdom. Such wisdom is not dependent on any other factors; it is naked wisdom itself. This wisdom is very general, and at the same time, very precise.*

I N SPEAKING of vajrayana, one cannot give a straight talk without making references to something else at the same time; it is a complete network. That is somewhat of a problem, but we try to do our best. There are many different ways of looking at the vajrayana, and a variety of traditional definitions exist. The vajrayana is referred to as tantra or *tantrayana, mantrayana, vidyadharayana,* fruition yana, *upayayana, guhyayana, dharanayana,* yana of luminosity, and imperial yana. These various categories are not particularly a hierarchy; they are simply different ways of looking at things for the sake of convenience.

## VAJRAYANA

In Tibetan, the vajrayana is called *dorje thekpa.* In Sanskrit *vajra,* or *dorje* in Tibetan, is "diamond-like" or "indestructible," and *yana* or *thekpa* is "vehicle"; so *vajrayana,* or *dorje thekpa,* means the "vajra vehicle" or "indestructible vehicle."

The vajrayana is known as the quick path to enlightenment. Such a path cannot be hampered by our general tendency to edit the world or our perceptions in terms of what we like or dislike, or to wander around within our state of mind, which is called discursive thought.

Entering the vajrayana is quite similar to the early level of entering the Buddhist path. When you take the refuge vow, you vow to enter the Buddhist path without being sidetracked by any other disciplines. You make a decision to follow the nontheistic tradition of Buddhism alone. Similarly, the vajrayana is a discipline that does not allow sidetracks. Rather than following any other cultures or traditions, you simply maintain yourself in the vajrayana discipline alone.

In the vajrayana, skillful means and knowledge are not regarded as separate, but as working together inseparably. This takes place by understanding sacredness: sacredness of vision and form, sacredness of communication, sacredness of the world, and sacredness of consciousness and the mind. By joining knowledge and skillful means, your body, speech, and mind can be coordinated—mind with body, body with speech, and speech with mind—to create the threefold vajra principle of vajra body, vajra speech, and vajra mind. This threefold principle is comprised of indestructibility, attributed to body; lucidity and a communicating or echoing quality, attributed to speech; and a penetrating, clear, concentrated, and shifty quality, attributed to the mind.

Vajrayana practice brings those three principles together, whether in formal visualization practice or in formless practice. Whatever it may be, they always come together. You see that solidness also speaks, that speech also thinks, that mind is also body, that body is also speech, that speech is also mind, and that mind is also speech. So there is a oneness to those three principles. The whole thing becomes very cohesive, workable, and intelligent, and at the same time somewhat efficient and enlightening. This way of working with the three principles together is only presented in the vajrayana tradition; that is where it is put into practice. So the three vajra principles are combined and made into a vehicle or working basis. That is why it is known as vajrayana.

## TANTRA OR TANTRAYANA

The vajrayana is also known as tantra or tantrayana. In Sanskrit *tantra* means "continuity," and *yana*, again, is "vehicle"; so *tantrayana* is the "vehicle of continuity." In Tibetan, tantrayana is called *gyü thekpa. Gyü* means "thread" or "continuity," and *thekpa* means "vehicle"; so *gyü thekpa* also means the "vehicle of continuity." *Tantra* is also a term for vajrayana texts, so it is similar to the Sanskrit word *sutra.*

*Vajradhara ("Vajra Holder"), the primordial Buddha.*

Tantra is the thread that runs right through the hinayana, mahayana, and vajrayana simultaneously. You never break that continuity. Meeting the elder, meeting the spiritual friend, and meeting the vajra master are all the same. You are meeting the same person, and you have the same kind of devotion throughout. You also have the same kind of sympathy for others—the same sympathy and the same sanity. So vajrayana is an expansion and continuation of greater sanity and greater sympathy.

In order to experience or have a glimpse of the vajrayana, you usually need to refer back to your hinayana and mahayana practices. On top of that, you need to understand and appreciate the aftereffect or fruition of those yanas. Then you are naturally and fully following the teachings of the Buddha.

Tantra means that the stream of your existence—your body, speech, and mind—has been linked together by this particular teaching, so you find that from beginning to end, there is a unity and a continuity. There is always a follow-up: things are never choppy, and the subject never changes. You continue with what you have, and what you already have is good enough. Therefore, we can work with you—including your extreme neurosis, your seeming neurosis, and any other problems you might have. We can actually handle them and work with them.

Gyü is continuous, like the thread that runs through your *mala* beads or like the fishing line that runs from the fisher to the fish. It is a continual process. What is the continuity? Very simply, it is that you begin to realize that your basic being, the means to develop your goal, and the goal itself are connected. That is the meaning of tantra, that they are all connected. They do not come separately: your basic characteristics are not separate from your goal, and the goal cannot exist without the path and the origin.

On the ground level, gyü means that the habitual patterns of body, speech, and mind are included as one continuous whole, without being broken down into separate things. On the path level, gyü refers to the continuous application of methods and techniques in order to overcome basic ego. Once the first technique has been introduced, successive techniques follow one after another quite predictably in a linear style, and those techniques and methods are easy to practice and easy to understand. The fruition aspect of gyü is that it gives you the realization of who you are and what you are. This is called attaining the state of Vajradhara, the final realization of the highest level of vajrayana.*

So the ground is who you are and what you are; the path is what you can do about it, or how you can accomplish your inheritance; and the fruition is that these two are linked together. With the fruition aspect, you are not changing yourself into somebody else, but you are simply becoming what you are. You realize what you are and who you are,

---

* According to the Kagyü tradition, *Vajradhara* ("vajra holder") is the primordial, or *dharmakaya,* buddha. He is blue in color with his arms crossed in front of his chest, holding a vajra and ghanta, symbolizing the inseparability of skillful means and wisdom.

which is a delight. There is continuity in that, and there is also continuity on top of that final fruition. At that level, you can combine your body with the body of the *tathagatas*, or realized ones, your speech with the speech of the tathagatas, and your mind with the mind of the tathagatas. Therefore, there is continuity from the beginning to the end. It is a seamless web.

The idea of continuity is like our life. We could say that our infancy, teenage period, young adulthood, middle age, and old age are all related with each other, as one continual growing-up process. Similarly, in tantra there is continuity because consciousness or awareness cannot be broken down into different departments, but moments of consciousness are all connected with one other. Therefore, when you have your first glimpse of fruition, you cannot just regard that as a warning. As soon as you tread on the path, you occasionally have an idea of how the fruition might be. You cannot disregard that, and you cannot view it as not really being the fruition. Continual continuity takes place.

The basic quality of the vajrayana teachings altogether is that there is a link from the origin, or yourself, to the path; and from the path, there is also a link to what might be. If you are planting an orchard, you have at least seen a photograph or a movie of an apple orchard or orange trees, even if you have not had the pleasure of actually touching the fruits, eating them, and experiencing them. You have some idea of what having a good time in the orchard might be. Because you have this particular idea in your mind, that inspiration acts as the path. It is not materialistic or corny or stupid, but just a vision you have had.

So your first glimpse of tantra includes your impression of what tantra might actually be like. It is like the impression you might have of your becoming a corpse in a coffin. In thinking about being a corpse in a coffin, your identification with what that might be like is happening right here and now; so in that sense, you are a moving corpse. Likewise, although it is just a bud, a bud is still a real flower; it is still a part of the flowering process.

This sense of reality is always there, although you cannot really grasp at that reality as you would like. It is not like grabbing the railing on the fire escape when the house is on fire. In tantra, you have a real glimpse as to what it might be like to become an awakened person. There is a faint warning or faint glimpse of that taking place constantly, which is very interesting and very powerful.

In this way, tantra is unlike the other yanas, which talk about how fertile you are and how much potential you have. They can say good things about you; they can say that you have potential. But so what? In the vajrayana, we talk about what you are, not what you are not. Talking about what you actually are is a very direct and actually lethal suggestion—and at the same time, it is inspiring. This is why getting into vajrayana practice is symbolized by a snake getting into a bamboo pipe. When the snake enters the tube, it can either face upward or downward. That is, you either go directly down or you attain enlightenment all at once. There is no ambiguity. It is very direct, very simple, and very meaningful. Tantra means business, and there is power behind it to support you either way, whichever takes place. Tantra is continuous. It is real and direct and very personal.

## Mantrayana

In the Tibetan tradition, when referring to the vajrayana, we usually use the term *ngakkyi thekpa. Ngak* means "mantra," *kyi* means "of," and *thekpa* means "yana"; so *ngakkyi thekpa* means "mantrayana."

This term is actually much more widely used in traditional circles than gyü, or tantra. If you say you are practicing gyü, that means you are practicing the texts of tantra; but if you say you are practicing ngakkyi thekpa or mantrayana, that means you are actually practicing the yogic traditions of vajrayana, the vajrayana itself. In the Tibetan understanding of the Sanskrit term *mantra, man* means "mind," and *tra* means "to protect"; so *mantra* means "protecting the mind." So the idea of mantra is to protect one's mind from obstacles; that is the basic definition.

Sometimes the path moves under you rather than your vehicle moving, and sometimes the path stops and you have to move. The vajrayana vehicle has nine forward gears.* It does not have a reverse gear and it does not have brakes; once you get in, your vehicle moves forward. It does have a steering wheel, thank heavens, and it doesn't need gas. It is very tough, almost like a tank. Therefore, it is known as mind protection, or mantrayana.

---

* A reference to the nine yanas of the Tibetan Buddhist path: shravakayana, pratyekabuddhayana, mahayana, kriyayogayana, upayogayana, yogayana, mahayogayana, anuyogayana, and atiyogayana.

## Mind Protection

When we say "mind," we are usually referring to the mind of emotions, the mind of subconscious gossip, the mind concerned with holding one's own territory. We mean the mind connected with taking care of the usual kingdom of one's ego and the subsidiary politics that revolve around it. So when we say that the mind is protected by mantra, it may sound as if what is being protected is an egomaniac, and what we would end up with is an egomaniac on a power trip, who does not know who they are. But the mind that mantra protects is not that mind of territoriality; what is protected is the intelligence alone.

When the mind is actually worked with and related to, what is protected is its intelligence and cohesiveness. So mind protection does not mean reinforcing the mind's defensiveness, but protecting its basic understanding and intelligence. However, while mantra is referred to as protection, it is not really protection as such. The practitioner of the mantra and the mantra itself work together as a kind of shell that protects the mind. So mantra does not magically protect the mind, but the protection comes naturally.

## Secrecy

This quality of protection is related with the understanding of secrecy, and the question of how to present the vajrayana teachings properly. The vajrayana should not be presented in an outrageous way or with a salesperson's approach, where you put out publicity about your secrets and say: "Join us in our secret mind-protection circle." When unskillful teachers on this continent have tried to proclaim the vajrayana in that way, it has been an absolute failure and deserving of punishment. So we have to use the right approach when we are presenting mind protection as a secret teaching.

Why is the vajrayana secret? It is very simple. The vajrayana is so secret that nobody can understand it other than by being tuned in to it properly. This is so much the case that traditionally it is referred to as self-secret. You might decide to ignore this quality and say that what you are doing is fine. But you get so involved with doing fine that you lose track of the message, and consequently you get attacked or killed. That is the kind of secret it is.

The vajrayana is secret, and at the same time it is a proclamation. It is the proclamation that brings the secret message, although there are no passwords or little chitchats going on through intelligence agents. If you understand it, you understand it; and if you do not understand it, you are liable to be extinguished. If you do not understand the vajrayana, even though you have studied it, you will be kicked out. But it is not only a question of understanding. The idea is that because you have listened to the vajrayana and misunderstood it, the vajrayana has turned out to be too lethal for you, so you should be kicked out to save your life.

## Protection from Comfort

At this point, there is still a need for protection from religiosity. There is a need for protection from too much piety. There is also a need for protection from the feeling that you have attained something, and therefore you do not have to give anything up. That is precisely why, when the Buddha taught the shunyata teachings, a lot of the arhats had heart attacks.

So mantra is protection from being comfortable in a given teaching. Once a teaching is received, whatever yana it may be, you might find that it is very comfortable and you can relax in it. That becomes a problem. With each new yana, you may have to give up the feeling of protection or security of the previous yanas. And you need to keep doing this until you have actually exhausted everything completely, until you no longer need to rely on any form of security. So even though the yanas are vehicles, you have to abandon those vehicles. You have to get into a diamond jet at some point.

## A Spell or Incantation

Mantra can also mean a spell or incantation—a positive or healthy spell. With this kind of spell, you are bringing the world together by means of one utterance. One thought brings all thoughts into one, and when you have that one thought, it liberates everything. One word elucidates everything; one thought, one perception, frees you from neurosis.

We usually recite mantras in Sanskrit, as opposed to translating them into English. For one thing, many mantras do not make any sense, so translating them would be pointless. Likewise, in visualization practice, we do not dress a deity such as Vajradhara in a suit and tie, but in his own medieval Indian costume, making primordial archetypal sounds, holding archetypal symbols, and wearing archetypal clothes.

Some people talk about mantras as vibration, but I do not think a mantra is just a vibration of sound. It is a psychological state, and each mantra has its own meaning. Mantras are not particularly objects of scholarship and the analytical process. Many mantras are simply ono-matopoeic enlightened sound. If your tantric deity, or *yidam,* burps, you might hear it as the syllable HUM.

There are also a lot of onomatopoeic sounds and meanings in ordinary language, but none of them are particularly threatening. They are usually very silly or playful. But you could develop threatening sounds or creative sounds as well, which is what is done with mantras. What do such mantras say that is so lethal, so powerful, and so dangerous? They do not make any conventional sense; therefore, they are powerful. A mantra changes your psychological state at once, as soon as you hear that particular sound. The closest thing to mantra I have heard is the howling of coyotes. Coyotes are constantly making mantric sounds. During certain parts of the day they do their tantric practice, or *sadhana,* and you are haunted by it.

## Joining Wisdom and Joy

Another definition of mantra is that it is the joining of wisdom and joy, or insight and bliss. Through that quality of mantra, we relate with magical powers; so mantra could be said to be the magical aspect of this world. We could say that tantra refers to the activity that takes place, and mantra refers to our state of mind in relation to that. One word for mantra is *slogan,* and another is *proclamation.* Mantra is also described as the combination of great pleasure and big mind, or in Sanskrit, *mahasukha* and *jnana.* According to tradition, great bliss and great mind (or wisdom) can work together.

## Overcoming Frivolity

The technique of mantra is continuous, linear, and ongoing. It is like you are on a long boat ride: you cannot suddenly get off and go to shore, but you have to flow along the whole way. That kind of continuous technique brings a quality of boredom. All vajrayana practices work that way. It is like your life: you actually cannot jump back and forth in it. Mantra is like eating a long meal without a break.

We usually do not want to be in one place all the time. We get bored so easily, and we are impatient. From that, we also become unreasonable. We demand so much from our life that we get divorced over and over, hundreds of times—at least we do so psychologically. We would like to change scenes all the time. The setting-sun society provides for that restlessness. There are all sorts of programs on television; there are all sorts of brands of cigarettes, in case you don't like your old brand; there are all sorts of places to go, new things to do, new cars to try. Everything is provided for you, so that you can say, "Wow! Look at that! Isn't that something!" You can always get into the next situation, and you go on that way constantly. There is a fear of being with yourself, which means that fundamentally you do not like yourself. You are always trying to escape from yourself, so you try some other occupation, some other entertainment, so that hopefully you can forget yourself for a while, as if you were somewhere else.

When you begin to look into your mind, you see that mind consists of every possible way of breaking the linear or evolutionary process of your growth. You are constantly jumping around all over the place, trying to get rid of any possible learning situation. For instance, you might suddenly come up with a bright idea and think, "Yesterday doesn't mean anything to me. I feel different today." But then you think, "This morning I felt one way, but now I feel different." Mind consists of that kind of fickleness. You are not willing to live with yourself at all.

When you study your childhood, teens, adulthood, and old age—or even when you study your yesterday, this morning, midmorning, noon, early afternoon, late afternoon, and evening—you usually do not actually relate to all that as one linear situation, although you have to go through quite an ordeal just trying to live through all those things. Instead, there is a kind of choppiness. That choppiness allows you to invite obstacles, because you are not regarding your whole practice, your whole life, as one piece, one gradual process, one big thing. That choppy or fickle mind is an obstacle in the vajrayana, and that same statement would be quite true even in the hinayana and mahayana. We like to pinpoint and celebrate, like a bird suddenly landing on a worm, eating it, then flying away, and that's that. And then we look out for the next worm. We do this all the time. That is mind's habitual pattern, and it is an obstacle.

Mantra protects your mind from that cheap scale of existence. It protects you so that you can relate to the whole process of your life as one piece, one theme. You can appreciate it and understand that there is a pattern to it. This is like the difference between a collage and an oil painting or watercolor. The collage approach is choppy; you just cut out some pictures and paste them on. In contrast, in a watercolor or oil painting, you start from the beginning with a sketch and then you apply your colors, so there is a sense of continuity. With such continuity, you are conducting your life, not with opportunism, but with grace and understanding. That is how mantra works. It protects the mind so that you can conduct your life fully and properly, and not just jump impulsively into situations from one minute to another.

The approach of working on your frivolity seems to be one of the definitions of tantra. People might think tantra is a very impulsive practice, with lots of drinking and lots of sex. They might think that you just say your mantras occasionally, here and there, and you have your little shrine setup, and everything is swell. But in fact, tantra is completely the opposite of that. Tantra is not frivolity, but seriousness with tremendous humor. This humor is brought out by compassion. The combination of gentleness, softness, and lust brings out and increases your sense of humor, so it becomes very simple and natural.

## Connecting with Magical Power

The tantric approach could be seen to have developed as a way to understand phenomena and oneself through the application of mantra, mudra, and various other techniques. It could be seen as a way to achieve magical power over the phenomenal world and oneself. Magical power in this case refers to knowing the sensitive focal points in the phenomenal world and in your own psychological world, which is saying the same thing, in a sense. You are able to pinpoint the stronghold of phenomenal power, the power the phenomenal world has been imposing on you for years and aeons and kalpas. You are a victim of that power, but finally you are able to pinpoint the heart or the brain of it by means of the application of mantras, mudras, visualizations, and so forth.

Mantra is the means or method of tantra. Your mind has developed many facets and sidetracks, but once you realize that and tune in to vajrayana practice, you begin to save yourself from circling or swimming

74

around in samsara or samsaric mind. At the same time, your mind has all kinds of reference points; it sees and perceives everything at once. Mantra protects that intelligence and understanding. So mantra could be described as protecting the intelligence of the mind, which is able to see the sensitive points of the phenomenal world.

The repetition of a mantra is not such a big deal. What *is* a big deal is the idea of protecting the mind, the intelligence, the buddha nature, that essential element that exists within us. Therefore, the vajrayana is known as mantrayana.

## VIDYADHARAYANA

Another definition of vajrayana is *vidyadharayana* in Sanskrit, or *rigdzin thekpa* in Tibetan. *Rigdzin* or *vidyadhara* means "wisdom holder"; so *rigdzin thekpa* is the "yana or vehicle of wisdom holders."

This definition is based on the understanding of visualizations and deities as expressions of ourselves and our personal energies and potentials. Because we identify with the particular deities that were given to us by our vajra master as expressions of ourselves, such expressions are met properly. We finally make friends with our own shadow. This removes our frustration, because we are finally able to speak to ourselves properly. This brings greater joy, not because everything is okay and fine, or because we no longer have problems or irritations, but because it brings a kind of orgasm.

In this situation, meeting your mind does not take place through somebody else meeting your mind. Instead, it is a meeting of your own mind with yourself, which cuts away all kinds of paraphernalia. The embellishment of trying to protect yourself goes away, so nakedness begins to dawn. You discover that you are naked, that you are your own expression, and that you need no embellishment, no clothing, and no ornaments. You are meeting your own good old self in a very special way, in a tantric way. You see yourself as you are very directly. Usually what happens with electricity when you put two wires together is that you get a short circuit. The fuse box cannot handle the power, it is too embarrassing, so the fuse box has to create a blackout. But in this case, in trusting your buddha nature, you have a stronger fuse box: you have vajra nature, a vajra fuse box. Therefore, your mind cannot shy away from itself; it cannot create a blackout or short-circuit anything at all.

That non-short-circuiting is known as *rikpa* in Tibetan, or *vidya* in Sanskrit, which means "intelligence." *Rik* means "perceiving," "seeing," or "touching," and *pa* makes it a noun; so *rikpa* means "that which perceives." In Sanskrit, rikpa is *vidya,* which can also be translated as "science" or "awareness."

Rikpa or vidya is self-existing conviction or understanding that never shies away from itself, and tantric practitioners are known as vidyadharas, the holders of that particular knowledge. Therefore, the vajrayana could also be known as the vidyadharayana, the vehicle for the great knowledge holders or crazy wisdom holders.

## FRUITION YANA

Another term for vajrayana is fruition yana, or *drebü thekpa. Drebü* means "fruition"; so *drebü thekpa* means the "fruition vehicle."

Generally, we start from the origin or the beginning, the root or the cause. But the approach of vajrayana is entirely different. Instead of beginning by studying the root or the seed, we study the end result as the inspiration, the way, and the starting point.

There are all kinds of ways by which we think we could make ourselves sane. It could be by swimming, racing horses, or cooking. There are endless ways to go about it. Some people think that if they play golf in an enlightened way, they could practice tantra, or if they ski in an enlightened way, they could attain complete enlightenment. The mahayana schools, with their *paramita* practices of transcendent virtue, have fallen into the same problem. They think that if you only practice your transcendental this or that, or if you understand the shunyata principle, you will be okay. In those kinds of approaches, we are stuck with our means being more important than the meaning behind the whole thing.

It is like planting a flower. The approach of starting with the seed is probably all right for the time being. But in order to be inspired to plant your flower seed, you first need to have seen a flower that has already blossomed. Then you will be inspired to plant the seed of such a flower. When you plant a seed, you want to know if you are going to get an iris or a chrysanthemum. You need to have a glimpse of the fruition; otherwise, if you just see a few little pellets in a bottle, it doesn't mean anything. If someone tells you, "It's going to become a good flower one day," all you can say is, "Sure, if you say so. But I have never seen a flower." That approach does not make any sense, and it requires enormous blind faith.

The idea of vajrayana as fruition yana is that you have already experienced what you might attain. Some glimpse has already developed, so the whole thing is not just a myth. The mahayana approach is seed oriented, and the vajrayana approach is blossom oriented. Vajrayana students have at least seen films of beautiful flowers, or photographs or drawings of them. Otherwise, they would not commit themselves into making big gardens, not knowing what kind of flowers they were going to get out of it. Therefore, there is enormous emphasis put on the result. So in the vajrayana, the seductive result is the inspiration, rather than the funky beginning. Therefore, the vajrayana could be seen as the yana of fruition.

## UPAYAYANA

Another term for vajrayana is *upayayana* in Sanskrit, or *thapkyi thekpa* in Tibetan. *Thap* means "skillful means"; so *thapkyi thekpa* is the "vehicle of skillful means."

In the mahayana, you learn to develop attitudes and behaviors based on the transcendent virtues, or paramitas. But up to this point, none of the lower yanas have attempted to present a true and complete psychological geography. There is no suggestion, other than in tantra, of tapping energy in unusual ways, such as by relating with the elements or the different emotions. So in tantra, you are part of the whole setup; you can see the whole psychological geography. Therefore, the lower yanas are inferior to tantra, because they fail to present greater skillful means. That is why tantrayana is called upayayana, the yana of skillful means.

## GUHYAYANA

Vajrayana is also referred to as the *guhyayana* in Sanskrit, or *sang-we thekpa* in Tibetan. *Sang-we* means "hidden" or "secret"; so *sang-we thekpa* means the "secret yana." When you try to understand or comprehend tantra, if you do not have enough preparation for it, it is self-secret. It is secret because in order to understand it, a personal process of ripening and freeing has to take place; otherwise, it does not make any sense, and the whole thing becomes gibberish.

Tantric teachings are sometimes deliberately kept secret from those who have not heard the message of vajrayana, because of the danger of confusing people and disrupting their path. People may think that the tantric path is outrageous, or even insane, which completely freaks them out; or they may think that because such an outrageously enlightened idea exists, their own path does not seem to make any sense. They may begin to think their own path is too limited. So the tantric path is both self-secret and deliberately kept secret at the same time, which seems to be absolutely necessary. Therefore, it is often known as sang-we thekpa, the secret yana.

## DHARANAYANA

Another term for vajrayana is *dharanayana* in Sanskrit. *Dharana* means "that which holds together" or "that which fastens things together," and *yana* again means "vehicle"; so *dharanayana* means the "binding or holding-together vehicle."

In dharanayana, what is held together are the body, speech, and mind of the practitioner. They are bound together, so there is no looseness and no confusion. Whenever you practice dharanayana, it holds your basic being together. It is like being a clean and well-dressed person who has taken a bath or shower and whose shoes and shirt and clothes all fit.

As the thread that binds together body, speech, and mind, dharanayana is similar to the idea of tantra. When your mind is synchronized with your speech and your body, it actually makes a bridge. Practices such as *oryoki*, or mindful eating, and vajrayana preliminary practices—such as the 100,000 prostrations and 100,000 mantras—are designed to synchronize body, speech, and mind so that there is no room for subconscious gossip, subconscious innuendo, or subconscious distractions. As the famous Zen saying goes: "When we sit, we sit, and when we eat, we eat." In fact, all of Buddhism teaches us how to synchronize body, speech, and mind thoroughly and fully as a way to overcome chaos and extend a sense of basic goodness.

## YANA OF LUMINOSITY

The vajrayana is also referred to as the yana of luminosity, or the self-perpetuating yana, because it does not require headlights or taillights.

In itself, the vajrayana is glorious and indestructibly self-sufficient. In Tibetan, the yana of luminosity is called *ösel dorje thekpa*. *Ö* means "luminous," *sel* means "clear," and *dorje thekpa*, again, is "vajrayana"; so *ösel dorje thekpa* is the "clear, luminous, indestructible vehicle."

Altogether *ösel* means a clear sense of existence, perpetually existing without beginning or end. So ösel is very much connected with self-existence, self with a small *s*. But this does not mean to say that you must have a self so that you can exist. Self-existence is a natural form of perpetualness, which you can experience through the practice of shamatha, or vipashyana, or tonglen, or for that matter whatever practice you are doing. It is natural and very basic self-existence.

## IMPERIAL YANA

Finally, the vajrayana is referred to as the imperial yana. It is a coming down rather than a going up, like relating with snowfall or rain, as opposed to relating with grass, flowers, and trees. Coming down is much more immediate and personal. The imperial yana is associated with the view that postmeditation practice is important. So the vajrayana actually works much more with postmeditation experiences of all kinds.

Altogether the vajrayana brings concentrated possibilities of wisdom. Such wisdom is not dependent on any other factors; it is naked wisdom itself. This wisdom is very general, and at the same time, very precise.

6

# Seven Aspects of Vajrayana:
# The Space before First Thought

*You already developed benevolence in the mahayana, but in this case you develop vajra bodhichitta, adamantine bodhichitta. It is adamantine because there are no cracks in your awareness or in your understanding of the vajrayana. Your conviction and pride in the vajrayana are of one piece. It is a diamond-like situation. There are no cracks where dirt could get in, so there is total awareness happening all the time. It is one piece, which is very precise and good, healthy and wholesome. Therefore, you are no longer subject to obstacles or hazards of any kind.*

ACCORDING TO Nagarjuna,* the vajrayana can be understood in terms of seven aspects. All seven are based on the idea of the space before first thought, on perception that does not allow the secondary cognitive mind to take place. That is, they are based on the first cognitive mind, which is actually no mind; they are based on mind that has not formed, and therefore has the quality of first shock.

---

* *Nagarjuna* (150–250 CE) was a renowned Buddhist logician and philosopher. According to Chögyam Trungpa Rinpoche, although ordinarily we know of Nagarjuna as a mahayana theologian, in the vajrayana tradition, Nagarjuna is known as a siddha and a great tantric practitioner.

The seven aspects of vajrayana are also based on the idea that the vajrayana is superior to hinayana and mahayana, and they are based on the nontheistic approach of paying further attention to relative truth, or kündzop. Basically speaking, the vajrayana approach to the emptiness of the phenomenal world is the same as that of the mahayana wisdom teachings, or *prajnaparamita*, but its view of the emptiness of self or individuality is different. In the vajrayana, the emptiness of individuality is seen not as emptiness alone, but in terms of mahasukha, or great joy. When the perceiver of shunyata has experienced great joy, it automatically makes the phenomenal world somewhat more cheerful than in the pure shunyata approach. Some kind of dance exists.

## MARKED WITH SAMANTABHADRA

The first aspect of vajrayana is that our vajrayana perspective is marked with Samantabhadra, which means that there is a quality of totality and basic goodness. Our perspective is that all dharmas, and the existence of oneself and others, are included in the *dharmakaya;*\* therefore, we find that the whole of phenomena is no longer subject to discussion about whether it is for us or against us.

With this aspect, we develop an understanding of the phenomenal world based on the union of emptiness and bliss. So when we look at a traffic light, for instance, we perceive its practical purpose; but at the same time, we perceive it with a sense of play, humor, and inner joy. When the two meet, there is genuine and good communication taking place. We begin to have reports coming back to us from the phenomenal world. For instance, when we see a red light, we put on our car brakes, and when we see a green or amber light, we go. In everything we do, including wiping our bottoms with toilet tissue, genuine communication is taking place. On one hand, that communication is based on the idea of total emptiness. On the other hand, there is also brilliance and joy and embryonic celebration taking place all the time in whatever we do in our life. Everything is included.

---

\* The *dharmakaya* ("dharma body") refers to enlightenment itself, the unoriginated primordial mind of the Buddha.

## POSSESSING ADHISHTHANA

The second aspect of vajrayana is that it possesses great blessings, or *adhishthana* in Sanskrit. The Tibetan word for adhishthana is *chinlap.* *Chin* means "atmosphere," a type of atmosphere that is overwhelming, and *lap* means "coming to you"; so *chinlap* means "being confronted by an overwhelming atmosphere." That is to say, you are receptive to that heavy atmosphere, and therefore you are "engolloped" by it. You are overwhelmed or swallowed up by it.

Chinlap has the connotation of producing heat. It is like entering a very clean room that is decorated with lots of gold and brocade, and in which a very powerful person is presiding. When you go into that particular room, you feel overwhelmed by the gold and brocade and everything. You feel hot. There is an overwhelming quality, and there is the potential that you might actually get melted on the spot. So chinlap, or adhishthana, is that kind of heavy atmosphere.

When we talk about blessings, we are not talking in terms of tokenism. It is not like saying that when you are touched with holy water, you are made kosher for no reason. In this case, the idea of blessings is that you are overwhelmed and engulfed, which has the connotation of mugginess. If it is very muggy and there is a lot of moisture in the atmosphere, when you walk outside you feel gobbled up by it; you feel heavy and heated. If you take a positive attitude toward that, you might feel that you are being made wholesome. But if you do not take a positive attitude, you just feel very sweaty. This kind of blessing is actually a quite different idea of blessing than that of the theists.

When you walk into an atmosphere of chinlap, you are exasperated throughout your entire being. You find yourself involved in that particular world because there is no other way. That is the vajrayana attitude toward blessings: you have no choice. You are swallowed up by the heavy atmosphere, and it is very full, very proper, and very good. Obviously, this quality of vajrayana arises from a vajrayana practitioner's previous training of hinayana and mahayana, as well as from the tremendous dignity that the practitioner possesses. Vajrayana practitioners, or *tantrikas,* manifest dignity and basic goodness, and that leads to the experience of adhishthana.

Adhishthana is somewhat present in hinayana, and much more so in mahayana. In the hinayana, there is reverence for the saneness of the elder, and a quality of awkwardness and tidyness in your conduct; in the mahayana, there is a quality of bigheartedness, goodness, compassion, and heroism. But nobody in those two yanas conjures up living magic. In the vajrayana, when you walk into a situation, you actually have magical energy happening, whereas in the earlier yanas, that was provided purely by innuendo.

The vajrayana is very special. It is respected even by the theists, because they see that there is something going on that is more than religiosity, more than purely wisdom of a common type. In the vajrayana, we regard the world as even more sacred than the theists regard it. Mystical theism talks about the world being blessed by its creator, but in our case we go further. From our point of view, the world is intrinsically good and sacred and celebratory and cheerful. This is true whether the cockroaches were designed by Jehovah or not—or, I should say, designed and manufactured. In the vajrayana, there is a quality of splendidness or terrificness. Our world is more than we can see, more than we can perceive, and there is tremendous splendor involved. According to traditional texts, it is said that gods such as Brahma and others respect the dharma because of that. In the Western style, we could say that Brahma, Allah, and Jehovah respect the dharma because of that.

## ACQUIRING SIDDHIS

The third aspect of vajrayana is that of acquiring siddhis. Having already experienced adhishthana, you begin to appreciate that kind of blessing as the blessing of the buddhas of the past, present, and future. In turn, you begin to experience siddhis. The Tibetan term for siddhi is *ngödrup*. *Ngö* means "real" or "proper," or sometimes it could mean "personally," and *drup* means "accomplishing"; so *ngödrup* means "actually accomplishing," which is the Buddhist notion of miracles.

In this context, the idea of miracles and magic is that from those overwhelming blessings, we begin to feel that we have accomplished something. We develop great dignity and fearlessness out of that. We begin to feel as if we could actually command the four elements to be at our service. And that actually does happen as we go on, which comes later, I suppose.

Chinlap is like rain, and ngödrup is like the rain after it has dropped onto the ground and you begin to grow your plants. Chinlap comes from the vajra master, yourself, and your trust in the teaching, which binds you together. When you are initiated into the vajrayana, you walk into a room that is filled with the vajra master's presence, as well as with the teaching atmosphere of the vajrayana, which we could say is the deities. So the deities, the vajrayana teaching, and the vajra master together are holding that particular glow.

In a vajrayana initiation, the vajra master creates a complete vajra world with the deity, and waits for you to come in. Then you come in from the outside and drink purified water as you enter. The idea is that you are supposed to be walking into a sort of vajra den, which is so powerfully heavy—or "heavy-ed"—that you get chinlap on the spot. This happens because you and the other students are open-minded; because the vajra master is open and loving and has tremendous affection for the students; and because the deities and the tantric teaching atmosphere are flickering and ready for you to zap into. So you just walk in and get mildly, quite pleasantly zapped. That is where the chinlap happens, when you are involved with that kind of humid atmosphere. So chinlap happens when you walk into the room, and then you get further blessings during the initiation as well. In the vajrayana, you are supposed to have an atmosphere of adhishthana happening all the time.

At the point when you are formally initiated into the vajrayana, there is no practice involved. But in order to get to that level, you need a lot of practice; and to go on from there, you also need a lot of practice. It is very natural, like the sun rising in the East every morning. The sun rises naturally, but you still have to lead your life in accordance with it. During the daytime, you should do your job, eat your lunch and your dinner, be awake and doing something. You cannot just lie around in the dark, because the sun has risen. It is that kind of logic. You do not just sit around and collect blessings all the time.

## CONFIRMATION

The fourth aspect of vajrayana is confirmation. Because vajrayana practice is so powerful and real, because it is so full of adhishthana and siddhis, or blessings and miracles, you begin to share that mentality or approach with the tathagatas, or *sugatas:* the buddhas of the past, present, and future. You begin to find that you are so uplifted that you have transformed yourself from an ordinary lower-level person. In particular, you have freed yourself from the lower existences: from the hell realm, the hungry ghost realm, and the animal realm. You are so uplifted, you are about to become superhuman or you have actually become superhuman; therefore, there is no fear of primitivism. You don't feel like a worm or cockroach, and you don't feel as if you are crawling on the floor in the dirt. Because you have experienced such strong blessings, you feel fully charged. You feel you are somebody. At least you are different from one of those beings that crawls on its stomach or walks on four legs, or one with a tail, or one with or without antennae. This means that you have been confirmed.

The Tibetan term for confirmation is very interesting and good: it is *ug jinpa*. *Ug* means "breath," and *jinpa* means "breathing"; so *ug jinpa* means "breathing the breath."

Ug jinpa means something like this: If you do not know who you are, you are just holding your breath, trying to find out. Then somebody tells you that you are Joe Schmidt, and you say, "Whew! At last I have found out who I am." Ug jinpa is that kind of relief. Finally you are confirmed in who and what you are. As much as the sugatas of the past, present, and future are confirmed, so you are confirmed as well. Therefore, vajrayanists, or tantrikas, can actually straighten their heads and shoulders much more than even the hinayanists or mahayanists. You can have good head and shoulders, good posture; you can walk upright and straight with delight and joy. Don't you think that's great?

## No Obstacles

The fifth aspect of vajrayana is the aspect of no obstacles. Having received confirmation, you then go beyond that. You begin to realize that confirmation means that your whole being is "vajra-fied," so to speak. Your body is no longer feeble and sickly, your speech is no longer stuttering, halfhearted and low-key, and your mind is no longer depressed or confused, but it is strong and cheerful. At this point, your whole being—your body, speech, and mind—is vajra-fied at the level of bodhichitta.

You already developed benevolence in the mahayana, but in this case you develop vajra bodhichitta, adamantine bodhichitta. It is adamantine because there are no cracks in your awareness or in your understanding of the vajrayana. Your conviction and pride in the vajrayana are of one piece. It is a diamond-like situation. There are no cracks where dirt could get in, so there is total awareness happening all the time. It is one piece, which is very precise and good, healthy and wholesome. Therefore, you are no longer subject to obstacles or hazards of any kind.

## NEVER VIOLATING SAMAYA

The sixth aspect of vajrayana is that of never violating *samaya*.* Because you begin to realize inward purity and spotlessness as well as outward purity and spotlessness, and because your world is seen as wholesome and you yourself experience wholesomeness, there is no reason why you should regard things as bad. The whole thing is built up, so at this point you feel you have nothing to fear and you have nothing to feel dirty about. You might not have taken a bath or shower for weeks and weeks, but still you feel clean and good. A sense of general goodness is taking place, so you can never break your samaya vow.

The reason you break your samaya vow is usually because you have doubts about yourself or your world. Either you feel that you are not good enough, or that your world is not good enough, or that the bad situation is made out of both you and the world, or that the bad situation is made out of neither you or the world. That makes four conclusions: you, your world, between you-yes, and between you-no. According to Buddhist logic, those four conclusions are called the four extreme beliefs.† You have you, you have the other, and you have you and the other put together, which sometimes proves to be good and sometimes proves to be bad.

Those are the four conclusions that you always work with in your relationship with your world. They are the four extreme beliefs in *madhya-maka* (middle way) logic—and at this point, you are free from all of them. You begin to develop the attitude that, although you might begin to impose those four extremes on the vajra world as well, in fact everything is fine, so there is nothing to worry about. Because you realize that the vajra master, the vajra world, and you are indivisibly fastened together, you begin to feel that you actually cannot violate samaya principles at all.

---

* The *samaya* vow is the third main vow of the Tibetan Buddhist path. It follows the hinayana refuge vow and the mahayana bodhisattva vow. The samaya vow establishes a bond between the teacher, the student, and the deity or yidam. For more on the topic of samaya, see part 5, "Complete Commitment."

† The *four extremes* of madhyamaka logic, attributed to Nagarjuna, are the four beliefs in existence, nonexistence, both, or neither.

## ALWAYS RESTORING SAMAYA, EVEN WHEN IT IS VIOLATED

The seventh aspect of vajrayana is that of always restoring samaya. Even though you might break the rules of your samaya vow with occasional doubts and occasional flickerings of thought, you can always restore it. Because you have experienced the previous six qualities of vajrayana, you have no problem in relating with your world or your life, so even if you have violated samaya, it can always be restored.

On the whole, the conclusion of these seven aspects of vajrayana is a quality of dignity and trust. That trust is inspired by maitri, or friendliness to oneself, and by karuna, or friendliness to others. So maitri and karuna are fundamental, and on top of that, there is also a quality of heroism, delight, and fearlessness. All seven aspects put together make the vajrayana workable. They do not apply only to advanced students, but to new students or amateurs as well. Therefore, vajrayana is very up-to-date. It is delightful to be in the vajrayana world and to experience the vajra world and vajra being. There is tremendous strength and joy taking place.

*Part Two*

# THE TEACHER-STUDENT
# RELATIONSHIP

# The Role of the Guru or Vajra Master

*The guru could shine brilliant hot sun on you or create a thunder-storm on you or freeze you to death or bake you into bread, because the guru has a relationship with every aspect of reality that there is, as far as your world is concerned.*

## THE TEACHER-STUDENT RELATIONSHIP

In the vajrayana, it is important and necessary to understand the relationship between the student and the guru, or vajra master. Having a guru might seem like a great idea, but it is necessary to know the function of the guru and how you are going to relate with him or her in terms of your own development. For example, somebody might think that getting married is a hot idea, but this person needs to first understand the role of a husband, the role of a wife, and how they are going to work together in their marriage. And when you relate to a guru, the guru has to relate with you as well. So you have to find a guru who does not change their mind in relating with you. That way you don't run into each other, like a car crash.

There are many teachers, but basically speaking you have one generator generating electricity, and then you have lots of bulbs. Which bulb you relate to depends on what room you are in. You can always walk into another room with a different bulb, where the chandelier seems better or the switch is more exotic. And if you need more light, you can turn on more bulbs, realizing that the fundamental generator never fails. The fundamental generator, or root guru, is omnipresent.

## The Hinayana Preceptor

The guru principle has different facets in the various yanas. In the hinayana, the guru is known as a teacher or preceptor, somebody who ordains you into the order, whether you are taking the basic refuge vow or monastic vows. So the hinayana teacher functions at the level of a preceptor. In Sanskrit, the word for a preceptor is *upadhyaya*. In Tibetan, the word *khenpo* refers to that kind of scholar and abbot, or professional master. The preceptor's role is to instruct the students, so a preceptor is somewhat like a schoolteacher. You are instructed and told about various levels of the teaching and given different ordinations. Basically, the hinayana teacher is acting as kind of a parental principle. There is no notion of craziness or wildness or penetration, particularly, unless you violate the rules and get told off.

## The Mahayana Spiritual Friend

At the mahayana level, you have the *kalyanamitra,* or spiritual friend. A kalyanamitra is more than a schoolteacher level: it is the level of a physician and friend at the same time. The kalyanamitra is more concerned with your basic nature, your basic makeup, and your state of being. So at the level of mahayana, the Sanskrit word *guru* also applies. *Guru* means "one who carries a heavy burden" or "one who carries a heavy load." The Tibetans use a slightly different word. Instead of guru, they say *lama* (which can be connected to *uttara* in Sanskrit). *La* means "above," and *ma* means "one who is"; so *lama* means "one who is above" or "one who is at the top." As a being on a high spiritual level, the lama has the panoramic vision of looking down on a student's development.

## The Vajrayana Master

In the vajrayana, the term or title for the teacher is "vajra master," or *dorje loppön* in Tibetan. *Loppön* means "teacher" or "master," and *dorje* means "vajra"; so *dorje loppön* means "vajra master." In Sanskrit the term for dorje loppön is *vajracharya.*

## Spokesperson for the Phenomenal World

The term *vajracharya* has the feeling of the teacher being a spokesperson for the phenomenal world. The relationship between the Indian mahasiddha Tilopa and his student Naropa is one example of a vajra master acting in this way. Naropa was a great scholar at Nalanda University who left to find his teacher. As Naropa was searching for his guru, he had twelve visions or experiences, all of which were actually the guru manifesting in various forms. But each time, Naropa failed to realize that what he was experiencing was a manifestation of the guru, because he was still clinging to his fascination. He took those experiences literally, as they appeared. For instance, Naropa came across a half-dead dog, and later he went to a freak show, but in both cases he missed the point, and the vision disappeared.

Each time this happened, Naropa would hear the voice of his teacher telling him how he had failed to understand the experience, and then his teacher would say, "Tomorrow we will do such and such or visit so-and-so." Then Naropa would go on to the next thing. He regarded what he was experiencing as an external world that was happening, rather than understanding it as symbolic language and recognizing it as the manifestation of the guru. If Naropa had understood what was happening, he need never have encountered the dog or gone to the freak show or whatever else.

So the vajra master is a spokesperson for, or even a manifestation of, the phenomenal world. Some of the stories about Don Juan that Carlos Castaneda told have a similar quality—that everything is the doing of the guru.[*]

## Surgeon or Executioner

The vajra master is a teacher, an executioner, a magician, and a surgeon. A doctor who does not have the training to perform surgery, but who has

---

[*] For more on the life and teaching of *Naropa*, see Chögyam Trungpa, *Illusion's Game: The Life and Teaching of Naropa* (Boston: Shambhala Publications, 1991). For more on *Don Juan* and *Carlos Castaneda*, see Carlos Castaneda, *The Teachings of Don Juan: A Yaqui Way of Knowledge* (New York: Simon & Schuster, 1976).

just learned to prescribe medicine and who tells you to discipline yourself, is somewhat at the bodhisattva level. But the vajra master is more like a surgeon, because they help you out thoroughly, and that thoroughness might present you with some pain.

It is similar to undergoing an operation in order to restore your health. You could say to the surgeon, "I want you to cure me, but I do not want you to open my stomach and look inside. I have a human right to proclaim that you do not have access to the inside of my stomach. You can recommend any diet you like, tell me what kind of food to eat and how to behave. You can give me medicine. But you can't get inside my stomach." But that kind of limitation seems to be ridiculous. In order for the surgeon to heal you, you have to let them get into you thoroughly and completely. So while the vajra master is a parental figure, this particular parental figure is a surgeon, somewhat of an executioner, a heavy-handed person who has good intentions. That is one of the important aspects of a vajra master.

The vajra master's compassion may manifest as kindness and softness in the background—or the foreground, for that matter—but that kindness does not become idiot compassion, or kindness without intelligence. Students need the chance to go through a lot of discipline. Being a vajra master is somewhat like teaching somebody parachuting. The teacher may have a soft spot for you in the back of their mind, but at the same time they do not prevent you from jumping. Teaching you to parachute is their profession; that is what they are supposed to teach. The vajra master teaches you to jump into nowhere, hoping that your parachute will open. No genuine teacher would say, "No, I cannot do this to you. You just come down with me in the airplane. You don't have to parachute."

The vajra master is the transcendent version of the bodhisattva, definitely. At the same time, the vajra master's principles and ways of working with their students are much more direct than the bodhisattva's. The bodhisattva creates some kind of hospitality, which does not exist in vajrayana unless you help yourself, in which case there is an enormous bank of wealth.

### Indestructible Teacher Who Is Never Put Off

It is impossible to put a vajra master off or to make a vajra master change their mind about working with you. You might think that if they become disgusted with you, they could say, "I'll go work with somebody else." But the more disgusting things the vajra master finds in a student, the more they find sickness or neurosis, that much more is the vajra master interested in you—in your problems and your sickness. Seeing the student's sickness is one of the ways that a vajra master becomes turned on, so to speak, and creative: "Ah, now there is a problem! Let's look into it; let's do tests. Piss in this bottle and shit in this container. Let me examine you."

The vajra master is interested in your problems, rather than disgusted. You are unable to put such a person off. That is one of the characteristics of a vajra master, and that is why this person is known as a vajra master, or indestructible teacher. The more icky stuff that comes out of you, the more the teacher is turned on to being a teacher who is willing and excited to work with you. This is one of the vajrayana principles: the vajra nature of the vajra master.

It is not so much that the vajra master is looking for a challenge, but the vajra master is highly inquisitive. They are highly inquisitive about investigating how this piece of shit may one day turn out to be a crystal clear *sambhogakaya* buddha.* The vajra master is fascinated that this wretched little stuff could be turned into a fantastic explosion of vajra energy. That kind of interest entertains the vajra master, and at the same time it entertains the phenomenal world and you as well.

So the activity of the vajra master is a somewhat more sophisticated level of compassion. It is not only how much you learn that interests such a teacher. In fact, the more you make mistakes, the more the vajra master is interested. So the nature of vajra masters is that they have the kind of exertion that never gives up hope.

## Crocodile Who Never Rejects Anyone Once They Are Accepted

Anyone entering into the vajrayana needs such a vajra master. It is said that you need a vajra master who is like a crocodile, who only knows how to accept. Once anybody enters into a crocodile's mouth, it accepts rather than rejects. The crocodile never lets go. Rejection is against the principle of crocodileship, and that quality of not letting go is also one of the vajra principles of the vajra master. You actually find that image

---

* The *sambhogakaya* (bliss body) is the speech or energy manifestation of enlightenment. Sambhogakaya buddhas represent different styles of enlightened manifestation.

in iconography. In the five-pointed vajra scepter, or dorje, the four outer prongs of the vajra arise out of the mouths of four crocodiles.

The principle of vajrayana is nonflinching; you never let go, but you accept and hold on. That is vajra nature. And the same thing applies to the vajra master, who is actually and literally the spokesperson of the vajrayana teachings. In fact, the vajra master is the only spokesperson. Even the books that present the vajrayana teachings cannot be regarded as independent from the vajra master. Books can speak, in some sense; but books have to be worked with, interpreted, and elucidated to be suitable for you.

## The Relative and Ultimate Vajra Master

The vajra master has two expressions: relative and ultimate. The relative expression is how the vajra master manifests according to kündzop, or the relative phenomenal world. Sometimes kündzop can fool you a great deal, and sometimes it can inspire you to see the flawlessness of the truth. In order to deal with your apparent phenomenal world, to deal with your fascination with this world of facade, you have an external guru, a kündzop guru. This external guru or vajra master of kündzop actually exists outside of your body and mind; this guru is manifested externally. The kündzop guru shares the same roof, the same sky, the same floor, and the same earth as you do.

The second type of guru, the ultimate guru, or töndam, appears from the memory or the example of the external guru. From that, you begin to have a sense of inner guru, or inner guidance. This is often subject to misunderstanding, because the inner guru could be misinterpreted as a part of your expectations. If you do not have a complete and proper relationship with the kündzop guru, you could misunderstand the inner guru according to your own wishful thinking.

The guru of kündzop is also called the guru of example or impression. When you have enough of an impression of the kündzop guru imprinted on your state of mind, then the guru of the ultimate reality within you can shine through. Otherwise, the inner guru could be regarded as just pure hoax, just your own expectations. That kind of inner guru is much phonier than the real kündzop guru who actually exists outside your body, physically or geographically.

*A vajra (Tib.: dorje) showing the prongs arising out of crocodile mouths.*

The way in which the kündzop guru becomes imprinted on your state of mind comes from something more than simply observing the guru or just gazing at the guru. Admiring him or her and hoping for the best somehow does not work. The impression the guru makes on you is a question of how much communication takes place between the guru and you. It is a question of how much the actual message is getting into you.

If we return to the analogy of the guru being like a crocodile, you could say that the impression the teacher makes on you is the same as when the crocodile has swallowed you, digested you, and shat you out, and afterward you still have teeth marks on your neck. As another analogy, it is a bit like relating to your dying father by having to put him in the coffin and put flowers around his corpse, rather than just watching the ceremony. You take part in the funeral service for your dead father, and it makes an impression on you. You have a sense of reality.

In talking about the kündzop guru, we are talking about a living guru. The guru is sending particular messages to you, and manifesting their liveliness to you in all kinds of ways. The living power of the lineage is taking place, channeled through your guru. Some of the guru's messages may be verbal, while others are communicated in silence. It could be any form of communication, but it has to be realistic rather than imaginary. You cannot stretch the logic by thinking that, since your guru gave you an apple this morning, you have attained some kind of fruition. The guru might give you an egg, but that does not mean you are in an embryonic state. The communication is more sophisticated than that. The guru is aware of your intelligence, and any communication has to work with that individual intelligence.

## FIVE ASPECTS OF THE GURU

The guru, whether relative or ultimate, is seen in the vajrayana as the embodiment of all the tantric principles. This is described in terms of five aspects: body, speech, mind, quality, and action.

### Body as Vajra Sangha

The form or body of the guru is a manifestation of the *vajra sangha*, the sangha of tantric practitioners. The guru is an example of somebody who has trod on the path, someone who has achieved and experienced sangha-hood. In this way, the physical existence of the guru can be seen as the vajra sangha.

## Speech as the Teachings

The speech of the guru is a manifestation of the teachings. Whether that speech is spoken or unspoken communication, both kinds of communication could be seen as manifesting the teachings.

When we talk about the importance or value of the guru's speech, it does not mean that the guru is a good speaker, a good lecturer, or highly articulate. Rather, the guru's speech has a quality or pattern that transforms the environment around you into an environment that is an utterance or expression of the teaching. A body without speech does not create such an atmosphere or feeling of a complete world; that sense of complete reality comes particularly out of speech.

If you see musical instruments just lying around on the floor, it is a very different experience than hearing musical instruments being played. However, if you have heard such musical instruments being played, and then you see the musical instruments lying on the floor, that still evokes an experience. So speech is not only words, or verbalization of the teachings alone, but speech is that which creates an atmosphere or environment of dharma.

## Mind as the Buddha

The mind of the guru represents the Buddha, the Enlightened One, the Tathagata. This connection is quite simple and direct. For one thing, the guru's mind is flawless, all-pervasive, and constantly keen. The guru's mind is the embodiment of the dharmadhatu principle of all-encompassing space. In addition, as in the example of the vajra master's fascination with the student and with the relationship that is taking place, the guru's mind is also connected with compassion.

## Quality as the Yidams

The quality or personality of the guru is that of the yidams. Yidams are personifications of your particular nature. They can be either peaceful or wrathful, male (called *herukas*) or female (called *dakinis*). The various deities that you identify yourself with on the tantric path are all embodied in the guru, but the yidam is not a guru. The yidam is your experience rather than a guru, because the yidam is an imagination of your mind, and the guru is somebody who tells you that the yidam is an imagination of your mind. The guru shows you how you should imagine the yidam. It is up to the guru; the guru manifests all five buddha-family principles to students,* depending on what particular nature they are receptive to.

### Action as the Dharmapalas

The action of the guru is constantly sharp, up-to-date, cutting, and powerful. The guru embodies the action of the *dharmapalas,* the protectors of the dharma.† The guru's actions are constantly pointing out various things. For example, if you are just about to jump off a cliff, an action of the guru could prevent you from doing so. This is quite simple and direct.

## GURU AS POSSESSOR AND MAKER OF ALL

In tantric literature, the guru principle is also described as the possessor and maker of all.

### Possessor of All Knowledge

The first point is that the guru is considered to be the possessor of all knowledge. The guru possesses complete knowledge of an individual's psychological development and the workings of their mind, as well as having a nationwide or cosmic scale of understanding about how the phenomenal world works. Because the guru is very much attuned to the phenomenal world, constantly and completely, the guru is never out-of-date. Therefore, the guru is the possessor of all knowledge.

---

* The *five buddha-family principles,* or five styles of awakening, appear throughout vajrayana teachings and practice. Yidams are generally representative of one of the five families. For more on the buddha-families, see chapter 26, "The Mandala of the Five Buddha-Families."

† *Dharmapalas* are usually portrayed in Tibetan iconography as fearsome, wrathful figures who are ruthless in protecting a practitioner's awareness and uncovering and destroying ego fixation. Vajrayana practitioners invoke the protectors in order to support them in their practice and to clear away obstacles to realization.

## Maker of Situations and Inspiration

In addition, the guru is the maker of all kinds of situations. In order to further a student's relationship with the dharma, the guru creates situations and inspiration. From a mundane way of looking at this, it is quite futile and needless to create such unnecessary hassles, but the guru does not hesitate to do so, even though these hassles are seemingly bizarre or unnecessary. And interestingly, those situations bring enormous insight to the student's mind.

When we speak of the guru setting up a situation for the student, it is not so much an actual biological or physiological setup; it is more of a psychological world. That is, the guru creates a psychological situation in which you are paranoid, or highly inspired, or whatever it may be. This has nothing to do with your basic karma. If you are born with a lot of bad karma, for example, the guru's role is to include that in the situation—and within that, they then create further situations, which are basically psychological. So the guru's actions are a kind of play.

The guru helps you to see things clearly, but before you can see things clearly, you might need to experience some kind of confusion. You might need some things to be turned upside down, to begin with—then you might turn things right-side up properly. Through the situations created by the guru, you are able to see this.

The guru is a spokesperson for the teachings; the guru's actions speak for the teachings and manifest the teachings for the student. The guru also has a direct relationship with the various energy principles or yidams that you are going to identify with. The guru can talk you out of the difficulties that come up on the path, and at the same time they can talk you *into* getting into those difficulties. The guru can use the power of the yidams, their wrathful or peaceful nature. The guru could shine brilliant hot sun on you or create a thunderstorm on you or freeze you to death or bake you into bread, because the guru has a relationship with every aspect of reality that there is, as far as your world is concerned.

The vajrayana teacher manifests as much more powerful, direct, and extraordinary than the hinayana preceptor or the mahayana spiritual friend. The guru not only has the key, but the lock as well. In order to understand tantric empowerments, or *abhishekas,* and any other aspect of the vajrayana, it is necessary for you to understand the principle of the tantric guru or vajra master.

It is important to appreciate how much power the guru has. Relating with the guru is like going directly to the bank manager, rather than just asking the teller to give you more money. If you really want to make friends with your bank account, you have to convince the bank manager that you are serious. Likewise, understanding the guru principle is a question of developing a certain attitude—one of awe and inspiration toward the guru and the vajrayana. When you are dealing with your guru, you begin to realize that you are dealing with the yidams and dharmapalas as well. In the tantric tradition, the vajra master is very important.

# The Root Guru as the Epitome of Freedom

*Sacred outlook is not only about thinking everything is good; it is the absence of imprisonment. You begin to experience freedom that is intrinsically good, almost unconditionally free. So the vajra world you are entering is basically good, unconditionally free, fundamentally glorious and splendid.*

## Self-Existing Sacredness

In the vajrayana, we develop an understanding of what is called sacred outlook, or the awareness that all phenomena are sacred. This understanding stems from the experience of mindfulness-awareness practice, or shamatha-vipashyana. The popular theistic view of sacredness is that certain things are blessed or influenced by external holiness; therefore, we feel that they are sacred. According to this view, you cannot make anything sacred; somebody else has to do so. But in the vajrayana, sacredness is self-existing. Although the term *self-existing sacredness,* or *sacred outlook,* is used in the vajrayana, it does not seem to appear in the literature of the early schools of Buddhism.

Sacredness is self-existing because in a healthy situation, if things are as they are, then there is no unwholesomeness involved—whether we are speaking of yourself, or your life, or whatever may exist. Sacredness means that situations are wholesome in the fullest sense. It means that experience is so sharp and penetrating, so powerful and direct, that it is like dealing with the naked elements; it is like holding a flame in your naked hand, or drinking pure water, or breathing air, or sitting on the earth. So sacredness is the psychological and spiritual one-hundred-percent whole-ness of experience. There is nothing more than that. No external holiness has blessed or influenced this experience in any way at all.

All situations have possibilities of sacred outlook. You develop an understanding of sacred outlook through your dealings with the phe-nomenal world, fundamentally. In dealing with your husband, wife, lover, father, mother, or enemy—in dealing with anything that occurs in your life or even in the cosmos—you begin to realize that all of these things are sacred. The dharmic atmosphere is the basic situation, and sacred outlook is the acknowledgment of that. For instance, while you are asleep, the sun might be shining all along—sacred outlook is opening your eyes and wak-ing up to that sunlight. It is opening your curtains so that you can witness the sunshine that already exists.

The guru is part of this sacredness because the guru is a one-hundred-percent guru and one-hundred-percent wholesome. The vajra master deals with you one hundred percent. Disobeying such a guru is the cause of all kinds of suffering. When you have violated the wholesomeness, you automatically catch a flu or sickness, or you have an accident, or whatever you can imagine. So from sacred outlook arises further and greater devo-tion to the teacher.

In turn, you begin to identify with the yidams, or tantric deities. That is, the experience of sacred outlook is embodied or manifested in the forms of the various deities that are described in tantric literature and teachings. These deities are not theistic entities, but they are various expressions of your own state of constant sanity. Each deity captures a certain quality of strength and wakefulness, related to the particular type of experience that an individual is going through. These yidams or deities begin to expand into vast possibilities of all kinds.

With an understanding of sacred outlook, and having developed unflinching, overwhelming devotion to the teacher, we request the teacher to include us even further in their world. We ask to be empowered so that we might be included completely and fully, as would-be kings and queens in the vajra world.

## THE ABSENCE OF STRUGGLE

That idea of sacredness is based on the principle of your environment providing natural gentleness. Because the world provides natural gentleness in your surroundings, things do not become too heavy-handed, but instead they are an easy, natural process. Therefore, you learn how to relax with your phenomenal world. Because you have learned how to relax, you do not have to struggle; and because you do not have to struggle, you begin to experience that there is intrinsic goodness everywhere. It is not just that your change of mind makes the world *seem* better, but the world in itself *is* better—it is intrinsically good.

Then because of that goodness, you begin to feel that even greater goodness exists. That greater goodness is called blessings. The reason the world is holy or sacred is because it does not bring out any aggression or outright struggle. Therefore, because you can slip in and relax with it, there is tremendous freedom. The definition of *freedom* here is the absence of struggle. You are freed from your oppression, your imprisonment. There is a pliable easiness and freedom, which makes things much more sacred. So anything sacred or holy is based on the absence of struggle, on freedom. That freedom is experienced further and further and at a higher and higher level.

## MANIFESTING FREEDOM

The product of such freedom, or the way in which such freedom manifests, depends on your particular temperament, your state of mind, your style of buddha nature. This freedom manifests and is presented to you in the form of deities. All tantric deities are manifestations of freedom. In tantra, that state of freedom is seen in terms of the feminine and masculine principles, the mother lineage and father lineage. The feminine principle is openness, and the masculine principle is application, or the pragmatic quality. The various levels of tantra are all expressions of total freedom.

## CONNECTING WITH FREEDOM

You might understand the concept of freedom in your head, but how can you actually go about connecting properly with this kind of freedom, which sounds so great? The interesting thing is that you cannot connect directly with such freedom. You might have a general idea of it, but you are still not altogether free. Somebody has to introduce that freedom, or in fact, somebody has to manifest it—and only the root guru can do that.

The root guru manifests as the symbol or epitome of freedom, as a deity as well as through being a teacher. So in the vajrayana, the one and only point—the key point— is to have one-pointed devotion to the root guru.

## SEEING THE PHENOMENAL WORLD AS A MANIFESTATION OF THE GURU

Through devotion, you realize that the world you are entering into, that freedom, is your freedom as well as the teacher's freedom and the freedom of the lineage. You experience a state of mind that is known as *tagnang*. *Tag* means "pure," and *nang* means "perception"; so *tagnang* means "pure perception." The best translation of *tagnang* my translators and I have come up with is "sacred outlook." The phenomenal world is seen as sacred because it is a manifestation of the guru, and it is also a product of your practice.

As far as this point is concerned, as students you do not have any other world. You might be visiting your parents or your rich uncle; nevertheless, those situations are all part of tagnang, or sacred outlook. They are a part of the vajra master's world. Your parents may be heavy-handed and overpowering, but they are still a manifestation of the guru.

The amazing point is that ego does not see, but the guru does see. Ego is regarded as blind, so if you really want to see properly, you have to see something other than what the blind see. But there is something other than the ego's vision of the world—there is true vision. With true vision, you see that the phenomenal world is already self-existing purity; you see that it is sacred. So ego's vision does not have very good credentials. The whole Buddhist path is like that: we try to shed any possibilities of ego's vision, a vision that is usually colored or distorted or completely blacked out.

The guru tells you the truth, and the truth can destroy anything untrue. That is the basic logic, or principle, of vajra nature. Somebody tells you the truth, and that truth is very powerful and penetrating. It creates a world of truth. Encountering the truth is like being in a dingy, dark room with a little hole in the window. First a little sunbeam comes through the window; then you decide to get up and get dressed; then you open your door and go outside and you discover there are sunbeams everywhere. Those sunbeams are an exaggeration of the first little sunbeam; it is the same thing, but it is everywhere. Likewise, seeing the phenomenal world as a manifestation of the guru is a further exaggeration of devotion, in a positive sense. One-pointed devotion is seeing the brightness of the sun through your peephole, and then multiplying that by hundreds of thousands as you step outside, where the sun is shining everywhere.

## THREE ASPECTS OF THE VAJRA WORLD

Along with that understanding of sacred outlook, it is very important for you to understand that the world has three aspects: the yidams, or principal deities; the teacher, or vajra master; and yourself. Combined, that threefold situation provides what is known as the vajra world. Sacred outlook is not only about thinking that everything is good; it is the absence of imprisonment. You begin to experience freedom that is intrinsically good, almost unconditionally free. So the vajra world that you are entering is basically good, unconditionally free, fundamentally glorious and splendid.

At the point at which you enter that world, there is bondage between your vajra master, your deity, and yourself; you are joined together. That provides a profound basis for vajrayana practice altogether. Without those three situations—without the vajra master or root guru, without yourself, and without the deities that you relate with, which are your own expression—you cannot practice vajrayana at all. That seems to be the basic idea of experiencing and understanding sacred outlook.

## FLASHING SACRED OUTLOOK

Sacred outlook comes to individuals in the form of a sudden flash. It can be discussed in terms of three lojong, or mind-training, slogans,* which are connected with vajra body, vajra speech, and vajra mind.

---

* In this discussion, Trungpa Rinpoche is looking at mahayana *mind-training slogans* from a vajrayana perspective. For more on mind training (lojong) and the fifty-nine related slogans, see Chögyam Trungpa, *Training the Mind and Cultivating Loving-Kindness* (Boston: Shambhala Publications, 2003) or volume 2 of the *Profound Treasury*, part 7, "Mind Training and Slogan Practice."

*Trungpa Rinpoche (ca. 1970–1971) at Tail of the Tiger (now Karmê Chöling) in Vermont.*

## Vajra Body

Vajra body is connected with how we relate to the phenomenal world. The lojong slogan that applies is: "When the world is filled with evil, transform all mishaps into the path of bodhi." This slogan means that whenever you are attacked or there is a setback, instead of going along with it, you flash sacred outlook, which only takes a fraction of a second.

The reason this slogan is connected with vajra body is that it talks about the environment. The environment threatens you all the time, and your own existence is dependent on it. But as a vajrayana student, you begin to feel that you are no longer undermined or intimidated by external obstacles. You are willing to relate with physical situations and obstacles. Therefore, you are able to transform mishaps into the path of bodhi. You are willing to do so because your shamatha-vipashyana practice has worked, and your lojong or slogan practice has also worked. So it is a linear situation, not an apple landing on your head.

According to this slogan, when the external environment is full of mishaps and problems, you divert or transform them into the path of bodhi. For instance, you may be living in a dirty apartment full of cockroaches, or you may not be able to go outside because of the pollution. But even so, you can begin to develop sacred outlook of the body, so the environment is respected and worshipped in the vajrayana sense.

As another example, if your house has caught fire all around you, you need to decide whether to sit in the middle of the house and let yourself be scorched, or step outside. Vajra body deals with questions like that, questions about how to relate with the environment. The idea is that when you are free from grasping and fixation, you can begin to handle your environment. In fact, by the power of bodhichitta, you could probably put out the fire in your house. That is the vajrayana twist. So when the external environment is full of mishaps and problems, you divert or transform them into the path of bodhi.

## Vajra Speech

Speech is that which acts as a pulsation between mind and body; it is what joins mind and body together. It is what feels and joins together the solidness of the body and the flying quality of the mind. If your mind is cold and your body is hot, speech is what is going to communicate those two to each other. Vajra speech is connected with becoming aware of your subconscious chatter and gossip. The slogan that applies to speech is: "Whatever you meet unexpectedly, join with meditation."

The idea is that whatever you come across, you suddenly flash sacred outlook, without discursive or intellectual answers. When unexpected situations occur, or when expected situations have finally caught up with you, you join that with meditation, or sacred outlook. This applies not only to the evil situations you meet in the environment, but to whatever you may encounter. You are able to join any unexpected situations or sudden surprises with meditation.

## Vajra Mind

Vajra mind means experiencing everything as shunyata protection. The related slogan is: "Seeing confusion as the four kayas is unsurpassable shunyata protection."* The idea is that whenever nonsacred possibilities occur in your mind and you begin to let yourself drown in them completely, you do not give in to that manipulation, but again you flash sacred outlook.

## THE PROBLEM OF RESENTMENT

In relating to the idea of devotion to the teacher or to the vajra master, your resentment may begin to become problematic. When you have mishaps of any kind, you automatically cringe and pass the buck to somebody else, and the most immediate person that you can pass the buck to is the teacher. You think it is because you are in the guru's environment that such things happen to you.

From the guru's point of view, any blame that you would like to impose on the guru will be accepted with delight. They are willing to accept fully any kind of blame that comes to them—all or none whatsoever, whatever

---

* The *four kayas* refer to the interconnected facets of enlightened manifestation. For a discussion of this slogan and the four kayas (the dharmakaya, sambhogakaya, *nirmanakaya,* and *svabhavikakaya*) in the mahayana context, see volume 2 of the *Profound Treasury,* chapter 38: "Point Three: Transformation of Bad Circumstances into the Path of Enlightenment."

you desire. But if you put the blame on the guru all the time, you will not be able to make any kind of forward movement. The whole thing will begin to become a vicious circle.

For example, practitioners in Western society often feel inadequate; they think that they cannot practice. At first they blame themselves, and then they begin to put more blame on the circumstances of the teaching environment and the demands of the organization they are a part of. Finally, they begin to blame the teacher, the one who created that organization. But that kind of resentment seems to become unnecessary at this point. You can use these descriptions of the role of the vajra master as an antidote for all that.

To introduce a fourth lojong slogan, basically the whole thing boils down to: "Drive all blames into one." At this point, you have to develop further vision, rather than just complaining all the time; and that further vision comes from having driven all blames into yourself. When you have done that, you begin to feel that some kind of freshness, lightness, and openness can take place in your life. For one thing, your mother sentient beings are regarded as objects of compassion and kindness.* Beyond that, you acknowledge the guru: the one who taught you to be kind to your mother sentient beings and to yourself, the one who taught you to drive all blames into yourself.

So as your lojong practice begins to work and to take effect, it creates a heightening of compassion for other sentient beings and a further appreciation of the guru, who is the author of that particular teaching. But appreciating the guru is not hero worship. You do not worship the guru for their looks or for their great standing; you simply appreciate what that person teaches and what they exemplify as the living dharma.

## APPRECIATING THE TEACHER AND THE TEACHINGS

There are five factors for developing appreciation for the teacher and the teachings: trust, faith, devotion, complete openness, and daringness.

---

* The phrase *mother sentient beings* expresses the view that over the course of many lifetimes, all sentient beings have been one's mother. The idea is that all beings are interconnected and worthy of loving-kindness and compassion.

## Trust

With appreciation of the dharma, you begin to develop a greater feeling not only of openness, but of longing. You develop utter appreciation, which brings about a trust in the teachings. You trust that what the teachings say is true and workable.

## Faith

Then, because of your trust in the teachings, you begin to develop faith in the teacher. This is an important point. In Tibetan, faith is *tepa*, which means "accepting what is there" or "accepting what has been taught." So with a nontheistic approach, faith is unselfish; you simply appreciate the teachings. But if you approach faith from a theistic perspective, although you still appreciate the teachings, at the same time you are always thinking about what you can get out of them.

## Devotion

One step beyond faith is devotion to the teacher. The idea of devotion is one of opening, like a flower. When rain falls on a flower, if the flower is humble and open, it can receive the rain; but if the flower has no longing for the rain, it does not open. So devotion is somewhat emotional. It is a longing to receive the truth that has been taught by the teacher—to receive it thoroughly. So a student with devotion is like a flower that is open to the rain: the flower allows rainfall to drop into it, and the rain makes the flower beautiful and gives it long life. The thunder and rain are connected with the teacher, and when the student opens up to that, the student can be alive and exist without neurosis. Therefore, devotion is very important.

This whole process is based on understanding the value of the truth that has been taught to you, rather than depending on blind faith. You feel that what has been taught to you makes sense, and that it is beginning to work on you. It does not matter whether it feels painful or pleasurable. Still, the teachings are beginning to crack you down to the possibility of non-ego.

## Complete Openness

Having developed devotion, the next level is what is called *lo-te lingkyur* in Tibetan. *Lo-te* means "trust." It refers to having a kind of trust that is a mixture of faith and devotion, and to having a firm commitment. *Ling* means "completely," and *kyur* means "abandoning" or "letting go"; so *lo-te lingkyur* means "to trust completely and be willing to let go." In other words, once you develop trust in the teacher and the teachings, you do not check your insurance policy. You may or you may not have an insurance policy, but in any case, you let go of that.

With lo-te lingkyur, you are actually trying to put your hand through your rib cage in order to take out your heart and hand it over to your guru. You hope that your guru will take care of your heart, both for yourself and for your guru. And having taken out your heart, you still survive beautifully. It is an extremely personal experience.

Surrendering to the guru is not necessarily confirmed by the teacher alone. You also begin to realize your own existence, your own space, your own situation. By surrendering, you become worthy of receiving further knowledge. It is a pragmatic approach, not particularly philosophical; it is an idea that comes through practice.

This type of devotion is very important, and quite ordinary, actually. When you are willing to take a chance and invest a million dollars with somebody, you have to trust that person. You sign your name on the dotted line, and you come up with the money. You say, "Here is my million dollars; I am going to invest it with you. Let's work together." Working with anybody or with any situation in any society is connected with that idea of trust. Becoming involved with major deals of any kind, handing over responsibility to someone else, spreading out your responsibilities, or working with anybody at all, is based on trust.

If you accept a ride in somebody's car, you are handing your life over to them. Likewise, you hand over your life to the pilot each time you fly in an airplane. You usually take that kind of thing very lightly. You couldn't care less who the pilot is. If you were really being careful, you would find out. But although you might be willing to jump into somebody's car even though you know they are a crazy driver, and you might even think that you are going to have a fantastic time by doing that, you do not usually regard spiritual situations in the same way. However, if you are willing to lend your life to some crazy driver, you should actually be able to trust a sane driver: the guru.

In any situation where you are not actually in control, you are signing your life away to someone else. That kind of trust happens all the time. But with the vajra master, you are facing the person to whom you are signing over your whole being. Although that situation is not particularly different, it seems to make a difference. So in relating to the vajra master, the idea is to develop trust, faith, devotion, and complete openness.

## Daringness

So there are several factors that enable you to bring the teacher into your life. And along with factors such as faith and devotion, you also need daringness. Daringness is more tricky. It is letting go of your own personal collection, the things that you have been holding on to for a long time. You have built a stronghold within yourself, a sand castle with guards and weapons and communication systems, so that nothing can ever jeopardize your project of holding on to the survival of your ego. So you might begin to panic about whether you are willing to give in, give up, or more likely, give out.

Letting go of that whole system is very daring, even threatening in some cases. But without making such a daring move to accomplish egolessness, any achievement of enlightenment is impossible. That is actually the definition of liberation: being liberated from yourself. It means that you are liberated from arrogance, panic, and deep-rooted attachment. So basically, what we are talking about here is that you have to tear open your heart. You do not literally need to commit seppuku, but psychologically it is very close to that. The possibility is there.

Having given up, having surrendered totally, thoroughly, and properly, you find yourself in a delightful situation: "What a relief! Whew! I got away from myself. I managed to abandon myself." In the process, you might sweat, you might shake, you might stutter—but it is a good stutter, a good shake, a good panic. Because you have been released from that particular imprisonment, you find yourself so meek. You begin to feel very humble. Therefore, you can actually relate with the vajra master.

At that point, you begin to find that there is no barrier between you and the teacher. You feel that finally your windows and doors have been opened, so that at last you can experience fresh air, which is so refreshing, so natural, and so good. You feel quite humble, but at the same time you feel so delighted. At last you can smile without pretense, and you can see your world in a different light. Such possibilities always exist.

## DEVOTION AS A MEANS OF RELATING TO THE VAJRA WORLD

Through devotion, you can let go of resistance and aggression and grow the seed of buddha nature.

### Letting Go of Resistance

Devotion allows you to relate with the vajra world, but usually, you would like to withhold something. You would like to maintain some kind of resistance, because you like your little corner, your little nook. That little corner may not be pleasurable, and it could even be quite painful; nevertheless, you have become so accustomed to your own pain that it feels almost comfortable to you. It is as if you have been living in the same one-room apartment in the same city for twenty years, and you begin to like your dirt, your dust, and your cockroaches. If somebody tells you to move out of your apartment—even if they say, "I'm going to give you a mansion"—you freak out. You may not particularly like your apartment, but you have become accustomed to it, to your roots. It is like having bad teeth and not wanting to have them pulled out.

So it is not so much that you do not open up because you want to stick with pleasure, but the pleasure comes from being accustomed to your pain. It is at least convenient and familiar, so the possibility of stepping out of that pain is a revolution indeed. The vajrayana approach of complete devotion is to *not* hold onto your little corner of privacy. It is very straightforward. Your hidden corners have to be given up.

### Dropping Aggression and Discovering Sacred Outlook

Aggression is thinking that your world is right and that others are wrong. But when you begin to project sacred outlook, there is no separation at all between this world and that world, so everything is pure. Aggression comes from not having developed enough awareness in relating with your shamatha-vipashyana practice. You want to remold your world to fit your version of things rather than just looking at your world, and when things do not go your way, you feel pissed off. But if you develop shinjang and vipashyana awareness completely, you begin to see the world very clearly and thoroughly. Then no attacks come to you: the world is hospitable as well as being a manifestation of the guru, which is saying the same thing.

Awareness produces gentleness and softness, and because awareness is not regarded as labor, all sorts of things develop: compassion, first of all, and beyond that, sacred outlook. The world is already sacred; otherwise, you could not discover this. You would be manufacturing the whole thing. But you are not manufacturing anything; you are just seeing clearly what the whole thing is all about. That is why we say that prajna comes out of awareness, or the vipashyana principle. With prajna, you begin to see clearly what the phenomenal world is like. That is how sacred outlook is discovered.

## Growing the Seed of Buddha Nature

In order to rouse buddha nature, you need two things: the first is the teacher, and the second is yourself. And according to various teachers, including the Tibetan scholar and historian Taranatha (1575–1683 CE), you not only have buddha nature, but you actually have a buddha inside you, alive and well. In order to rouse that buddha nature, you need two things: the first is the teacher, and the second is yourself. So you have a seed, which is yourself, and because you have this seed, the teacher causes the seed to grow properly. That teacher may be inside of you as well as outside of you. Relating to the teacher is like seeing the bright sun. If you are blind, you cannot see the bright sunshine, so the sunshine depends partly on your perception, and at the same time, the sun exists in the sky as the other.

When you plant a seed in the ground, in order to grow your seed, you need a certain atmosphere and weather. The vajra master is like the weather: rain, sunshine, and wind are all embodied in the teacher, who in this case is also the earth itself, as well as the gardener. The vajra master ripens the seed that you have planted, which in this case is somewhat fully blossomed already.

So the vajrayana style of relating with the teacher, or vajra master, is quite unusual or extraordinary, compared with the hinayana or mahayana. It is necessary for you to have a teacher who not only teaches but who creates an entire atmosphere. Good devotion combines the three yanas together. The main point of devotion is that in both your thoughts and behavior, you should follow the teachings of the vajra master.

## THE PROCESS OF OPENING UP

Basically, we are talking about expanding, or opening up, your body, speech, and mind so that they can become vajra body, vajra speech, and vajra mind. We are doing so with the help of the first three slogans we discussed, and beyond that, we are doing it with the ideas of devotion, longing, and openness. It is very simple logic, and very straightforward.

Because what you have been taught works, you begin to trust that there is some connection already. Out of that kind of trust, you develop faith. You realize that guidelines such as shamatha-vipashyana practice are actually beginning to work in your existence, your whole being, and so you develop faith in the teachings. From that, you begin to realize that the one who teaches those teachings is valid as well, and you begin to feel a fantastic connection with the teacher. Therefore, you develop devotion. And having developed devotion to the guru, you begin to experience an atmosphere of complete openness.

The same logic applies to any situation. With Indian food, for example, at first you hear that Indian food is good. Then you go to an Indian restaurant, and you meet the chef, who cooks you a good meal. Since you like the food, you invite the chef to your home, and finally you ask the chef to stay with you and be your chef for the rest of your life. Your devotion to the chef is not so much because that chef is a great man or a great woman, but because they are a good cook. A chef produces good food in the same way that a teacher produces good teachings. So you can relate with the whole thing very naturally. You finally begin to open up in that way. Then there is a further situation, which is that your cook begins to become your boss! Your cook begins to tell you what to eat. But that comes much later.

On the whole, if you want to become completely soaked in vajrayana discipline, there is no other way than by surrendering or giving in to the vajra master. There is no other way, because without that, the magic and openness could not occur. If there is no devotion, no magic, and no openness, then the rest of the vajrayana is irrelevant.

Once this magic happens in your life, a little effort is needed, but most of the process is based on mutual understanding. As a person entering the vajrayana journey, you have come to the conclusion that there is no other way to do it. It is like flying in an airplane. Once you walk in and take your seat, you realize that there is nothing else for you to do except fly along with the captain. In that sense, the whole thing is incredibly simple. We make it very complicated, but it is actually very simple.

## 9

# A Total Surrendering of Samsaric Logic

*In order to enter the vajrayana, it is necessary to have a vajra master. Moreover, self-indulgence has to be cut through by means of vajrayana discipline. In other words, in order to wake up, in order to wake the human mind of hinayana and mahayana, it is absolutely necessary to have an object of surrender beyond logic and beyond any philosophy, even beyond a measure of kindness.*

VAJRAYANA MIND protection can only occur when you have a vajra guru. Then you and the vajra guru in combination perform particular vajrayana disciplines, and as a result of having done them, you attain utter final enlightenment.

## TRANSFORMING THE THREE GATES

In vajrayana discipline, the emphasis is on working with body, speech, and mind. These are known as the "three gates" of entering into the vajrayana. Physical existence or body is the first gate; speech or intellect is the second gate; and consciousness, or mind and memories, is the third gate. Basically, human beings possess those three gates as three different aspects of their psychological existence.

The body looks for physical comfort and for confirmation of its existence. Speech provides further territory; it is a means of communication by which you can actually tell somebody to go away or ask them to come back to your home. Mind or consciousness provides a quality of manipulation whereby you can function in a world where some people love you and others hate you, and you love and hate other people as well. By working with body, speech, and mind together, you can conduct all of your business, whatever comes up. That is our ordinary state of being, the ordinary way we work with body, speech, and mind.

In the vajrayana, you are transcending those three mundane states through your discipline and through your connection with the vajra master, so that everything is regarded as sacred. Your body, your speech, and your mind are regarded as a sacred and holy environment. Bringing about such an atmosphere or holy environment is dependent on each of you individually. But to begin with, evoking that quality of sacredness depends on someone who can actually initiate that possibility. This initial provocation is provided by the deities of vajrayana. These various vajrayana principles or deities are basically natural reflections of your own vajra nature, but they manifest as the power source at the beginning.

Secondly, there is the need for a teacher, or vajra master, who pushes you into the situation. And, thirdly, there is you yourself, the student who can be provoked into that sacredness altogether.

To understand this better, let's use an analogy: If you are going to jump off a cliff very ceremoniously, very properly, very deliberately (supposing such a situation exists), you yourself, as the person who is going to jump, walk toward the cliff. You also have a person who will help you jump off the cliff, someone who encourages you and maybe has to give you an extra push. That person is the vajra master. We could say that the cliff itself and the space beyond it represent the deities.

These three principles could also be exemplified by the analogy of someone committing hara-kiri, or ritual suicide. In this analogy, you are the person who is going to commit hara-kiri; the sword is like the deities; and the court or audience that encourages you, watches you, and expects that you could actually do so, is the vajra master.

## Opening the Door to the Vajrayana Teachings

It is completely impossible for a beginning student to relate with any of the vajrayana teachings without the vajra master opening the door of vajrayana to that student. So the vajra master plays a very important part: the vajra master opens the experience of vajrayana to you.

The reason the vajra master is so important is that your existence is still wrapped up in the mahayana realization of the egolessness of dharmas. You have soaked yourself in the benevolence of the mahayana, but you are unable to go beyond mahayana saviorship. Although you may be perfect on a mahayana level, there is an extraordinary magical power—in other words, ultimate enlightenment—that you are still not accepting. That is precisely the reason why you are held back; it is why you are not a completely enlightened person.

You may be a good mahayanist, but that does not mean very much at this point. You are willing to clean a lot of diapers for sentient beings, you are willing to work in a lot of social situations, and you are kind to others—but from the point of view of vajrayana, so what? You are missing the point unless you are able to click further, and to give up such territory altogether and join the vajrayana band, or the vajrayana hordes. But if you can just dive in, the heroic aspect of mahayana could become vajra-like and monolithic.

Mahayanists might begin to feel that their realization is not diamond-like enough, not vajra-like enough. They may have heard about or experienced vajra samadhi, but a furthering of that adamantine quality has not been made available to them, so they are still hungry. It is as if the hinayanists had a good breakfast, and the mahayanists had a great lunch, but now they are looking for a fantastic dinner party. They are not completely fulfilled. Things have been executed heroically, but still something is lacking. You can never quite be in the world if you are always regarding samsara as something to be gotten beyond. The idea of transmutation has not yet taken place.

## SURRENDERING

In order to enter the vajrayana, it is necessary to have a vajra master. Moreover, self-indulgence has to be cut through by means of vajrayana discipline. In other words, in order to wake up, in order to wake the human mind of hinayana and mahayana, it is absolutely necessary to have an object of surrender beyond logic and beyond any philosophy, even beyond a measure of kindness. At this point, you are surrendering everything. Everything is included—all your reservations, including poetic license, which everybody has. That total surrender is actually seeing things as they are.

For that to happen, for that to actually take place, the illogical master begins to come into your life. At that point, there are a lot of possibilities for you to cut the samsaric logic altogether. In other words, if there is no vajra master, it is impossible for students to click into the vajrayana path, because they are still involved in reasoning. Although the hinayana and mahayana are trying their best to cut through the student's reasoning mind, that cutting-through process has itself become reasonable.

The vajra master becomes the unreasonable figure who does not buy any of your trips, not even the holiest of the holiest of your trips. But at the same time, your mind—your vajra-essence mind—is protected by the vajra master. That is why vajrayana is referred to as mantrayana, because your mind is protected. That protection has two sides: your clicking to the vajra master, and the vajra master clicking to you. That makes a definite bond.

Your unreasonable mind—or reasonable mind, for that matter—would have lots of expectations as to what vajrayana might be. But in order to actually get into vajrayana, it is necessary to give up those expectations. A lot of giving up is involved. Therefore, your mind is protected from expectations that would interfere with the actual surrendering process. By protecting the student's mind, the vajra master also acts as an agent for the deities. These various tantric deities, which come from nontheistic vision, provide a great deal of miracle and power.

If you do not have enough faith in the vajra master, but you are still trying to con your teacher, it can be dangerous. The vajra master's view is a totality, and your view is another totality. You might try to say: "Who's who and what's what? What do you know?" Or you might think: "Who's cheating whom? I'm cheating him, and he knows I'm cheating him; therefore, he is cheating me. So I cheat him, then he cheats me, blah, blah, blah." Your same old logic could go on and on. If you cannot get away from that, it will be disastrous for you in the vajrayana. You will end up in a realm where there is no reference point of pleasure and pain; you will end up in a realm of utter pain and claustrophobia.

So the role of the vajra master is crucial and much larger than that of the spiritual friend at the mahayana level. The vajra master does not try to do a good job or interpret the teachings. The approach of being your psychologist or therapist, or trying to do good things for you, does not apply to the vajra master. The vajra master is also not using vajrayana to get a credential. Trying to use vajrayana to establish your credentials or create possibilities for yourself is disastrous. Trying to make yourself into a homemade teacher, let alone a homemade student, does not work.

The whole relationship between vajra master and student has to be professional, by the book, a business deal. It is a businesslike attitude, a business approach, because very simply, everything involved in your life is your concern. You have to relate directly with your suit and tie or your skirt and blouse, because the world we have is the world that is: the world of vajrayana. It is the vajra world, so everything in your life is part of your business. You cannot say that this portion is my business, and that portion is somebody else's problem. You take everything on yourself—all the energies of the world—and that involves tremendous responsibility, daring, and heroism.

## STICKING WITH TRUE DHARMA

Vajrayana is a very bold statement and a bold experience. What has been said was said because it is real. Nothing is left up to interpretation. If you try to do that, it means you are in bad shape. You should not try to rationalize the vajrayana. You cannot afford to interpret and reinterpret and re-reinterpret the world of vajrayana at all, whether philosophically, psychologically, poetically, or however you might do it. You have to stick with the true dharma. There is no choice. You should remember that.

I do not want anyone to become my interpretive spokesperson, editing what has been said. In presenting the vajrayana, I am trying to be as genuine as possible, according to the teachings. You should not create obstacles to hearing that by saying, "Well, he said that, but he didn't *mean* that. He meant something more delicate, something more poetic or psychological." You should not pervert the teachings. If you do, you will be eaten up.

When you are studying the vajrayana teachings, and especially when you are preparing to become a vajrayana student yourself, you can question or investigate anything you want, as long as you are not reinterpreting to make yourself comfortable. Everybody brings along their wishes as to what the teachings should mean, which is a problem. But if you just consider what is being presented, that is okay. In other words, what I am saying is: Don't bring your past into it, but bring your present. Don't say: "I have been a psychologist, I have been heroic, I have been a poet, and

I have been a bartender." Trying to use whatever you may have been to give validity to the teachings in your own way is not the way—it is your own distorted way, which is not so good. In that case, you are perverting the teachings.

At this point, you should just try to understand what is being said—that's all. Just study. Study, and discuss what you study with others. Relate to how you feel, rather than how you have been decorated by your background. When you are receiving the vajrayana teachings, no one has any background. Everybody is just a student, a gray dot, and everyone's past has been forgotten for a while. You are just studying the dharma, nothing more. So do not try to play one-upmanship or prove that you are smarter than others. When you study the vajrayana, keep it simple. You are just a student of the dharma, that is all.

# 10

# The Power of Devotion

*Devotion is somewhat like a spiritual love affair. You are longing to learn from a learned and enlightened person, like a schoolchild. Without devotion, there is no possibility of learning or studying vajrayana teachings of any kind. Devotion is what leads to transmission.*

## VIEW OF OURSELVES IN THE THREE YANAS

Devotion is an important topic in the vajrayana, but in order to relate with devotion, we first need to look at ourselves as the recipients of the teaching. It is necessary for us to realize who we are and what we are, particularly when we begin to practice and study the vajrayana.

In the hinayana, we know who we are: we are an abundance of pain and an abundance of heaps that do not coordinate with each other, except in a neurotic way.*

In the mahayana, we find that we are an abundance of fixations. We find that we are holding on to ourselves and that we could be liberated by realizing and transplanting bodhichitta into ourselves. We see that working with bodhichitta loosens everything up, and we begin to become loosened up as well.

In the vajrayana, we also regard ourselves as an abundance of neurotic fixations, and we find that we are constantly uptight and self-conscious.

---

* *Abundance of heaps* refers to the combination of five constituents of ego, called *skandhas*, or "heaps."

However, we also find that we are more than that. In particular, when we begin to listen to the vajrayana teachings, we find ourselves terrified and fearful. We develop tremendous fear of the profound meaning and profound subjects that are taught in the vajrayana.

## FEAR AS THE GROUND OF DISCOVERING SACREDNESS

The experience of sacredness begins with fear. It begins with your resentment, fear, uncertainty, and your feeling of being unable to understand— but then you give in to that. There is both fear of fear, and fear of walking into the sacredness. First you experience fear of the profound meaning; then we tell you to jump in because of your fear. And when you jump in, you experience fear of the sacredness. In the vajrayana, we begin with experience, not logic. We only use logic after you have understood the experience, after it has actually come to seem logical to you.

Fear is an obstacle when you do not give in to it; but after you have given in, fear becomes kindling, an encouragement, and a pilot light. Once you have given in, you develop so much reverence for the vajra master, the one who actually created that particular situation and the whole experience. If the sacred world is the world as it is, the world as it has always been, you might ask, "In what sense does the vajra master create it?" But who actually knows the world as it is? Tom, Dick, and Harry do not really know the world as it is. The one who does know is the vajra master.

So in order to become devoted students, we have to start out with terror and awe. It seems that this is the only way we can begin. We have to start with the kind of fear that people develop when they begin to have an idea of what the vajrayana actually means. When people have studied the hinayana and mahayana, they begin to develop respect for the vajrayana as being a very special case. People who have studied something about the vajrayana, and particularly those who are contemplating becoming vajrayana practitioners, begin to feel terrified. It is not that the presentation of the vajrayana teachings is terrifying; it is that the consequences of embarking on the whole tantric journey become terrifying. It is on the basis of that terror and fear, that unwillingness or uncertainty about giving in, that we begin our practice.

So fear is our starting point. And from that initial terror and fear, we begin to discover what we are terrified of. If we look into the depths of our mind, into that mind of terror and fear, we find that we are afraid of the sacredness of vajrayana. It is as if we were dressed in T-shirts and jeans, and suddenly we were invited to Buckingham Palace. We feel as if the teachings are beginning to mock us. More precisely, we are exposed as sloppy, unwholesome individuals who are still carrying our handbags of habitual patterns and neuroses with us. We are like kangaroos carrying our little pouches of resources, our little neuroses, in case we need further reinforcement to hold on to all our stuff. We are unwashed, smelly, shaky, nervous, untidy, and unwholesome; and when we begin to walk into the vajrayana world in that style, we obviously feel both dirty and unpresentable.

## Awe and Reverence

At this point, however, instead of placing too much emphasis on your dirtiness and unpresentableness, you could shift to a different state of mind: one of awe and reverence. When you look around at your world and see that everything is sacred, holy, wonderful, colorful, dignified, and powerful, you experience the contrast between yourself and the vajrayana world. Because of that contrast, you begin to be awe-inspired. You pick up on the awe-inspiring and fearsome nature of the world, and you develop a feeling of reverence for it. So the perception of sacredness comes from the mind's experience of contrast.

In terms of fear, fear of oneself is self-consciousness, and fear of sacredness is other-consciousness. When you first enter the vajrayana world, you should not necessarily just feel your own self-consciousness. You should use your self-consciousness to review the rest of the environment, so that this self-consciousness is imposed on the whole perspective rather than purely on yourself. Out of that, you might pick up some reverence for the sacredness of the vajrayana world and the sacredness of your experience itself.

In the example of Buckingham Palace, walking into that palace creates fear of oneself, or self-consciousness. But actually you are both self-conscious and other-conscious. You are conscious of the surroundings, so altogether it is a fear of sacredness, which implies oneself and other at the same time. It is like being in a plane. If you are flying in an airplane, simultaneously you are self-conscious of being in the plane and being in space. You look down and you realize that there is a big drop, and at the same time you also realize that you are flying in the airplane. It is a similar experience here.

The sense of sacredness is the key to how you can get further and further into the vajrayana. This particular vajra Buckingham Palace, this sacred world that we are talking about, is created by the vajra master and by the lineage of the vajra master. When you develop faith or trust in that sacred world and in the teacher, who is the creator of that world, you realize that you do not have to stick to your jeans and T-shirts, which is a joy.

At this point, since you have not run back to your former home, quite possibly the best thing to do is to take off your T-shirt and jeans, take a shower in the compound of the palace, and present yourself, naked and clean. That is how you enter the vajra Buckingham Palace. And as you enter, you still feel as if you are yourself—as if. So devotion in this case is the fearlessness of coming as you are, properly showered and cleaned up, without your T-shirt and jeans. Once you enter, the king or queen and the occupants of the palace appreciate you and recognize you as a brave guest. They acknowledge that entering this space takes courage and conviction. So devotion in the vajrayana sense is not just trust and worship, but it is having a wholesome attitude toward yourself.

## AAH! THE SPACE BEFORE FIRST THOUGHT

In the vajrayana, the expression of that wholesome attitude of devotion comes from the space before the first thought; it happens before the first thought. When you have a thought—for instance, "column" or "ceiling"—that thought is already fully formed. But before you have the thought "column" or "ceiling," you have openness—*aah!* So there is openness—*aah!*—then "column" or "ceiling." As long as there is a gap of openness—*aah!*—there is no problem. As practitioners, you are supposed to pay attention to that *aah!;* you are supposed to look at it. After that, this *aah!* might become "column" and "ceiling," which at that point is: So what?!

*Trungpa Rinpoche opening a Japanese fan. Aah!*

Experiencing the openness of *aah!* leads to reverence for the vajra master who created your awareness of this situation. Your experience of *aah!* could be sparked by anything. It could be like the opening of a Japanese fan. The first stage of seeing the fan is just—*aah!* Then you see the fan as a "fan," which is the second stage. And the first experience of devotion occurs just like that. It is not about bureaucracy, or loyalty, or territory. But having started out with fear of the profundity, with being awe-inspired, you then go *aah!*—and after that you click into the situation.

Through your connection with the vajra master, you can experience openness early on, often right at the beginning of the vajrayana path; and as you go on, you are still doing it—*aah!* You keep doing it, on the spot. From that, loyalty begins to develop. Loyalty means having a sense of oneness with that openness—*aah!* You are loyal to that. You find that as a student of the vajrayana, you are beginning to share the mind of the vajra master. You begin to catch glimpses of the vajra master's mind on the spot. Whatever the experience may be, whether it is a memory or a confirmation—*aah!*—you have it.

## Mögü: Joining Longing and Respect

Devotion, or *mögü* in Tibetan, can be divided into two aspects: *möpa* and *küpa*. *Möpa* means "longing" or "wanting," and *küpa* means "humility," "respect," or "being without arrogance." With küpa, you are not pretending to be somebody who has reached a higher level of wisdom. So in devotion, longing and humbleness are put together. That state of mind brings openness to the teacher and to the dharma.

With möpa, there is so much longing. There is a very passionate longing for the vajra master and the lineage. An analogy for this kind of longing is when two people are about to make love. While they are in the process of taking off their shoes and shirts and becoming naked so they can jump into bed together, they look longingly at each other. Möpa is similar to that process of anticipation and longing. Such longing needs to have already been inspired early on by the sense of *aah!*

With küpa, the longing of möpa does not become purely an emotional indulgence or demand on the part of either the student or the teacher. The devotion of küpa is the respect or sacredness that comes from that experience of *aah!* Küpa arises because every highlight in your life has always been touched by the sacredness of vajrayana, even before you knew it.

## A Spiritual Love Affair

Devotion is somewhat like a spiritual love affair. You are longing to study with a learned and enlightened person, like a schoolchild. Without devotion, there is no possibility of learning or studying vajrayana teachings of any kind. Devotion is what leads to transmission.

### Rock Meets Bone

In the Kagyü tradition, there is a traditional verse that says: "When you intensify devotion in your heart, rock meets bone in insight, and the ultimate lineage blessing is received.* You could say that the lineage is the

---

* This quote is found in the collection of vajra songs of the Kagyü gurus. See *The Rain of Wisdom*, translated by the Nalanda Translation Committee under the direction of Chögyam Trungpa (Boston: Shambhala Publications, 1980).

rock, and your practice is the bone. When your determination is very hard and bony, it begins to meet the rock-solidness of the teachings, and they begin to agree with each other. When the two meet, two hard cores are put together, and your bone becomes rock, and rock becomes bone. There is no frivolity. You do not need blood, skin, or flesh anymore. You are planted properly and completely in your practice and discipline. There is no other lingering experience.

## Driving an Oak Peg into Hard Ground

A similar expression says that devotion is "like an oak peg in hard ground." Again, the sense is that your entire core is meeting another entire core. When you have a peg made out of oak and you hammer it down far enough into hard ground, you cannot take it out. It is so solid and so real, so ordinary and so tough.

## UNREQUITED LOVE

When you first meet your guru, you have been making your living by cheating everybody. That is how you have made yourself wealthy. Then you see another wealthy person, the vajra master. But the vajra master's way of becoming wealthy is by being genuine all the time. So you have a mind-boggling revelation: previously you thought that you could not actually become rich except by cheating, and then you find that somebody else has done the opposite—they have become rich by being genuine and honest. That is the meeting of different minds. The product of kleshas, which is your search for pleasure, has met with nondual wisdom, and finally you are shocked to find that by being genuine, you could become wealthy. That is the starting point of the explosion. You actually see that you can practice dharma properly, and that you can actually attain enlightenment. It is an interesting discovery.

Usually, according to our ordinary concepts, if you don't cheat, if you are not trying to make a dollar out of fifty cents every minute, you will end up with nothing. You never think that anybody could get rich just by being rich in their natural state. And for the first time, you have met a vajra master who has never tried to cheat; they have never even heard of cheating. Earning wealth, from a vajracharya's point of view, is entirely different from your way of becoming rich.

There are a lot of stories about this in *The Life of Milarepa.** In one story, Milarepa meets a huntsman and says to him, "Hunting is not the only pleasurable thing you can do. Why don't you practice? Then you can hunt your own mind, your kleshas, and you will become a better hunter." The huntsman did what Milarepa advised, and he became a great yogi.

Our lifestyle and our values are always based on either making love or killing, and in between these two activities, we get confused and fall asleep. Those are the only three possibilities taking place in our life: murdering, mating, and falling asleep. There is passion, aggression, and ignorance, to a greater or smaller degree, in whatever we do. That is our logic of happiness, whether in the form of socialism, democracy, capitalism, or what have you. Then we are confronted by somebody who has done something other than seeking happiness in those ways—but by being bored, by just sitting, by just being, by not resorting to any form of entertainment at all, but just remaining like a statue. It is mind-boggling. None of us expected that anyone could do that. Nonetheless, we begin to realize that it has actually happened, and it has turned out to be much more powerful than we had expected, much better than our version of business.

It is a question of seeing the contrast. In the first moment of that meeting, in the first flash, you are paralyzed or shocked, and then you are amazed. You begin to feel doubtful of your ego; you begin to crumble. And when you resort to memory, you find that your memory is a collection of bad news or insults. You are revolted. But as we say in the *Supplication to the Takpo Kagyü:* "Revulsion is the foot of meditation."† So this revulsion essentially becomes a bank of energy.

When the meeting of minds happens, the residue may be that the student falls completely in love with the mind of the master. There is a feeling of unrequited love. That unrequited love is very healthy; it is the path. The more unrequited you feel, the better. Traditionally, unrequited love means that you have been rejected, that you have no future with your lover. But unrequited love in the vajrayana sense is the best love. It means that you have a path together, or along with, your vajra master. You feel unrequited all the time; there is never enough. Even the hinayana tradi-

---

* *Milarepa* was a renowned teacher of the Kagyü tradition known for his deep practice, his austerity, and his teaching in the form of poetry and song. For more about this great poet-saint, see Lobsang P. Lhalungpa, *The Life of Milarepa: A New Translation from the Tibetan* (New York: E. P. Dutton, 1977).

† The *Supplication to the Takpo Kagyü* is a profound and well-loved aspirational chant written by Pengar Jampal Sangpo as a summary of the essence of the Kagyü path.

tion talks about unrequited love. In referring to the Buddha, *The Sutra of the Recollection of the Noble Three Jewels* says, "One never has enough of seeing him."* The idea that one never has enough of seeing the Buddha is a form of unrequited love. There is a hunger and appreciation for this giant world, this wonderful world, and that hunger is absolutely good. It allows us to practice and to get more into the world of the teacher all the time. At this point, the ground really becomes the path.

Personally, in terms of my relationship with my teacher, Jamgön Kongtrül of Shechen, I still want to tell him what I have been doing. Fundamentally speaking, he knows what I am doing. He knows how much he taught me, and he has great confidence in me. He made me his regent, believing that I would make no mistakes. But I wish he could actually see what we are doing here. I want him to meet every one of my students so that he could see their discipline, their devotion, and their dedication.

That is the kind of unrequited love that goes on in the Kagyü and Nyingma traditions. It is sad and real. It is even sadder because the teacher becomes very lonely. I personally feel extremely lonely. I have no one to talk to, no one to tell, "Look! Joe Schmidt is a great practitioner. He had a nice background, and now he has joined us. He has practiced a lot, and now he is beginning to understand coemergent wisdom.† He is beginning to understand the wisdom of beyond beyond, and he is beginning to click."

That is the kind of unrequited love we are talking about. Nonetheless, that love can make us feel quite satisfied. We can become intoxicated on our unrequited love and also inspired, as though we had been given some kind of liquor to drink. When we were translating *The Life of Marpa,*‡ I was actually thinking, "If only Marpa were here." If he could see how the English-speaking people are practicing, it would be very interesting for him. He would probably cry once again, and he would probably create a *ganachakra,* or vajra feast for us, in order to celebrate what we are doing.

---

* This sutra is included in full, with commentary, in volume 1 of the *Profound Treasury,* part 1, "Entering the Path," in the section titled "Reflecting on the Three Jewels."

† *Coemergent wisdom* refers to the simultaneous arising of samsara and nirvana, which gives birth to wisdom.

‡ Chögyam Trungpa formed, and worked closely with, a translation committee called the Nalanda Translation Committee, in order to translate Tibetan texts and liturgies into English. This story is about their work on *The Life of Marpa the Translator: Seeing Accomplishes All,* trans. by the Nalanda Translation Committee under the direction of Chögyam Trungpa (Boston: Shambhala Publications, 1995).

*Part Three*

# THE TÜLKU PRINCIPLE
# AND THE TRUNGPA TÜLKUS

# II

# The Tülku Principle

*Once they are born, such blessed tülkus still have to study and go through various trainings. Otherwise, if each incarnation were either already totally enlightened when they were born, or had to begin all over again, it would defeat the purpose of the tülku system. If in each life a teacher had to struggle from the ground up, it would seem to contradict the perpetuation or furtherance of the development of enlightenment.*

H AVING DISCUSSED the principle of the vajra master, or guru, we could discuss the Trungpa lineage and how the idea of *tülkus*, or incarnate lamas, fits into our discussion of the vajrayana.

The principle of lineage is very important. It is our heritage; it is what we have received. In particular, we have received the Kagyü and Nyingma traditions. These two traditions both emphasize practice methodologies. In these practice lineages, whether you are in the world or in retreat from the world, you are in retreat all the time.

Kagyü vision is like seeing the colors, and Nyingma vision is like focusing, which helps you to see the precision of the colors. The Kagyü and Nyingma are almost like one tradition. It has been said that they are like using two eyes in order to see. Forms, such as the way the shrine is arranged, the way *thangkas* are hung, and the way meditators sit cross-legged, are not made up. They are part of a twenty-six-hundred-year-old tradition that is still being followed today.

## The Three Kayas and the Tülku Principle

The tülku principle is connected with the guru and the yidam principles, and in particular with the vajrayana concept of the *trikaya* or the bodies of enlighenment: dharmakaya (Tib.: *chöku*), sambhogakaya (Tib.: *longku*), and *nirmanakaya* (Tib.: *tülku*). The idea of the three bodies or *kayas* is very simple: it is that the enlightened state has three levels. The dharmakaya is ultimate being, the origin of everything, formless and all-pervasive. The sambhogakaya is the manifestation of the activities of dharmakaya into the visible level of energy and play. The nirmanakaya represents actual earthly connections and energy materializing on a physical plane, particularly as human beings.

The term *tülku* is the Tibetan translation of nirmanakaya. *Tül* means "emanation," and *ku* means "body"; so *tülku* means "emanated body." There are several types of tülkus. Gautama Buddha, the historical Buddha, or the Buddha on earth, is considered to be one type of tülku. Images of the Buddha are also known as tülkus, as art tülkus. Another type of tülku is one who continues to be reborn again and again in order to help beings on various levels.

The good intentions of the buddhas extend to all the world realms, but in general the enlightened ones find that human beings are the most workable. Humans speak languages; they have developed intelligence; they have complicated social systems; and they also experience pain more acutely than the beings in the other realms. The beings in the other realms are said to be dissolved much more into their own confusion, and therefore they are more freaked-out than human beings. So the human realm is the most workable of all the realms.

## The Tibetan Tülku System

The Tibetan tradition of discovering tülkus involves identifying incarnate lamas, or proclaiming that somebody is the tülku of so-and-so. In this system, there are various types of incarnate lamas and various types of rebirth taking place. For example, one kind of tülku incarnates before the previous incarnation has died, several months or even years earlier; another kind of tülku takes rebirth directly after the previous incarnation has died. In general, we can say there are three types of tülkus: blessed, anonymous, and direct.

## Blessed Tülkus

Among the various types of incarnation in Tibet, the most prominent seems to be the form of tülku called a blessed tülku. In this case, the teacher chooses someone to bless. They may choose the person who is closest to them, or bless some passing bodhisattva who has not quite attained the highest of the bhumis. The teacher, or current tülku, blesses that person by taking a certain type of spiritual energy that transcends ego, and then transferring this energy to the chosen person. This person then comes back in the next life as the incarnation of that previous tülku. So although he or she is a different person, there is spiritual continuity taking place.

Blessed tülkus have to be raised and educated; they have to go through training and practice. Since they are recognized as a tülku of some previous teacher, they have more potential for realization than an ordinary person who is not pushed or encouraged in the same way, and who hasn't had anything injected into them. So these young tülkus have a great deal of potential, but they have not quite realized it; therefore, they have to go through training and education. With training, and because such spiritual energy has been put into them, they can then begin to come up to the level of their previous incarnation.

While this transfer of spiritual energy is possible, we ordinary people cannot transfer energy in this way because we believe ourselves to be one entity, in spite of philosophical indoctrination about egolessness. So we find it very difficult to split our personality, unless we become schizophrenic, which is not a very pleasant or enlightened way of splitting oneself. The principle of the blessed tülku shows us that there may be a higher level of splitting personality—not into just one person, but into many. In this splitting, usually the body, speech, mind, quality, and action aspects of a particular being are transferred, so you end up with five different incarnations of one previous teacher. Some may specialize in scholarship, and others in contemplation, and others in the activity of propagating the dharma, and so forth.

His Holiness the Dalai Lama, His Holiness the Karmapa, and all the other tülkus you may be familiar with seem to be the blessed tülku type. Each of them was recognized by their predecessor, who blessed that person as somebody who was already making progress in some way. The previous incarnation encouraged them or pushed them in a certain way, so that they could reincarnate as the next Karmapa or the next Dalai Lama.

But once they are born, such blessed tülkus still have to study and go through various trainings. Otherwise, if each incarnation were either already totally enlightened when they were born, or if they had to begin all over again, it would defeat the purpose of the tülku system. If in each life a teacher had to struggle from the ground up, it would seem to contradict the perpetuation or furtherance of the development of enlightenment.

## Anonymous Tülkus

You might ask what happens to those people who have already injected their essence and their wisdom into somebody else. What happens to the original people? Where do they go? It seems that those original people also come back to this world, not as their official reincarnation, but anonymously or incognito. They may come back as farmers or fishermen or businesspeople or politicians or whatever. Anonymous tülkus do not necessarily have to come back into a Buddhist environment, because the teachings of enlightenment could be taught in many different forms, and people can be helped at all kinds of levels.

The point of anonymous tülkus seems to be that it is possible to meet people who have never heard or thought about any form of the Buddhist teachings, but who somehow are realized in themselves. In such cases, some memories exist within them, and they have some idea of their basic being. But they see no point in advertising that eccentricity, particularly if they are going to communicate with the ordinary world.

Such secretly real incarnate persons have no problems at all. Their sanity cannot be undermined, because anything that happens in their life is a reminder of their intelligence or their enlightenment. Anything that happens reminds them that they are completely realized beings, so nothing can undermine them, nothing whatsoever. In the same way that the sun is never influenced by the clouds, anonymous tülkus are unconditioned in their basic being, so any condition that comes up is superfluous.

## *Direct Tülkus*

In addition to blessed tülkus and anonymous tülkus, there are also what are called direct tülkus. With such tülkus, very little training is needed. A genius in the family could be that kind of direct incarnation.

There are extraordinary stories about such tülkus. When they are being brought up and they are still children, maybe only six years old, they are already very articulate. They seem to know everything, and they just continue to get better all the time. Their parents begin to feel very inferior to their own children, who seem to function much better in the world than they do. Such children may not yet have been taught reading or writing, or maybe they have gotten just a hint of it, but they pick these things up very fast, and they even correct their teachers as they go on. Similar stories are told about Mozart, who was supposedly composing music when he was only six years old.

Direct incarnations do exist, but they are rare. So the idea of direct incarnation is not often discussed. However, sometimes a teacher is known to be a direct incarnation. For instance, the great Khyentse Rinpoche, Jamyang Khyentse Wangpo, was actually a direct incarnation. But that does not seem to be the case with any of the present incarnate lamas.

Direct incarnations need a lot of special attention. It is interesting to see what happens when an incarnate lama who is recognized as a direct incarnation rejects his life completely. When I lived in Tibet, I met a local king in the neighborhood next to mine who had five sons, and one of them was a direct incarnate lama. The king did not want to let go of this son, because he did not want him to face hardships such as being mistreated by tutors. So his son was held back and kept home, and eventually he married. But then that son went completely insane. People had to restrain him to keep him from jumping out of windows and things like that. Somehow, when you do not meet that kind of karmic demand from higher authorities, you either explode or turn into a vegetable.

## MEMORIES OF PREVIOUS LIFETIMES

As the eleventh Trungpa tülku, I am sometimes asked if I have acute memories of previous lifetimes. Being a blessed tülku, I am not the real tenth Trungpa, Chökyi Nyin-je. I am not him exactly, but I may be a part of his memory, part of his being. Goodness knows who I am! I could be a gentleman from Osaka, or one of the tenth Trungpa's disciples, or whatever. Still, there are memories, which I was usually forbidden to talk about, for some reason. I suppose that is understandable, since people may begin to trip out on the whole thing. So I was only allowed to tell such memories to my tutor when I was young.

Those memories continued until I was about thirteen. Usually, at the level of puberty, such memories begin to disappear and you do not get flashbacks anymore. This point is very significant, because at the level of puberty you begin to relate with the world. You become a man or woman of the world. Before that, you are still a past-oriented infant, somehow. These kinds of memories seem to be based on something much purer than just the seventh consciousness.* The seventh consciousness is impermanent and is liable to be forgetful. The process of going through your birth and your death shocks you so much that you forget your past, which is what usually happens to ordinary people.

I do not think there is any harm in telling you a few stories. For instance, I remember visiting the place where the tenth Trungpa died, a local lord's house. There was a particular place for his bedroom, for the shrine, and for everything else. When I arrived, people were busy organizing my welcome party outside, and I was helped off my horse and I walked inside. Traditionally, there was somebody with incense to lead me in, but somehow they did not get their act together, so nobody was leading me. I had to walk in, because there were a lot of people waiting and it was getting rather late.

As soon as I walked through the door, I knew exactly where to go and which room to enter. My attendant, who had never been to the house before, followed me. All the doors were closed, so he said, "Maybe we should get somebody to help."

And I said, "Well, let's find out first. How about here?" We then walked into exactly the same room as the tenth Trungpa had when he arrived. It was arranged in exactly the same way, in exactly the same pattern.

Another time, we were looking for a particular village, and we got lost in the rain and mist. We were traveling toward some nomads with their tents set up in various camps, and there was a certain fork in the

---

* In Buddhist psychology, consciousness can be described as having eight aspects. In this schema, the *seventh consciousness* represents the basic identity in the dualistic sense of self and other. It is referred to as the afflicted, or klesha, consciousness.

road you were supposed to take. Everybody was completely bewildered, and cold and upset and hungry. The monk in charge of discipline with his loud voice was getting really hungry, and whenever he got hungry he got mad. Everybody was feeling completely down, and they began to curse the people who had invited us to this strange place.

I wasn't quite sure, but I thought I knew the way. I thought everybody knew it—but then suddenly it clicked with me that nobody knew. Somehow I had some memory of having been there before. I did not even bother to ask the question, "Have I been here before in this life?" Maybe when I was an infant they took me there, but as far as I could remember, I had never been there in this body.

In a ceremonial procession, there was usually a guy who rode on a white horse to lead the procession, and then there was a guy with flags, and then a guy who carried the umbrella behind me. The rest of the people were supposed to follow after me. Everything was set as to who comes next. Although the whole atmosphere was very miserable, the ceremony still continued.

But then I said that I would like to break the rule; I said that I should go to the front, with the guy on the white horse. My attendant did not know what to do. He said, "Okay. Maybe we could do it, but we shouldn't tell anybody."

So I told my attendant not to tell anybody, and I broke the rule and rode with the guy on the white horse at the head of our procession. I told the guy, "Let's go this way. If we go this way, there is going to be a pass. Then we are going to go by a village, which is not our place, and we are going to go by a second one, which is not our village either. There is a bridge on the other side, and beyond that, seemingly hidden in a sort of dimple in the meadow, you can see the village, the smoke going up and everything." So we were able to get to the village. Actually, I expected that somebody would be surprised about that, but nobody said anything.

Those are a few stories from my days in Tibet.

# 12

# The Early Trungpas

*Trung Ma-se began to attract many prominent students. . . . Among these, there were eight very close students, who were known as the eight mystics. The Tibetan word for mystic is* togden, *which means "someone who is realized" or "endowed with realization." Along with the eight mystics, there were the three idiots, who were the closest students of all, and the first Trungpa was one of these idiots.*

## The Line of the Trungpas

In connection with the tülku principle, we could discuss a specific lineage of blessed incarnations: the line of the Trungpas.* The word *trungpa* means "being nearby to the teacher," which refers to an attendant: *trung* means "nearby," and *pa* makes it the "one who is nearby."

The lineage of the Trungpas began around the fifteenth century and continues to this day. Altogether, there have been eleven Trungpas; so the lineage is comprised of the first Trungpa, Künga Gyaltsen, and ten incarnations. As the eleventh Trungpa, I am the current holder of this particular lineage.†

---

* In this chapter and the next, Trungpa Rinpoche is introducing his students to his own personal spiritual lineage and tradition, as well as giving an example of how the Tibetan tülku system works.

† There is now a twelfth Trungpa Tülku. Trungpa Rinpoche passed away in 1987, and four years later, His Eminence Tai Situ Rinpoche recognized a two-year-old Tibetan boy, Chökyi Senge Rinpoche, as the twelfth Trungpa Tülku. The twelfth Trungpa is presently engaged in the traditional intensive study and training needed for his position as the current lineage holder.

## THE LINE OF THE TRUNGPAS

Trung Ma-se (15th century)
*Teacher of the first Trungpa, who was one of the "three idiots"*

1st Trungpa / Künga Gyaltsen (early 15th century)
*Student of Trung Ma-se, Surmang encampments*

2nd Trungpa / Künga Sangpo (b. 1464)
*Student of Trung Ma-se*

3rd Trungpa / Künga Öser (15th–16th centuries)
*Incarnation of Dombipa, established Dütsi Tel*

4th Trungpa / Künga Namgyal (1567–1629)
*Chö practice, great mahamudra scholar*

5th Trungpa / Tenpa Namgyal (1633–1712)
*Political leader, teacher of Chinese emperor, said to have created rain*

6th Trungpa / Tendzin Chökyi Gyatso (1715–1734 est.)
*Died young*

7th Trungpa / Jampal Chökyi Gyatso (1743–1768 est.)
*Poet, also died young*

8th Trungpa / Gyurme Thenphel (b. 1771)
*Incorporated Nyingma teachings, propogated* The Tibetan Book of the Dead, *adopted protector Ekajati*

9th Trungpa / Tenpa Rabgye (19th century)
*Known for being ordinary*

10th Trungpa / Chökyi Nyin-je (1879–1939)
*Student of Jamgön Kongtrül the Great, rebuilt Surmang*

11th Trungpa / Chökyi Gyatso (1940–1987)
*Vidyadhara Chögyam Trungpa Rinpoche*

12th Trungpa / Chökyi Senge (b. 1989)
*Current lineage holder*

Dates for the Trungpa Tülku lineage are based on information provided by Dr. Michael R. Sheehy, Head of Research for the Department of Literary Research, Tibetan Buddhist Resource Center, Cambridge, Massachusetts, in consultation with Derek Kolleeny.

## Trung Ma-se and the Origins of the Trungpa Lineage

The Trungpa lineage traces its origins back to the fifteenth-century siddha, Trung Ma-se, who was the teacher of the first Trungpa.

### Birth and Training

It is said that Trung Ma-se was born at the time when the king of Minyak was making a pilgrimage to Lhasa, and that Trung Ma-se's mother was part of the traveling party. His birthplace was in what would become the region of Surmang, which is where the Trungpa lineage was later based, and in the same area where the Surmang monasteries would be established in the future. So Trung Ma-se was born in the far east of Tibet, as a prince. When I was at Surmang, there was a certain field, which we referred to as the place where the king of Minyak had set up his encampment. It was there that this child was born.

Trung Ma-se happened to be illegitimate, and he was the youngest child in the family. There was some resentment of him because he was illegitimate, but the family still paid him a certain amount of respect, honoring him simply because he was born into their family. The area of Tibet where he grew up was predominantly Nyingma, the earliest school of Tibetan Buddhism, so in that area the students were taught the culture and the meditative traditions of the Nyingma school. When this child grew to be about fifteen, he became a very learned and powerful person of that particular principality.

Trung Ma-se was raised in both the spiritual and secular disciplines that had evolved at that time. When he was older, he wanted to leave his homeland, and with the permission of his parents, he journeyed to Central Tibet. He had already received the atiyoga teachings of the Nyingma school as part of his upbringing. Then, in Central Tibet, he visited the fifth Karmapa, Teshin Shekpa (1384–1415), and received instruction in the Kagyü tradition from him. Trung Ma-se remained there practicing for something like seven years.

### Trung Ma-se's Reed Hut and Teaching Activity

After that, the fifth Karmapa sent Trung Ma-se back to his home ground where he had been born, and told him to settle anywhere he could find a place suitable for practicing and teaching. So Trung Ma-se came back to eastern Tibet and settled down. He practiced meditation there in a hut made out of reeds. He spent a long time doing sitting meditation practice, something like six years, and he had very little to eat, but nobody discovered who he was.

Eventually Trung Ma-se began to feel that he was able to relate with students and that he was in a situation to do so. So he decided to go back and ask his guru's permission to teach. He set out to see the Karmapa, but on the journey he somehow got a message before he had a chance to ask his teacher for permission. Some merchants brought mail for him that said, "Don't come back; go ahead," or something like that. He understood this to mean that he did not have to ask if it was okay for him to teach or not, and having realized the meaning of the message, he went back to eastern Tibet. He had already built his reed hut there, so he began to teach in that hut. In particular, he began to teach the six yogas of Naropa and the *anuttarayoga* teachings connected with that.*

Trung Ma-se was also well-known as a holder of an important "ear-whispered" or hearing lineage within the Kagyü tradition. He received the complete teachings on Vajrayogini, Chakrasamvara, and Four-Armed Mahakala, and these became the special transmissions that he was to hold. It is said that when Naropa transmitted the teachings of Vajrayogini to Marpa, Naropa told Marpa that these teachings should be kept as a transmission from one teacher to one student for thirteen generations, and then they could be propagated to others. This kind of transmission is called *chiggyü,* which means a "single lineage" or "single thread" transmission. Since Trung Ma-se belonged to the thirteenth generation, he became the first guru to transmit this particular lineage of mahamudra teachings to more than a single dharma successor, and in fact he taught it widely.†

---

* *Anuttarayoga,* or mahamudra, refers to the highest teachings of the New Translation school of Tibetan Buddhism. For more on anuttarayoga, see part II, "The Tantric Journey: Mahamudra." The *six yogas of Naropa* are a set of advanced tantric practices attributed to Naropa that include the yogas of: inner heat, illusory body, dream, luminosity, transference of consciousness, and the intermediate state.

† According to Trungpa Rinpoche: "The first Trungpa, Künga Gyaltsen, was one of Trung Ma-se's disciples who received this transmission. As the eleventh Trungpa Tülku, I received the Vajrayogini transmission from Rölpa Dorje, the regent abbot of Surmang and one of my main tutors." See *The Collected Works of Chögyam Trungpa,* ed. Carolyn Gimian, vol. 3 (Boston: Shambhala Publications, 2004), 426–427.

Trung Ma-se was an expert on those teachings, and he gathered a large number of disciples. People in the local principalities also began to take an interest in his teachings and in his being. As Trung Ma-se's teaching situation became stronger and clearer, his students requested that he give a name to his establishment. Trung Ma-se suggested that they could name the establishment after his reed hut. It had a lot of corners, because a reed hut needs a lot of support, which is provided by the corners. Therefore, they called the place "Surmang." *Sur* means "corner," and *mang* means "many"; so *Surmang* means "many cornered." It was quite arbitrary; Trung Ma-se was not particularly concerned with creating a glorious name.

## The Eight Mystics and the Three Idiots

Over time, Trung Ma-se began to attract many prominent students. Eventually, he was teaching a public audience of several thousand students. Many hundreds of his devotees, something like 360 of them, were considered close students. Among these, there were eight very close students, who were known as the eight mystics. The Tibetan word for mystic is *togden,* which means "someone who is realized" or "endowed with realization."

Along with the eight mystics, there were the three idiots, who were the closest students of all, and the first Trungpa was one of these idiots. The Tibetan word for "idiot" is *ja. Ja* is actually a local idiom that means "moron," or someone "lower, flat, and very naive," like a sitting duck.

So there were three idiots or morons. The reason they were known as idiots was because they were so stubborn and so earthy that they did not flinch at anything at all. They simply set their minds to one thing at a time. When the teacher told them to do something, they just did it. They became known as the idiots for their stubbornness. The eight mystics were quite good in their idiotness, but they did not quite qualify to be known as idiots. They were somewhat good students and nice people.

## THE FIRST TRUNGPA: KÜNGA GYALTSEN

The first Trungpa, Künga Gyaltsen, lived during the early fifteenth century, and was born into the family of one of the local lords.

## The Meaning of Trungpa

*Künga Gyaltsen* means "All-Joyful Victory Banner," and the word *trungpa* is an honorific term, which means "attendant." Ideally, when somebody serves their guru twenty-four hours a day, they begin to get some glimpse of the workings of the teacher's mind. They begin to get messages and reminders of awareness and things like that. So the best way to develop is to be the guru's servant. That is the tradition.

## The Training of the First Trungpa

Künga Gyaltsen was raised as an educated person. In his youth, he worked with his father ruling the country, collecting taxes, and fighting with hostile neighbors. But when he heard the name of Trung Ma-se, he left his kingdom and abandoned his home to find this teacher. He settled in with him and spent almost twenty years practicing meditation.

Künga Gyaltsen received a lot of teachings at the beginning. He was taught the various levels of Chakrasamvara tantra—the external, the internal, the secret practices, and so forth—and he studied and practiced the six yogas of Naropa. Then his teacher sent him away, saying, "You have received enough of what I have, so now you should find your own monastery and teach other people."

## The First Trungpa and Adro Shelu-bum

When Künga Gyaltsen left Trung Ma-se, he visited various places. As he traveled around eastern Tibet, he came to the fort of Adro Shelu-bum, who was the local landowner and local lord. When Künga Gyaltsen arrived, he was repeating a line from a very famous Manjushri text, the *Manjushri-nama-sangiti* (*Chanting the Names of Manjushri*). In the text there is a phrase, *chökyi gyaltsen lekpar dzuk,* which means "Firmly plant the victorious banner of dharma." So he arrived at the door of Adro Shelu-bum's castle with that particular verse on his lips, and he repeated that line three times. For that reason, at my principal monastery in Tibet, Surmang Dütsi Tel, we always repeated that same line twice when we chanted the text. And here in the West, that line has been made into one of the main slogans of Naropa University. We have translated it in that context as "We firmly plant the victory banner of dharma."

Künga Gyaltsen was well received by Adro Shelu-bum and became his teacher, and Adro Shelu-bum offered his fort and his castle to Künga Gyaltsen as a monastery. Without very much interest, Künga Gyaltsen, the first Trungpa, accepted the gift of the castle, but he did not remain there; he just continued his travels.

## The Second Trungpa: Künga Sangpo

The second Trungpa, Künga Sangpo (b. 1464), lived during the fifteenth century. He was also a traveler. There are very few stories about him, but after the first Trungpa's death, the second Trungpa was discovered by the Karmapa, as usually happens. Künga Sangpo was discovered as an incarnation of the first Trungpa. But he created no monastery, no establishment. He just became a student of a student of Trung Ma-se.

## The Third Trungpa: Künga Öser

The third Trungpa, Künga Öser, lived during the fifteenth and sixteenth centuries.

### The Surmang Encampment

During the time of the third Trungpa, Künga Öser, something important happened: Künga Öser established a set location for the Surmang monasteries, which had previously not been located in one place. Before this, going back to the time of Trung Ma-se, the monks usually camped around. As far as Tibetan monasticism goes, the age of encampment extended from the fourteenth century into the late sixteenth century. These monastic camps were constantly moving. It was a much more grandiose level than nomads, and much more powerful than military camps. The Surmang encampment was called Surmang Garchen, which means "Surmang, the great camp."

In those days the monks traveled in caravans, covering great distances throughout eastern Tibet. Their libraries were on pack mules; the shrine was a large tent; and the monks' and the abbot's quarters were tents as well. In Künga Öser's group, there were about 140 people. The pattern of the culture was to travel in the highlands during the summer when the highlands were not too cold, and to travel in the lowlands in winter when the climate there was relatively reasonable.

The monks set up temporary monasteries in each place they camped. Their practices were conducted in the camps, and student newcomers could be instructed there. As local students began to join the camp and become accepted as novices, the camps became larger. That was the pattern in Tibet for quite a long time. Tsurphu, the Karmapas' monastery, was itself conducted in that same fashion. It was called the "great camp of Karmapa." So for several centuries, in most of Tibet the Tibetan monastic system was not in permanent dwelling places, but in tents.

## The Story of the Skull Cup

Finally, at the end of Künga Öser's life, the Karmapa had a sudden insight. He sent an invitation to Künga Öser to come and visit him. So Künga Öser took a journey to Central Tibet, which usually took about six months. When he arrived, the Karmapa told him of the prophecy of the mahasiddha Dombipa.

Dombipa was a great tantric master who lived in India during the fifteenth century. One evening at the end of his life, as he was drinking out of his skull cup, he decided to transplant his tantric teachings somewhere other than India. He prophesied that in about ten lifetimes, he would go wherever his skull cup landed. Then he threw his skull cup into the air, and it flew across India and landed on a particular hill at what would become Surmang.

The Karmapa told Künga Öser that Künga Öser was the incarnation of Dombipa, and that he should establish a permanent monastery on that site. The place where the skull cup landed happened to be the location of the castle of Adro Shelu-Bum, and since then it has been called Dütsi Tel. *Dütsi* means *amrita,* and *tel* means "hill"; so *Dütsi Tel* means "hill of amrita" or "hill of blessed liquor." Apart from that story about how the third Trungpa, Künga Öser, received instructions to establish a permanent monastic residence, nothing very much is known about him.*

---

* The story of the skull cup and the founding of Surmang has many variations. In one story, the founding of Surmang is attributed to the first Trungpa, who is said to have thrown a cup of beer into the air, based on a dream in which he was acknowledged as an incarnation of Dombipa. For variations, see Chögyam Trungpa, *The Mishap Lineage: Transforming Confusion into Wisdom* (Boston: Shambhala Publications, 2009), 31n2.

## THE FOURTH TRUNGPA: KÜNGA NAMGYAL

The fourth Trungpa, Künga Namgyal (1567–1629), lived during the sixteenth century.

### Chö Practice

Künga Namgyal was well-known as a teacher throughout the Kagyü tradition. He was the only person who actually received what is called the *shi-je* tradition, one of the contemplative schools of Tibetan Buddhism associated with the teachings of *chö*. Künga Namgyal composed texts for the practice of chö that have remained the most important such texts in the Karma Kagyü tradition. This practice is sometimes known as the Surmang chö. He also established something like 108 retreat centers, supposedly in haunted places.

The basic philosophy of chö is that, instead of asking for protection from the *mahakalas* (wrathful deities) or your guru, you offer up your negativities and your security. You ask the enemies or the demons, whoever they are, to consume you. Chö practice usually takes place in the evening or at night. For many people, chö practice is very revealing, particularly in dealing with death and with life's sickness and chaos. This practice is actually something that the contemplative tradition extracted from the *Prajnaparamita Sutras*. There is a touch of tantric outrageousness as well; you are stepping on your problems, stepping on your threats.

### Leaving the Monastery with a White Yak

During the time of Künga Namgyal, the monastic setup became the central focus of society, much more so than in the past. At that point, the principality or kingdom around Surmang began to hand over both the administrative and spiritual duties to the Trungpas. The Chinese emperor acknowledged Künga Namgyal as an important political leader, and formalized that acknowledgment by presenting ceremonial seals of all kinds. In his youth, Künga Namgyal was horrified by his political role, unlike the Trungpas who came after him. In fact, at the age of twenty-four, Künga Namgyal actually left his monastery and handed over the political administrative duties to his brother, who became an important and powerful local ruler.

Having bestowed the rulership of his monastery on his brother, Künga Namgyal rejected any services from the monastery and decided to travel around the country by himself. He had a domesticated white yak without any horns so that it wouldn't be temperamental, and with a ring through its nose so the yak could be led wherever Künga Namgyal wanted. In the treasury of our monastery we used to have that ring, a wooden loop, as well as the thighbone trumpet that he used in chö practice to call the haunting evil spirits to eat him up.

## The Nedo Kagyü Subsect

Künga Namgyal was also one of the great teachers of the subsect of the Kagyü tradition called the Nedo Kagyü, which is not included in the four great and the eight lesser schools of the Kagyü lineage.* This subsect developed based on the idea of the pure land. Like the pure land tradition in Japan, it placed enormous emphasis on the worship of Amitabha.

## Six Years in Retreat

After traveling for several years around the countryside, Künga Namgyal found a cave in a valley just north of Dütsi Tel and meditated in it for six years. The cave was apparently very primitive and had a lot of leaks. It is said that sometimes Künga Namgyal's body was completely soaked in water up to his waist. According to the stories, he sat so still that birds made nests in his hair, which is not quite believable. He moved so little that he became part of the architectural design of that particular cave, like a tree.

Being an important person, Künga Namgyal had one attendant who was always there with him, but he distrusted anybody who came to see him from the political administration of Surmang. Going to see him was terrible because he was so nasty to visitors.

After practicing for six years, Künga Namgyal collapsed and lost consciousness. When he recovered from his collapse, he suddenly woke into a different frame of mind altogether. Some people thought he was com-

---

* The four greater schools of the Kagyü tradition are the Karma Kagyü, Barom Kagyü, Tsalpa Kagyü, and Phagdru Kagyü. The eight lesser schools are the Taglung, Drukpa, Drikung, Martsang, Trophu, Yelpa, Yabsang, and Shuksep Kagyü.

pletely crazy, and other people thought he had attained enlightenment. Seemingly, according to the favorable stories, he attained enlightenment on the spot. He behaved entirely differently after his collapse; he was more fearless and powerful.

## A Great Scholar of Mahamudra

One of the outstanding aspects of the fourth Trungpa, Künga Namgyal, is that he was a great scholar. He wrote a three-volume commentary on mahamudra, each volume containing about a thousand pages. At that time, nobody in the Kagyü lineage had ever written a commentary on mahamudra, except for a few manuals on visualization and other topics. But this particular commentary on mahamudra was straightforward; nothing else like it had ever been written. According to the stories, one of the Karmapas was very shocked that Künga Namgyal could say so many things about mahamudra. He said that Künga Namgyal's skull must be bursting since he had so much to say about mahamudra.

The example set by Künga Namgyal became one of the landmarks of the Trungpa lineage. His work led to the line of the Trungpas becoming more powerful. In addition to all the practice he did, he was also very scholarly and learned. He composed something like twenty volumes of writings. He wrote about the history and social science of the Tibetan tradition of that time, and he wrote commentaries on all kinds of books. He was also a great musician; he composed a lot of monastic music and developed various chants. But above all, he was a great contemplative person.

## THE FIFTH TRUNGPA: TENPA NAMGYAL

The fifth Trungpa, Tenpa Namgyal (1633–1712), lived during the seventeenth century. He was born into a noble family and was trained as a teacher. He became the ruler of his principality as well as a powerful spiritual leader. Tenpa Namgyal was known as an expert on Buddhist philosophy, and he also promoted the contemplative disciplines existing in the Surmang tradition. In those days, Surmang was very much a contemplative community, and the monasteries there were almost like retreat centers. There was very little need to set up any extra contemplative discipline.

*A seal given to the fifth Trungpa, Tenpa Namgyal, by the Chinese emperor, brought from Tibet by Chögyam Trungpa Rinpoche.*

## An Imperial Teacher

Tenpa Namgyal continued the process of transforming the traditional tent-culture approach into a well-established, permanent setup. His court, as well as the fort of Adro Shelu-bum, was incorporated into the monastery. Tenpa Namgyal received what is known as *hutoktu,* a Mongolian title for a spiritual teacher, which is an honorary degree or post as the teacher to the emperor of China. After this appointment, his political power grew much larger.

At Surmang, we had the official seals that were presented to Tenpa Namgyal at that time. I was able to rescue them and bring them with me from Tibet. These seals, presented by the Chinese emperor to Tenpa Namgyal as an imperial teacher, are quite impressive.

Surmang Province was one of twenty-five provinces in the kingdom of Nangchen. The king of Nangchen was the ultimate power in that area, and Tenpa Namgyal, being an imperial teacher, also had a great deal of power over that kingdom. He was well respected, and he had a particular talent for dealing with the local rulers.

At that time, the Kagyü lineage was going through a transformation. The Kagyüpas were beginning to realize that in order to have higher spiritual participation in the country, they also had to have higher political participation as well. That process of combining the two was natural in Tibet. So the Kagyüpas became politically active. In this case, the Kagyü statesman, Tenpa Namgyal, had the inspiration and vision needed by the people of that locality. As the leader, he was taking an active role in the spiritual welfare of the people, as well as taking care of their psychological and economic welfare. That is what was known as a politician in those days.

## Political Problems and Imprisonment

Because of Tenpa Namgyal's approach to dealing with the economy of the local villages and families, the Surmang Province became very powerful and wealthy. The economy was built on timber and salt exports, and there were many talented businesspeople and statesmen of all kinds. Consequently, Tenpa Namgyal became both a very affluent person and a very enlightened person.

At that time, Surmang was in Nangchen, an entirely separate kingdom, both politically and economically, from the Central Tibetan Government. But the Central Government, which usually had nothing much to do with the region of Surmang, was quite shocked by Surmang's affluence. One of the main Surmang monasteries had a gold roof and a gigantic shrine room painted in gold leaf. In the shrine room, there was an image of the Buddha drawn in vermillion paint over the gold. The Central Government said that this was illegal, and that no monastery, no one in Tibet at all, was allowed to make such an ostentatious display of their wealth without receiving permission. So troops were sent out to invade and ransack Dütsi Tel and Namgyal-tse monasteries.

After the invasion, Tenpa Namgyal was imprisoned with a number of others for five years in Chamdo, the district capital. When he and his regent, many abbots, and other monks were imprisoned, the kingdoms in that area did not lend him any support. The local government was afraid of possible warfare with Central Tibet, so they did not help Tenpa Namgyal and his friends and colleagues.

## Making Rain

From the first year of Tenpa Namgyal's imprisonment, there were constant droughts and mishaps with the harvests in that province. By the end of the fourth year, everybody was getting very confused and concerned about a possible famine taking place. And in the fifth year, famine actually did take place in that area. People were starving. They did not have grain to eat, and they had nowhere for their cows to graze. The whole country became completely dry. Supposedly, this was the first time in history that a famine had occurred in this area.

One of the cabinet ministers of the province said, "Maybe we should ask the Trungpa people to do something about this. Maybe we should ask them to create rain." Some people said, "Well, they are just a bunch of schmucks in prison, so what can they do?" But others said, "We have heard that they are very powerful. Maybe it is because we imprisoned them that this chain reaction happened." All kinds of discussions took place.

Finally, they decided to approach Tenpa Namgyal and his colleagues. However, the prisoners had achieved immense discipline in their practice at that point, and they did not want to be disturbed. They were having a great time in prison. Tenpa Namgyal had been able to finish three hundred million recitations of the Avalokiteshvara mantra.[*] His friend, Chetsang Sung-rap Gyatso Rinpoche,[†] who was also in prison, was painting thangkas. He had completed something like one hundred beautiful thangka scrolls. We actually had these in our monastery; they were

---

[*] OM MANI PADME HUM.

[†] The sixth *Chetsang Rinpoche,* the first having been one of the eight mystics and a very great teacher.

beautifully painted. Another prisoner, Garwang Rinpoche, had written several volumes of commentary on mahamudra experience. So they were having a great time, and they did not particularly want to be disturbed.

Then somehow, in the late summer of that year, this request from the government came: "You should make rain for us. Otherwise, we are going to keep you in prison much longer, and you might be executed."

So Tenpa Namgyal said, "Yes, sure. I could create rain for you." He asked to be taken to a local spring, saying, "I could go there and do a little something, if it helps." They took Tenpa Namgyal to the spring. He washed his mala in the water and sat there for a while, and after that he went back to jail. Supposedly a lot of smoke arose, a sort of cloudy mist came out of the fountain and created clouds in the sky, and there was fantastic rainfall.

The local people were very excited to finally have rainfall after five years. Everybody rejoiced and wanted to find out what had happened. And when they heard that it was Tenpa Namgyal who made it rain, everybody unanimously demanded that he be freed from his imprisonment. He was not particularly happy about that; prison was his retreat place. But he was given a pardon, and he had to leave his retreat. The government returned all his privileges and his monastery.

So Tenpa Namgyal, the fifth Trungpa, was victorious, and he was still respected by the Chinese emperor as an imperial teacher. There were no further highlights to his story, and he passed away peacefully.

## 13

# The Later Trungpas

*Although I have no intention of continuing the Trungpa line, the energy is still there. When you give this energy to someone else, you do not give it away, you radiate it. But having done so, you have the same amount of energy left, exactly the same volume. So energy is not a separate entity. A sunbeam coming through the window is not different from the sun itself.*

## THE SIXTH TRUNGPA: TENDZIN CHÖKYI GYATSO

The sixth Trungpa, Tendzin Chökyi Gyatso (1715–1734 est.), lived during the eighteenth century. Very little is known about him. He died when he was very young. Some time after he was discovered as the Trungpa tülku, when he was about eighteen or nineteen years old, one of his students was carrying him in order to help him cross a bridge. They both slipped and fell, and the sixth Trungpa died on the spot. So much for the sixth Trungpa.

## THE SEVENTH TRUNGPA: JAMPAL CHÖKYI GYATSO

The seventh Trungpa, Jampal Chökyi Gyatso (1743–1768 est.), lived during the eighteenth century. He was a very intelligent person who studied a great deal. But he also died young, around the age of twenty-five. When he was an infant, his mother accidentally dropped him on the floor, which caused a concussion, and after that he was sick throughout his life.

There is no particular monument that he left behind, except that he wrote a lot of poetry. Many of his poems were lost, but some of them were kept in the archives of the Surmang monasteries. It was a very romantic type of poetry, somewhat adolescent, but insightful neverthe-less. It was not particularly good as poetry, because he was still develop-ing. If his life had been prolonged, he could have written many more poems and become a great poet-saint.

## THE EIGHTH TRUNGPA: GYURME TENPHEL

The eighth Trungpa, Gyurme Tenphel (b. 1771), lived during the nine-teenth century. He was a very eccentric person and a great artist. Gyurme Tenphel used to love drinking a very thick tea, and he was very kind and gentle. He spent a long time practicing meditation, something like ten years, locked in the top part of his castle, which had been given to him and his lineage earlier on. He also paid a visit to the fourteenth Karmapa.

### The Tibetan Book of the Dead

According to Surmang tradition, when *The Tibetan Book of the Dead** was first discovered by the fourteenth-century tertön, or treasure discoverer, Karma Lingpa, he presented it to Gyurme Tenphel and asked him to take care of it. He said that Gyurme Tenphel should help in promoting this particular teaching. And the eighth Trungpa became a very power-ful source in presenting the teachings of *The Tibetan Book of the Dead*. So Surmang people, we regard *The Tibetan Book of the Dead* as a part of our tradition, and as one of our contemplative disciplines.

### Ekajati†

Gyurme Tenphel incorporated a great number of Nyingma teachings. His role was similar to the role of the third Karmapa Rangjung Dorje

---

* *The Tibetan Book of the Dead* describes an after-death journey through the bardo of forty-nine days, with each day providing another opportunity for awakening. One opportunity after another one comes along, and each time you have the option of either awakening into greater freedom or continuing to perpetuate samsaric imprisonment.

† *Ekajati* ("one single lock of hair") is a female protector important to the Nyingma lin-eage. She is said to be the protector of the highest tantric teachings, known as maha ati.

in unifying the Kagyü and Nyingma teachings. Gyurme Tenphel actually adopted the Nyingma protector Ekajati as a protector of Surmang Monastery. Before that, the Kagyüs did not have Ekajati.

## Artistic and Literary Activity

Gyurme Tenphel was a gentle, artistic, and well-meaning person. Supposedly, he had only two fights during his whole life. The first time, a cat jumped on his dish of food and was trying to lick his soup. He pushed the cat aside and got very angry. The second time, his attendant cut his bamboo calligraphy pen in the wrong way, and Gyurme Tenphel again lost his temper. So he lost his temper twice in his life. Isn't that shocking?

Gyurme Tenphel was a very articulate person in terms of visual dharma. I have seen some of his illuminated manuscripts and artworks, and they were fantastic and very beautiful. His handwriting was impeccable. He was a great calligrapher and a great painter, and he was also a great composer who produced music for monastic chants. He collected and edited the works of the previous Trungpas and of the Surmang tradition, and he also collected the songs and life stories of Trung Ma-se. He compiled the library of Surmang, which was later destroyed at the time of the tenth Trungpa.

We had some of Gyurme Tenphel's art in our monastery. We used to have some of his handwriting, calligraphies, and thangkas. Some of those thangkas were similar to the ones I have seen depicting the kings of Shambhala. He also painted little thangkas of the eighty-four siddhas. They were very beautiful Gardri school paintings and fantastic works of art.

Gyurme Tenphel's taste was extraordinarily rich, in terms of creating mountings for these thangkas. He would buy brocades and use them to mount the scrolls, and he would cover books with silk scarves of all kinds. His taste was impeccable and very rich and wealthy, with a somewhat aristocratic flavor. In fact, he was supposed to have come from a wealthy aristocratic family.

## THE NINTH TRUNGPA: TENPA RABGYE

The ninth Trungpa, Tenpa Rabgye, lived during the nineteenth century. He was supposedly a very shameful person. He was not shameful in the sense of being wild or anything like that, but he just spent his life sitting around outside in the sun, chatting with people and taking anise snuff. He was very peasant-like. The only thing he composed in his life was a four-line offering to Mahakala, which we used to chant in our monastery, and which does not say very much. It goes like this:

Chief protector of the teachings,
I supplicate you, Mahakala, the four-armed one.
Accept this offering.
Fulfill the four karmas.*

He was very ordinary. I think at the time there was not very much learning or intellectual work going on, and there was also not very much practice going on. So Tenpa Rabgye just existed. However, his death was supposed to have been quite interesting. He announced, "Tomorrow I am going to die. Since I am going to die tomorrow, at least I'm going to die in a dignified way." So he called his attendant to come and take off his old clothes and put on his yellow robe. Then he sat up in the cross-legged vajra posture, and he was gone. That was the only testament that Tenpa Rabgye, the ninth Trungpa, knew what he was doing.

## THE TENTH TRUNGPA: CHÖKYI NYIN-JE

The tenth Trungpa, Chökyi Nyin-je (1879–1939), my own predecessor, lived during the nineteenth and early twentieth centuries.

### Leaving the Monastery

The tenth Trungpa was quite a different person from the ninth. He was born to a local chieftain of Surmang, and he was raised with very strict discipline by his uncles, as well as his tutors, his bursars, his secretaries, and others. In the early part of his life, he took everything in the Kagyü teachings extraordinarily seriously. He took his ngöndro practice, his

---

* The *four karmas,* or four activities, refer to the actions of pacifying, enriching, mag-
netizing, and destroying. Iconographically, these four are symbolized by the protector
Mahakala's four powerful arms. For more on the four karmas, see chapter 48, "Yogayana:
Empowerments and Practice."

shamatha-vipashyana practice, and everything else very seriously. He did every practice step-by-step very successfully.

Chökyi Nyin-je did not like being told what to do. In particular, he felt that people were trying to make him into a good moneymaker. In those times, it was traditional for the monastery to set up a winter trip, a summer trip, and an autumn trip to collect donations from the locality. During the summer trip, the monks would collect dry cheese and butter. In the autumn, they would collect turnips, potatoes, and vegetables. And during the winter, the monks would collect grains, predominantly wheat and barley, with some beans and peas, or whatever was available. So the poor tenth Trungpa was pushed to make these trips all the time; it was always time to make the next round.

That became problematic for Chökyi Nyin-je, and he did not like it. He wanted to practice instead of constantly involving himself with the work of collecting donations. One night, he decided to leave his monastery and his camp, and try to seek teachings from Jamgön Kongtrül the Great. (This is all written about in *Born in Tibet*.* You can read the story of the tenth Trungpa there, which is quite colorful.) Chökyi Nyin-je managed to do this, and he decided to stay with Jamgön Kongtrül for a long period of time, continuing his practice, his discipline, and his study. It was a very rare situation to become a student of Jamgön Kongtrül the Great, and as a result, Chökyi Nyin-je became one of the world-renowned teachers of the Kagyü tradition.

Chökyi Nyin-je was very short of funds at that time, but the monastery wanted to lure him back, so they did not give him any resources. There was not even enough butter for him to create a butter lamp so that he could read the scriptures in the evening. He had to buy sticks of incense in order to try to read the texts, studying and memorizing them by the glow of an incense stick. Supposedly, when Chökyi Nyin-je was memorizing texts and trying to practice, he tied his hair to the ceiling with a cord, and he stuck nettles around himself. If he dozed and started to fall over, he would be pulled up by his hair or he would be stung by the nettles. He kept himself alive by practicing constantly under Jamgön Kongtrül the Great.

---

* Chögyam Trungpa, *Born in Tibet* (Boston: Shambhala Publications, 1995).

## Political Problems and Court Case

Chökyi Nyin-je also had his political problems. The same old problem kept coming back again and again in our province: our monastery kept being attacked by a local Geluk monastery. The Gelukpas raised legal points questioning Surmang's power over them, and Chökyi Nyin-je spent something like three months in the local capital, Jyekundo, arguing his case. There were no lawyers, like we have these days, so he had to create his own case by writing out each point, one by one. He had to write everything out at night and present the points during the day. Chökyi Nyin-je spent three months presenting the case for the survival of Surmang Monastery, fighting for its existence.

Chökyi Nyin-je asked his friends for suggestions and help. He also asked those who were well versed in Tibetan law to contribute. One of the local chieftains gave him advice that became famous. He told him, "It is okay even for a lama to argue a court case. That is fine. But you must accept one thing, which is that you should tell the body of truth with the tentacles of a lie. Otherwise, if you are constantly truthful and honest, you will not win." This was actually very helpful to Chökyi Nyin-je in winning his court case.

When he won the case, a lot of the local people were infuriated. His monastery was attacked by the troops of the Tibetan Central Government, and was completely burnt down and looted. The tenth Trungpa was taken prisoner, although he was eventually rescued by friends. The general of the Central Tibetan Government, who was also a local king, the king of Lhatok, saved him. It is interesting that the political neuroses of the country were still taking place even as late as the 1920s.

## The Rebuilding of Surmang

After Surmang and its libraries had been looted and burnt down, some people said that it was great that the monastery had been destroyed, because then they could create a fresher and much grander one. And that actually was the case at Surmang. Having recovered control of his monastery, Chökyi Nyin-je rebuilt it completely and fully, much better than it had been before.

In rebuilding the monastery, the ambition of the tenth Trungpa was to change the shape of the situation altogether. Instead of having

*Chögyam Trungpa wearing the robe of his predecessor, the tenth Trungpa Tülku, one of the few relics that Trungpa Rinpoche managed to carry out with him from Tibet.*

a monastery alone, he also established a community center for contemplative practice and study. Through this process, Chökyi Nyin-je reestablished monasticism and contemplative discipline at the same time. He was a great and dedicated contemplative, who united all this in one situation. Because he was so powerful, open, and fearless, he was able to hold on to his basic integrity in spite of all the chaos that occurred in his life. I have been told that he had fantastic integrity.

Chökyi Nyin-je died at the age of sixty-three, still trying to raise funds for the monastic establishment. The tenth Trungpa was an example of a hard worker and a political visionary. He was a powerful person who was able to win people over and conquer other people's false concepts.

So those are the Trungpas. And as we discussed previously, all the Trungpas were blessed tülkus, blessed incarnations, rather than a one-shot deal.

## THE ELEVENTH TRUNGPA: CHÖKYI GYATSO (CHÖGYAM TRUNGPA RINPOCHE)

[Editor's Note: A brief biography of Chögyam Trungpa Rinpoche is included at the end of this volume. For an account of Trungpa Rinpoche's early life and training, see his autobiography, *Born in Tibet*.]

## THE SURMANG KAGYÜ TEACHINGS

In some accounts of the various Kagyü sects, the Surmang Kagyü is considered to be a separate sect, of which the Trungpas are the head. There are certainly some unique aspects of the Surmang teachings. For example, as noted above, the eighth Trungpa incorporated a lot of Nyingma teachings and he adopted Ekajati as a protector. And earlier, the fourth Trungpa's chö teaching made him very special. Other characteristics of the Surmang Kagyü include the research work done on the six yogas of Naropa, and the many studies on mahamudra, particularly the fourth Trungpa's commentary.

Based on that, the Surmang people had a great deal of information about mahamudra: they were experts on that. In fact, the fifteenth Karmapa, Khakhyap Dorje, invited Surmang Tendzin Rinpoche to teach him the Surmang Kagyü's ideas about mahamudra. But soon after, the fifteenth Karmapa died and Tendzin Rinpoche also died, so there was no chance to do that. So mahamudra seems to be one of the Surmang Kagyü specialties, in which they are expert. Altogether, not in a particularly flashy or extraordinary way, but in a very subtle way, the Surmang people have managed to maintain their intelligence and wisdom.

Bringing the Nyingma tradition into the Kagyü is also a Surmang specialty. The tenth Trungpa, Chökyi Nyin-je, was very emotional about the Nyingma tradition. He visited Shechen Monastery to see Shechen Gyaltsap Rinpoche, who was Jamgön Kongtrül of Shechen's teacher. Chökyi Nyin-je and Shechen Gyaltsap had a sort of spiritual love affair. The tenth Trungpa would say, "I wish I was born in your monastery," and vice versa.

It was a very moving experience when Chökyi Nyin-je left and they parted. He and Shechen Gyaltsap went up to the roof. They sat together and chanted a tune of invocation to Ekajati, so that Ekajati would keep an eye on them after they parted and they would still be together.

## CHAKRASAMVARA DANCES AT SURMANG

The Surmang tradition includes a version of the complete Chakrasamvara sadhana translated into a form of dance.* This dance was the discovery of the first Trungpa's teacher, Trung Ma-se.† The Chakrasamvara dance is very elaborate. It has 360 moves or themes, and the performance usually lasts about a day and a half. There is a three-hour performance first, which is the preparation of the ground; then there is a five-hour performance that establishes the shrine and creates the mandala; and finally there is a twenty-four-hour dance, concerned with the actual mandala itself. As you chant and dance along, there are certain movements connected with taking refuge and with the bodhisattva vow. Then there are movements for exorcising the hostile environment and for calling upon

---

* The *Chakrasamvara* (Skt.: binder of the chakras) *Sadhana* is an important meditative practice of the Kagyü tradition. In general, sadhanas, or vajrayana ritual practices, include formless meditation, visualization practice, music, mantra recitations, and physical gestures, or mudras.

† In another account, based on an interview between Carolyn Gimian and Surmang Khenpo, it is said that the first Trungpa received this dance directly from Chakrasamvara and Vajrayogini. See Chögyam Trungpa, *The Mishap Lineage*, 116n6.

blessings. And then you have visualizations. All of these are in the form of dance.

This Surmang dance is different from basic Tibetan dances that you might have seen in films, where the dancers are wearing robes. In this Chakrasamvara dance, everybody wears the same costume. In a certain part of the dance, all the dancers are divided into pairs. In this section, the rhythms are the same for you and your partner, but the movements are opposite, so it is very difficult to do. This is the part when you visualize Chakrasamvara and his consort.

The dancers are all dressed in heruka costumes, with bone ornaments and crowns, usually made from ivory, or mule or horse bones, and carved and inlaid with jewels. This is supposed to represent the various yogic exercises, and it is the hatha yoga part of the practice. The idea is that there are what are known as the "fast dance" and the "slow dance." The slow dance is like competing with a cloud; you are barely moving at all. And in the fast dance, you speed that up.

The Chakrasamvara dances are a complete practice, and as you dance you begin to get into it more and more. I started to learn to dance when I was about sixteen. And not having had enough exercise previously, the first three days my whole body completely ached and I had the flu. And my tutors said, "You shouldn't just lie down. You should come down and do at least three hours of practice." And I kept hanging on, and finally I felt much better and I was able to get into the rhythm and energy of the whole thing.

Chakrasamvara dances are more like tai chi than traditional Tibetan dance, which is jumpy and very fast. Instead, the movements in these dances are very slow. You have a drum in your right hand and a bell in your left hand, and you have to learn to use them properly. After every full beat, you ring your bell. So everybody—the orchestra and all the dancers—have to be synchronized. And it is very defined, six beats of one movement, and seven of another, and then ten more repetitions. The leaders of the dance make certain moves, which indicate which part of your body you are going to use at the beginning as a main movement. It is very much like the feeling of Chakrasamvara: you dance all the time and you radiate out passion, constantly. You relate with your passion, and the more you relate with your passion, the more you get into it.

The Chakrasamvara dance is based on a great feast. So there is a great feast offering in the middle of the dance circle, which is eventually distributed to everybody. There is a blessing of the feast, in which you visualize yourself and the altar table holding the feast as part of a great mandala. And you bring in the *jnanasattva* with a certain dance movement.* Usually that part is very slow.

I was able to dance only about six times, because this dance happens only once a year. I began to enjoy it more every year; I was not particularly approved the first year as a good dancer, but as I went on I had memorized the whole thing completely. People used to carry little instruction books attached to their ornaments or dance costumes, but I didn't have to do that. I was very good at it. I had become such a good dancer that I was about to be able to teach it. Every six years you recruit new dance students, and you spend three months training them, teaching the movements and the disciplines first, and then the actual themes and songs and everything. I was going to begin teaching the next year—and then I had to leave Tibet.

The dance movements are very precise. I found that first you have the hassle of learning the dance and how to do it properly, and after that you begin to know the implications behind it. And what used to happen is that when you sounded your bell a certain way, or the monk in charge of chanting sounded his bell a certain way, it was a tea sound. This means they brought tea around as you danced. And there was another sound you made that was the liquor sound. So you would have tea and liquor alternately. So you were actually allowed to drink while you danced; you could drink some kind of beer, such as barley beer, or *chang,* or even *arak,* which is a more concentrated kind of alcohol.

## SUMMARY AND PREDICTIONS FOR THE TRUNGPA LINEAGE

In conclusion, since we have already exposed the mystique of incarnations, I thought I should make myself very articulate about my own situation and intentions. If one were to ask whether this Trungpa is real or unreal, we might say, who cares? Based on an understanding of blessed incarnations, even the tenth Trungpa was not really "real." Even the first Trungpa was not real, as soon as he became the second. There is always duality.

---

* In visualization practice, the *jnanasattva,* or "wisdom being," is the wisdom power that descends into and enlivens the visualization.

I do not think the Trungpa line is going to continue beyond this life-time. I don't even know if I am going to be a Buddhist in my next life. I would be, at least in essence, but who can tell? If there are no more Trungpa tülkus after me, then what happens to that energy, that Trungpa tülku energy? Does it just die? I suppose in this case, although I have no intention of continuing the Trungpa line, the energy is still there. When you give this energy to someone else, you do not give it away; you radiate it. But having done so, you have the same amount of energy left, exactly the same volume. So energy is not a separate entity. A sunbeam coming through the window is not different from the sun itself.

I may individually embody the Trungpa energy, but not independently. The Trungpa energy sucks up different people at different times. Actually, I was hoping to come back in Japan as a scientist. Maybe when I come back, one of my students will introduce me to the books *Meditation in Action* or *Cutting Through Spiritual Materialism.** And then we could go on from there.†

---

* Chögyam Trungpa, *Meditation in Action* (Boston: Shambhala Publications, 2010); *Cutting Through Spiritual Materialism* (Boston: Shambhala Publications, 1987).

† In spite of this prediction, four years after Trungpa Rinpoche passed away in 1987, His Eminence Tai Situ Rinpoche recognized the two-year-old Tibetan boy Chökyi Senge Rinpoche as the twelfth Trungpa Tülku. For more detailed information on the Trungpa tülkus and the Kagyü lineage, see Chögyam Trungpa, *The Mishap Lineage* (Boston: Shambhala Publications, 2009).

*Part Four*

# ESSENTIAL TEACHINGS

# 14

# *Unconditional Ground*

*Yeshe cuts your thoughts on the spot, so there are no thoughts. It is like the experience of eating a jalapeño: it numbs any possibilities of wandering mind. It is a one-hundred-percent experience, or even two-hundred-percent.*

## INDESTRUCTIBLE BEING

In tantric Buddhism, we talk about vajra existence or vajra nature, as opposed to the vajra-like samadhi that the mahayanists talk about. At the same time, none of the experiences of vajrayana can occur if you do not understand the idea of tathagatagarbha from the point of view of mahayana. Vajra nature of dorje kham refers to an indestructible quality that we maintain and possess intrinsically in our being.

### *Neither Beginning nor End*

If you ask how egolessness and emptiness fit together with the topic of vajra indestructibility, the answer is that this intrinsic quality of our being is completely indestructible because it is not existent. If it were at the level of existence, there would be no question of indestructibility, because it would have a form, and anything that has existence or form cannot possess vajra nature. The Sanskrit word for form is *rupa*, which refers to that which has substantial existence and which could therefore be destroyed at any time. Vajra nature, on the other hand, does not have its own entity, its own existence; therefore, it is indestructible. So vajra indestructibility equals nonexistence, because it has neither beginning nor end.

## Existence and Manifesting

Samsara is nirvana, from that point of view. Whether something is garbage or a blade of grass, it is the same. Anything goes; it is all sacred. You see everything as the manifestation of the guru's world, which allows you to relax and maintain your upliftedness. Even if you are sleeping in the midst of a garbage heap, you can then build up from that and work with whatever is workable. You can clean up whatever has to be cleaned up. But before you clean anything up, the point is not to fight with the ugly or unpleasant things, because that means you are labeling them as something to get rid of, as something outside of your capable world. So charity begins at home. That is why we have maitri practice first, and compassion practice later on. Unless you have developed maitri, you cannot develop compassion.

Vajra nature is a state of complete invincibility. It is a complete state and completely invincible because you do not need an essence to work on. You are fully developed. You might ask, "Then why is it necessary to practice?" The answer is that the point of practice is to try to bring out the hang-ups of the mahayana. Although you experience and learn a lot in the mahayana, at the same time it also provides you with deceptions and hangovers of all kinds. The mahayana is enormously helpful, but its hangovers are problematic.

In order to experience the true form of vajra existence, that you are already buddha in any case, you need two aspects: *ku* and *yeshe*. Ku, or the body aspect, is solidity; it is the ground of sanity. Yeshe is the shining out or the celebrating of that particular situation. In Sanskrit, ku is *kaya*, as in dharmakaya, and yeshe is *jnana*. Kaya and jnana cannot be separated; existence and manifesting always happen together, like positive and negative electricity.

## Glimpses of Vajra Nature

The vajrayanists' approach to vajra experience is that you are there already, although it may be just in a glimpse, whether a short glimpse or a long glimpse. But even those glimpses have become arbitrary, and we do not pursue them. The idea here is that glimpses are workable, and since they exist within us already, we do not need to pursue them. In the mahayana, such glimpses have to be cultivated and brought about constantly. But in the vajrayana, they are already fully developed, although we might have to push ourselves to experience them. The only problem is in how long these gaps or glimpses could be experienced.

In the mahayana, it is also possible to experience gaps, but those gaps are clouded with conflicting emotions. In the vajrayana, they are not. In the mahayana, it is as if you have a thick shield of glass in front of you, but in the vajrayana those gaps are real, a sheer drop. At first those gaps are very quick, and then you begin to expand the gaps so that you are not dependent on just glimpses. That is how you build vajrayana insight.

The experience of vajra nature is more than perception; it is just what we have. Perception means that you perceive something, but here there is no separation between perception and perceiver. So the experience of vajra nature is not even an experience; it just happens. Vajra nature is nonconceptual and happens without perception, and without collecting further reference points or recording anything in the subconscious mind. Vajra nature just happens.

## Letting Go of Grasping and Fixation

Because we have such a wonderful foundation, we can turn to ourselves and begin to realize what happens when we surrender, when we give up our ego. When we let go of our grasping and fixation altogether, we realize that there is greater vision beyond grasping and fixation. This vision is very firm and definite, no longer just a wishy-washy idea. In fact, there is no idealism involved with this vision; it is realistic.

The absence of grasping and fixation provides something extremely firm. It is not firm in the style of grasping or fixation, but it is the firmness of pure ground. It is like flying in an airplane. We take off and we fly up, and when we rise above the clouds, we begin to realize that upstairs there is blue sky all the time. We realize that the sun is always shining, even when it is cloudy and rainy down below. There is blue sky all the time, twenty-four hours a day, whether it is light or dark, and that blue sky is free from clouds.

That kind of solidity or firmness is beyond the level of ego-clinging, because at that point, we are not harassed by our desire. For that matter, we do not hold on to our identity as such at all. When we let go of grasping and fixation, we find pure ground, which is all-pervasive and spacious. It is firm, not because there is a reference point, but because there is no reference point.

The realization of nonreference point is connected to being without hesitation; it is connected with firmness, but in this case firmness does not refer to anything solid. It could be called lucidity rather than firmness, and it could even be called shiftyness. If you look up into the middle of a completely blue cloudless sky, you could say that it is very shifty, and at the same time, that it is very firm. It is firm because the sky is blue all over. But because the sky is so vast, you cannot focus your eyes on it. You cannot focus your eyes on the blue sky because there is nothing to focus on, so it is shifty as well as firm. Any glimpses you experience become a letdown, because there is nothing to hang on to. And if you sustained your glimpses, you would be experiencing that letdown continuously.

There is nothing very mystical about this whole thing. Firmness simply means that you cannot grasp anything. If you are a lost astronaut floating in outer space, that space is very firm, because you have nothing to hang on to. So we are talking about a different kind of firmness than hanging on to a column or crushing your pillow in your arms.

## Glimpsing Threefold Vajra Being

When we are able to take off that far, we begin to catch a glimpse of what is known as the threefold vajra nature: vajra body, vajra speech, and vajra mind. I think that *vajra nature* is the wrong term, however, because nature implies something that is still embryonic. It is like tomorrow's sunshine as opposed to today's sunshine. Instead, we probably should use the term *vajra being*. Vajra being is something that is already exposed, already existing. Vajra being, or in Sanskrit, *vajrasattva,* means "vajra existence."

When you give birth in the vajrayana, you give birth to a fully grown person, not to an infant. By means of vajra vision, or your understanding of the absence of grasping and fixation, you develop vajra being. Vajra body, speech, and mind are the expressions of that complete freedom from grasping and fixation. So firmness is nonreference point, and that firmness is threefold.

## The Necessity of Mind Training

Threefold vajra being develops out of your lojong practice. In lojong, or mind training, the word *training* implies that effort is involved. Nothing comes out of a dream; you cannot simply expect to find gold coins in your Christmas stocking right away. So vajra body, speech, and mind are the products of exertion. They are the products of sending and taking completely. If you are truly, fully trained in lojong, your body, speech, and mind turn into vajra body, vajra speech, and vajra mind. That allows you to remain in the vajra world physically, to hear the vajra teaching, and to experience glimpses of vajra mind.

Lojong is limitless. Each time a student reaches a certain level of training, our standards get higher. Some students may think that they could go beyond the mahayana ideal when they became tantrikas, but that is completely wrong. If you do not have a good understanding of tonglen, as well as of lojong, you cannot become a good tantrika because you have not really experienced any kind of absence. When you do sending and taking, you experience absence. Nobody is actually there to do the exchanging; it just happens between space. There is a kind of enlightened confusion, in which you do not know who you are, whether you are the receiver or the sender. You have a gap, which is a very interesting point. So the study of lojong will help you to understand the vajrayana much more clearly.

The vajrayana is very definitely a product of mind training. I think that everybody in the lineage would approve of that particular remark. That is how your mind becomes one with the dharma, and the dharma becomes the path. So you could work with lojong and the mahayana slogans from the vajrayana point of view. When you actually discover your own basic gentleness, your intrinsic goodness, you begin to realize that your hesitations have gone far away. You develop a vision based on fearlessness, gentleness, compassion, spaciousness, and invincibility. Lojong begins to become a vajrayana-like situation at that point.

The basic point, which I would like to make clear, is that you have to prepare yourself first; then you can respond to what you have prepared. Natural preparation also exists outside of your own existence. That is to say, your own readiness to receive and understand the vajrayana, and the vajrayana world of the lineage, which exists outside of you, are both included. So it is a question of relating with two situations: the vajra world, and the vajra nature that exists within you. When you put those two together, you begin to have a basic understanding of entering into the vajrayana altogether.

## Attaining Freedom from the Kleshas

The meaning of tantra is continuity. There is continuity from the beginning of the journey—from when we become refugees on the hinayana path, through when we become helpers of others, or would-be bodhisattvas on the mahayana path, and through the greater sanity that arises as we go on to the vajrayana. Throughout, the point is to attain freedom from the kleshas.

This freedom is twofold: it is freedom from both samsara and nirvana. That is, we do not dwell in the peace or cessation of shamatha, nor do we dwell in ego-centered grasping and fixation. Freedom from grasping and fixation is freedom from samsara; freedom from fixed notions of peace and contentment and from pure shamatha tranquillity is freedom from absorption in nirvana. We tend to have already developed that kind of attitude when we take the bodhisattva vow and begin to practice the mahayana discipline of twofold bodhichitta.

## Yeshe: Primordial Wisdom

Even at the earliest stage of the vajrayana, we have to study and understand jnana, or *yeshe* in Tibetan. The meaning of *ye* is "primordial" or "original," or it could be "a long time ago," and *she* means "familiarity," "comprehension," or "knowing"; so *yeshe* means "primordial knowing." It could be regarded as root knowledge or basic knowledge. In the related term *ngo-she*, *ngo* means "face," and *she* means "knowing"; so *ngo-she* means "I know somebody." It means "I know their face," or in other words, "I am familiar with that person, I have met them before."*

Yeshe, or primordial knowing, is the definition of wisdom. Such wisdom is a very important and intrinsic aspect of the vajrayana; it runs right through the vajrayana presentation from beginning to end. In the vajrayana, all sorts of wisdoms are discovered, introduced, and realized. So

---

* The knowing quality of *ngo-she* has the implication of recognizing one's true nature.

yeshe is a very important term, one that we are going to use forever and ever.

According to the *Oxford English Dictionary*, the term *wise* refers to someone who comprehends knowledge. It refers to someone who is accomplished, either by training or through natural talent. But the concept of being wise is somewhat theistic; it means that you *possess* your wisdom, which is a concept we do not use in the Tibetan tradition. For instance, we do not say *yeshepa*, which would mean "one who possesses wisdom," or a "yeshe-ist." We do not say that, but we could use the word *chang*, which means "holding." So we could say *yeshe changwa*, which means "one who holds wisdom," as in *dorje chang*, which means "one who holds the vajra." Chang, or holding, seems to be different than possessing. Holding means being adorned with or endowed with. For instance, you might hold the title of *father*.

## Experiencing Reality

When we say that yeshe means fundamentally comprehending, you might ask: Comprehending what? In English, of course, we always have to qualify things. If you like, we could say comprehending the nature of reality. But what is the nature of reality? The nature of reality seems to be something that cannot be changed or manufactured by concepts or philosophical speculation. The nature of reality is without a watcher; it does not require anyone to observe it or look at it. In other words, we could say that reality is unconditional. Reality cannot be put into pigeonholes, metaphysical categories, computer chips, or data of any kind. That cannot be done. Since the nature of reality is free from observation, it cannot be spoken of in conventional words. However, it can be experienced; it can be experienced very strongly, very thoroughly, very fully and fantastically.

## Protection from Conditionality

When you experience the nature of reality, then that particular wisdom, or yeshe, has the possibility of protecting you from conditionality. It takes your mind away from further involvement with conditionality of any kind. What we have, therefore, is mantra: the protection of mind, the protection of consciousness, the protection of awareness.

Mantra is that which is able to protect itself from others, which is why it is said to be synonymous with yeshe. It is a natural situation of the mind through which your existence cannot be attacked, defeated, or overpowered. This protection could be through any one of the three principles of body, speech, or mind. So although mantra is often referred to as incantation, such as when you say a mantra, it is not necessarily just things you say. Mantra is something more than that; it is the natural vibration that exists when you have such an experience within yourself.

Mantra is protection from boundaries. It is connected with boundaries and with anything that boundaries cannot conquer. By means of mantra, you can dispel the negative forces coming from boundaries; therefore, there is protection. For instance, you could be protected from the boundaries of the three times. There is also a boundary between your experience of sanity and insanity. As you go out from where you are, your sanity becomes thinner and thinner. You begin to lose your grip on sanity, and you begin to experience insanity. You begin to question your existence and why you are practicing at all. If you go outside of that boundary, you lose your conviction and wonder why the dharma is true. Sanity is simple, and also quite terrifying in a sense, so it is easy to make that kind of choice.

The ordinary samsaric pattern is always, without exception, to maintain its existence, even on the subconscious or unconscious level. Conditional mind is a mind that constantly looks forward. It is always looking out for its own survival, and generating further possibilities of maintaining ego. But now as we look back, it makes sense that mind protection is possible. It is possible because we have understood yeshe, the unconditionality that protects us from conditionality. Mantra, which could be said to be synonymous with yeshe, is protecting a particular way of thinking in which we do not stray into ego-centeredness, and therefore do not reproduce the volitional actions of karma.

Once the wheel of karma is set in motion, it is like a potter's wheel: it goes on and on, again and again. Once we have "I" existing, we just keep on going. When a potter has a little clay sitting on their wheel, they begin to fashion it with their hands until finally it becomes a nice, neat pot. Until then, they won't stop. That is exactly how we fashion our karma, which sometimes makes us happy, sometimes makes us sad, and sometimes leads us into trouble. So mantra protects us from that; it protects our mind from conditionality.

### Protection from Habitual Patterns of Transmigration

When our mind is protected from conditionality, this also tends to over-come the habitual pattern of transmigration, or *phowe pakchak* in Tibetan. *Phowa* means "transmigration," "changing," or "departing from one place to another," changing *phowa* to *phowe* makes it "of that," and *pakchak* means "habitual patterns"; so *phowe pakchak* means "habitual patterns of transmigration."

Habitual patterns of transmigration happen to us when one thought begins to die and we start looking for the next one. For instance, when we begin to lose interest in our orange juice, we would then like to order our coffee, which is the next thing. That is precisely the pattern of habitual transmigration. As soon as we get one thing, we would like to change it to something else. Throughout our life, we keep jumping like grasshoppers in that way. We would like to exchange one thing for another.

With phowe pakchak, we also have the tendency to be bored. This particular type of consciousness or habitual pattern is what allows us to miss the reference point of understanding what is known as the fourth moment. The first three moments are the past, present, and future; and then there is a fourth moment that transcends all three. This moment is a pure moment that is not connected with what you have missed, what you are experiencing, or what you expect is about to happen. The fourth moment is a pure state of consciousness; it is clear and pure and free from habitual tendencies.

Phowe pakchak does not contain the fourth-moment state of mind. In other words, phowe pakchak allows no abruptness; it does not like shocks of any kind. You would just like to relax a little bit and take your time. You would like to have your juice and then your coffee, and maybe a cigarette afterward; you would like to just lounge around and have a pleasurable life. With phowe pakchak, you would just like to lead your life in accord with the habitual patterns you used to enjoy. You would like to re-create them all over again.

Phowe pakchak makes it difficult to practice patience, particularly in the vajrayana sense. The mahayana notion of patience is purely the ab-sence of aggression, while the vajrayana notion of patience also includes the idea of waiting. You are just waiting, and by doing so, you are being the master of time. So vajrayana patience involves proper timing. There is greater precision in the experience of appropriateness: you know the time to proceed and the time not to proceed; you know the time things are ripe and the time they are not ripe. The idea of mastering time has nothing to do with aggression; you just have to tune in to the way situations develop and mature.

Phowe pakchak is one of the outstanding problems that keep you from being able to receive proper transmission. When a student receives transmission from a vajra master, that transmission is usually abrupt. Transmission cuts thought; it cuts mind abruptly, on the spot. But the habitual tendency of phowe pakchak goes against that completely: you would just like to socialize a little bit more with your samsaric mind. Mantra, or yeshe, cuts through that.

## VAJRAYANA RENUNCIATION

In order to get the pith instruction of vajrayana, you need to understand the pithiness, abruptness, and directness of shamatha and vipashyana as best and as fully as you can. This is necessary in order to understand, even for an instant, that you are not just theorizing that samsara is bad because it gives you pain, but samsara really *is* bad and difficult. It is not pleasurable to indulge in it even for an instant. Indulging in samsara gives you a very muddled and muddy state of mind, composed of preconceptions and habitual patterns, which together bring kleshas of all kinds.

We understand how bad and painful it is to be in the hungry ghost realm; how bad and painful it is to be speedy; how bad and painful it is to live in the samsaric world. But we do not seem to be able to understand or click into that properly and fully. We do not understand that we are flipping back and forth, even at this very moment. At first, the samsaric state of mind seems inviting and comfortable, and we get into it. Our preconceptions and habitual patterns seem somewhat soothing. But then that state of mind begins to engulf and smother us, and we find ourselves, for no reason, in the middle of helplessness. We find that we have lost our connections somewhere, and we begin to feel loneliness, sadness, and pain. Suddenly, in an instant, or in a second or two, we get a tremendous attack of samsaric-ness.

However, although we understand the pain of samsara, we do not see samsara as so bad that we just have to forget all about it. Instead, you might say we see it as somewhat bad. By understanding samsara, it might teach us a lesson; we might learn how not to be in samsara. So we could study samsara the way we study poison and how it affects us. Poison is not bad, per se; but eating poison might be bad. Likewise, studying poison is not necessarily bad; doing so might give us more understanding about how to deal with it.

In the vajrayana, we talk about renunciation in terms of the samsaric state of mind rather than samsaric life, which we already seem to understand. It is not that the samsaric world at large is particularly bad, but it is our pleasure-oriented attraction to samsara that is the problem. The attraction of our mind to that mentality is quite shocking—and we are accustomed to re-creating that mentality again and again, constantly. The purpose of renunciation is to reverse our mind from that particular situation and tune it in to something else. This may be somewhat discomforting in the beginning, because we do not get the grandmotherly kind of comfort or reassurance that we are used to getting. Nonetheless, renunciation is much fresher. Renunciation is regarded as fresh and good, basic and excellent.

As a vajrayana student, or tantrika, you can develop this kind of renunciation by following the examples of the lineage and the vajra master. You can do so by appreciating their journey and their example, and by emulating that.

## RIKPA: INSIGHT

Yeshe is that which is free from the habitual patterns of ordinary mind, or *sem* (that which projects to other), and from yeshe there arises what is known as insight, or rikpa. Rikpa is a clear way of looking at a situation, a kind of built-in perception for yeshe. It is also a seed of prajna, although prajna operates more in relationship to other, and rikpa relates more to yourself. With rikpa, you are your own disciplinarian, so you do not stray.

Rikpa is able to perceive yeshe. But we cannot call this kind of perception a watcher. It is like your own tongue: when you eat food, you cannot call your tongue the watcher of your food. There is no strain in having a tongue in your mouth while you eat food. But if you did not have one, you might have a problem with eating. Likewise, you cannot call your eyelids the watchers of your eyes because you blink. So rikpa is a built-in situation, like your tongue.

## Prajna: Clear Perception

Rikpa is the basic approach we are trying to work with in order to maintain or get in touch with yeshe. But in order to realize yeshe, we also have to realize prajna; and in order to realize prajna, we have to experience vipashyana. Vipashyana gives us a quality of gentleness, so we do not become too harsh and clever and we do not stay in the higher realms alone. It brings us down to the level of compassion and softness. Yeshe is all-knowing, and prajna is the communication system that goes with yeshe. Prajna enables you to relate with your world altogether. So prajna and yeshe happen together, simultaneously. Prajna is like the limbs, and yeshe is like the body.

Prajna perceives what is there, which is not very much, so prajna is the perceiver of absence. But if you go beyond that, you have the perception of brilliance because of the absence, which is getting into yeshe. Shunyata, or emptiness, still has a slight notion of boundary. Why do you have to say "empty" once you are in the middle of it? You seem to be saying "empty of something," so it is a somewhat defensive concept. The idea of being empty of something is a slightly early level and is connected with the path rather than the fruition. That is why in the vajrayana tradition we talk more about luminosity than emptiness, because the concept of emptiness is always crossing the boundaries of full and empty.

## No Boundaries

Yeshe cuts your thoughts on the spot, so there are no thoughts. It is like the experience of eating a jalapeño: it numbs any possibilities of wandering mind. It is a one-hundred-percent experience, or even a two-hundred-percent experience. Yeshe does not have any boundaries. So you cannot exactly experience yeshe, but you are there already. It is almost as if you are without a physical body, or you had a physical body a long time ago, so you no longer need to maintain it. You do not even have to be fearful of death; it is as if you are part of the elements already.

With yeshe, the reference point—if you can call it a reference point—is that there is no experience other than *That. That* is the epitome of nontheism. If there are no discursive thoughts, you have intense devotion. If there are no clouds in the sky, you have intense sunshine. But here I am not speaking from the point of view of students, but from the point of view of the climate.

With ordinary consciousness, you have gaps of unconsciousness, or ignorance. You fall asleep or go unconscious, and then that is short-circuited by consciousness, and you wake up. But after you wake up, you might relapse; it is possible to fall asleep, lose consciousness, or become forgetful. Yeshe is altogether different. The stage of yeshe is reached once you have understood or clicked into the possibility of being able to break through fundamental falsity altogether. So it is even more than indestructible; with yeshe there are no possibilities of making mistakes anymore at all. Driftwood cannot become plastic wood.

## GOING BACK TO SQUARE ONE

To approach the stage of yeshe, we first have to experience the shamatha level of taming ourselves, which once again brings us back to square one. When you have tamed yourself by means of shamatha, you begin to realize that you can be more decent and genuine in expressing warmth, which in the vajrayana is connected with devotion. Shamatha is connected with humbleness. But this does not mean that you feel low and bad, belittled and uninspired. Rather, you are humble and simple because you begin to feel that you are like tilled soil, which has been plowed so many times that it feels soft and humble and ready for a seed to be sown.

Next, with vipashyana we find ourselves ready for further communication, for actually sowing a seed, which in vajrayana terms means meeting the guru. Vipashyana is also connected with hearing the dharma. When there is humbleness and tameness and the willingness to open up, you spend your energy on hearing the dharma, rather than worrying about what you should do with yourself. If there were no gentleness and no tameness, there would be no possibility of hearing and experiencing the dharma; you would become like an upside-down pot.*

---

* A reference to a traditional analogy in which students are compared to pots. If the pot is upside down, the teachings cannot enter; if the pot is leaky, the teachings will not stick; if the pot is dirty or poisoned, the teachings will be distorted or deadened; but when the pot is open and upright, the teachings can enter without distortion.

## Dropping the Watcher

At the beginning, on the primitive shamatha level, you have to develop your watchfulness. But as you begin to master shamatha, you require less watchfulness. Your mindfulness becomes a natural pattern. And when you develop shinjang, watchfulness is no longer necessary. You do not need feedback; you just know what is happening.

As you evolve into vipashyana, you develop more of an awareness of the situation, rather than constantly having to check back and forth with headquarters. So you need less watching, and more just being on the spot. In fact, the more you keep checking back, the more you lose your vipashyana; therefore, in vipashyana you should be on the spot all the time, each time.

From there you go further, and you begin to experience shunyata. You practice tonglen and become much more intense about developing compassion, gentleness, and kindness to others. Since you are concentrating on the pain of others and on developing generosity for them, you do not have to be so watchful of yourself all the time. You do not have to congratulate yourself about what a good person you are. As you put more exertion into your practice, you need less congratulation. Instead, you need more of a one-to-one relationship with your actual experience of the meditation technique, and you need to simplify yourself. Since you are dealing with the techniques very simply, you need less commentator, which is the voice of watchfulness, and more just seeing things very clearly. You are doing that properly and fully, on the spot.

As your confidence, discipline, exertion, and patience grow further, you finally get to the level of yeshe. It seems to be quite a long way, actually. At this point, you begin to feel that there is no need for a watcher. There is not even a question of being watched. If you had a watcher, it would actually be more of an obstacle. So finally, you do not need a commentator. That is the last thing you want! You just do it. That is called *nowness*. You do not need the past or the future to mind your business, but you are right here—and the fourth moment is even more so.

This whole process of dropping the watcher is like martial arts training. You need help at the beginning to make sure that you do not hurt yourself with your sword, and to make sure that you do a good job. But at some point, your assistants begin to become obstacles because they cut down your confidence in yourself, so they need to go away.

Eventually you do not need anybody at all. You begin to pick your-self up.

## BASIC GOODNESS: THE GATEWAY TO YESHE

In terms of yeshe, basic goodness is like kindling, or starter wood. The Tibetan for basic goodness is *künshi ngangluk kyi gewa*. *Künshi*, or *alaya* in Sanskrit, is the "basis of all," *ngangluk* is "natural state," and *gewa* is "goodness" or "virtue"; so *künshi ngangluk kyi gewa* means the "natural virtue of alaya."

Basic goodness is a glimpse of wakefulness or reality in which uncondi-tionality is possible; but it is still based on a certain amount of dichotomy or separate reality, on *this* and *that*. It has been said that the experience of yeshe cannot be born out of dualistic mind, or sem, because yeshe is a completely non-ego experience, while sem still involves the reference point of self and other.

Künshi ngangluk kyi gewa is inferior to yeshe, because it still has the reference point of virtue, as opposed to non-virtue. However, I am afraid that you might nonetheless have to approach yeshe through künshi ngangluk kyi gewa. So basic goodness might accompany you up to a cer-tain point—but then it is not there anymore, and you are left on your own with yeshe, completely. Even the absolute bodhichitta practice of lojong, or resting the mind in the nature of alaya, is a starting point rather than the ultimate reality. It is similar to the European custom of parents put-ting a small measure of wine in a glass of water, and presenting it to their children at the dinner table so their children can learn how to drink. Later on, when their children learn how to drink properly, they can have a whole glass.

## BEING SOAKED IN ALL THREE YANAS

When all of this has taken place, the vajrayana aspect of taming is very simple and direct. First of all, you have been already fully and thor-oughly trained in the basic Buddhist tradition of hinayana. Secondly, you have also learned to develop your ability to relate with others through mahayana practicality and through tonglen. Because you have thoroughly and fully developed in those ways, any leftover habitual tendencies and remains of samsaric pre-Buddhist training have been removed without a trace. And even if there were such a trace left over, it would not be difficult to remove the problem, because you have already been thoroughly trained or shinjanged.

It seems to be very important for a vajrayana student to be soaked in all three yanas and become thoroughly Buddhist, rather than just becoming a vajrayana practitioner alone. We are talking about how to become a real Buddhist—about how to become a real hinayanist in the fullest sense of being tamed properly and thoroughly, and how to become a real mahayanist so that you have no problem with letting go and experiencing warmth.

With that ground, you will be able to share your gratitude and devotion to people such as the guru, the lineage, and the teachers from whom you receive your teachings. When you have become quite proficient in shamatha-vipashyana and lojong, you will begin to understand and develop unconditional wisdom, or yeshe. You will be able to identify and emulate the style and mentality of the enlightened ones fully and completely. That enlightened mentality will cease to be a myth and will instead become a real living tradition.

# 15

# Transcending Mental Concepts

*When you wake up from ignorance, you discover rikpa. Rikpa is the first notion of wakefulness, not necessarily in the sense of enlightenment, but as contrasted to slothfulness or confusion. So rikpa is a sort of spark, as opposed to dullness and sleepiness. It is intrinsic sharpness, penetratingly bright.*

I N THE vajrayana, we are freeing ourselves from habitual tendencies, which brings about the transcending of mental concepts. That freedom from habitual tendencies and mental concepts seems to be the basis for bringing the three yanas together. It is the height of vajrayana possibilities that exist in us naturally. Such freedom is the result that derives from being thoroughly processed or shinjanged. It comes from full accomplishment of shamatha and vipashyana, and from the thorough and full development of tonglen practice.

## LO: METHODICAL MIND

The term for "mental concept" in Tibetan is *lo*. *Lo* is quite a vast term and it is used in several ways. Generally, *lo* means "mind" or "minding," in the sense of "minding others." When mind minds others, it begins to achieve the clarity of lo.

Lo is not a question of sanity, particularly, but of being methodical. You may achieve temporary or seeming sanity by being very methodical and orderly, but that's it. You cannot go beyond that. You cannot put lo on a pedestal and say that it has greater potential than that. At the same time, lo is not at the klesha level, which is somewhat more mean. Lo is very innocent. It just tries to gather information and come to conclusions about where you are. Lo seems to be the first level of trying to figure out where you are, the primordial-ego level.

Being methodical or meticulous is what lo does: that is lo's function. Your body does the same thing in the sense that no matter how much you abuse your body, it always has a way of correcting itself. Physically, certain things are disposed of and certain things are maintained on an almost mechanical level. Psychologically and mentally, lo does the same thing: what needs to be kept is kept and what needs to be rejected is rejected. Lo is always faithful. It is the basic mechanism that exists in all of us always that keeps us going. Even though we might feel crazy, lo makes sure we do not do anything crazy, that we don't jump off the roof or turn on the hot water and burn ourselves.

Lo is almost on the animal instinct level of just being decent. It is the most decent aspect of regular mind. Lo takes care of you. Even though you might be depressed or excited, there is still some moderation principle going on in your mind, and that which moderates your mind is lo. Consequently, that lo needs to be trained, and that training is called lojong. So lo is not theoretical. It is simply minding what you would or would not do to yourself, on the day-to-day functional level.

## Two Types of Lo

There are two types of lo: ordinary lo and transcendent lo.

### Ordinary Lo: Reference-Point Mind

Ordinary lo provides a reference point. It enables you to get feedback as to whether your projections are reaching whatever you are projecting to and whether your projections are achieving something. Obviously, this kind of lo is purely samsaric. Nonetheless, it is very businesslike, and in the conventional sense, very sane and regular. When the mind minds others, when it projects to others, it may discover either tenderness in them or harshness. So ordinary lo refers to the mind that discovers love and hate and so forth, the mind that expresses various emotions.

### Two Types of Ordinary Lo: Lopham and Lo-Te

There are two types of ordinary lo: *lopham* and *lo-te*. *Lopham* means "disappointment" and *lo-te* means "trustworthiness." *Lo* is "mind," and *pham* means "defeat," so *lopham* means "defeated lo," or "disappointment." Similarly, in the word *lo-te*, *lo*, means "mind," and *te* means "directing"; so *lo-te* means "directing your mind," which in this case means to trust somebody.

In the vajrayana we are transcending ordinary lo altogether. We are transcending both lopham, or defeated lo, and lo-te, the lo of accomplishment, fulfillment, or trustworthiness. We are developing lo that is free from habitual tendencies altogether. However, in being free from ordinary lo, we are not actually giving up lo itself: lo itself is maintained.

### Lodrö: Transcendental Lo

There is a third type of lo, called transcendental lo, or *lodrö*. *Lo* as before means "minding," and *drö* means "satisfied" or "established," so *lodrö* means "established minding." Literally, *drö* means "advice," or "counsel." Lodrö is almost a synonym for *prajna* or intellect in the higher sense, so higher lo is close to prajna. Particularly in the case of the vajrayana, *lodrö* is more likely to refer to the transcendental form of lo, which is definitely free from habitual patterns as well as free from regular, discursive lo. With transcendental lo, freedom from the love-and-hate or hope-and-fear type of lo seems to be the outcome.

### LO AS THE PRODUCT OF CONCEPTUAL MIND OR SEM

Lo seems to be the result of sem, or conceptual mind. Sem searches and cultivates, and lo achieves some sort of outcome. With lo, you come up with something hopeful, something passionate, something aggressive, or whatever. So lo is the product of sem, it is what sem discovers. Lo could be deceptive, but it is still just a discovery of mind. It is the conclusion of sem, and as such, lo is definitely conceptual. However, when sem is tired of working, it tends to produce lo.

In a way, when you go beyond habitual patterns of mind, you are going beyond lo. The term for this is *lo-de*, which means "beyond lo."* That is, lo itself does not go very high; for lo, there is nothing higher than lodrö. But transcendent sem goes beyond lodrö.

## THE DISCOVERY OF TRANSCENDENT SEM OR RIKPA

Sem is generally regarded as ordinary, as samsaric. But there is an interesting term for sem, "transcendent sem," which is said to have been coined by the great nineteenth-century Nyingma master, Mipham Rinpoche. In Tibetan, transcendent sem is called *nyuk sem*, or "primordial sem," which is the same as rikpa.

Rikpa is the clearest and most precise discovery. Before sem even begins to work, rikpa has a first glimpse of reality. We have referred to this first glimpse as "first thought, best thought."† Traditionally, rikpa means a discovery beyond ignorance. That is, when you wake up from ignorance, you discover rikpa. Rikpa is the first notion of wakefulness, not necessarily in the sense of enlightenment, but as contrasted to slothfulness or confusion. So rikpa is a sort of spark, as opposed to dullness and sleepiness. It is intrinsic sharpness, penetratingly bright.

Rikpa is not dualistic: it could see everything. But rikpa is very hard to get hold of, which is why it is placed very high. In the vajrayana tradition, the *vidyadhara*, or *rigdzin*, the "holder of knowledge" is placed even higher than the *vajracharya*, or "vajra master." So rikpa is regarded as the highest development, more or less on the level of yeshe, or wisdom.

At the same time, rikpa is somewhat of a student's or a practitioner's point of view. In this case, rikpa is path oriented. On that path you could have a perception or rikpa of dharmakaya. The related term *prajna* could refer to either a faculty or to what you perceive. When prajna is what

---

* *Lo-te (blos gtad)* means "directing the mind," whereas the similar term *lo-de (blo 'das)* means "beyond lo."

† This phrase comes up in many contexts in Trungpa Rinpoche's teachings. For more on this quality of "first thought, best thought," in terms of the mandala principle, see chapter 27, "The Outer Mandala."

you perceive, that prajna is perceived by rikpa; whereas, when prajna is regarded as a faculty, prajna, like rikpa, is a path or journey. In that case, prajna is called *prajnaparamita*, which means "knowledge gone beyond." So prajnaparamita is different than simple prajna.

## YESHE: PRIMORDIAL KNOWING

A further kind of knowing is called yeshe. Yeshe is primordially knowing. It is the universal monarch or fruition level; therefore, it is even free from the path. But what we are talking about here is simply becoming free from habitual patterns, or transcending lo. So we are coming down to a much cruder and more detailed level. Saying that lo is the path or working basis for the practitioner is like saying that in order to be rich, you have to work harder. It is not yet at the level of saying that in order to be a universal monarch, you have to stop begging.

The term *yeshe* is related to the notion of dharmakaya, which is actually a shortened form of *jnana dharmakaya*. Likewise, the Tibetan word for dharmakaya, or *chöku*, is an abbreviation of *yeshe chöku*. So *dharmakaya* means "being in the state of yeshe."

In the hinayana, the term *dharmakaya* refers simply to the body of dharma, such as the teachings of the four noble truths or whatever other dharma is being taught. But in the vajrayana, yeshe chöku or jnana dharmakaya means "full of wisdom." So in order to experience dharmakaya, you have to be filled with yeshe. That is, yeshe *is* what dharmakaya *has*. In order to be known as someone who is rich, you have to have lots of money. In this analogy, the money is like yeshe, and being rich is like the dharmakaya. So if someone calls you a rich person, it means you have lots of money, and if someone calls you dharmakaya, it means you have lots of yeshe.

# 16

# *Fundamental Magic*

*The world is a healthy world in its own way. Even if you are sick or unhealthy, even if your bathwater turns out to be full of rusty clogs from your pipes, still it is healthy. Because of that vajrayana approach of basic healthiness, you actually are able to cut through the original root kleshas, which is the best magic of all.*

## THE UNIFICATION OF EMPTINESS AND COMPASSION

Emptiness and compassion provide the basis for the student of vajrayana; as potential vajrayana persons, we are expected to have already understood shunyata, as well as karuna. We should have that much understanding to begin with in order to practice vajrayana. In vajrayana, we take the attitude that our basic nature is already in the process of full realization; we do not regard it as an essence or potentiality. Out of that, and due to our practice of the hinayana path and the bodhisattva way, we begin to experience the unification of emptiness and compassion.

## LUMINOUS EMPTINESS

First comes emptiness, or shunyata. Shunyata is the emptiness of *küntak*, or "random labeling," and of dualistic fixations of any kind. It is also the emptiness of oneself and of one's basic core of bewilderment. That original primordial ignorance is also empty. Understanding that quality of emptiness, or twofold egolessness, we begin to develop a quality of brilliance. As we begin to see beyond dualistic fixations or hang-ups, we also begin to understand their absence. We realize that this absence is not empty or vacant in the ordinary sense, but there is a tremendous spark or brightness taking place. When we recognize that brightness, we develop what is known as "vajra pride" in traditional vajrayana terminology. Vajra pride is based on affirming that not only have we begun to see the emptiness or absence of all those hang-ups, but we have also begun to see the brilliance. We begin to take a fearless attitude toward all that, and we begin to hold that kind of posture.

That brightness or brilliance is very basic. It is like daylight. It shines into your life so that you develop clear perceptions. You know what to perceive, how to follow situations, and how to prevent obstacles. It is almost at the level of prajna; but in tantric language, instead of referring to it as prajna, we refer to it as luminous emptiness. It is empty because it is free from fixations and hang-ups; it is luminous because after all the fixations are removed, what is left behind is fully realized experience, which is outstanding.

So in the vajrayana, you are able to separate what should be rejected on the path from what should be accepted on the path, in the fashion of prajna. But not only are you able to discriminate what to accept and reject, you also experience brilliance, which brings delight and heartiness, and a somewhat macho style. It brings vajra pride.

Immediately after the experience of emptiness, there is a quality of fullness. So emptiness is not regarded as a loss. In the vajrayana, your experience of shunyata is not as if part of your brain or heart has been taken away, but more as if the first layer of tissue on your brain and heart has been taken away because it created an obstacle. You feel that now your brain and heart are functioning extremely well, that they are actually functioning much better. You feel that at last the whole thing is working properly and as it should.

In the vajrayana, you are not relating to emptiness as if you were a patient recovering in a hospital to regain your strength. In this case, the patient was never sick. Even though you had to go to the hospital to have some obstacles removed, fundamentally speaking you never got sick. The experience of emptiness is more like going to a barber to get a haircut when your hair is too long or needs shaping. When you get your hair cut, you come out better, but it is not an ordeal. The whole thing is straightforward and quite delightful.

## Compassion as Transcendental Indulgence

After emptiness comes compassion, which is soft and gentle, with an aspect of wrath. That is to say, in the vajrayana, compassion is no longer regarded as kindness in the conventional sense. It is not even kindness in the conventional mahayana sense. There is no particular norm of how to be kind in the vajrayana. Instead, compassion is an expression of the union of emptiness and luminosity.

This kind of compassion sometimes has a threatening aspect, but it is only threatening because we want to gain something from ego's point of view. It is threatening because if an unreasonable situation occurs, this kind of compassion would answer that with its own unreasonability. This makes the whole thing into a good deal; it balances both situations. It could sometimes happen the other way around, of course, but that depends on what your shunyata vision has provided for you.

Vajrayana compassion is based on fundamental lust and passion. So much warmth is expressed to fellow sentient beings and to yourself that you begin to feel almost romantic about the whole thing. In the bodhisattva path, you are not allowed to look at the romantic aspect, particularly; you are just performing good deeds all the time. You become a bridge, a highway, a ship, or a reservoir. You become whatever you possibly can in order to accommodate everything.

In mahayana compassion, there is little possibility of indulgence, but in vajrayana compassion, indulgence somehow comes back. This is quite a dangerous thing to say, I suppose, but I hope you understand what I mean. I don't want to produce any egomaniacs. In vajrayana compassion, indulgence means taking pride in your gentleness and softness, which is also harsh and flavored with aggression. But in this case, it is obviously transcendental aggression. Vajrayana compassion is like drinking milk that has been cooked over a slowly burning fire until it has begun to thicken and condense. That milk has lots of honey and sugar in it, but you then add a few drops of Tabasco sauce, which makes it both sweet and chipper, tasty, but with a reminder. You cannot just get into the smoothness and simplicity of it, but there is a touch of bitterness at the same time.

Transcendental indulgence is very simple, but you cannot understand this if you don't do it. When you have the clarity and precision of shunyata along with a feeling of compassion, then you begin to develop who you are and what you are. Your identity, so to speak, becomes absolutely clear. What direction you should be going in and what you should be doing are certain, so you just go and do it. You proclaim yourself with no doubts and no depression. It is very simple that way. If you beat around the bush, there will be endless problems.

All of this—how to clarify this situation and actually be able to see this fully and properly—is based on the principle of devotion. When you have enough devotion and loyalty to the lineage and to your vajra master, when you actually begin to do what has been said by the teachings, this provides tremendous confirmation. You can be arrogant in the positive sense.

## ABRUPTLY CUTTING THOUGHTS

There is magic in vajrayana practice and in vajrayana altogether. People often think that magic is the ability to do things like change fire into water, or float up toward the ceiling and then come down again, or make tomato ketchup into cream cheese. But we have a better understanding of magic than that; what is actually happening is better than those things. We are not talking about magic in the style of a conjuring magician on the stage, but we are talking about fundamental magic. This magic is always based on the profound effect that we have discovered from the hinayana discipline of one-pointedness and the mahayana discipline of openness and compassionate nonterritoriality. Out of that comes vajrayana magic, which is that we are able to cut our thoughts abruptly and directly. On the spot!

### Trust

There seem to be several stages to that process of cutting thoughts. The first is an attitude of trust in your vajra master and in his or her wisdom. Whether your vajra master is a vajra lady or vajra lord, in any case, the vajra master becomes a source of magic to cut your thoughts. When a vajrayana student begins to think of the qualities of the vajra master, that student should have an experience of hot and cold simultaneously. You experience hot because it is so fiery that it burns every deception and doubt, and you experience cold because it puts out the fires of emotional eruptions and emotional blazes.

## Cutting Discursive Thoughts

When a student has some idea of the vajra master as the author of that power to cut thoughts, the vajra master in turn begins to instruct that student and tell them how to go about this. Because the vajra master is already an accomplished yogi and has gone through this experience themselves, their teaching is much more applicable and understandable to ordinary students.

In tantric iconography, the herukas and dakinis are wearing garlands of freshly severed heads, which represents cutting through mental contents. That is the first thing we come across: cutting through our mental contents. So the truth of the matter is that first you cut the fringe thoughts, or what are known in Buddhist psychological writings or *abhidharma* literature as the mental contents. Mental contents are divided into good ones and bad ones. That is to say, some of them are virtuous, such as faith, and some of them are wicked, such as anger and laziness. Nevertheless, they are all mental contents. There are said to be fifty-one or fifty-two of these mental contents, depending on which text you follow—but there are definitely at least fifty.*

## Seeing Thoughts as Unborn, Unceasing, and Completely Empty

Before you actually cut the guts of ego in yourself, first you cut the mental contents by direct measure. Following the instructions of the vajra master, you look at the mental contents and realize that they do not come from anywhere; then you experience that they do not have any content; finally, when you look at them further, you realize that they do not go anywhere. The traditional way of saying this is that thoughts are unborn, unceasing, and completely empty.

The magic of cutting your discursive thoughts or mental contents actually happens as they dissolve and you see that they do not exist, and as they arise and you see them as complete shunyata. In other words, thoughts are free from past, present, and future. Toward the end of realiz-

---

* In Sanskrit, *mental contents* are called *samskaras*. In English, they may also be referred to as "formations" or "concepts." The samskaras are one of the five skandhas, or five "heaps," that constitute the ego, and they are also one of the twelve nidanas in the chain of interdependent origination. See volume 1 of the *Profound Treasury*, chapter 9, "The Painful Reality of Samsara."

ing that thoughts are free from the present, and the beginning of realizing that they are free from the future as well, there is that kind of [*snaps his fingers*]. That is definitely magic; you are able to cut your thoughts very abruptly and very precisely.

In the mahayana, you try to quell your aggression and hatred for yourself with maitri, and you quell your hatred toward others with karuna. You have already had an experience of shunyata; you have already seen things as free from concepts, and you have already seen your thoughts as transparent. In the mahayana, everything depends on attitude, and everything is done with diplomacy. But in this case, you cut thoughts abruptly, on the spot. You do not even take an attitude. Taking the bodhisattva vow is committing yourself to an attitude, but in this case you are not committing yourself to an attitude; you are committing yourself to the real thing. You just do it. It is very direct and precise. In the vajrayana, you confront thoughts right away—bang, bang, bang, on the spot. You just do it.

How to cut your thoughts in this manner would obviously be the next question. But there is no particular way to do it. The only thing I can say is that having developed genuine loyalty to the teachings of vajrayana and dedication to the vajra master, you just jump, on the spot, at your own thoughts. That is the only magic there is. No gunpowder or ingredients are involved, but cutting thoughts is the first way of blowing up the samsaric world.

This combination of abruptness and devotion and actually being able to do it is the very important first step. So when you practice vajrayana, the main point that runs through all the traditions, through every level of vajrayana practice, is that you are able to cut your mental contents directly and abruptly.

## CUTTING THE CAUSE OF THOUGHTS:
## PASSION, AGGRESSION, AND IGNORANCE

Having cut mental contents, we go beyond that, slightly further, to cutting the cause of the mental contents.

### Paralyzing Kleshas

At this point, we are basically working with passion, aggression, and ignorance: the three root kleshas, or three poisons. Cutting the three root kleshas abruptly on the spot is much more dynamic than cutting the mental contents, which is easier. Cutting the mental contents is like a sneeze: you just pounce on your mind, you just cut it. But the three poisons are deep-rooted.

The way to work with the three root kleshas is to paralyze them. The basic bewilderment is already a paralyzed situation that is trying to spew out passion, aggression, and ignorance, so you are trying to overparalyze beyond that. You are trying to throw out a much bigger zap—[*gasps sharply*]—which comes from understanding the sacredness of the vajrayana world.

## *Experiencing Sacredness*

In the vajrayana tradition, drinking, eating, sleeping, walking, sitting, and whatever we do in our whole life is sacred. It is sacred because inherently there is no reason for it not to be sacred. It is actually as simple as that. We do not have to build up reasons for why it is holy, or say, "It has been blessed by the Father, the Son, and the Holy Ghost." We also do not have to say that everything is sacred because it has been blessed by a great Buddhist, like the Karmapa. We don't have to go through any little logic like that—things are just intrinsically sacred.

When we touch an object, it is purely an object from our somewhat half-awakened point of view. We touch an object; it is an object that we are touching; therefore, it is good to touch the object. When we listen to a sound, it is good to listen to the sound. When we taste, it is good to taste. That kind of goodness is intrinsic goodness. There is no reason why it should not be, by the very fact that we are not particularly angry or pissed off at phenomena, but we actually accept our world simply as it is. The world is very definitely as it is. There is no reason either to be pissed off at it or to boost it up. It is just a simple world, which is a full world, a bright world, a shining world, a brilliant world.

The world is a healthy world in its own way. Even if you are sick or unhealthy, even if your bathwater turns out to be full of rusty clogs from your pipes, still it is healthy. Because of that vajrayana approach of basic healthiness, you actually are able to cut through the original root kleshas, which is the best magic of all. Usually passion, aggression, and ignorance occur through the inspiration of cheapness. You are angry, you are passionate, and you feel stupefied. Because you do not explore, you do not experience any of the room around you; you do not experience any atmosphere. That is very unintelligent. It is as if you were to go to a restaurant, sit at a table and eat, and find that your plate is the only world there is. You don't even recognize that there is salt and pepper in front of you, let alone notice the music or the decor in that particular restaurant. You just do your thing and devour your food. With that point of view, you find yourself sitting on your plate and consuming your little world. You are not even sitting on your chair.

## Ransacking the Kleshas

That small-world approach of passion, aggression, and ignorance could be called setting sun, quite definitely so. And that smallness is cut by the largeness of the expanse of space outside of it. It is cut by a sense of vastness and openness, and also by a sense of accomplishment. Magic happens at the level when you begin to loot the privacy of passion, aggression, and ignorance. You begin to search and loot. You go over your whole property, open all your drawers and cabinets, and throw everything out. Then, naturally and obviously, after searching and looting, you begin to find quite good delight. You feel delight that finally you were able to loot, or to ransack, your stronghold, which has given you problems for a long time.

The process of ransacking is not like the police coming to your home and intruding, or like your enemies or the Mafia ransacking your house. In this case, ransacking is sacred activity, much more so than what you have done already. The whole thing is very sacred; it is basically sane. Whatever you do, whether you do it abruptly or slowly, it is sacred.

## Complete Looting

When you cut thoughts on the spot so thoroughly, you are cutting karma. But then, because of habitual patterns and because you have not yet cut your basic alaya principle, you come up with further karmic actions. You can cut that by developing a sense of magic, or complete looting. When you have complete looting, there is not a next moment. Situations come from your own mind rather than from somebody else. When you control your mind, when you are able to loot your mind fully, then there is no other world to put garbage into your mind. There is no karma at that point. You have cleaned up the whole thing. Everything is in here, so once you begin to clean that up, there is no problem at all. Making decisions on the spot has no karma. You cannot make a wrong decision.

Interestingly, during sitting meditation in the vajrayana, you practice the hinayana style of shamatha-vipashyana, which reinforces the state of healthiness of your mind. Then in the postmeditation experience, when you have finished your sitting practice and are going about your regular business, you can zap into that state of mind. You can always do that; it is what has traditionally been improvised. That is the only way to combine hinayana, mahayana, and vajrayana together. This means you have to be awake and aware all twenty-four hours of every day.

Particularly with beginning vajrayana practitioners, there is no relaxation at all, none whatsoever, and you cannot have a good time. But you are being fed by the energy that exists around you, which could be the equivalent of relaxation. That energy is your personal passion, aggression, and ignorance; it is the five-buddha-family principle of energy.* So you are not exactly relaxed, but you are being fed constantly by this energy. Because of that, you begin to realize that you can give up and let go very easily.

## Vajrayana Sayings

In the vajrayana, there are several sayings related to the discovery of transcending habitual patterns, which might be helpful at this point.

### Rikpa Free from Sem

The first saying is "Rikpa free from sem." In Tibetan it is *sem tang tral-we rikpa*. *Sem* means "mind," *tang tral-we* means "free from," and *rikpa*, again, means "insight"; so *sem tang tral-we rikpa* means "insight that has departed or separated from the mind." It means rikpa that is free from the mind. This is one of the definitions of vajrayana insight: it is insight that is free

---

* The *five buddha-families* refer to five styles of energy, which can manifest in either confused or enlightened ways. This grouping of five, arranged in the center and four cardinal directions of a circle, or mandala, is found throughout tantric teachings and iconography. For more on the five buddha-families, see chapter 26, "The Mandala of the Five Buddha-Families."

from thinking about something else, free from perceiving the other. In other words, it is nondualistic; it is just direct perception.

## Buddha without Breath

The second saying is "Buddha without breath," which is rather difficult. In Tibetan it is *uk tang tral-we sang-gye*. *Uk* means "breath," *tang tral-we*, as before, means "separated from" or "without," and *sang-gye* means "buddha"; so *uk tang tral-we sang-gye* means "buddha without breath." "Buddha without breath" means that the Buddha does not gasp or become short of breath. A buddha does not depend on saying "Phew!"

This saying is connected with being wakeful. You can become a buddha whether you are dead or alive. Whether you breathe or not, you can become a buddha. So we have insight without mind, then buddha without breathing.

## Meditation without Thought, but Luminous

The third saying is "Meditation without thought, but luminous or brilliant." In Tibetan it is *sella tokpa me-pe gompa*. *Sel* or *ösel* means "luminosity," *tokpa* means "thoughts," "thinking," or "discursive mind," *me-pe* means "without," and *gompa* means "meditation"; so *sel-la tokpa me-pe gompa* means "meditation without thought, but luminous."

The idea of luminosity here is opposed to just emptiness or the absence of duality alone. When we begin to look beyond duality, we see that it is not just empty and nonexistent. We begin to realize that beyond egohood, there is still tremendous aliveness, vitality, strength, and energy. This aliveness and energy is luminous and bright, and it contains tremendous wisdom. This is the basic point of the vajrayana approach to emptiness or egolessness: it is not purely annihilation, but it goes beyond annihilation. That is what is meant by meditation without thought, but still brilliant.

## Action without Fixation or Desire

The fourth saying is "Action without fixation or desire." In Tibetan it is *dzinchak me-pe chöpa*. *Dzin* means "holding" or "fixation," *chak* means "desire," *me-pe* means "not having that," and *chöpa* means "action"; so *dzinchak me-pe chöpa* means "action without fixation or desire."

Usually when we act, we act in order to get something. We do not usually do something without getting something back. That is the samsaric approach to action. But in this case, we are talking about spontaneous action. Spontaneous action is related with skillful means; it is related to bodhisattva activity, or working for the sake of others. This kind of action is not based on ego fixation or the desire for our own attainment of any kind of pleasure. It is action without pleasure fixation or ego fixation. Therefore, it is pure action.

## View without Desire

The fifth saying is "View without desire." In Tibetan it is *shedö me-pe tawa. Dö* means "wanting," and *she* is another word for *lo*, so *shedö* means "mind of desire," *me-pe* means "without," and *tawa* means "view," referring to a metaphysical view or attitude; so *shedö me-pe tawa* means "view without desire."

These five sayings are all the blessings of the guru. The guru is the one who bestows the insight free from mind; makes you buddha without breath; teaches you the meditation without thought, but luminous; shows you the action free from fixation or desire; and shows you the view free from desire.

There are a lot of blessings here, but I do not think these blessings are regarded as a kind of zap. Rather, when students develop these qualities, the teachers can tune in to them more. And in that way, in fact, students can short-circuit their past, present, and future, and begin to see the fourth moment on the spot. That seems to be the idea of blessings here. The guru is able to control the environment, because you and the guru share a world together. Because you share the same world, you both click at the same time, which is known as the meeting of minds.

These five sayings seem to be the basic reference points of vajrayana. They are the commentary to our previous discussion of ordinary lo, transcendental lo, and freedom from habitual patterns. The idea is that when there are no habitual patterns, there is always insight free from mind; buddha without breath; meditation without thought, but still luminous; action without fixation or desire; and view without desire.

Even at the beginning of the journey, these sayings are basic reference points for how we can attain freedom from habitual patterns and mental concepts. They are not necessarily the fruition, but they describe how we begin at the beginning, at the ground level. These sayings are more at the level of motivation. When we have such motivation, we definitely become nontheistic, because we are not really referring to ourselves. We do not say, "I want this and I want that." We begin to see through our wantingness and desire.

Wantingness and desire are the biggest problems and blockages of all. We have a problem with wanting and desire, with wanting to achieve something and wanting to refer back to our habitual patterns to make sure that what we are doing is right. On the basis of all five vajrayana sayings, and because we begin to see through our wantingness and desire, the four reminders arise: our precious human birth, free and well-favored; impermanence; the cause and effect of karma; and the suffering of samsara.*

---

* The practice of the *four reminders*, the first stage of vajrayana preliminary practices, is discussed in chapter 30, "The Four Reminders."

# 17

# The Play of Space and Form

*When we talk about enlightened ones as opposed to unenlightened ones, that vocabulary of enlightenment has actually developed from the samsaric point of view rather than from the view of ultimate perfection. Ultimate perfection transcends the definition of enlightenment. It is purely space, purely dhatu or ying.*

BEFORE WE get into the details of the various yogas of tantra, I thought we should talk about the idea of space in tantra. The Tibetan term for space is *ying,* and in Sanskrit it is *dhatu.* The word *dhatu* can be used to mean "realm" or "essence," but in tantra it means basic psychological space. I suppose the word *realm* is appropriate as well, meaning the particular environment you are in, so dhatu is your environment as well as space. The word *ying,* or *dhatu,* is a very prominent and important principle of vajrayana understanding.

## RIKPA AND THE LEVELS OF SPACE

Your practice of shamatha at the hinayana level and your vipashyana and shunyata experience at the mahayana level have together brought this particular notion of space into the situation. The tantric way of looking at the whole thing brings in a different perspective, which is that there are various levels of space. Basically, we are trying to relate with the origin of the origin of the originator and of origination itself. But we are not talking in the theistic sense of the maker of the world. Instead, we are talking in terms of transcendent intelligence, or rikpa.

There are various definitions for rikpa. There is rikpa according to vipashyana experience, and rikpa according to higher tantric experience. At the vipashyana level, rikpa still has some kind of plan or strategy. But in the vajrayana, rikpa is not equated with discriminating one from the other, or "me" and "my world." It is not operating from the point of view of the dualistic split, but it is more like a beam of light that shines constantly. And because that beam of light or beam of intelligence shines constantly, it is known in the tantric literature as the dawn of Vajrasattva. It is the dawn, the awakening, the crisp-winter-morning aspect of clarity and sharpness.

At the same time, rikpa creates space. Rikpa is indivisible with space. Rikpa does not have any plans; it does not decide to become enlightened or not to become enlightened. Rikpa is a self-existing situation. It has also been said that the basic nature of tathagatagarbha is self-existing. Tathagatagarbha has limitless functions. It is not aware of itself, but at the same time it is also not ignorant of itself. So it is self-shining or self-luminous.

The basic principle here is that when tantra speaks of enlightenment, it means basic being. The idea is that you have already arrived at the final end result, except that you have clouded it over. But each time there is a gap between the clouds, you begin to see your attributes clearly. It might take only a fraction of a second or a microsecond, and it might only be a glimpse; nevertheless, it is still a glimpse of what it should be in the long term, the final term.

## The Four Levels of Space

In connection with rikpa, there are various levels of space and form, or dhatus and kayas. First we'll discuss the four levels of space: indestructible space, self-existing wisdom, primordial space, and intricate space.

### Vajradhatu: Indestructible Space

The first level of space is *dorje ying* in Tibetan, or *vajradhatu* in Sanskrit, which means "indestructible space." Vajradhatu is regarded as the basic space that accommodates everything, samsara and nirvana. Nothing can challenge this space. In spite of its clarity, or discriminating wisdom, it is still indestructible.

Generally when we talk about space, we are talking about psychological space, but vajradhatu is not particularly psychologically oriented; it is just basic experience, basic being. Vajradhatu is completely distinctive and completely clear, and at the same time, there is immense space and indestructibility. The basic quality of this space is that it is immovable. It is immovable because of its spaciousness, because of its all-pervasiveness.

## Rangjung Gi Yeshe: Self-Existing Wisdom

The next level of space, according to the great fourteenth-century Nyingma master Longchen Rabjam and Jamgön Kongtrül the Great, is called *rangjung gi yeshe*. *Rang* means "self," *jung* means "arising" or "coming into existence," *gi* means "of," and *yeshe* means "wisdom"; so *rangjung gi yeshe* means "self-existing wisdom."

After the indestructibility of vajradhatu, there is wisdom. There is a sense of being learned, a sense of comprehending all kinds of things, a sense of scrutinizing the phenomenal world in a very spacious way. The reason this wisdom is known as "self-existing" is because there is no reason. There is no reason, no purpose, and no particular attitude. But there is enormous clarity—clarity born from nothing.

## Dö-me Ying: Primordial Space

The next level of space is called *dö-me ying*. *Döma* means "primordial," *dö-me* makes that "of primordial," and *ying* is "space"; so *dö-me ying* means "primordial space."

Based on the perspective that you have already covered the indestructibility of vajradhatu, you then experience primordial space as well. Here, a concept of time and space begins to come into being in the psychological state of the practitioner. This particular idea of mind is not new, and it is not a newly discovered experience. You have not been talked into it or led into it by metaphysical concepts. But you begin to realize its oldness, that it existed a long time ago. There is a quality of primordial space and time—time in the sense of endless beginning. You begin to feel that the beginninglessness is more important than what is happening now—and what is happening at this point also depends on that beginninglessness, so it too is primordial.

So the idea of primordial is not just at the level of prenatal or pre-historic, but it goes far beyond that. It is old wisdom that is still new at the present moment. Old space, or dö-me ying, is still up-to-date at this moment.

When we talk about beginninglessness, we have to be very clear that we are not saying that something started at the beginning, and that this beginning is far away from us. We are talking about beginninglessness. Beginninglessness is why it is primordial rather than just very old, like an antique piece. It is very old because it does not have a beginning. Therefore the old and the young could be together at once, because it is up-to-date now and it is also very old. In that sense, primordial space is beyond age; it transcends age. And that brings us to the next level, or dharmadhatu.

## Dharmadhatu: Intricate Space

After the space of beginninglessness, the next level is dharmadhatu. With dharmadhatu, because so many dharmas exist, because so many norms and styles exist, that crowdedness becomes the space element at the same time.

Dharmadhatu provides further clarification in terms of understanding separate realities: me and my perceptions, me and my relationships, me and my concepts of the phenomenal world, and so forth. At the same time, there is a sense of norm, or law. The functions and workings of the phenomenal world begin to come into being, but there are so many styles of working, so many ways of being, that the whole thing is completely endless and completely beginningless. Therefore, the space of dharma-dhatu is known as the space of the complete and very intricate galaxies of intelligence and styles operating in the phenomenal world. But in spite of its crowdedness and nonspaciousness, dharmadhatu creates another space. So dharmadhatu is also a level of space.

## THE THREE KAYAS AND THE LEVELS OF FORM

Now we'll discuss the next three levels, which are the levels of form: the dharmakaya, the sambhogakaya, and the nirmanakaya.

## Dharmakaya: The Body of Dharma

The next level is dharmakaya, the body of dharma. I would like to make it clear that with dharmakaya, we are beginning to get more into form than space.

At this level, intelligence begins to appear in terms of the awakened state, or enlightenment, as opposed to samsara. *Awakening* as a dualistic term begins to appear. So at the dharmakaya level, there exists a separate reality apart from samsaric confusion and nirvanic liberation, and this is where the actual awakening aspect begins. So with dharmakaya, there is still an entity or a personality of some kind. Therefore, when the Buddha first attained enlightenment under the *bodhi* tree in Bodh Gaya and claimed that he was the enlightened one, he touched the earth and said that the earth was his witness. He said, "I sat on the earth and I attained enlightenment."

According to the tantra *Rikpa Rangshar Chenpö Gyü (Tantra of Great Self-Arising Awareness)*, the utterance of the dharmakaya is: "I am unborn; therefore, I am intelligent. I have no dharma and no form. I have no marks. I am the charnel ground where all existence is exposed.* Since I am the origin of kindness and compassion; therefore, I have transcended the definition of shunyata or any ideology. I shine brilliantly; therefore, I have never known the darkness." Those are the utterances of the dharmakaya Buddha.

This quote begins with "I am," because of its kaya-ness. Because of its dharmakaya quality, there is definitely an entity, an enlightened being. So with dharmakaya, there is the origin of the idea of an enlightened being who knows all the norms of the phenomenal world. That enlightened being also knows all the norms of the phenomenal world's jargons. Enlightenment should therefore be equal to saying: "This. That is that, and this is this. Therefore, I am this, and so on and so on."

This "I" has nothing to do with ego particularly; it is just the utterance of space. When space is ignored or you begin to lose track of space, you begin to knock pots off your table. Space accentuates its voice of "I do exist." Therefore, breaking your pot is a message from space. When

---

* The charnel ground is a cemetery where dead bodies are placed to be devoured by wild animals. It is a powerful symbol used throughout vajrayana literature and iconography.

THE PLAY OF SPACE AND FORM

you begin to get crowded or confused, and you lose track of space, space makes you break pots. That is dharmakaya.

## Sambhogakaya: The Body of Joy

From dharmakaya, strangely enough, comes the sambhogakaya, the body of joy. *Sambhoga* means "joy" or "bliss"; so *sambhogakaya* is the "body of joy." In this case, the body of joy has nothing to do with pain or pleasure, but it is the body of stimulation. Everything is completely stimulated and heightened. All kinds of perceptions could be experienced from the stimulation that comes from the dharmakaya of the origin. It is stimulated so completely that the body of joy is synonymous with stimulation.

In the sambhogakaya, expression comes out in terms of speech and movement. You experience the sense perceptions very clearly and precisely, and you understand them as they are. When you see red, red is very red; and when you see yellow, yellow is very yellow. Black is very black, and blue is very blue. There is no blurry vision, and everything speaks for itself. This is not particularly mystical, as in the feeling that red should mean compassion, or yellow should mean richness, and it is not particularly intellectual or conceptual. But in seeing the phenomenal world, the experience is very direct, definite, and clear.

## Nirmanakaya: The Emanation Body

The next level is the nirmanakaya, or tülku. *Tül* means "emanation" or "multiplicity," and *ku* means "body"; so *tülku* means "emanation body." It is like mistakenly bringing an anthill back home, thinking it is bread: when you break it open, you find so many ants coming out. There is such minuteness and so many things happening at once; it is a sudden shock. There are bodies of emanation all over, but each has its own little style.

Emanation bodies, or tülkus, appear in this world as craftspeople, teachers, business leaders, and politicians. There are all kinds of tülkus, and all of those beings are equally enlightened. It is like the story of the eighty-four mahasiddhas. Each had their own function, their own occupation, but somehow they all still seemed to be siddhas; they were all still nirmanakaya buddhas.

Nirmanakaya buddhas are resourceful, and they never cause a nuisance to society. Not only that, but they also tend to create further expansion and further realization by teaching other people. Because you are not a nuisance to society, because you have your trip together, you can also communicate. You do not have to ask society for any favors, so there is a sense of freedom or liberation. You know what you are doing.

The nirmanakaya level is another kind of space, actually, and it is more interesting than any of the others, as a matter of fact. If you look in detail, you see that the skillful means, compassion, and resourcefulness of these nirmanakayas are all expressions of the teachings. And nirmanakayas are visible to the eyes of ordinary sentient beings who are unable to see the other kayas and the other levels of space.

## FURTHER THOUGHTS ON KAYAS AND DHATUS

The dhatus are not particularly hierarchical. They are more accentuated and expressive. So the dhatus are not a progression particularly, but they are rather different manifestations of space. It is like seeing a building during darkness, dawn, sunrise, midday, and evening: you are seeing the same building in different perspectives, different lighting. However, each time we go to the level of the next dhatu, it is much closer and more communicative and understandable to the samsaric world. That is the only pattern.

The kayas are closer to the samsaric world than the dhatus because there is a form to relate with, although the dharmakaya refers to a buddha who attained enlightenment and who has no form. From this point of view, vajradhatu is more distant from enlightenment, because enlightenment is a samsaric concept. When we talk about enlightened ones as opposed to unenlightened ones, that vocabulary of enlightenment has actually developed from the samsaric point of view, rather than from the view of ultimate perfection. Ultimate perfection transcends the definition of enlightenment. It is purely space, purely dhatu or ying.

The basic approach to space throughout the whole tantrayana is based on the three kayas. The dharmakaya is the origin or nonexistence body that is the creator of everything. The sambhogakaya is the body of excitement of intelligence, and the willingness to play with the phenomenal world. The nirmanakaya is the body that is actually communicating with the sunset and sunrise, daytime and nighttime and everything. It is in that acceptance of the universe, within that particular frame of reference, that the nirmanakaya buddha functions.

In tantric disciplines, what we will largely be working with is the sambhogakaya buddha principle. For instance, all the yidams are sambhogakaya buddhas. They are also part of your own basic being, basic expression, and basic mannerisms. Your innate nature is the sambhogakaya buddha principle.

For practitioners, what happens is that there is a developmental journey, which starts with being in the nirmanakaya, then experiencing sambhogakaya, and finally experiencing dharmakaya. But then you have to break through your kaya-ness, your formness, and begin to experience the dhatus. The reversal of that is the expressive journey, which goes downward. In this journey, having attained dharmakaya already, you experience the dhatus, then you come down to sambhogakaya, and then the nirmanakaya.

Basically, your world is questionable, so you keep searching. There is some body, some kaya, evolving itself into the samsaric world, acting as a benevolent bodhisattva or as a very sane arhat. Whether as a sane teacher or an outrageous one, some expression begins to take place. But the whole approach is offhanded. Nothing is planned and nothing is strategized, but there has to be some brilliance or intelligence, some accuracy and skillfulness, in order to be offhanded. Probably that is what the word *self-liberated* means: offhandedness in the enlightened sense.

## Relating with Vajrayana Language

In the mahayana, even if someone completely attained the mahayana through the eleventh bhumi, although they could imagine looking down and although they have the intelligence to experience that, they are still journeying upward. But we are now speaking the vajrayana language, which is a view from above as opposed to a view from below. The view from above would say that the city is behind a cloud, and the view from below would say that the sky is covered with clouds. So we are talking from the point of view that cities are covered with clouds, not that the sun is behind a cloud, or the moon is behind a cloud. That is why the vajrayana is referred to as the imperial yana. It is like being on top of a mountain and looking down on the small hills and being able to see the whole thing. So it is a different approach altogether.

Relating with the various definitions of space is a question of expansion, of how many territories or areas have been covered or conceptualized.

These definitions exist because of us confused people; that is why these definitions unfortunately happen to exist. But they do not really mean anything, actually, if we can even say that. The whole point is that you cannot trust the definitions, because once you begin to trust the definitions, you begin to solidify them. When you say "vajra," it means all kinds of things. So unless you know the limitlessness of the definitions of dharma from the highest tantric point of view, you cannot really trust in any concrete term for anything. That is why all these definitions are called ying or space: nothing is concrete, and nothing is dependable. The fact that basic being cannot be depended on may be a refuge. It could mean cutting your own throat, but at the same time, it could mean putting a new head on your body.

# 18

# The Eight States of Consciousness
# and the Trikaya Principle

*According to the vajrayana tradition, every journey that we make throughout the entire path is based on the trikaya. It is based on the achievement of the perfect trikaya principle: the basic physical state, or nirmanakaya; manifestation, or sambhogakaya; and finally, the fundamental nonfixation and nonduality of "I" and "other" altogether, or dharmakaya.*

## THE TRIKAYA PRINCIPLE AS THE
## BASIS FOR VAJRAYANA PRACTICE

Having discussed the play of space and form, we could look into the trikaya principle as the basis for vajrayana practice. *Tri* means "three," and *kaya* means "form" or "body"; so *trikaya* means "three bodies." Basically, the three kayas are the different subtleties of enlightenment. First, there is the vacant state of dharmakaya; then there is the energy level of sambhogakaya; and finally there is the practical level of nirmanakaya. So basic egolessness is dharmakaya, and out of that basic egolessness comes sambhogakaya, and out of the sambhogakaya comes the functional, pragmatic world of the nirmanakaya.

### Dharmakaya: Mind without Fixation

The first kaya is dharmakaya, or in Tibetan, *chöku*. Mind plays a very important part in dharmakaya, because mind is the cognitive means for perceiving things as they are. All our thought processes and all forms of discursive mind are regarded as dharmakaya. The dharmakaya is related with the idea of mind, with or without thinking. With no praise and no blame, we accept and realize our thought process as it is—but with a touch of nonfixation and without holding on to thoughts.

When your mind is completely with your breath, that is dharmakaya at the shamatha level; breath flows, and mind occurs. Between the breath and the mind, between your perception of body and mind, there is no dichotomy; there is no other thought at all. You are completely synchronized with your mind and body, and your mind and breath are together. At that point, mind is nonmind. That is the state of dharmakaya; it is as simple as that.

When you are not mindful, you do not experience dharmakaya. And when you are lost in a daydream, although the nature of thoughts is said to be dharmakaya, you are not experiencing dharmakaya. You are not on the path; you are just on the ground. But whenever a flash of mindfulness takes place, there is no wavering; there is just the occurrence of mind and mindfulness at the same time. Mindfulness does not mean looking at your mind, but rather it means that you are being mind-ed. You are minding yourself on the spot. At that point, there are no kleshas and no thoughts. It is a one-shot deal all the time. For instance, if you hear a sudden *boom!* you do not even think "boom," but booming and hearing are one: your mind has joined them together. At that point, there is dharmakaya. It is very immediate and precise.

## Sambhogakaya: Clear Perception of the Phenomenal World

Out of that state of being without fixation and not holding on to your thoughts, there arises a clear perception of the phenomenal world. There is the kaya of manifestation, or sambhogakaya. In Tibetan, sambhogakaya is *longku*. *Long* means "enjoyment," and *ku* means "body"; so *longku* is "enjoyment body." The sambhogakaya is called the "body of enjoyment" not so much in pleasure-oriented terms, but simply because when you exist as what you are, you thrive on being alive.

The sambhogakaya is connected with speech and the interchange between oneself and others. Whatever we see (reds, blues, yellows, pinks, purples, and greens); whatever we taste (Roquefort cheese or blue cheese); whatever we feel (silk or cotton or polyester); whatever we hear (classical music or rock music or the sounds of nature); whatever we smell (expensive perfume or the smell of sewage)—whatever passes through our sense perceptions is all regarded as one. It is all the expression of the nonthought of dharmakaya. Therefore, in terms of both discursive thoughts and our personal experience of things as they are, we find that there is no conflict, none whatsoever. That is the sambhogakaya.

## Nirmanakaya: Natural Existence

Beyond that, we have the nirmanakaya. This is the kaya that can be perceived by our individual reference point. It is created existence or manifested existence. The Sanskrit term *nirmanakaya* (or *tülku* in Tibetan) also refers to individuals who have created their own manifestation in the world, such as Shakyamuni Buddha himself. The nirmanakaya is a more earthbound situation, in which communication with others becomes very natural and extraordinarily ordinary.

You have already had training in sending and taking. You are tireless, and you practice tremendous exertion, dedication, and generosity in relating with others. You are highly disciplined. Beyond that, as a product of realizing and experiencing the trikaya principle, there is a general sense of being tamed as a Buddhist.

Buddhists walk softly, they talk softly, they behave gently, they turn around slowly, they reach for things with respect. That is the mark of being a true Buddhist. The way Buddhists wear clothes is dignified, even if they are wearing rags. When they wear little pieces of jewelry, they look elegant. When they gaze at the sun and the moon, their gaze is sure and profound; they are not just dreaming in the setting-sun style. You have that Buddhist outlook, and the principles of Buddhism have seeped into your system, so you conduct yourself magnificently, precisely, and so beautifully. You are an elegant Buddhist.

## OBSCURATIONS VEILING THE TRIKAYA

Generally, we are bound by being unable to see the three kayas as they are, properly and thoroughly. We are veiled by obscurations or anxieties, which are known in Tibetan as *drippa*, which means "obscuration." It is like having cataracts in your eyes, which shadow your vision. We are bound by the kleshas, or *nyönmong* in Tibetan. A nyönmong is a nuisance and a pain; it is a nuisance-pain. The term literally implies the quality of unnecessariness.

Kleshas are organized and developed through the eight states of consciousness, up to the level of the storehouse consciousness, or *alaya-vijnana*.

## The Eight States of Consciousness

Altogether there are eight states of consciousness: the five sense consciousnesses, the mind consciousness, the klesha consciousness, and the alaya consciousness.

THE FIVE SENSE CONSCIOUSNESSES. To begin with, we become fixated on and fascinated by our five senses. We are fascinated by seeing things; by hearing words, music, and other sounds; by smelling our environment; by tasting our food; and by feeling various physical sensations of touch, temperature, and so on. Those five senses are the first five states of consciousness. They are natural animal instincts, and they seem to be very basic.

The eyes of a vulture see a corpse from a great distance, and automatically the vulture knows that it should fly to the corpse and eat it. The ears of a jackal hear a rustling in the jungle, and automatically the jackal knows that it should pursue that rustling, that there is something to prey on. The nose of a dog sniffs out the presence of food, so automatically the dog knows to look for food. The tongue of a shark tastes through the medium of water, so automatically it knows that there is something in the ocean it should pursue. The bodies of all animals that pursue their prey tell the animals if there is an environmental problem, or if they can go along with their pleasure-seeking process. For example, in Colorado we see a lot of moose coming down to the highway in the springtime in order to experience the luxury of fresh green grass and warm weather. And when we take the saddles off horses and mules, they roll around on the ground, experiencing their environment.

MIND CONSCIOUSNESS. The sixth consciousness is what is known as the mind consciousness, which seems to be connected with human beings alone. It is that which dictates our policy toward sight, sound, smell, taste, and touch. Mind asks: Are these sense perceptions temporarily good? And if they are temporarily good, are they fundamentally good? So the mental faculty, or the sixth state of consciousness, edits the first five. But it does not necessarily do so from the point of view of love and hate. At this point, it is purely a survival principle that we develop.

KLESHA CONSCIOUSNESS. It is the seventh consciousness, the klesha consciousness, that actually does the final editorial job and declares that this is good and that is bad. It says, "We should stick with the pleasurable, and we should stay away from pain." It is a final sorting-out process that relates with all the previous six consciousnesses. It is an editorial situation, and because of that editorial process, kleshas are manifested. But the term *klesha* as it is used in the seventh consciousness is not necessarily a reference to the primary kleshas. Klesha consciousness simply makes reference points. It acts as a spokesperson, as the intelligence that knows how to sort things out.

ALAYA CONSCIOUSNESS. After that sorting-out process, the information is stored in alayavijnana, the last of the eight consciousnesses. The alayavijnana becomes the bank of memory, the bank of habitual patterns. You remember that you used to like this, therefore you should pursue it, and you remember that you used to dislike that, therefore you should not pursue it. In that way, you keep referring back all the time to your alayavijnana.

Your mind begins to develop its own bank account, or we could say that it develops its own library. Probably the word *library* is much more accurate. This library consists of index cards of all kinds. That is what is called alaya consciousness, or alayavijnana. In the alaya library, you collect information on what is good, what is bad, what should be cultivated, and what should not be cultivated. You see ugly sights, which give you problems or interfere with your pleasure, and you see good sights. You experience good smells and bad smells, good tastes and bad tastes, good feelings and bad feelings. All of those are collected in a kind of library. We could say it is almost like a computer system. It is a collection of all the discoveries that you have made because you have sight and all the other senses.

That combination of eight consciousnesses is what supports the workings of kleshas, or nyönmong, altogether.

## Transcending the
## Eight Consciousnesses

Absolute bodhichitta and künshi ngangluk kyi gewa, the basic goodness of alaya, transcend those reference points. They are beyond memory, beyond the alayavijnana. The alaya that is beyond memory is somewhat naive; it does not care for securing or not securing.* It is just cognitive mind, which is very close to the nature of sugatagarbha. Sugatagarbha, which is also beyond memory, allows us to make a connection with our root guru and with the oral instructions of our guru. When we connect with the root guru in this way, when we hear the guru's name or see them, we say, "Wow! Wonderful! How excellent to see such a person, whose state of mind is so different from ours."

That state of mind beyond memory is the connection that allows you to discover the possibility of trikaya. You cannot just say that synchronizing the past, present, and future is a problem. You have to be quite careful and precise. You know that the past occurred because of memory, that the present exists because of uncertainty, and that the future is reflected because of fear or aggression or wanting. So you see past, present, and future, and you see the possibilities in all of them, and you do not panic and you do not make them into an exciting game. You just cut your thoughts and try to relate with absolute bodhichitta.

## Realizing the Trikaya

According to the vajrayana tradition, every journey that we make throughout the entire path is based on the trikaya. It is based on the achievement of the perfect trikaya principle: the basic physical state, or nirmanakaya; the manifestation, or sambhogakaya; and finally, the fundamental nonfixation and nonduality of "I" and "other" altogether, or dharmakaya.

The three kayas are persons we can actually communicate with, or begin to learn how to communicate with; they are persons we can begin to experience. Such communication is not theoretical, like relating with a god principle; it is communicating with things that you actually possess. The teachings are being taught to us by those three kayas, those three

---

* Trungpa Rinpoche is contrasting alayavijnana, or alaya consciousness, with alaya, which is the fundamental ground giving rise to both samsara and nirvana.

buddha-like natures, which we also happen to be in tune with ourselves. So relating with the three kayas is not a matter of somebody telling us how to relate with something alien or outside of ourselves, but it is a natural phenomenon that takes place within us. In the same way that if we are hungry we are attracted to food, if we are thirsty we are attracted to drink, and if we are cold we are attracted to warm clothes, perceiving the three kayas is very natural. Because they arise within our existence, we do not have to strain ourselves in order to relate to the buddhadharma in that way.

The vajrayana is an organic process; it is not alien to us. Vajrayana teachings are connected with our intrinsic outlook, our intrinsic being. They are self-existent, not superstitious hoo-ha. In relation to this, there are concepts like *rangdröl,* which means "self-liberated." Rangdröl means that liberation is self-liberated by itself, rather than by our imposing anything extra on ourselves. It is quite a relief for us to know that this is the case. In the vajrayana, liberation is intrinsic, which raises the possibility of maintaining ourselves at that level.

As we practice the best alaya, the virtuous alaya, the naive alaya, we begin to see that there are possibilities of realizing the trikaya. We see that we can go beyond the neurosis of our eight states of consciousness. First, we begin to hamper the schemes and products of the eighth consciousness, or alayavijnana—we go beyond the alaya consciousness, the storehouse of reference point. Then we realize that the seventh consciousness, the mind that edits, can also be overcome. And because we can overcome the mind that edits, we also begin to touch our sixth consciousness, or sense-consciousness mind, which acts as a spokesperson for the remaining five consciousnesses: sight, hearing, smell, taste, and feeling. We begin to overcome their fixations, their neuroses, and their grasping quality altogether.

When we go back through all eight consciousnesses in that way, it does not mean that we cease to see, hear, smell, taste, or feel. In fact, all those capabilities—our vision, our hearing, our sense of smell, and the rest—become doubled or tripled. They are a hundred times sharper because there is no messenger running back and forth trying to see: "Is this good? Is this bad?" That messenger no longer exists, so our perceptions become very direct, as if our pupils were dilated. We begin to see true color and hear true sounds, properly and fully. Thus we begin to appreciate the vividness of the phenomenal world.

Because we are not involved in defending our territory, we begin to like our phenomenal world; we begin to develop maitri and compassion. We develop a loose heart, an open heart, a naked heart. We also begin to appreciate our root guru much more, because the root guru has shown us this vivid world completely.

Because of that, we are able to see that the dharma is not an alien teaching, but a real teaching. We can actually perceive the dharmic world altogether. Therefore, we are able to see all thought patterns as dharmakaya, free from preconceptions of any kind. We begin to have a clear understanding, a precise and very real one. And obviously, needless to say, there is no kidding involved. That experience of clear understanding is what is known as transmission. In transmission, the mind of the teacher is transmitted to the student properly and without any further obstacles.

## THE MEETING OF MINDS

The idea of the eight states of consciousness may seem somewhat complicated and even theoretical, but once you understand the case history of the eight states of consciousness—how they evolve, how they become fixated, how they begin to be solidified, and how you can undo them step-by-step by going back through them—this idea will become more real. Once you have a basic understanding of the concept of kleshas and of anxiety, which is referred to in the hinayana tradition as the *duhkha* principle, or the truth of suffering—once you realize what duhkha is made out of, why it arises, and how it functions—you will then begin to realize that this state of mind can be altered and worked with. You see that although there may be habitual patterns happening all along, those habitual patterns can be raided and punctured. You begin to be able to see beyond the world of your kleshas. At that point, transmission is possible.

The Tibetan word for transmission is *ngotrö*. Ngo means "face," and *trö* means "introducing" or "synchronizing"; so *ngotrö* means "introducing the face." Transmission is showing you the absolute possibility that when you begin to open yourself through shamatha-vipashyana training and lojong practice, you can actually transcend unnecessary pain and anxiety. You can step forward—or backward, however you would like to look at it—and achieve the precision of the best of alaya. And through that, you can meet the transcendent, awake, and joyful mind of the root guru or vajra master. Then, to your surprise, you realize that your mind and the vajra master's mind are the same.

The first stage of the process of transmission is obviously the awareness of "I" and "other," "I" being the student and "other" being the teacher. You realize that the teacher is going to show you their mind, and you and the guru begin to meet. In the second stage, the next flash, you realize that "I" and "other" are one, that they are not two. That is the definition of transmission. And out of that, you can begin to practice vajrayana disciplines of all kinds.

*Part Five*

# COMPLETE COMMITMENT

## 19

# *Samaya: Making a Commitment*

*In the hinayana, in taking the refuge vow, you are bound to the dharma for your lifetime. . . . In the mahayana, in taking the bodhisattva vow, you are bound together with mahayana teachings, commitments, and the kalyanamitra until the attainment of enlightenment. . . . Vajrayana is entirely different. With the samaya vow, the bondage lasts until ultimate sanity is completely achieved.*

## THE HAUNTING QUALITY OF COMMITMENT

The moment you open your eyes and say to yourself, "I am going to become involved in this discipline of individual salvation. I am going to work with myself; I am going to practice shamatha discipline; I am going to sit," you are already haunted. Beyond that, when you say, "Now I am going to transfer my personal care for myself to others, and I couldn't care less about me. Therefore I am going to do my tonglen practice," you are further haunted, almost ridiculously haunted. Beyond that, when you begin to practice the vajrayana and say, "I am going to let loose. I am going to let go of all my preconceptions of any kind and enter into this particular journey, which nobody knows," you are even more haunted. And that seems to be all right.

Your basic commitment is to yourself. Beyond that, your commitment to others and to your teacher will arise naturally. For instance, if you are serious enough about wanting to have a good education, then your commitment will naturally go beyond that: you will extend the education you receive toward others; and beyond that, your education will actually take effect. You can build an airplane that flies in space, or you can invent a medicine that cures headaches. Your purpose is already fulfilled.

The development of commitment is a natural process; it is a path. Commitment is not based on creating any new magic or any new tricks. Basically, your commitment is intact as long as you are committed to yourself in practicing your daily routine.

## SECRECY

It is quite rare to hear the vajrayana, and it is also difficult to understand the vajrayana because of its secretness. It is not kept hush-hush in the way ordinary people talk about secretness, but it is self-secret. You have to understand the meaning behind the whole thing before you can actually conceive an understanding of vajrayana secretness. At the same time, the secret teachings of the mandala and working with that secretness become sacred; secretness and sacredness are one thing.

The word for "secret" in Latin is close to the English; it is *secretus,* which means "hidden." The ancient Greek root is *cryptos,* from which we get the words *cryptography, cryptic,* and *crypt.* The word *mystery* comes from a Greek root also. In the fifth or sixth century BCE, the hidden spiritual teachings were called mysteries, and the word *mystery* simply meant "something hidden." Nowadays a mystery is something that a detective has to figure out, but in the middle ages, mysteries were secret spiritual teachings that were not public.

In Sanskrit, *guhya* and *gupta* mean "secret," "hidden," or "cryptic." *Cryptic* and *mysterious* seem to imply something very immediate and are connected with speech, and *hidden* is much more connected with body and mind. *Guhya* means "hidden," in the sense that your private parts are hidden. In the vajrayana, secrecy does not mean that something is hidden because it is criminal, but it means something that is inconceivable to others. They would not understand it; therefore, it is hidden until they see it.

## DEMOLISHING THE HIDDEN CORNERS OF SAMSARA

It is important to understand why a person would tread on the path of vajrayana at all. The reason to tread on such a path is not just because you are going to get a good deal. It is not because you hope to receive secret magic and mantras so that you could very cynically play games with people. You might want to use magic and miracles on people you like in order to invite or subjugate them, or on people you dislike in order to terrorize them, but that is not what we are talking about. We are talking about using the possibilities of the vajrayana path in order to liberate all sentient beings from their samsaric trips and their samsaric hidden corners. We are treading on this path in order to bring people out of their tendency to rest in their neuroses.

If you are treading on this path, it is very important for you as a student that you and your vajra master to come to a mutual conclusion. You have to reach a mutual understanding with each other that you actually have to demolish the hidden corners of samsara. You have to demolish the devastating tricks that exist and that you have been able to maintain for such a long time.

Maintaining samsara has become the natural situation for most of the world. So as students and teachers of vajrayana and the other teachings of the Buddha, the Compassionate One, you are the only ones who would actually like to expose the world's samsaric tricks. You want to expose those samsaric tricks and go beyond them in order to help people learn how to expose their own and others' neuroses altogether. That is why the vajrayana is a very powerful mechanism: it does not depend on people's tricks or deceptions. That is why it is necessary to have a vajra master who is your personal link and who never keeps anything secret from you. Once you understand the secret yourself, once your own secret has been revealed, the vajra master never keeps anything secret from you. That is the mutual appreciation and mutual bond that is set up by practicing the vajrayana.

But before you embark on your study of the vajrayana, it is necessary to understand why vajrayana is important. Why don't we just stop at the hinayana or mahayana, where we already have the best of enlightened attitudes happening? It might be good enough for you just to hang on to that, but for some reason you realize that is not quite enough. The reason it is not quite enough is that until you get into the vajrayana, you have not actually understood basic phenomena properly.

When we talk about phenomena, at this point we are talking in terms of actually integrating enlightened mind as essence with enlightenment as reality. As far as the vajrayana is concerned, enlightenment is actual existence, actual reality. It is our actual situation. You might ask, "If that is so, then why do we have to study?" And the answer is that the reason you have to study is that you have not actually faced that particular truth. Therefore, in order to understand that this is the case, you have to use a language that allows you to understand what is happening.

## Indestructibility and the Symbolism of the Vajra

According to tradition, the vajra is the scepter of Indra, the king of the gods or *devas* and the lord of the celestial kingdom. Once Indra found a *rishi*, or saint, meditating. This rishi meditated so much that when he died and his body decayed, his bones turned to diamond because of his powerful meditation. So Indra ordered his craftspeople to carve a weapon from one of the saint's bones, and it came out shaped like a vajra.

The properties of the vajra are such that, if the right person uses it, it always strikes with deadly accuracy; once it strikes, it always destroys; and having destroyed, it returns to your hand like a boomerang. The vajra represents the idea of the indivisibility of power and wisdom. It evokes the sense of a very powerful force that cannot be cracked or seduced or conned. The prongs of the vajra, which are usually fivefold but can be as many as one hundred, open up when you are about to strike, and when the vajra has fulfilled its function, it returns back to the user's hand with its prongs closed. So a vajra is a celestial, diamond weapon; it is one that no other weapon can overcome.

The word *dorje*, which is the Tibetan equivalent of the Sanskrit *vajra*, has a slightly different meaning. *Do* means "rock" or "stone," and *rje* means "noble" or the "highest"; so *dorje* means "noble rock" or "noble stone," which is another word for diamond.

When you combine *vajra* and *yana*, you get *vajrayana*. The vajrayana is diamond-like, for once you enter into this particular vehicle, it is indestructible; it cannot be destroyed by saboteurs who would like to maintain their own personal secrecy.

When *vajra* and *sangha* are put together, you get *vajra sangha*. The vajra sangha is indestructible because it develops a bond with the vajra master. In this bond, what you are binding together are you and your vajra master, along with your practice and discipline. You yourself, your behavior pattern, and your existence are bound together with the vajra master in the form of a very strict vow.

When *vajra* and *master* are combined, you get *vajra master*: the vajra-

*The vajra and ghanta (scepter and bell), ritual implements symbolizing skillful means and wisdom. This set is from Trungpa Rinpoche's personal shrine.*

charya or dorje loppön. In the vajrayana, the teacher is called a vajra master, because they also have that indestructible quality. You can never intimidate, buy, or corrupt such a person by offering them money, or by means of sense pleasures. You cannot bribe the vajra master into buying your ego trip. The vajra master does not like trips of any kind.

The teacher plays an extremely important part in vajrayana. In fact, the vajra master is not just a teacher at this point, but more of a vajra warrior. Their role is similar to that of a master warrior in the samurai tradition: they are going to be tough with you. We could say that the vajrayana level of training students is like training the vajra master's henchmen or henchwomen. And for students, the point is to develop fearless devotion. If your devotion becomes fearful, then there is still something that needs to be cut through.

## THE SAMAYA VOW

Once you have understood the vajra master, or the dorje loppön principle, you can begin to understand the samaya principle. We do not have a good translation for samaya, so we would like to work the word *samaya* into the English language. I am sure it will be in *Webster's Dictionary* in a few years. In Tibetan, samaya is *tamtsik*. *Tam* means "holy" or sometimes "tightness," and *tsik* means "word" or "commitment"; so *tamtsik* means "sacred word." Although *tamtsik* is often translated as "sacred word" or "sacred oath," it boils down to meaning the same thing as samaya: something by which you are bound together.

In Tibetan we use honorific terms instead of ordinary ones when talking about samaya, because samaya is very special and extraordinary; it is sacred. In Tibetan, when we refer to something in honorific terms instead of using ordinary terms, the person we are talking to automatically knows what we are talking about. There is an entire vocabulary of honorific terms. If you are talking about the guru's ear or the king's ear, you use different terms than you would if you were speaking of your own ear. So the honorific form is not just a dead language, and it is not simply an imperial or autocratic form; it is a form particularly applicable to dharma terms, since dharma terms are sacred.

To begin with, samaya involves making a commitment or taking a vow. The samaya principle is a kind of verbal agreement or oath. It is like signing your name on the dotted line. Once you understand the samaya principle, you can learn how to hold your pen in your hand and write your name on a piece of paper. Before that, you could not even sign your name because your hand was too shaky. The foundation of samaya is the practice of shamatha-vipashyana, which quells your discursive thoughts. Without that foundation, you would not have a chance of paying attention to anything. You would be blown here and there by discursive thoughts; you would be completely disturbed or interrupted.

With the samaya vow, the teaching, the teacher, and the students are bound together in one particular project. Nobody can make a commitment of this kind without relating with a vajra master who is a holder of the lineage, and who is the individual's actual vajra teacher. Nobody can get a ticket without going to the booth. Samaya may seem to be purely a command out of nowhere, like the Ten Commandments. However, they are not really the same, for although you could say that the Ten Commandments came from God and Moses, there was no dorje loppön principle, no binding vow, and no personal relationship with a vajra master.

## COMMITMENT IN THE THREE YANAS

In Tibetan the refuge vow, the bodhisattva vow, and the samaya vow are all referred to as *dompa*. They are regarded as things that bind, like a belt that binds your clothes to your body. But samaya is unique to the vajrayana, and the level of commitment in the vajrayana is different from that of the other yanas.

### Hinayana Commitment

In the hinayana, in taking the refuge vow, you are bound to the dharma for your lifetime. You are taking refuge in the Buddha as the example, in the dharma as the path, and in the sangha as companionship. In the hinayana, the idea is to prevent yourself from physically being a nuisance to yourself and others. It is to prevent yourself from indulging in pleasures or frivolousness that might produce further nuisance. You are trying to keep your life simple.

### Mahayana Commitment

In the mahayana, in taking the bodhisattva vow, you are bound together with mahayana teachings, commitments, and the kalyanamitra until the attainment of enlightenment. You are saying that henceforth you abandon your own personal enlightenment, and you commit yourself to sentient beings. The mahayana vow is based on an understanding of the six paramitas: generosity, discipline, patience, exertion, meditation, and prajna (wisdom).* There is a quality of positive heroism in relating with yourself and others. Constant communication provides a working basis;

---

* For more on the six paramitas, see volume 2 of the *Profound Treasury,* part 6, "Bodhisattva Activity."

and as you work with people and with yourself, the feedback you receive becomes a way of expanding and perpetuating your bodhisattva activity.

## Vajrayana Commitment

Vajrayana is entirely different. With the samaya vow, the bondage lasts until ultimate sanity is completely achieved. Your training has already happened, and your ideas and attitude have developed through hinayana and mahayana discipline. But you have not looked at discipline as total experience, rather than purely as discipline; when you see discipline as total experience, discipline becomes complete practice, and your entire experience becomes discipline. The samaya vow is that which binds together your life and your mind.

In samaya, you are signing over your life to the vajra master and to the tantric deities: you are signing over your neck, your brain, and your heart. Also, needless to say, you are signing over or giving up your possessions and relatives. But having given up so much, you get something in return, so you cannot just give up and relax. It is like filing your taxes and getting a refund—but with samaya, what you get in return are responsibilities.

When you first begin to practice the vajrayana, you are just committing yourself loosely to the vajrayana. But when you take part in a vajrayana abhisheka, or empowerment ceremony, you drink what is called the samaya oath water.* At that point, you are actually taking the formal samaya vow. When you take the samaya vow, you surrender your sanity completely to the teacher and the lineage with ultimate devotion and faith.

At that point, if you try to take your vow back due to resentment, confusion, and ignorance, what you get back is vajra neurosis. Because you have violated samaya, you go utterly crazy. If you go against your samaya oath—that is to say, if you go *completely* against it—you are destroyed and made into dust. You go really crazy. The vajra master is always helpful in such difficult situations, but if you do not let the vajra master be helpful, in either the wrathful or peaceful fashion, you have a problem.

---

* An *abhisheka* is an empowerment or formal initiation into the vajrayana path. In the context of such an empowerment, the student takes the samaya vow and makes a formal commitment to the vajra master and to the tantric path. For more on the topic of abhisheka, see part 8, "Empowerment."

## USING POISON AS MEDICINE

The mahayana approach to discipline is based on working less with aggression and more with compassion and generosity, whereas vajrayana discipline is based on working directly with kleshas such as aggression and passion, which are considered to be poisons. In vajrayana, you do not have to con phenomenal experiences and you do not have to destroy them; the phenomenal world is entirely workable and open. It is quite different from the bodhisattva concern that you should be kind to the world, or generous to it, or patient with it. In the vajrayana, the phenomenal world provides its own resources for you, so the whole of phenomena is very much *there* actually. Very much so.

The vajrayana approach is based on enormous conviction and enormous trust. That trust could be provoked by the example of your guru and your yidam, and by your basic being. In the vajrayana we say: "I am going to use this poison as medicine. I am going to transmute it into medicine." That particular oath is very powerful. In fact, it is absurd. To say that poison is medicine is absurd, but poison *is* medicine from the vajrayana point of view. There is no medicine other than poison.

If you do not fight against the medicine-poison duality, then poison is medicine and medicine is poison. They are one flavor. In the case of mahayana, medicine might be poison if you become a bad bodhisattva, if you regress. But in the vajrayana, poison is medicine because there is no poison as such. This idea goes against the survival approach, in which working directly with aggression and passion is considered to be very poisonous. But by seeing poison as a medicine, based on the inspiration of your guru and your yidam, your samaya becomes extraordinarily alive and lively. The inspiration for this comes from dedicating yourself to a guru of a particular lineage, and regarding the guru's inspiration as a resource for creating real miracles.

## NOT TRUSTING NORMAL LOGIC

In the vajrayana, you have a chance to create miracles because you do not particularly trust in normal logic. This seems to be quite different from the logic of the Zen koan tradition. The question, "What is the sound of one-handed clapping?" is still feeble logic. The assumption is that there *should* be the sound of a one-handed clap, so in presenting the impossibility of this, there is still logic involved. But in the vajrayana, there is no logic at all.

Our sense of basic "yes" or "no," which seems to be the essence of samaya, is not concerned with logic. Usually, we keep trying to figure out the right logic: "Supposing I said 'yes,' then would I be cornered by all kinds of challenges if I said 'no'? And supposing I said 'no,' then would I be cornered by saying 'yes'? Could I be pushed into demanding situations?" That is the general ethical dilemma. And the ethical approach would usually be that even if you are cornered, you should still say "yes" or "no" based on whatever you committed yourself to right at the beginning. You should stick to your original idea, to what you are *supposed* to say.

If you believe in the validity of a certain king and his citizens, even if your enemy has cornered you and threatened you with death, you still say, "I do believe in my king"; you say this even if you could be saved by saying, "I do not believe." You are willing to go as far as that. But in the vajrayana, that whole logic does not work. In the vajrayana, if you are cornered and will be killed if you say that you believe in the king, and therefore you say that you *do not* believe in the king, you are still not going to be saved. Your lie begins to bounce back on you in either case.

The vajrayanist does not have to stick to any logic. You could say "yes" or "no" at random, because when you say "yes," that means "no." When you ask a question that seems related with a "yes," it could mean "yes" or "no." It is not quite random, however. There is still some logic involved. The seed of this logic is that if there is any kind of lie, it will bounce back on you. The vajrayana is the most highly supersensitive lie detector that ever existed in any yana. Even the mahayanists do not have such a highly sensitive lie detector. The mahayana works very vaguely with trusting in the karmic consequences, and the hinayana works very basically with the level of suffering and personal neurosis. But the vajrayana acts as a police officer. The consequence comes back to you very sharply. It is like feeling pins and needles in your legs when you sit for a long time.

## BONDAGE AND FREEDOM

Samaya has nothing to do with maintaining a particular territory. That is why understanding the meaning of samaya is so important. Samaya is a territoryless-ness that is able to cut through falsity and lies of all kinds. Because there is no territory, there is no gain or liberation. The guru is the executioner from that point of view, and at the same time the guru is the person who inspires you. The guru is the initiator or the preceptor of the abhisheka, the one who could bring you into the realm of the body, speech, and mind of your inherent buddha nature. The guru could bring your buddha nature to the surface.

The full experience of samaya can only fully occur when a student receives empowerment. Nevertheless, the basic samaya principle comes up when you are about to enter into vajrayana discipline altogether, when you are about to begin your practice. At that point, there is a basic bond already, which consists of your trust in the truth of the teachings, and the teacher's trust in your genuineness. Combining those two aspects of trust—that of the student and that of the teacher—creates the vajra world. There is a sense of commitment, and there is the willingness to accept the vajra world and jump into it. That commitment seems to be very important, even before a student decides to practice ngöndro, or any other preliminary practices.

The samaya principle is bondage; it is an oath that exists between the teacher and the student. Basically, the vajra master and the student of vajrayana are joined together in a love affair instigated by the various tantric deities. In vajrayana, you study and work with different deity principles and you actually become a part of their world, but it is not based on the worship of any god. Tantric deities are part of your innate nature, which is shining through and being experienced. In the vajrayana, you are celebrating that experience properly and fully. It is very moving.

The strength inherent in the samaya bond is based on the fact that nobody is deceiving anybody else. It is reality in the fullest sense. The vajra master and the vajra student have taken their mutual vow, and if either the vajra master or the vajra student violates that, they will suffer in the lower realms: the animal realm, the hell realm, or the hungry ghost realm. So that particular bond, or samaya, is very important and very powerful.

The interesting thing about the samaya bond is that the more freedom you experience, that much more bondage takes place in you. The more you develop openness and a letting go or shedding of your ego, that much more commitment there is to the world of sanity. Therefore, student and teacher are bound together eternally.

Samaya binds you not only from the outside, like a belt you put on, but at the same time it binds you from within. If you let go of that bondage, you will find that you are on the top of a garbage chute and that you will go right down the drain. But if you constantly maintain the bondage and stay bound together, you will go further and further on your journey together. You can actually go along and uplift yourself with delight, confidence, and sanity in the vajra world. And finally, you transcend the vajra world and go beyond even the dharmakaya level and attain absolute sanity. At that point, the bondage is dissolved, and you become one with coemergent wisdom.

## 20

# Positive Entrapment

*At the beginning, you have a devotional inspiration to get into the vajrayana, so you commit yourself into the samaya trap. Your approach is open; you decide to commit yourself. But having committed yourself, the vajra gate closes, and you are included in the vajra world. This could be regarded as imprisonment or as entering into the vajra world. In either case, it is somewhat the same.*

## ENTERING A CROCODILE'S JAW

The initial vajrayana samaya is the starting point. It is where we gain some understanding of how dangerous the vajrayana is. Deciding to get into vajrayana is like entering into a crocodile's jaw. A crocodile will not let you go; all the crocodile's sharp teeth are pointing inward, so you cannot get out. Likewise, once you get into samaya, there is no way out.

The earlier yanas present liberation; vajrayana provides entrapment. That seems to be the basic point of the vajrayana. We could say that vajrayana equals a trap that entraps you into the higher yanas. That trap is provided by your guru and by your yidam, and your own basic being is the subject of the entrapment. So you could regard the vajrayana path as a gigantic entrapment, but it is also possible to regard it as dance or play.

## THREEFOLD NAILING

Samaya has also been described as a kind of vajra nailing in which you, your guru, and your yidam are bound together by your guru in order to make a sandwich that you cannot separate. The diamond or vajra nail that binds together your guru, yourself, and your yidam is like the nail that is put in the sole of your shoe, binding the first, second, and third layers of the sole. Samaya is very direct and simple and powerful. You cannot regress, and you cannot step back. Even the thought of regressing or stepping back suggests violation of the samaya vow.

Tantra is called "vajrayana" because of that diamond quality. However, the vajrayana is not so much a yana at this point, so referring to it as a yana may be misleading. It is no longer regarded as a yana, or as a journey, but as a vajra command. You accept the process by which your teacher, yourself, and the yidam or deity that you are going to work with are bound together by the nail. That is the command. You are bound together and nailed down by the guru. So there is a very blunt approach in the vajrayana; it is very brutal and blunt.

## The Guru

In the vajrayana, we do not talk about the kalyanamitra, or spiritual friend; we simply say guru or lama. The lama is not a heavenly being at the spirit level, but a human being who lives above you. That is to say, the lama has achieved the hinayana, mahayana, and vajrayana disciplines. The lama or guru also has the power to use their nail and hammer to nail you and the guru together into the teachings. You are bound together by the threefold tantric samaya of technique, devotion, and being beyond technique.

The guru's attitude to relating with the student is somewhat suicidal, you might say. They are not afraid of being stuck with you for the rest of their being. If a guru decides to nail themselves to you and the teaching, then that teacher is not a very practical person; but this seems to be the tantric approach, which is very blunt. That threefold nailing is precisely the meaning of empowerment, or abhisheka; you bind yourself to the practice.

In an abhisheka, you are bound together by the body of the guru, the speech of the guru, and the mind of the guru. You are bound together by the vajra nail of indestructibility. If the guru decides to chicken out, they are going against that nail, the same as if the disciple decides to chicken out or if the yidam decides to chicken out. But actually, your guru and your yidam have a pact—they will not chicken out, although quite possibly you yourself, as an insignificant part of the sandwich, might do so.

## The Yidam

The yidam is a deity that you agree to take on as a manifestation of your basic being. It is the psychological manifestation of enlightened mind in a form you can relate with, connected to your particular style and energy. In the word *yidam, yi* means "mind," and *dam* is related to "samaya"; so *yidam* is "mind samaya." The longer word for yidam is *yikyi tamtsik*, the "samaya of your mind." The yidam is a part of your basic being that your mind finds applicable or that you could relate with. It has nothing to do with Yiddish!

Having a yidam gives you a way to relate with or express your samaya. In visualization practice, you visualize the yidam as an expression or manifestation of your basic being. This visualization is referred to as the samayasattva. *Samaya*, again, is "sacred word," and *sattva* is "being"; so *samayasattva* is "samaya being." By means of the samayasattva, you can relate with your guru, yourself, and your basic being as the yidam. So the samayasattva is a way of making a link with the basic discovery of the spiritual path. By the samaya vow of dedication to your own being or nature, your basic neurosis or basic sanity is visualized as the yidam. So the yidam is related with your self; but in this case, when we talk about your self, we are talking about the utterly confused or distorted self.

## The Distorted Self

You may think that you can relate to your self as a tangible being, but it is a distorted being. This distorted self is the middle of a sandwich; it is the overripe chicken or overripe pork that exists between your yidam and your guru. It is a confused being, stinking and paranoid and ignorant. You have the guru on the topside of the sandwich and the yidam on the bottom. So the guru is a part of your basic being; they are another kind of yidam, not purely a teacher who tells you what to do. The guru is not quite involved with you on that level. But the guru is highly involved with you in that your guru's basic being is connected with your basic being, and with your particular mentality or psychological approach. That is why we call the guru a heavy-handed and superior being, rather than purely a spiritual friend.

## THE TANTRIC EXPLOSION

It is important and necessary for you to understand the outrageousness of this. So let me use another analogy. In this analogy, your basic being is like the gunpowder in the middle of a hand grenade; your yidam and your guru are forming a shell around that gunpowder; and the samaya bond represents the fuse. When you pull the ring out of the hand grenade, the grenade explodes, and at that point you become one: you are united with your guru and your yidam at the same time. The guru is no longer a separate entity from you and your yidam. The guru *is* your yidam, and the yidam *is* your guru, from that point of view. They are in league, and they are conspiring against you from the point of view of tantra. So you should regard the tantric approach as explosive. It is producing an explosion in which the basic shell is broken and expanded.

## COMMITTING YOURSELF
## INTO THE SAMAYA TRAP

From the tantric point of view, devotion is extraordinarily important. If you have no attitude of appreciation and no understanding of the vajrayana preceptor as the guru rather than as a kalyanamitra, then you will have no way of actually getting into the discipline of vajrayana. The starting point of vajrayana is to realize that all the different samayas are based on the samaya of devotion.

Samaya could be regarded as a booby trap, a net, or a vajra prison. But actually, it is less like a prison than a mental institution. In a prison, you have no choice about committing yourself, but in a mental institution you do have the choice. So samaya is more like a mental institution in that you commit yourself. At the beginning, you have a devotional inspiration to get into the vajrayana, so you commit yourself into the samaya trap. Your approach is open; you decide to commit yourself. But having committed yourself, the vajra gate closes, and you are included in the vajra world. This could be regarded as imprisonment or as entering into the vajra world. In either case, it is somewhat the same.

Once you have entered the vajrayana, you have no choice. There is no opportunity to manipulate your deceptions. On the bodhisattva path, you have the possibility of manipulating your experience, and exposing and demonstrating your characteristics. There is still showmanship at the bodhisattva level. You have a good chance of becoming a star, and if you become a *mahasattva,* or "great being," there is a good chance of becoming a superstar. But in the vajrayana, there is less chance of becoming a superstar and more chance of becoming an inmate of a vajra dome. Like a geodesic dome, the vajrayana is a round world. It is no longer square, because square worlds give you too many chances to hide behind something.

## The Role of the Yidam

The guru's power goes beyond your desire to create a league with the teacher as a personal friend who could save you from whatever mistakes you make, as someone who could transmute your mistakes by saying that they are misunderstandings rather than mistakes, and then communicating that message to headquarters or to the yidam. Samaya is very important, but it does not mean committing yourself to the guru so that the guru will save you if you go wrong. In fact, there is a possibility that your guru will not be able to save you if you go wrong. That is why there is the need for the yidam. The yidam comes in if you have gone so far away that the guru's love, dedication, and kindness cannot save you. So the yidam seems to be another expression of imprisonment.

A person who enters into the vajrayana must be highly inspired so that they are not afraid of entering this realm of vajra imprisonment. By means of samaya, you are bound to this particular realm and you realize that you have no way out. At first, the guru can point the way for you and show you how to handle your yidam. But at the level when you have identified with your yidam completely and thoroughly, the guru can no longer control the situation. It is as if the guru has sold you a pet lion, and then that pet lion grows up and eats you. The person who sold you the lion has no control over what happens; it purely depends on your way of handling that particular pet. If the lion eats you up, the guru says that it is too bad, but this is all they can do.

21

# The Different Types of Samaya

*Without the relationship with the vajra master, there is no vajra-yana at all. That is quite definite. The vajra master is the buddha, the dharmapalas, the dakinis, and everything else at the same time. So it always comes to the same point: in order to have electricity, you have to have both a negative and a positive pole. In this case, you could say that you are the positive electrical element; you are putting energy in. But there is also the negative element, somebody who subtly plays with the energy you put in—that is the vajra master.*

WHEN YOU take part in an abhisheka, or empowerment ceremony, and you take the samaya vow, you are empowered to be a tantric practitioner and the holder of a certain lineage. You are entered into a particular sadhana practice. The holiness and fullness of the lineage, the sacred word, and the magical aspect are all transformed into you personally, step-by-step. So abhishekas are an aspect of the sacredness and wholesomeness of samaya.

In addition to the samaya vow taken during abhisheka, there are other types of samaya commitments that one can assume, such as the samaya of making offerings, the samaya of reciting mantras, and the samaya of visualization. The samaya of mantra is connected with the principle of wholesomeness as it applies to utterance or words, and to the mantric quality of experience altogether. There is the samaya of realizing the world as being beyond the petty world, and the samaya based on the wholesomeness of your relationship with the yidam as a symbolic or psychological entity that has inspired your fullness. Another samaya is based on the sacredness of vajrayana formless meditation practice. This samaya is similar to the mahayana meditation experience of shunyata, but it is more playful and more realistic than the experience of shunyata. A sense of openness, playfulness, vividness, and inquisitiveness in vajrayana formless meditation practice brings the shunyata experience into the mahamudra level. Another samaya is the samaya of experiencing everything as completely sacred in vajra nature.

## THREE ASPECTS OF SAMAYA

Samaya has three aspects: seed samaya, upaya samaya, and fruition samaya.

### Seed Samaya

The first aspect of the samaya bond is known as the seed samaya. The essence of this samaya is that all dharmas—that is to say, whatever is perceived or heard—are regarded as self-existing wisdom. When the seed-samaya principle comes into your system, you realize that you already have self-existing wisdom, which is very basic and prominent. So you are not trying to get better, particularly, but you are trying to realize your own nature.

### Upaya Samaya

The second aspect of samaya is known as upaya samaya, the samaya of skillful means. In the context of samaya, the idea of skillful means is that all the different techniques that have been developed for overcoming the conceptual mind in its rough and refined aspects are now transcended in the greater skillful means of visualization practice, or *utpattikrama*.

### Fruition Samaya

The third aspect of samaya is called fruition samaya. In fruition samaya, whatever occurs, whatever has occurred, and whatever is about to occur in your phenomenal world—everything that there is—is regarded as a part of the body and wisdom of the buddhas. Here "body" refers to the tangible reactions that take place in relation to whatever is cluttering the mind, particularly your emotional response to the world. It is the actual visible personal and emotional level. Wisdom goes beyond the emotional level; it is more comprehensive. You see basic phenomena and general frames of reference as expressions of wisdom. Body refers to both speech and physical manifestations, and wisdom refers to more ethereal phenomena and insights—but in fact, they are both saying the same thing.

### Samaya and the Vajra Master

All three aspects of samaya depend on the vajra master. The seed cannot take place without the vajra master, skillful means cannot take place without the vajra master, and fruition cannot take place without the vajra master. The vajra master is the lover, the master, and the conqueror of your particular wretchedness. In any aspect of samaya, the vajra master is very important, absolutely important, for conquering you and bringing you into the situation. This seems to be one of the recurring themes in the vajrayana.

Without the relationship with the vajra master, there is no vajrayana at all. That is quite definite. The vajra master is the buddha, the dharmapalas, the dakinis, and everything else at the same time. So it always comes to the same point: in order to have electricity, you have to have both a negative and a positive pole. In this case, you could say that you are the positive electrical element; you are putting energy in. But there is also the negative element, somebody who subtly plays with the energy you put in—that is the vajra master. By combining those two, you come up with vajra tape recorders, televisions, and telephones.

### THE SAMAYA OF THE BUDDHAS

In order to understand the samaya principle, you have to understand the two principles playing together in your life: "samaya-ee" and "samay-a." The samaya-ee is the practitioner, and samay-a has to do with the rules imposed on the practitioner.

We could look at this in terms of the symbol EVAM.* In EVAM, the

---

* The symbol EVAM is one of the seals of the Trungpa tülkus. The Sanskrit EVAM, or "thus," is used at the beginning of all sutras, which begin: "Thus have I heard." In EVAM, the stillness of E and the activity of VAM are in an inseparable balance.

EVAM, *one of the seals of the Trungpa Tülkus.*

samaya-ee corresponds to E, and samay-a to VAM. Together they make EVAM. Here, E is basic space, while VAM is the basic energizer. We could say that E is connected with the feminine principle, the giver of birth, and VAM is the son that comes out of the feminine principle.* In the EVAM symbol, the two aspects of E and VAM, samaya-ee and samay-a, are brought together by skillfulness. Trained students, because of their experience, their understanding, and their intellect, are able to bring the two aspects together; this is known as the samaya of the buddhas.

---

* The *feminine principle* has many layers of meaning. It does not simply refer to the female gender, but to the quality of boundless space and emptiness from which all phenomena arise. See Chögyam Trungpa, *Glimpses of Space: The Feminine Principle and* EVAM (Halifax, Nova Scotia: Vajradhatu Publications, 1999).

## THE SAMAYA OF THREEFOLD VAJRA NATURE

Samaya is the only way to make the tantrika's whole world sane. It is connected with the deities you are practicing and with the vajra master's body, speech, and mind. The samaya of vajra nature comes in three categories: samaya of vajra body, samaya of vajra speech, and samaya of vajra mind. As far as vajra body is concerned, the phenomenal world is viewed as a self-existing vajra world; in regard to vajra speech, all utterances are regarded as self-existing vajra speech; and in regard to vajra mind, all thought processes are regarded as vajra mind completely and utterly.

### Samaya of Vajra Body

The samaya of vajra body, or the samaya of mudra, is based on the idea that any apparent phenomenon you experience is connected with the sacredness of the total environment: you do not have any doubt as to whether your world is sacred or not. The Tibetan word for this is *chaggya kü tamtsik*. *Chaggya* means "symbolism," "mark," or "mudra," *kü* is the honorific term for "of the body," and *tamtsik*, again, is "samaya"; so *chaggya kü tamtsik* is the "samaya of body." With this samaya, your total world or existence develops into sacred outlook. All forms, whether visual, auditory, olfactory, tastable, or touchable, evolve into the sacred outlook of form. The notion is that whatever you perceive can be transformed into sacredness.

Body refers to forms or images. So when we talk about body, we also mean the room or space in which experience takes place, like the room you are in, or the room where your meditation cushion is placed. The samaya of vajra body means that you do not hang on to any solid substance, but you continuously and devotedly involve yourself with vajra form. This means respecting and beautifying your body and, at the same time, regarding phenomenal activities and experiences as part of the mandala setup. Because of that, you could not write such a poem as: "Ugly New York truck drivers fucking themselves and producing pollution." That would be disrespecting New York City, which is sacred.

Body samaya means that you begin to see everything as a sort of adornment. You actually can work with what is known as shunyata form. In the tantric tradition, shunyata form means something more than in mahayana. Shunyata form in Tibetan is *tongsuk,* which means "empty form," or form that is intrinsically empty and nonexistent. According to this samaya principle, you are actually supposed to relate to form in that way. You do not lay heavy interpretations or heaviness of any kind on things: you simply see form. You perceive table-ness, chair-ness, food-ness, car-ness, ceiling-ness, and floor-ness—the "ness" quality of all these things—as manifestations of transparency. At the hinayana level, you see the transparency of küntak, or random labeling; at the mahayana level, you see the transparency of aggression; and at the vajrayana level you see the transparency of *that* and *this,* of fixation of any kind, of hanging on to anything.

It boils down to this: even when you drink a glass of water, you usually lay a tremendous trip on it. You think, "I need this glass of water. I'm drinking it now because I am so thirsty." There are so many, many conditions involved with it. Likewise, you think, "I'm hungry; I'm going to eat," or "I feel chilly; I'm going to fetch a sweater," or "I feel lonely; I'm going to find a companion." Everything you do has an exaggerated aftereffect. If you are cold, it is okay to go and get your sweater, but you are making the sweater-ness more meaningful than just going to your room, getting your sweater, and putting it on. There is that aftereffect.

Each time you conduct an activity in your world, in your life, you bring along your hang-ups—and not only your hang-ups, but your hangovers. Each time you do something, it is as if you have had a heavy drink and now you have to suffer for it. Having put your sweater on, you still suffer from the hangover of the sweater; having had a glass of water, you still feel hung over from it. Maybe that is why tantrikas are supposed to drink and find out about hangovers, for in everything you do, you are inviting hangovers all the time. Whatever you do, you feel bad. You may even feel too warm and comfortable. But in any case, your mind is completely bursting into something else: you are drifting all over the place in a completely unreasonable way.

Initially, you may simply have a need for some comfort, like a glass of water or a nice sweater. At that point, you are very reasonable, because you feel constricted by your demand. But when you have put on your sweater or had your glass of water, you go crazy. You no longer seem to have any binding factor of sanity at all, absolutely not. Instead, you think of the past, future, and present. You might emulate your past or complain about the present or do something else with the future. Your mind goes all over the place. The point of the vajrayana teachings is to keep you away from those little indulgences.

With the body samaya, you can actually keep yourself very tight and tidy. If you need a sweater or a glass of water, you can go ahead and get what you want. You have the body samaya already, so you can maintain yourself. You can remain very tight and dignified and, if necessary, you can prevent yourself from farting or burping. You just hold tight.

We are not particularly talking about the Victorian style, but about tantric Victorian style, which is necessary. Often we have been slaves of ourselves, as everybody knows very well. You should do something about that. You should never become a slave of yourself; that is the worst slavery of all. The United States of America has achieved freedom from external slavery. That is fantastic! Great! But what about the internal slavery inspired by democracy? By promoting the democratic ideals of individual freedom and individual salvation, and by trying to help others sociologically and politically from the point of view of ego-centeredness, we have actually achieved imprisonment. If a political group would like to put in its two cents' worth to promote the cause of freedom from self and how we can free ourselves from ourselves, that should rouse the biggest cry, the biggest proclamations, and the biggest demonstrations, with posters and everything!

## Samaya of Vajra Speech

The second samaya is the samaya of vajra speech. It is the samaya of the *ghanta,* or tantric bell. The Tibetan for this samaya is *trilbu sunggi tamtsik. Trilbu* means "ghanta," *sung* is the honorific word for speech, *gi* means "of," and *tamtsik* is "samaya"; so *trilbu sunggi tamtsik* is "the samaya of speech or sound."

The samaya of vajra speech is related with passion and with communication. It does not just mean talking, but it includes emotional communication. Passion is said to bind together form and emotion, so communication could take place by means of body, by means of sight, by means of smell, by means of sound, and so forth. At this point, we could regard all the emotions, including the kleshas, as forms of fundamental, subtle communication, which, for that matter, could also be very crude.

The meaning of this samaya is that speech is invincible, which means that when you communicate, you actually communicate. Every word you say—"hello" or "goodbye" or whatever might occur to you in whatever state of mind—is always mantra. So your communication or speech becomes extremely powerful, and at the same time it becomes bondage or samaya. Speech is about the intellect and about communication. If you respect the sacredness of vajra speech, you could not write such a poem as: "Illiterate mumbo-jumbos hanging themselves as spiders on webs." That would be mocking the world, mocking the universe.

The samaya of speech occurs on the level between mind and body. It is connected with the idea that any utterances and thoughts are sacred. Subconscious gossip or ongoing discursiveness is transformed into sacredness, so there is no chatter. In the past, you may have been told to drop subconscious gossip when it appeared in your shamatha practice, but here, subconscious gossip is transformed into energy. The fickleness of subconscious gossip is used as enlightened energy. This only happens when you drop the neurosis associated with subconscious gossip. When you do not negate your subconscious gossip, but just drop its neurotic aspect, its energy is still maintained in your basic being. So although neurosis creates subconscious gossip, the inquisitiveness that exists in subconscious gossip could be described as having the possibility of prajna.

The samaya of speech means that you relate with speech as sacred. Whatever you say or talk about, whatever you utter, including your sneezes and burps, is sacred because it indicates that you are actually relating with the world, communicating with the world. If you are by yourself in a retreat, or alone in your own bedroom, you might only burp or fart, but that is communication. It has its own sacredness, glory, and goodness. You are an individual person, and in the case of vajra speech, you are an individual person communicating a relationship to the world. You are actually doing something to the world; you are communicating to it.

The reason you are able to communicate in that way is that, if you first take the basic attitude of pre-thought—*aah!*— you find that every expression you make in relationship to the world makes sense. If you start with pre-thought, each sound you make, each word you say is unconditional. From the mahayana point of view, this is shunyata expression.

When you say, "Hello, how are you?" it usually does not particularly mean anything. But saying "Hello, how are you?" does not have to be a small-talk approach. With the samaya of speech, you begin to experience that something more is being said than "Hello, how are you?" You realize that something more than that is being said all the time. We always undermine our speech. When we say, "Hello, how are you?" we think that is just a tiny little thing that we just burped. But somehow, as you project that to the world or to your partner, it means a big "Hello! How are you?!" It actually magnifies to double, triple, a hundred times the size.

There is always that kind of projection going on. This does not mean that you should project all kinds of neurosis. Sometimes you may do that, but you are breaking your samaya vow by making such a proclamation of neurosis. If you shout "I feel shitty! Who are you?!" you begin to pollute the world of speech. But when you respect the sacredness of speech, speech is regarded as invincible. Once you have said something, you have said it. That kind of speech comes from a mind that is in a state of impartiality.

### Samaya of Vajra Mind

The samaya of mind is the basic space in which the other two samayas can take place. States of mind such as delusion or wakefulness are in this category of samaya. The samaya of vajra mind is known in Tibetan as *dorje thukkyi tamtsik*. *Dorje* is "vajra" or "indestructible," *thuk* is the honorific term for "mind," or in this case, "enlightened mind," *kyi*, again, is "of," and *tamtsik* is "samaya"; so *dorje thukkyi tamtsik* is the "samaya of vajra mind." It means that the vajra mind samaya is invincible and unchanging. That is to say, within the state of mind of the first impulse—*aah!*—from that reference point, when we look at objects we begin to feel the objectivity or solidity of things. This includes our body, our world, and our relationships to the whole society. Whatever we feel and whatever situations we encounter become very solid.

By mind, we mean wakefulness; we mean that day and night you realize the awakening and falling asleep of your thought process. In terms of vajra mind, you could not write such a poem as: "This is my mind so crazy, I'm completely upside down." Such a poem would disrespect the phenomenal world, which is already sacred, powerful, and beautiful.

Situations are usually and ordinarily very solid. Our body is very solid and our world is very solid, and we maintain that notion of solidity. But on top of that, with this samaya, we begin to develop further solidity, or vajra solidity. That is, when we look out, we feel that we are totally *here.* It is like waking up and feeling yourself breathing the air, inhaling and exhaling, and experiencing your solid world properly. You think about eating breakfast in the morning, or lunch at midday, or dinner in the evening. You think about taking a walk or taking a shower. You think about relating with your personal thingies and phenomena such as making a telephone call. In whatever you do, you have that sense of thingness. You sense that in all your activities, you are dealing with solid things. When you are walking into a building, changing your sheets, taking a shower, or eating food—in whatever you do there is a thingness involved.

In the vajrayana, relating with this kind of thingness is based on the understanding that thingness is very genuinely solid. This is not because we would like to gain security from that solidness, particularly, but we simply feel that the objects around us are workable. This solidity is the same kind of perception through which we experience the Great Eastern Sun. It is direct perception, with no bureaucracy involved, very clear and precise. Things feel good and solid. You do not feel at all claustrophobic, and you do not perceive things as confirmation. You are simply seeing things as they are.

This is particularly so when your mind is crystallized in first thought, or actually in what is previous to first thought: in "prime thought." When you have prime thought as you look at objects, things are much more solid, real, and good. They are absolutely good and beautiful at the same time. We could almost deify such a world as being a heaven filled with all the deities that one could imagine. That is the samaya of oneness with the mind, in which there is joy and solidity.

Usually when we experience solidity, we feel either depressed or excited, but in this case we are even-tempered. Whatever we see, any solid world we experience is fine, no problem. We are dealing with a solid world, but that vajra world has a kind of light-handedness in it. The usual heaviness of depression is not involved; therefore, the vajra mind is unchangeable or invincible.

With this samaya, you are using your senses to work with all sorts of forms, such as visual, perceptual, or olfactory forms. It is your world, the solid world: when you bang on something, you hear it and feel it at the same time. You feel thingness or solidity, which is okay and good. It feels as if you are driving in a luxury tank that has guns and catapults on its outside and is made of solid metal, but on the inside the tank is very comfortable, with a leather interior. You do not feel particularly aggressive, you are just driving this luxury tank—and you feel transparent. That is how a student of vajrayana should feel: you should feel good and solid. So the samaya of vajra mind is connected with the idea of indestructibility. It never allows any possibilities of neurosis to enter into your state of mind, because the whole world is sacred and blessed already with the bondage of abhisheka, the mutual bondage of student and teacher.

Samaya of vajra mind frees us from from any conceptions that would cause us to regress. Without it, we could regress into a lizard, an ant, a snake, or a worm. For that matter, we could regress into an amoeba, just one cell reproducing by itself with no mate, which is supposedly the lowest form of existence that is still regarded as a sentient being.

To avoid regressing, you could develop more patience. As a result of patience, you will learn to have exertion in the dharma; as a result of exertion, there will be peace of mind. In the beginning you need to have a sense of wonder and devotion. But if you have no exertion, there will be no wonder, and your mouth will not be able to smile. The vajrayana dharma is like that: there is a sense of humor.

If you work with situations in the style of enlightenment, in accord with the samaya principle, you not only cease to regress, but you also experience further development. You are finally cutting through. It is the same kind of experience as when the physician cuts your umbilical cord after you are born. You begin to experience the mixing of your mind with the vajra master's mind. And having mixed your minds together, you begin to experience an intense, extraordinary orgasm.

Joining together the three samaya principles—samaya of body, samaya of speech, and samaya of mind—brings about your understanding of the cosmos and of the universe altogether. You have the sense that you are not going to follow your neurosis, but you are going to see through it. At the same time, you keep the essence of neurosis, which at this point is no longer neurotic. As is said in the *Supplication to the Takpo Kagyü*, "The essence of thoughts is dharmakaya." That is the basic idea here.

### Samaya of the Vajra Master

In addition to the samayas of body, speech, and mind, there is a fourth samaya, called the samaya of the vajra master. We have already talked about the vajra master as your only life strength or life potency. If you need energy for your life or to survive, you need the vajra-master samaya to work with that. When you reject the samaya of the vajra master, then you deflate into a sort of dead-rat level or the level of a feeble bat.

The vajra-master-samaya principle is itself divided into samayas of body, speech, and mind, which are connected with the samayas we just discussed. Here, "body samaya" means that your body and the vajra master's body are combined to form a team, so that you could actually win liberation or enlightenment together. Your speech and mind principles are also combined with the vajra master's. So you are not actually doing the whole vajrayana path single-handedly, but you are doing it along with your vajra master.

The vajra master is your best partner. Your vajra master is your financier in terms of energy consumption, so you never run out of energy. If vajrayana students run out of energy, it is usually because they have no relationship with the vajra master or the vajra dharma. It is quite simple: if you reject your vajra master's reinforcement, you automatically feel deflated.

All these samayas have a connection with patience in that they are regarded as practices rather than simply as occurrences. When you see the three samayas as your practice on the path, they become a journey rather than just experiences. As with the mahayana *lamkhyer* slogans, you bring the environment, your subconscious chatter, and your state of mind onto the path.* You use all that as the basis for relating with the energy of vajrayana.

But in the case of vajrayana, it is not just that everything is workable. It goes beyond workability—it is so! Therefore, you do not even have to say, "If I step on this ice, there will be water down below, and I might sink into this ocean or this lake." You do not even have to test it out. It is so! Just go ahead and do it! The question does not exist, but even that is needless to say. The question is long gone!

---

* *Lam* means "path," and *khyer* means "carrying"; so *lamkhyer* means "carrying whatever you encounter onto the path." For more on lamkhyer as it is used in the mahayana, see volume 2 of the *Profound Treasury*, chapter 38, "Point Three: Transformation of Bad Circumstances into the Path of Enlightenment."

# Maintaining the Samaya Vow

*You are an idiot if you do not feel terrified in the vajrayana. Likewise, if you feel okay about jumping into midair in a parachute, then you do not know what is going on. . . . But there is a need for idiocy! Once you jump, your fearfulness creates—aah!—first thought. This is a very important point; you catch yourself before the first moment. You catch yourself at that zero situation where you have some kind of wakefulness.*

## THE DISCIPLINE OF SAMAYA

The samaya principle has many functions; it refers both to the samaya vow at the beginning of the abhisheka, as well as to the commitments the student makes as part of receiving the empowerment. Samaya is based on the understanding of sacredness as its inspiration and working basis. It is based on the experience of wholesomeness and the one-hundred-percentness of the whole situation.

The samaya principle provides intelligence or guidance in the vajrayana teachings, and it is one of the important disciplines in the vajrayana. Therefore, samaya is also referred to as *samayashila*, which combines the word *samaya* with *shila*, or "discipline." Samayashila refers to your individual discipline with regard to the tradition or the practice. It is realizing and carrying out the mutual bond that you and your vajra master committed yourselves to together. The discipline of samaya involves being directed toward basic sanity.

The bond of samayashila is threefold: first, you are bound to work on yourself; second, you are bound not to create suffering for yourself or your fellow sentient beings; and third, you are bound to overcome your passion, aggression, and ignorance, and all the rest of your neuroses and kleshas. It is very important, absolutely necessary, to keep the samaya vow. Such things as not properly transmuting or working with negativities and emotions, developing laziness, or exhibiting cowardice can all cause the violation of samaya.

However, samayashila is not based on rules or behavior alone, but on your attitude. It is based on openness and on surrendering or submitting, which binds you to the practice and to the instructor of the practice. Samaya is based on a feeling of awe toward the teaching and the teacher combined, which creates magical power. A lot of things are hidden in the vajrayana, and that hidden quality is not revealed until a quality of basic sanity evolves in a tantric way, which comes from openness and the willingness to be completely groundless.

## Two Levels of Discipline

In the vajrayana, we talk about two levels of discipline: workability, and the union of great joy and wisdom.

### Workability

The first level of discipline is workability. It is taking the attitude that the dualistic fixations and habitual patterns that exist in your mind can be accommodated or worked with. They can be refrained from or they can be transmuted, depending on the level of your ability.

### The Union of Great Joy and Wisdom

The second level of discipline is realizing that in order to work with these things, the intrinsic nature of your existence can no longer be regarded as a "nature," but as reality. This reality is the unity or indivisibility of jnana and mahasukha, wisdom and great joy.

Jnana, or yeshe, is an all-knowing, all-comprehensive experience of reality that does not need any feedback or reassurance. It is self-existing openness and precision.

*Great joy* is a term that can be found in the language of a number of spiritual traditions, particularly theistic traditions. The Hindu tradition also uses the term *great joy,* and we find similar language in Christianity and Judaism for the experience of the pleasant, beautiful, and seductive side of the face of Jehovah. But in the vajrayana, when we talk about great joy, we are not talking about any blessing descending on us. Instead, the idea is that we have to invoke mahasukha ourselves, personally.

You might ask, "How do I do that?" or "Can I do it?" And the answer is: "You can do it." You might then say, "If you tell me the technique, then I can do it." However, that is not how it works. Great bliss can only be evoked on the basis of realizing that kündzop is no longer a hang-up, and töndam is no longer a promise. When you realize that neither kündzop nor töndam is a big deal, there is bound to be a sort of cosmic orgasm taking place, an experience in which power and realization take place automatically. That kind of cosmic orgasm can take place in situations such as the time between life and death, when a mother is giving birth to a child, in the state of panic, and in the experience of sexual orgasm. So a cosmic orgasm can take place in sexual union, as well as the petty orgasm that usually takes place.

This approach to tantra may seem dirty, but we have to use these kinds of analogies. I hope any highly genteel people who may be reading this will not be embarrassed. I would like to ask your permission to speak in this manner so we can preach tantra. Of course, vajrayanists themselves would not regard these things as dirty. As for the theists, there may be issues of morality to be considered, and they may prefer a more genteel approach. However, using sexual analogies does not mean that our approach is cheap or perverted now, or that it might have been perverted in the past, or might be in the future. We are just using natural, simple language.

The idea of cosmic orgasm is that everything is one and many at the same time. The logic is: if you experience oneness, you also experience multiplicity at the same time, because of the oneness. This is very simple logic, actually. If you want to be alone in your little cabin, in one little room, the reason is that you are aware of the multiplicity of all the societies around you. That is why you appreciate oneness. At another point, you may feel very lonely and need company. If you call to your spouse, "Come down! We have company!" that is an expression of loneliness at the same time. So again, you are feeling both the oneness and multiplicity. But in neither case is there quite the realization of the unity of the one and the many. However, in cosmic orgasm, there is the experience of the one and the many being indivisible. In mahasukha, because of the experience of the one and the many put together, there is immense openness, an immense feeling of multiplicity, and an immense sense of inauguration.

Mahasukha takes place on a relationship level. It is not particularly connected with the hinayanists, who are leading their frugal lives and trying to work with the truth of suffering in their homespun style, one stitch at a time. Nor is mahasukha connected with the mahayanists, who are trying to develop joy out of nothingness, or shunyata, and who are debating with one another on a dialectical level. Those approaches are not applicable here. But since we have already gone through these trainings, which have provided us with enormous background, we now have an immense, open style. We have the skill of understanding natural phenomena in their own right, in their own exuberance, in their own expansiveness and extravagance. That is joy, or mahasukha.

To review, the first level of discipline in vajrayana is regarding dualistic fixations as the basis of practice. What follows from this is that we work with dualistic fixations in the unity of mahasukha and jnana. In discussing vajrayana discipline, we are not talking about dreamworlds. We are not dreaming about what we will do when we become enlightened, or thinking that when we are enlightened we will become great people and do great things. Instead, we are talking about our own actual personal and ordinary situations. That seems to be the basis of the vajrayana.

## Maintaining Your Discipline

Sometimes in practice, you may experience fear. Fear might simply be arising in your stream of being, but you might then project onto it the idea of having broken samaya, without having really done so. However, if you begin to separate one little aspect of practice from another, it is going to be very difficult to sort them out. You would need a great logician like Nagarjuna to come along and tell you which part of your practice is on the right track, and which part is on the wrong track. So it is better to regard your practice as one whole, one situation.

At this point, since you do not have Nagarjuna, you should simply let go with the transmission that has been given to you by your teacher. You should dissolve these concerns and maintain your discipline. In other words, do not be concerned with too many details, or with whether or not you have violated your samaya. Simply let go of that situation, and maintain your samaya discipline. Your single-minded discipline is very important. It is sometimes known as the fourth moment—beyond the three moments of past, present, and future. Maintain that. By doing so, it is possible to keep up your discipline and training when the inevitable stormy waves of strong sickness and turmoil overwhelm you.

A basic samaya principle is not to completely lose sight of what you are doing, and not to be overwhelmed by the kleshas. You should not be subjugated by physical ailments or problems on the physical level, but you should stay above those and maintain a sense of sanity. You can develop cheerfulness and joy, in spite of your sickness. You need joy, because dealing with sickness is difficult. But even if you are sick, you do not have to feel that you are completely trapped. There are gaps, moments in which you can cheer yourself up and celebrate the existence of life.

When you have a lot of physical ailments, and there is a moment of lightening up or humor, it is an opportunity to come back to your discipline precisely. I think you are strong enough to do that. You can actually cure physical ailments by simply returning to your discipline. When you are really rolling in the waves, you can just come back. Absolutely! I am not talking from a secondhand point of view, but from firsthand experience. I have done it myself, and it is possible. It is important to continually come back and never give up. In the vajrayana, we are not cheating the world, but we are promoting some kind of goodness.

## Protecting the Vajra Dharma

I would like to apologize for using so many traditional terms. These terms come out of the texts and scriptures and philosophical writings of my Buddhist heritage, and they are loaded with meaning. However, in this discussion, they are not particularly meant to be philosophical terminology, but experiential terms referring to experiences that actually exist. In presenting the vajrayana, I also do not want to create the impression that everything is over your head, so that there is nothing you can actually do. That would be like telling fairy tales, which seems to be the wrong approach. If I did such a thing, I would be personally punished by the dharma protectors, such as our friend Ekajati, who would be very angry with me.

As far as the role of the teacher is concerned, it is considered criminal to teach vajrayana by presenting it as ordinary. It is also said that trying to convert individuals directly into vajrayana without preparation would be criminal. According to the *Hevajra Tantra* and many other tantras, students should first be taught hinayana and mahayana, and only then should they be shown the path of mantra, or vajrayana. If teachers ignore that tradition and lead students into the vajrayana immediately, it is quite possible that chaos will result, and a lot of neurosis will take place.

The *Guhyasamaja Tantra* says that to begin with, a person should receive the complete hinayana disciplines; then they should receive the complete mahayana disciplines; and finally, they should be received into the vajrayana. People in the past have recommended quite strongly that hinayana is the preparation, mahayana is the further direction, and vajrayana is the final crescendo. Without that kind of prior development, vajrayana can be destructive to both the vajra master and the student. So before entering the vajrayana, there needs to be immense respect for the hinayana practice of shamatha-vipashyana, and for the bodhisattva's paramita practice and their glimpse of shunyata experience. Having had that training, the worthy person can then enter into the vajrayana properly.

Entering the vajrayana is like boarding a vajra airplane. You will be welcomed and received by the vajra master, as well as by vajra hostesses and hosts of all kinds: "Welcome aboard the vajrayana. Captain So-and-So is directing this diamond airplane. If there is anything we can do, please call on us." Once you get onto this particular flight, it is quite an odyssey, but it does not seem to be all that easy to do. It is necessary to realize the crimes that can be committed, both by an incompetent vajra master (who hardly could be called a vajra master, but should be called a salesperson, which basically means a charlatan) and by a frivolous student who would like to collect powers and techniques and wisdoms of all kinds (which they are not going to get out of a real teacher). So both teacher and student should be very firm in understanding that unless the student has some experience of the hinayana and the mahayana, they are not going to be accepted into the vajrayana.

The teacher at this point is regarded as an immovable person, someone who cannot be shaken by little jokes, little tricks, little scenes, little insults, or little criticisms. That person has a very solid basis in vajra dignity. They also embody the lineage of the past completely, every one of the individuals in the lineage. There may be a thousand people in the lineage, but all their wisdom is transmitted and communicated properly by that one particular person: the vajra master.

Presenting tantra is a very sacred matter and very dangerous. If we were off by a quarter of an inch, somebody would tell us that we were doing something wrong. So we are relying a lot on messages from the phenomenal world, and at the same time we are relying on our own intelligence. This discussion of vajrayana is being closely guarded by visible forces and invisible forces. But it is not as if a ghost is hovering around dressed in a white sheet with holes for the eyes. Actually, there is something much more powerful than a ghost guarding this situation. Nonetheless, we can still discuss everything nonchalantly, as if nothing is happening.

## GROUNDLESSNESS

The willingness to be groundless could be called the seed of being outrageous in a tantric way. In other words, you are willing to let the threat to security break through. Unless there is that kind of bravery, you are not apt to hear the vajrayana teachings. The more that people without bravery hear the teachings, the more confused or completely terrified they get. They cannot take it.

Usually, the ground is something that you can push against in order to escape. If somebody is trying to catch you with a lasso, you can save yourself from being caught by standing steady on the earth and pulling back on the rope. But with groundlessness, you have nothing to stand on and no way to free yourself. From the tantric point of view, you are caught already and you cannot pull back, so groundlessness has a quality of no escape. Ground, from this point of view, is negative. It is a way to chicken out.

Groundlessness is as if your experience is taking place in outer space. It is like a city in the air. It is like being in a jumbo jet, which is a world of its own. It is like being in a plane that has nowhere to land, but still continues to fly. If you want to go back to your home, you cannot do it; and if you jump out of the plane, it is suicide. It seems to be too late even by the time you buy the ticket.

The important point about samaya is not how much you have achieved, but how much you are willing to "be achieved," how much you are willing to be a victim of something or other. Before taking samaya, a student of tantra has not developed completely and fully, but at the point of samaya that student is consciously willing to become a victim. You are willing to submit. That is the basic samaya principle.

Samaya involves both sacredness and respect. It is much more than just taking a vow: it is the attitude of letting oneself be exposed in this way. You do not hold a grudge against anything; and even if you have a grudge, it is not regarded as a problem. You are a willing student, rather than someone who is being pushed. It is your own choice, so you end up, basically speaking, with no choice, and therefore there is no grudge. You cannot kill the past. Samaya is very direct. You still might have resentment, confusion, and so forth while you are on the path, but those things are not regarded as terribly bad. They are workable—highly workable, in fact. They are the juice of the meal, and it is delicious!

Resentment is very different from fundamentally violating the samaya vow. Resentment is a temporary experience, although it could develop into a permanent experience, which *would* be violating samaya. When you are resentful, normally you do not just decide to leave the whole practice environment; you just feel resentful that you are there. However, the thought of stepping out onto the fire exit and making a run to the nearest airport is beyond resentment. It is beginning to get very heavy. You are getting into the area of going against the sacredness or wholesomeness. That is connected with self-destruction. You are actually executing some scheme, which is a suicidal process.

Samaya is not the style of a compassionate bodhisattva. The experience of nonreference point in the mahayana is very sane and domesticated, and coached by compassion constantly. And in the vajrayana, the experience of nonreference point is also coached by compassion, but here compassion is turned into ambidextrous skillful means. It is turned into resourcefulness, rather than just being kind and nice, gentle and polite. That seems to be the difference. It takes more guts; you are willing to be fearless, although you may feel extremely cowardly.

We could use the analogy of the mouse who tried to become an elephant. In this analogy, the mouse held its breath, thinking it could expand into an elephant. But the mouse waited too long, and it burst into pieces. Such is the case if you are without a vajra guru or the teacher principle. The guru shows you when to hold your breath in order to imitate an elephant, and when to be a cunning mouse. Nevertheless, you have to be brave, fundamentally and basically brave.

Samaya is an attitude that brings trust. It is based on awe and feeling awe-inspired. The attitude of samaya is one of wakefulness. It is not wakefulness on the level of hysteria or insomnia, but in the sense of fearlessness. You do not need any compliments or confirmation, and at the same time, you are willing to relate with the messages and directions that come to you.

## THE TANTRIC UMBILICAL CORD

Samaya makes connections. When you enter into vajrayana discipline, it is as if you have been given another birth. In a sense, you are newly born, but this birth is slightly different from ordinary birth. When you are born into the vajrayana realm, nobody cuts your umbilical cord. For that matter, your umbilical cord never dries. You are born as a separate individual, but you have a link with your guru, and you have a link with your yidam. So becoming a vajrayanist is like growing up with an umbilical cord that is still fresh.

You are obviously still alone on the vajrayana path. Aloneness or loneliness is always there, but there is still an umbilical cord in the vajrayana, so there is still communication taking place. This means that although you are alone, you cannot get away; you have to remain in the vajrayana environment. The umbilical cord is the connection you have with the teachings and the teacher and yourself at the same time. But this connection is necessarily within the realm of loneliness. You could still be lonely even with an umbilical cord attached to you.

## VAJRA PARACHUTING

Samaya is like deciding to jump out of a plane with a parachute. You may feel both pain and pleasure at the same time. On one hand, you experience pain, because there is a lot of terror involved. You realize that if you decide to let go of your cord, you will go down and make a mess on the ground, to say the least. On the other hand, there is also pleasure. An accomplished or confident parachutist would appreciate the experience of floating through the air. Such a parachutist would enjoy the sport of parachuting, and appreciate the landscape as they float down.

### The Power of Fear

You are an idiot if you do not feel terrified in the vajrayana. Likewise, if you feel okay about jumping into midair with a parachute, then you do not know what is going on. Anybody without wings—which is all human beings—who jumps out into midair in a parachute without fear is a bit of an idiot. But there is a need for idiocy! Once you jump, your fearfulness creates—*aah!*—first thought. This is a very important point; you catch yourself before the first moment. You catch yourself at that zero situation where you have some kind of wakefulness.

In this process of vajra parachuting, you are bound by your conviction and by the discipline, which is the open parachute. You are inspired by the wind of the vajra master's acceptance of you. If there is the slightest doubt that the vajra master is accepting you into the vajra world, the wind will never inflate the canopy of the parachute. Even though you are committed, and you are willing to get into the vajrayana teaching, you could still puncture holes in your parachute. In turn, your parachute could be torn apart by the wind of the vajra master and become shredded; and since there would then be no canopy to hold you up, you would go down—*plop!*

### Turning Your Back on Your Commitment

Your total commitment to the vajrayana teachings is what provides you with a parachute. Without that parachute, you would have nothing to hang on to. You are completely dependent on the chute, the cord, and yourself, which are all very vulnerable. That seems to be basically what you should understand about the principle of tamtsik, or samaya.

With that understanding, the details of how to be in the vajra world, to be inspired by the vajra master, and to be accepted as a member of the vajra sangha seem to be very simple and delightful. The only problem is when there is no faith in the vajra master, who represents the lineage, the sanity, and the teachings of twenty-six hundred years of Buddhism. When that trust and faith begins to break down, you develop doubts about the structure of the yanas altogether. You become like a student sitting with their back to the shrine.

When you become a student of tantra, you are acknowledging the Buddha's ultimate and fullest enlightenment, which resulted in the vajrayana. As a tantrika, you cannot have allegiance to hinayana if there is no allegiance to vajrayana. If you think that you can get some wisdom out of Buddhism without acknowledging the whole path, or by completely giving up on the possibilities of the vajrayana teachings, you will find yourself like that student, sitting with your back to the shrine.

If you cannot stand the dangerous path of tantra, you may prefer to think that Buddha was simply a hinayana chap who made everything okay; you may prefer to stay on a safer path. You may find that you actually agree enormously with the hinayana. You find the hinayana understandable and the mahayana very sensible, but when you come to the vajrayana, you say to yourself, "Oh, boy! How could I get away from this? How could I find something else to do? Maybe I could become the best hinayanist or the best mahayanist. Then I would not have to go through this whole ordeal." That is, again, like the student sitting with their back to the shrine. Once you have entered the vajrayana, it is too late for that kind of approach, and it does not help. You have to face your mind; that is the basic point.

## Landing in the Vajra World

The samaya principle binds together you and your vajra master, who is your lover and who loves you, and the teachings, which strike so much at your heart. For a long time, you have felt so lonely. You have been lonely, without a love affair, lonely with yourself, and at last you have a chance not to be lonely. You have a chance to get into the vajrayana teachings and be included in some kind of bigger world. So it is time for you to pull up your socks or your trousers—or as we say in Tibet, "It is time to hitch up your *chuba.*"

With the samaya principle, we are bound together in the vajra parachute. If you ask where we are trying to land, the answer is that we are trying to land in the vajra world. To come to the vajra world, you cannot use any other form of transportation, none whatsoever. The only way you can land in the metropolis of the vajra world is by parachuting, and each parachutist has to navigate their own canopy and cord and self. In turn, we can begin to create an enlightened society. In this enlightened society, all the citizens enter by that same process; and because they never crawl in, but instead use their parachute, they become good citizens.

## 23

# *Enlightenment and Its Opposite*

*Enlightenment and vajra hell are like the two ends of a vajra: when you hold a vajra, prongs go up and prongs go down.*

## BREAKING SAMAYA

Once you have taken samaya, you are not allowed to leave the vajra castle. There are big pits and holes around it. If you try to escape, you find that there is no bridge, and if you try to swim across the moat, you drown because there are crocodiles who pull you down into the water. If you break your own commitment, it is devastating, suicidal. If you decide to abandon the vajrayana, you will be roasted alive, unable even to die on the spot. You will find yourself in what is called vajra hell, or *vajra naraka,* where you attain a perverted version of enlightenment in which there is the ever-present experience of pain. That pain is without a gap. It is nondual pain, coemergent pain. You are in so much pain that you cannot even experience pain, and you cannot get out of it.

Vajra hell does not refer to literally being boiled in water or roasted in fire. Rather, it is that one's mind is so completely consumed by kleshas that there is no possibility of escape. In English, this is known as claustrophobia. So vajra hell is the individual's mind being trapped in pain. Once you are trapped in pain, neither the guru nor anyone else can extract you from that monolithic situation. No one can save you.

## THE SNAKE IN THE TUBE

It has been said in the scriptures that a person entering the vajrayana path is like a snake entering a bamboo pipe. Once the snake has entered the tube, it will either face up or down; it all depends on how the snake enters the tube. So entering into samaya is a question of motivation, to begin with. If you want to snuggle into your old habits, you go down; if you want to play a more adventurous game, you go up. It is a question of giving up territory or not giving up territory. If you want to give up your ego, or if some ventilation is possible in your ego situation, you go up; if not, you go down. It is not a negotiable situation; it is a dictatorial situation.

## VAJRA HELL

If your approach to the vajrayana is wrong, you are going to be like that upside-down snake and end up in vajra naraka. In vajra naraka, you will have no saviors; neither the generous bodhisattvas nor the good hina-yanists can save you. The big secret about vajra hell is that there is no end to it: once you enter vajra hell, there is no way out, no escape from the karmic consequences. Vajra hell is an experience that constantly per-petuates itself. In that way, it is almost comparable to the experience of enlightenment, which also perpetuates itself. Enlightenment becomes greater vision in the realm of the three kayas, and in vajra hell an equiva-lent three kayas perpetuate themselves.

There is no way out of vajra hell. You are stuck because your vision, which is actually your neurosis, seems to be constantly growing stron-ger. Therefore, you perpetuate being in that particular realm. You have a notion of sanity, but you have no notion of neurosis, and that perpetuates the pain enormously. The pain you experience in vajra naraka is said to be the opposite, but equivalent, of what a person who attains buddhahood would experience. People attaining buddhahood experience spontaneity and openness—and to an equal degree, people in vajra hell experience claustrophobia and imprisonment.

Vajra hell is a devastating poison that you cannot use as medicine. It is total poison. Vajra hell is the other end of the stick from enlighten-ment. It is the opposite experience in almost a mystical way, a fantastic super-samsara. The experience of pain is so complete that you do not even have the relative reference point that you are the one experiencing your pain. You are stuck there completely. There is not even a buddha teaching there. Vajra hell is so impenetrable that it even walls off the buddhas. The vajra quality usually refers to cutting off ego, but in this case it is the opposite: the ego cuts off enlightenment. It walls off everything completely. Even the teaching that all the constituents of being are transitory would not apply to vajra hell. That is why it is called vajra hell, and why it is extraordinary.

The pain that ordinary samsaric people experience has gaps of buddha mind, or the meditative state. But in the case of vajra naraka, it is all black. There is no hope of even a glimpse of enlightenment. It is as if you are covered all over with tar, and you have no breathing space. You might wonder how something can stay black, if there is no reference to white. But that is the whole point; that is why you remain. In vajra hell, there is no reference to anything else, which is why the whole thing is so painful.

Vajra hell is a consequence that we enter into when we die. It is something that we end up in for millennia or for millions of years, without even a reference point of how long we are there.

That is the very definite understanding of vajra hell. It is what I understood myself, and I do not want to alter it to make it presentable to Americans. Vajra hell is too touchy a subject to make it presentable. I just have to lay it out flat: a person might be a candidate for vajra hell. As long as the idea of enlightenment is eternal, the opposite is also true. Vajra hell is not just samsara; it transcends samsara. In the realm of vajra hell, as in the realm of enlightenment, the truth of samsara and nirvana being the same still applies. Enlightenment and vajra hell are like the two ends of a vajra: when you hold a vajra, prongs go up and prongs go down.

In terms of discipline, vajra hell and enlightenment are completely different. Enlightenment is the result of the discipline that you have developed and applied. Because of that discipline, you have a sense of achievement, creativity, and openness, and you have sentient beings to work with. But vajra hell comes about because you have no dedication to anything. It gives ego the opposite result: there is a feeling of being completely down, completely and thoroughly in blackness, with no breathing space. It is total imprisonment.

We could say that in the state of enlightenment, there is total pleasure and total freedom. There is pleasure without any reference point, there is total spaciousness and openness. You could display all kinds of sam-bhogakaya manifestations. But in the case of vajra hell, there is a feeling of complete imprisonment and utter suffocation. And because there is no reference point, it is not that you still see black as opposed to white, but you are in blackness.

All dharmas are like mirrors, and on those mirrors anything can be reflected: vajra hell can be reflected, and vajrayana buddha fields can be reflected. You begin the path on the ground of your individual merit, and what happens after that depends on your exertion. When your merit and exertion are joined together, complete liberation is possible. Such libera-tion is not dependent on hope and fear, so it is possible for the guru and you to share ground.

## Reasons for Going to Vajra Hell

The reason you get into vajra hell is because you ignore the warnings that you receive from the phenomenal world. You begin to be enormously self-righteous and very selfish. You feel that you are correct, so any warn-ings are regarded as unnecessary and insignificant. You think it is just your thinking process and your fear that prevents you from doing something. So you override those strong messages and warnings, thinking, "Oh, that's nothing. I'm still going to do it." With that approach, you are actu-ally disrespecting the phenomenal world.

That is precisely what ego means: disrespecting the messages of the phenomenal world. You are centralized in yourself, just doing what you want to do, what you feel like doing, and you do not pay attention to anything around you. That is the definition of aggression, passion, and ignorance all lumped together.

But you have to be a powerful person to end up in vajra hell, some kind of VIP. You are a candidate for vajra hell if the powerful statement you make with your life is distorted. You may have a fair amount of infor-mation and experience and ideas, but all of them are based on ego. When that happens, there is a possibility that if you have an incompetent guru, that guru will not be powerful or awake enough to give you a warning. It is also possible that you will leave your teacher and develop your own cult. You may begin to interpret things your own way, based on what you would like to hear from yourself. In that case, you may end up in vajra hell and find your guru down there with you, saying "Fancy meeting you here!"

Slipping up or making mistakes is not regarded as problematic, because you still have good intentions. It is the general sense of losing heart and disregarding any possibility of truth in the vajrayana that seems to make one a candidate for this particular region. If you violate samaya deliberately, then you go downhill altogether. However, if you do something that violates samaya out of ignorance, there is room for that, because if you are just ignorant, that can be corrected.

As long as there is any trace of ego remaining, there is always going to be some doubt. There are different levels in your development: there is the complete destruction of ego, there is being unable to be seduced by ego, and there is ego fixation. If there is just plain old ego, it's fine; in that case, there are simply problems of hot and cold. But if there is any tendency to become a revolutionary trooper and go against the vajra force, this is the path that leads to vajra hell.

Vajra hell arises from perverting the teachings, and going against them with deliberate consciousness. So you get into vajra hell not because you are ignorant or cowardly, but because you are brave in the sense of being willing to completely disobey your samaya vows. If you are not practicing enough sitting meditation when you do vajrayana practices, or you are simply experiencing resistance, that seems to be a purely mahayana sin, rather than a vajrayana sin.

Whether you are a candidate for vajra hell or not depends on whether you develop a philosophy or logic for why you do not sit. For example, you may think that it is okay that you do not sit because what you are doing is in accordance with the dharma. You may think that your reason for not sitting is logical, that it is based on quotations from the scriptures, that there are ideas and philosophy behind it. But in creating a big deal out of your resistance to sitting, you are digging your own grave. The simple experience of resistance has become a philosophical ego trip. Once you develop principles to justify your behavior, it becomes a problem in the long run. That kind of philosophical justification is an application to vajra hell. I am sure that in vajra naraka there are more poets and philosophers than farmers. Even bankers don't make it to vajra hell! But I cannot give you the whole answer as to how vajra hell works. I am not particularly the janitor of vajra hell.

## An Example of Someone Who
## Ended Up in Vajra Hell

One example of a person who is supposed to have gone to vajra naraka is a teacher who lived in the eighteenth century, in the reign of the fifteenth Karmapa. This teacher produced literature on tantric abhishekas and initiated a lot of students. But he was making a kind of Satan worship out of vajrayana doctrine, and he turned his students into vicious, aggressive people, which began to cause a lot of pain and suffering in the vicinity where he lived.

This teacher was celebrating his victory one day, and for this celebration he had set up a tent, and he invited his friends over for a feast. But during the feast an earthquake occurred, and simultaneously, supposedly, there was the utterance "Vajra naraka!" echoing in the sky. Everybody in attendance fell through a crack into the earth. So the teacher's students went with him.

Some pilgrims who came to visit my monastery had seen the place where this happened. They had seen the big crack in the earth where the earthquake occurred and the people went downstairs. For a few years, no crops would grow in that area. The whole place became very dry, famine stricken, and desolate. People began to call it Death Valley.

## The Story of Rudra

The classic example of someone who went to vajra hell is Matram Rudra, a student who killed his own vajrayana teacher. When Rudra's teacher told him that his path was wrong, but his brother's path was right, Rudra killed his teacher and ended up in vajra hell—and he is still there. If you want to meet him, I am sure he will wait for you there!

The story of Rudra is that he and a fellow student, a dharma brother, were studying with the same master. The teacher said that the essence of his teachings was spontaneous wisdom, and that even if a person were to indulge himself in extreme actions, they would become like clouds in the sky and be freed by fundamental spontaneity.

The two disciples understood these teachings on spontaneity entirely differently. The first disciple went away and began to work on his own characteristics, positive and negative. He became able to free them spontaneously without forcing anything, neither encouraging nor suppressing them. The second disciple went away and built a brothel. He organized a big gang of his friends to make raids on the nearby villages, killing the men and carrying off the women.

After some time, the two disciples met again, and both were shocked by the other's kind of spontaneity. Each of them was sure that he was right, so they decided to go to the teacher and ask for his opinion. When the teacher told the second disciple that the first disciple was right and that he was wrong, the second disciple became so angry that he drew his sword and killed his teacher on the spot. Because he did not like what his teacher had to say, he decided to eliminate him. That disciple was eventually reborn as the demon Matram Rudra.

There is a powerful link between rudra-hood and the relationship with the teacher. According to the vajrayana, the worst thing you can do is to kill your teacher, to kill the dharma. If you destroyed all life in the universe, that would still be a much lighter sin than destroying the dharma or the teacher. From that perspective, you could say that in comparison, even dictators like Hitler are very mild cases of rudra.

## RUDRA AND THE PRINCIPLE OF ABSOLUTE EGOHOOD

Rudra, or the principle of absolute egohood, is the opposite of enlightenment. The vajrayana teachings warn that it is actually possible to attain this state of total egohood. Such absolute egomania requires an incredible amount of precision and intelligence, yet there is no ability to communicate. In other words, you are completely walled in. Basically, rudra-hood is the same as vajra hell. With rudra, you actually go through experiences and training in the same way that ordinary people headed in the direction of enlightenment go through their training, but instead of going in the direction of enlightenment, you get sucked into vajra hell and experience constant struggle, pain, and punishment. Because of the intense punishment, pain, and resentment that exists in vajra hell, you turn into a rudra, a cosmic monster who can destroy individuals' lives.

The teaching and the practice of rudra is to try to make everything a part of your own personal trip. It is a power trip without any wisdom, the epitome of egohood.

## 24

# Perfecting the Samaya Vow

*The samaya principle is not exactly positive, but it is an utterly delightful process. It is utterly delightful because you begin to realize the depth of reality by experiencing it fully and crudely, and you begin to realize the surface of reality by experiencing it as vast, empty, and fantastic.*

### DESTROYING OUR OWN
### THEISTIC PRECONCEPTIONS

When we talk about vajrayana, we should be very careful: we should understand the difference between theism and nontheism. In the vajrayana you visualize various deities, which could be misunderstood as the re-creation of a kind of god principle. Therefore, it is very important for you to realize the meaning of nontheism at the beginning. In order to relate to the yidams and the protectors and the various liturgies, you have to understand that they are not the product of defending our territory or proclaiming our religion.

Once a basic samaya bond is established between student and teacher, and we are joined together with the vajra master, we have a scheme for destroying any possibility of theism. That seems to be the basic bondage. The idea of destroying theism may seem quite outrageous, but our style of destroying theism is not like the Islamic style of chopping off the heads of statues of gods, or destroying churches. What we are destroying is our own preconceptions of the savior notion in our own mind.

According to the nontheistic approach, we are not going to be saved by the other. However, we are going to be helped by the other, or the guru principle. The guru's blessing and the blessings of the lineage can enter into our system. We are not going to create a fourth world war to propagate nontheism; the path of nontheism is based on how we can actually conquer ourselves. We have our daddy, our mommy, our guru, and our friends and family. How can we relate to them properly? We have to be free from leaning on any source of help, but at the same time we can be inspired by the power and the blessings that are always available to us, which is an interesting dichotomy.

You may think that you understand very generally how theism works, but you have to try to understand it more precisely. Theism is ingrown in us. Because of our previous encounters with theism, it sits somewhere very deep within us. It even shows up in the kind of vision that leads to the creation of shopping centers, or supermarkets like King Soopers in Colorado. Anything of that kind is a vision of theism, as opposed to having a dairy farm or a vegetable garden or a bazaar. In that sense, theism is something manufactured.

Everything in our world has been stamped by theism. In our society and culture, we do not go to the butcher, but we buy packaged meat at the supermarket—that is a manifestation of theism. We do not want to do things manually or to handle things directly in our messy world. Theism is the laundromat and fast-food approach. Overcoming that theistic approach is why we do oryoki at practice programs in our community. Oryoki makes everything very simple: we do our eating, our cleaning, and our dish washing properly.

Samaya, the basic bondage of student and teacher, destroys any possibility of theism. Theism is based on comradeship, the idea that you and I will try to fix this world together. But according to the samaya principle, you alone are supposed to fix this world, without anybody else. You cannot call your plumber to fix your plumbing; you have to do it yourself. That is the practicality of samaya.

Samaya as command, samaya as bondage, and samaya as a rule that you cannot violate means that you have to do it yourself. You cannot use any other reference point, any other quotations, or any other ideas, but you have to be genuine and true to yourself. It is comparable to life and death. When you were first born, nobody helped you; you did it yourself. Your mother pushed you out of her cervix and you were born. Later you will die. Nobody makes you die; your breath just stops, and you die on the spot. Everything is raw and rugged, as precise as putting a knife in a sheath.

Samaya is very personal, very individual. It is like being sick. When you are sick and you look around, you see that nobody else is sick, only you. And if you need surgery, you have to go through the operation yourself. Nobody can do it for you; it wouldn't help. You alone are put in the ambulance and driven to the hospital, nobody else. You alone are examined by your doctor and told that you have appendicitis. Everything is personal, always. You cannot borrow or substitute anything for anything, but you have to do everything manually. Our lineage has done that, and you have to learn to do that as well. It is very direct. So the samaya bondage is essentially to oneself. The bondage is to personal experience, which is very lonely. It is based on not blaming, not lying, not trying to fiddle with things—and not trying to get reinforcement.

Once you are committed to samaya, if you violate that commitment, it could send you into complete neurosis or psychosis, so that you have no relationship with your body, mind, and logic at all. You could become completely psychotic, beyond Mussolini and Hitler, because they still had some understanding about reality, even if it was based on psychotic logic. The samaya principle is a powerful bond. Taking the samaya vow is signing one's name on the dotted line. In doing so, you are saying that you will either go toward absolute complete freak-out, or you will return to fundamental sanity completely.

## UPROOTING THE SAMSARIC WORLD

Taking the samaya vow is the way to completely uproot the samsaric world. It is how you can understand and uproot the conflicting emotions, or kleshas. So if you want to be uprooted completely, it is necessary for you to understand the samaya principle. The samaya principle is very important, and the consequences of violating such a principle are quite severe. It is possible that you might find yourself stuck with one or two of the kleshas, or maybe all of them, and be unable to bail yourself out. You might be boiled in that pot of kleshas eternally, which does not make a good soup for you or for your friends.

Not all emotions are conflicting emotions, or kleshas. Emotions like delight, sympathy, and tenderness have more to do with basic goodness than with any kind of obscuration. By overcoming the kleshas, we do not mean that everybody should become like jellyfish, without any good or bad emotions whatsoever. We are not talking about that. We are talking about what actually causes samsara to be perpetuated altogether.

Some thoughts and emotions are much more keenly directed toward basic goodness. These are acceptable, and they actually become crutches, helpers, or guidelines. The kind of emotions that are not causations of samsara are called *lhaksam,* which is another term for vipashyana. *Lhak* means "superior," and *sam* means "thought" or "thinking"; so *lhaksam* is "superior thinking." Lhaksam refers to the good kind of kleshas. The closest word I can think of for this is *kosher.* These kleshas are kosher and good.

However, emotions are tricky. Emotions are also quite prone to being grasped, and they could flip into the lower realm of emotions. But as long as you are able to stay on a very tight rope, as long as you can remain unattached, but still care for others, then it should be all right. With the kleshas, if a nondwelling quality is there, that nondwelling is their transformation into wisdom. By nondwelling, you are overcoming the kleshas altogether.

If we regard the kleshas as fuel, then absolute bodhichitta is what ignites them. Because whenever a feeling of sympathy or an immediate kindling of kindness occurs, you feel tremendously raw all the time. In the vajrayana, we speak about mantra as protecting the mind—but the heart is left alone, by itself. Mind needs to be protected, because mind is capable of jumping to conclusions of all kinds, but the heart is always pure. Cultivating that tender heart invites quite a lot of pain, but that is all right; it is a part of the process. We have to bear that kind of pain. It is like a young child growing up: a child experiences all sorts of pain, including diaper rash, and that is all right.

Buddhist teachings say that attaining a precious human birth is the only way we can attain enlightenment. And yet in the human realm, there is a whole range and richness of human emotions that everybody experiences, whether they practice or not, and these experiences seem to have value. So there seems to be value to human life, even if people are not able to hear the dharma. Even if people are capable of being wicked, they still have possibilities of basic goodness in them. Anybody who can respond to pain or pleasure is worthwhile, and they are able to hear the dharma, if there is someone to teach it to them. Nonetheless, people do need to hear the dharma, for then they can actually develop a very profound and deep kindness, and a compassionate attitude toward others. Otherwise, this depth of compassion would be impossible.

## PROFUNDITY AND VASTNESS

The samaya principle is not exactly positive, but it is an utterly delightful process. It is utterly delightful because you begin to realize the depth of reality by experiencing it fully and crudely, and you begin to realize the surface of reality by experiencing it as vast, empty, and fantastic. This is a similar process to the mahayana idea of joining profundity and vastness. So at this point, having already been introduced to basic vajrayana principles, you can begin to look at the profundity and vastness of the vajrayana teaching.

### Profundity or Depth

If you take even a short, small glance at the vajrayana, you discover its depth and profundity. Depth, in this case, means that the vajrayana teaching allows us to utterly destroy our ideal scheme of self-preservation, which is known as ego.

FIXATION AND GRASPING. According to the Buddhist tradition, self-preservation is described by two terms: *fixation* and *grasping*. In Tibetan, first we have *sungwa,* which means "fixation," and then we have *dzinpa,* which means "holding" or "grasping." We fixate on ourselves because we are afraid to lose "I" or "me."

Fixation and grasping follow the same logic as seeing and looking, which we have talked about before.* First you find some kind of ground to fixate on; then, having found ground to fixate on, you begin to grasp it and make it into a permanent situation. It is like the negative perspective of marriage, in which first you fall in love, and then you possess your

---

* In his book *True Perception,* Trungpa Rinpoche discusses the process of perception in terms of seeing and looking. In the chapter "State of Mind," he talks about perception starting with seeing, followed by looking. In the chapter "Joining Heaven and Earth," he says that from the nontheistic point of view, the order is reversed so that first we look, and then we see. See Chögyam Trungpa, *True Perception: The Path of Dharma Art* (Boston: Shambhala Publications, 2008).

mate so that there is no room for anything else. Similarly, in terms of ego, first you fixate, and then you grasp or hold on. At that point, everything becomes glued together. Having sungwa first and dzinpa second reflects how ego actually arises: first we fixate with our mind, then we try to grasp our world.

GRASPING AND FIXATION. When the order is switched so that grasping comes first and fixation comes second, this reflects a path orientation. We start with dzinpa or grasping because it is the part of twofold ego, the ego of self, that we cut through first. Sungwa, the second half of twofold ego, or the ego of dharmas, is talked about second because it is more basic and more difficult to cut through. It is not yet cut through on the hinayana path.

The meaning of dzinpa and sungwa, from the path point of view, is that first you experience yourself grasping, or holding on to something, and then you actually try to possess it. Holding on is a pathetic gesture. In spite of the care and help you have received from your parents or your local rabbi, priest, guru, *sadhu,* or whatever you have, you feel so lonely and so lost that you immediately want to grasp something. In theistic terms, you want to be saved. That desire to be saved is apparently why Billy Graham had such successful campaigns. In fact, when Billy Graham was presenting Christianity in England and he asked, "Who wants to be saved?" my mother-in-law walked up and said that she wanted to be saved. So grasping is about the desire to be saved, about wanting to have a hold on freedom or on reality. And the second part of the process is fixation, which is slightly different.

Reality is crude to its very core, just pure mere lust that cuts to the core of reality. For a long time, depending on how old we are or how much heritage we have received from our particular culture, we have assumed that we have actually been perceiving the reality of the phenomenal world—but we haven't quite. The depth remains untouched, as something more than what we have experienced. We have never touched reality properly in terms of profundity, at all.

## Vastness

We have not yet experienced real vastness completely either, because we have been so stupid. We have only been thinking in terms of what the vajrayana teaching is in reference to our sunny-side-up ego and the philosophy around it. Don't you think that is slightly perverted and so limited? We have not actually related even with the light of fireflies, let alone with the brilliance of something like the Great Eastern Sun.

## Going Deeper

Both vastness and profundity are mind's creation; they are your mind's creation. Profundity means getting deeper, so that you can cut the thickness of stupidity. Vastness means that you can expand, so that you can go beyond the territoriality of possessiveness. From the point of view of vastness and profundity, samaya means greater thinking, or greater vision. It means greater punishment and greater reward. Perhaps it is not so much reward, but rather the absence of punishment as reward. And finally, you gain magical power.

We are talking of the depth of the depth of profundity: nobody has gone to that depth completely. We are talking of the vastness of the vast of the vast: nobody has expanded that much. If you go too deeply into the vajrayana, ordinarily you will be hurt, and you might say, "Ouch!" And if you become too vast, you will be so stretched that you might again say, "Ouch! I don't want to be stretched that far." In fact, Matram Rudra's body was so stretched out that it became the basis of the charnel ground and the basis of all the mandalas that we build.* The heart of Matram Rudra was so pierced that he shouted, "Ouch!" And out of Matram Rudra's utterance sprang the shout of Vajrakilaya, the penetrating dagger.†

The samaya principle allows you to go deeper, deeper, and deeper. It is like surgery. The samaya instrument is the practice, and the user of that instrument is the vajra master, who is like a surgeon in that they are very well-meaning, but seemingly mean. Exploring the depth and vastness is part of the surgical operation. It is necessary for your mind to be stretched and penetrated. Why is that necessary? It is because we are so thick and so

---

* For a discussion of the mandala principle and the charnel ground, see chapter 25 of this volume, "The Sphere of Self-Born Wisdom."

† A *kilaya* is a three-bladed dagger used symbolically to cut through passion, aggression, and ignorance. The deity *Vajrakilaya* ("Indestructible Dagger") wields such a dagger in order to destroy deceptions and obstacles to the path of awakening.

clumsy. We are so thick that the depth has to be experienced, and we are so clumsy that the vastness has to be experienced at the same time.

Pre-vajrayana students still have little rudras, or touches of ego. They still have all their little tricks happening. So they need to have an operation by the great surgeon, the vajra master. The vajra master's role is to stretch you out and exasperate you in every possible way. The idea is to penetrate and puncture your skin at the same time as stretching your whole existence, so that the phenomenal world no longer means anything to you except being awake all over the place. That is recognizing vajra nature; it is seeing the rising sun of the East.

The samaya process is pushing and pulling you at once. In terms of vastness, if you are about to be stretched and you chicken out by trying to run out of the operating room into the street, you will look so funny, half-stretched and trying to run away. You will die or be run over by cars. Quite possibly you will be arrested by the police force, because you look so funny and stretched-out and indecent. So you cannot chicken out of the vastness.

And as far as the depth goes, if you are about to be profoundly penetrated and you chicken out and run away, you will end up in the mental hospital. There you will be treated by psychologists, who are like cosmic vultures. Because they need their salaries, they need to keep you in the hospital. So it seems much better to stick with the vajrayana, in spite of all the trials and tribulations.

In the vajrayana, you are protected from psychological cults, from ultimate and temporary world-pain, and from all sorts of drugs and mental breakdowns. You are finally included in this very beautiful world of sanity that nobody seems to have heard of. But actually, somebody *has* heard of it and experienced it: it is the great twenty-six-hundred-year-old tradition of vajrayana, which actually goes back to even before that time. This world is so beautiful, so warm, so indestructible, and so unshakable. In this world, you are actually protected and served. You are invited to enjoy yourself in the diamond castle of the vajra world.

*Part Six*

# THE MANDALA PRINCIPLE

# 25

# The Sphere of Self-Born Wisdom

*The experience of self-born wisdom, or the awakened state of mind, is the transmission you receive from the teacher when you receive abhisheka. That is when your superficial ordinary mind ceases to exist, and therefore, your further ordinary mind becomes powerful.*

## CENTER AND FRINGE

Having presented an overview of samaya, we can discuss the mandala principle. *Mandala* means a "society" or "group"; it means a "complete world." The Tibetan word for mandala is *kyilkhor. Kyil* means "middle" or "center," and *khor* means "fringe," "surroundings," and also "circling" or "revolving around"; so *kyilkhor* means "center and fringe" or "revolving around the middle."

The word *khor* has many meanings. It is the word for "wheel," as in *shingta khorlo,* which means "wagon wheel." *Khor* is also found in the word *khorwa,* which means "samsara," or that which spins around itself continuously. The idea is that when you are confused, you also make others confused. Therefore, we also have a term called *trülpa pangwa. Trülpa* means "going astray" or "delusion," and *pangwa* means "giving up"; so *trülpa pangwa* means "giving up delusion." So altogether, the mandala principle works like a wheel; but in this case, when the wheel rotates, your delusions can be transmuted into wisdom. So hopefully, the khor of kyilkhor is a better message than the message of samsara.

We are not going to discuss all the mandalas that exist in the vajra-yana tradition. Goodness knows, we have thousands of abhishekas and mandalas, and it would take many pages to discuss all of them at great length. So I am simplifying this for the readers' sake, to make sure you do not get overwhelmed.

## SELF-ARISING WISDOM

Another definition of mandala is *rangjung gi yeshe,* which means "self-arising wisdom." *Rang* means "self," and *jung* means "coming into existence" or "arising"; so *rangjung* is "self-arising" or "self-born." *Gi* means "of," and *yeshe,* again, is "wisdom"; so *rangjung gi yeshe* means "self-born or self-arising wisdom." And if you ask what self-arising wisdom is, the definition of *self-arising wisdom* is the "awakened state of mind."

The basic understanding of mandala principle is stated in one particular Tibetan phrase, *nangsi yeshe kyi khorlo shepa,* which means the "knowledge that all phenomena are included in the sphere of wisdom." *Nang* means "phenomena," *si* means "existence," and *yeshe* means "wisdom"; so *nangsi yeshe* means the "existence of all phenomena within yeshe." *Kyi* means "of," *khorlo* means "wheel" or "sphere of the mandala," and *shepa* means "knowing"; so altogether, in discussing the mandala principle we are talking about knowing that all phenomena are included in the sphere of wisdom. That is one definition of mandala.

Self-arising wisdom has two qualities: it is free from speculation, and it is unchanging and therefore spontaneous. This means that your metaphysical concepts cannot change what you perceive. This statement might surprise you. When you first study Buddhism, for example, the concept of the five *skandhas** may seem to be a metaphysical concept that can very much change your perception. But if you look beyond the concept, you begin to realize that the experience is real, rather than purely metaphysical. It is not secondary, but it is real, it is physical. When you experience the skandha of form, you really have form; when you experience the skandha of feeling, you really have feeling.

At the beginning of our studies we are learning things by theory. It is like wearing a coat with pockets but having no idea where to put things. The very first time you put the coat on, you had no idea it had pockets, but then somebody told you there were pockets to put your things in, and

---

* The *five skandhas* ("five heaps") are the components giving rise to the false presumption of a separate and independent self or ego.

you realized that you were actually wearing a coat with pockets. At first, the idea that you could put things in pockets was just a theory; then you actually began to put things in the pockets; and after a little while, your pockets become real to you rather than theoretical.

The experience of self-born wisdom, or the awakened state of mind, is the transmission you receive from the teacher when you receive abhisheka. That is when your superficial ordinary mind ceases to exist, and therefore your further ordinary mind becomes powerful. Because you forget or stop the functioning of past and future concerns, and because you are no longer in the present, your mind is no longer anywhere. Therefore, you are self-born wisdom. You do not need any reference point of where, when, or how you got there. It doesn't matter. Self-existing yeshe can be realized or experienced in a body that is a result or leftover of karmic cause and effect, but you do not have to hang on to that solid concept of body. Self-existing yeshe does not come out of ignorance, and it does not need a potter's wheel to spin. It does not have to spin; it just blossoms out.

## THE ICONOGRAPHY OF THE MANDALA

The mandala's iconography breaks down into three separate parts: the charnel ground, the center deity palace, and the four directions.

### The Charnel Ground

The mandala principle involves a lot of symbolism. To begin with, the ground of the mandala is the charnel ground, a place of births, deaths, old age, and sickness.* Most readers will never have seen a real charnel ground, because the Western world is so tidy and cleaned up. The closest thing to the charnel ground in the West might be a hospital, since it is where many people are born and die. However, you can imagine an actual charnel ground as the place where you leave your dead, or where you bring placentas when you have finished giving birth. Such charnel grounds did exist in India, other parts of Asia, and South America, as well as in other parts of the world.

---

* The quality of *charnel ground* is evoked quite beautifully in Trungpa Rinpoche's prose-poem "The Charnel Ground." See appendix 3.

*The Kalachakra mandala, an example of a three-dimensional mandala.*

The concept of a charnel ground is a place where you have no room for conceptualization, no possibilities of going anywhere. It is the place where life begins and ends; it is that which sustains the whole universe, as well as that which kills everything. The iconography depicting the charnel ground includes rivers, trees, dancing skeletons, sages, pagodas, and wild animals tearing apart bodies. From the outside, a charnel ground seems rather gloomy and unpleasant; but from its own point of view, it is self-existing, extremely rich and fertile. So the mandala begins with the charnel ground.

## The Center of the Mandala

In the middle of the charnel ground, there is a big palace or castle for the yidam or deity. This castle has a wall around it and four gates, one in each of the four cardinal directions. Inside, it has little cubicles for the various attendants or servants of the central deity, and there is a central chamber where the deity abides. So it is a palace-like structure, and the central figure, whoever it might be—such as Avalokiteshvara, Vajradhara, or Chakrasamvara—abides in the middle.

The central figure represents your basic, natural, self-existing wisdom; it represents your bodhichitta. In this case, bodhichitta literally means a seed of enlightenment; it is where you begin. You are in the center of the mandala, and from there you see the East, South, West, and North. From there you see the sun rise. It is very simple and straightforward. The center is wherever you are; you are always in the middle of the palace.

## The Four Directions of the Mandala

The four directions are also important, and each is colored differently. The East is white,* and refers to the dawn of vision or the first sight of mandala power. The South is yellow, and represents richness. The West is red, and represents magnetizing or comforting and a sense of joy and pleasure. It is the subsiding of phenomenal desire or samsaric thoughts. The North is green, and represents action. It is complete fearlessness and the willingness to ward off any obstacles to the path wherever they happen to occur. That is how the mandala of natural phenomena is structured.

The iconography of the mandala is not just somebody's concept or clever idea. It developed through twenty-six hundred years of tradition. People have actually experienced and realized such situations. They have gone inside the mandala and witnessed the charnel ground. They have also witnessed the guardians at the doorways of the four directions. The mandala principle is like another world, but it is not like another country that you can travel to—it is right here, right now. Quite possibly you are already sitting in it. And if you are thinking of running away from it, it may already be too late.

## SEEING THE WISDOM IN SAMSARA

Although the mandala principle is very available to us, we should understand that the samsaric world is definitely not a mandala-type situation. There is no such structure in samsara, no such hierarchy. Instead, everything that happens is very casual. The only samsaric mandala is that of

---

* Sometimes the East is white and the center is blue; at other times the center is white and the East is blue.

*His Holiness the Fourteenth Dalai Lama ritually slashing through a painted-sand Kalachakra mandala. After these elaborately constructed mandalas are used in an abhisheka, they are dismantled and offered into a flowing stream or over the edge of a cliff.*

the six realms, a linear situation in which you go up and down.* That is the closest thing to a mandala in the samsaric world.

However, when you are introduced to the mandala principle, you actually can see the whole world as mandala and work with that. You can see the potential in the samsaric world. It begins to join in and participate in the mandala principle. Once you develop your rangjung gi yeshe, your self-born wisdom, you begin to see that there is an undercurrent of mandala existing in the world already. In that sense, there is wisdom in samsara.

It might seem as if all this is a long way from the beginning of the path as we have described it. It seems a long way from the first experience of shamatha practice and a little glimpse of a gap, to the experience

---

* The *six realms* of existence are: the hell realm, the hungry ghost realm, the animal realm, the human realm, the jealous god realm, and the god realm. In samsaric existence, one continually cycles up and down through these six ways of being.

of becoming the central figure of the mandala. The iconography of the mandala is so full-blown and seemingly solid, compared to that original gap, that little glimpse. In some sense, however, the full-blown-ness of the mandala principle is already present, and it is in relationship to this full-blown-ness that you experience a glimpse or gap. You need to have something to have a gap from. Otherwise, you would not have any place to breathe. So mandala possibilities exist already.

When you sit, you should be thankful that you have a front, a right side, a back, and a left side. When you sit on your meditation cushion, you are already sitting in the middle of the mandala. So with the first gap of shamatha, the sense of being in the middle of the mandala is already there. Front, back, left, and right are everywhere. So you are your own mandala. That is precisely where shamatha and vipashyana come together.

From the point of view of sacred outlook, the whole world could be seen as mandala. Let's say you see a samsaric situation that is full of suffering; this could be seen as the mandala of the first noble truth. When the Buddha sits in the middle, and the arhats sit around him, this is also a mandala of its own. So you could have a hinayana mandala with the four gates and everything, and all sorts of bodhisattva-like mandalas could happen, too.

In the vajrayana, when suffering happens, the experience of the sufferer and the suffering become one at some point. You do not separate them into two. You are right in the middle; you are already the central deity. So in the vajrayana, we see the world as sacred, as a sacred mandala. And as long as we are humble and understanding to others, then even people who have not heard about the dharma can tune in to this experience as part of the mandala principle.

## SHAMATHA-VIPASHYANA AS INDIVISIBLE EMPTINESS AND LUMINOSITY

The experience of the mandala principle is based on having received abhisheka. It is based on realizing the nonduality of shamatha and vipashyana as the body, speech, and mind of the guru, and recognizing that as indivisible vajra nature. So in discussing the mandala principle, it is most important to realize that the discovery of ultimate wisdom derives from the indivisibility of shamatha and vipashyana.

Shamatha-vipashyana is sometimes referred to in vajrayana terms as the indivisibility of emptiness and luminosity. Emptiness is connected with shamatha, for slowly but surely, by means of shamatha practice, we try to eliminate the things that are not necessary to us. Discursive thoughts are not necessary, so we try to avoid them; therefore, we attain emptiness, or vacancy of some kind. Luminosity is connected with vipashyana. It means seeing brightly and clearly. By means of vipashyana, awareness begins to pick up what needs to be done.

Shamatha-vipashyana is also known as the combination of emptiness and skillful means. Emptiness, again, is the shamatha process of eliminating mind's occupations and preconceptions, slowly removing them altogether. "Skillful means" refers to vipashyana awareness, which sees all the possibilities of the environment around oneself. So as you can see, shamatha-vipashyana is a very powerful discipline and a very definite experience.

In the vajrayana, shamatha and vipashyana are indivisible. We are not practicing just one or the other alone, but we are trying to join together emptiness and its brightness, emptiness and its skillfulness. So the vajrayana practitioner begins to feel that situations are being handled, but without being regarded as a dualistic feast, pleasurable to mind's duplicity and fickleness. Therefore, indivisible shamatha-vipashyana is known as ultimate. It is ultimate because we have practiced it and we have achieved the result: we have achieved freedom from the fickleness and duplicity of mental activities.

In the nondual experience of shamatha-vipashyana, we have achieved the ultimate shunyata or the emptiness possibilities of shamatha, free from all preoccupations; and with the vipashyana aspect, we have achieved brightness and luminosity as well. Because such an achievement has taken place already, on the spot, it is real and definite. Because it is real and definite, it is known as the ultimate wisdom, or *töngyi yeshe*. And because of the achievement of ultimate wisdom, we can experience the results of abhisheka.

## 26

# The Mandala of the Five Buddha-Families

*Without understanding the five buddha-families, we have no work-ing basis to relate with tantra, and we begin to find ourselves alien-ated from it. . . . There could be a big gap between tantric experience and day-to-day life. But by understanding the five buddha-families, it is possible to close the gap.*

THE TANTRIC approach is not just to make sweeping statements about reality and to create calmness and a meditative state. It is more than learning to be creative and contemplative. In tantra, you relate with the details of your everyday life according to your own particular makeup. So the question in this chapter is how to relate your own ordinary existence or daily situation to tantric consciousness. Tantra is extraordinarily special; it is extremely real and personal.

## FIVE PRINCIPLES OF BUDDHA NATURE

The tantric discipline of relating to life is based on what are known as the five buddha principles, or the five buddha-families. These principles are traditionally referred to as "families" because they are an extension of yourself in the same way that your blood relations are an extension of you: you have your daddy, you have your mommy, you have your sisters and brothers, and they are all part of your family. But you could also say that your motherness, your fatherness, your sisterness, your brotherness, and your me-ness are experienced as definite principles that have distinct

# Five-Buddha-Family Mandala

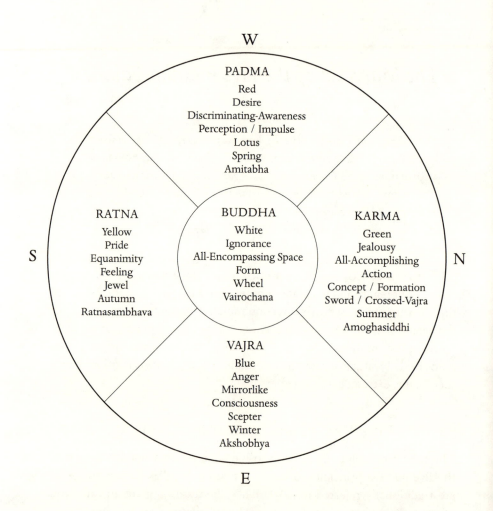

W

**PADMA**
Red
Desire
Discriminating-Awareness
Perception / Impulse
Lotus
Spring
Amitabha

**RATNA**
Yellow
Pride
Equanimity
Feeling
Jewel
Autumn
Ratnasambhava

**BUDDHA**
White
Ignorance
All-Encompassing Space
Form
Wheel
Vairochana

**KARMA**
Green
Jealousy
All-Accomplishing
Action
Concept / Formation
Sword / Crossed-Vajra
Summer
Amoghasiddhi

S

N

**VAJRA**
Blue
Anger
Mirrorlike
Consciousness
Scepter
Winter
Akshobhya

E

characteristics. So the tantric tradition speaks of five families, five principles, categories, or possibilities.

The five buddha-families are called: vajra, *ratna*, *padma*, karma, and buddha. These five families are quite ordinary; there is nothing divine or extraordinary about them. It is just that at the tantric level, people are divided into these five types. Everyone we come across is a member of one or more of these five families; everyone is partially or completely one of these five. You and the people you meet and all aspects of the phenomenal world are made up of one or more buddha-families. The five buddha-families are five principles of buddha nature; they refer to the buddha qualities in all of us. So everyone is a fertile person, a workable person who could be related with directly and personally. From the tantric point of view, when we encounter different types of people, we are actually relating with different styles of enlightenment.

In the bodhisattva's approach, everything has to be kept cool and skillful, steady all the time. The paramitas rely on the central logic of realizing that you have buddha nature in you, so you can be generous, patient, and so forth. But in the vajrayana, you are not expected to be uniform and regimented, to be ideally enlightened and absolutely cool and kind and wise. Tantra does not have that kind of one-track mind.

In tantra, there are many variations that you can get into, based on the different perspectives of the five buddha families. You can identify yourself with all or one of these, or partially with any of them. The five buddha principles are different expressions of basic sanity; they are five different ways to be sane. But in actuality, they are not five separate principles, but one principle manifested in five different aspects. They are five different manifestations of one basic energy in terms of its richness, its fertility, its intelligence, and so forth. So although we refer to five families, we are talking about one basic intelligence or one basic energy.

There is no reason why there are just five buddha-families; it just organically happens that way. In the tantric texts, we sometimes find references to 100 families and even to 999 families. But those are exaggerated forms of the five basic principles.

The five buddha principles are not a Buddhist version of astrology, and they have nothing to do with fortune-telling. They are more like guidelines to perception or experience. That is, you perceive and experience things in relationship to the five-buddha-family principles. You appreciate the five buddha-families as reference points for perception and for the realization of phenomena in the complete sense.

Psychologically, vajrayana permits the openness to work on all kinds of elements that you have within you. You do not have to tune yourself in to only one particular ideal, but you can take pride in what you are, in what you have, in your basic nature. By perceiving the energies of the buddha-families in people and in situations, you see that confusion is workable and can be transformed into an expression of sacred outlook. A student must reach this understanding before the teacher can introduce the tantric deities.

The five buddha-families, or five principles of buddha nature, are the working basis of tantra. Each family is associated with a particular deity or yidam. These tantric deities represent the different energies of the five buddha principles. They represent the wisdom associated with each family and the possibility of overcoming or transforming the main neurosis or *klesha* associated with that family.* So the yidam is the ruler of the wisdom aspect of that family. In tantric practice, you identify with a yidam of the buddha-family that corresponds to your own nature. So yidams should not be regarded as external gods who will save you, but as expressions of your true nature. The buddha-family principles provide a link between ordinary samsaric experience and the brilliance and lofti- ness of the yidams' world. By understanding the buddha-families, you can appreciate the tantric deities as embodiments of sacred world, and you can identify yourself with that sacredness.

The buddha-family or families associated with a person describes that person's fundamental style, their intrinsic perspective or stance in perceiv- ing the world and working with it. Your buddha-family is associated with both your neurotic and your enlightened style. The idea is that the neu- rotic expression of any buddha-family can be transmuted into its wisdom or enlightened aspect. As well as describing people's styles, the buddha- families are also associated with colors, elements, landscapes, directions, seasons—with everything.

---

* The *five wisdoms*, or the awakened aspects of the five buddha-families are the wisdom of all-encompassing space (dharmadhatu), mirrorlike wisdom, the wisdom of equanimity, discriminating-awareness wisdom, and the wisdom of all-accomplishing action. The *five kleshas* are ignorance, anger, pride, passion, and envy.

## ICONOGRAPHY AND THE MANDALA SETUP

In tantric iconography, the five buddha-families are arrayed in a mandala, which represents their wisdom or enlightened aspect. The buddha-families make up a five-part mandala, with buddha in the center, and vajra, ratna, padma, and karma at the four cardinal points. In any mandala, everything breaks into those four sections, along with the middle. Of course, you can invent numerous directions, but even if you had a hundred directions, they would still be based on the logic of the four cardinal directions. That is just how things work.

### The Center

Traditionally, the buddha family is in the center, and is symbolized by a wheel and the color white.* It is connected with basic coordination and wisdom.

### The East

Vajra is in the East, because vajra is connected with the dawn. It is connected with the color blue and is symbolized by the vajra scepter. Vajra is the sharpness of experience, as in the morning when we wake up. We begin to see the dawn, when light is first reflected on the world, as a symbol of awakening reality.

### The South

Ratna is in the South. It is connected with richness and is symbolized by a jewel and the color yellow. Ratna is associated with the midday, when we begin to need refreshment and nourishment.

### The West

Padma is in the West and is symbolized by the lotus and the color red. As our day gets older, it is time to socialize, to make a date with our lover. Or if we have fallen in love with an antique or with some clothing, it is time to go out and buy it.

----

* Sometimes the East (vajra family) is blue and the center (buddha family) is white; at other times the center (buddha family) is blue and the East (vajra family) is white.

*Symbols of the five buddha-families: wheel (center), vajra (East), jewel (South), lotus (West), and crossed-vajra (North).*

## The North

The last family, karma, is in the North. It is symbolized by a sword or crossed-vajra and by the color green. Finally we have captured the whole situation: we have everything we need, and there is nothing more to get. We have brought our merchandise or our lover back home, and we say, "Let's close the door and lock it." So the mandala of the five buddha-families represents the progress of an entire day or a whole course of action.

## QUALITIES OF THE FIVE FAMILIES

To better understand the qualities of the buddha-families, we can look at each of them and how they manifest in one's experience, in both neurotic and enlightened ways.

### Vajra Family

In the East of the mandala is the vajra family, the family of sharpness, crystallization, and indestructibility. The buddha of this family is Akshobhya. The term *vajra* is superficially translated as "diamond," but that is not quite accurate. A vajra is a celestial precious stone that cuts through any other solid object. So it is more than a diamond; it is complete indestructibility. Incidentally, the use of the term *vajra* in such words as *vajrayana*, *vajra master*, and *vajra pride* does not refer to this particular buddha-family, but to basic indestructibility.

The symbol of the vajra family is a vajra scepter, or dorje. This vajra scepter has five prongs, which are related to the five emotions of aggression, pride, passion, jealousy, and ignorance. The sharp edges or prongs of the vajra represent cutting through any neurotic emotional tendencies; they also represent the sharp quality of being aware of many possible perspectives.

The indestructible vajra is said to be like a heap of razor blades: if you naively try to hold it or touch it, there are all kinds of sharp edges that are both cutting and penetrating. The idea is that vajra corrects or remedies any neurotic distortion in a precise and sharp way. In the ordinary world, the experience of vajra is perhaps not as extreme as holding razor blades in your hand, but at the same time, it is very penetrating and personal. It is like a sharp, cutting, biting-cold winter day. Each time you expose yourself to the open air, you get frostbite instantly.

Intellectually, vajra is very sharp. All the intellectual traditions belong to this family. A person in the vajra family knows how to logically evaluate the arguments used to explain experience. They can tell whether the logic is true or false. Vajra-family intellect also has a quality of constant openness and perspective. For instance, a vajra person could view a crystal ball from hundreds of perspectives, according to where it is placed, the way it is perceived, the distance from which they are looking at it, and so forth. The intellect of the vajra family is not just encyclopedic; it is sharpness, directness, and awareness of perspectives. Such indestructibility and sharpness are very personal and real.

The klesha or neurotic expression of vajra is anger and intellectual fixation. If you become fixated on a particular logic, the sharpness of vajra can become rigidity. You become possessive of your insight, rather than maintaining an open perspective. The anger of vajra neurosis could be pure aggression, or simply uptightness because you are so attached to your sharpness of mind.

Vajra is associated with the element of water. Cloudy, turbulent water symbolizes the defensive and aggressive nature of anger, while clear water suggests the sharp, precise, clear reflectiveness of vajra wisdom. In fact, vajra wisdom is traditionally called mirrorlike wisdom, which evokes this image of a calm pond or a reflecting pool.

## Ratna Family

The next buddha-family, in the South of the mandala, is ratna, which means "jewel," "gem," or "precious stone." The deity of the ratna family is Ratnasambhava. Ratna is a personal and real sense of expanding yourself and enriching your environment. You make yourself at home with collections of all kinds of richness and wealth. It is expansion, enrichment, plentifulness.

Such plentifulness could also have problems and weaknesses. In the neurotic sense, the richness of ratna manifests as the klesha of greed, and as being completely fat, or extraordinarily ostentatious, beyond the limits of your sanity. You expand constantly, open heedlessly, and indulge yourself to the level of insanity. It is like swimming in a dense lake of honey and butter. When you coat yourself in this mixture of butter and honey, it is very difficult to remove. You cannot just remove it by wiping it off, but you have to apply all kinds of cleaning agents, such as cleanser and soap, to loosen its grasp.

In the positive expression of the ratna family, the principle of richness is extraordinary. You feel very rich and plentiful, and you extend yourself to your world personally, directly, emotionally, psychologically, even spiritually. You are extending constantly, expanding like a flood or an earthquake. There is a quality of spreading, shaking the earth, and creating more and more cracks in it. That is the powerful expansiveness of ratna.

The enlightened expression of ratna is called the wisdom of equanimity, because ratna can include everything in its expansive environment. Thus ratna is associated with the element of earth. It is like a rotting log that makes itself at home in the country. Such a log does not want to leave its home ground. It would like to stay, but at the same time it grows all kinds of mushrooms and plants and allows different animals to nest in it. That lazy settling down and making yourself at home, and inviting other people to come in and rest as well, is ratna.

## Padma Family

The next family, in the West, is padma, which means "lotus flower." The symbol of the enlightened padma family is the lotus, which grows out of the mud, yet still comes out pure and clean, virginal and clear. The deity of the padma family is Amitabha.

Padma neurosis is connected with the klesha of passion, a grasping quality and a desire to possess. You are completely wrapped up in desire and want only to seduce the world, without concern for real communication. You could be a hustler or an advertiser, but basically you are like a peacock. In fact, Amitabha Buddha traditionally sits on a peacock, which represents subjugating padma neurosis. A person with padma neurosis speaks gently, fantastically gently, and they are seemingly very sexy, kind, magnificent, and completely accommodating: "If you hurt me, that's fine. That is part of our love affair. Come toward me." Such padma seduction can sometimes become excessive and sometimes become compassionate, depending on how you work with it.

Padma is connected with the element of fire. In the confused state, fire does not distinguish between the things it grasps, burns, and destroys. But in the awakened state, the heat of passion is transmuted into the warmth of compassion. When padma neurosis is transmuted, it becomes fantastically precise and aware; it turns into tremendous interest and inquisitiveness. Everything is seen in its own distinct way, with its own particular qualities and characteristics. Thus the wisdom of padma is called discriminating-awareness wisdom.

The genuine character of padma seduction is real openness, a willingness to demonstrate what you have and what you are to the phenomenal world. What you bring to the world is a sense of pleasure. In whatever you experience, you begin to feel that there is lots of promise. You are constantly magnetizing and engaging in spontaneous hospitality.

The quality of padma experience is like bathing in perfume or jasmine tea. Each time you bathe, you feel refreshed and fantastic. It feels good to be magnetized. The sweet air is fantastic, and the hospitality of your host is magnificent. You eat the good food they provide, which is delicious, but not too filling. You live in a world of honey and milk, but in this case it is a very delicate experience, unlike the rich but heavy experience of the ratna family. Fantastic! Even your bread is scented with all kinds of delicious smells. Your ice cream is colored by beautiful pink lotus-like colors. You cannot wait to eat it. Sweet music is playing in the background constantly. When there is no music, you listen to the whistling of the wind around your padma environment, and it becomes beautiful music as well. Even though you are not a musician, you compose all kinds of music. You wish you were a poet or a fantastic lover.

## Karma Family

The next family, in the North, is the karma family, which is symbolized by a sword or a crossed-vajra. In this case, when we speak of karma, we are not talking about karmic debts, or karmic consequences: here *karma* simply means "action." The buddha of the karma family is Amoghasiddhi. The enlightened aspect of karma is called the wisdom of all-accomplishing action, which is the transcendental sense of the complete fulfillment of action without being hassled or pushed into neurosis. It is natural fulfillment in how you relate with your world. The klesha or neurotic quality of karma is jealousy, comparison, and envy. But in either case, whether you relate to the karma family on the transcendental level or the neurotic level, karma is the energy of efficiency.

If you have karma-family neurosis, you feel highly irritated if you see a hair on your teacup. First you think that your cup is broken and that the hair is a crack in the cup. Then there is some relief. You realize that your cup is not broken; it just has a piece of hair on the side. But when you look at the hair on your cup of tea, you become angry all over again. You would like to make everything very efficient, pure, and absolutely clean. However, if you do achieve cleanliness, then that itself becomes a further problem; you feel insecure because there is nothing to administer, nothing to work on. You constantly check every loose end.

In the karma family, being very keen on efficiency, you get hung up on it. If you meet a person who is not efficient, who does not have their life together, you regard them as a terrible person. You would like to get rid of such inefficient people, and certainly you do not respect them, even if they are talented musicians or scientists or whatever they may be. On the other hand, if someone has immaculate efficiency, you begin to feel that they are a good person to be with. You would like to associate exclusively with people who are both responsible and clean-cut. However, you find that you are envious and jealous of such efficient people. You want others to be efficient, but not more efficient than you are.

The epitome of karma-family neurosis is the desire to create a uniform world. Even though you might have very little philosophy, very little meditation, very little consciousness in terms of developing yourself, you feel that you can handle your world properly. You think that you have composure, and you can relate properly with the whole world, and you are resentful that everybody else does not see things in the same way that you do.

Karma is connected with the element of wind. The wind never blows in all directions, but it blows in one direction at a time. This represents the one-way view of resentment and envy, which picks on one little fault or virtue, and then blows it out of proportion. But with karma wisdom, that resentment falls away, and the qualities of energy, fulfillment of action, and openness remain. In other words, the active aspect of wind is retained so that your energetic activity touches everything in its path. You see the possibilities inherent in situations, and you automatically take the appropriate course. So action fulfills its purpose.

## Buddha Family

The fifth family is called the buddha family. The symbol of the buddha family is the wheel, and the deity of the buddha family is Vairochana. This family is in the center of the mandala, and it is the foundation. The buddha family is associated with the element of space. It is the environment or oxygen that makes it possible for the other principles to function. Buddha-family energy has a sedate, solid quality. Persons in this family have a strong sense of contemplative experience, and they are highly meditative.

The buddha neurosis or klesha is the quality of ignorance. It is being spaced-out rather than spacious. It is often associated with an unwillingness to express yourself. For example, you might see that your neighbors are destroying your picket fence with a sledgehammer. You can hear them and see them; in fact, you have been watching your neighbors at work all day, continuously smashing your picket fence. But instead of reacting, you just observe them, and then you return to your snug little home. You eat your breakfast, lunch, and dinner, and you ignore what they are doing. You are paralyzed, unable to talk to outsiders.

Another quality of buddha neurosis is that you couldn't be bothered. Your dirty laundry is piled up in a corner of your room. Sometimes you use your dirty laundry to wipe up spills on the floor or table, and then you put your laundry back on the same pile. As time goes on, your dirty socks become unbearable, but you just sit there.

If you are embarking on a political career, your colleagues may suggest that you develop a certain project and expand your organization. But if you have a buddha neurosis, you will choose to develop the area that needs the least effort. You do not want to deal directly with the details of handling reality. Entertaining friends is also a hassle. You prefer to take your friends to a restaurant rather than cook in your home.

And if you want to have a love affair, instead of seducing a partner, or talking to them and making friends, you just look for somebody who is already keen on you. You cannot be bothered with talking somebody into something.

Sometimes you feel you are sinking into the earth, the solid mud. Sometimes you feel good because you think you are the most stable person in the universe. You slowly begin to grin to yourself, to smile at yourself, because you are the best person of all. You are the only person who manages to remain stable. But other times you feel that you are the loneliest person in the whole universe. You do not particularly like to dance, and when you are asked to dance with somebody, you feel embarrassed and uncomfortable. You want to stay in your own little corner.

When the ignoring quality of buddha neurosis is transmuted into wisdom, it becomes an environment of all-pervasive spaciousness. This enlightened aspect is called the wisdom of all-encompassing space. In itself, it might still be somewhat desolate and empty, but at the same time it has a quality of completely open potential. It can accommodate anything. It is spacious and vast like the sky.

## Looking at the Buddha Families in Terms of Depth and Expansiveness

Another way of looking at the buddha-families is in relationship to the five skandhas. The five skandhas—form, feeling, perception, formation, and consciousness—represent the structure of ego, as well as the evolution of ego's world. Skandhas are also related to blockages of different types—spiritual blockages, material blockages, and emotional blockages. The first skandha, form, is the sense of there being something definite and solid to hold onto. The second skandha, feeling, is the projection onto phenomena as being either pleasurable or painful. The third skandha, perception, is the impulse to grasp what is pleasurable and reject what is painful. The fourth skandha, formation, is the tendency to accumulate a collection of mental states as territory. The fifth skandha, consciousness, is the subtle fulfillment of the entire skandha process and is the mental undergrowth of the thought process.

From the point of view of the skandhas, whenever we function, we function with all five principles at once. So in this case, we are viewing the buddha-families as having various levels of depth or weight. We are looking at the buddha-families in terms of depth and expanding from that depth, or as a process of going from heaviness to lightness. It is like rising out of the depths of the ocean, and slowly floating up to the surface.

In this approach, there is no allegiance to a particular buddha-family that you cherish as your one-and-only style. That view would tend to give you a two-dimensional experience of the buddha principles. In order to see the whole thing as a three-dimensional experience, you have to approach it as a process from depth to expansion.

### The Buddha Family and the Skandha of Form

You start with the buddha family, which is the heaviest of all. This is the most solid family, that which clings to ego or relates to the wisdom of all-pervasive space. It is the core of the matter. The buddha family brings a sense of solidity and basic being, and at the same time, it brings a quality of openness, wisdom, and sanity. The buddha family is related with the skandha of form.

### The Ratna Family and the Skandha of Feeling

From there, with the ratna family, you move out slowly to the skandha of feeling. This brings a quality of intelligent expansiveness, like tentacles or antennae.

### The Padma Family and the Skandha of Perception

Next is the padma family. The padma family is connected with the skandha of perception or impulse, because of its sharpness and quickness, and at the same time its willingness to seduce the world outside into relationship with itself.

### The Karma Family and the Skandha of Formation

Fourth is the karma family, which is connected with the skandha of concept or formation. This principle happens very actively and very efficiently.

## The Vajra Family and the Skandha
## of Consciousness

The fifth is the vajra family, and the skandha of consciousness. Here there is a type of intelligence and intellect that operates with very minute precision and clarity, so the whole thing becomes extraordinarily workable. Once you are on the surface, you know how to relate with the phenomenal world.

The five skandhas are components of our basic makeup, our being, both from the samsaric and nirvanic points of view. Therefore, we are constantly manifesting the five types of buddha nature within ourselves directly and precisely, with a certain amount of style. Because of that, the five types of energy are completely available to us and workable. It is very important to realize that.

## THE BUDDHA FAMILIES AS THE
## WORKING BASIS OF TANTRA

We need to understand and relate with the five buddha principles before we begin tantric discipline, so that we can start to understand what tantra is all about. Without understanding the five buddha-families, we have no working basis to relate with tantra, and we begin to find ourselves alienated from it. The vajrayana is seen to be so outrageous that it seems to have no bearing on us as individuals; we feel that it is purely a distant aim, a distant goal. If tantra is a mystical experience, how can we relate it to our ordinary, everyday life at home? There could be a big gap between tantric experience and day-to-day life. But by understanding the five buddha-families, it is possible to close the gap. Therefore, it is necessary to study the five buddha principles, because they provide a bridge between tantric experience and everyday life.

By working with the buddha-families, we discover that we already have certain qualities. According to the tantric perspective, we cannot ignore those qualities, and we cannot reject them and try to be something else. We each belong to certain buddha-families, and we each have our particular neuroses: our aggression, passion, jealousy, resentment, ignorance, or whatever we have. We should work with our neuroses; we should relate with them and experience them properly. They are the only potential we have. When we begin to work with them, we see that we can use them as stepping-stones.

## Developing the Ability to
## Perceive Mandalas and Families

The sitting practice of shamatha meditation develops basic sanity. It develops solidness and slowness, and the possibility of watching your mind operating all the time. Out of that, you develop vipashyana expansiveness and awareness. You become more perceptive, and your mind becomes more clear, like an immaculate microscope lens. You develop awareness without conditions, just simple, straightforward awareness itself, awareness being aware without putting anything into it. Out of that clarity, various styles of perception begin to develop, which are the styles of the five buddha-families.

Awareness is the key point. Clarity is the microscope that is able to perceive the mandala spectrum and the five buddha-families. With that kind of clarity, the buddha-families are not seen as extraordinary but as matter-of-fact, and the basic mandala principle becomes very simple and straightforward: it is that everything is related to everything else.

On the solid, sane, open, fresh ground of hinayana, the mahayana gives you directions about how to act as a good citizen; and in the vajrayana, there is an enormous possibility of becoming a genius. Basic sanity has developed, a proper lifestyle has been established, and there are no hassles or obstacles. At the vajrayana level, having removed the fog of any dualistic barrier, you begin to have a clear perception of the phenomenal world as it is. That is the mahamudra experience, in which there is no inhibition, and things are seen precisely and beautifully. In this experience, you begin to see the workings of the universe in its ultimate details. You are such a genius that you see everything completely. This genius is described as jnana, or wisdom, of which there are five types, corresponding to the five buddha-families.

## THE FIVE WISDOMS

So within the clear perception of the mahamudra, you develop the ability to experience the wisdoms of the five buddha-families. That is the kind of cosmic genius we find in the vajrayana.

### The Wisdom of All-Encompassing Space

In the center of the mandala is all-encompassing space, also known as the wisdom of dharmadhatu, or the wisdom of clear space. It consists of a quality of utter and complete spaciousness, where the coming and going of thought patterns, as well as the phenomenal world and everything else, could be accommodated completely, thoroughly and fully.

### Mirrorlike Wisdom

In the East, there is mirrorlike wisdom, which is connected with the dawn, with the morning. This is the experience of shining and brilliance, along with a sense of great joy.

### The Wisdom of Equanimity

In the South, there is the wisdom of equanimity. It is the one-taste experience of wisdom, seeing that sweet and sour are one. You are not particularly attracted to the sweet or repelled by the sour, but there is a quality of equilibrium.

### Discriminating-Awareness Wisdom

In the West, there is discriminating-awareness wisdom. You are able to see pain as naked pain, and pleasure as naked pleasure. Therefore, you are no longer magnetized by the pleasure or repelled by the pain, but you see them as they are.

### The Wisdom of All-Accomplishing Action

In the North, there is the wisdom of all-accomplishing action, which is the idea of achievement without being a busybody. It is the natural

## ATTRIBUTES OF THE FIVE BUDDHA-FAMILIES

| ATTRIBUTE | BUDDHA | VAJRA | RATNA | PADMA | KARMA |
|---|---|---|---|---|---|
| TATHAGATA | Vairochana | Akshobhya | Ratnasambhava | Amitabha | Amoghasiddhi |
| WISDOM | All-Encompassing Space | Mirrorlike | Equanimity | Discriminating-Awareness | All-Accomplishing Action |
| KLESHA | Ignorance | Aggression | Pride | Passion | Jealousy |
| BASIC ENERGY | Spaciousness | Precision | Richness | Seduction | Activity |
| COLOR | White | Blue | Yellow | Red | Green |
| DIRECTION | Center | East | South | West | North |
| SEASON OF YEAR | Continuity | Winter | Autumn | Spring | Summer |
| TIME OF DAY | Present | Dawn | Mid-morning | Sunset | Night |
| ELEMENT | Space | Water | Earth | Fire | Wind |
| QUALITY OF ELEMENT | All-pervasiveness | Cohesion, fluidity | Solidity, fertility | Heat, light | Lightness, motility |
| SKANDHA | Form | Consciousness | Feeling | Perception | Formation |
| SENSE PERCEPTION | Touch | Sight | Taste | Smell | Sound |
| NEUROTIC EXPRESSION | Dullness, avoidance | Anger, intellectual fixation | Pride, hunger, poverty mentality | Grasping, clinging | Resentment, envy, excessive speed |
| AWAKE EXPRESSION | Openness, accommodation | Clarity | Expansiveness | Appreciation, compassion | Accuracy, energy |
| BRAHMAVIHARA | | Maitri | Equanimity | Compassion | Joy |
| KARMA | | Pacifying | Enriching | Magnetizing | Destroying |
| ABHISHEKA | Name | Vase | Crown | Vajra | Ghanta |
| BUDDHA ACTIVITY | Body | Mind | Quality | Speech | Action |
| MUDRA | Meditation | Earth-touching | Generosity | Meditation | Fearlessness |
| BUDDHA'S EMBLEM | Dharmachakra | Vajra | Jewel | Lotus | Crossed Vajra |

achievement of seeing that each situation, each color, each sound, and each taste has room or space of its own. You do not just reorganize the universe according to your own wishes of what you would like to see, but you see things as they are.

These are the five buddha-family wisdoms. Of course, all these wisdoms come from strict training and experience in shamatha and vipashyana, and also from softening yourself by means of tonglen practice and developing compassion. Having had those experiences already, you will then be able to experience these five types of wisdom.

## 27

# The Outer Mandala

*When you experience total sacred outlook, there is no grudge against any situation and no overindulgence in possessiveness and wanting. Physical existence and the forms you see in the outer world are seen as the heavenly realm of the deities; speech is experienced as mantra; and the psychology of the world is experienced as awakened clarity.*

T HE MANDALA principle is threefold: outer, inner, and secret. Of these three principles, the first we encounter is the outer mandala, or the mandala of the phenomenal world. The outer mandala includes our country, our province, our district, our immediate household, and so on. It is the world of our projections.

## FOUR STYLES OF ENTERING INTO REALITY

The phenomenal world is conducted or perceived by the media of the sense faculties, by the *ayatanas* and dhatus. We then make use of cognition, and going further, a deeper form of perception.

### Ayatanas

The ayatanas are the sense faculties: the sense organs and their objects. In Tibetan, the word for ayatana is *kye-che*. *Kye* means "being born," and *che* means "flourishing" or "burning"; so *kye-che* means "being born and igniting." An ayatana is like a fire that ignites and flourishes. The twelve ayatanas are comprised of the six sense organs of eyes, ears, nose, tongue, body, and mind; and the six sense objects of sights, sounds, smells, tastes, touchable objects, and mental objects. They are your mental and physical capabilities.

Altogether, the ayatanas make it possible for us to propagate our physical being. Because of the ayatanas, we can eat and drink and smell and see and feel. It is all happening right now. If you feel uncomfortable with the temperature in the room, you might open a window; that is the ayatanas in action. It is because the ayatanas are functioning that you are able to project the outer mandala, or the world outside. That world outside is your projection; it is a projection of sight, sound, taste, smell, and so forth. So in the outer mandala experience, your projections begin to work as they should work. They work in the sense that you can see or hear. But beyond that, they do not work. Later, at the level of the inner mandala, you begin to see that your projections do not actually work.

## Dhatus

The eighteen dhatus are comprised of the same six sense organs and the same six sense objects, with the addition of the six corresponding sense consciousnesses: seeing consciousness, hearing consciousness, smelling consciousness, tasting consciousness, touching consciousness, and mind consciousness.

The ayatanas were the six basic sense faculties and objects. With the dhatus, the six sense consciousnesses are added in because they are the final perception of your surroundings.* With the dhatus, you have the consciousness to make judgments about what you see. You see good things, bad things, and mediocre things; you see things that you couldn't care less about, and at the same time you see things that you care for so much. Through the ayatanas and dhatus, you become complete and perfect, capable of experiencing the reality that goes on around you in the form of sights, sounds, feelings, tastes, and smells. When you have good ayatanas, then you should also have good dhatus at the same time.

---

* Simply having a sense organ and a sense object does not mean that a perception will necessarily register. The addition of a corresponding sense consciousness is necessary for a sense perception to arise as a conscious experience.

## Cognition

Once we have the sense perceptions, we then make use of cognizing faculties of all kinds. As human beings, we perceive pain, pleasure, and indifferent sensations by using any one of those sense perceptions to cognize or re-cognize. We develop our mode of behavior patterns, including such things as the feeling that we want to cry, we want to complain, we want to absorb, we want to take advantage of things—the simple, ordinary level of experience. We conduct ourselves in that way.

## Deeper Perception

Then we go beyond that a little bit, if we can. Along with those perceptions that happen to us, and the cognizing faculties that we possess, we cannot reject that there is deeper perception taking place. That deeper perception is full perception; it is the fresh experience of all of those perceptions. We begin to use smelling, seeing, hearing, and every perception not only as one of our sense faculties, but to experience some clarity. Ordinarily, hearing is often conflicting with tasting, smelling is conflicting with feeling, and thinking is conflicting with smelling. But we begin to experience the clarity and precision beyond those senses—beyond smelling, beyond hearing, beyond tasting. We begin to experience a kind of clarity that can govern all of those situations.

Ordinary experiences could be regarded as sometimes having a clouding effect. Hearing too much or tasting too much might have a numbing effect. But here, we are talking about going beyond that. Beyond ordinary perception, there is supersound, supersmell, and superfeeling existing in our state of being. This kind of perception can only be experienced by training ourselves in the depths of the hinayana. It can only be developed through shamatha practice, which clears out that cloudiness and brings about the precision and sharpness of the perceptions of hearing, smelling, tasting, feeling, and all the rest.

In shamatha practice, we develop the precision of experiencing our breath going in and out; and in walking meditation, we experience the movement of our heel-sole-toe. That begins to bring out precision that goes beyond the cloudiness of seeing, smelling, and tasting. Meditation practice brings out the supernatural, if I might use that word. By supernatural, I do not mean that you are going to see ghosts or become telepathic or anything like that, but simply that your perceptions become super natural. You feel your breath; it is so good. You breathe out and dissolve your breath; it is so sharp and so good. It is so extraordinary that your ordinary techniques become superfluous. Usually we think of how to become smarter than somebody else, but with shamatha, we simply see better, hear better, and smell better.

Through shamatha, the best cognition begins to arise in your system and elevate your sense of existence. This happens purely through the means of being with your body, mind, and breath, through simply surviving on your meditation cushion. This process starts in the hinayana, so even at that point, your path is tantra already. Like tantra, the hinayana is continuity; it is dharana, or binding together. The continuity is already there, and the clarity and precision begin to come out of that continuity.

By experiencing the clarity and the precision of the hinayana, we begin to find ourselves in the realm of utter, complete, and thorough reality. You might ask, "What is reality?" Reality, in this case, means seeing absolutely clearly and thoroughly. You can clearly see how you conduct yourself, how you manifest yourself, how you perceive, how you see, how you hear, how you smell, how you taste, how you feel, how you think, and so on and so on. You might say this is nothing particularly extraordinary; it is how you operate anyway. You might even say that you could get the same result out of any form of training. But that is not quite so. You do not begin to experience the mandala principle automatically, without this kind of training.

## SEEING THE OUTER WORLD AS A MANDALA

The mandala approach could apply to many situations in life. It is not particularly alien to us, but it is natural and automatic in a sense. We will work with the mandala principle after our death, in how we experience our *bardo*,* and we will work with it before we die, in how we experience sickness and turmoil. We are constantly working with those four styles of entering into reality.

However, the ordinary world that we project out to is usually divided into friends, enemies, and neutrals, so we see the phenomenal world as

---

* *Bardo,* or "intermediate state," refers to the period between death and rebirth, traditionally described as a journey lasting forty-nine days.

either desirable, undesirable, or else we couldn't care less. But at this point, having received transmission and developed at least a basic understanding of flashing sanity out to the world, we begin to realize that the distinction between friends, enemies, and neutrals is not that solid.* So in relating to the outer mandala, you could refrain from such projections. Moreover, beyond simply refraining from solidifying those projections, you could transform them. That world of friends, enemies, and neutrals could be transformed, and the entire phenomenal world could be regarded as the heavenly realm of the mandala.

Projecting sacred outlook in this way does not mean that your friends become enemies, your enemies become friends, and the ones you are indifferent to become either friends or enemies. You do not have to switch everything around completely. However, you become more accepting of how your friends are, in their own right, because they are sacred already; and that also applies your enemies, and to those to whom you are indifferent. Because of your sacred outlook, you do not have to stress either good or evil attitudes.

When you experience total sacred outlook, there is no grudge against any situation and no overindulgence in possessiveness and wanting. Physical existence and the forms you see in the outer world are seen as the heavenly realm of the deities; speech is experienced as mantra; and the psychology of the world is experienced as awakened clarity. In that way, the outer world is completely transformed by means of a greater understanding of sacred outlook.

## First Thought as the Center of the Mandala

The mandala principle is based on the idea of having a first glimpse of something, and then having the rest of your impressions revolve around that. For example, somebody might say, "Hey, who are you?" That statement is the first proclamation. Then, when that information has come to you, you try to answer the question, and your answer revolves or circulates around that person who was saying, "Hey, who are you?"

So you have a first thought, a flash, and then you have that which confirms it. That which confirms the first thought is the set of thoughts that

---

* This idea is discussed quite extensively in volume 2 of the *Profound Treasury*, part 7, "Mind Training and Slogan Practice."

revolves around that first thought, or the conclusion that follows from the first proclamation. In other words, this is a more enlightened version of the discussion of "I am," or twofold egolessness, which is found in hinayana teachings.* Here when we say, "I am," the "I" is our starting point, and the "am" is what confirms our I-ness. So there is a basic situation, and there is also a secondary situation revolving around it, which confirms the initial situation. This is how the mandala principle operates in our everyday perception and interaction with others.

From this point of view, "first thought" could be regarded as the center of the mandala. However, the term *first thought* does not literally mean the first thought you have when you get up in the morning. It refers to any first fresh thought that comes at the end of some babbling. At the end of a string of little babblings, you have a fresh beginning, a new first thought happening. You have the conceptuality of *blobbidy bla,* and then you have first thought—*tshoo!*—coming out of that. So first thought could happen at any time. And once it happens, there is the realization of that first thought, which is connected with the fringe principle. It is like saying "kingdom." You have a "king" first, and the "dom" comes later, which makes a whole world; so altogether, it is a mandala.

To describe this pattern of perception, Allen Ginsberg and I developed the phrase "First thought, best thought."† The center of the mandala, or kyil, is first thought, the first perception of reality; the surroundings, or khor, are what make first thought best. That first thought of awareness, which brings you into sanity altogether, could be either your own vajra state of being and awareness or that of your vajra master. In a mandala, there is no dichotomy between your own state of existence and the vajra master's. You are in the vajra master's world, in the sanity of the vajra master altogether. When sun is sun, there is always sunshine.

You have a first perception of reality. For instance, you might look at an open Japanese fan, or *suehiro,* which is silver on one side and gold on

---

* See volume 1 of the *Profound Treasury,* chapter 68, "Cutting Through the Numbness of Ego."

† Chögyam Trungpa had a long and close connection with Allen Ginsberg, and he was Mr. Ginsberg's principal vajrayana teacher. At Naropa University, Trungpa Rinpoche worked closely with Anne Waldman and Mr. Ginsberg in the development of Naropa's school of writing and poetics, called The Jack Kerouac School of Disembodied Poetics.

*Trungpa Rinpoche brandishing a gold and silver fan.*

the other. The first thought is seeing either a silver fan or a gold fan. Then you might see the fan upside down, but it is still first thought. You might then see the silver side down and the handle up; then you might see a gold fan with the handle up. At the same time, it is still just first thought.

## BEST THOUGHT AS THE FRINGE OF THE MANDALA

Out of first thought (kyil) arises best thought (khor), the fringe or surroundings of the mandala. Usually what happens with those of us who are not realized is that we are possessed by what we project out. So ordinarily speaking, out of that first thought come passion, aggression, ignorance, jealousy, stinginess, and all sorts of other kleshas. But in this case, we do not regard those things as particularly wicked or terrible. The idea is that reality is always there. The texture of the phenomenal world always plays with you and rubs against you, and whether you feel up or down does not really matter. That is the meaning of khor.

In speaking about the Buddha, *The Sutra of the Recollection of the Noble Three Jewels* says, "The dhatus have no hold on him. His ayatanas are controlled." So the idea is not to be possessed by the dhatus, not to be possessed by your surroundings. "Not being possessed by projections" means that you do not go along gullibly with your idea that your perceptions are wicked. When you begin to see things as they are, you just accept them as they are, on the spot, and you do not try to edit your world. You have a sense of humor; you realize that things are not all that serious and not all that consequential, but they are simply the display of your khor, your perception. In *The Sadhana of Mahamudra*, there are lines that say: "Now pain and pleasure alike have become ornaments which it is pleasant to wear." That is the same notion as not being possessed by dhatus.

In relating to the sense perceptions, to the ayatanas and dhatus, instead of trying to understand all this intellectually, the best approach would be to try to investigate and see how the dhatus relate with you personally. This lineage is called the practice lineage, not the intellectual lineage. We always try things. We just go out and look and find out for ourselves.

## SHUTTING DOWN THE FACTORY OF SAMSARA

Altogether, this discussion of the meaning of *kyilkhor* is reminiscent of our discussion of *sang-gye* in the hinayana teachings.* Here, we said that *kyil* means "centering," "precision," and "clarity," and *khor* means "surroundings"; and in discussing *sang-gye*, we said that *sang* means "clarified" or "purified," and *gye* means "expansion" or "blossoming." So there is a correlation between *sang* and *kyil*, and between *khor* and *gye*.

Generally, the kleshas are connected with all kinds of mental contraptions, but with khor or gye, such contraptions are undermined and made unworkable. The whole factory of samsara is shut down. There is a sense of completely stopping the world, while at the same time still functioning in the world. If the factory of samsara is shut down, the kleshas can no longer operate. The kleshas occur because of your state of mind, because of the way the factory is operated. But in this case, metaphysics and logistics are no longer obstacles, so you can start a better factory.

This is connected with the idea of creating an enlightened society. If we are creating an enlightened society, we do not shut down the lights, or

---

* See volume 1 of the *Profound Treasury*, chapter 13, "The Buddha."

stop serving meals, or vacuuming our floors. But an enlightened version of lightheartedness, as opposed to heavy-handedness, can take place.

Presently, a lot of people feel aggression; they feel that they have been put in a situation in which they cannot celebrate anymore. But such a situation could be lifted up. There could be a change in the psychology of the factory administration, and the workers could begin to take joy in working at the factory, which would be wonderful. When the mechanisms and machinery of the factory are no longer problematic, they are like the sunrise and sunset.

## Mantras as Expressions of Mandala Principles

The structure of mantras also reflects the mandala principle. In a mantra, traditionally we put OM ( ཨོཾ ) first, we put the name of the deity in the middle, and we put SVAHA ( སྭཱ་ཧཱ ) at the end. For example, we could have OM Joe Schmidt SVAHA or OM Ginsberg SVAHA. So a mantra begins with OM and ends with SVAHA, and you are in the middle.

In mantras such as OM MANI PADME HUM, OM is first thought. That first thought of OM is made up of three steps: The first is A, the feminine principle; the second is O, the masculine principle; and the third is M, the union of the masculine and feminine. So masculine and feminine are joined together in OM, in first thought. That is kyil, the center of the mandala.

Ending with SVAHA is like saying "amen" or "let it be so." However, SVAHA does not just mean "let it be that way" alone. It is slightly more than that. The idea is that having begun something, how you end it is also very important. So in a mantra, as in the mandala principle, the center or first thought is kyil (OM), and the surroundings or what we then perceive are khor (SVAHA).

## Entering the Mandala

Iconographically, the mandala structure is shown with four gates, surrounded by a wall of flames, beyond which there is the charnel ground. The flames keep away those who would like to enter purely on the basis of being possessed with dhatus. They force the practitioner to enter properly.

When you enter the mandala, you enter through one of the four gates. The Eastern gate represents entering peacefully, the Southern gate represents entering with richness, the Western gate represents entering with passion, and the Northern gate represents entering the mandala with aggression. But all of those ordinarily samsaric styles are transformed by the time a person actually enters into the mandala.

We could apply this same principle to how you personally enter the vajrayana path altogether. If you want to study the dharma, you have to go to a center somewhere to do that. For instance, you might go to a monastery or to a practice center, where there is already a mandala setup. You will not actually see a wall of flames and a palace with four gates, but psychologically you have to prepare yourself to enter such a situation. And as soon as you register for a program, you begin to manifest your own style. You might use a yielding or peaceful mentality, entering by the Eastern gate. You might use a quality of richness, entering by the Southern gate. You might enter with politeness and courtesy in the style of the Western gate. Or you might enter from the North, saying, "I have the right to be here." Entering a particular mandala of the teachings, no matter what its outer apparent form, presents the same issues as how you enter into the visualized mandalas of the divinities in vajrayana meditation practice.

# 28

# The Inner Mandala

*The inner mandala is based on working with or overcoming the
kleshas. But when we talk about overcoming the kleshas, we do
not mean throwing them out the window or getting rid of them.
Particularly in the vajrayana tradition, we do not get rid of anything, but we work with whatever arises and whatever we have.
We use such material as the kleshas; we work with them. The
kleshas are regarded as the fuel for attaining enlightenment.*

HAVING DISCUSSED the external or outer aspect of mandala,
now we can discuss the internal or inner mandala principle. In
the inner mandala, the five kleshas are transformed into five wisdoms.*
So in the inner mandala, we add our emotional life and the kleshas to
the world of perception that developed in the outer mandala. The inner
mandala includes the practice of transmuting the kleshas: consuming
the neurotic aspect of them, and transforming the rest into energy and
wisdom. This mandala is called the inner mandala, because it deals with
our emotional life as opposed to our perceptions, which are part of the
outer mandala.

---

* For a description of the wisdoms and kleshas, see chapter 26, "The Mandala of the
Five Buddha-Families."

## SACREDNESS AS THE BASIS FOR
## UNDERSTANDING INNER MANDALA

Holiness, or sacredness, is one of the main points of the inner mandala. It is important to recognize yourself as sacred. In the vajrayana, the idea is that things are sacred because, no matter what we experience by means of the ayatanas, dhatus, and mental contents, at the same time we begin to see that our world is uplifted.

One of the problems in realizing the mandala principle altogether is the feeling that we are divided or separated from sacredness, that we are not sacred anymore. It is very easy for this to happen if we have a theistic view. The samsaric world and our regular, ordinary, samsaric ayatanas and dhatus tend to bring us down into depression, unless we are given toys. We become depressed unless we can play with passion, aggression, ignorance, and all the other samsaric toys. Otherwise, we are like babies without toys, who always feel down; we cry when we are hungry or thirsty or when our diaper is full and wet. We react to all sorts of things in that way. If we regard ourselves as infants, we will find all sorts of ways to disregard the possibility of sacredness.

### The Idea of Sacredness

The root of the English word *sacred* is the Latin word *sacer*. *Sacer* refers to something that should not be trampled on or touched in a crude way. Although something sacred could be regarded as a regular, ordinary world phenomenon, *sacer* could also mean something secret or taboo. The idea is that those who do not know the secret should not touch it. The English word *holy* comes from the Anglo-Saxon *heilig*. Heilig is connected with health and with what is whole or wholesome. In English, we also speak of a *sanctum* or a place of sanctuary, which comes from the Latin word *sanctus*. The related Christian term *spiritus sanctus* means "holy spirit."

In the Tibetan tradition, the idea of "holiness" is the same as the "best." In fact, *tampa*, the Tibetan word for holy, means "best." Another word that is often used for best is *chok*. For instance, there is a phrase *choktu kyurpa*, which means "becoming the holiest of the holy, the best of the best, the supreme of the supreme." So like tampa, *chok* means the "best" or "excellent." Yet another word for holy is *pal. Pal* means "glory," which contains much more of a sense of richness.

## Te-kho-na-nyi: "That Itself, Alone"

The internal mandala is based on the vajrayana understanding of sacredness and holiness as a primordially or constantly uplifted situation. *Te-kho-na-nyi,* "that alone," is the attitude you need to develop in order to experience that sacredness. It is the ground of carrying out the transmutation of the neurotic aspect of the kleshas into wisdom.

*Te* means "that" or "this" or both, because at this point there is no distinction between "that" and "this." Therefore, *te* is almost like saying "it." One way of translating *te* is "that which is" or "this which is." *Kho* means the "other" or "that," *kho-na* makes it "that alone" or "only," and *nyi* means "itness" or "-ness"; so *te-kho-na-nyi* means "that itself, alone." The experience of "that itself" is the beginning of the inner mandala. So we might look at the discovery of the inner mandala in terms of the te-kho-na-nyi experience.

Out of "that itself" come the constituents of the inner mandala, which are the five skandhas, the five kleshas, and the five wisdoms. But in the inner mandala, the first flash is to perceive this situation as a one-shot deal, as one experience: te-kho-na-nyi, or "that itself." After that, there will be a second take on the whole thing; this second take works with the five wisdoms, in accordance with your nature, your possibilities, and your style. So you branch out after the first initial "that itself."

Te-kho-na-nyi can sometimes actually be translated as "you alone," meaning it is your own experience rather an experience shared with somebody else. Te-kho-na-nyi can also mean "only for the few." Te-kho-na-nyi is for the few because it is not necessarily public, in the sense that anybody who comes in the door will experience it. People first have to go through the process of realizing shamatha-vipashyana, tonglen, and all the rest of it. So it is only for the few, from that point of view. But as far as your own experience is concerned, it is only for you; it is for you alone.

We all experience such loneliness. I feel tremendously lonely myself. We cannot really come up with the ideal occupation that will entertain us completely. There is always some kind of gap where we have to experience a sense of loneliness. I feel that a lot, but I feel joyful, too, just being myself. You cannot expect one-hundred-percent hospitality anywhere at all. That is precisely the meaning of liberation or freedom: freedom from both the loneliness and the hospitality of the world. With that freedom, you begin to find a new strength, a new dimension. You do not have to lean to the right or the left anymore, but you could stand on your own two feet, or one foot, whatever you possess. The ability to do that comes completely out of practice.

## Using the Kleshas as the Fuel for Enlightenment

The inner mandala is based on working with or overcoming the kleshas. But when we talk about overcoming the kleshas, we do not mean throwing them out the window or getting rid of them. Particularly in the vajrayana tradition, we do not get rid of anything, but we work with whatever arises and whatever we have. We use such material as the kleshas; we work with them. The kleshas are regarded as the fuel for attaining enlightenment.

*Nyönmong*, the Tibetan word for klesha, means "drowsiness." *Nyön* is related to the word *nyal*, or "sleep"; *mong* makes it actually falling asleep, and can also mean "made stupid"; so *nyönmong* means "drowsy and made stupid." The five types of nyönmong or kleshas—passion, aggression, ignorance, jealousy, and pride—are the basic material or the firewood that we work with in understanding the inner mandala.*

Working with the kleshas means that, when you first come across a klesha, you do not abandon it. For that matter, you do not regard it as an obstacle or as problematic. Instead, you work with the mandala practice of the particular deity that has been given to you, as a way of relating to that klesha. You work with the deity and the deity's five wisdom possibilities. So through practice, you look at the kleshas and work with them. In doing so, it is not a question of the kleshas becoming the five wisdoms; it

---

* The list of primary *kleshas* can vary. In terms of the five buddha-families, Trungpa Rinpoche usually lists them as ignorance (buddha), aggression (vajra), pride (ratna), passion (padma), and jealousy (karma). In relation to the six realms of being they are anger (hell), greed (hungry ghosts), ignorance (animals), passion (humans), jealousy (jealous gods), and pride (god realm).

is a question of the kleshas being realized as the five wisdoms. There is a big difference between "becoming" and "being realized as."

In working with the mandala practice of the deity, you are relating very directly to the energies of the kleshas. You are experiencing this energy as sacredness, because that is so much what it is. There is a quality of "that itself alone" to the kleshas, so there is an experience of simplicity and directness in working with them. Because of that, there is tremendous richness in the world. You realize that the world is much bigger and richer than you had thought. In fact, the main point of working with the threefold mandala principle is to develop that sense of universality. The point is to have larger vision, a greater perspective.

You work with the kleshas through the practice of sadhanas and through visualizing vajrayana mandalas of all kinds. But it goes much deeper than that. When you practice, you begin to realize that you are not hanging on to one particular identity. You give up your personal identity as such. When you begin to give up the identity of "me-ness" or "I-ness" altogether, you realize that meeting with a guru, or with a deity such as a heruka or dakini, is no longer a big obstacle. It is a question of having a firm and unwavering state of mind while you are practicing—and the way that this will be established is by first practicing shamatha properly, practicing vipashyana properly, and practicing tonglen properly. By means of those practices, you begin to find that you have established your stability on the spot.

For beginning students, trying to use this understanding of the kleshas in your shamatha practice may be impractical. It is not possible to do so if you have not yet gone through the stages of vajrayana discipline properly and thoroughly. As a beginner, you may not be able to tell the difference between working with the kleshas and just being somewhat sloppy about getting back to the breath. So I think it would be better if you just stick with your breath.

There may also be some confusion about working with the kleshas in everyday life. It may feel possible to work with the kleshas in terms of shamatha and vipashyana while you are doing your sitting practice. On the meditation cushion, you are just sitting there, and whatever comes up is your stuff, your kleshas. So it may seem workable or straightforward. But it is not so straightforward in the world outside of the practice situation, particularly in relationships. When there are other people and you are working together and being together, there is a great deal of potential confusion. The passion, aggression, ignorance, jealousy, and pettiness are all in operation very strongly and energetically. So in everyday life, I would suggest that you sew your cushion to your pants, as it were.

## THE SACREDNESS OF THE BODY

The inner mandala also has to do with the sacredness of our personal physical body. Basically, our body has become a prominent reference point for our projections of sanity and insanity about ourselves. Particularly in the modern world, technology has provided every possible comfort for the body, which makes these projections more exaggerated and more painful in some sense.

### Viewing Pain, Pleasure, and Indifference as Sacred

In relating to the inner mandala, or the sacredness of the body, we experience pain, pleasure, and indifference in much the same way as we relate with enemies, friends, and neutrals in the outer mandala. That is, pain, pleasure, and indifference are also regarded as sacred, so we do not react so violently to our personal feelings about our body. The food we eat, the drinks we consume, the clothes we wear, the places where we sit or sleep—any experience that we might go through is sacred. Whether it is sexual ecstasy, complete torture, or an indifferent situation, whatever we go through could be regarded as sacred outlook. This tones down our sudden jumpiness in relating with our body.

In the Shambhala tradition, we talk about how in the confused world of the setting sun, we use pleasure as a drug to secure ourselves, which actually creates tremendous pain for us. We create pain in the various ways we have to take care of ourselves in the modern world, including our numerous diets, our invention of electric toothbrushes and hot water bottles, our use of drugs to soothe ourselves or to perk ourselves up, and all the rest of our improvisations.

A lot of our industry goes into taking care of the body, and a lot of neurosis comes out of that as well. Much more energy goes into taking care of our bodies than into building roads, bridges, or houses. In fact, we might say that seventy percent of all industry goes into taking care of the body. In turn, the possibility of actually doing so is quite hopeless. The more we try to take care of our body by means of this and that, the more we find that our body is deteriorating nevertheless, and becoming very spoiled from all that pampering. So the more we relate with our body, the more ways we find of experiencing discomfort that is disguised as pleasure.

## Prana, Nadi, and Bindu

When we remove that kind of passion, aggression, and ignorance in relating to our body, we begin to see the body as sacred. We see it as having possibilities of sacred outlook; we see it as the inner mandala. From the point of view of the inner mandala, the three constituents of the body are *prana, nadi,* and *bindu.*

PRANA. Prana is the circulation and breath. It is connected with gravity or with wind, with the wind of existence. Whenever we sweat or breathe or hiccup or burp or sneeze, whenever we inhale or exhale, we are fundamentally maintaining our existence. That is the basic idea of wind, the prana principle.

NADI. The nadi principle is connected with the channels in the body: the veins and arteries through which our blood circulates, as well as our lymph, muscular, and nervous systems, which provide communication from the top of our head to the soles of our feet. Nadis refer to the systems that relate and transmit messages constantly. If you put your finger on a hot plate, your brain picks that up. This kind of message and telecommunication system that goes through the body is called nadi.

BINDU. The bindu principle is connected with a basic essence. Your body is sustained by a kind of strength, a basic core that maintains health. Bindu sustains your existence by means of bringing prana and nadi together. You have the circulation; you have the channels through which the circulation passes; and you have the basic strength to maintain or sustain the circulation and keep it up-to-date in your body. Those are the three basic principles of the inner mandala.

Working with the three principles of prana, nadi, and bindu is regarded as one of the main points in practicing vajrayana, particularly in the study of yogic disciplines. We do not have to become too analytical or complicated about it. Prana, nadi, and bindu are the basic situation and mechanism of the body, and they are workable. You do not have to panic in order to maintain your body, nor do you have to become too easy and reject possibilities of maintaining your body. With the inner mandala, there is a sense of sacredness and respect for your body. Your body is regarded as being equally as sacred as the world outside.

## Taking Care of Your Body

The vajrayana directions for taking care of your body are to respect it and treat it well, but without going through the neurosis of pampering it. You could do this by wearing good clothes, performing ablutions, eating good food, and practicing meditation. Such things are all supposed to be good for the body. Similarly, the Buddha said in one of the sutras that eating food, sleeping, taking care of your body, and practicing meditation are all practices that glorify your body. He said that if the first three are in balance, then practicing a lot of meditation will not cause your body to deteriorate.

From this perspective, things like combing your hair properly or wearing perfume or makeup do not seem to be a problem. They are not regarded as marks of arrogance, but as expressions of authentic and genuine respect for your body. When you dress up, you are not dressing up for anybody else: you are dressing up and taking care of your body out of natural dignity. Because of that, you take care of your body. That is how you maintain sacred outlook.

## Preparing the Ground

To prepare the ground for working with the inner mandala, it is important to work with the ayatanas and dhatus, understand shamatha awareness and vipashyana tranquillity, and understand tonglen.

## The Ayatanas and Dhatus of the Outer Mandala

Natural possibilities of working with the body mandala, or inner mandala principle, arise because you have already worked with the outer mandala. If we were to discuss the inner mandala without your having understood the external mandala, you might find the discussion very difficult to understand. But with the help of your work with the ayatanas and dhatus of the outer mandala, you begin to find yourself able to work with the inner mandala in its own way. In fact, understanding all three mandalas is related with learning how to deal with the ayatanas and dhatus that go through your mind.

## Transforming Kleshas through Shamatha-Vipashyana

On top of that, it is also very helpful to understand the experiences of vipashyana awareness and shamatha tranquillity. Without that understanding, you will have difficulty in relating with or experiencing the five wisdoms.

All five wisdoms originate from the basic wisdom called dharma, and the definition of dharma is passionlessness. The opposites of dharma are grasping and holding oneself as more important than others. So in this teaching, we are reminded once again that not grasping comes from the hinayana practice of shamatha-vipashyana, and we are reminded that not holding oneself as more important than others comes from the mahayana practice of exchanging self for other. When you are so adaptable that you begin to realize that you could change places with other people, and that pain and pleasure could be exchanged, you will no longer have any difficulty understanding the universality of the five wisdom principles. So in order to understand vajrayana thoroughly and fully, both the hinayana and mahayana are extraordinarily important.

It is necessary to understand that shamatha and vipashyana are also vajrayana techniques. Even at the level of vajrayana, they play a key role. Through shamatha and vipashyana, you can realize the sacredness of the Buddha, the sacredness of the dharma, the sacredness of the sangha, and their indivisibility.

At that point, the kleshas could arise: you breathe that in. Then as you breathe out again, with the beginning of the out-breath, you surrender your holding on. So as the breath goes out, it is actually transforming the kleshas. At the end of the out-breath, the kleshas are being transformed into sacred world.

## Tonglen and Understanding the Pain of Others

In order to understand how to become a true tantrika and how to bring the three yanas together, you also have to understand tonglen and be willing to let go and give up your own desire to have a cozy experience. Hanging on to your personal heirlooms, by yourself, without sharing with others, is wicked. So the ability to understand others' pain, and the personal experience of letting go of your own pleasure and receiving others' pain, is extraordinarily important. The purpose of Buddhism altogether, and the reason why it is nontheistic, is that it enables us to thoroughly understand other people's pain. On the Buddhist path, we work for others in order to save them from the pain that comes from neurosis of all kinds.

On the basis of the hinayana and mahayana, we can understand and appreciate the regality and richness of the vajrayana very easily. If we had not heard of hinayana or mahayana, and simply jumped the gun and got into vajrayana, we would have a great deal of difficulty. Quite possibly we might not get it at all. So in studying the meaning of outer and inner mandala principles, you will understand much more about mandala and about vajrayana altogether by understanding that you first have to tame yourself by means of hinayana and help others by means of mahayana.

## 29

# *The Secret Mandala*

*The secret mandala is quite simple and straightforward: it is the idea of transmuting neurosis into wakefulness.*

## RELATING TO YOUR MIND
## AS A SACRED MANDALA

The third mandala principle is the secret mandala. The Sanskrit word for secret is *guhya,* and the Tibetan is *sangwa,* which means "secret" or "hidden."

The secret mandala is known as secret, not in the sense of top secret, but in the sense that you alone can understand it. So this mandala is not necessarily all that secret, or a trick of any kind. It is called "secret" because it is based on an individual's understanding of reality. Experiencing the secret mandala does not mean that you have actually developed or advanced from the outer mandala to the inner to the secret. It is more a question of preparing the ground and going through the depths of reality as a tantric practitioner, or a tantrika.

Basically, the secret mandala is based on relating to your mind as the mandala principle. Any kleshas that occur are regarded as the mandala of the five wisdoms. So if any emotionalism or sheer klesha state of mind arises, that is not regarded as either a problem or a promise, but as a source of wakefulness. It is regarded as a source of understanding the fourth abhisheka of *That*.* The secret mandala is quite simple and straightforward: it is the idea of transmuting neurosis into wakefulness.

When neurosis occurs, we begin to feel that it is putting us to sleep or making us deaf, dumb, and mute. But we can transcend that total stupidity altogether when we realize that there is wakefulness beyond the threshold of the doorway, beyond that twist. When we put our foot inside the doorway of the mandala, we begin to realize that there is an entirely different story, and we cannot help appreciating that. There is a quality of sacredness, and the sacredness of smell, sight, sound, and feelings begins to dawn. Once again, there is the fundamental principle of sacred outlook.

A mandala is a complete world, which possesses a center and a fringe, a beginning and an end. A mandala could be made up of master and servants, commander and troops, warlords and their machine guns, fountains with water, flowers with the seasons, winter with the snow, autumn with the harvest, spring with blossoms, hair with barbers, publishers with writers, equestrians with horsemanship and saddles, fishing with hooks and worms, taking a shower with dirt, shoemakers with feet, doctors with patients, dentists with teeth, and electricians with domestic conveniences. Many of these things are connected with the secret mandala and with the secret aspect of the guru principle.

In the secret mandala, the guru principle is experienced more intimately than the principle of te-kho-na-nyi in the inner mandala. The relationship between teacher and student is like that of a doctor and a patient: you are regarded as a patient, and the guru is referred to as the physician. In the inner mandala, te-kho-na-nyi is a kind of directness; but in the secret mandala, te-kho-na-nyi becomes warmth. The secret mandala is very personal. You are sharing the guru's heart, which is "that itself." The inner mandala may be impersonal, but the secret is very personal.

In some sense, the process of realizing the kleshas as wisdom is carried to its completion at the level of inner mandala. But there are various levels of fruition. It does not work quite like the ordinary Western concept of getting married, which is that once you get married, you are married forever. It is more a question of first being engaged, and then getting married. Using this analogy, the inner mandala is like being engaged, and the

---

* For a discussion of the four main abhishekas, see chapter 37, "The Four Main Abhishekas."

secret mandala is like getting married. So the secret mandala could be considered the fruition of the inner mandala.

This has to be so, for at the level of the secret mandala, there is no further need for working with the inner mandala. You have already done that, so at this point the inner mandala is no longer necessary. However, the outer mandala involves working with sentient beings, so you always need that. You cannot abandon that, unless you liberate the whole world. So you have to keep working with the outer mandala for the sake of sentient beings. The outer mandala goes on, always.

## Busting Secret Samsara

When you study the secret mandala, you also have to understand secret samsara at the same time. Secret samsara refers to your secret individualism. It is your not wanting to give up anything at all, unless it is in the name of pleasure or the glory of your own existence. With secret samsara, you experience pleasure if you have a little bit of money or a little bit of resources; and you feel glorious if you have even more money, which provides you with much more flair to magnetize the rest of your world to you. The teacher cannot let you keep your secret samsara, and then teach you the secret mandala on top of that, so you keep a double secret.

This description of secret samsara might make it sound as if everybody is being somewhat wicked—and from some point of view, you have been wicked. You have not wanted to give away your little corner of secretness that you have been holding on to so dearly. It is very precious to you. You hold your little Joe Schmidt treasure or your Jane Doe treasure. It is your secret treasure that you really do not want to give to anybody at all. You want to hold on to it. You always want to hold on to it, and you never want to give it away; you never want to reveal it.

With respect to the kyil and the khor principles that we discussed already, in the secret mandala the kyil is the guru principle, and the khor is the little secret you want to hide. In vajrayana, the role of the secret mandala is precisely and obviously to raid that secrecy. This might be regarded as an intrusion, but let it be an intrusion. Regard it as an uncompassionate way of busting your little stash. Let it be so; it is the case.

Having been busted, you are not put in prison, and you are not seen as a terrible person who has committed a major crime and has a long criminal record. Instead, once you are actually able to expose that little secret of yours and let go of it, you and your vajra master and your vajra brothers and sisters could share a feeling of pleasure and joy and a sense of humor. You could meet each other once more, and say to one another, "Hello, how do you do?"

In the secret mandala, you are relating to the teacher in a very intimate way. You are working with your hesitation and with holding back in those little, personal areas. Generally, you are holding on to that little piece of yourself that you think you are, and without which you feel that you are not anything. Even if it is something painful, you still hold on to some little corner of it. But you have to give that up; you have to offer it as a present. That seems to be the only way, and I have done it myself.

You might have one little secret or many little secrets; nonetheless, all those secrets have to go. Your secrets may have to do with hiding from your vulnerability, with the wish to boycott the pain of others, with all sorts of things. The way to give all that up would be to connect to your heart without any secrets, very simply. If you give up your secrets, you do not find any problems. In fact, you begin to realize that it costs you more to keep your little secrets. It costs a lot to try to maintain those secrets: You have to pay them little rents. You have to feed them, and you have to wash them and groom them. Keeping those little secrets is a source of inconvenience and financial drain. They become very demanding tenants. So when you feel hesitation come up, you could just give that hesitation away. You should not do so naively or with blind faith. You could do it with intelligent faith, because of the trust that has developed from your shamatha, vipashyana, and tonglen practice.

Giving up your secrets is like cleaning your mandala plate. When you establish or set up a physical mandala, you first clean the background.* This process is related with developing peacefulness and tranquillity. You relate to every part of the mandala as being innately good, clean, and pure. Out of that come the vajrayana possibilities of never giving in to your hesitation and never running away from reality. In the vajrayana, you

---

* In the vajrayana preliminary practice called mandala offering, students offer heaps of rice onto a plate, which symbolizes offering the entire universe. The first step of the practice is to wipe the plate clean. This sequence of cleaning and offering rice is repeated many times. For more on preliminary practices, see chapter 31, "The Four Preliminaries."

just stick with reality. When you experience difficulties, you do not just throw them into the dishwasher because you cannot cope with cleaning them up manually—you clean the mandala by hand. You do not give up on anything. You do not throw your neurosis and chaos into the dishwasher. Instead, you keep things very simple and very direct, and you take things step-by-step.

## The Bond between Student and Teacher

The secret mandala is connected with devotion to the teacher, the guru. In this case, the definition of the guru is someone who lives and sees with panoramic vision, someone who has the highest perspective on their students' state of being. The Tibetan term *lama* means the "one who holds the highest virtues of all," and the Sanskrit term *guru* implies the "one who carries the heaviest load of all." That load is put on the lama by the students, by their neurosis, so the lama could be regarded as the most dedicated and courageous porter. The guru is willing to carry the load for you that you cannot carry.

Such a guru is intimately connected with the secret mandala because they are willing to share your vision and your inadequacies completely. The guru is willing to carry you out and willing to see you through. If necessary, the guru will carry you out of samsara. Without the guru principle, the secret mandala does not mean anything. And as we go on further, we will continue to discuss the mutual bond that exists between student and teacher.

## The Mandala of the Buddhas

Because of your devotion, trust, and appreciation of what you have experienced already, you begin to realize an additional mandala: the mandala of the buddhas. This mandala actually extends over or permeates all the other mandalas. With the buddha mandala, you begin to experience sacredness everywhere. You could be too localized in experiencing the outer, inner, and secret mandalas without this connection to greater sacredness. But with the buddha mandala, there is an overall sense of the messages that you might receive in dealing with the threefold mandala. So with the mandala of the buddhas, you experience a pervasive sense of sacredness, whether it is connected with your outer, inner, or secret mandala.

At this point, you are including the adhishthana principle, the guru principle, and the principle of devotion. The reason you can actually let go into such a larger space is because of the buddha mandala, which is a combination of intense devotion and a slight pain in the heart. The experience of buddha mandala is somewhat painful and sad, but at the same time it brings out tremendous delightfulness. It is analogous to falling in love: when your lover's name is mentioned, you feel heartache, a slight hurt, but at the same time it is a pleasurable sensation.

When you have this pain, it is a feeling of empty heart. This empty-heartedness is different from an "Oy vey!" or complaining type of pain. It is not a pain of blame. Instead, it is the pain that comes out of hardship. It is amazement. You think, "Good heavens! For a long time, for a very long time—eternally!—I have been fooled by something or other. How come I am not fooled now?" You do not feel resentful, but you realize that you had become a professional samsaric person. And now suddenly, you have finally realized that you do not have to be that way. You do not have to carry that kind of burden anymore, so there is a sense of relief.

This is like finally falling in love. When you fall in love, your seeming incapability of falling in love suddenly changes into your being completely capable of falling in love. That provides a feeling of pain and delight at the same time, as well as a sense of relief, because there is no blame.

Ironically, such an experience always comes to you by driving all blames into yourself. Because you drive all blames into yourself rather than onto others, you begin to realize that *this* is the only problem—and *this* is very easy to pop. You have finally caught this nasty thing, and you can pop it. You do not have to chase after anybody else so they can try to pop it for you or with you. You have it with you right here and you can pop it, which is at once painful and pleasurable.

The heartfelt principle of the mandala of the buddhas is one of complete and total fullness. Because you are so full, you want to expand completely into your three worlds: your outer world, your body, and your state of mind. There is a respect for situations and experiences throughout. So for example, you do not step on or over teaching objects, such as texts or practice materials. You recognize that it is necessary to respect such seemingly small or insignificant principles. You learn to appreciate the sacredness and the magical aspect of those norms and admonitions.

## MAGIC AND SURPRISES

The magical aspect of vajrayana is not cheap magic—presto! Instead, in this case we are talking about something much more profound. Magic is the reason that you connect with the dharma or the vajrayana altogether. Encountering the vajrayana is a fundamentally magical situation. Meeting a teacher is also a magical situation: you would never, ever have expected to meet a teacher who communicated the truth. It is a magical situation that a teacher and a student come together. It is magical to be able to hear the teachings. If you reflect back many years to before you even heard these teachings, you realize that you would never have thought then that you would ever be doing such a thing. Finally, practice is a magical situation: you would never have thought that you would be practicing anything like this at all.

When you enter the vajrayana, all sorts of surprises come up. There are changes in your relationships and changes in your outlook on the phenomenal world. You begin to feel that you may actually be able to overpower the phenomenal world by means of complete understanding and total wakefulness.

You might think that this description of the vajrayana is somewhat tame and ordinary, but believe it or not, once you enter the vajrayana, there is no doubt that you will have all sorts of magical experiences. However, I am not saying that you should dwell on these experiences and try to make a great magician out of yourself. Instead, you should become a great practitioner, and save becoming a magician for later.

*Part Seven*

# PRELIMINARY PRACTICES

# 30

# The Four Reminders

*We practice the four reminders by having a greater sense of connection with the lineage, with the disciplines that are inspired by the lineage, and with our own discipline. Therefore, we begin to have devotion to the authentic guru, and we understand that studying with such an authentic guru is the only way that we can actually do these four practices properly, fully, and truly. We begin to realize that we are worthy people, and because we are worthy people, we find that our guru is also a worthy person.*

## RIPENING STUDENTS

In the vajrayana, we talk about students being ripened. We say that a student's potential to be free depends on their level of ripeness. From this point of view, every fruit has the potential of becoming ripe, but it is very tricky. Your level of ripeness depends on how long you have been sitting in the fruit basket. It depends on when you were picked off the tree: what season, what day, and what month. And it depends on what temperature you were stored at after you were separated from the branch of your tree in your particular orchard.

The ripening process is based on the pre-vajrayana disciplines of shamatha and vipashyana. It is based on practicing the two bodhichittas and tonglen. We have to go through that training fully and thoroughly, to transcend hesitation and be fully shinjanged. In fact, teachers of vajrayana usually recommend that students entering the vajrayana should be two-hundred-percent shinjanged; they say that one hundred percent is not good enough.

We have been told that such training is particularly important as we get further and further into the dark age, a time when there is less sacred outlook in the world, and there is no help in maintaining our sanity. When insanity reigns constantly and we have to overcome the external world's neurosis, a complete cleaning and sweeping process is necessary. Therefore, it has been recommended that we attain two-hundred-percent hinayana and two-hundred-percent, or even three-hundred-percent, mahayana. The degree to which we are properly prepared for vajrayana discipline determines whether we are workable or unworkable as vajra-yana students.

So workability is not based on whether we are Jewish or Gentile, or whether we are made out of ivory or plastic. It is based on how much we have actually attained through practice and study, and on how thoroughly we have been processed by the previous yanas. Whether you fill a bucket with water from a lake, a river, or a waterfall, it will make the same base for your stew. Likewise, as a vajrayana student, it does not particularly matter where you come from. What really matters is how much you have attained through practice and study.

We begin to become workable when we finally accept ourselves. We start by giving up our spiritual shopping and by taking refuge in the Bud-dha, the dharma, and the sangha. We begin by synchronizing our mind and body through shamatha-vipashyana, and by developing friendliness to ourselves. Having begun by paying attention to ourselves, we then find that others are also important. So in the mahayana, we develop com-passion by means of tonglen practice and by working with the lojong slogans. We relate to both relative and absolute truth, and we realize ultimate bodhichitta.

## RELATING WITH THE TEACHER

In our approach to the vajrayana, we also relate to both absolute and relative truth. We begin to relate with reality very literally and directly. In fact, at the early level of vajrayana practice, we do not try to provoke or invoke any form of magic. We simply humble ourselves, and the only way to humble ourselves is to have devotion to the teacher, to the guru. At this point, there are possibilities that our whole egotistic scheme could collapse.

As we progress to the next stage, we might begin to talk about how to relate with the world, but we first need to relate with what we have discovered from practicing ultimate and relative bodhichitta. We have to put ultimate and relative bodhichitta together; we need to become very pragmatic and practical.

When we enter the vajrayana, ideally we will have gone through such good training already that we will have run out of any resentments or doubts. We will have a solid understanding of the path, and be fairly certain that what we are doing is right. We may still feel that we are always stumbling and stuttering—there is always that kind of awkwardness happening—but at the same time, we begin to feel thankful and appreciative of the lineage. We are particularly appreciative of our own personal teacher, who has managed to bring us up, and who has had enough patience to watch us through our ups and downs, through our complaints and whatever else. So there is an appreciation of our teacher, our spiritual friend.

At this point, the teacher begins to become much more than purely a spiritual friend. We begin to appreciate their profound authority in the teaching situation, as well as their teaching style and skillful means. We begin to really appreciate the dharma that our teacher has taught us, and the upbringing that they have given us so far. We begin to feel very appreciative of all that. Therefore, we are ready to turn to the further extension of mahayana, which is tantrayana. But if there is no discovery of the root guru, a personal teacher with whom we can relate, entering the vajrayana is said to be like a blind man seeing the sun: it is impossible.

By the time we encounter the vajrayana, we have learned to appreciate the teachings as precious. We have understood that it is a unique situation to come across a teacher, and we realize how important it is to relate with a teacher who has both methodology and patience. Therefore, as we enter the vajrayana, in order to learn how to be humble we practice what is known as the four means of discipline, or the four reminders.

## REVERSING YOUR ATTITUDE

The Tibetan term for the four reminders is *lodok namshi. Lo* means "attitude," *dok* means "reversing," *namshi* means "all four"; so *lodok namshi* means "four ways of reversing one's attitude." *Dok* in particular refers to reversing your previous naiveté, your belief that you just happened to come across such a thing as Buddhism haphazardly, and that the reason you are practicing is purely by chance. With that point of view, there is no appreciation. But your encounter with the dharma is not purely by chance. Therefore, there is this practice of reversing that naiveté.

## Precious Human Birth

The first reminder is to realize that your precious human birth is free, well-favored, and difficult to find. The Tibetan for this is *taljor nyeka*. *Tal* means "free" or "having time," *jor* means "plentifulness" or "everything coinciding at the right time," *nye* means "finding," and *ka* means "difficult"; so *taljor nyeka* means "free and well-favored, difficult to find."

FREE. You are free because you are not subject to any handicaps. According to *The Jewel Ornament of Liberation*, being free means that you are not hampered by the eight unfavorable conditions, and therefore you are free to practice.* "Free" is the basic idea of how and why you are able to practice. Your physical body functions perfectly, and you have no obstacles to hearing and practicing the dharma.†

WELL-FAVORED. Along with being free, you are well-favored, which refers to the circumstances that brought you to the dharma. According to *The Jewel Ornament of Liberation*, there are ten positive circumstances.‡ We could add an eleventh, one extra: you are brought to the dharma because of the Chinese communist invasion of Tibet. So we should practice sending and taking for old Mao Tse-tung.

---

\* *The Jewel Ornament of Liberation* by Gampopa describes the *eight unfavorable conditions* as: (1) living in the hell realm, (2) the hungry ghost realm, or (3) the animal realm; (4) being a barbarian uninterested in spirituality, or (5) a long-life god attached to temporary happiness; (6) holding wrong views; (7) being born at a time when the Buddha is absent; and (8) being stupid and unable to express yourself. See Gampopa, *The Jewel Ornament of Liberation*, trans. Khenpo Konchog Gyaltsen (Ithaca, N.Y.: Snow Lion Publications, 1998).

† This should not be construed to mean that people with disabilities cannot practice the dharma. But at the same time, Tibetan pragmatism reminds us that real physical obstacles can arise at any time, making practice difficult. The point is to take advantage of our good circumstances while they last.

‡ The *ten positive circumstances* include five personal ones and five external ones. The five personal ones are: being human, being born in a country where one can meet holy persons, having all the senses, not reverting to evil deeds, and having devotion to the teachings. The five external circumstances are: that a Buddha has appeared in this world, that a Buddha has taught the dharma, that the dharma continues to be taught, that there are followers of the dharma, and that there is love and support from others.

DIFFICULT TO FIND. The basic point of the first reminder is that the reason you meet up with the dharma is by no means purely an accident. In a way, it is predetermined that you are encountering the dharma and you are able to practice it: each situation is brought about by a cause, in terms of cause and effect. At the same time, there is a quality of accident, in the sense that things just come together. This is what is called auspicious coincidence, or *tendrel*. You have the basic situation, which is not purely an accident, but somewhat predetermined; then, in order to light up that predetermined situation, you have a seeming accident. It is quite natural. If you buy a stove with a pilot light, when you turn on one of the burners and the flame goes up, it seems to be an accident. But the only reason you can turn on your stove is because there is a pilot light.

A free and well-favored human birth is very difficult to find. There are millions of people who have not had the unique opportunity of hearing and practicing the teachings, and actually being able to do so properly and thoroughly. You may try to jump over or avoid this portion or that portion of the discipline. Nonetheless, whether or not you are trying to bypass something, your opportunity is still magnificent and extraordinary.

One of the first things that anybody who practices the vajrayana should realize is how extremely unusual this situation is, how difficult it is for us to find, and how fortunate we are. We could discover the measure of our good fortune by looking back to before we even heard the vajrayana teachings. If we look back, we can see how well-trained we were in the practices of hinayana and mahayana. We can see that we have been well prepared. Because of such preparation, our situation is so good that now we are ready for the vajrayana. So we are appreciative of the whole path.

Appreciating our human birth is the first means of reversing the naiveté of our attitude of smugness or arrogance, thinking that since we have our free and well-favored human birth, we can just take our time. Earlier, in the presentation of the mahayana teachings, we spoke about the naiveté of *pagyang* as simple, carefree, or loose. That kind of naiveté is more path oriented. Here, naiveté is different altogether; it has possibilities of arrogance. Because we feel that our human situation is quite fine, we think that we can drink and have a good time instead of listening to the teachings. We take our human birth as a casual thing. Some people even say they are resentful that they were born. I heard a story about a young man who took his parents to court in order to sue them for giving birth to him. But in the case of the first reminder, it is completely the opposite: we are grateful for our human birth.

## Death and Impermanence

The second reminder is *chiwa mitakpa* in Tibetan. *Chiwa* means "death," *mi* is negation, or "not," and *takpa* means "permanence"; so *chiwa mitakpa* is "death and impermanence." Just because we have been able to get ourselves into such an unusual situation due to our previous karma and our own fortunate existence, we cannot simply take it easy. You cannot just relax and say, "Isn't it wonderful that I have a free and well-favored human birth? Now I can relax." But it is impossible to relax, because our fortunate situation might vanish. We could be struck by sudden death at any time. We could choke to death right now from laughing at this discussion.

For more than twenty years after I left Tibet, I had no news at all about my family. Then one day, I received the news that my mother, my brothers, and my sisters were alive and well. I heard that from a Tibetan gentleman who traveled to Tibet and then returned to the West. He had visited a place near my mother's village and learned that she was still alive. He also brought me a letter from one of the monks in my monastery, who said that everybody was alive and well. But when I read the letter, I thought, "This letter was written six months ago. Anything could have happened since then. Maybe my mother is no longer alive. Maybe all of them are dead."

That may be a gloomy way of looking at things, but when we begin to think of the preciousness of our good fortune, we should feel even more the importance of not losing that opportunity. When we handle diamond chips wrapped in a piece of paper, we are very careful not to let the paper pop up because we don't want the diamonds to jump into the rug and get lost. In the same way, we have to be very appreciative and careful of our precious human birth.

The situation is perfect now for you to practice, but anything could happen. You cannot relax in this situation. One phone call from someone or other, and your whole life could be turned upside down. Your situation may suddenly become unfree and un-well-favored. Anything could happen. You might make one visit to the doctor for a physical checkup, and they might have bad news for you: "You are going to die tonight or tomorrow or maybe next year." You might take one nice pleasure ride down the road, and you could meet with a bad driver and be finished on the spot. You could drop dead in the middle of your sentence.

During an early visit to California, I was in a car with my wife and child, the driver, and one other person. We were going to visit Alan Watts, and we were quite happily driving down the street.* In fact, we were talking about mindfulness. The driver was asking me about the four foundations of mindfulness, and suddenly there was a *boom!* Our car hit something. Apparently, while the driver was talking about mindfulness, he ran through a red light and crashed our car. For a few minutes I couldn't speak. My ribs had been completely fractured, all of them. I was going "Hoo hoo"; I couldn't breathe. And people were asking me, "Are you all right? Are you all right?" I could not even answer them. I was *not* all right.

Anything could happen. Such a pessimistic attitude is necessary and good—in fact, excellent. We do not want to lose this very precious situation that we have. We do not want to lose this wonderful opportunity. There are excellent descriptions of impermanence in *The Jewel Ornament of Liberation*, which are very helpful to study. The point is that death is always imminent. For that matter, change is always imminent. That is the second reflection practice, or chiwa mitakpa.

The second reminder is also connected with the mahayana dialectical studies of shunyata, and with the mahayana and vajrayana practices of realizing egolessness. We cannot cling to our ego all the time. Shunyata, or emptiness, means that there is no real substance to hang on to. Everything could be and would be and should be subject to decay and change.

The term for form, or existence, is *rupa* in Sanskrit and *suk* in Tibetan. The definition of *form* is something that is perishable; otherwise, you cannot have form. Everything is manufactured in one way or the other. Anything we see, anything we perceive in our entire world—including our own mind, space, and outer space as well—is a form. Forms accommodate each other; they exist by coexistence or by coincidence. By making reference points with each other, things begin to become suk, to become rupa. Things assemble themselves together, but then they decay; because they decay, therefore they can exist. In other words, anything that

---

* Alan Watts (1915–1973) was a pioneering and well-known popularizer of Buddhism and the Zen tradition. He was a prolific writer, and his books *The Way of Zen* and *Beat Zen, Square Zen, and Zen* brought an awareness of Zen to the larger public.

we perceive in our life, including thought patterns, is all subject to decay. There is no eternity of any kind.

The reality of impermanence is one of the strongest and most interesting arguments for the falsity of theism. According to nontheism, you cannot attain a state of eternity, and you cannot relax in so-called heaven. Whether things are modernized these days or not, you are still subject to decay. Theists say that you can attain eternal life: they say that first you are a regular noneternal person, and at death you are suddenly transformed and attain everlasting life. But nobody can change objects into space, or space into objects. Since accommodation and existence cannot be reversed—it has never happened—the theists' logic is wrong. They have forgotten the vision of impermanence and have become involved in a race to eternity. Such logic can be exposed by understanding the wisdom of impermanence. The wisdom of impermanence is the essence of the teachings, because it reveals the truth of egolessness and the truth of nontheism. It also allows the possibility of practice and the attainment of enlightenment.

## Karmic Cause and Effect

The third reminder is the appreciation of karma, or cause and effect, which in Tibetan is *le gyu dre*. *Le* is the Tibetan word for "action," *gyu* means "root" or "cause," and *dre* means "fruition"; so *le gyu dre* means the "cause and effect of actions." It is the understanding of the root and fruition of karmic possibilities.

We cannot avoid karma as long as we have continual thoughts and continual subconscious gossip. As long as we have a liking-and-disliking state of mind happening all the time, we cannot avoid karma at all. It is quite straightforward. The idea of karma is that virtuous actions, or good karma, produce good situations, which are somewhat predetermined; and bad actions, or bad karma, produce bad results, which are also predetermined. But at the same time, we can prevent sowing further seeds of karma altogether by realizing that there is a level where karmic seeds are *not* sown, which is the nonthought level. That is why we meditate. It has been said that sleeping, dreaming, and meditating, or developing awareness, are the only states in which we do not sow further seeds of karma.

The cause-and-effect mechanism of karma is very accurate and extremely precise. In fact, it is much more precise than our bank account.

Sometimes tellers or even bank managers make mistakes, but karma always provides tit for tat, constantly and naturally.

## The Torment of Samsara

The fourth reminder is realizing the torment of samsara, which is due to bad karmic situations. The Tibetan term for this is *khor-we nyemik.* *Khorwa* means "turning around," "circling," or "spinning around." It is a vicious circle—khorwa, khorwa, and khorwa. Replacing the *a* on the end of khorwa with an *e* makes it "of spinning around." *Nye* can mean "ill intention," "wrongdoing," or "bad planning." It also sometimes means "sin," but I prefer not to use that term, because it has theistic connotations of good and bad, which is somewhat misleading. *Mik* means "reflecting" or "conception." Altogether, *khor-we nyemik* could be translated as the "wrong purpose of samsara."

The torment of samsara is a natural situation, one which happens to us all the time. Whenever we engage in misconduct, we get direct feedback always. Even though the situation may be quite innocent and clear, and even though there are no problems, we suddenly begin to indulge in our habitual patterns or our kleshas. When we get into certain situations, we would like to have a so-called good time. Strangely, we might have a semi-good time, but after we indulge, we begin to be hit by all sorts of sudden neurotic attacks, or *döns;* we get hit by all sorts of punishments.

Such punishment results from violating the sacredness of the world. Appreciating the sacredness of the world is a fundamental point that I have been stressing in my presentation of the Shambhala teachings.* In the Buddhist tradition, although the texts do not quite say it directly, there is also the idea of sacred world. It is taught that you have to realize and respect that world.

Not only should you respect the world, but fundamentally and above all, you should respect karmic cause and effect as it is taught in hinayana, which is also very much applicable in the vajrayana. This process of karmic punishment is very direct and ordinary. It is the result of not taking care of ourselves properly. Appreciating our existence as human beings

---

* For more on the *Shambhala teachings* on the path of warriorship and the cultivation of enlightened society, see Chögyam Trungpa, *Shambhala: The Sacred Path of the Warrior* (Boston: Shambhala Publications, 2009).

is sometimes a hassle: eating properly can be a hassle, and even taking a shower may be a hassle. We sometimes forget to do those things. We begin to abuse our body and mind just to get a temporary kick out of something or other. But patterns of misbehavior of any kind will result in immediate feedback. Overindulgence always gives you feedback.

Beyond that, greater overindulgence in the samsaric world of passion, aggression, and ignorance always has the result of sending you down to the lower realms. You find yourself being scorched in the hell realm, hunger stricken in the hungry ghost realm, and made stupid in the animal realm. The hungry ghost realm and the hell realm are states of mind in which you are locked in certain situations and you cannot even get out. You are stuck in your particular vacuum. Because of your intense desire to maintain your habitual patterns, you replay your own cassette tape again and again.

This kind of realm is not necessarily a literal colony that has been set up and run by somebody. It is more that you are in a state of existence in which you are stuck, and you cannot come back to the human realm, or even the animal realm. Even the animal realm would be better, in some sense, but you are stuck in the hell realm or the realm of the hungry ghosts. I think some people might get a glimpse of those possibilities by taking psychedelic drugs: you find yourself locked in your mind, and you create your own world.

When you are stuck, you also find that your old friends are in that particular state of being stuck as well. You and your cronies are both stuck. You see each other, and you are stuck together in that state of blockage, very intensely replaying your trips, again and again. You could live in such a state for thousands of years, because you have missed the possibilities of practicing dharma, changing your karmic seeds, and not planting further karmic seeds in this life.

Once you begin to avoid any kind of discipline, once you neglect your discipline, once you begin to feel that practice and discipline do not need to be respected and that the command of your teacher does not need to be respected, you are blocked. It is like being in an eternal washing machine that cannot be opened by anybody.

In the hell realm, you are being scorched and cooked. You watch yourself being cooked and scorched, but you cannot even manage to faint. You cannot pass out for the very reason that you may no longer even have a body You are stuck with your own mind; it is a mental creation. If somebody is being highly tortured on the physical level, they will obviously pass out, faint, or collapse, which is a tremendous relief. But in this case, that is impossible. The hungry ghost level is similar: you have tremendous hunger and thirst, and nothing at all can satisfy you.

The result of samsaric torment is very real. We are talking about our immediate experience, our state of mind right now—and this state could continue after our death as well. It is shocking, isn't it?

## Appreciating the Teacher, the Teachings, and Your Own Worthiness

These four reminders, or four ways of reversing one's intention, are the beginning of the vajrayana teachings altogether. At this point, you have already gone through the preciousness and power of the hinayana and mahayana journeys, and now you are ready to hear and practice vajrayana. Therefore, devotion is very important.

In order to relate with your free and well-favored human birth, you have to appreciate your teacher. It is like inviting Einstein to America to teach science: you appreciate his brilliance. Likewise, you appreciate the teacher, who brought you the preciousness of dharma. You realize that the teacher is the spokesperson or author of the dharma. You appreciate your teacher further because of the teachings on impermanence, the consequences of karma, and the torment caused by the wrongdoings of the samsaric world. At this point, you are extremely careful because you understand karmic cause and effect, and you are still more careful because of the possibility of ending up in the blockage of the lower realms. You see that only the guru principle can save you from torment.

We practice the four reminders by having a greater sense of connection with the lineage, with the disciplines that are inspired by the lineage, and with our own discipline. Therefore, we begin to have devotion to the authentic guru, and we understand that studying with such an authentic guru is the only way that we can actually do these four practices properly, fully, and truly. We begin to realize that we are worthy people, and because we are worthy people, we find that our guru is also a worthy person.

The four reminders are the footing, or the ground level, of how the new student of vajrayana first begins to find their way into the mandala.

## 31

# The Four Preliminaries

*The four preliminary practices are very important, but you cannot practice them without first receiving an initial vajrayana transmission. They cannot be done before you have a complete theoretical understanding of the tantric path. You have to be aware of the consequences, because all four of these practices are actual tantric practices. Prostrations and the repetition of the refuge formula are tantric practice, the repetition of the Vajrasattva mantra is tantric practice, and the mandala offering is tantric practice.*

H AVING UNDERSTOOD the four reminders and the five vajrayana sayings, we go back once again to shamatha discipline. But in this case, it is a much more vigorous discipline than sitting on a cushion and simply working with your breath. Here the practitioner works quite hard on the ngöndro, or preliminary practices. *Ngön* means "before" or "front," and *dro* means "go"; so *ngöndro* means "that which goes before." So before you go into vajrayana practice altogether, you need to complete a series of preliminary practices, or ngöndro.

The four preliminary practices you need to complete are: 100,000 prostrations, 100,000 recitations of the refuge formula, 100,000 recitations of the Vajrasattva mantra, and 100,000 mandala offerings. Since each of these four is repeated 100,000 times, that makes 400,000 in all. In addition to

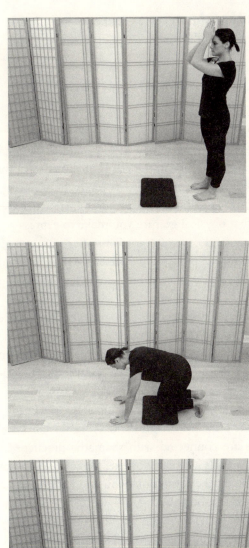

*An example of a student performing a full prostration.*

these four preliminary practices, as further preparation for the vajrayana the practitioner engages in the practice of devotion, or guru yoga.*

## PROSTRATIONS AND REFUGE

In the first preliminary practice, you offer prostrations 100,000 times, and as you do so, you repeat the refuge formula 100,000 times. In the vajrayana, in addition to taking refuge in the Buddha, the dharma, and the sangha, you also take refuge in the gurus of the lineage, the yidams, and the protectors of the dharma.

In Tibet, offering prostrations is a traditional practice. When you meet a teacher, the first physical gesture you make to express your dedication, devotion, respect, and commitment is to offer a prostration. It is also a way of introducing and presenting yourself. In the case of ngöndro, when you meet both the vajrayana teachings and the teacher, you offer 100,000 prostrations.

At the point that you begin ngöndro practice, you should already have a thorough understanding of hinayana and mahayana, and a preliminary idea of what visualization practice is all about. You should have some idea of the visualized deity or *samayasattva* and the blessing deity or jnana-sattva principles, and you should have the basic aspiration to connect with a yidam. You should also know something about the lineage you are joining and about the principle of abhisheka.

Prostrations are connected with shamatha practice. Like shamatha, offering prostrations is a repetitious exercise, and you always come back to the same spot. At the same time, you are dealing with any irritations that arise. You have a body and you have to relate with your body, the same as you relate with the breath. In prostration practice, you are trying to burn up the fuel of restlessness. Although prostrations do not exactly develop calmness, they are working toward calmness. So they are correlated with the shamatha discipline of making sure that there is a sense

---

* In describing the ngöndro, Trungpa Rinpoche here lists the four practices as prostrations, refuge formula recitation, Vajrasattva-mantra recitation, and mandala offering. He refers to guru yoga as an additional preliminary practice, as well as a continuing practice. At other times, he lists the four practices as prostrations (with refuge formula recitation), Vajrasattva-mantra recitation, mandala offering, and guru yoga.

of peace, harmony, and gentleness in us, because there is no arrogance and pride.

The reason we do prostrations at the beginning of ngöndro, as the first thing, is to make sure that our pot is not upside down. In order to receive something inside, we have to turn our pot right-side up. If our pot is upside down, it is because we are arrogant and full of ego reservations. We are trying to maintain ourselves, so we do not want to put anything of anybody else's inside. We are quite content with our emptiness, which is the wrong type of emptiness. So at this point, prostrations turn our pot right-side up 100,000 times.

We make sure we have the pot right-side up by reversing our arrogance and pride and by surrendering. We might feel we have worked hard to become good at something. We may have come up with all sorts of credentials to present to the teacher and the teachings. Nonetheless, we have to let those credentials go in order to receive the vajrayana teachings. So we prostrate 100,000 times to make sure we have our pot right-side up.

In prostration practice, you visualize the teachers of a particular lineage. It could be the lineage of the Gelukpas, the Sakyapas, the Kagyüpas, or the Nyingmapas. Some traditions have the lineage sitting on a tree, called a refuge tree; some traditions have the lineage sitting on big lotus petals; some traditions have the lineage sitting on clouds; and some traditions just have them sitting on each other's heads, one on top of the other. But whatever the visualization may be, the idea is to develop a sense of the guru and the lineage. You can witness your lineage, and you can surrender yourself to the lineage and its wisdom. Prostrations and the refuge formula, which take place together, make up 200,000 of the 400,000 things that you count when you do ngöndro.

In my tradition, you visualize the lineage in a refuge tree. The Kagyü lineage traditionally starts with Vajradhara at the top of the tree, representing the dharmakaya aspect of the guru. Below Vajradhara, you visualize all the teachers in the Kagyü lineage. You visualize yourself sitting in front of the refuge tree and prostrating to the lineage and to your teacher. When you visualize yourself sitting in front of the tree and prostrating to it, you are not visualizing in the sense of imagining, but you actually feel the presence of the gurus. They are right there, receiving

I take refuge in the glorious holy gurus—the kind root guru and
the lineage teachers.
I take refuge in the divine assembly of the mandala of yidams.
I take refuge in the buddhas, those who are victorious, virtuous,
and transcendent.
I take refuge in the holy dharma.
I take refuge in the noble sangha.
I take refuge in the assembly of dakas, dakinis, dharmapalas, and
protectors who possess the eye of wisdom.

—*Translated by the Vajravairochana Translation Committee
under the guidance of Chögyam Trungpa.*

*The Kagyü lineage refuge tree with the sixfold refuge formula.*

your prostrations. So the fundamental idea is to develop a feeling of the guru, and a feeling of the lineage of teachers and the teachings to which they belong.

A sense of your samaya vow should be present in your awareness of visualizing the refuge tree. The samaya vow is very important. A teacher cannot present such a practice as prostrations at the hinayana level or the mahayana level. When you do prostrations, it has to be *absolutely* mahayana, which means vajrayana. You need to have a feeling of the sacredness of the guru and an understanding of the samaya principle in connection with the guru. You need to have guru awareness, and recognize that the lineage is made out of heavy-handed people by the hundreds of dozens who are very powerful. Your root guru or your personal guru is heavy-handed and personal, and the other gurus have multiplied by the hundreds, so they are heavier and more powerful. As the generations go upward, your imagination expands.

## VAJRASATTVA MANTRA

The next preliminary practice is Vajrasattva mantra recitation. In Vajrasattva practice, you recite the one-hundred-syllable Vajrasattva mantra 100,000 times.* By doing so, you are purifying yourself by identifying with Vajrasattva, which is a very powerful thing to do. *Vajrasattva* means "indestructible being," and the deity Vajrasattva is associated with the dharmakaya and with purity.

As with prostrations, unless you know the basics of tantra, you cannot do this practice. In particular, with Vajrasattva mantra you should be very familiar with the ideas of purity and immovability.

In Vajrasattva practice, as you recite the mantra you visualize Vajrasattva emitting a milk-like amrita as the elixir of life and purity, which enters into your body and purifies your body as well as those of all sentient

---

* The *Vajrasattva mantra* is:

OM VAJRASATTVA SAMAYAM ANUPALAYA / VAJRASATTVATVENOPATISHTHA / DRIDHO ME BHAVA / SUTOSHYO ME BHAVA / SUPOSHYO ME BHAVA / ANURAKTO ME BHAVA / SARVA-SIDDHIM ME PRAYACCHA / SARVA-KARMASU CHA ME CHITTAM SHREYAH KURU HUM HA HA HA HOH BHAGAVAN / SARVA-TATHAGATA-VAJRA MA ME MUNCHA / VAJRI BHAVA MAHASAMAYASATTVA AH.

*Vajrasattva ("Indestructible Being").*

beings. So this practice involves not only the recitation of the mantra, but it also involves the visualization and your state of mind. Mantra practice occupies body, speech, and mind, all three of them at the same time. You do not have any spare parts left over, so you cannot occupy yourself with anything else. Your whole body, your whole being, is employed, so you do not have the time to reproduce bad karma at that point.

You do this second stage of ngöndro practice to acknowledge your shortcomings. Even if your pot is turned right-side up after the surrendering process of prostrations, it still might not be clean. Your pot might have some poison inside, so you might not be able to put anything into it, or cook food in it, or eat out of it. Therefore, you have to clean it properly.

In order to do that, the proper dish-washing process is needed. By reciting the Vajrasattva mantra, you take the attitude 100,000 times that you are basically and intrinsically pure. You do this by identifying yourself with the intrinsic goodness and purity of Vajrasattva himself and the Vajrasattva mantra altogether. You also develop the vipashyana quality of general awareness of the environment. You are completely aware of your blockages and your habitual tendencies and neuroses, and through this practice you look into all that. You realize that even having surrendered your arrogance and pride, you still have more cleaning up to do.

Purification plays a very important part in ngöndro. Such purification is not a question of how many mantra repetitions you do, but it is a question of continuity. When you take a shower, you do not ask how many water drops have to come along in order to clean your body. You do not regard the shower as a repetition of water drops, but just as a lot of water falling onto you. That is the approach. It is a question of volume, and of realizing that your body can be clean because you are basically not dirty. You may have temporary dirt and grease on your body because you have not washed for a while, but you can be as clean as the other people across the alleyway or next door.

## MANDALA OFFERING

The first three preliminaries (prostrations, reciting the refuge formula, and reciting the Vajrasattva mantra) were connected with what to refrain from: arrogance, personal neurosis, obscurations, and so forth. The remaining two preliminary practices are connected with what to

*A simple mandala offering plate with heaps of rice signifying Mount Meru
and the four continents.*

cultivate: the richness of the mandala-offering, and the devotion of guru
yoga.* These two practices are fundamentally a continuation of the previous disciplines.

When we refrain from arrogance, we witness the impurities existing
in us, and we begin to purify those problems. We discover our intrinsic
purity by means of the Vajrasattva mantra. However, the notion of purity
might leave us with some residue that we try to hold on to, which has to
be overcome. So there is still something to be cultivated. What needs to
be cultivated is further richness, the realization that we are capable of
giving offerings. So the next preliminary practice is the offering of the
mandala.

In mandala practice, you are giving offerings to the lineage and to the

---

* A discussion of *guru yoga* in the context of vajrayana preliminaries is found in the following chapter.

spiritual teacher or vajra master. By doing so, you begin to attain the two accumulations: relative and absolute. The relative accumulation is material wealth, and the absolute accumulation is the attainment of yeshe, the possibility of sanity.

In this preliminary practice, the mandala being offered is very simple. First you create a mandala in the form of heaps of rice on a round mandala-offering plate, representing the world; then you offer the mandala to the lineage, which is visualized in front of you. This way of depicting the world is quite ancient; the world is symbolized in the form of a central mountain called Mount Meru, which is surrounded by four continents.*

The idea is that such a mandala has a global quality, like Japan being in Southeast Asia and Europe being in the West. So you are not just offering your mandala as a goodwill token to your lineage, but you have to give up everything. You have to give up the outer mandala, which is the physical, geographical setup; the inner mandala, which is your physical body; and the secret mandala, which is your emotions. The whole thing has to be given up.

From the vajrayana perspective, you need to give your total world to the lineage, rather than a partial world. You need to be entirely generous. You might give up your last shirt and your last underpants to your guru, but that is not quite enough—you still have your body to give. The idea is that if you do not have any sense of the subtle world and subtle experience, if you have no identification with your yidam, then in the mandala offering you will just be giving a few of your things to somebody, rather than giving the entire world and exposing yourself completely.

The basic notion of mandala offering practice is to offer yourself completely to the lineage and to the spiritual friend or vajra master. This means you are offering even the offerer. You do not give with the hope that you will enjoy the elaborate gift you have made, or that you will enjoy any congratulations or thanks. You actually give the giver as well as the gift, so there is no one to receive thanks, no one to be appreciated, and no one to be congratulated for giving such a gift. That is a very important point. At the same time, there is still someone to count your mandala offerings on your mala. There is still rikpa, which could become both

---

* In a simple mandala offering, *Mount Meru* is represented by a central pile of rice, and the *four continents* are represented by piles of rice in the four cardinal directions.

more relaxed and critical. So you do not have to give up your comptroller, but your policy maker could be let go.

If you give a gift with something behind it, with an ulterior motive that you feel good about, then you are still planting habitual patterns in the back of your mind. You are not quite transcending conceptual mind, or lo. Therefore, you are once again accumulating conceptual seeds in your eighth consciousness, or alayavijnana. You are using the donations that you offer to your teachers as a part of your mental collection. But in the mandala offering, when you give gifts you should not expect anything in return. You simply give. Even in the hinayana or mahayana traditions, it is necessary that the style of your gift be an absolutely ideal one.

There is a Tibetan expression or slogan concerning this style of gift, which is *len tang nammin la rewa mepa*. *Len* means "answer" or "response," and refers to the reaction to your generosity, the fact that people will say, "Thank you so much for your gift. We appreciate it very much." *Len* is the response to your gift, *tang* means "and," *nammin* means "result" or "karmic consequence," and *la* means "for." *La* applies to both the response as well as the karmic consequence. *Rewa* means "hope," and *mepa* means "without." So altogether, *len tang nammin la rewa mepa* means "without hoping for responses or results." In other words, we are saying that generosity should be without hope of karmic consequences or good responses.

Having given something, you automatically hope to have a good karmic result. This result would happen organically in any case, but hoping for it is something else. Ideal generosity, the ideal gift, should be free from any such expectations. That is the idea of giving even on the hinayana or mahayana levels; and in the case of the mandala offering on the vajrayana level, it is much more so, because we are beginning to offer our ego as well.

At this point, we begin to find ourselves in no-man's-land. Once we have given the giver, we find ourselves floating in nowhere. We are hardly even able to witness whom we are giving to, because we have given ourselves away as well. As we previously discussed in the section on the five vajrayana sayings in chapter 16, we begin to discover insight free from mind, buddha without breath, meditation without thought but luminous, action without fixation or desire, and view without desire.

We begin to find ourselves in a situation where everything is translucent, and no claims can be made. We cannot say, "This is my deed; therefore I have a right to own it." This situation is much more extreme than the mahayana vows of egolessness, or even the idea of exchanging one-self for others. In this case, we are uprooting the whole thing, the giver as well as the gift. In exchanging ourselves for others, we might expect some kind of a good result to come out of it. But here we are uprooting that expectation as well. That is the idea of "giving" in the vajrayana sense.

Mandala offering is definitely a shamatha discipline. You are training your mind not to expect anything in return, but instead you are constantly giving, giving, giving. Therefore, this practice is very much related with the out-breath, much more so than any of the other ngöndro disciplines. This emphasis on the out-breath means a lot. In order to breathe out, we naturally have to breathe in, but we do not put any emphasis on the in-breath. Instead, we constantly go out again and again. By doing so, we discover natural dignity and richness. We see that we are intrinsically rich. We have basic richness because we are capable of giving lots of gifts, and we have a lot to give because we have nothing to lose. If we had anything to lose, we would have lost it already in the previous yanas and in the earlier parts of the discipline. So at this point, we have nothing left to lose. And because we have nothing to lose, we have lots to gain.

The four preliminary practices are very important, but you cannot practice them without first receiving an initial vajrayana transmission. They cannot be done before you have a complete theoretical understanding of the tantric path. You have to be aware of the consequences, because all four of these practices are actual tantric practices. Prostrations and the repetition of the refuge formula are tantric practice, the repetition of the Vajrasattva mantra is tantric practice, and the mandala offering is tantric practice.

# 32

# Guru Yoga

*Prostrations allow you to disembody or disarm your arrogance or your ego. Mantra practice allows you to experience your neuroses and to connect with a quality of purity. Having purified yourself, in the mandala offering you learn how to give further, to give everything. Finally you can actually mix your mind with the teacher's mind.*

H AVING COMPLETED the four preliminary practices, the next practice is guru yoga, or *la-me naljor*. *Lama* means "guru," *la-me* makes it "of guru," and *naljor* means "yoga"; so *la-me naljor* means "guru yoga."

Guru yoga is not exactly part of the ngöndro, as such. However, it is sometimes referred to as the fourth ngöndro discipline. Since reciting the refuge formula goes along with the prostration practice, it could be said that prostrations and the refuge formula recitation, the Vajrasattva mantra recitation, and the mandala offering are the first three preliminaries, and guru yoga is the fourth. Guru yoga discipline is more of an intermediary step to the actual practice of vajrayana discipline, but since it is referred to as a preliminary practice, it can be put in the category of ngöndro, which means "prelude."

Guru yoga definitely goes along with *lhakthong*, or vipashyana, discipline. It comes after mandala practice, because when we begin to offer everything fully and completely without expecting anything in return, not even thanks, we begin to experience faith, trust, and longing. We experience the validity of the teacher and the teachings, and we automatically begin to appreciate them.

Guru yoga practice itself is very simple. In the Kagyü tradition, once again we visualize the lineage, this time arrayed in a stack on top of our head, and we repeat a short mantra calling upon the lineage and the holder of the lineage; in the Kagyü lineage, this is the Gyalwa Karmapa. This short mantra is repeated 1,000,000 times.*

## THREEFOLD LOGIC OF DEVOTION

The practice of devotion is based on three elements: blessing (*chinlap*), changing your perception (*nangwa-gyur*), and nonthought (*tokpa gak*).

### *Chinlap: Blessing*

By practicing the guru yoga discipline, we realize that we are capable of receiving blessings, or chinlap. Earlier we defined the Tibetan term *chin* as "atmosphere," though it could also be defined as "intensity." It is the intensity of your devotion to the teacher, along with the atmosphere created by that devotion. The warmth of chin is like being in a very hot climate, such as India or Africa. In such a climate, not only do you find heat in the atmosphere, but even the furniture and the telephone and any other objects that you touch radiate heat. Everything is permeated with heat, so central heating is not needed. There is that kind of radiation or atmosphere.

With chinlap, you are engulfed in an atmosphere of intense devotion. With such devotion, you are like a little chick sitting under the large wings of an eagle. The eagle has large wings to stretch, so even if you are the ninth chick, the eagle's large wings still stretch over you and cover you. The nest may be big and you may be the farthest away of all the chicks, but still you are never left out.

I am not quite sure exactly what *adhishthana* literally means in Sanskrit, word by word, but I find that the Tibetan translation, *chinlap*, is quite close to the true meaning. The early Tibetan translators had quite a vivid understanding, because they practiced a lot in those days. So when

---

* In the Kaygü tradition, the short guru yoga mantra is KARMAPA KHYENNO ("Karmapa, hail!").

they translated *adhishthana* from Sanskrit to Tibetan, they translated as practitioners.*

## Nangwa-Gyur: Changing Your Perception

Chinlap is that which influences you, that which causes you to change your outlook. The Tibetan word for changing your outlook that applies here is quite a good one: *nangwa-gyur. Nangwa* means "perception" (*nang* means "what you see," and *wa* makes it a noun), and *gyur* means "changing"; so *nangwa-gyur* means "changing what you see" or "changing your perception."

Chinlap, or blessing, is what causes you to change your perception, and nangwa-gyur is the path of doing so.

## Tokpa Gak: Nonthought

The fruition of chinlap and nangwa-gyur is *tokpa gak. Tokpa* means "thoughts," and *gak* means "stop" or "cease to exist"; so *tokpa gak* means "thoughts cease."

So there are three things happening here: because of adhishthana, or chinlap, you change your perceptions, which is nangwa-gyur; and finally, nangwa-gyur causes you to stop your thoughts, which is tokpa gak. Nangwa-gyur stops samsaric motion altogether, which seems to be the essence of guru yoga discipline. When you begin to practice this discipline, there is tremendous longing for the guru's mind, devotion to the guru, and love for the guru. Your good connection to the guru brings about chinlap, which causes you to change your perceptions, so your thought patterns cease to exist in the ordinary sense. That is the basic notion of guru yoga.

Usually you feel quite confident that you can keep on going, but when you are practicing guru yoga and you begin to meditate on these teachings, you begin to find yourself running in a different direction. You find you are running backward, and then dissolving altogether. There is a gap. I

---

* The literal meaning of the Sanskrit term *adhishthana* is "standing over" or "resting upon."

do not know whether you would say that the gap is in your thoughts or in your consciousness, and it does not mean that you just black out, but your rational mind ceases to exist. It is not that you are stopping thoughts, but thoughts simply cease to function. There is a gap in your mind. We cannot even say that we are seeing through thoughts, which would mean that there is still a see-er. And it is not that somebody else is seeing through. It is just seeing through by itself. Therefore, the seeing sort of short-circuits itself. Many of the vajrayana songs of Marpa talk about space copulating with itself, or about flowers that blossom in the middle of nowhere, in space, or the dreams of a mute who cannot express anything. Images like that express this idea of the ceasing of thoughts.

Thoughts cease to exist; thoughts cease to happen. This is so, not because you are incapable of thinking or because you are forgetful, but simply because your practice is so direct. That directness allows your mind to flourish somewhat. But at the same time, because your mind flourishes, because it is given such freedom to move around, it does not know where to go. Therefore, it ceases to happen. So the ceasing of thoughts is a result of liberation. You feel that you are no longer constricted. You feel you can do anything you want, but at the same time you let yourself go. You do not know where to go; therefore, you cease to exist. You do not have anywhere to go, but that seems to be the only way that you can have a good time.

## UNITING WITH THE GURU

*Guru yoga* means "uniting with the guru" or "being one with the teacher." So how do you mix your mind together with the guru's mind? Having received transmission and identified yourself with the tantric path, you automatically develop an appreciation of the guru. Particularly the root guru or your personal guru is appreciated enormously. Your personal guru becomes the embodiment of all the buddhas in the world and beyond the world. You identify with the guru principle, and you receive any transmissions or abhishekas with that sense of identification. That is the actual mental process of receiving transmission. You identify with the guru as the spokesperson of your lineage. You visualize the guru sitting on your head, you eat food as an expression of the guru eating food, you speak as the expression of your guru speaking, you walk as the expression of the guru, and you work as the expression of your guru. So there is pervasive guru-awareness.

## THE GURU AND THE YIDAM

Having related with your guru as your object of devotion, you go through another stage of devotional practice when you receive abhisheka. You expand your devotion to the yidam, so that your yidam is also an object of devotion. If you have difficulty identifying with your yidam, you find that your guru is the closest thing to a yidam that you can relate with. In fact, since the guru gave you your yidam, the guru is the yidam, and the yidam is your guru. The yidam might be regarded as something transcendental and extraordinary, in the realm of the gods, but your guru's activities can be seen in the ordinary world. The guru is an actual physical, corporeal being who you can relate with as an expression of your yidam. So relating with the guru is the closest way to bring an awareness of your yidam.

Guru yoga is very important in vajrayana. It is not only the practice itself that is important, but there is enormous importance placed on samaya, or commitment. In samaya, the idea is that you are joined together with your guru and your yidam as one. You feel that the guru is no other than the yidam, and that the guru can grant you siddhis of all kinds. Guru yoga involves enormous devotion. You feel that the guru is the embodiment of all yidams and is the central figure of the mandala. It is that kind of awareness.

You might think that you are able to mix your mind with the guru's mind right at the beginning of the path, even at the first moment you meet the teacher. In some sense, you may have done that on an early level, maybe just on a metaphorical level or on the level of an example. Even seeing a photograph of the teacher might cause you to experience certain things of that nature. But the real thing, actually changing your perception, cannot happen until you have gone through all four ngöndro practices. Prostrations allow you to disembody or disarm your arrogance or your ego. Reciting the refuge formula and the Vajrasattva mantra practice allow you to experience your neuroses and to connect with a quality of purity. Having purified yourself, in the mandala offering you learn how to give further, to give everything. Finally you can actually mix your mind with the teacher's mind. Until you have gone through the whole ngöndro process, you cannot do the real thing absolutely ideally.

You might read books that make mixing your mind with the teacher's seem very easy. Even when you read this chapter on guru yoga, at first you might think such a thing would be simple to do. You might think that you could make the connection right away, but it is very difficult to do so personally, properly, and fully.

Mixing your mind with the teacher's is one of the merits and virtues of the ngöndro. These vajrayana preliminary disciplines all come from training your mind, naturally, and also from being willing to let go of habitual tendencies. To practice the ngöndro, you need to let go of lo, to let go of any fixation or holding back, as well as any holding forward or expectations.

*Part Eight*

# EMPOWERMENT

# 33

# *Transmission*

*When the teacher gives the student an empowerment, the student begins to realize and understand a total and utter feeling of authentic sacredness. The mind of the teacher and student meet together to appreciate authentic presence. Authentic means not being influenced by kleshas or second thoughts, and presence means that nothing is by innuendo, but everything is direct. So in an empowerment, there is direct communication between the student and the vajra master.*

I N O R D E R to get into vajrayana discipline, it is necessary to develop one-pointed devotion toward the vajra master. Along with that, it is necessary to receive a vajrayana empowerment from the vajra master, who is the embodiment of everything at that point. So there needs to be communication between the student and the teacher. In such an empowerment, the best of the student's ability and the best of the teacher's ability begin to communicate together. This communication is the source or the path of ultimate realization.

## PLAYFULNESS AND GENEROSITY

In order to relate with the vajrayana and with the vajrayana teacher, we could say that two things are necessary: a sense of humor, or playfulness, and being generous in offering one's body, speech, and mind. *Giving* can mean exchanging something in order to get something back, but *offering* is sacred in that when you offer, you do not expect to get anything back.

Offering is a psychological attitude as well: you do not expect to be complimented. For example, when you hear the dharma, you may ask a question and receive an answer. The microphones, used by you and the speaker, belong to nobody, but there is communication, nonetheless. The teachings are always there. You receive a teaching from the teacher, appropriate to your being, but there is no confirmation.

## TRANSMISSION IN THE THREE YANAS

The ideas of surrendering and of a mutual journey are connected with one of the fundamental teachings of the vajrayana, and of Buddhism altogether, which is known as transmission. Transmission means providing real understanding from one person to another. It is often referred to as a love affair: there is a mutual love, acceptance, and softness. The process of transmission has three levels: hinayana, mahayana, and vajrayana.

### Hinayana Transmission

The first level of transmission is hinayana transmission, which takes place by means of shamatha practice. If you had not experienced shamatha, you would have no idea that a transmission from teacher to student was possible. In the hinayana, you become humble. You are learning from a teacher, or elder, someone who is learned, thoroughly trained and disciplined. So in the beginning, you humble yourself, and then you begin to become appreciative, but somewhat fearful.

Studying with an elder is not exactly the same as dealing with a schoolmaster, but you begin to enjoy the practice of sitting with the teacher. You enjoy meditating together, listening to their teachings, and sharing a sense of humor with such a person. When the teacher teaches you, you develop respect and reverence.

### Mahayana Transmisison

At the mahayana stage, you begin to relate with the teacher as your spiritual friend. But this friend is not on the level of a buddy. In the mahayana, it becomes more joyful to learn from your teacher. You begin to learn how to relate with others, how to relate with yourself, and how to appreciate the world.

Mahayana transmission is nonconceptual—there is a slight quality of being "zapped." According to the traditional teaching, you are zapped six times by the six paramitas. You learn how to be open and generous, how to discipline yourself, how to be patient and control your aggression, how to develop exertion, how to control your subconscious gossip through the development of meditation, and how to read and hear the dharma, or teachings. You learn how to experience egolessness.

## Vajrayana Transmission

In vajrayana transmission, you learn how to give up everything totally, how to completely surrender your body, speech, and mind. You learn how to relate with the teacher, and you give in thoroughly and utterly. Giving in or surrendering means not holding back anything that you cherish: any personal pride, personal anger, personal jealousy, personal passion, personal ignorance or delusion. Once you let go of all that, you begin to feel a sense of relief and joy. It is as if you had taken off your heavy sweater in the hot sun of midsummer—you begin to feel coolness.

SPIRITUAL ORGASM. Giving in or giving up does not happen just because the student wants to give in on an intellectual level. Something else has to happen: as you give in, you have to have an orgasm, so to speak. That is, vajrayana transmission happens in one powerful shot. It is not a process of intellectual decision-making, but rather it is a kind of spiritual orgasm. This happens because of the student's relation with the vajra master; it certainly would not happen otherwise. In the process of giving in, it does not rain if the rain clouds don't gather. Or you might also say that the rain clouds don't gather if it does not rain. Intellectually, that does not seem logical, but on the level of experience, it makes sense. That is the orgasm.

The interesting point about orgasm, if I may say so, is that the experience happens now, but the realization of it comes later. When an orgasm happens, it shocks you. Whether you want it or not, it is a shocking thing. But it is pleasurable nonetheless. However, it makes you smile after it has occurred, not during. You may not understand what is happening right at the moment, but you do not have to understand. First the orgasm has to happen; then you will understand.

In some sense, an orgasm is very ordinary and not a big deal when it happens. It is intrinsic, built into you. Likewise, with this kind of spiritual orgasm, we do not put any new things into you. It happens by itself, because you have it intrinsically. The teacher makes a contribution, but essentially the teacher is just telling you about it and helping you to see what is there.

GIVING UP PRIDE AND RESERVATIONS. The vajrayana approach to relating with the teacher is like relating with an emperor. It is based on giving up our pride and our reservations. Without doing that, we cannot receive transmission. In the process of surrendering or giving in, we might feel that too much is being demanded of us. It may almost feel as if we are being raped. Personal pride and personal anger are extremely valuable to ordinary people. We are willing to pay lots of money in order to keep those so-called family heirlooms. But if we look closely at ourselves, we see that we are simply cherishing our pain. However, this is something you have to experience for yourself, rather than just hearing somebody tell you about it some kind of message.

## REMOVING YOUR GLASSES

All aspects of transmission occur due to finding the teacher and completely surrendering your body, speech, and mind and following that teacher's teaching. Without that connection, we cannot understand or experience reality. We were born wearing glasses, and we have never seen the real world: we have to take off those glasses in order to have true vision.

The idea of being born with glasses on is that we have been conditioned, right from the beginning, from the first time we took milk from our mothers. This leads to obscuration or bewilderment. We do not know where we are or who we are. Therefore, when we are born, we cry for the first time. We complain about the rest of the world and we do not, or rarely, smile. The idea of glasses is quite different from the concept of original sin, which would be more like having bad lenses in your eyes, which are a part of you. In this case, the glasses or obscurations can be removed.

## RESHAPING IRON WITH FIRE

After you receive vajrayana transmission, you may have to suffer or go through an arduous process of transformation, so devotion and respect for the teacher are very important and necessary. The process of transformation is like reshaping iron. When you want to reshape a piece of iron, you first have to put it into the fire, so that the blacksmith can use a hammer to reshape the iron while it is still hot. That might be a horrific analogy, but at the same time, it is a story of relief.

## ABHISHEKA: SPRINKLING AND POURING

A vajrayana empowerment is a kind of baptism or coronation. It is the coronation of the student as a would-be king or queen. The Sanskrit word for empowerment is *abhisheka*, which means "anointment." Specifically,

*Trungpa Rinpoche bestowing the Vajrayogini abhisheka.*

*abhisheka* means "sprinkle and pour": sprinkle means "to bless," and pour means "to accept the blessed substance into your system."

In an abhisheka ceremony, you are sprinkled and washed, with water poured from an abhisheka vase. In that way, you are included in the guru's world and in the world of the deity, which is saying the same thing in some sense. The idea of sprinkling and pouring water is similar to the practice of christening somebody in the Christian tradition: it is a form of purification. The Jewish practice of *mikvah* is a similar concept. In the mikvah, you are completely naked, and you get into holy water that has been blessed and provided for you. You are completely and thoroughly soaked in holy water.

In Tibetan, an abhisheka is referred to as a *wang*, which means "power" or "strength." The Tibetan word carries more weight than the Sanskrit; it goes beyond sprinkling and pouring. In the Tibetan tradition, when we say abhisheka, we are talking about performing an empowerment. This is slightly different from the Sanskrit meaning, but it does not contradict the original notion of abhisheka at all.

## THREE CONFIRMATIONS: WANG, LUNG, AND TRI

An abhisheka is one of three types of confirmation: *lung, wang,* and *tri.* The first one, *lung,* confirms that you have access to the powers of a particular abhisheka. The second one, *wang,* is the abhisheka itself, which means that you not only have access to powers, but you also have the potential to become a teacher yourself in the future. The third one, *tri,* is the detailed instructions on how to proceed. Ideally, you receive the lung first, so that there is a chance for someone to tell you how to conduct yourself in the wang. And after the wang, you receive the tri, or the instructions.

These three confirmations are very important. Usually what happens in a lung nowadays is that the teacher reads a book very fast and you just listen. People attending a lung bring their own little things to do: they could be doing handicrafts or crocheting or writing or typing or some other thing. So the students just sit there and the teacher does the whole thing. But the original idea was to listen and to try to make sense out of what you heard.

A lung is the first kind of confirmation. It confirms that you have possibilities, that you have the okay from the lineage, and that you have begun your approach towards tantra. Beyond that, you have to go through the abhisheka, or wang. Finally, having gone through the abhisheka, you receive further training in how properly to conduct yourself so that you do not miss the point of the abhisheka or initiation. So with the tri, you receive the actual practice instructions.

## BEING CONFIRMED AS ROYALTY

By the time you receive abhisheka, you have already begun to become a part of the royal family of vajrayana practitioners, as either a prince or a princess; and in the abhisheka ceremony itself, you are confirmed as a king or a queen. Royal in this case means victorious: you are victorious over the five skandhas and the five kleshas. That is the general abhisheka process.

## DRINKING THE SAMAYA OATH WATER

At the beginning of the ceremony, before you become a would-be monarch, you take a vow that you will not discuss the teachings you are receiving with people who have never experienced such a thing. You take the samaya vow by drinking what is known as the samaya oath water. This vow binds together the teacher and the student. If you violate your samaya vow, that oath water becomes poison or melted iron: it burns you from within and you die on the spot. But if you keep your vow and your discipline, the oath water acts to further propagate your sanity and your experience of the glory, brilliance, and dignity of the vajra world.

In an abhisheka you are bound by the samaya of the guru, yourself, and the deity. The samaya vow is a way to bind yourself to the tantric discipline and to the vajra master, or guru principle. If you go through an abhisheka ceremony without taking the samaya vow, it is just a blessing: it is just a confirmation on a light-handed level.

## RECEIVING A PRACTICE

When you receive abhisheka you begin to realize that your basic, intrinsic goodness could be manifested as the five buddha principles. As part of the abhisheka, you usually receive the transmission of a tantric *sadhana* or "practice." Each abhisheka and sadhana is connected with the mandala of a particular yidam, and sometimes with more than one yidam.

The Tibetan word for sadhana, or *druppa*,* also means "practice" or simply "being industrious." It means working along with the particular practice or technique that is given to you. A sadhana or druppa is a practice that binds together the world, oneself, and the mind. A person who practices a sadhana is known as a *sadhaka* in Sanskrit, or in Tibetan, a *druppapo*. (The *po* is added to *druppa* to make it "a person who is doing the druppa.")

## The Meeting of Minds

When the teacher gives the student an empowerment, the student begins to realize and understand a total and utter feeling of authentic sacredness. The mind of the teacher and student meet together to appreciate authentic presence. Authentic means not being influenced by kleshas or second thoughts, and presence means that nothing is by innuendo, but everything is direct. So in an empowerment, there is direct communication between the student and the vajra master.

An abhisheka is performed at the point when the student is ready and receptive. Before receiving abhisheka, students usually will have accomplished the four preliminary practices. They will have practiced guru yoga and attained a sense of devotion and commitment to the lineage and to the lineage holder. They will have made a commitment to their personal root guru: to a living teacher or vajra master. Having made such a connection, students receive confirmation of that in the form of an abhisheka. Such an abhisheka is performed by a vajra master and is received by students of the vajra sangha. It confirms students as being on the appropriate path in their relationship with the teacher and as being in the proper state of mind. That confirmation takes place by the meeting of two minds: the mind of the teacher and the mind of the student.

## Receiving Powers

Transmission could be regarded as a kind of coronation or enthronement. It is as if one monarch places a crown on your head and enthrones

---

* The most common Tibetan word for sadhana is *drup-thap*, which translates as "means for accomplishing"; it can also mean "group practice." *Druppa* is a less formal version of this term.

you as another monarch, so that you receive the power to rule a particular country. Transmission is like putting your finger in an electric socket: you get shocked. It is like the traditional story about Tilopa hitting Naropa on the cheek with his sandal.* It is quite mysterious.

Transmission is connected with particular kinds of power. Those powers are known as deities such as Vajrayogini or Chakrasamvara or Kalachakra, among others; however, they are not simply deities, or gods and goddesses, but principles of energy. They are embodiments of energy, power, and wisdom, and they contain intelligence, richness, passion, action, and stillness. When a teacher gives transmission to a student, the student receives those powers.

Having received transmission, you have to maintain that bond with both the teacher and that particular power. If you do not, you will wind up in a state of eternal pain. The bond with the teacher is so powerful that the pain of breaking it is much worse than the pain that comes from divorce or the pain of going to jail. So you have to think thrice about what you are getting into, and about what you are committing yourself to. Personally, I have committed myself to the vajrayana path, and I have never violated any of its principles.

The vajrayana is very powerful. You may be entering a realm of great joy, great pleasure, or you may be entering into great pain, depending on whether you practice it properly or not. It depends on you. You cannot put the blame on anybody else. There is no attorney to present your case, no court, and no judge. It is simple reality, like time: if you are late, you cannot sue time.

---

* It is said that after many arduous trials, Naropa attained realization the moment his teacher, Tilopa, hit him with his sandal. See Herbert Guenther, *The Life and Teachings of Naropa* (London: Oxford University Press, 1963) and Chögyam Trungpa, *Illusion's Game* (Boston: Shambhala Publications, 1994).

# 34

# *Surrendering*

*Fear, doubt, and feelings of inadequacy are all part of the abhisheka process, but when you experience them, they should be crushed on the spot. You can do so by means of the unified power that comes from the mandala and the vajra master being one. Together the mandala and the vajra master form a scepter of power, a vajra in your hand, and with that vajra, your uncertainty, fear, and resentment are crushed as obstacles to the path.*

## Relating with the Vajra Master

When you enter the vajrayana, you are expected to completely turn over all of your capital and every resource to the vajra master. Then the vajra master can actually edit your energy—some of it is bad, some of it is good—and proceed. It is as simple as that. You give every bit of energy to begin with. Then the teacher says, "Keep that as your capital, you'll need it later. Keep that as your interest payment." You may have read about Marpa the Translator, how Marpa wrote a little note for his student Milarepa and told him, "Don't open this note now, you'll need it later on when you encounter obstacles. So keep it."

Faith in the vajra master comes from the fact that the vajra master is capable of ransacking your kleshas. The vajra master has great accuracy, and they can actually be in touch with the energies of situations. You bring along your world to be with the vajra master and to study with them, and then at some point a meeting takes place.

The procedure of going through hinayana, mahayana, and vajrayana is necessary and important. First there is the hinayana elder level, then the mahayana spiritual-friend level, and finally you come to the vajra-master level. They somehow mix together, and before you know where you are, you begin to give all your secrets, everything, to the vajra master, although you did not mean to do such a thing at all. You ask to be accepted as a student of sadhana, as a tantrika.

At that level, something flips with a tremendous shock. You begin to realize that you have actually given up your seed syllable, which is "me," "my," and "I." In turn, although the vajra master does not want to do it or mean to do it, the vajra master begins to know your secrets, your seed syllable, your world, and your desires. The vajra master begins to develop wrath. In talking about the idea of the guru being wrathful, we have to be very clear that we are not involved with such notions as the wrath of God. The guru's wrathfulness is simply not being willing to buy your trip. There is no terror or horror involved, so *unreasonable* might be a better word than *wrathful*.

In relating to the vajra master, you have to take the right attitude. The vajra master is not devouring you right and left and becoming satiated with all your funny trips, but the vajra master is actually trying to help you. It is important to realize this; it is very obvious. You have to keep that in mind, rather than feeling that you are dealing with a monster whom you respect, which is a terrible idea! It is a very gentle thing, basically. The whole thing is absolutely gentle and very well-meaning.

## TRUST AND FEAR

You cannot become part of the vajrayana circle unless there is trust. In terms of abhisheka, you need to have complete, unshakable trust in the vajra master, as well as complete trust in your trust of the vajra master. That trust is based on some kind of fear; it is based on the fear of the vajra master and of the divinities of the vajra realm of whatever sadhana is presented to you. This fear is part of the natural awakening process of bodhichitta, but it is also a fear of your own inadequacies and shortcomings. Such fear is brought forth here very strikingly, very ordinarily, and absolutely directly.

You work through that fear; there is a progression. But you should not deceive yourself by thinking that everything is going to be okay. You have to stand on the edge; you are sitting on pins and needles in any case. You should not remake that into a comfortable philosophical statement that everything is going to be okay. Nevertheless, everything *is* going to be okay as long as you stand on the edge and sit on pins and needles at the same time. That is why there are different abhishekas, because you conquer one fear, and then there is another.

## THE GREAT EAST AND THE SETTING SUN

Fear is positive in the sense that it gives you more dignity, more aware- ness, and more sharpness. The mandala arises out of the setting sun of the West, out of death, out of the charnel ground. Around the mandala is the setting sun, the Occident, which is death, and the center of the man- dala is the Orient, which is enlightenment. One cannot exist without the other; you have to have both the setting sun and the rising sun.

In the center of the mandala, everything is birth, and on the edge of the mandala, everything is death. So if there is enough death-ground where the mandala is built, then there is enough birth taking place. *Occident* comes from the Latin word *occidere*, which means to "fall" or "go down," as in the sun going down. So the Occident is the area or the direction in which something falls down, and *Orient* simply means "rising."

The fear of the setting sun, of one's confusions and conflicting emo- tions, is a healthy situation. However, the fear of the death of one's ego is a very Occidental experience. We do everything we can to try to survive that death of ego. We adopt various psychological points of view, and we import all sorts of pretty teachers from the Orient to try to help us, so that our egos do not die. That is what is called spiritual materialism. The Occident, which is death, tries to borrow from the rising sun in every possible way that might enable it to survive.

In the vajrayana, we are not worried about the setting sun; we are actu- ally more worried about the rising sun. We might have problems working with the rising sun. We have to keep up with the possibilities of sanity, or the rising sun, all the time, so we might tend to feel inadequate.

## CRUSHING FEAR ON THE SPOT

The mandala principle is bounded by fear. There is no relief at all; there is energy and uncertainty. Yet that very fear is also known as the instrument of awakening. In the abhisheka ceremony, that fear is represented by the teacher holding a golden stick with which to open your eyes. It seems as if the teacher is going to put the golden stick through your eyes in order to open them. So there is some kind of fear.

But *fear* may not be such a good word. You could say *airiness* rather than *fear*. You have not actually seen the whole thing, but you are about to do so, so there is airiness, as if you have not quite landed on earth. There is that dot of waiting, the pins-and-needles feeling of something waiting for you elsewhere. But you are not particularly waiting for something else to happen; it's happened already. It is as if there is the possibility of being shot, but you have not actually made an enemy of anyone, so you never know where that shot could come from. It is that kind of airiness, which is not quite fear.

Airiness means that you feel you are already awake. You do not want to curl up, but you would like to stick your neck out. It is the dawn of a fresh, cold winter morning with icicles hanging outside, and you can't go back to sleep. It is as if a cosmic porcupine is about to roll onto you, which is a very delightful experience, actually. I have had it myself. You feel so awake and so good to begin with, which is fantastic—but on top of that, you never know. Something is actually happening somewhere, including below you, so you cannot actually say "Whew!" and relax.

Something is about to happen, but you are not trying to defeat it. There is a sense of reality somewhere, a sense of *Tai Tung*, the Great East. Great means that when you sit up, there is a quality of wakefulness and delight taking place, a feeling of being on pins and needles all the time throughout your life. It is very powerful, but there is no fight involved. East means that when you wake up, you assume your posture of wakefulness, sanity, and dignity beyond psychosomatic and neurotic problems. You hold your posture in any case. You need to have continual devotion, faith, and respect. You even have to make physical gestures of having such devotion; you have to hold your hands together and bow as an expression of your openness.*

The obstacle of fear manifests on all sorts of levels, in the form of diseases, colds, and sicknesses, as well as psychological depressions, but these manifestations can be crushed by the experience of the preparatory practices, or ngöndro. When such obstacles and doubts have been crushed, a student is able to receive abhisheka. Fear, doubt, and feelings of

---

* A reference to a traditional gesture of respect in which the hands are held together in front of the heart, as in the Western prayer position or in the Indian greeting of *namaste*.

inadequacy are all part of the abhisheka process, but when you experience them, they should be crushed on the spot. You can do so by means of the unified power that comes from the mandala and the vajra master being one. Together the mandala and the vajra master form a scepter of power, a vajra in your hand; and with that vajra, your uncertainty, fear, and resentment are crushed as obstacles to the path.

As a student approaches transmission, a lot of things begin to come out. There is so much happening in the minds of the students: there is so much longing, so much trying to reach, and so much trying to maintain. The students begin to regard the vajra master as the only vajra master, whether by power of suggestion, by personal understanding, or whatever else. They begin to form attitudes toward the vajra master, very fixed attitudes. They have all sorts of fixations, and all of them have to be popped like fat ticks. When you start to crush fear and other obstacles on the spot, it means that something has happened to you. You are suddenly so absolutely resentful about the whole thing that you cannot wait, or you cannot wait because you are so touched. Somebody has tickled your heart, and it creates either hate or love. It is tough, but those things have to be crushed.

Every tantric student has to fall in love with the vajra master fully and completely. Some love affairs are personal, and other love affairs are ways of trying to reach something. There is both push and pull: push is trying to reach, and pull is also trying to reach. The love for the vajra master occurs in different styles, and the idea is to pop all of these styles of fixation like ticks that are fattened by too much blood. Until those things are popped completely, you cannot receive transmission utterly and fully.

Having popped, there is further devotion and further love. It is like when you make love to someone, and the two of you have a mutual orgasm. When the vajra master meets with the student, it is the same kind of clicking. The manifestation of illusion has occurred already, so the joke is on you: on the vajra sangha and on the vajra master at the same time. A mutual orgasm takes place, and after that there is no problem. Love has already manifested; it is already apparent. The flower has already blossomed; the sun is already shining.

But we have to be very careful when we talk about illusion in the vajra-yana. We do not mean "illusion" in a pejorative sense; when we say that everything is illusion, we are talking on a complimentary level. Everything is real as illusion, which is good. Illusion refers to the goodness, softness, and transparency of everything.

When students have finished the four stages of ngöndro and are doing their guru yoga practice, their fixations have to be popped and crushed. As a result of that squashing, or that squashedness, they begin to find a new aroma, a new sense. A new feeling begins to dawn, which is a sense of the yidam. It is very real and personal, absolutely personal. When that energy of letting go has happened, it is possible to perform the abhisheka.

So in the vajrayana, everything is based on the idea of transmission, which basically has two levels. The first level of transmission is the idea of popping your previous reserves. When you have popped those, there is a quality of messiness and interaction. So the second level of transmission takes place at that point of interaction and messiness. That is when you are introduced to your own freshness and ordinariness; ordinary mind is introduced at that point.

## SHARING THE REALITY OF BUDDHA'S WORLD

The idea of abhisheka is to further bind you and your vajra master together. In abhisheka, you share the utmost sacred and secret of mandala possibilities or principles between you. It is as if the vajra master were you, and you were the vajra master. It is in that sense that the vajra master shows you the innermost secrets of everything. Namely, the vajra master shares with you their attitude toward form, speech, and mind.

In terms of form, you are shown the actual physical reality, or form, as the vajra master sees it. You are shown how the deities of the mandala see form. In terms of speech, you are shown speech as the vajra master uses it. You are shown how the incantation of words and symbolism can be uttered and experienced in the most powerful way. In terms of mind, you are shown how the mind of the vajra master works, and how the mind of the particular mandala setup feels.

While performing abhisheka, the vajra master is bestowing Buddha into the student's hand. The student is receiving Buddha in the palm of their hand completely. At that point, what the student actually experiences, sees, and feels becomes real, the utmost reality. The student is sharing the reality of the Buddha's world from the beginning to end. The world of Vajradhara is completely shared, completely experienced, and thoroughly felt. Abhisheka is the only way to convince you to experience the actual miracle that exists on the spot—this very experience, this very spot.

The discipline of abhisheka is connected with samaya bondage. In samaya, you are binding together your personal experience of reality, the experience of reality of the vajra master, and the experience of reality of the deities of the mandala. At that point, every possibility of help is given, and every wakening process is exercised and formed. So you have no other way of speaking but in a straightforward direction.

Abhisheka is further sunrise, further East, further dawn of Vajrasattva, further Tai Tung. Abhisheka enables you to be among the tathagatas and sugatas, the Victorious Ones, and their sons and daughters of the bodhisattva path. It enables you to join together the invincible powers that exist: the vajra, ratna, padma, karma, and buddha possibilities. That strength and way of conquering the universe can only be realized by receiving abhisheka. Without receiving abhisheka, there is no power. Without receiving abhisheka, studying the vajrayana is purely paying lip service.

Receiving abhisheka is proclaiming that in the future, you will be "So-and-So Tathagata," or "Lord of the Universe So-and-So." Those who receive abhisheka are the future candidates for being "Lord of the Universe" of the various buddha-families. Because these students are completely unified, and because they have given their complete devotion, understanding, and service to affirming the teacher's wish, therefore the will of vajrayana power has been fulfilled. In other words, receiving abhisheka means that you have become, finally and completely, one with the will of the vajrayana. You no longer exist as an independent little person, but you have become a part of the vajrayana altogether.

## Taking Pride in Vajra Training

In the same way, I myself always feel that I am no longer a person, no longer a human being at all. I realize that I am a subhuman being, a subindividual. I am the lowest of the lowest of the fleas, and I have the youngest flea's mentality. I do not exist. I am a mere vehicle. I possess the body of a human being in an Oriental form, and I have been able to receive the wisdom of the Great East. I use my existence here as nothing other than a vehicle of the dharma. Other than that, I am the lowest of the lowest beings. I cannot even add numbers well enough to be a good busboy. I could be the lowest of the lowest slaves of the universe, but at the same

*Khenpo Gangshar and Trungpa Rinpoche.*

time I rise up as the universal emperor. This is possible only because I possess the teachings; without them, I would be nothing.

I have been blessed, confirmed, and acknowledged as such a ruler purely because I am just a human being, not anything else. Being such a naive, basic, Tibetan highland peasant has provided me with lots of strength and power—just because I am so insignificant. I was called Abi by my mother before I was recognized as a tülku. I was just little Abi, a

tiny little person, a sweet little baby. Because of such a humble upbringing, because it was so delightfully simple and basic, Chökyi was able to
rise as the Ocean of Dharma. Because of that, I was worthy enough for
transmission to take place.*

My teachers were kind to me because I was so confused, and at the
same time, very smart. Because I was so confused, I was *more* smart. They
thought I was great because I was able to catch every angle. I was able to
defend every aspect of my life, and my teachers took advantage of every
defense mechanism I could bring up while I was studying and learning. I
was so smart and at the same time so stupid, defending every corner of
myself. Every one of my teachers, and especially the two main people
in my life—Jamgön Kongtrül of Shechen and Khenpo Gangshar—were
always able to catch me.† Whenever I came up with little spikes or sparks
of every possible way of making myself well-known and maintaining my
ego, they would throw a web or net of some kind over me. At the time
it was very miserable and painful. I felt that instead of such torture, why
didn't they just execute me on the spot? I requested them to do so many
times, but they said, "You will be more useful later on if we don't kill
you." It seemed sadistic, but it became true.

More recently, the Nalanda Translation Committee and I were working together, and I was very moved by the whole thing. I was able to
understand every sentence with heartfelt understanding. Every word that
we translated had very profound meaning to me. So I feel very moved and
appreciative of the savage and crude discipline that people like Jamgön
Kongtrül of Shechen, Khenpo Gangshar, my tutor Apho Karma, and all
the rest laid on me personally. They were very powerful and helpful to me.‡

I remember one time when I was doing my calligraphy, writing
Tibetan strokes, and I had a cut on my finger. My thumb was infected
and beginning to swell up because I had touched a naked, sharp knife
and cut myself. It was a very wet winter with snow falling outside all the
time, and I was practicing calligraphy with my sore thumb. Then in addi-

---

* One of Trungpa Rinpoche's names is Chökyi Gyatso, which means "Ocean of Dharma."
The name "Chögyam" is a contraction of Chökyi Gyatso.

† Khenpo Gangshar Wangpo (b. 1925) was one of Trungpa Rinpoche's primary teachers.
For more on Khenpo Gangshar and his teachings, see Khenchen Thrangu, *Vivid Awareness:
The Mind Instructions of Khenpo Gangshar* (Boston: Shambhala Publications, 2011).

‡ In his autobiography, *Born in Tibet*, Trungpa Rinpoche tells many stories of his strict
tutelage under the direction of Apho Karma and others.

tion, I touched the fire and burnt my middle finger so that I couldn't hold my bamboo quill. But I still had to practice calligraphy and hold the quill in my hand. I could not make the strokes properly. I was drawing two strokes that are known as *kum* and *she*. The *kum* stroke is a corner design, and *she* is a cut design, or a drawing down. I was unable to do those things properly, and I felt so stupid and clumsy. Actually, I felt more clumsy than stupid, with my hurt fingers and the winter so cold that the ink was beginning to freeze into a layer of ice that I had to dig into with my quill.

I was in my study trying to do all those strokes with my bamboo quill, and I felt so painfully inadequate. Not only inadequate, but I felt that since my tutors wanted me to do the strokes perfectly, why couldn't they choose another situation in which my thumb and middle finger were not hurt? But still they made me go on, and whenever I made a mistake, my tutor went *wham!* At one point he picked up the whole ink bottle and hit my head. The ink bottle was made of four carved snow lions holding a pot of solid silver, and it was very heavy. So the ink poured all over my face and the silver hurt me so badly that I couldn't even sleep that night or rest in order to draw my next calligraphy stroke. Such was the discipline I received, and that kind of discipline is very meaningful.

Nowadays, students do not have to go through that kind of individual discipline. For example, at our seminaries we have only general disciplinary guidelines, and even with that level of discipline, students can follow these guidelines or not. If students feel bad or depressed, they can always go to their bedroom. They know they are not supposed to, but they still can do that. Nobody is pushing them back, and nobody is hitting them with an ink bottle to make them do a stroke of calligraphy.

At this point, Westerners are babies. They receive all the best treatment everywhere. When they go to theistic teachers, they are fed with milk and sugar all the time. But you could tighten up your discipline. Fundamentally, you need to tighten up your mental discipline so that there is no room for doubt and no room for joking around with yourself. Everything has to be included. You need to tighten up the possibilities of poetic indulgence, psychological indulgence, humanistic indulgence, and the fixation on having a good time. Everything needs to be tightened up completely. That actually works, but you have to take it step-by-step as you go on.

I wanted to describe what I myself have gone through personally, because although it is not great, not fantastic, I think it is also adequate for you to go through. I want you to share that level of discipline. There is a lot of pride involved with such discipline. The pride we are talking about here is not chauvinism, but a positive arrogance. It is absolutely necessary to take pride in order to enable the vajrayana to continue in the West. In spite of the untrustworthy smiles of politicians, we could continue the vajrayana in this land. We must take pride so that transmission can take place in this land properly and fully. We must take pride so that some kind of real smile takes place here.

## 35

# *Entering the Vajra Mandala*

*The one and only binding factor that allows you to be so fortunate as to receive abhishekas at all is that you begin to realize that you are in the service of sentient beings. All the abhishekas develop because of this basic principle. . . . So in receiving abhisheka you no longer hold territory purely for yourself; your territory is completely gone. Your attachment to little personal pleasures has also disappeared. That is why what is known as enlightenment is possible—at last! Whew!*

### REQUESTING ABHISHEKA

After you do ngöndro, you can request abhisheka. But none of the abhishekas come automatically; it depends on the ripeness of the student. The abhisheka ceremony is usually given in one piece, and you request it when you are ready for all four parts of it.* Your worthiness to receive abhisheka is not a question of whether you should get the first part first, or the second part second. The question from the start is whether you are worthy to receive the fourth abhisheka. If you are worthy to receive the fourth abhisheka, then you might be invited to take all of them.

What makes you worthy is your understanding that you cannot solidify, or will not solidify, your experience into ordinary samsaric mind. It is

---

* The four main abhishekas are the outer abhisheka, the secret abhisheka, the prajna-jnana abhisheka, and the formless abhisheka or abhisheka of *That*. For a description, see chapter 37, "The Four Main Abhishekas."

your understanding that you will never use the experience of adhishthana that you receive from the guru as a way to solidify your ego. Guru yoga is very much a matter of surrendering, and it is also very much a matter of giving up your comfort. That is how your guru yoga experience is judged.

## GRADUAL PATH / SUDDEN ENLIGHTENMENT

In the abhisheka process, there is an element of sudden enlightenment, which goes pretty fast. But in order to express sudden enlightenment, you have to go slowly, which is very difficult. A teacher cannot just grab somebody off the street, pull them in the door, and say, "I'm going to give you abhisheka right away. Wake up!" It might work, but it might not. The person might think they have been mugged. So in an abhisheka, there is always the element of effort. The blessings are always there, always available, but you have to learn how to respond to them. That is the difficult part.

In an abhisheka, there is a need for devotion, but there is also the need for an appreciation of your own existence. If you have devotion, but feel that you are a bad person, this sort of self-torture might take a long time to clear up. Before receiving abhisheka, situations like that have to ripen properly. Eventually you begin to feel good about yourself, and you also feel good about the lineage, and the whole situation is somewhat hunky-dory. You begin to feel that everything is all right. At that point, you can sit down and relax, receive abhisheka, and have your fourth moment.

## JOINING THE VAJRA WORLD

In an abhisheka, students who are ready for vajrayana discipline or practice are empowered to enter into the world of the guru, or the guru mandala, and the mind of the student and the teacher begin to meet. At this point, the difference between the mind of the student and the mind of the teacher is that the mind of the student is still uncertain about whether they have actually heard the message, or whether they have really understood the abhisheka principle.

Once you have achieved a royal position, confirmed by abhisheka, then you obviously have to practice according to what you have been told. That is to say, you have to join the vajra mandala or vajra society. In this case, *mandala* means "society," and *vajra* means "indestructible"; so *vajra mandala* means "indestructible society" or "vajra world." The vajra world is a world in which the teacher and the students share one mind together. The Tibetan term for this is *tönkhor gongpa yerme*. *Tön* means "leader" or "teacher," *khor* means "disciples" or "retinue," *gongpa* means "mind," *yer* means "separation," and *me* means "without"; so *tönkhor gongpa yerme* means that the minds of the teacher and students, or master and servants, are unified completely and inseparably.

I should warn you: this does not mean that the student is going to become the teacher, or that the teacher is going to become the student. We are simply saying that the participants of the mandala are of one flavor: the teacher's mind and the students' minds are completely one-flavored. In other words, the attitude taken by the teacher is reflected in the students as well. Everything has equal qualities: the central deity, the teacher, and the student. That particular student could be a garbage collector or a minister in the highest ministry, but they still share that oneness in the wisdom of mahasukha, or great joy.

The idea of the mandala principle is that there is equality, but individuals have their own particular functions. For instance, in tantric sadhanas, we have doorkeepers on the fringes; we have deities of all kinds sitting in the East, South, West, and North; and finally we have the main deity in the middle—but nobody fights with one another. The whole setup is not based on assigned posts, but everything is psychologically fitting. The gauris are as sane as the central deity who presides in the middle of the mandala.

The mandala principle is very organic. In terms of the mandala of your body, your arms and your fingers would never fight to become your brain because they want more control over your body, your heart would never fight to be your brain, and your blood would never fight to become your liver. So your whole system operates very harmoniously. Likewise, people can feel attuned to their own place in the vajra mandala when they know their own nature. This does not necessarily mean that you have to stick to one place for the rest of your life, but you begin to feel the goodness of your own little mandala. Nothing is regarded as important or unimportant, but everything is based on what you can do on the spot.

That is the idea of enlightened society in a nutshell. In such a mandala, students or servants do not resent their situation, they do not get excited about their situation, and they do not get bored with their situation, because there is that sense of oneness. Therefore, people function in their appropriate places. If a person becomes a door, they are a door; if they become a column, they are a column; if they become a ceiling, they are a ceiling; if they become a floor, they are a floor. The floor does not resent the ceiling, the ceiling does not resent the columns, and the columns do not resent the doors. Everything has become harmonious in oneness or togetherness. Everyone functions in their own particular style, their own particular way. Everything has its own particular power. For instance, the mandala of garbage collectors is unique, and this mandala has its own power.

## SERVING SENTIENT BEINGS

The one and only binding factor that allows you to be so fortunate as to receive abhishekas at all is that you begin to realize you are in the service of sentient beings. All the abhishekas develop because of this basic principle. In the liturgies of the various abhishekas, you are encouraged to work with the rest of the world. Sometimes you might even receive the vajracharya abhisheka, which presents how to be a leader of the world. So in receiving abhisheka, you no longer hold territory purely for yourself; your territory is completely gone. Your attachment to little personal pleasures has also disappeared. That is why what is known as enlightenment is possible—at last! Whew!

The final enlightenment requires a lot of giving away of *this* and *that.* You have to give away *that* as opposed to *this;* give away *this* as opposed to *that;* give away *that* as opposed to *that;* and give away *this* as opposed to *this.* You might wonder, "If *this* is a certain way, how does *that* work in connection with *this?* If all of *this* is a certain way, how do we understand *this* and *that* put together? And if we were able to put *this* and *that* together, then how and why, for heaven's sake, would we be able to figure out who is who and what is what?" My explanation may seem to be a somewhat free interpretation; however, it is actually taken directly from the vajrayana texts.

As another example, consider this *doha* that I composed:*

---

* A *doha* is a traditional Tibetan poem that expresses awakened mind.

## WHAT THE BUDDHA TAUGHT

When *this* is beyond words,
How does *that* work?
How do we know *that* works,
If we don't understand what *this* is all about?
When we transcend *this* and *that* altogether,
How do we perform bodhisattva actions,
Which would seem to suggest having a full understanding
of *this* and *that* combined?
If *this* and *that* are simply mirage-like,
Pure conception alone,
How do we understand that *this* and *that* are in the state of
one taste?
How do we realize that they are coemergent?
Nonetheless, realizing *this* and *that* are one in every sense,
We begin to find vast space that has neither beginning
nor end.
Hey ho!
Why don't we come together in that particular state,
Which is free from *that* and *this*?
Let us experience the ultimate joy, which transcends any
petty joy.
Let us think bigger.
Let us develop greater vision,
Which consists of a mixture of intense blue and vermilion
red.
Let us sing and dance.

See if you can make heads or tails out of that!

## 36

# Stability, Luminosity, and Joy

*When you receive abhisheka, it is not so much that you are relaxing, but that your mind is relaxing with the mind of the vajra master and the mind of the lineage altogether. . . . There is a sense that the ordinary hang-ups of the phenomenal world, which are heavy and painful, begin to dissolve. They are no longer dragging you down, and because there is no fixation or feeling of being imprisoned, you are uplifted. You are not completely blissed-out, but you feel somewhat lighter. Your dirt and your obscurations have been removed.*

## JOINING SHAMATHA AND VIPASHYANA

Throughout the path, shamatha discipline produces one kind of experience, and the vipashyana experience furthers that particular situation. For instance, the shamatha aspect of mandala offering brings about the vipashyana aspect of guru yoga. So all along the way, you alternate shamatha and vipashyana, the development of steadiness and awareness.

Steadiness is the way to be on the spot thoroughly and fully, as much as possible. It is developed by means of vajrayana techniques, such as mandala-offering practice. So shamatha is the skillful means, the discipline; and that type of discipline tends to bring about the vipashyana aspect of vajrayana practice. It brings greater awareness, devotion, and longing for the teacher. Through vipashyana, you unify your emotions with your appreciation of the teacher.

That union, or bringing together of the teacher and yourself, makes it possible for you to work together. It is the experience of tokpa gak, the cessation or stopping of thoughts. By stopping thoughts, we are not talking about becoming zombies. You have to be quite careful about that. We cut conceptualization, but the natural, functioning mind and general awareness still goes on continuously. In fact, it is cultivated further by the vipashyana experience. Later on, it becomes the upaya of the vajrayana disciplines as well. So that particular aspect of mind could be sharpened. There is never a need for conceptual thinking. Nobody needs it. It is absolutely unnecessary because it produces pain and the unnecessary fortification of ego. That is what conceptual mind is for: to build your ego fortification. It is for "me," for "I." It is about how to be "I," how to build "myself" up—and that is not necessary. There could be a world without "I."

## STABILITY AND LUMINOSITY

The abhisheka experience is a combination of shamatha and vipashyana put together completely. At the point when you receive abhisheka, you do not have any separation of those two at all. When you begin to share your reality with the vajra master, when you begin to enter into the vajra master's world, your experience becomes very dynamic, direct, and basic. You have the solidness and stability of shamatha, and at the same time you are not completely solidified in hanging on to your ego. Therefore, an expansion of vision takes place on the level of *prabhasvara,* or luminosity. That luminous quality goes along with your vipashyana practice. So things become bright and luminous, and at the same time they are very steady, direct, and simple.

These abhisheka principles are very much connected with transforming your ordinary mind and your ordinary concepts into another form of ordinary concept. When you see, hear, or think about things, your first glimpse might be extraordinary; you might hear something extraordinary or you might think something extraordinary. But when you go beyond that, when you do a double take, you begin to realize that things are not so extraordinary after all. That comes as a kind of relief. It is not a relief because there have been any misunderstandings or problems, but rather because a fundamental relaxation or fundamental freedom takes place. Finally, you can relax.

However, when you receive abhisheka, it is not so much that you are relaxing, but that your mind is relaxing with the mind of the vajra master and the mind of the lineage altogether. Your mind is relaxed with the minds of Tilopa, Naropa, Marpa, Milarepa, and all the rest of the lineage teachers, including the Buddha and Vajradhara as well. There is a sense that the ordinary hang-ups of the phenomenal world, which are heavy and painful, begin to dissolve. They are no longer dragging you down, and because there is no fixation or feeling of being imprisoned, you are uplifted. You are not completely blissed-out, but you feel somewhat lighter. Your dirt and your obscurations have been removed.

At this point, you begin to realize that the inanimate and animate worlds could be seen as the living mandala principle on the spot. In other words, that situation is no longer mythical; it has become very real and very direct. Abhisheka is the first entrance into the world of the yidams and the world of the guru's mind altogether. It is the point at which we have finally joined the shamatha and vipashyana principles together. That is the way we are able to receive abhisheka fully and thoroughly.

Luminosity is vipashyana, and steadiness is shamatha. This combination of shamatha and vipashyana shows up in Tibetan terms such as *nangtong,* or "appearance-emptiness," in which the *tong,* or emptiness part, is shamatha, and the *nang,* or appearance part, is vipashyana. It shows up in the term *traktong,* or "sound-emptiness," in which the *trak,* or sound part, is vipashyana, and the *tong* part is shamatha. Shamatha is an expression of emptiness, and vipashyana is an expression of luminosity. Shamatha is overcoming complications, which is a kind of cessation or negation, while vipashyana is something positive and vast. Vipashyana is the absence of fixation; it is that which sees egolessness. It is postmeditative awareness.

In the vajrayana, it is said that skillful means come out of luminosity, which is considered to be synonymous with compassion. So prajna and shunyata develop into compassion and skillful means; that is the combination of shamatha and vipashyana on the highest level. Shamatha and vipashyana produce each other automatically. If you have a feeling of tremendous space, that automatically bring a sense of detail, and the unity of the two is the abhisheka itself. You cannot have Vajradhara without shamatha and vipashyana.

## WORKING WITH THE TRIKAYA PRINCIPLE

The combination of shamatha and vipashyana is also connected with the trikaya principle. The practice of shamatha brings the dharmakaya, and the practice of vipashyana brings sambhogakaya and nirmanakaya.

Broken down that way, the three kayas are sometimes known as the two kayas: the formless kaya and the form kayas.

It is interesting that at the beginning of the path, we think we are working on a very crude level when we do shamatha practice: we just learn how to breathe, how to stop our thoughts, and things like that. It seems to be quite a primitive level, but in fact we are actually working with the dharmakaya, or with potential dharmakaya, which is very advanced. The dharmakaya is a very high level, particularly from the vajrayana point of view. It is jnana-dharmakaya, the wisdom aspect altogether.

So first we have to manifest dharmakaya, and after that there are the postmeditation experiences or awareness practices, the sambhogakaya and nirmanakaya principles. We have to rescue the pure strictness of shamatha by relating with our day-to-day living situation through vipashyana experiences, which are luminous and bright.

## RELATIVE TRUTH AS THE DANCING GROUND OF GREAT JOY

Receiving abhisheka depends largely on the students and their motivation, as well as on the vajra master's willingness and friendship with the students. Between the two, they provide the abhisheka situation by inviting the wisdom deity, or *jnanasattva*, to confirm the deity as visualized by the student, or *samayasattva*. The jnanasattva and vajra master are somewhat linked; they are in league together. For the student, on the other hand, there is the potential for the jnanasattva, as well as the actual experience of samayasattva, as far as the tantric logic of kündzop is concerned.*

In the vajrayana, kündzop brings a further experience of great bliss. The ordinary kündzop of the hinayana level or the mahayana level simply refers to the factual phenomenal world. That is *yang-dak-pe kündzop*, or pure kündzop. But in the vajrayana, kündzop is seen as the potential dancing ground of great joy, or mahasukha. The Tibetan word for great joy is *dewa chenpo yi yeshe*. *Dewa* means "joy," *chenpo* means "great," "grand,"

---

* The references to jnanasattva and samayasattva have to do with the practice of visualization, and the relationship of the vajra master and student to the sambhogakaya deities, or yidams. For a discussion of visualization practice, see chapter 38, "Visualization and Sadhana Practice."

or "big," the *yi* makes it possessive, and *yeshe* means "wisdom"; so *dewa chenpo yi yeshe* is the "wisdom of great bliss." That is the object as well as the subject of abhisheka.

That experience of yeshe would be realized, or experienced, in a body that is a result of karmic cause and effect—a leftover. But you do not have to hang on to that solid concept of body. That concept might have been resolved a long time ago. That is why in the vajrayana we can have sacred objects, and why we can be blessed. That is why we can have abhishekas like the vase abhisheka. The abhisheka vase is made out of actual metal, and we can drink the actual water. Objects like that vase are made by silversmiths. They are not the result of hardship; they are the result of freedom.

By going through the process of ngöndro, you develop devotion. When you have already accomplished complete devotion to the vajra master, without fear and without doubt, you are ready for abhisheka. At that point, as a student of vajrayana, you begin to experience that your vajra master is not just your lover, not just your schoolmaster, not purely a dictatorial leader, not purely a simple king, and not simply a professor. Instead, the vajra master is seen as a unique and extraordinary person, the guide who leads you on this journey.

You see that the vajra master is a great teacher who has power over their students. If you are no longer willing to ransack your root kle-shas—your passion, aggression, and ignorance—the vajra master does it for you. The vajra master minds your business very thoroughly. With that kind of confidence and dignity, the vajra master can actually bring down the jnanasattva and join it with the samayasattva, and so make you, the student, a worthwhile person.

The vajra master joins heaven and earth to establish human society, to establish the vajra world. The jnanasattva, or heaven, and the sama-yasattva, or earth, are joined together, which makes a perfect human. The vajra master is the person who can actually do that for you. We could say that the wisdom of great bliss can be brought out because the jnanasattva principle already exists in the student's mind. That is to say, vajra nature is in everyone. Everyone has fear and wisdom and precision. Outrageous-ness as well as insight exists in everyone. Whether or not you are exposed to that kind of vajra world, it is still possible to experience wisdom. So the wisdom of great bliss could be awakened anytime.

## Two Levels of Great Joy

There are two levels of great joy: the mahasukha of example, and the mahasukha of reality.

### Mahasukha of Example

The first level of great joy is the mahasukha of example. It is the reference point, or the flint stone that sparks the fire. Intrinsically and fundamentally, great joy means a state of mind that is without doubt or fear, a state of mind that experiences total love. Love here means rejoicing. It is ghastly, completely exasperated rejoicing. With this kind of rejoicing, there is a feeling of being intrinsically gay and festive. When you open a door and look down a narrow, dark hall, you don't feel depressed, but you feel delighted: "Ha ha! There's a narrow, dark hallway!" When you see a pile of shit on your plate, you don't say, "Yuck," but you think, "Why not?" And when you see a beautiful flower or bright green grass, you take the same attitude, which is very easy to do. There is a feeling of total and absolute celebration, and there is also a sense of humor. You can smile at your own depression with tremendous genuineness.

### Mahasukha of Reality

The second level of great joy is the mahasukha of reality, the actual, real mahasukha that occurs when you cut your thoughts. Usually you do not want to cut your thoughts. You feel so wrapped up in them, and you enjoy indulging in your neuroses and making love to them. Even though that is shitty and smelly, it is what you always do.

That kind of indulgence in depression can be overcome by a feeling of sadness and loneliness. Sadness is the recognition that you are the only person who can actually experience your own world, which is fine. It could be ego-centered, but it is still basically fine. And loneliness is finding that you are your only companion, apart from your vajra master. This loneliness is a very intrinsic loneliness, because you have no way to express your emotions. You experience the nonexistence of emotionality, and you begin to feel very empty, ghastly, completely ransacked. But some kind of energy is still taking place. It is very simple.

Then, having realized your loneliness, there is an element of being intrinsically tickled by that very notion. If you take your loneliness with a vajrayana sense of humor, which is like having salt and pepper with your meal, then you begin to feel that it could become delightful. You begin to see trees, water, mountains, snowfall, raindrops, highways, your apartment and kitchen stove—everything—in that way. Those things make you lonely, but that loneliness is titillating. It is sad and happy put together, somewhat. At least you have found a companion. You never know where the loneliness is coming from, but there is some kind of companionship taking place there, which actually cheers you up. That experience makes you smile to yourself; you do not need an audience. There is depression, then suddenly there is [*snaps fingers*]—*pfff!*—and it flips. *Aah!* The air is filled with a heavy-cream cloud of joy—or bliss, in fact.

When you begin to take that attitude of leaping or stepping over, then that flip becomes real, and you have what is known as mahasukha. This may sound a little bit artificial; however, it is true. You begin to find out what an artificial approach is later, but the point is that painful strongholds have finally been broken through. You flip over, and you find a home as opposed to imprisonment.

When that flip takes place, you begin to open yourself simultaneously to the vajra master and to the vajra world. And at that point, the whole world, the whole atmosphere, is filled with jnanasattvas, along with your vajra master and your personal sense of great joy.

# 37

# The Four Main Abhishekas

*With ultimate sacred outlook, there is nobody to flash sacred out-look, and nobody to open to sacred outlook: the doer and the doing are dissolving into one. There is a feeling of basic shock: the possi-bilities of conventional mind are dissolving into nothing. Wakeful-ness is a choiceless state. You cannot help but be wakeful, as long as you do not try to follow it up or to sustain it.*

THERE ARE many different levels of abhishekas, but basically there are four main abhishekas: outer, secret, prajna-jnana, and formless.* These abhishekas are all connected with experiencing the phenomenal world as a sacred mandala. Checking in to a hotel does not mean you check in to any old hotel, just like that. First you decide what kind of hotel you want to check in to, and then you find out which floor your room is on. You can get a suite, a single bedroom, or a double bedroom, a private bathroom or a public one. There could be a restaurant.

Likewise, there are a lot of possibilities and different levels of abhishekas. Each abhisheka is unique, and each abhisheka is connected with a particular sadhana, and with particular mandalas and deities, or yidams. The deity or yidam of the mandala is the agent of the vajra mas-ter, and this deity is your agent as well, so you are a part of that yidam and mandala.

---

* Trungpa Rinpoche also sometimes refers to the *four main abhishekas* as outer, inner, secret, and That.

# The Outer Abhisheka: Coronation

An abhisheka or empowerment ceremony begins with the outer abhisheka, which is like a coronation, confirming you as a king or queen. In this abhisheka, you are given purification water. Then you are crowned and given a scepter, or vajra, in your right hand, and a ghanta, or bell, in your left hand. Finally, you are given a name. Your name is changed from your ordinary name into the name of a would-be king or queen, a master of the mandala.

In the outer abhisheka, you begin to identify yourself with a particular yidam, or deity. You visualize yourself in the form of whatever deity is chosen for the particular empowerment you are receiving. Such deities are not regarded as theistic deities or external beings, but as expressions of your own innate nature.

## The Five Steps of the Outer Abhisheka

There are five steps to the outer abhisheka: the water abhisheka, the crown abhisheka, the vajra abhisheka, the ghanta abhisheka, and the name abhisheka.

WATER ABHISHEKA. The outer abhisheka begins with the water abhisheka. It begins with purification and bathing. The water abhisheka is related with the idea of indestructibility or immovability. So before you put on your royal garments or wear your crown, you take a bath and are purified with holy water. Then, having been purified once, you are further purified in order to exorcise any of the little demigods or little ego friends that you may have brought along. You also reconfirm your refuge and bodhisattva vows.

CROWN ABHISHEKA. Once you have been purified, and you are fully dressed in your royal garments, the second step is that you are crowned. The crown abhisheka is related with equilibrium and a sense of rulership.

VAJRA ABHISHEKA. Once you have been crowned, you receive a vajra scepter to hold. This is the vajra abhisheka, which represents transcending passion and developing discriminating-awareness wisdom.

GHANTA ABHISHEKA. Next you receive a bell, or ghanta. This is a proclamation of the extent to which you can actually fulfill all your actions.

NAME ABHISHEKA. Finally, you are given the name abhisheka, and you receive a royal name. You are actually confirmed and declared an enlightened person. You are told that, having received these abhishekas, you are actually going to become a buddha known as "Tathagata So-and-So." The name abhisheka is related with the idea of all-encompassing space.

## The Five Wisdoms

The five steps of the outer abhisheka are connected with the five wisdoms. Before the coronation, you first bathe and clean yourself so that you may develop mirrorlike wisdom, which sees the transparency of everything. Then you are given a crown, so that you may develop the wisdom of equanimity. Next, you are given a scepter so that you become entitled to develop discriminating-awareness wisdom. Then you are given a ghanta, or bell, so that you may proclaim the wisdom of all-accomplishing actions. And having done all that, you receive your royal name, which is connected with the wisdom of all-encompassing space.

Through the five outer abhishekas, you actually become royalty. You are no longer a commoner like the bodhisattvas, the arhats, and the rest of the world of sentient beings.

## A Further Empowerment

Sometimes if a student is completely ripe, that student is also empowered to transmit power to others. But this part is reserved for last, because after you have made somebody a king or queen, they have to be watched to see how they perform as the head of the country. You have to see how they relate with their own power structure, before you give them the power to create further kings and queens.

## THE SECRET OR INNER ABHISHEKA: MUTUAL INTOXICATION

The secret or inner abhisheka is connected with the idea of mutual intoxication. In this abhisheka, you are presented with amrita, or liquor, from a skull cup. This liquor represents the juice derived from the union of the particular deities that you are being introduced to. Drinking the liquor intoxicates the confused mind into a higher level of existence.

With the secret abhisheka, the boundary between confusion and wakefulness begins to dissolve. When that boundary is dissolved, confusion and wakefulness happen simultaneously. The problem with sanity is that it is bounded by insanity. That is, sanity is usually based on comparison, because there is also insanity. But when you dissolve both sanity and insanity, they both become, "So what?"

Here we are not talking about small sanity; we are talking about greater sanity. If you open up your mind to greaterness, then you dissolve small sanity and small insanity into greater sanity. Relying on small sanity is like trying to read a book by flashlight during the day. When it is nighttime, there is a difference between using your flashlight and not using your flashlight to read a book. But when the sun is shining, you do not have to use a flashlight; in fact, a flashlight becomes an obstacle. So you have to think bigger.

The secret abhisheka transforms your existence completely. Reality is no longer regarded as an obstacle, and you no longer have difficulty communicating. Your passion, aggression, and ignorance are transformed into greater wisdom, so the fickle aspect of duality is conquered. This abhisheka has to do with how you can amalgamate the nirvanic, enlightened point of view together with the samsaric, confused point of view. If you are able to digest this particular teaching, the effect is that your whole body becomes a sacred existence.

## THE PRAJNA-JNANA ABHISHEKA: BLISS

The secret abhisheka is followed by the prajna-jnana abhisheka. This abhisheka is connected with understanding your reality and the relationship between you and your world. It is connected with how to relate with your consort, your family, and your world. Because of the wakefulness of intoxication, you begin to experience joy. You experience a sense of uniting with the world, a sense of orgasm.

Such a relationship is often developed by means of *karmamudra,* or sexual union practices, which show how the experience of orgasm can be related with that of sudden enlightenment. So the general notion of this abhisheka is that the experience of orgasm is actually a way of opening yourself to the phenomenal world. In this abhisheka, you are allowed to use your passion at last, not as a source of aggression or possessiveness or self-indulgence, but as a source of raising the greatest joy in your life.

The prajna-jnana abhisheka changes your mind and body completely; you become able to relate with the phenomenal world. You are able to copulate with the phenomenal world, to make love with the phenomenal world thoroughly and fully. You no longer experience inhibitions of any kind; therefore, you can actually open yourself up completely. By doing so, you can conquer any attacks, negativities, or negative powers that come to you.

## The Four Types of Bliss

In the prajna-jnana abhisheka, you work with four types of bliss.

BLISS OF FREEDOM FROM EGO. The first bliss is the bliss of freedom from ego, which is like taking off your heavy coat on a very hot day. It is a tremendous relief.

BLISS OF BEING CAPABLE AND WORTHY OF FREEDOM FROM EGO. The second bliss is the appreciation that you are capable of dealing with that level of bliss or freedom; you feel you are worthy of it.

BLISS OF DROPPING INHIBITIONS. In the third bliss, you boost yourself up further to the point that you begin to have no inhibitions about going beyond that bliss or freedom, even if you then have greater freedom.

BLISS OF TRANSCENDING FREEDOM AND BLISS. With the fourth bliss, you go beyond freedom and you go beyond the experience of bliss. You do not have to experience the freedom or the bliss, so you are transcending freedom and bliss altogether. You are *it* already: you *are* the freedom; you *are* the bliss. You are united with it; you are one with it. It is nondual experience.

That uniting with bliss, that being beyond bliss, is regarded as the bliss of the wisdom of example, which we call *peyi yeshe.* So the third abhisheka is also known as the abhisheka of the wisdom of example, or the wisdom of analogies.

## THE FORMLESS ABHISHEKA: *THAT*

After the bliss of the third abhisheka, you have the fourth abhisheka, which is something more than that—or maybe less than that. After peyi yeshe comes *töngyi yeshe,* or "actual wisdom." *Tön* means "ultimate," "pith," or "final," *kyi* means "of," and *yeshe* is "wisdom"; so *töngyi yeshe* means "ultimate wisdom."

The fourth abhisheka is very ordinary, but it is not particularly a big comedown. It is known as the mahamudra abhisheka, or the abhisheka of *That. That* traditionally refers to suddenly stopping the mind, suddenly stopping thoughts so that there is a gap. Ordinary mind is then introduced as *very* ordinary mind, and the idea of abhisheka as something special is cut through. Therefore, ordinary mind is experienced very directly. Once you have seen real ordinariness—the superordinary, the absolute ordinary—you realize that the regular world is not all that ordinary. Its ordinariness is purely superficial; you have not really deepened into it.

The point of this abhisheka is to realize that none of those processes you have been going through are based on a subject-object relationship. It is no longer a matter of "this" and "that," "I gain" or "I lose." You are simply introduced to the understanding that past, present, and future are one. Again, this is what is traditionally known as the fourth moment. The fourth moment consists of warmth and power and strength. I don't think I can actually explain it to you until you have received these abhishekas, but roughly speaking, there is a quality of warmth, strength, joy, and tremendous delight, because at last you are freed from being stuck to the past, present, and future.

This also means that you are freed from "I" and "other," "me" and "my belongings," and all the rest of it. Usually, we find all of that schmuckiness so annoying, but at the same time, so pleasant. Because we feel so much pain from those fixations, we begin to enjoy them. But in the fourth moment, you begin to be given freedom from conceptualized enjoyment. You are given an experience that is no longer yours as a possession, but belongs to the cosmic world. That is why this is known as the fourth moment, because it is free from past, present, and future. You begin to appreciate that.

The fourth moment accommodates all the rest of the abhisheka empowerments. It is the conquering of the entirety of space altogether; it conquers the entire time-and-space speculation. Our notions are not exactly changed, but they become bigger. When we talk about time and space, we usually think in very small measures. When we talk about time, we talk about minutes and hours; and when we talk about space, we talk in terms of yardage, meters, and miles. The measurement of the fourth moment transcends such measures altogether, and at the same time it comprehends them all at once. It is the all-encompassing space, definitely so, which includes both time and space. So although the fourth moment is talked about in terms of "moment," which you might think means time alone, the fourth moment includes both space and time.

That is why we can actually breathe in and out when we have a shamatha experience. We are beginning to transcend our small and limited world a little bit; we are beginning to go slightly beyond. Sometimes students find that they are regressing, because for the first time they are beginning to measure their realization of time and space. But if we go beyond that and begin to measure less, we get a greater quantity. We begin to feel less passionate, less measured, and less heavy. So we are going slightly beyond always keeping track—at the beginning, we do this just slightly, but in the end, we do it entirely.

But this does not necessarily mean that you lose the context of those measurements or limits; they are still included. It is like having a gigantic mound of sand in your storage bin. You know every grain of sand, and you also know the mound as a whole, but you are neither belittling each small grain of sand, nor are you giving greater credit to the larger pile of sand. You are bringing the two all together, which makes you both free and joyful. It makes you smile.

When you come to the fourth or formless abhisheka, real wisdom is transmitted. The teacher's mind and the student's mind actually meet together properly, completely, and thoroughly. With the fourth abhisheka, the mind of the teacher and the mind of the student become one, and the student is able to have a direct glimpse of dharmakaya.

The fourth abhisheka is known as the abhisheka of *That* with a capital *T*. You do not have to dwell on the past, present, or future. You could just wake yourself up on the spot. That particular spot is very ordinary; it is often called ordinary mind. Your mind is opening into ultimate sacred outlook. But at the same time, with ultimate sacred outlook, there is nobody to flash sacred outlook, and nobody to open to sacred outlook: the doer and the doing are dissolving into one. There is a feeling of basic shock; the possibilities of conventional mind are dissolving into nothing.

Wakefulness is a choiceless state. You cannot help but be wakeful, as long as you do not try to follow it up or to sustain it.

However, in discussing the vajrayana, I think I had better not elaborate too much. You need to experience it yourself, personally. That is much better than having it told to you. The vajrayana has to be a firsthand experience. For instance, if you were told about the process and the stages of orgasm by a professor, then when you had a date with your lover for the first time, you would be looking for all those things. You would be completely confused, rather than having a real orgasm of any kind. So in the same way, I would prefer not to talk too much. But I will indicate that there is definitely a situation that is free from space and time—and it makes you smile.

## Abhishekas with and without Elaboration

Abhishekas are said to be with or without elaboration. The Tibetan term for "with elaboration" is *trö-che*. *Trö* means "complication" or "elaboration," and *che* means "with"; so *trö-che* means "with elaboration." The term for "without elaboration" is *trö-me*. It is the same *trö* to begin with, but instead of *che* we have *me,* which means "without"; so *trö-me* means "without elaboration." Trö-che usually refers to the first three abhishekas, which require you to visualize lots of things. Trö-me refers to the fourth abhisheka, the one without elaboration.

The idea is that first you must have trö-che, or abhisheka with elaboration, in order to be able to experience the contrast, or trö-me. So first you must be educated and trained in trö-che, and then you begin to get something out of it. After trö-che, you have trö-me, or the abhisheka without elaboration, which is the fourth abhisheka of *That.* Capital *T*— *That!* [*Trungpa Rinpoche opens his hand suddenly, palm up, as he says,* That!] It is very ordinary.

*Part Nine*

# VAJRAYANA PRACTICE

## 38

# Visualization and Sadhana Practice

*Visualization is simply active mind putting its attention toward and identifying with basic sanity, symbolized in the forms of various deities. . . . Visualization is a catalyst for seeing the phenomenal world in an enlightened way.*

### SADHANA PRACTICE

Taking part in an abhisheka is like receiving meditation instruction, and sadhana practice is like meditating. In an abhisheka, you are being initiated by the guru into a mandala. So first you receive an abhisheka, and having received that abhisheka, you are then allowed to perform certain sadhanas, or practices.

*Sadhana* means "practice" or "sacred act." A sadhana is a discipline of some kind; it means doing things completely. For instance, you could have the sadhana of cooking, which means that from the time you start cooking until you serve the food, you have not finished your sadhana. If you are a good cook, you complete your sadhana by cooking a good meal. If your sadhana is laziness, you complete it by going to sleep.

A sadhana has a beginning, a middle, and an end, so the whole thing is a complete job, whatever job that might be. In vajrayana sadhana practice, from the time you begin your practice by taking the refuge vow until you finish the whole thing, that sadhana is your practice, your situation. So sadhana is a constant commitment.

The texts of some sadhanas are sixty pages or longer, with the whole practice taking many hours to perform, and other sadhanas are short.

Ideally, the practitioner would know the contents of the sadhana they were practicing precisely. But unfortunately—for instance, in Tibet—the whole thing can become a matter of just reading through the text and trying to finish the pages without really understanding it. That is the kind of corruption that naturally takes place.

The collection of abhishekas edited by Jamgön Kongtrül the Great consists of sixty-three volumes in Tibetan, and includes something like seven thousand different mandalas, sadhanas, and deities. All of them are categorized according to the six levels of tantra: kriyayoga, upayoga, yogayana, mahayoga, anuyoga, and atiyoga. So there is an infinite number of abhishekas. Before Jamgön Kongtrül edited and compiled these books, he received an abhisheka for each individual practice from each lineage, and he performed each individual practice in its entirety.

In sadhana practice, you have the root guru; you have the yidam; and you have the protector deities, or mahakalas, appropriate to the school or the particular buddha-family that the deity comes from. For instance, the six-armed protector Mahakala is connected with the Kalachakra sadhana.

## VISUALIZATION AND NONVISUALIZATION

There are two stages of vajrayana practice: the visualization or creation stage, and the nonvisualization or completion stage.

### Visualization: The Creation Stage

The first stage of vajrayana practice is visualization. Visualization practice is called *kyerim* in Tibetan. *Kye* means "manufacturing" or "making something," and *rim* means "level" or "stage"; so *kyerim* means "level of manifesting" or "stage of manufacturing." The Sanskrit equivalent is *utpattikrama*. *Utpatti* means " giving birth" or "creation," and *krama* means "stage"; so *utpattikrama* means "creation stage."

Visualization practice is based on imagining a certain image, figure, or person in your mind. This image or being that you are visualizing is the highest ideal of its type that you could possibly come up with. This being, or yidam, is sparkling clean and dressed in an elaborate costume or outfit, adorned with all kinds of ornaments, and holding scepters or other items. The idea is to identify with such figures and to work with them as if they actually existed individually. The yidam brings the experience of the unoriginated, unborn quality of you, which is completely unconditional, neither good nor bad.

Although the idea of a central deity or yidam is not exactly the same as the theistic concept of divinity, there is still a tangible object of your visualization. Your visualization is tangible in the same way as your lust is tangible when you are horny, or your aggression is tangible when you are uptight. So the visualization is tangible in the way lust and anger are tangible, rather than being anything outside of you. When we are highly lustful, we do not usually believe that we are controlled by somebody else. Rather, we experience our own lust developing within ourselves. When we are very angry, we do not think in terms of being possessed by somebody else, but we experience our own uptightness in the buildup of our own emotions. We should understand that the visualization of deities is the other end of that same stick. It is just our vision or our insight being formed into a particular format, picture, or image in our mind.

## Nonvisualization: The Completion Stage

The second stage of vajrayana practice is nonvisualization, or formless practice. It is called *dzogrim* in Tibetan, and *sampannakrama* in Sanskrit. *Dzogrim* means "completion stage." *Dzog* means "final" or "completion," and *rim*, again, means "stage." In the Sanskrit term *sampannakrama, sam* means "completely," *panna* means "gone," and *krama* means "stage"; so *sampannakrama* means "complete practice."

*Dzogrim* is the absence of visualization. It refers to a meditative state that is a sophisticated form of shunyata experience, probably on the level of mahamudra. So in vajrayana practice, we have both utpattikrama and sampannakrama, or kyerim and dzogrim, the creation and completion stages.

## THE ROLE OF THE YIDAM

A yidam represents your particular characteristic, your basic being. It is something that you can identify with. For instance, depending on whether you have an attachment to food or to entertainment, depending on whether anger, pride, passion, envy, or ingorance is your basic characteristic, the corresponding yidam will be situated in the center of the mandala, so you have that connection.

The choice of yidam is made during the abhisheka by throwing a flower onto a specially created mandala with conviction. This process is like flipping a coin with confidence. With such confidence, if you constantly say that it is going to be heads in your favor, it happens that way. You cannot make a mistake, because you are getting into the energy level of what you are, who you are, and where you are, all at once.

Your particular view of the world can also be seen in terms of the five buddha-families. Depending on the buddha-family to which you belong, you will have a certain innate emotional style. The function of the yidam is to bring out that style—to bring out that desire, ignorance, aggression, pride, or envy. The yidam represents the clear or vajra form of your emotions, and your actions become an expression of that process. But the yidam might also include your negative, confused aspects, because that might be the only available medium you have. Your yidam is predominantly an expression of your own buddha-family, but at the same time each yidam has elements of all five buddha-families.

Emotions are usually an expression of dullness or confusion, and you are usually drugged by your emotions. But in relating with the yidam, you are developing a different approach. You are revealing the wisdom aspect of the five buddha principles by means of discriminating awareness. So the yidam is more sympathetic to your particular style in the confused world, while the activities of the five buddha principles represent a more glorified version of you.

The tantric yanas are not quite linear, but as far as the practitioner is concerned, you are supposed to receive your own basic yidam first, and that allows you to practice the rest of tantra. The yidam you receive is usually connected with your guru. That is, your guru has their own yidam, and is highly accomplished in the practice associated with that yidam, so their students also supposedly have a karmic connection with that same yidam.

Furthermore, throughout the whole path, from the hinayana up to the mahayana level of vipashyana practice, you have been churning out your emotions onto the surface. Your teacher has been seeing you a lot, completely, in your very real nakedness. That allows you to be given a yidam appropriate to your emotional style or destiny.

First you receive your own basic yidam, and then you may be introduced to other yidams. For example, to develop knowledge, you may relate to Manjushri, and to develop long life, you may receive White Tara. But to begin with, you have your own basic yidam. That yidam stays the same—and traditionally, you keep it a secret.

## Two Aspects of Yidam: Samayasattva and Jnanasattva

There are two aspects of the yidam: the samayasattva and the jnanasattva. The samayasattva is the image visualized by you. *Sattva* is "being," and *samaya* is the "discipline of tantric practice"; so the *samayasattva* is your version of the deity that you have visualized. Samayasattva is what you create with your visualization

The jnanasattva is what legitimizes your visualization by descending into it. *Jnana* means "wisdom," and *sattva* again means "being"; so *jnana-sattva* means "wisdom being." In visualization practice, you invite the greater wisdom forces to descend into your visualization. Both aspects of the yidam, the samayasattva and the jnanasattva, are given to you by the guru. Before you get into the full practice of sadhana, you first identify your yidam as your guru; you look up to the yidam as the guru. Then at a certain point, you view your yidam at eye level, and your yidam becomes less than a guru. But each sadhana has to begin with guru yoga, with guru devotion.

The samayasattva is like creating merchandise, and the jnanasattva is like finally putting a price tag on it and selling it. Or we could say that the samayasattva is like being born into a rich family, and the jnanasattva is like finally inheriting the money from your parents. Because of the descent of the jnanasattva, the samayasattva is legitimized. It has real value, real responsibility, and real goodness.

The jnanasattva is a final confirmation. But again, I would like to make it clear that the jnanasattva is not regarded as external, outside, or even subtly or semi-outside. It is not as though a divine being were entering into your system, or as though you were being possessed by the Holy Ghost. The jnanasattva is a very basic and subtle thing; your own sanity begins to possess your visualization. In some sense, we could say that when you begin to visualize, you are on a trip; you are just imagining all sorts of colors and forms. But finally, when the jnanasattva descends, you are "untripped." Your trip is transcended. You are finally confirmed and blessed, so you do not have to imagine anymore. What you have imagined becomes a real vision, rather than a fantasy. So the difference between the samayasattva and the jnanasattva is the difference between a trip and a vision.

With the samayasattva, you are trying to visualize as well as you can, but the visualization is still made by you. Because the visualization is homemade, you might feel that there is some kind of dirt from your hands on this sacred object. The samayasattva is somewhat related with a guilt complex. You are still a wretched person trying to visualize this ideal, so it is an imperfect ideal. The ideal is imperfect because it is connected with guilt and an element of the fall of humanity.

The jnanasattva is a replica of what you have visualized. It is the unvisualized form that descends on you, the pure form of the deity. When the jnanasattva enters into the samayasattva, it takes out all the doubts. It legitimizes what you are doing completely. The jnanasattva makes it so that this particular vision or inspiration is no longer homemade, but heavenly made. The jnanasattva is not made by you or by anyone. It just comes to you. From where? From nowhere. It comes from under, from the side, from above, from everything, from everywhere.

The jnanasattva descends on you from the realm of what is called *kye-me*, or "unborn." It has no makeup, but it still has a form. As the jnanasattva descends, it then becomes one with you. This is possible due to the encouragement of the lineage, who have a relationship with the jnanasattva and who authorize you to bring down those things that come from nowhere. And when the jnanasattvas descend, they don't come down on diamond stepladders, but they come down like snowflakes falling into a lake and melting.

It is important in tantric practice to understand the meaning of samayasattva and jnanasattva. It is an important point for tantric practice. The jnanasattva is anything that makes your ordinary little mind exasperated. It is like an explosion from inward. It is just there—unmade, unborn, unoriginated. The jnanasattva is the transcendental aspect of the deity; it is shunyata and wisdom. It embodies the five wisdoms and anything good that you think of.

The jnanasattva is not a spirit, and it is not exactly shunyata. If it were purely shunyata, there wouldn't be anything or there would be everything, so it would be very confusing. And in the absence of confusion, it would still be very confusing. If it were an external deity coming down, it would be very difficult to dissolve it like a snowflake melting into a lake.

Something would still be left. So jnanasattva is quite different from the idea of spirit, and it is different from the idea of God descending or, for that matter, the Holy Ghost functioning.

The jnanasattva is a result of your wakefulness. Because you are so awake, you begin to see things very sharply. For instance, if you are awake, feel good, and have good health, you see everything vividly. You have good eyesight, so you don't need glasses; you have good hearing, so you don't need a hearing aid. You don't need any of those things. You are a healthy human being, very sharp and interested. With youthful exuberance, everything is penetratingly sharp. You are not sleepy, either. You are awake, and you begin to see that things are very vivid and clear, and at the same time you see that these things are a part of your world.

There is no question about that, and no alienation. There is no particular grudge against anybody. That is the kind of state we are talking about. We could describe it in another way by saying that it is like being a person who is falling in love. When you fall in love, you even lose your sense of possessiveness because you begin to melt like butter on a stove. You don't exist, and that doesn't exist—you just melt. You tingle with pleasure at even the thought of the person you are in love with. This is another example we could give; falling in love is a valid analogy for dissolving the jnanasattva into the samayasattva.

We are not talking about a mysterious force or energy. It is your receptivity, your state of being, that determines how transparent the jnanasattva could be. If you are self-conscious, if you are holding on to your ego and your defense mechanisms and are a clumsy old fool, the jnanasattva will be a clumsy old fool in the disguise of a jnanasattva. Such a jnanasattva is very difficult to dissolve. It just drops into the water, and if you drink that water, probably you will get indigestion. So the more purified and open your state of being, that much more smooth and flexible is the jnanasattva. It is you who gives it life. It is your own life, very much so—as much as the sun is your sun, and the moon is your moon.

In tantra, there are no visualizations without the samayasattva and the jnanasattva. We should be very clear about that. The samayasattva-jnanasattva relationship destroys the clinging of ego. Without that, the visualization becomes purely imagination. In fact, it has been said in the tantras that if you visualize without the jnanasattva descending, or if you visualize without the awareness of shunyata, you achieve rudrahood, the building up of ego. The result of the samayasattva being visualized without the jnanasattva is that you become highly centralized in your ego, and you begin to make a more than necessary big deal of yourself.

Your yidam becomes a valid yidam when the samayasattva receives the jnanasattva. That is when it becomes a one-hundred-percent yidam instead of a fifty-percent one. If it weren't for the samayasattva and jnanasattva, your visualization could become an ego trip, because you are just imagining yourself to be a yidam, which you are actually not. There is nothing to give and nothing to open to. In samsaric-style visualization, you would like to visualize something good. You would like to visualize yourself as some kind of god, and you would like to keep your territory intact, whereas the jnanasattva coming to you cuts down the possibility of keeping any territory of your own making. It cuts the misunderstanding that the visualization is made by you alone. So the visualization has greater, more open, and more spacious qualities.

## Visualizing Yourself as the Yidam

The samayasattva is a samsaric projection of yourself. But if you were actually visualizing a samsaric projection of yourself, you would not visualize yourself as a yidam, the symbol of enlightenment. Instead you would visualize yourself indulging in an enormous meal in a restaurant, or having a big orgy, or dancing, or drinking yourself to death, or driving a sports car, or anything else that you can think of. Those are the kinds of common visualizations everybody has.

However, visualizing yourself as a yidam is a really eccentric visualization. You are visualizing somebody who has an entirely different mode of behavior. A yidam behaves either in a completely angry form or a completely peaceful form. Yidams hold various scepters, like monarchs do, and they emanate all kinds of good vibrations, even though they may be frightening or terrible or overpoweringly good. It is for that reason that such images as herukas and dakinis developed, and you can visualize them. They represent the basic philosophy of tantra, which is the idea that your basic makeup is like that of the herukas and dakinis.

When you study the five buddha-families and realize what buddha-family you are, this gives you enormous hope that your style of being messed up could actually be related with the wisdom of enlightenment. It is not just a vague hope, or the idea that you are going to be okay eventually; but it is the belief that your particular hang-ups are connected with certain types of wisdom. There is actually a link. Some kind of dialogue was taking place before you knew who actually was holding the dialogue. Your absentminded mind and your nonexistent enlightenment potential had a dialogue before you knew where you were, and they decided to make you into a yogi, or practitioner.

If you have any knowledge of the buddha-family principles, even at the neurotic level, it is a stepping-stone. You realize that there is something that is happening that is more than just samsara alone. For instance, if you think you are karma family, that automatically means you are going to become the yidam Amoghasiddhi. That is what you are actually saying. When you identify yourself with a certain family, it is not like having an astrological chart made for you that determines what fate you might have as you go on with your life. You are actually saying something fantastic: you are saying that you belong to a particular family, and therefore you are going to become one of the five buddhas. In fact, once you identify yourself with one of those buddhas, you are actually one of them already. On one hand, that is somewhat presumptuous; but on the other hand, it is not presumptuous, because you are identifying with your neurosis at the same time. As long as you have those elements of neurosis, you are naturally bound to get the other side as well.

## PROPER VISUALIZATION

In order to visualize properly, there needs to be some kind of mental training at the beginning. You need to have some reconciliation with your thoughts and emotions, and you need to allow them to come through. In vipashyana experience, anything that occurs in your mind is not rejected and not accepted. The basic accommodation of free-flowingness, carelessness, or detachment has developed. Having developed that—not necessarily constantly, but having had an occasional glimpse of that—then the visualization becomes less a collection, and more a matter of things developing in the space within that awareness. So visualization depends on a person's previous training in the three yana disciplines.

Visualization is a catalyst for seeing the phenomenal world in an enlightened way. But this does not mean that you see blue Vajradharas walking down Wall Street. It is much more subtle than that. When you visualize, you are visualizing your particular version, concept, and understanding of a particular deity. Therefore, a philosophical and spiritual understanding of that deity is important. Otherwise, you are just throwing yourself into a foreign culture. Without having some idea of the deity's significance, you have no way of relating with it. So before you visualize, you have to come as close as you can to knowing the complete story of the figure in question.

For instance, if you are visualizing Avalokiteshvara, the bodhisattva of compassion, you need to have some feeling about compassion, and what compassion actually means. You have to know what the Buddhist tantric view of compassion is all about, and how this differs from the ordinary understanding of compassion. Once you understand that and begin to have a feeling about it, you are then in a position to visualize Avalokiteshvara. A similar process applies to all the rest of the visualizations in vajrayana practice.

The idea of visualization is to catch a glimpse of personal feeling and an environmental feeling, not just of the objects of visualization themselves, but also what surrounds those forms. By visualizing in that way, you begin to develop some understanding of the deity you are visualizing. You understand the physical and psychological environment of that deity, and the tradition out of which that practice comes.

## The Purpose of Visualization

The purpose of visualization is not to re-create longing concepts, or concepts that have to do with what you want to happen. It is not like when you are hungry and you visualize chocolate cake or a fat steak. It is much subtler than that. Visualization is simply the active mind putting its attention toward and identifying with basic sanity, symbolized in the forms of various deities. It incorporates your own personal emotional experience.

For instance, if somebody has been lecturing you, saying the same things over and over again, you might express that feeling visually as somebody dressed in gray clothes droning on in a monotone and putting you to sleep. If you feel angry, you might have a visual sensation of blazing fire. If you feel lustful, you might picture yourself swimming through cool water with a tinge of sweet in it. Your emotions play a part in visualization in this way.

The kinds of visual perspectives that exist in your ordinary life continue in visualization practice. But visualization is not a matter of your feeling dingy, dark, wet, and cold, and since you feel you need bright

VISUALIZATION AND SADHANA PRACTICE

sunshine, you suddenly picture tropical isles and the seaside. It is not as simple as that. But often people do think about visualization in that way. In particular, there are examples of that approach among people who are trying to visualize on the basis of only elementary training in the tantric tradition of either Hinduism or Buddhism. Such students try to visualize great, beautiful, and glorious things, but that approach is based on simply wanting to escape. These students want to get rid of their problems, so they try to visualize the opposite of them. That is actually more a neurotic problem than an insightful technique.

There is always that problem of trying to use visualization as a way of calming down, or as a way of feeding your expectations with a complete dream world. If you feel thirsty, you visualize a Coca-Cola bottle or a nice cool drink. If you feel cold and wet, you visualize a nice, warm house with a nice fire in the fireplace, or a nice down jacket. If you feel terribly poor, you visualize making lots of money. Those are little tricks we play when we don't like what is happening. They are the ordinary visualizations arising out of boredom, neurosis, and pain that many Americans experience. The creation of Disneyland is a dream come true, a visualization come true. In Disneyland, there are lots of rides and you can get into all kinds of funfairs. But that is not quite what we are talking about. We are not talking about a vajrayana Disneyland, or simply trying to quell our neurosis or quench our immense thirst.

It is possible to regard the deities as completely beyond the trikaya, as simply the energy of outer space, simply part of human consciousness. When you visualize, the whole idea is that you are trying to break through something. Eventually, you are supposed to transcend the deities that you visualize. The deities are not regarded as objects of worship or objects of accomplishment. It is the same with shamatha practice: eventually you are supposed to transcend your focus on the breath. So a visualization is a kind of temporary measure, another Band-Aid. It may be a colorful one, but you are still supposed to take it off when the wound is healed. A visualization is a kind of prop or trick. That is why we refer to it as upaya, or skillful means.

The best way to prepare for visualization is through regular sitting practice, rather than by playing with your perceptions or with phenomena. The only exception would be cultivating a sense of humor. Humor makes you begin to see the world in a different perspective. You see the differences between being in a retreat hut and coming into the city. This perspective on the colors and powers that exist is natural and obvious. It has a powerful impact on you. But apart from that, I wouldn't recommend anything other than just sitting meditation.

## GIVING BIRTH TO THE VISUALIZATION

Visualization practice is connected with the realization of things as they are in terms of symbolism. In this practice, you have a sense of the presence of the particular deity—and at the same time, the absence of the deity is also the presence of the deity.

You start with formless meditation, or dzogrim. In formless practice, you empty yourself out completely into the charnel ground, which is the birthplace and death place of everything. You begin with a basic understanding of shunyata, which is called the shunyata deity, and from there the visualization takes place in stages.

Next, having contemplated and meditated on shunyata, you visualize and experience the seed syllable, or *bija mantra*. This step is called the divine principle of letter, character, or written form.

So first you visualize the bija, or seed syllable, and from there you transform yourself into a deity. This is like human birth: when you are first conceived, there is an egg, or bija, and from there you have to develop. So bija is connected with birth and with the evolution of life; bija is the seed or the egg of your birth. In visualization practice, you are dealing with different types of birth and purifying them. You are purifying birth from an egg, birth from a womb, birth from moisture, and spontaneous birth.*

Bija mantras can also be used as a spell. Once you have achieved a particular sadhana and identified with the deity, you can use the bija mantra as a creative or destructive spell.

Next you visualize the divine sound principle, sending forth rays of light from the bija mantra that you have visualized, and fulfilling all the actions of samsara and nirvana.

Having heard the sound of the bija mantra, which could be OM, AH, HUM, or anything of that nature, that is then transformed into visual symbolism. For instance, you might have the symbols of the five buddha principles: the vajra for the vajra family, the jewel for the ratna family,

---

* According to the Buddhist tradition, there are four modes of birth: birth from an egg, from a womb, from moisture, or spontaneously.

the lotus for the padma family, the sword or crossed vajra for the karma family, and the wheel for the buddha family. Some symbol of that nature occurs in your mind.

So the bija mantra is much more than just a word, it is an onomatopoeic symbol. And that symbol then turns into an anthropomorphic image. So there are two stages of creating an image. When you hear the word *sword,* for example, you first hear the sound *sword,* and having understood the sound, you simultaneously get a picture of a sword in your mind.

In the final stage of the visualization process, a particular form takes shape from the symbol or seed syllable. You create the visualization itself. This is called the divine principle of form.

Then various mudras, symbols, or scepters are placed in the hands of the visualized deities, which is called the divine principle of mudra.

Once the visualization is complete, you practice the repetition of a mantra in which you bless or consecrate yourself as a complete mantric being or mantric principle. This is called the divine principle of mark or sign. At this point you are completely involved in the practice, which is a question of becoming an actual deity rather than purely a principle. You have twenty-four-hour awareness of what you are and who you are in that particular practice.

When you have completed a session of visualization practice, everything is dissolved back into the charnel ground.

After your meditation, you remain in the charnel ground continuously. You practice meditation in action. At this point you do not need to continue the repetition of the mantra. In postmeditation, you should have an awareness or imprint of the mantra repetition taking place as part of your thought process, rather than actually doing it on the spot.

## The Importance of Mental Clarity
## in Visualization

In visualization practice, there is a quality of total awareness and clarity. That is one of the most important points of this practice. If you have mental clarity, you will automatically pick up on hang-ups. You do not pick up on only the good aspects, but you pick up on the heavy-handed and confused ones as well. You work with the confused aspects the same as you work with the good ones. It does not make any difference.

Visualization is not a matter of thinking: "I would like to visualize Vajradhara," and suddenly—wham!—he's out there holding his bell and dorje. That seems to be much too crude and illiterate an approach to visual perception. It lacks dignity and a sense of process. Usually in vajra-yana disciplines you do not have sudden visualizations, except in the high-est levels of tantra. In the earlier yanas, it is a training process. In order to have form, there first has to be the potential of form. The potential of form leads to the possibility of form, and after that the actual form appears. The potentiality is the seed syllable, the possibility is the symbol, and the fruition of the process is that the actual visualization occurs.

You might think this is unnecessary red tape or some kind of dogma, but that's not true. This is how our mind usually works. We have a sud-den insight, very sudden and direct, and if we are very speedy, we just flash on that idea. But if we actually dissect our process of thinking in slow-motion, we see that the process of suddenly flashing on an idea is actually very gradual. First there is the seed of the idea, the seed syllable or sound; then that begins to develop; and finally there is the full image. And then we begin to operate on the basis of that image.

As an ordinary example, if somebody says, "How are you?" we con-dense that whole phrase into a single little unit of sound and meaning— "howareyou." We have some idea of that person asking, "How are you?" Then we begin to formulate that into a shape or a symbol. It becomes visual, or imagery. And finally we have the whole picture very fine and clear, so that we know how we are going to react to that person. Depend-ing on the situation, we might say, "I'm fine, thank you" or "Not doing so well."

The mental process always takes place in stages. It is like taking a pho-tograph. When you press the button, the first exposure of the film to a particular object is like the bija-mantra level. Then the type of film and the length of the exposure work together, creating a definite impact on the film, and finally the picture has been taken fully. This is the kind of three-stage process that we always go through. This is not dogma; it is actually how we handle our mind.

It is very precise and extraordinarily beautiful how the vajrayanists studied human perception so completely. They made the way we handle our world into transcendental wisdom. They made the way we perceive into a vajra religious-type approach, and then translated it back to us, so we could learn in the manner that we are describing here. So this three-stage process is not to be regarded as superstition or just doctrinal—it is personal experience that develops spontaneously. The seed, the mudra or symbol, and the form develop in that way, and the relationship of the practitioner to the visualization harmonizes with this approach.

You develop immense concentration when you begin to visualize in that way. Very strict concentration begins to develop, and having developed greater concentration and realization, you begin to attain the level of crazy wisdom, the vidyadhara level. You begin to attain a glimpse of Vajradhara, the tantric name for Buddha as the teacher of the vajrayana. At the same time, you continue to practice shamatha-vipashyana along with visualization practice, which helps you to visualize properly. One of the important tantric vows is not to look down upon such lower-yana practices.

## STRAIGHTFORWARD PRACTICE

In visualization practice, there is no other purpose than to have proper contact with reality through whatever deity was given to you as part of your practice. You just work with that very simply. It is not all that subtle. You have your own particular patron saint, and you just work with that. It may seem to be very unsubtle and crude, but it is very direct. You just do the visualization you were given. You develop your own identification with that particular deity. Simply that.

It's like buying clothes. If the clothing fits well, you wear it, and if it doesn't fit, you don't wear it. It's like buying a pair of spectacles. If you can see through them, you buy them, and if you can't see through them, you don't buy them. You follow your own inclination as well as the vajra master's recommendation. The eye doctor might recommend a certain kind of glasses, so you just wear them and use them. You are buying something that you do not yet have, but at the same time it is something you are somewhat familiar with. Otherwise, you wouldn't be buying it. You would be too nervous to be willing to spend money on it.

## THE CONTINUITY OF MEDITATION
## AND POSTMEDITATION PRACTICE

In the postmeditation state, you see and hear and think in the same way as the deities that have been given to you. Postmeditation is considered formless because you have dissolved the ritual activities and visualization. So there is an alternation between the meditation, which is in the form of visualization, and ordinary life, which is formless.

A further possibility is what is known as the indivisibility of those two states. This has to do with being able to handle the phenomenal world and your state of mind at the same time, which should be regarded as the ideal form of visualization. That kind of visualization comes out of a basic awareness of shunyata running through both visualization and formless practice, so there is some kind of continuity, or tantra.

# The Importance of a Nontheistic View

*The vajrayana approach to deity is very simple and basic: it is that there is no external salvation. Although in vajrayana we speak a great deal about the experience of blessing, or adhishthana, and we invoke all kinds of power and energy, those things do not come from some entity existing either within us or outside of us. We do not invoke blessings from any entity at all.*

I T IS timely to review the difference between theism and nontheism, at this point, for we will continue to speak of the divine principle or *devata* throughout our discussion of vajrayana, so it is important to understand the nontheistic idea of divinity. The view of the deity in tantra is often thought of as the same as in the theistic traditions. The simple fact of having all kinds of deities, gods and goddesses, devas and *devis,* is completely misunderstood. However, in the vajrayana teachings, the concept of deity has nothing to do with messengers or representations of some kind of external existence. We do not talk in terms of God, Godhead, or God-ness. There is no reference in vajrayana to celestial beings. Rather, we are talking about a higher level of energy, a higher level of wakefulness. But even that is not a definite reference point. Keep this in mind for future reference.

Deities in tantra have a purely situational existence, which brings our insight to its fullest point, but they are not regarded as external existents. Buddhist tantric deities are simply expressions of our mind. So although the word *divinity,* or *devata* in Sanskrit, is used quite widely in the Hindu tradition as well as in the Buddhist tradition, there is no mutual understanding of divinity between the two traditions.

## DIVINITY IN THE THREE YANAS

To understand the nontheistic approach to divinity, it would be helpful to examine the notion of divinity in each of the three yanas.

### The Hinayana Approach to Divinity: Prajna

There is a link to the vajrayana concept of deity starting from the hinayana. On the ordinary level, before even embarking on the path, there is a sense of self. Then in the hinayana, we have an experience of renunciation and of loneliness. We feel that somebody is actually experiencing suffering and pain. In that situation, we develop admiration for the Buddha as an example of freedom from suffering. That is the seed of the realization of deity in the Buddhist sense.

The seed of the deity principle in Buddhism is not based on a sense of self, or on any kind of tangible or intangible mystical experience. It is based on prajna, on insight. It is like the story of the arhat practicing in the charnel ground. The arhat saw a piece of bone and began to contemplate where it came from. He saw that the bone came from death. Then he asked, "Where did death come from?" He saw that death came from old age. The arhat went on in his contemplation, which led him through the entire cycle of the twelve nidanas. Finally, he realized that the whole process depends on ignorance, and that in order to dispel ignorance, one needs insight. At that point, the arhat began to develop prajna. That prajna principle, which is the insight that runs through all the yanas, is the basic idea of divinity.

### The Mahayana Approach to Divinity: Buddha Nature

Prajna is the starting point for the idea of deities in Buddhist tantra, and it continues through the mahayana and expands into the vajrayana. On the mahayana level, the deity comes into the picture, not as an external deity or Godhead, but as a feeling for the existence of buddha nature in you. When you have opened to that possibility and have some understanding of buddha nature, or tathagatagarbha, that is the notion of deity on the mahayana level.

Once again, the deity is not seen from the point of view of self, nor is it seen as an existence or concept outside of yourself. Divinity is your experience of a basic and subtle inner nature, which comes with the experience of prajna. In the mahayana, prajna becomes more intelligent and expands out to a greater degree. Prajna continues in the mahayana in the realization that one has buddha possibilities in oneself.

## THE VAJRAYANA APPROACH TO DEITY: NO EXTERNAL SALVATION

The vajrayana approach to deity is very simple and basic: there is no external salvation. Although in vajrayana we speak a great deal about the experience of blessing, or adhishthana, and although we invoke all kinds of power and energy, those things do not come from some entity existing either within us or outside of us. We do not invoke blessings from any entity at all. The whole experience of invoking the deity is on a nonentity level. That is a very basic point.

In the vajrayana, we do not start with matches in order to light a fire. We just light the fire, and the fire just burns. That may sound impractical, but it actually does happen that way. There is no set point or spotlight to work with or work up to; there is no existing thing that constitutes the spotlight or focus. There is not any kind of basic reference point. Even if such a point of focus were equated with something psychological, such as the highest degree of awareness or the highest degree of confusion, it would not make any difference. We do not start from anywhere. When we invoke deities, there is no reference to a special existence. That is the difference between Hindu tantra and Buddhist tantra. In Buddhist tantra, we do not start from anywhere. We do not start from a word or by developing a name.

Bhaktivedanta was an Indian teacher who came to this country as the head of the Hare Krishna movement. In his teaching, he equated the mantra syllable OM with the Christian idea that "In the beginning was the Word, and the Word was God," which is quite accurate in a sense. He said that because of the truth of the belief that the Word is God, all the Hare Krishna disciples chant their devotional mantric incantations. Furthermore, Bhaktivedanta said that this truth was universal—and in the theistic world, it *is* universal, but it absolutely does not apply in the nontheistic world, or in the humanistic world, for that matter.

In Buddhist vajrayana, we do not have such a Word. We do not have a Word that is God, and we do not have God. We do not have anything.

There is nothing to be made out of God, and nothing to make anything out of. In theism, I suppose the Word has a feeling of energy, proclamation, and brightness, and God is the basic accommodator and the fantastic overviewer that is within us or outside us, depending on the particular approach. But as far as Buddhist tantra is concerned, we do not have any of that.

The nontheistic view is crucial to the vajrayana. In hinayana, the question of nontheism is not particularly important. You do your little practice and you have your particular discipline. Everything is based on morality and discipline, on monastic rules and individual salvation. On the mahayana level, the theory of God or gods still does not play a very important part. You engage in compassionate action, and there is the inspiration from within concerning your buddha nature and so forth. But in the vajrayana, knowing the real differences between theism and nontheism is absolutely crucial.

It is very tricky. It has been said in many of the tantras that whatever the deity, if you visualize the image of the deity on the basis of blind faith or one-pointed belief, you are cultivating egohood. So nontheism is a very important point. You have to understand the difference between the theistic and nontheistic view. You have to understand both the similarities and the differences.

## BUDDHISM AND WESTERN MYSTICISM

In the past, the finest Christian mystics were afraid they might be beheaded, cooked, boiled, and crucified for speaking the heresy of nontheism. They actually had to fear for their lives if they spoke out. People had that kind of fear in the past and, though less extreme, that fear still exists. Even today, Christian mystics have to watch their step and think in terms of diplomacy. This situation has prevented a true, real mystical tradition in both the Christian and Judaic traditions from shining through properly. It has prevented mysticism from coming into the picture in the fullest sense, with the fundamental realization of divinity as just a phantom. But nonetheless, there has still been a lot of personal insight occurring and being expressed by Christian and Jewish mystics.

In Christian and Judaic mysticism, the concept of God is often qualified with some kind of subtlety, such as calling God the "kingdom of heaven within us." For instance, the German theologian Meister Eckhardt

(1260–1327) described God in terms of the Godhead principle. That idea is very close to the idea of divinity in Buddhist tantra, but there is still a faint little tissue of difference between the two; in Meister Eckhardt's view, there is still the faintest idea of a kind of power that comes from somewhere else.

In his writings, Meister Eckhardt does not refer to the Godhead as being completely outside of us or completely beyond us, nor for that matter does he quite say that the Godhead is completely in us. He somehow dances on that razor's edge. It is as if he could see the possibility of nontheism very clearly, but he was hesitating, torn between theism and nontheism. It seems as if he wanted to say that no-God is the greatest experience, but at the same time he did not quite want to say so. So although Meister Eckhardt understood and experienced things in a completely vajrayana way, he was still afraid to break from theism, so he ended up by speaking in terms of Godhead.

Father Thomas Merton (1915–1968), the prominent Catholic mystic, who was a great friend of mine, was also going in the nontheistic direction. In private we agreed on everything, and he understood nontheism completely. We met over a few gin and tonics in a hotel in Calcutta, India, and he was in complete agreement with me, and not just because he was influenced by the gin and tonics. He was very good, and we understood one another. But even at that point, his last words were that he was concerned about whether he would be quoted by me for what he had said. There was a little panic about that on his part.

A similar thing happened when I gave a meditation workshop in a nunnery at Stanbrook Abbey in England. I met with the abbess and the rest of the senior nuns, divided from them by an iron grill. The hall for public talks was divided into two sections: outsiders sat outside the grill, and the nuns sat inside. We discussed meditation and the existence of God, and the nuns went along completely with the nontheistic view. They understood fully. But then one little nun in the corner of the room panicked, and suddenly distance set in.

The point of these stories is that in the theistic mystical traditions, people do understand the concept of the nonexistence of the divinity principle outside of one's existence. They understand fully and completely. But in order to stay in the church, in order to make the appropriate confessions, they are still very shy about the whole nontheistic approach.

I am not trying to show that the theistic mystical traditions are wrong. I am just saying that they are bound by their religious orders and laws and by their hierarchical problems. Many very radical and true writings and teachings of those theistic mystical traditions have been shut down simply because they are unorthodox. Such is the case with the doctrine of reincarnation, or the principle of continual consciousness, which was shut down very powerfully by the early Roman Catholic Church. And things like that can still happen. So Western mystics have to watch their step about speaking out; they have been told to be careful. We should sympathize with those people, who actually would like to say much more, but who are unable to do so because of the constraints of their particular hierarchy and political situation.

The principle of divinity in Buddhism has nothing to do with deifying anything, as it does in Christian and Judaic mysticism. As far as the non-theistic tradition of Buddhism is concerned, we have nothing to lose, and we just speak out very fully. We might lose a few audience members in the Christian world, but nevertheless, there is fundamentally nothing to lose. We have no hierarchical setup saying that you should worship a deity like Vajradhara or a great teacher like Padmasambhava as God. Even if some unenlightened hierarch decided to impose that idea on us, we could always challenge that view by saying, "If you believe in egolessness, you are wrong to take the theistic approach."

*Part Ten*

# THE TANTRIC JOURNEY: LOWER TANTRA

40

# *Kriyayoga:*
# *Trust in Reality*

*The function of kriyayoga is to abandon the notion of töndam as something to be attained or looked forward to. Instead, you pay homage to kündzop and try to relate with its usefulness. You try to relate with the insightfulness of the phenomenal world properly and fully. You can take water as water, and it cleans you inside and out, including your psychological problems. The point is that you need to drop any hesitation about actually getting into kündzop.*

## THE TANTRIC YANAS

The tantric yanas can be explained in terms of the nine-yana system or the four-yana system.

### The Nine-Yana System

The three-yana journey can be described in terms of nine yanas. The nine yanas are *shravakayana, pratyekabuddhayana,* mahayana or bodhisattva yana, kriyayogayana, upayogayana, yogayana, mahayogayana, anuyogayana, and atiyogayana. Of these nine, the first two are a part of the hinayana, the third is the mahayana, and the remaining six are within the vajrayana. These last six yanas are known as the tantric yanas, which are divided into lower and higher tantra. The first three (kriyayoga, upayoga, and yogayana) are referred to as lower tantra, and the second three (mahayoga, anuyoga, and atiyoga) are referred to as higher tantra.* The Old Translation school,† which are the teachings introduced to Tibet at the time of Padmasambhava, is associated with the three higher yanas, and with the approach known as *dzokchen* or maha ati.

## MAHA ATI AND MAHAMUDRA TRADITIONS

| MAHA ATI / DZOKCHEN | MAHAMUDRA (GREAT SYMBOL) |
|---|---|
| HINAYANA<br>1. Shravakayana<br>*The vehicle of hearers* | HINAYANA<br>Shravakayana<br>*The vehicle of hearers* |
| 2. Pratyekabuddhayana<br>*The vehicle of solitary realizers* | Pratyekabuddhayana<br>*The vehicle of solitary realizers* |
| MAHAYANA<br>3. Mahayana / Bodhisattvayana<br>*The vehicle of compassionate warriors* | MAHAYANA<br>Mahayana / Bodhisattvayana<br>*The vehicle of compassionate warriors* |
| VAJRAYANA<br><br>Lower Tantra<br>4. Kriyayogayana<br>*The vehicle of purification* | VAJRAYANA<br><br>The Four Orders of Tantra<br>Kriyayogayana<br>*The vehicle of purification* |
| 5. Upayogayana<br>*The vehicle of conduct* | Upayogayana<br>*The vehicle of conduct* |
| 6. Yogayana<br>*The vehicle of union* | Yogayana<br>*The vehicle of union* |
| Higher Tantra<br>7. Mahayogayana<br>*The vehicle of great union* | Anuttarayogayana / Mahamudra<br>*Supreme yogayana* / Great Symbol |
| 8. Anuyogayana<br>*The vehicle of passion* | |
| 9. Atiyogayana<br>*The ultimate vehicle, the great completion* | |

---

\* The first three tantric yanas are also referred to as "outer tantra," and the last three as "inner tantra."

† The *Old Translation school* refers to Buddhist teaching introduced to Tibet in the eighth century by masters such as Padmasambhava and Shantarakshita. The Nyingma tradition is based on this early translation period.

The six tantric yanas are not highly structured and linear like the ten bhumis of the bodhisattva path. The tantric path is more random and temperamental. I find it very difficult to discuss tantra after the mahayana because the whole thing is so illogical. It doesn't make much sense. As I read Jamgön Kongtrül the Great's writings, every sentence makes sense and every word makes sense. But when I try to pick up the basic geography, a lot of things sound absurd. I often have to look back and find out what something means. So I discovered I have to give up any hope of understanding the tantric path in a linear way. Instead, I just take the merit of each yana as it is. I realized that I do not understand tantra if I try to understand it.

## The Four-Yana System

The tantric path is also described in terms of four tantric yanas, called the four orders of tantra: kriyayoga, upayoga, yogayana, and anuttarayoga. Here, along with the gradual psychological development through the first three levels of kriyayoga, upayoga, and yogayana, there is a fourth stage of tantra, known as anuttarayoga. According to the New Translation school, which was introduced at the time of Marpa, anuttarayoga is regarded as the highest of the tantric teachings.* This approach is referred to as mahamudra ("great symbol").†

The first two tantric yanas—kriyayoga and upayoga—are about how to begin our life as tantric practitioners. It is the beginner's level, so we are dealing with a very early stage of tantra. We are not yet concerned with the drama of tantra or the larger scale of tantra. This stage has to do with the discovery of basic purity and impurity and the realization of immovability, and it stays on that level. At the same time, it is the starting point for discussing time and form, and it is the basis for more advanced tantric practices.

Kriyayoga is referred to as the tantra of action. The Tibetan term for kriyayoga is *cha-we gyü. Cha-we* is "action," *gyü* is "tantra"; so *cha-we gyü* is

---

* The *New Translation schools* base their traditions on teachings brought to Tibet in the eleventh century by translators such as Marpa. Of these schools, the Kagyü, Sakya, and Geluk traditions are the best known.

† Chögyam Trungpa Rinpoche taught from the perspective of *mahamudra* and his Kagyü heritage, from the perspective of maha ati and his Nyingma heritage, and from the perspective of the inseparable union of the two.

"action tantra." The word *gyü* has many meanings: It can mean "continuity" or "thread." *Gyü* is also the Tibetan word for "lineage." *Gyü* can refer to family lineages or blood relationships, such as between grandparents and grandchildren. It can also refer to dharma lineages such as the Kagyü, which is the lineage of *ka,* or the "sacred word."

In terms of an understanding of relative truth, it has been said that those who have a rudimentary understanding of kündzop are ready for kriyayoga; those who have more understanding are ready for upayoga; those with more understanding still are ready for yogayana; and those who have complete understanding are ready for anuttarayoga.

In terms of the emotions, ignorance is connected with kriyayoga, aggression is connected with upayoga, uncertainty or random movement among those emotions is connected with yogayana, and passion is connected with anuttarayoga

In still another approach, a person appreciative of cleanliness and purity belongs to the first category, or kriyayoga; a person who tends to relate with the dharmata, or the absolute, and who is not concerned with external rituals belongs to the second category, or upayoga; a person who is prejudiced directly against practicing external rituals and is highly dedicated to the inner practice belongs to the third category, or yogayana; and a person who is highly open to the samaya of indulgence and to applying skillful means and knowledge in their life belongs to the fourth category, or anuttarayoga.

## BYPASSING THE EARLY YANAS

Traditionally, the early tantric yanas are not taught unless a particular teacher feels that a person should receive more training, or should be slowed down in getting into the higher yanas. What usually happens instead is that, having gone through the mahayana experience, a person then comes directly to the higher tantras, in other words, to the mahamudra or maha ati level. They just bypass all the rest of it.*

It is possible that an ordinary person who is not even a bodhisattva could practice anuyoga or even atiyoga, but they would need to have some kind of three-yana training. Training in the three yanas is linear,

---

* Trungpa Rinpoche clearly thought it was valuable to study the full progression of tantric yanas, even though the earlier tantric yanas are often overlooked.

but this does not mean that a person has to attain the tenth bhumi before they can practice tantra. A person on the path of accumulation with an advanced state of mind could also practice tantra. A person with good practice in shamatha and vipashyana, or good practice in shunyata and prajna, could practice tantra. Such a person could make a kind of nine-yana journey within the path of accumulation. They could make a sort of mini-journey, but with the same kind of experience and understanding.

That is the tradition, but some people are diligent enough to go through all the yanas. Such a practice would probably take about eight years in retreat. In the first part of the retreat, or kriyayoga, you lead a vegetarian life and you don't wear any leather products. Then as you go on, you begin to change your diet and your outfit, and you begin to wear clothes made from animal skins. So you start with kriyayoga, but you gradually go beyond that level. That has been known to be done, but not very frequently.

As I have said before, it is very important to have the hinayana and mahayana as a foundation before moving on to vajrayana. But somehow, once you have the tantric approach, it does not make all that much difference where you begin. You do not first need to develop the lower tantric yanas as a foundation. You can build anything on bodhichitta and the experience of shunyata, because you have already experienced transparency. If you started from the hinayana, skipped mahayana, and then tried the vajrayana, you would have absolute chaos; but if there is a real understanding of shunyata experience, there is no particular problem.

Tantra is not regarded as a linear process. You begin with hinayana and go on to mahayana, but when you get to the third yana, or vajrayana, you could choose whichever tantric yana you feel directed toward, so there is some freedom. Particularly in the three higher yanas, it is very much pick and choose. You can choose what particular sadhana to do directly from the bodhisattva level. But kriyayoga makes an enormous impact on people, so it is sometimes recommended that students who have already developed an understanding of the practice of mahamudra or maha ati go back to do a few months of kriyayoga practice. It is regarded as an interesting contrast. In that case, although you do the kriyayoga visualizations and meditation, it is highly influenced by maha ati practice.

Even though the lower yanas are not taught that often, at the same time it is necessary to study each yana in detail. This is absolutely necessary because, in order to understand the vajrayana, you have to get a feeling for the experiences of the different tantric yanas. You not only have to learn the vocabulary and the concepts, but you have to pick up the feeling, particularly the element of craziness that exists in each yana. It is important to pick that up, and to do so, you have to practice.

The higher yanas of mahayoga, anuyoga, and atiyoga also have their way of dealing with beginning students. It is not just a big bomb, and it is not just at the level of yes or no, but there is a gradual way to begin to adapt yourself and get used to that level. And depending on the particular yana you enter, once you are in it, you can build on it. If a traveler arrived at lunchtime, you would not make them eat breakfast, but they would be served lunch. If that traveler arrived at night, you would serve them dinner. You would not try to serve them breakfast *and* dinner *and* lunch, just because that traveler was a newcomer.

Altogether, the idea is that once you have experienced shunyata, you are free to embark on any of the yanas. You might start at the atiyoga level or you might start at the kriyayoga level—it doesn't really matter. It depends on your personality or your state of being.

In discussing the tantric yanas, there will be lots of references to the union principle, or yoga, which is very powerful. Sometimes the emphasis on union causes problems, because people would like to see things as being completely one. The idea of union or being united with something may also bring with it the idea of separateness. That creates an object of the various emotions, which can become a problem. But that problem is dealt with in tantra.

## Ground of Mahayana

The mahayana tradition deals purely with very abstract ideas. It is concerned with things such as paramitas, ethical codes, and shunyata, and focuses on understanding the nature of reality and one's relationship to the world, rather than on forms and symbols. It could be said that the mahayana approach to understanding the phenomenal world, or buddha mind, is like buying a caldron to boil water in; whereas the approach of kriyayoga and the other tantric yanas is not just to buy a caldron, but to buy a pot with a handle. The vajrayana approach is based on the realization that when you have boiled the water, you are going to pour it out as well, so a pot with a handle is more practical than a caldron. The practicality of the vajrayana is very powerful.

## THE IMPORTANCE OF KÜNDZOP / RELATIVE TRUTH

In vajrayana, the relative or primary truth is the most important truth. According to the vajrayana, you cannot attain enlightenment by rejecting the relative world or relative truth, but you need to work with phenomena. When a person is involved with the primary truth, there is a lot of conviction, which is somewhat on the level of *prabhasvara* in Sanskrit, or *ösel* in Tibetan, which means "luminosity." There is a quality of interest or inspiration that manifests as luminosity. This comes from realizing that experiencing the fullness of the manifested world has more truth than looking at it as empty. So in the vajrayana, you have to review the absolute and the relative truth all over again.

In the mahayana, kündzop is seen through, and töndam, or shunyata, is attained. In the Mind-only, or *yogachara* tradition of mahayana, you might see the world as your mental projection, and at the same time you view the world as real, workable, artistic, definite, and colorful. However, there is still an enormous emphasis on mirage or illusion. The difference between the mahayana approach and the vajrayana approach is that in tantra, there is no notion of mirage or illusion. Relating to the relative truth, or kündzop, is not a problem; in fact, kündzop is more important than töndam. It is absolutely important. So in terms of the two truths, the kriyayoga attitude toward the world is different from that of the mahayana.

The function of kriyayoga is to abandon the notion of töndam as something to be attained or looked forward to. Instead, you pay homage to kündzop, and try to relate with its usefulness. You try to relate with the insightfulness of the phenomenal world properly and fully. You can take water as water, and it cleans you inside and out, including your psychological problems. The point is that you need to drop any hesitation about actually getting into kündzop. So kriyayoga's commitment to kündzop is very powerful. It is more than a commitment; it is an inspiration. In kriyayoga, you realize that kündzop is no longer problematic.

Kriyayoga is one of the best ways of seeing things as they are. Water really means water; water is water; it has everything in it as waterness. Water could clean anything you could think of. That trust in reality is one of the very refreshing points of kriyayoga. The only problem would be if you overemphasize the sacredness of reality and make it into a trip of some kind. But in the original practice of kriyayoga, the sacredness is not quite the point: the point is precision.

## Two Approaches to Kündzop

There are two aspects to the kriyayoga approach to kündzop: purity of action and purity of attitude.

### Purity of Action

The first aspect of the kriyayoga approach stresses purity of action. Your body and your speech are regarded as manifestations of deities, of divine beings, so you are offering your body and speech in ultimate, complete purity.

In order to meet that particular demand and to satisfy that vision of purity, you are supposed to bathe three times a day, change your clothes three times a day, and eat what is known as white food—that is to say, just milk products and no meat. You are also supposed to eat sweet food. Traditionally, this means foods sweetened with brown sugar, white sugar, or honey. So the approach here is somewhat similar to that of Hindu kriyayoga, with its focus on being vegetarian and leading a clean and pure life.

The reason for doing all that is to connect with the inherent purity that exists already. You lead that kind of clean life in order to meet the demand of inherent purity, in order to actually get close to it, to attain that level. This is not a particularly far-fetched idea, although we could say it may be somewhat pedantic or too literal.

### Purity of Attitude

The second aspect of the kriyayoga approach to kündzop has to do with the importance of attitude. The importance of attitude is explained in terms of three categories: form, speech, and mind.

ATTITUDE TOWARD FORM. The first category is your attitude toward form. All the forms that exist—tables, chairs, vases, pillows, ceilings, floors, rugs, and whatever you have in the world—are regarded as expressions of kündzop. It is real kündzop, pure kündzop in its own purity, without any hang-ups, without any room for dualistic fixation. It is just simple, pure, good kündzop. Table is table; chair is chair.

Having been trained in hinayana and mahayana, students already have an understanding of the logic of shunyata. Since they have gone through their training of completely transcending dualistic fixations with regard to kündzop, they now have a fantastically fresh and absolutely powerful vision. So the tendency in the previous yanas of trying to kill kündzop or make it into a crude truth no longer exists in kriyayoga. Everything is fine. Fundamentally, there is no problem with kündzop at all.

The approach of kriyayoga is one of trusting kündzop completely. It is one of loving kündzop: loving pure food, loving pure clothes, loving a pure body. But the acceptance of kündzop is not naive or "love-and-lighty." On the level of form, we relate with kündzop as tangible things, the solid things that we have in our world. The basic, very solid and resounding things that exist around us are not regarded as a hassle anymore. They are regarded as expressions of purity, expressions of their own dignity. Vajra nature exists in the form aspect of kündzop, so we want to seize onto form completely. We want to relate with the images of the deities or sambhogakaya buddhas, because basic principles exist in those forms.

In kriyayoga, you no longer have a fixed idea of the one or the many; you transcend that. If you have as your reference point the idea that one thing is clean and another is dirty, then you have lost your vision of cosmic purity completely. On the other hand, if you think everything is clean, there is too much security, and too much make-believe, goody-goody thinking. Even the vision that everything is clean is actually a further dirtying. Therefore, you transcend both the one and many. You begin to see, without the qualifications of one or many, that this world is simply a clean world, a pure world. You are no longer talking in terms of pollution or dirt, but in terms of the intrinsic purity that exists in this world. This understanding can only come to be by trusting kündzop, the phenomenal world. Relative truth in itself is right and clean and pure. There is vajra nature in relative truth.

ATTITUDE TOWARD SPEECH. The second category in the importance of attitude is the attitude toward speech. This category is connected with transcending intellect. However, although the power of sound or voice transcends intellect, it does not mean that you are opposed to intellect. In particular, speech transcends the four logical possibilities of existence, nonexistence, both, and neither—the four extremes that you tend to get into when you have uncertainties about reality. When you are uncertain about something, you usually say it is yes, or it is no, or it is both, or it is neither.

To transcend those extremes, you need pure emotion, pure speech, pure voice. You have to manifest properly without being entangled with those four problems. To do so, you need trust or conviction in the power of voice to transcend those extremes. If you utter something, you utter it with a true voice rather than falling into one of those categories. True speech is unhesitating.

This kind of pure voice is called *vach* in Sanskrit. It is also called *shabda*, or "sound." Shabda is the idea of cosmic sound, which has nothing to do with the tangible world particularly or, for that matter, with the intangible world. Basically, the idea of vac is that everything you hear is the sound of the teachings. We could also say that everything you hear is the sound of mantra—or the sound of Atisha's mind-training slogans. Shabda is that which, through combining together the body and the mind, produces utterance in the phenomenal world. There is a quality here of divine utterance or cosmic utterance as an expression of pure energy. Kriyayoga makes a big deal about shabda.

ATTITUDE TOWARD MIND. The third category of attitude is concerned with the thought process. It is said in the tantric texts that thoughts are the scepters of the tathagatas, the divinities of a particular mandala. Scepters are signs of authority. For instance, a king holds his globe and his staff, which mark him as king. An editor might have a pen and paper on her desk as her scepter; a general might hold a stick or whip; a murderer might hold some kind of weapon. Scepters are reminders, marks, highlights. All thoughts that exist have that character; thoughts are our scepters, rather than just merely our thoughts.

We do not actually have thoughts all the time, but we have thoughts whenever we need them. So our thoughts of this and that change our manifestation all the time. Thoughts are regarded as scepters or symbols from that point of view. At the same time, thoughts go on continuously, and those thoughts are regarded at this point as perfect meditation, perfect awareness. All thoughts are equally pure. Dirty or clean thoughts, or whatever thoughts you have, are all regarded as perfectly pure and ordinarily insightful. Thoughts have the quality of the vision of the nidanas in the higher sense, as the expression of the interlocking of different situations taking place all the time. Thoughts are also expressions of vajra nature. They are pure and sacred.

## THE SACREDNESS OF ORDINARY PHENOMENA

Sacredness in kriyayoga is related to purity, but purity does not particularly refer back to sacredness. Sacredness is regarded as purity, because when things are sacred, they are inherently faultless. They stand on their own; there is no question about that. In kriyayoga, there is an appreciation that whatever appears in the way of ordinary phenomena turns into perfect purity, and therefore whatever appears is very sacred.

The emphasis on the importance of vegetarianism and other expressions of purity in this yana is not a neurotic hang-up or a food trip. It is not an ideology that you try to lay on other people because you yourself still feel unclean. In kriyayoga, nobody is forcing you to eat anything. Rather, whatever you do and however you live, that life is fundamentally pure and grand, clean, magnificent, and dignified. That is the kind of purity in kriyayoga—unconditional purity without condemnation. Nobody is condemned as being a bad girl or a dirty boy, but even the dirt itself is regarded as inherently pure dirt. So you cannot use the kriyayoga philosophy of the Buddhist tradition to impose your ideas of ecology, antipollution, or anything like that, which is a great relief.

## THE DEVELOPMENT OF PURITY

We can discuss the development of purity through relative bodhichitta, absolute bodhichitta, and the union of relative and absolute bodhichitta.

### Relative Bodhichitta

From the kriyayoga point of view, the experience of relative bodhichitta is like something entering into your system. You feel that you are relating with a definite intelligence, as opposed to an abstraction. There is a feeling of real ground, which comes from having experienced an absolute division between pure and impure, and the possibility of making a choice. There is a quality of purity in following all the rules and disciplines of conduct that are given to you. So the whole approach seems to be based on not taking in anything impure. Any impurity you take in is regarded as bad or unhealthy, and a cause of further pain. So instead of taking in any impurity, it is best to clean any impurity out.

## Absolute Bodhichitta

The experience of absolute bodhichitta entering into you is said to be similar to taking the refuge vow. You feel that some kind of belief or conviction has entered into your system. At the beginning of the path, you have a belief that calls you to become a refugee or a follower of the Buddha. Then in the refuge vow ceremony, as you are repeating the last of the three refuges—"I take refuge in the sangha"—the element of refuge enters into your system.

In the vajrayana, something similar takes place. Once again, a quality of appreciation and faith enters in, but in this case it is much more delicate and less crude. Very curiously, at the same time some kind of crudeness or samsaric mind begins to enter. But in this case, samsaric mind is disguised as absolute bodhichitta, the conviction and trust in the purity of being cleaned and stripped and perfectly well-dressed.

## The Union of Relative and Absolute Bodhichitta

With the union of the absolute and relative principles, you begin to see the purity of the phenomenal world overall. You see that whether it is pure or impure, it is all the same. How this idea of purity develops in this particular yana is very different from what happens at the bodhisattva level. In kriyayoga, things become much more clear and precise. At the highest level of kriyayoga, there is a hint that purity and impurity are one. But there is just a hint of that, rather than the full experience. A minute seed of crazy wisdom is beginning to develop, which is extraordinary and encouraging. If somebody moves very slowly from hinayana to mahayana, and finally embarks on the vajrayana, they begin to see a seed of craziness. That is a very powerful experience.

## INHERENT PURITY

The great Nyingma teacher Longchen Rabjam said that kündzop is unborn and unoriginated. That is the attitude toward reality in kriyayoga.

But it is hard to believe that; it is a very radical thing to say. Usually we believe that kündzop is born and originated. We think that things such as vases and tables and chairs are born and originated. But in this case, they are seen as unborn and unoriginated. Why? Because of their inherent purity.

As an example, however much we might like to romanticize the nature of childbirth, giving birth is a very messy job. You have blood coming out of you, you have pain, you have contractions. You are attacked by this sudden sickness called childbirth. You may like to sugarcoat the experience and say, "It was fine, fantastic, a real experience. My child was born by natural childbirth, and it was great!" But let us be very honest at this point. Although you may try to think of reality as some great natural wonder, although you may romanticize it, reality has its messy qualities always.

In kriyayoga, it is not that there are no messy qualities; the messiness is obvious. Reality is very messy! Nevertheless, that messiness is in itself inherently pure because it is a pure messy quality! It is truly messy, and that's fine. The mess is one-hundred-percent mess, so it is pure. That makes it unborn. Shit is one hundred-percent shit; therefore, it is inherently pure.

I would like to emphasize that this particular yana has a lot of wisdom. Good things come from developing that sense of purity completely. In the kriyayoga concept of purity, everything is sacred and everything is profane. And as long as there are no exceptions, it appears that it does not matter whether we call something "sacred" or "profane." The idea is that since everything is profane, therefore everything is very sacred.

The kriyayoga approach is realistic, rather than insight based. That is the difference between kündzop and töndam: in töndam, you take a superficial view at first, then you try to see inside it; but with kündzop, everything is taken at face value. Water is water; therefore, water is sacred. In kriyayoga, purity is seen to be an absolute, inherent quality of kündzop. That is where the very powerful vision of kriyayoga comes from.

# 41

# *Kriyayoga:*
# *Purification*

*In terms of [kriyayoga] purity, you are not just washing out dirt.*
*You are cleaning your skin and flesh and muscles and bones and*
*marrow and everything in your body so that it becomes transparent.*
*. . . Because you have cleaned everything out completely, including*
*having surrendered your ego, you have nothing left but pure trans-*
*parency, which is a tantric version of the bodhisattva path.*

## ROOTS IN HINDUISM

The tantric approach in Buddhism is based in part on Hinduism. In order
for Buddhist tantra to establish its own ground, it had to make use of the
existing tantric culture of Hinduism; and since kriyayoga is the first stage
of tantra, Hinduism and Buddhism could work together in kriyayoga.
So in kriyayoga, Buddhist and Hindu tantra share a cultural similar-
ity, which is unavoidable. If we look at kriyayoga from an anuttarayoga
point of view, we see a preoccupation with form, ritual, and other highly
symbolic activities. And at the level of anuttarayoga and the three higher
yanas, Hindu and Buddhist tantras are entirely different. But kriyayoga is
the starting point of all tantra, and at that level there are similarities and
meeting points.

The path of Hinduism is purely a tantric path; in Hinduism, there
are no such things as hinayana and mahayana. The Hindu ideal of total
human development in terms of the social setup—from one's upbringing,

professional pursuits, and relationship with the world, until one's final retirement as a *sannyasin,* or monk—might be the equivalent of the stages of hinayana, mahayana, and vajrayana. However, there is no definite or direct teaching of the three yanas within Hinduism.

The approach of Buddhist tantra is very closely related to Hinduism, but from the Buddhist perspective, worshipping Hindu deities is a form of ignorance. In particular, kriyayoga is considered to be a way of transcending the worship of Brahma, which is connected with ignorance; upayoga is considered to be a way of transcending the worship of Shiva, which is connected with aggression; and anuttarayoga is considered to be a way of freeing those who believe in the doctrine of passion, which is associated with Vishnu. The idea is that the basic qualities of those three Hindu deities seem to have developed into expressions of cosmic or national emotions and confusion. So kriyayoga, upayoga, and anuttarayoga can almost be seen as being dedicated to working with or overcoming the basic Hindu conflicting emotions, or kleshas.

## PHYSICAL PURITY AND HINDU TANTRA

Kriyayoga could be interpreted as being a pragmatic approach to life. What is the first thing to do when you are giving a tea party? You wash the teacups. That is precisely analogous to what happens in kriyayoga. Kriyayoga has a quality of practicality. It puts great emphasis on external actions and on physical and verbal discipline. It has to do with taking care of your body and your voice, and having an understanding of sound.

The idea of action in kriyayoga is very close to the Hindu approach of physical purity. In Hindu tantra, much of the discipline has to do with acts of physical purification. The means of purifying yourself include bathing, eating vegetarian food, and doing the *agni puja,* or the fire-offering ceremony. We should be very careful not to think of such Hindu physical purification practices as merely superstitious. There is a lot of wisdom in them, although the wisdom is somewhat one-sided from our point of view.

The Buddhist approach to physical purity differs from Hindu kriyayoga practice, although externally they appear to be almost the same. One reason they are not quite the same is that in the nontheistic Buddhist tradition, there is no belief in an external power, so there is no fear from that angle. However, neurotic eruptions could still develop within you and cause chaos, so you keep yourself pure in order to prevent such chaos. Whether in a group or alone, the mentality of purity is strongly present, so there is very little room for ignorance—but there is still room for a sudden attack, skirmish, or border fight of ignorance. A sudden attack of confusion and chaos, an attack of samsaric mind, almost at the blackout level, is still possible. Therefore, there is a feeling of vulnerability, which brings out the need for purity. You feel that you cannot be attacked if you keep yourself clean and pure.

In the previous yanas, the hinayana and mahayana, there is the same approach. You sit and meditate in order to attain enlightenment, in order to avoid being vulnerable to klesha attacks. The purity of kriyayoga is another way of retreating from such problems.

In Buddhist kriyayoga, the response to living in an impure world is not so much that you conquer it. There is a lot of paranoia involved in the principle of victory. So in Buddhism, there is less emphasis on conquering or victory as compared to the Hindus, who talk about victory a great deal. In Buddhist kriyayoga, it is just that if you are dirty, you wash. You have acquired a vajra soap, and you have it available to you, so you do not have to make a big deal about it. Purity is in itself the practice, rather than focusing on impurity as something that you should dispel. There is actually a problem with our language, in that when we talk about purity, there is automatically the idea that impurity has to be dispelled, that we are attacking impurity or dirt. But that is not the case here. In Buddhist kriyayoga, we are indulging ourselves in purity without reference point. The purity itself becomes a way of life.

In Buddhist kriyayoga, even baby shit could be seen as an object of purity. It is washable, so there is no fear of permanent damage. The world is inherently pure. If you put a few little ingredients of purity into the world and apply water, the world will speak for itself in its own purity. The purity will begin to relate with you. It is as if you shine a flashlight on the sun when the sun is hidden behind a cloud, and then the sun dispels the cloud because you shone your flashlight on it. The sun begins to communicate with your light, and the sun is very happy. But this has nothing to do with victory.

You might think that although the sun is pure and the flashlight is pure, there is still the cloud, which is impure. But in the view of Buddhist kriyayoga, clouds are temporary phenomena. They are not something you have to struggle with or destroy. Such obstacles do exist, but they are not particularly a big problem. You experience impurities, but you know they are temporary and could be dissolved. That is the hope, the enlightenment. According to Buddhist tantra, from the beginning of the path we are already enlightened. We just have to realize it, and it is realizable.

In kriyayoga, trust and faith are developed in how you handle yourself, within the notion that everything is transcendent. But such a transcendental approach can still only take place in kriyayoga at the level of physical gestures. And the basic physical gesture of the transcendental approach of kriyayoga is physically keeping clean, which includes maintaining a vegetarian diet, taking three baths a day, and eating pure food.

## Kriyayoga in Japan, Tibet, and the West

In Tibet, in order to perform the kriyayoga sadhana of Vairochana, we have to be trained in the five hundred mudras of that particular deity, as well as learning the forms and ideas associated with that sadhana, and memorizing the text. When you are receiving the abhisheka and practice this sadhana, you get up very early, you do not eat any meat, and you do not even put peacock feathers on the abhisheka vase. You just put *kusha* grass on it. You do not wear leather or fur products, but just simple wool.

The sadhana is very severe, and memorizing the mudras is very confusing. In fact, in my monastery one of the examinations that the monks had to go through, including myself, was to sit in the middle of the assembly and perform the mudras that relate to a particular five-page section of the text. In the verse in that sadhana where the visualization occurs, it talks about how Vairochana holds a vajra and a three-bladed ritual knife, or *phurba,* in his hands, and he is churning out little wrathful protectors, or mahakalas. You have to do all the mudras that go along with that, which each have their own form.

Kriyayoga seems to be taught differently in Japan than in Tibet. In the Japanese tantra of Shingon Buddhism, which is largely based on kriyayoga, there are two main mandalas: those of Garbhadhatu and Vajradhatu. In Japan, there is less emphasis on purification and more emphasis on mudras and forms of all kinds. I think it is necessary to have forms of that nature, but for Tibetans, mantra practice is the main form. However, in doing the practice, the hand gestures, visualizations, and mantras are universal. It has nothing to do with culture.

In terms of introducing kriyayoga in the West, there are very few cultural reference points to such purity practices. Although certain diets and forms such as yoga could be seen as purification practices, they tend to be heavy-handed, and any practice involving aggression does not quite work. However, as long as we are not obsessed with such disciplines, they could be useful in kriyayoga. Beyond that, we could introduce kriyayoga forms of mudras, mantras, and music, which are absolutely necessary.

## The Symbolism of Water

In kriyayoga, you are beginning to understand vajrayana symbolism. In particular, you are beginning to relate with water. Water plays an important part in kriyayoga. It is not so much that you are disgusted with your dirt, but rather that you are relating with the feeling of cleanliness. There is a respect for the cleansing power of water. There is respect for the magic of water and the magic of cleanliness. This is reflected in the practice of symbolic cleansing at the start of a ceremony, which begins in kriyayoga and continues throughout tantra.

Kriyayoga is a very interesting yana, because it has the sophistication of all the previous yanas, but at the same time it has also collected the paranoias of the previous yanas. Everything is based on action, on physical evidence of your commitment. You are involved with particular physical practices, and you understand the symbolism. It is good symbolism to take three baths a day and keep a vegetarian diet so that you do not associate yourself with the animal realm. In particular, kriyayogins avoid eating such things as the tongues, hearts, and brains of animals. If you must be a nonvegetarian, it is better to just eat an ordinary steak.*

In kriyayoga, purity is an act of cleanliness, and at the same time purity is self-existing. You are already pure and clean, but if you have doubts about that, you might take a shower or two. In the hinayana, purity is loneliness and simplicity. In the mahayana, purity is benevolence. So the purity of kriyayoga is a natural progression.

We should not look down upon hinayana or kriyayoga as being a

---

* In some Buddhist ethical systems, it is said that if you eat meat, it is better to eat a portion of a large animal rather than many small animals, for you are causing the loss of fewer lives.

limited or fixed view. That is absolutely not true. If you do kriyayoga practice, it might actually turn your head around, in contrast to the tameness of just discussing it. You would be surprised how much power it has. Purifying yourself in this way is great. It is a fantastic and worthwhile experience. You actually do feel that you are changing your system completely, that you are becoming clean and pure.

In kriyayoga, we could even go so far as to say that that you worship water as the mark of purification. One problem with Buddhism is that if we just stop at the level of madhyamaka, we end up sounding so dry and impersonal that we do not even have a path anymore. That is precisely why Naropa and others left their monasteries and decided to take a different approach altogether.*

In our practice community, Karmê Chöling, we try to meditate at least three times a day. But this does not mean that we are paranoid about going insane, and so we are trying to regroup ourselves constantly. We just regard meditation as our way of life. We just do it. And the same thing is true with kriyayoga. Taking a bath is regarded as holy activity, sacred activity. You just do it. That is your lifestyle, your discipline. It is not because you are afraid of getting dirty. The fear of being dirty seems to be a more Hindu approach, but such paranoia can be a form of intelligence. As our discussion of tantra continues, you will find that we are going to use the word *paranoia* more and more. But we do not mean just any good old paranoia. We are talking about intelligence that is so sharp that it begins to cut through itself.

A kriyayoga person has an understanding of the nature of water. You understand not just that water cleans physically, but you have a sense of psychological waterness. You realize that the purity of water does not just wash away your dirt. But this idea is not like the theistic belief that if you bathe in the river Ganges, your sins will be washed away. Buddhist practitioners of kriyayoga are not fooled by that kind of thinking.

It may seem to be a bit ironic that a person who has reached the level of the highest form of mahayana Buddhism and the sophistication of the

---

* Naropa left his distinguished university post at Nalanda University in order to seek a genuine teacher, recognizing that intellectual understanding alone was insufficient for true dharmic awakening. For more on Naropa and his studies with his teacher Tilopa, see Chögyam Trungpa, *Illusion's Game*.

middle way, or madhyamaka, could still be involved with such trivialities. That may be, but it still makes enormous sense. You begin to get a great deal of benefit out of this kind of symbolism. Water means water; fire means fire. Symbols make sense to basic being. They can be the manifestation of the awakened state of mind or of confusion; therefore, it is much better to be on the safe side.

According to kriyayoga, impurities are not regarded as lethal or poisonous, but they are regarded as a way of delaying final perfection. Therefore, people have to watch themselves: what they do, what they eat, and so forth. In terms of purity, you are not just washing out dirt. You are cleaning your skin and flesh and muscles and bones and marrow and everything in your body so that it becomes transparent. That is one of the most powerful points about kriyayoga. Once you have put your thoughts through the washing machine, you might still have thoughts, but they are transparent thoughts, pure thoughts. Because you have cleaned everything out completely, including surrendering your ego, you have nothing left but pure transparency, which is a tantric version of the bodhisattva path.

## Two Types of Surrendering

Kriyayoga is highly and skillfully organized. I cannot imagine who actually thought of it. You are a little clean thing and you have all these visions coming to you, but you still have to submit. The hangover of hinayana and mahayana still continues at the kriyayoga level, so the mental discipline is still one of surrendering. It is one of offering ego and purifying ego. There is a quality of not holding anything back, a feeling that everything has been washed or cleansed.

Two types of surrendering take place here: surrendering the gross ego and surrendering the refined ego.

### Surrendering the Gross Ego

Surrendering the gross ego is based on identifying yourself with relative bodhichitta. It is based on practicing kindness, not being selfish, and practicing virtues such as being gentle and patient. It is a sort of external gentility and kindness. In surrendering the gross ego, you take a vow to accept relative bodhichitta.

## *Surrendering the Refined Ego*

Surrendering the refined ego or minute ego is based on taking the absolute bodhisattva attitude, which is also an inheritance from the mahayana. You are willing to see the phenomenal world in terms of absolute bodhichitta. However, you have never actually visualized yourself as a deity, so although the ego is dissolved, the shell remains. In other words, the experiences of relative and ultimate bodhichitta can be achieved by keeping the rules and disciplines of the kriyayoga tantra, but you still have a sense of *this* and *that,* which does not particularly belong to either the gross or the refined level of ego. The sense of *this* and *that* remains, because you still have not identified yourself personally with any of the tathagatas or tantric deities.

At the higher levels of kriyayoga, there begins to be some true identification with the deity. But generally in kriyayoga, you are viewing the deities as external objects of reverence that you could open to, but not truly identify with. So although you are cleansed, there is still a sense of *this* and *that.* In order to have true vision, you first wash your eyeglasses immaculately so you can see *that* and *this* properly. You begin to relate with the deities by purifying the medium, and before you go in, you also take a bath and put on fresh clothes. You begin at the level of purification. In turn, the deities watch you and regard you as a worthy spectator. They see that you are also pure. Therefore, you could be in their particular realm; otherwise, you could not. However, one shortcoming of kriyayoga is that there is not enough vajra pride or identification with the deities.

## CLEAR PERCEPTION

In kriyayoga, there is still a hangover from the hard work of the hinayana and mahayana. We find that there is still more dirt to clean up. Our hinayana and mahayana training helped us get rid of our basic dirt, and having gotten rid of that heavy-handed rubbish, what remains is quite workable. That is why we evolve into a practitioner of kriyayoga tantra: to clean that up. It is as if we have already gotten rid of the basic garbage and dirt from our house, and the only thing left is just to vacuum the floor and do a light dusting.

The mentality of the kriyayoga practitioner is still one of paranoia. It is not paranoia in a pathological sense; rather, at the level of yogic practice, there is still fear, hope, uncertainty, and a light amount of anxiety. The paranoia of kriyayoga seems almost nonexistent from the point of view of the lower yanas, but when you are at this level, it is quite outstanding. And there is one further problem in kriyayoga, which is the fear of profound teachings. There is a fear of going deeper or involving yourself in a deeper situation.

A basic psychological shift takes place after the mahayana experience of shunyata. You realize that you have to clean up properly and perfectly, and there seems to be enormous inspiration to do so. The shunyata experience brings a quality of simultaneous emptiness and fullness, and once that begins to happen, you also begin to see further vistas. You see all kinds of things. Once you are really engaged in the shunyata experience, you begin to see that there are various little areas not covered by shunyata. These are not areas to be conquered, but more like the little bubbles left in a glass bowl or little specks of dust on a table. You begin to see that you are covered with freckles, and that they are washable.

Once you begin to get into vajrayana mentality, your perspective is more perky. You begin to stick your neck out much more than the subdued bodhisattvas—and the more you stick your neck out, the more bubbles you begin to see. You clearly see the bubbles, which may be filled with pollution, and you wash them out without taking a bath. You clear them out. You pierce them. And the technique you use is identifying with the deities in the mandala. You do so by identifying with the principle of surrendering. Mahayana practitioners do not even see the bubbles. They bathe in soda water, and they think everything is okay. But kriyayogins do not bathe in soda water; they bathe in real water.

So it could be said that the problem you are working with in kriyayoga is not dirt at all, but the paranoia that comes from feeling that your perception is twisted. It is a question of working with the quality of your perception. You are trying to make your perception so clear that you no longer perceive any dirt.

## 42

# *Kriyayoga:*
# *Empowerment*

*In order to enter into the experience of kriyayoga, you begin by receiving abhisheka. Having gone through a kriyayoga abhisheka, you develop a feeling of cleanliness and purity. It is very refreshing, fantastically refreshing, and it gives you a sense of enormous health and freshness and—if I may go as far as to say it—happiness.*

### THE FOUR PRELIMINARIES

Before starting to practice kriyayoga, you need to complete the four foundation or preliminary practices of the ngöndro; the 100,000 prostrations, the 100,000 refuge formula recitations, the 100,000 Vajrasattva mantra recitations, and the 100,000 mandala offerings.

Vajrayana disciplines cannot be practiced without undergoing a great deal of preparation in the form of surrendering, purifying, giving, and all the rest of it. Going through these preparatory practices is like being put through a washing machine. You are crumpled up, pushed into the machine, the lid is closed, the water is turned on, soap is put in, bleach is added, and then you are cycled through the washing process completely. You come out at the other end somewhat clean and presentable, but still needing to be ironed. The ironing process is called guru yoga practice, which comes at the end of the ngöndro practices and brings complete union with the guru or guru principle. Kriyayoga and the other tantric yanas are all on a level of practice that comes after a person has already gone through all this preparatory training, after they have been ironed and become wearable clothing.

In guru yoga practice, you visualize the guru, but you do not visualize yourself as anything. You worship the guru, and the visualization of the guru dissolves into you at the end; but you are still separate from the guru, and that mentality continues in kriyayoga. In the transition from ngöndro into the kriyayoga level, you begin to have the possibility of identifying completely with the yidams. However, the experience of seeing yourself as the deity or merging with your visualization does not begin until the next yana, or upayoga. In kriyayoga, you are just a respectable spectator in this particular theater. If you go to France but you do not speak French, you can still respect their culture and their food. Eventually you might become more like a French person. You might dress like a French person, learn the language, and be ready to jump in, because you have seen how they handle their world in a French way.

## RECEIVING ABHISHEKA

In order to enter into the experience of kriyayoga, you begin by receiving abhisheka. The word *abhisheka* has a connection with water and the idea of anointment, and in kriyayoga you have many different waters to relate with: water at the beginning of the abhisheka, water from the yidams, water from the hinayana practitioners, the *shravakas* and *pratyekabuddhas,* water from the bodhisattvas, and water from the Buddha. There are many waters to relate with, and they all seem to be different because your attitude and the water-giver's attitude toward each water is different. But although each kind of water may give you a different flavor, it is still the same water from the same jar or tap.

Having gone through a kriyayoga abhisheka, you develop a feeling of cleanliness and purity. It is very refreshing, fantastically refreshing, and it gives you a sense of enormous health and freshness and—if I may go as far as to say it—happiness. It is possible that such an experience of purity could develop even at the lay bodhisattva level, not only after the eleventh bhumi level. That is why tantra is communicable.

Empowerment in the kriyayoga abhisheka is similar to that of the higher tantric yanas. Through the abhisheka, power is transmitted from your guru and through the power of the yidams to you. In this case, you are receiving the empowerment to perform a particular kriyayoga sadhana. By means of the abhisheka, the basic sanity principle is being awakened within your system. So a kriyayoga abhisheka is a transmission, but the transmission is rather weak. The kriyayoga notion of abhisheka is not that you are enthroned as a given deity or a lineage inheritor. Instead, an abhisheka is viewed as a form of purification. It is viewed as a mark of entering into the tribe or the tribal structure. In that sense, an abhisheka is similar to anointments and rituals, such as circumcision, which have been developed in other mystical schools.

## THE KRIYAYOGA ABHISHEKAS

In a kriyayoga abhisheka, the definitions and categories are actually quite simple, compared with the upcoming yanas. The abhishekas are: preliminary abhisheka, water abhisheka, crown abhisheka, water purification and protection abhisheka, and enriching abhisheka.

### The Preliminary Abhisheka: The Abhisheka of the Vajra Disciple

The preliminary abhisheka is called the abhisheka of the vajra disciple. In this abhisheka, the first thing that occurs is that the disciple throws a flower onto a specially created mandala, either a mandala made of sand or a painted mandala. The disciple throws the flower with concentration and trust in the reality of the nowness of that particular world, which is a world without deception, a world without further dreams.

The mandala is divided into a pattern based on the principle of the kriyayoga buddha-families, and when you throw your flower, you hit a certain part of the mandala. By throwing the flower and seeing where it lands, you discover your own deity or yidam. So you have a role in actualizing that. If you do not trust in that particular primary truth completely, or if you lack an understanding of the whole process, then it is possible that you will not be able to throw the flower onto the mandala. Your flower might jump out of the mandala. This would show that you have no recognition of the reality or truth constituted by the power created by your vajra guru in the vajra relationship that exists between vajra guru and vajra disciple.

## The Main Kriyayoga Abhishekas: Water and Crown

Having discovered your particular family, you receive the two main abhishekas: the water abhisheka and the crown abhisheka.

THE WATER OR VASE ABHISHEKA OF DHARMAKAYA. The first main kriya-yoga abhisheka is the abhisheka of water, or the vase abhisheka (which is another way of saying the same thing, since a vase contains water). In the water abhisheka, you are given water from a vase full of water that has been blessed by the vidyadhara or vajra guru. The guru has performed their own sadhana practice over the water to bless it, so the water has been influenced by the thought power of that person.

When the water is given to you, first the base of the vase is put on your head, then you are given water in the hollow in your hand as a symbol of pouring water over your head, and then you drink the water from your hand. You have now been christened in this particular tradition.

Water is connected with the dharmakaya, which is the original purity, the original cleanliness, and the perfect transparency that you are. In drinking the water, there is complete appreciation that reality is finally workable. Even on the level of dharmakaya, reality is workable. At this point we are not talking about anything transcendental, but in going through the previous yanas, you have developed a lot of resistance to accepting reality simply as it is. The dharmakaya, in this case, is a purification of that resistance. You are accepting that there is a space or opening in you already—and that space can be discovered by means of the example of water, by your vajra master, and by your taking part in this water abhisheka ritual.

FIVE VASE INITIATIONS. Traditionally there are five vases of water and five vase initiations in kriyayoga. Kriyayogins seem to be "hydro-maniacs."

*Opening water abhisheka.* The first vase empowerment is known as the opening water abhisheka. It is entering into the abhisheka and preparing yourself to receive the empowerment. Basic empowerment or basic power is created, which is a neutral situation.

*Water abhisheka of all the deities.* The second vase empowerment is the water abhisheka of all the deities, or all the yidams. It is connected with being willing to commit yourself to the deities, and to relate to these particular deities and to the concept of deities. You are willing to relate to the sambhogakaya buddhas.

*Vase of the shravakas and pratyekabuddhas.* The third vase empowerment is the vase of the shravakas and pratyekabuddhas. It is the acceptance of the lower yanas as part of the vajrayana process. Having been accepted into the mandala and recognized as a worthy student, you have to go back to the hinayana. You have to acknowledge that the journey you are taking is not purely at the vajrayana level, but you are also accepting the complete teachings of Buddha.

The visualization that your vajra master gives you at this point, and that your vajra master has also done, includes all kinds of arhats and other forms of hinayana iconography, which all dissolve in tantric style into the water in the vase. The water is then given to you in the same way as before. At this point, the hinayana is turned into vajrayana as a magical process. In case you have not already received the magical transformation of the hinayana, you now receive that particular magical transformation from the power of the arhats and the hinayana saints and the hinayana awakened state of mind.

*Vase of the bodhisattvas.* The fourth vase empowerment is the vase of the bodhisattvas. In the same way as the previous empowerment, the mahayana principle and the various bodhisattvas are visualized, and they dissolve into the water in the vase. The vase is put on your head, and again water is poured into your hand. By drinking this water, you connect with the basic sanity of the bodhisattvas, and you receive the magical power of the bodhisattvas in the tantric fashion.

*Vase of the Buddha.* The fifth and final vase empowerment is the vase of the Buddha. From the kriyayoga point of view, the Buddha is actually the dharmakaya. In fact, all the water abhishekas are regarded as dharmakaya abhishekas. The symbolism of water and the basic quality of water is that it can contain all the elements. Likewise, the dharmakaya can contain shravakas, pratyekabuddhas, and bodhisattvas. All thinkable entities are included in it. Like water, the dharmakaya contains all the elements at once. So the water or vase abhisheka is the kriyayoga abhisheka of dharmakaya.

THE CROWN ABHISHEKA OF SAMBHOGAKAYA AND NIRMANAKAYA. The second main kriyayoga abhisheka is the crown abhisheka, which is merely a confirmation. The crown abhisheka is also called the abhisheka of mark or emblem. In kriyayoga they do not always use an actual crown, as they do in the upcoming yanas. Instead they use some form of identification, such as a headband, to mark that you have been given the honor of belonging to a particular family and receiving such an abhisheka.

The crown abhisheka is connected with the kayas of form: the sambhogakaya and the nirmanakaya. Finally you are crowned, not as the great master or great king or anything like that, but as a true member of the tribe. By means of this coronation, you now take pride that you have finally decided to give in to reality. Reality is workable and it speaks to you, rather than you having to speak to reality in order to be accepted as a part of it. Reality comes toward you, and it acknowledges your existence and the validity of the activities taking place between your vajra master and you as the vajra disciple.

The abhishekas of water and crown are the main abhishekas within the overall ceremony. Having received the water abhisheka and the crown abhisheka, you have now become a son or daughter of noble family. You are part of the whole mandala principle, and you have received the five types of kriyayoga purification. So you have actually conquered the world of purity. You have received the power of transmission and the power to practice. That is the basic abhisheka.

## Two Further Abhishekas

After the main abhisheka, there are two further abhishekas, which are purely paraphernalia or embellishments. It is like cooking your food properly: if you think that the food might taste bad, you add a few spices. You might also put salt and pepper on your table in case you need them.

WATER PURIFICATION AND PROTECTION ABHISHEKA. The first of the two further abhishekas is the water purification and protection abhisheka. It pacifies all obstacles, all evil forces. It pacifies the evil spirits and harmful imaginations that capture your state of mind. Having already gone through the main abhishekas, you still need to be confirmed further. At this point, you might be thinking, "Have I been initiated or not?" The purpose of this abhisheka is to dispel that question, and even that doubt.

This abhisheka is, again, a water abhisheka. In this case, the guru sprinkles water all over your body. He pours water over your head, and he gives you a portion of the water, which you are expected to take back to your home as protection water. He may also give you a protection cord.*

It may seem that when you receive this water protection abhisheka, not a great deal happens. But there will definitely be communication and connection transmitted. In particular, at the level of the water purification abhisheka, you are relating with a magic potion of some kind. It may be your imagination or your psychological state, or it may be because you are receptive to suggestion, but at the same time it is somehow very real. It is real because you have opened your mind to that situation. You are afraid of it, and at the same time you hope you might get something out of it.

That simultaneous mixture of fear and hope produces enormous openness. With that combination, you are open to the virus of kriyayoga. So the people who get hit the hardest, in terms of receiving some kind of message or energy, are the people who are afraid and open at the same time. Things have more effect on them than on people who are fully afraid or fully open.

After the water and crown abhishekas, a very feeble but well-meaning watcher is left.† But when you receive the water protection abhisheka of kriyayoga, quite possibly your watcher is the target. This abhisheka is to protect you from that watcher, to purify you from that watcher. The vajra master has the power to dispel your watcher. And in this case, at the level of the water protection abhisheka of kriyayoga, you are pacifying evil spirits—and the watcher is an evil spirit, if you would like to put it that way. Psychologically, once you receive this abhisheka, you feel that you have been washed. You feel as if you have been stripped, and completely and utterly cleansed.

ENRICHING ABHISHEKA. The final kriyayoga abhisheka is the enriching abhisheka. Having purified everything and having given up everything, you still need to have a roof over your head, and you still need food to

---

* A *protection cord* is a colored string with a special knot in it that has been blessed by a vajrayana teacher. It is worn around the neck or kept in a special place as a form of protection, and as a reminder of one's practice and one's link with the teacher.

† The *watcher* is a reference to the self-conscious factor in sitting meditation, that which keeps track. For a discussion of the watcher, see volume 1 of the *Profound Treasury*, part 3, "Meditation / Samadhi," in the section entitled "The Four Foundations of Mindfulness."

eat. There are still physical needs. Therefore, you need the power to make yourself comfortable, so that poverty does not hassle you in your life. In order to provide that power of enrichment, the same eight types of ingredients that were presented to the Buddha by various people at the attainment of his enlightenment are presented to you by the vajra master. The ingredients given to the Buddha were a kind of insurance so that having attained enlightenment, he did not have to suffer from poverty, and the offerings given to you in this abhisheka are a continuation of that tradition. With this abhisheka, you are provided with that magical power of enrichment.

The eight ingredients are usually presented to you as pictures. It would be preferable to have the real things, but generally nobody takes the trouble to do so. But whether you are presented with the ingredient itself or with a picture of it, this is saying the same thing, since whatever you see is a color postcard in any case.

EIGHT INGREDIENTS OR OFFERINGS. The first ingredient presented to you is a *milk drink,* which is in the form of a picture that the vajra master puts in your hand.* The next ingredient is a *kusha grass mat,* symbolizing the spot where Buddha sat after he was given the milk drink. The third ingredient is a *sesame seed,* which gives protection from evil spirits. The fourth ingredient is the *gallbladder of an elephant,* which has all kinds of medicinal powers, such as reducing high blood pressure. The fifth ingredient is *litri,* or red lead, a mineral or orange-colored stone that is ground and used quite widely in India. Litri has the power to reduce high blood pressure; it also acts as a laxative and cleanses the circulation. The sixth ingredient is *bamboo.* It is not hollow bamboo but solid bamboo, which is very strong, and which is also used for medicinal purposes. The seventh ingredient is a kind of fruit known as a *wood apple.* This type of fruit is used more as an ornament than as actual food. The eighth and last offering is a *mirror,* symbolizing the mirror that was presented to the Buddha by a goddess as a confirmation of his health. If you feel sick and you look in a mirror, you may very well look sick. But once you have taken all these ingredients and you feel good, when you look in your mirror, you look good.

---

* This offering mirrors the *milk drink* offered the Buddha by a milkmaid at the crucial turning point in his path, when he decided to drop the practice of austerity and sit by himself under the bodhi tree until he attained realization.

EIGHT AUSPICIOUS SYMBOLS. Having received the eight auspicious ingredients, the quality of wealth developed in this abhisheka is enacted through the presentation of the eight auspicious symbols: the *lotus,* for speech and for purity; the *knot of eternity* for your heart, for your awareness, and for harmony; the *umbrella* for protection; the *conch shell* for proclamation; the *victory banner* for overcoming obstacles; the *golden fish* for fearlessness; the *dharma wheel* for knowledge and realization; and the *treasure vase* for prosperity and long life.

Having already stripped away all doubts and washed out any dirt you had on you, you are finally confirmed. You are given fundamental wealth or richness. It is as though you had washed, abandoned your rags, and finally are given a royal costume. However, although you have been given a royal costume, you are not yet enthroned as a king or queen. There is no notion of actually becoming royalty at this point. This empowerment is still very much concerned with making you a good citizen in the tantric tribal setup.

## KRIYAYOGA SAMAYA

The samaya process in kriyayoga is very direct and safe, in the positive sense that you could be ideally healthy, both psychologically and physically. In kriyayoga, the samaya vow is connected with surrendering, while in later yanas, samaya involves an identification with all the deities, which gives you a quality of vajra pride.

The commitment in kriyayoga is related to purification, so it involves a task or action. You may feel that as a burden, but this burden is good. It is a journey. Even in the experience of enlightenment, or complete purification, if you have enough compassion you will still have this sense of burden. However, if you regard enlightenment as a good vacation, then you are far back on the path.

# Kriyayoga:
# Practice

*Kriyayoga is the first yana beyond mahayana, and it is a great exposure to the vajra world, which is fantastic. But you need to keep it cool. The idea is to be humble.*

## CREATING THE MANDALA

The basic principle of kriyayoga is spotlessness. In Sanskrit this is *vimala*, or "purity." Spotlessness is a quality of the peaceful deities, since dirt can never perch on such deities. According to kriyayoga, there is definitely such a thing as a clean mind, and it is very possible to achieve that pure mind. Spotlessness does exist, and you could achieve it. There is absolute purity.

In kriyayoga, you need to be completely cleansed and purified. You should radiate purity. As we mentioned earlier, vegetarianism is important in kriyayoga because it is thought that taking in anything impure is very improper, and eating flesh is considered to be a form of taking in impurity. So vegetarianism in kriyayoga has nothing to do with the principle of nonviolence toward animals. It is simply a form of tantric kriyayoga chemistry. Kriyayoga also shares the Hindu idea of the sacredness of the cow. So in creating the physical mandala of kriyayoga, you purify the ground of the mandala with what are called the five ingredients of a cow: dung, urine, milk, snot, and saliva.*

---

\* In some commentaries, this list is given as dung, urine, tears, snot, and saliva.

Kriyayoga is one of the most meticulously ritualistic yanas. Ritual is the basis of kriyayoga's connection with tantra, and it is also a basic philosophy of kriyayoga. One example is the sand mandala. The details of creating elaborate colored-sand mandalas were transmitted to Tibetan kriyayoga practitioners directly from India by the tantric kriyayoga masters. Some people say that the Tibetans have a cultural link with the Native Americans, because native people also make sand paintings. However, such a link is more wishful thinking than reality.

In a kriyayoga empowerment ceremony, the space in front of you will usually be organized as a shrine, with a mandala created out of colored sand, which is the prescribed form of a mandala in kriyayoga. The various ritual objects that are connected with kriyayoga principles and deities are then placed upon that mandala. The kriyayoga tantra says that it is necessary to understand the proportions and colors of the mandala properly. Upon that mandala the various ritual objects, the objects connected with kriyayoga principles and deities, are placed.

In the lower tantric yanas, a sand mandala is considered the best mandala to use. If you cannot do that, you can use a painting of the mandala, and if you cannot manage that, you can arrange heaps of grain in the shape of the mandala. In the higher tantric yanas, it is the opposite. According to the three higher tantras, the best way to create a mandala is by arranging heaps of grain; the second-best way is by using a painting; and the third and worst way is by creating a sand mandala. So in the lower tantric yanas, a more meticulous approach is best; and in the higher tantric yanas, which lean toward simplicity, less elaborateness is best.

## FAMILIES OR BUDDHA PRINCIPLES

Kriyayoga does not yet have five buddha-families. It is too early on the tantric path to get into that level of sophistication. Here there are six families divided into three transcendent and three worldly families. The three transcendent families are the tathagata family, the padma family, and the vajra family; the three worldly families are the family of jewels or wealth, the family of prosperity,* and the family of the ordinary.

---

* Trungpa Rinpoche also referred to the second worldly family as the family of hungry ghosts.

## Three Transcendent Families

In terms of correspondence with the five buddha-family principles, the tathagata family corresponds with the buddha, ratna, and the karma families jumbled together; the padma family corresponds with the padma family; and the vajra family with the vajra family. The reason kriyayoga does not include the ratna or karma families as separate families is that the kriyayoga mentality and approach is so puritanical and cleanliness oriented. It has not developed the power of ratna or the speed of karma. Therefore, you only have three transcendent families in kriyayoga: the tathagata family, the padma family, and the vajra family.

As for the principal deities or inhabitants of the transcendental world, the tathagata family includes all the buddhas, although at this point they are not named as the five buddhas, but are just a collection of buddhas. For the padma family, you have the bodhisattva Avalokiteshvara, and for the vajra family, you have the bodhisattva Vajrapani.

## Three Worldly Families

The three worldly families represent the lower realm, the worldly shadows of the previous ones. The jewel family is related to the tathagata family, the prosperity family to the padma family, and the ordinary family to the vajra family. The jewel family is connected with the Vaishravana, the god of wealth. The prosperity family is connected with the hungry ghosts, or the feeling of poverty, and also, according to the books, with seeking for joy. The ordinary family is connected with any sort of *brahmaloka*, or god realm, which is the traditional dwelling place of Hindu deities such as Brahma and Krishna, as well as mythical beings such as *garudas* (birds), *gandharvas* (messengers), and all the rest. You also have a touch of the tathagatas and of Avalokiteshvara and Vajrapani, but the sense of the transcendental families is not quite complete.

## ENTERING THE MANDALA

In kriyayoga, you enter the vajrayana mandala from the front door, which is in the East, according to the mandala principle. The East is connected with the vajra family, so you start with the vajra family. That is definitely the first family you come across. Kriyayoga seems to be particularly suited to the vajra family, because it has so much to do with water. Akshobhya is the buddha of the vajra family, and his consort is Mamaki, who in this case is connected with the earth, or with enriching.* So kriyayoga has a lot of connections with the vajra family.

## Mandala Deities

In a mandala, the principal deity appears in the center, and is called the owner or proprietor of the mandala. Surrounding the central deity are the proprietor's consort and the protective deities, or bodyguards. There are wrathful gods and goddesses, as well as masculine and feminine messengers, and masculine and feminine servants. Those are the general categories of deities found in a mandala, and it is the pattern of deities that we have in kriyayoga.

As an example of a kriyayoga mandala, if you study the *Mahavairochana* mandala of the Japanese Shingon tradition, you will see that there are something like forty-two gods, including wrathful gods, peaceful gods, messengers, servants, and so forth. All of those deities are connected with the six buddha principles: the three transcendent and the three worldly families. The central figure is connected with one of the three transcendent families: the tathagata, padma, or vajra family. The other figures, such as the servants and messengers, are connected with the three worldly families. They are from the jewel, prosperity, or ordinary families, and may include worldly gods, garudas, Vishnu, Shiva, and others.

## Deities and Cleansing

In kriyayoga tantra, the central deity of the mandala is a peaceful one. The deity manifests a peaceful state of purifying, tranquillizing, and opening—a pacified state of being. The yidam's consort, the feminine principle, represents enriching. Symbolically, the combination is like having a massage after taking a shower. Once you have thoroughly bathed or showered and steamed yourself in order to purify yourself, all the oils that exist in the pores of your skin are completely cleansed and washed out, as if you had gone through a washing machine. Therefore it is necessary to have yourself massaged with oil.

---

* *Mamaki* is more often associated with water and with pacifying.

So cleanliness alone is not the way, but you have to regain the energy of the purity that comes from such cleanliness. That energy has to be re-created. For example, if you give a bath to a corpse, it gets clean, but it does not shine with liveliness or cleanliness. However, if you give a bath to a living person, their healthiness shows. The principle of bathing and then being massaged with oil also represents the magnetizing quality of the consort. So the consort of the deity represents both the magnetizing and enriching qualities at this point.

The peaceful and enriching central kriyayoga deities are accompanied by several wrathful deities or protectors. The wrathful principle in kriyayoga is not quite the same as in the other tantric yanas. Here the idea of wrathfulness is just extra coloring, which creates a definite boundary or territory. It is as if, having bathed and properly massaged your body with oil, you put your bright clothes on. The wrathful principle is protection against dirt; the wrathful deities are saying that this is an area of purity that no one can touch.

## Visualization Practice

Visualization practice is a way of actualizing or experiencing certain realities by following the specific instructions given to you. In kriyayoga visualization practice, proper preparation and trust are essential.

### Proper Preparation

Kriyayoga includes the practice of visualization, but there is a danger if you try to jump into this form of the creative use of imagination before you have developed shamatha and vipashyana practice, which makes you more peaceful and aware. Without shamatha-vipashyana, visualization practice could be a very big ego trip. Unless you have some understanding of mind control or ego control and the experience of relating with neurosis and boredom and so forth, none of these tantric practices will actually be workable at all.

You would go completely haywire if you just started with visualization. You might be floating in the air, doing offerings and uttering your mantras, but so what? What does that visualization mean to you? Visualization practice is supposed to be good for you, but where does the goodness come from? Unless there is an understanding of basic goodness and basic sanity, unless you can actually relate with your sanity properly, there will be no goodness coming out of anywhere. The whole thing will be chaos and aggression.

It is necessary for you to acknowledge your journey as a solid journey. It is necessary that you know your breath, that you know your body, and that you know your thoughts. This is an enormous relief. It is a relief to know that your breath makes sense, and that your thoughts make sense or do not make sense; when you know this, then the whole thing becomes less of a dream. That is very important, otherwise you cannot take the true kriyayoga approach to reality. You cannot take part in the water abhisheka, let alone the crown abhisheka. You cannot take part in any of those abhishekas unless you have an actual understanding of things directly and thoroughly as they are.

We had a lot of problems in Tibet with people collecting abhishekas and initiations. They would just extend their hands, get the blessed water, drink it, and then leave. If you asked them, "What was that abhisheka all about?" they would reply, "I don't know. It doesn't really matter. It was given by a great teacher, and I managed to drink the water, so I don't have to be particularly careful about what commitment I'm making."

### Externalizing Trust

A particular characteristic of visualization practice in kriyayoga tantra is that you do not visualize yourself as one of the deities. Instead, you worship the yidams as external helpers. This is similar to what you find in Hinduism, where you visualize external deities as objects of worship. So although Buddhist kriyayoga is a nontheistic approach, there is a still quality of reverence. A Buddhist practitioner of kriyayoga still carries with them a quality of externalized trust from the day that person took the refuge vow. They maintain the idea of taking refuge in the Buddha as an example. So in kriyayoga visualization practice, it is felt that you personally cannot identify yourself with a particular yidam.

Because of this, it is said that in kriyayoga there is appreciation, rather than the vajra pride that comes from complete identification with the deities. Therefore, kriyayoga has sometimes been described as having no joy. Although there have been various disagreements about the approach to visualization practice in kriyayoga, several esteemed teachers, including Karma Trinlepa, Karmapa Rangjung Dorje, and Jamgön Kongtrül the Great agree that practitioners of kriyayoga should not visualize themselves as deities.*

Kriyayoga is complementary to the preexisting tantra of Hinduism, and kriyayoga is generous in trying to work with Hindu tantra, but that kind of generosity may also bring a kind of primitiveness. It may lead to the flaw or limitation of not being able to identify yourself with the deities in the later tantric yanas. You are simply a spectator of all those happenings, which reflects a quality of inadequacy. You just watch the deities, but you never think of doing such things yourself. According to kriyayoga, if you think of yourself and how you should handle yourself, that is too ego-centered. You should not think about who you are at all. But this approach ignores or forgets that you are also one of the deities.

The reason there is no visualization of yourself as the deity is based on the same principle as vegetarianism. That is, you should not indulge in the forms of divinities in the same way that you should not indulge in eating flesh. You have the deities out there, and you simply worship them and watch what is happening. So kriyayoga seems to be an utterly devotional approach, based on outer devotion. The vibrations of the bijas (seed syllables) and the sounds of mantras give you some kind of benefit, but you yourself do not jump into the visualization and enter into that world. The phenomenal world in kriyayoga takes place by itself, without your being in it. Kriyayogins would say that when you are excited by watching a movie, you do not jump into the screen and dance with the forms there—you just sit and watch. You do not get carried away, which is sensible. This is a way of defining the boundary between imaginary reality and you. In kriyayoga, that boundary should be respected.

## KRIYAYOGA VISUALIZATION PRACTICE

The visualization practice of kriyayoga includes the same six types of gods, or divine beings, that we described earlier in terms of the steps of

---

* *Karma Trinlepa* (1456–1539) studied with the seventh Karmapa and was one of the eighth Karmapa's teachers; *Rangjung Dorje* (1284–1339) was the third Karmapa.

giving birth to a visualization.* In all these cases, you do not visualize yourself as the deity, but you watch these things happen as if you were gazing at them on the full moon. You take advantage of seeing the pleasure of the buddhas.

## The Divine Beings of Shunyata

The first divine beings, the divine beings of shunyata, represent the principle of shunyata and the practice of meditating on bodhichitta. Here the understanding of bodhichitta is slightly different from that of the mahayana. In kriyayoga, bodhichitta has a sense of appreciating that you can see the real world as it is. There is a hint of mahamudra in the kriyayoga understanding of bodhichitta.

## The Divine Beings of Syllables

The second divine beings, the divine beings of syllables or letters, represent the bija mantras, or seed syllables. Practitioners of kriyayoga are usually very artistic. When they visualize the seed syllables of the three transcendent kriyayoga buddha-families (tathagata, padma, and vajra), they may visualize the syllables alone, or they may visualize the full moon with the seed syllable sitting in the middle of it. They take a syllable such as OM, or whatever seed syllable they are using, and put it on the full moon. The full moon is very much connected with bodhichitta, the awakened state of mind; it is connected with openness and being completely, fully all right.

We actually had this kind of practice presented to us in 1971 at our retreat center Tail of the Tiger (which was renamed "Karmê Chöling" by the sixteenth Karmapa in 1974) when Professor Yoshito S. Hakeda visited.† He made all of us visualize the full moon, and we put the symbol AH in the middle of it. Later, he told us that we could put any symbol we liked on it. So there is definitely a living kriyayoga visualization practice in Shingon Buddhism.

---

* See chapter 38, "Visualization and Sadhana Practice."

† *Professor Yoshito S. Hakeda* was one of the elite scholar-priests sent abroad after the Second World War by the Japanese Shingon sect. He came to visit Tail of the Tiger from New York City, where he lived for many years and taught as a professor at Columbia University.

## The Divine Beings of Sound

In terms of the divine beings of sound, having established your syllable on the moon, the moon echoes that syllable, and the sound of the syllable vibrates and repeats its own mantra as a part of your visualization.

## The Divine Beings of Form

With the divine beings of form, having visualized the seed syllable on the moon, you radiate light out from the syllable in order to alleviate the sufferings of all sentient beings, and to make offerings to the buddhas of the past, present, and future. After that, the light comes back, having fulfilled all its purposes, and you begin to visualize the form of the deity.

## The Divine Beings of Mudra

With the divine beings of mudra, after you have visualized a particular deity sitting in front of you on the full moon, you create what are called mudra deities or armor deities. That is, you make certain hand gestures or mudras that go with the visualization, which represent what is called putting on a suit of armor. By means of these mudras, you offer protection to the psychic centers of the central deity's body by visualizing little deities sitting on the appropriate parts of the central deity's body: the forehead center, throat center, chest center, navel center, genital center, and so forth.

## The Divine Beings of Mark

With the last deity, called the divine beings of mark, or the divine beings of seal or symbol, you dissolve the visualization back into emptiness, back into the nonexistence of confusion. When you dissolve the visualization into shunyata, that visualization is no longer solid. Dissolving the visualization into shunyata is a way of reducing the visualization into nowhere.

At the same time, there is subtlety in the approach to shunyata that is present in kriyayoga. Shunyata has dissolved the visualization, but pride of some kind continues. You begin to see that the deities exist independently without being visualized. You see that your friends are the form of Vairochana or some other deity, and that your friends' speech is the mantra echoing. You see that your thought patterns happen within the realm of that deity. So the divine attitude of mark is a kind of meditation in action. The deity is being felt and seen and thought of in the same way as you feel and see and think of your friends around you.

## Samayasattva and Jnanasattva in Kriyayoga Practice

VISUALIZATION PRACTICE. In the kriyayoga tantra, although you do not identify with the deities by visualizing yourself as one of them, you still have the two sattva principles: samayasattva and jnanasattva.

Samayasattva is the basic visualization. You begin by understanding the symbolism and creating the visualization. You visualize the deity as a samayasattva outside of you, in front of your body. Then the jnanasattva descends on the samayasattva and becomes united with it, and the samayasattva is blessed by the presence of the jnanasattva. The empowerment you receive from your guru during the abhisheka is what makes the jnanasattva listen and accept your invitation to descend. In the abhisheka, you actually have a chance to meet a jnanasattva properly for the first time.

The jnanasattva is the reality or the wisdom of that which has been invoked. So as you visualize, you suddenly invoke the jnanasattva, which is the actual experience of the enlightened principle in the form of a sambhogakaya buddha, and the jnanasattva dissolves into the visualization, or samayasattva. At that point, the visualization becomes powerful energy. In kriyayoga, you just witness all this in front of you. In your purely ordinary body, you watch these things taking place.

The relationship between samayasattva and jnanasattva changes throughout the various tantric yanas. As far as kriyayoga is concerned, the practitioner regards the samayasattva as a personal creation. That actually remains the same throughout the yanas, but the relationship to the jnanasattva changes. In kriyayoga, relating to the jnanasattva is like relating to something outside of oneself. You regard yourself as a servant, and you regard the deity that you invoke as lord or master. That attitude is actually very helpful in this underdeveloped level of vajrayana. Otherwise, you could trip out completely.

At this stage, it is necessary to develop humility. Kriyayoga is the first yana beyond mahayana, and it is a great exposure to the vajra world, which is fantastic. But you need to keep it cool. The idea is to be humble;

the things that you see are not actually yours. You are merely an observer who still remains wretched in spite of your purity. You are just a clean little thing watching those visualizations happening over there. You are relating with the jnanasattva principle as lord or master. By regarding the jnanasattva like that, you transcend unnecessary obstacles of ego-boost and rudra-hood.

You also begin to receive all kinds of miraculous powers. But at this point, you do not wait for or look toward realization or the attainment of miraculous powers. Realization, final vision, final insight, or final liberation is not particularly regarded as a highlight or the "real thing." You are completely satisfied with your clean pure life—with your clean body, clean speech, and clean mind. You are that purity anyway, since you are relating with these deities. So the approach to visualization in kriyayoga is one of integrating the higher realm of thinking with the lower realm of thinking.

POSTMEDITATION PRACTICE. In kriyayoga we almost always talk about the jnanasattva in terms of practice, but the jnanasattva exists in the postmeditation experience as well. Actually, that is usually when the jnanasattva is present. The samayasattva and jnanasattva are more separate during the meditation itself, when you are doing sadhana practice, than in everyday life. In daily life, the experience of jnanasattva would be somewhat the equivalent of a sense of humor, in that the jnanasattva enlivens experience and gives you a fix of reality. It could be an experience of space, or a breathing space, or it could be very claustrophobic, because you cannot get out of it. It is haunting, but at the same time it is immensely spacious and fantastic.

## MANTRA

There are two types of mantra in kriyayoga tantra: secret mantra and knowledge mantra.

### Secret Mantra

The first mantra is *sang-ngak* in Tibetan, or *guhyamantra* in Sanskrit. *Sang* means "secret," and *ngak* means "mantra"; so *sang-ngak* means "secret mantra." Secret mantra is based on the idea of invoking the magical aspect of purity.

## Knowledge Mantra

The second mantra is a necessary accompaniment to the first one. It is called *rig-ngak* in Tibetan, or *vidyamantra* in Sanskrit. *Rig* means "knowledge" or "insight," and *ngak,* again, means "mantra"; so *rig-ngak* means "knowledge mantra." It is quite the opposite of the guhyamantra. Here, trust is not based on the magical aspect alone, but on intelligence and on the suddenness and spontaneity of the mahamudra experience.

## PEACEFUL ACTION WITH A HINT OF CRAZINESS

Kriyayoga involves pacifying. The act of pacifying is something you do. It is not passive, but you are pacified. You pacify as much as you can in kriyayoga, and anything that is still left to pacify is dealt with in the coming yanas. As you go on to further yanas, you actually become more and more aggressive. You become more thought provoking, more powerful, and more angry. In the case of kriyayoga, there may be a more timid or tiptoey quality. Nevertheless, it is very genuine and very powerful.

You might think that such a timid or peaceful quality makes it almost contradictory to call kriyayoga the yana of action. But there is no problem with that. In kriyayoga, action is peaceful action. If you eat a vegetarian diet, you just do it—flat. You take three showers a day—flat. You have visualizations—flat. That is one of the characteristics of kriyayoga tantra.

At the same time, even though in kriyayoga it seems that you are trying to be sane, there is still craziness. Your eccentricity in kriyayoga has a seed of enlightenment in it. Although kriyayoga is just the entrance to the vajrayana, there are already mahamudra-like experiences at this level. This does not mean, however, that the practitioner of kriyayoga is someone who already has experience with anuttarayoga. It means that although you could begin the path of tantra with kriyayoga, your experience will still have an element of anuttarayoga. Kriyayoga is tantra, and if you are practicing tantra, you always automatically have some mahamudra aspect taking place.

44

# Upayoga:
# Unadorned Perception

*Upayoga involves greater compassion and greater individual salva-*
*tion at the same time. . . . There is a quality of purity, openness, and*
*diligence in practice, related with seeing things clearly. . . . That is,*
*compassion is not something you are taking on as a further burden,*
*but it is a stripping away of your own burden—and the more you*
*take away your burden, the more compassionate you become.*

## THE TRANSITION FROM KRIYAYOGA TO UPAYOGA

The second tantric yana is upayoga. *Upa* refers to conduct, so upayoga is the yoga of application or practice.* The Tibetan word for upayoga is *chögyü. Chö* is "practicing" or "performing," and *gyü* means "tantra"; so *chögyü* is the "practicing tantra." You are continuing the purification practices of kriyayoga tantra, and at the same time you are practicing ideas borrowed from the next yana, or yogayana. In upayoga, half of its practice is identical to the practice of kriyayoga, and half of its practice is like that of yogayana.

---

* The Sanskrit term *upa* seems to be a shortened form of *ubhaya,* which means "both," indicating that this yana has qualities of both kriyayoga and yogayana. Upayogayana is more commonly called *charyayana. Charya,* like the Tibetan *chö* (spyod), means "conduct" or "practice." (Not to be confused with *chö* [chös], which means "dharma.")

The qualities of appreciation and psychological clarity become much greater at this point, because you have been thoroughly trained in kriyayoga. Kriyayoga has made you more aware of the phenomenal world, and its purity and impurity are completely known. This automatically allows you to turn your attitude more inward than outward. You develop further confidence and free-flowing trust in the yidams. To relate with them and work with them becomes very important. Kriyayoga is like buying the land and dealing with the water and sewage system, and upayoga is like constructing a house. Upayoga has greater vision, but this greater vision cannot develop unless you know who you are and what you are. The practicalities have to be worked out in detail.

At the level of kriyayoga and upayoga, there is a quality of great surprise rather than great joy. If you are involved with these two yanas, you find yourself enormously refreshed. It is as if you were traveling in a new country and discovering all the different aspects of that particular country. You may not know who you are or how you are doing, but a quality of spaciousness is always there, which is very refreshing. You feel somewhat alien and cultureless, and at the same time you are pushed into corners. You are not certain whether you can get into this new culture or not, which helps enormously. That is one of the most interesting aspects of this particular yana. I am afraid that when you get into the next yana, the culture changes its flavor, becoming perhaps too concrete and too hospitable, too fascinating and realistic.

As far as purity is concerned, upayoga is very close to kriyayoga, but a kind of mental carelessness is taking place, so you are transcending kriyayoga. Therefore, fewer mudras are practiced. Here, mudras are just a delicate way to handle the deities' hands so that the deities are not clumsy or crude. In upayoga, deities are expressing the delicacies of enlightenment, but they still have solid earthiness. They are like well-bathed princes who are also peasants. In upayoga, the purification itself is the earthy element. You are getting rid of dirt, but you also have more connection with dirt. It is like being a farmer: if you are plowing, harvesting, or threshing, you tend to collect more dirt, and you take more baths for that reason, not just because taking a bath is pleasurable.

In upayoga, practical living situations such as a vegetarian diet and taking showers are not regarded as the main point, but more as helpful suggestions. In contrast, in kriyayoga tantra, purification is very important.

It is not just matter-of-fact, not just trying to get rid of your dirt, but it is the main principle and your main occupation or practice. But in upayoga, the practice of purity is not your main occupation. Purity is just a side credential that you have inherited from the previous yana. In upayoga, you combine purity with carelessness. That carelessness brings purity: you can be careless and clean at the same time. Just focusing on being clean does not seem to be the point, and for that matter, casualness is not the point. But you bring them together, so you have relaxed cleanliness. That is the approach of this particular yana.

The upayogayana brings an uplifting quality that tends toward anuttarayoga and maha ati. Those yanas are yet to come, but somehow this practice is closely related. There is no ambition, but you keep purification as part of your behavior. That is what one generally does anyway. If you have finished eating your dinner, you wash your plate so you can eat on it again in the future. You clean up every night and every morning, you vacuum the floor and tidy up your room because you want to use it again. There is a concern about the future, and a sense of an ongoing process taking place.

The feeling that you are actually leading your life is very much a principle of this particular yana. You are leading a life, and you have considerations and concerns about how to handle your life. You are concerned about your purity as well as your freedom, so you get the best of both worlds.

Upayoga begins to reach toward yogayana and anuttarayoga. It is as if upayoga has found a secret message. Therefore, you are not too concerned about your purity alone, but you begin to know that something else is happening. It is as though your grandchildren are rich and can give you money, but at the same time you realize that your great-grandparents are also rich and that they can help you as well. So you are bounded by two richnesses simultaneously.

## SYMBOLISM

You cannot talk about reality without symbols, even in the ordinary sense. For example, if your children ask, "What does visiting daddy mean?" you say, "That means daddy is going to be right in front of you." That is the direct experience of how things work. You could hardly say that this is only symbolism. So symbolism involves having a direct experience. Tantric symbolism should be like experiencing an apple: if you understand an apple thoroughly and completely, you understand your deity.

If you do not have an understanding of and respect for symbolism and the necessity for symbolism, then you cannot understand and respect tantra. Without an appreciation of symbolism, the means of communication would be neglected, and you would be concerned solely with the aftereffects. Instead of watching the whole movie, you would just like to know what happened at the end, whether the good guys won or the bad guys were destroyed. This kind of approach blinds you to the appreciation of the importance of symbolism.

Our parents, our toys, our enemies, our friends, buying a car, getting money, eating our food, and wearing clothes—all of these are symbols. Such symbols make sense to us because we appreciate them. Without symbols, there is nothing left. Everything we do, everything we have, and the ways we behave are all the activities of symbolism. That is why our world is called the world of mirage or the relative world.

Unless you understand the symbolism, there is no means of communicating with the ground of tantra, no means of understanding the principles of tantra. You have no way of identifying with those principles or meditating on them. At the tantric level, we do not seem to make any distinction between philosophy and experience. You may have a philosophy of symbolism; that's fine, but it should also entail an intuitive understanding of symbolism, otherwise you do not have good philosophy. So experience and theory go side by side. The tantric approach is more like learning how to be a good cook rather than learning how to be a good philosopher. It is very much connected with communication with reality and survival.

Using symbols does not mean that you do not understand the facts, so you have to come up with some image instead. With tantric symbols such as scepters, wheels, swords, bija mantras, and the rest, you are not just relating with particular forms, images, or names. You relate with a symbol like a wheel, or a sword, or a jewel as something immediate, something that applies to your passion or your confused nature. In visualization practice, that sword or other symbol is transformed into the appropriate buddha. So a sword could mean your karma family aggression, and it could also mean the karma family wisdom of the fulfillment of all actions. That type of symbol is an immediate synopsis of your basic being. And when you refer to buddhas such as Vairochana or Vajrasattva, that is a more glorified expression of belonging to a particular buddha-family.

At the level of upayoga, you are expected to have a relationship with things as they are. You are expected to know the vividness of everything completely. Because of that, you are encouraged to indulge in sense perceptions and sense pleasures. This is not particularly a revolutionary idea that goes against hinayana principles of morality. It is more than that. Every experience in your life, all your sense perceptions, your pleasures or your pains, each has its own particular flavor and characteristics. And all of these experiences are manifested by the deities; they *are* the deities. So visualizing the deities helps you to illuminate those qualities in everyday experience, and it helps create an appreciation of the deities' cosmic aspect as well.

## A CONSTANT LETTING-GO PROCESS

The significance of upayoga is that it goes beyond the emphasis on and respect for the ordinary level of kündzop. It transcends that level in such a way that you are able to understand a need for greater practice. You realize that you have to do more than just view everything as sacred. In order to actually realize sacredness, you have to go beyond just taking that view.

In upayoga visualization practice, there is a feeling of equality between you and the jnanasattva that you visualize. There is also a recognition of the importance of the abstract level, or formless meditation, which goes beyond the visualization itself. So in upayoga, the emphasis, apart from purity, is on sampannakrama, or formless practice.

In this yana, when you perceive things in the phenomenal world, everything is translated into an understanding of unadorned perception. The Tibetan word for that is *tsen-me*. *Tsen* or *tsenma* means "mark" or "adornment," *me* means the negation of that; so *tsen-me* refers to "unadorned experience." In order to realize the vajrayana, you do not need gimmicks that make things in your life colorful. The upayoga understanding of purity goes somewhat further than kriyayoga, in that purity is not regarded as an adornment, but rather as a statement of the absence of adornment. It is a statement of expressionlessness, marklessness, reference-point-lessness.

Upayoga involves greater compassion and greater individual salvation at the same time. In some ways, they are the same thing. There is a quality of purity, openness, and diligence in practice, related with seeing things clearly. The tantric logic of compassion is generally related with the unadorned approach. That is, compassion is not something you are taking on as a further burden, but it is a stripping away of your own burden—and the more you take away your burden, the more compassionate you become. It is not at all like the mahayana idea of being a good guy, and it is not a matter of obligations. There is more spontaneity. According to upayoga, the more you unmask and unclothe, the more compassion comes along.

In upayoga, you perceive the world in your own way and on the basis of whatever training you have had, but you are not trying to hang on to your view. Everything happens within a kind of constant letting-go process. When something occurs in your mind, you let it occur. You let it come, and you let it develop its purity. You do not try to grasp anything, and you do not try to take hold of anything in order to learn something. You just let everything go in its own way.

## IMMOVABILITY

Another important factor in upayoga is the emphasis on *achala*, which means "immovability" or "stability." Upayoga sadhanas make frequent reference to immovability, and the principle of vajra anger begins to come alive at this point, although at the upayoga level it is a very mild form of vajra anger. There is more anger at the crazy-wisdom level, but here it is more like stubborn determination to take part in the confused world, rather than real anger. In upayoga, the idea of immovability is connected with the deity Achala, who is represented as a wrathful figure holding a mace and a lasso. In kriyayoga, no central figures were wrathful. All the central figures were peaceful, although the guardian deities or messengers could be wrathful.

In the Shingon Buddhism of Japan, there are also frequent references to Achala, or Fudo as he is called in Japanese. Interestingly, Zen Buddhists are also fascinated by Fudo. Some Zen masters wrote poems on Fudo as a symbol of immovability, but those poems are not like the poems of tantric practitioners. Zen Buddhists connected that quality of sternness with Bodhidharma, the fifth-century monk who is said to have introduced

Ch'an or Zen to China. So in the Zen approach, Fudo simply represents toughness and immovability, rather than being threatening or wrathful in the tantric sense.

## EMPTINESS / FULLNESS

In these first two tantric yanas, nothing specific is happening in terms of emptiness, or shunyata, but it is slowly building up. These yanas do not yet have an approach to the idea of sexuality or the feminine principle, or even the mother principle. Their version of relating with shunyata is purely based on sampannakrama, or formless practice. Beyond visualization, there is a kind of quiet moment when you do not have visualizations in your mind, but you begin to pick up on the essence of the deities. That is the idea of shunyata in upayoga.

According to the followers of madhyamaka, this is not really true shunyata; but according to the tantrikas, it is real shunyata because emptiness is at the same time full. It is because of its fullness and richness that the emptiness notion happens. Fundamentally, the reason emptiness happens is that there is no ego and no divine being.

It depends on the practitioner, actually, but the texts say that in upayoga, visualizations are also subject to the philosophy of the unadorned approach. Once you are unadorned, you could have as much adornment as there is. So being unadorned and having the adornment of all the textures are the same. It is like the analogy of the desert. In the midst of all the grains of sand in the desert, one little grain of sand sticks its head up and says, "Hello." The idea is that if you take away the ego, there is still somebody there. So there is the multiplicity of all the little grains of sand, and at the same time you are left with the desert.

## INTERMEDIATE YANAS

In the tantric traditions of upayoga and kriyayoga, there is an emphasis on individual practice, while in later tantra, group practice is more common. Because of that, we could say that this yana is still on the level of the pratyekabuddhayana. We could say that it is close to the rhinoceros tradition of solitary realization, because practice is done individually and privately. You find a similar situation in the Shingon Buddhism of Japan. They have assembly halls to congregate in when they do group practices, but each practitioner has a little table in front of them with a little shrine so they can practice by themselves. Likewise, in the Tibetan kriyayoga and upayoga traditions, practitioners have their own meditation cells to study and practice in. Doing individual practice seems to be important because you are not yet fully developed. Therefore, you practice independently without outside distractions or problems. The fact of doing your own personal practice by yourself indicates that the vajrayana version of mahayana group practice has not yet developed.

There are a lot of practices in this yana, of course, but most general writings have very little discussion of them. In fact, Tibetans do not practice kriyayoga and upayoga all that much. Maybe they are spoiled by having anuttarayoga practice, or maybe they just do not like water or bathing, and find it difficult to take three showers a day. Tibetans have their vision set on the higher tantras, the last three yanas. Therefore, the lower yanas seem to be too primitive, and Tibetans prefer to bypass them. Nevertheless, many kriyayoga and upayoga practices are still regarded as important for getting some perspective on the whole tantric path.

Kriyayoga and upayoga are not really all that essential. They are not as essential as the shravaka and pratyekabuddha yanas. It is absolutely necessary to have the understanding of basic Buddhism that is found in the hinayana. Teachings such as the truth of suffering, the twelve nidanas, and so forth are basic, and it is necessary to understand all that. But kriyayoga and upayoga are just steps toward breaking the ice and becoming more familiar with the vajrayana tradition in general. So the early tantric yanas are a kind of intermediate step.

# 45

# *Upayoga:*
# *Empowerment*

*The main point of upayoga is to develop further sophistication and respect for your basic being. It is like building a house on purified ground. In kriyayoga, you have less confidence in the phenomenal world because you perceive it as being dirty. But now that you have the knowledge of how to clean it up or purify it, you feel more relaxed and comfortable. So with upayoga, you have more confidence in the phenomenal world.*

I N UPAYOGA, the abhisheka is more than just an anointment ceremony accepting you into the tribal structure, but it is still not up to the point of being a coronation. You are accepted into the tribe, and you are told the laws and the meaning of being involved with the tribe.

In kriyayoga, the main abhishekas were the water abhisheka, connected with the dharmakaya, and the crown abhisheka, connected with the kayas of form, the sambhogakaya and the nirmanakaya. We had three transcendent families, or buddha principles. But in upayoga, we have all five buddha principles, so some additional symbols are used in the abhisheka ceremony. In addition to the water and the crown, we have the vajra, the bell, and the vajra and bell fastened together in the form of a cross.

## Five Main Abhishekas

It is important to remember that upayoga maintains its kriyayoga purification practice, but it also includes the yogayana practice of freedom, although not completely. The abhishekas reflect that same pattern. There are five main abhishekas—water, crown, bell, vajra, and name, and one additional abhisheka called opening the eyes.

### Water / Vase Abhisheka

First there is the water or vase abhisheka. The vajra represents discriminating-awareness wisdom, because you hold the vajra scepter in your hand as a way of communicating to others. This is similar to the vase abhisheka that we discussed in kriyayoga, but it is not so highly based on purity and it has a slightly different and more sophisticated form.

Within the water abhisheka, there are four further abhishekas. The first one is to purify the fixations of the lower realms. The second one is to completely uproot any samsaric seeds. The third one is to develop or bypass the bhumis from one to ten completely. It is known as creating the seed for the two accumulations: merit and wisdom. (In this case merit is achievement rather than just credit, which is how the term is usually used.) The fourth one sows the seed for one to become the regent of the vajra master. These four abhishekas are all part of the first abhisheka.

### Crown Abhisheka

The second abhisheka is the crown abhisheka. The crown abhisheka is to attain certain attributes of the Buddha's form, such as richness, opulence, dignity, and so forth.

### Bell Abhisheka

The third abhisheka is the abhisheka of sound or bell. Its purpose is to attain the attributes of the Buddha's speech. Buddha is said to have possessed sixty variations of articulation, depending on the audience. He achieved a way of communicating to students completely and provocatively, which is symbolized by the bell. The bell represents the wisdom of all-accomplishing actions, because the sound of the bell terrifies and puts a stop to thoughts. Since the problem of being unable to fulfill your actions is caused by preoccupation with thoughts, when your thoughts have been stopped by the sound of the bell, you become one with your actions, and your actions are automatically fulfilled.

## Vajra Abhisheka

The fourth abhisheka is that of the vajra, which represents the mind of the Enlightened One. Seeing and knowing are the two types of insight that exist in the mind of enlightenment. Seeing is perceiving things as they are, and knowing is knowing things as they are. Together, they represent the mind of the Buddha, which is symbolized by a vajra.

## Name Abhisheka

The fifth abhisheka is the abhisheka of name, in which the symbolism is that of the bell and vajra put together in a cross and tied up with a ribbon. The bell and dorje fastened together represents the dharmadhatu wisdom, or the wisdom of all-encompassing space. The teacher rings this bell above your head and proclaims your vajrayana name, declaring that from today onward you shall be known as the "Tathagata of Non-returning," or the "Self-Liberated Rainbow," or whatever it may be. The teacher proclaims your particular buddha and the family name of your particular tantric discipline. That confirms that you are a ruler of the threefold world.

Those are the five main abhishekas that take place in upayoga.

## Opening the Eyes

Following the five main abhishekas, there is an extra abhisheka that is not included in the main abhishekas, which is called opening the eyes. This abhisheka is somewhat different in that it is not so much for your development alone. It is based on the teacher's openness in relating with students and interpreting and explaining the meaning of the various mandalas and their symbols. So it is an action abhisheka, which seems to be the basic point of this particular yana.

In this abhisheka, the teacher uses a ritual stick called an eye stick, or *mikthur*. *Mik* means "eye," and *thur* means "stick"; so a *mikthur* is an "eye stick." Traditionally, the students all blindfold themselves, and the teacher removes their blindfolds with the eye stick. When all the blindfolds are transferred to the eye stick in this way, the teacher points out that confusion has been removed. Then the students are shown the meaning of the symbolism that is being used.

At this point, the teacher holds the eye stick in his hand and uses it to point out the various facets of the mandala that you are receiving. In the center of the mandala, the teacher has placed the crossed bell and vajra, representing the abhisheka of name. In the East quarter of the mandala, the teacher has placed a vase filled with water; in the South quarter, a crown; in the West quarter, a vajra tied with a red ribbon; and in the North quarter, a bell tied with a green ribbon. The vajra master uses the eye stick to point out the different areas of the mandala and tell you what all of them mean. We could say that this is the first time the tantric student receives the actual introduction to the five buddha-wisdom principles, and has their characteristics explained.

### The Inner Abhisheka

There are some references to the inner abhisheka in this tantra, but it is not explained in great detail. The idea of abhisheka is simply that your mind is completely churned into the tathagatagarbha of your particular deity, which is the expression of the purest form of your being. But in order to relate with the purest form of your being, you must also relate with the impure form of your being.

The inner abhisheka enables you to bring your problems and your development into your visualization of particular deities. You visualize the deities in certain forms and colors as mental images, and these deities are then transmuted into a higher form of mental images. So the deities are a form of hope, and at the same time they are a way of clearly seeing your confusion. Problems are no longer problematic because they become symbols and deities. They become transcendent problems, so there are no solid problems as such. This seems to be the inner or higher form of abhisheka. The teacher recommends that you practice this, and empowers you to practice it from this point onward.

In upayoga, the abhisheka principle is usually not so much about what you are going to become, but some hint of possibility is given to you so that you feel you are capable of becoming something. By practicing the sadhana of this yana, you develop potentiality. You are collecting enough gunpowder to shoot your cannonballs beyond the hill. So an upayoga abhisheka is about potential, about how much gunpowder you collect. That is the idea of abhisheka—encouragement and empowerment.

## FAMILIES AND MANDALAS

There is disagreement as to the number of families in upayoga. According to the fourteenth-century historian Butön (1290–1365), upayoga can be divided into three families, based on vajra body, vajra speech, and vajra mind. Vajra body is connected with the vajra family, vajra speech with the padma family, and vajra mind with the buddha family. However, the great scholar Taranatha (1575–1684) says that upayoga includes all five buddha-families: vajra, ratna, padma, karma, and buddha.

Those two possibilities can occur concurrently, and both are workable. Although little details like that may seem arbitrary, all the commentators agree on the importance of the symbolism; they agree that it is very powerful and alive. There is no disagreement at all on that basic point.

In terms of the mandala principle, from upayoga onward, there is an emphasis on the importance of the inner mandala as well as the outer mandala—the outer mandala being the shrine and the physical setup outside your body, and the inner mandala being your own physical body. In contrast, in kriyayoga there was very little reference to the body mandala.

## UPAYOGA SAMAYA

The upayoga samaya has three categories.

### The Samayas of Surrendering the Ego

The first upayoga samaya category is the surrendering of the gross ego, which is related to relative bodhichitta, and the second upayoga samaya is the surrendering of the refined ego, which is related to absolute bodhichitta. These are the two surrenderings of the kriyayoga, which we discussed earlier.

## The Samaya of the Dharmachakra Mudra

But a third samaya vow is added to those two, called the samaya of the dharmachakra mudra. With this samaya, you are able to see that all form is Vajrasattva's form, all speech is Vajrasattva's speech, and all thought process is Vajrasattva's thought process. So there is a sense of all-pervasive intelligence, openness, and wisdom continuing all the time. This extra samaya combines kriyayoga and mahayoga, which are the previous yana and the next yana.

The main point of upayoga is to develop further sophistication and respect for your basic being. It is like building a house on purified ground. In kriyayoga, you have less confidence in the phenomenal world because you perceive it as being dirty. But now that you have the knowledge of how to clean it up or purify it, you feel more relaxed and comfortable. So with upayoga, you have more confidence in the phenomenal world. The whole purification system is known to you, and you are capable of constructing your own building. That is why this yana is known as half kriyayogayana and half yogayana.

# 46

# *Upayoga:*
# *Practice*

*In tantra, we are unfolding the mysteries of reality, or kündzop, and that unfolding is enormous, it is endless. To really become somebody who has gained mastery of the world, someone who has learned to live in the world and to enjoy pleasure thoroughly and completely, demands enormous wisdom. It is a huge task. Yet that seems to be one of the promises of the worldliness of tantra.*

## Making Contact with the Yidam

In the vajrayana, you cannot relate with the phenomenal world as a whole from the ultimate point of view unless you relate with the details. You need to relate with a particular aspect of the world, with a certain buddha-family, symbol, or deity. In this case, the term *deity* has nothing to do with the idea of an external deity coming to you; a deity is an expression of reality.

At the level of vajrayana, no experience is ineffable or nameless, and nothing is beyond description. Everything is capable of being described in a very practical way. That is why the accuracy of vajrayana is far superior to ordinary ideas of doing good, or having insight without being able to put a name to it. One of the merits of the vajrayana path is that its practitioners would never say that in order to express such and such, even the Buddha's tongue is numb. The vajrayana practitioner would not make such a pathetic remark, suggesting that the speaker's ignorance is to be equated with Buddha's ignorance. In the vajrayana path, you have constant reference points. You have constant colors, images, and energies to relate with. That is why it is very powerful and very accurate.

## Regarding the Yidam as Your Friend

An important aspect of upayoga is the attempt to make contact with the yidam through sadhana practice. In the case of kriyayoga tantra, the deity was regarded as a lord or master, but in this case the deity is regarded as a friend, somewhat on an equal level. So a sense of friendship is taking place between yourself and what you have visualized. But at this point, you still do not identify the visualization with yourself, particularly. It seems to be too early to get married; a courtship would seem to be more efficacious. Nevertheless, there is trust and friendship taking place between the deities and yourself. The yidam can accommodate all your aspects. You do not have to think in terms of the better part of you being the yidam, but all of you is included. Otherwise, you cannot have the samayasattva and the jnanasattva becoming one.

## Samayasattva and Jnanasattva

In upayoga, you visualize the internal samayasattva in your own body, in your being, and you also invite the external samayasattva in front of you. So your visualization is in the form of two sets of mandalas: inner and outer. You are in the center of one mandala, and there is another visualized mandala on the shrine, which is the dwelling place of the yidam.

Then you invite the jnanasattva to come to you, and the jnanasattva dissolves into the samayasattva that you are visualizing in your own body, as well as into the version that you are visualizing in front of you on the shrine.

Inviting the jnanasattva is not like inviting a god from heaven. The transcendental aspect of your body and your shrine is invoked, which seems to help enormously in assuring that your visualization does not become just imagination, but rather is true visualization. You are inviting a feeling of that particular deity. It is very intimate.

To take an example, you might visualize a beautiful dish of food in front of you, but at some point the whole thing looks a bit funny. You visualize so thoroughly that the whole thing becomes artificial, as if it were made out of plastic. But then you tune your mind in to a different level. You tune in to your love of food, and you bring your love of food to that particular dish that looks like plastic—and finally it becomes eatable! You actually feel that the food is alive and fresh.

Visualization becomes much more powerful and realistic when there is that quality of feeling. Just extending your hallucination is not the point of visualization in the tantric approach. The important point about visualization is that you have a feeling of Akshobhya or Vairochana or whomever you are visualizing. You tune in to their emotions, their senses, their particular approach. You do not need to watch yourself, because you are completely involved. You do not have to make sure that you are doing it right, because you are there already.

The upayoga style of visualization is said to have three principles of unification: unification of body, speech, and mind. Your body, speech, and mind are united with the yidam. In terms of the inner and outer mandalas, not only is there unification of the three principles in your physical body, but there is also unification in your visualized body or external shrine. So your physical body is the dwelling place of the yidams, just as the shrine is the dwelling place of the yidams. There is a definite sense of trust and faith that your whole setup—your physical being and the place you are living—has the characteristics of the particular yidam that you are working with.

In upayoga visualization, the six types of gods that we discussed in kriyayoga are exactly the same: the gods of shunyata, syllable, sound, form, mudra, and mark. So the visualization is almost identical, except that in upayoga there is more confidence and more personal identification.

## JOINING PRACTICE WITH DAILY LIFE

One of the interesting points about tantric practice is that you do not impose your philosophy or moral principles on anything. You just accept wholeheartedly the social norms that take place in society. On top of that, you color that situation by your own insight and your own craziness. So it does not make any difference where you work: you could work in a missile factory, or an atomic energy plant, or in a slaughterhouse. One of the fascinating things about tantric practitioners is that you are able to work in any of those ways, because you have a relationship with what you are doing.

Tantric practitioners couldn't care less about their dogma. There is no dogma, none whatsoever. The dogma is their world. They cannot change their world, and at the same time they conquer the world. It is a very powerful twist. Acceptance also means conquering. You do what you have to do. So even if your work is in a slaughterhouse, you go ahead and do it. Nothing is wrong with this work, absolutely not. You are still a tantric practitioner.

The world can be seen very humorously and very concretely at the same time. Mahasukha comes from precisely that point. You do not have to try to fit everything into your little book of rules and regulations. The only book is your behavior. If your behavior or psychological state does not fit the phenomenal world, you are punished and you get into enormous danger. You become self-destructive or subject to execution because you have failed fundamentally, rather than because you have failed to keep to the dogma. That is the whole point. The whole thing is very direct; it is absolutely direct.

## FACADE OF RESPECTABILITY

Kriyayoga and upayoga are more directed toward passion or desire than toward anger. There is a quality of indulgence, a sense of committing yourself in various ways and becoming one with the cosmos. But becoming completely one with what you are doing needs a certain amount of wildness in a deeper sense. In kriyayoga, as well as upayoga, there is still an element of the Indian Brahmanical tradition. That shadow of the medieval Indian approach continues. You follow certain rules and regulations, such as keeping clean or reciting mantras as you go about your life. Nevertheless, behind the whole thing, wildness and craziness take place.

In tantra, there is not respectability all the time. You could be a respectable person, but at the same time you are slightly offbeat. Within being clean, you could be very strangely clean. You could be clean and crazy at the same time. The insight or wisdom in that craziness is based on knowing that you could tap the secret. You are not afraid of that or of anything.

Usually when people keep very strict, very virtuous rules and regulations, they have little clue as to what they are getting into. Therefore, there is a fear of losing that clue. So they keep following those rules very puritanically. But in tantra, people do have some kind of clue, so they know that they cannot lose in any case. You may still maintain a facade of respectability, but at the same time, there is a little twist taking place because you know you cannot lose. You have gotten the hang of it. That twist is self-existing; you are not told to develop this twist. If you were told that, then you would try to manufacture it, which would be pure guesswork. But in this case, it is very simple and direct. You begin to pick up the message, the spirit of the pun.

## CRAZY WISDOM

Someone able to do all that is a called a vidyadhara, according to this yana. Our way of translating *vidyadhara* is "crazy-wisdom type." The idea of the vidyadhara, the holder of insight, begins to come along much more vividly at this point, but still very meekly. There is just a hint of it. There is crazy wisdom only to the extent that there is some connection with Vajradhara. Simply that. So the unadorned state of mind has the potential of crazy wisdom, but it hasn't actually happened yet to the extent that it comes into play in the three higher levels of tantra. It all depends on how much you can actually unmask or unclothe your ego. It depends on how courageous you are about that. It is the same old Buddhist logic.

The idea of the vidyadhara, of crazy-wisdom insightfulness, is that you take your own stance. You do not need help or support or any adornment, and you are quite content with that. You are somewhat direct and precise in the sense that for you, things do not need a reference point in order to be understood. Things just present themselves as they are.

## ENDLESS UNFOLDING

Tantra is not merely a question of knowing how to indulge in sense pleasures. That is not quite enough; that is not quite tantra. We may think that we know the five colors and how they are connected with the five wisdoms, but that is also not quite enough. There are infinite varieties and profundities involved with even knowing the five colors or the five emotions. Tantra has much greater depth than that.

In tantra, we are unfolding the mysteries of reality, or kündzop, and that unfolding is enormous, it is endless. To really become somebody who has gained mastery of the world, someone who has learned to live in the world and to enjoy pleasure thoroughly and completely, demands enormous wisdom. It is a huge task. Yet that seems to be one of the promises of the worldliness of tantra.

47

# *Yogayana:*
# *Complete Union*

*Yogayana is referred to as the embodiment of a great prince. This embodiment does not refer to tathagatagarbha, but to self-existing bliss or joy. Joy exists on this path because the dichotomy of physical or external practice and internal practice has been solved. There is complete union, complete oneness.*

## ONENESS AND POWER

The third yana of the vajrayana is yogayana. The word *yoga* means "union," and the particular importance of this yana is the experience of power and complete union. Yogayana is on the borderline of anuttara-yoga, also known as mahamudra, but although there is an element of mahamudra in yogayana, it is not the full experience.

In yogayana, the physical discipline is borrowed from kriyayoga, and there is still an emphasis on purity, but psychologically yogayana is much more mahamudra oriented. There is an appreciation of the direct simplicity of things as they are. The previous yana, upayoga, is said to combine the external action-oriented practice of kriyayoga and the internal meditation-oriented practice of yogayana. However, that is not quite regarded as real union; it is a combining together rather than a union in the fullest sense. But with yogayana, there is real union.

Here, union is not about two pieces put together; rather, it is oneness with two expressions. That is the real meaning of union: oneness with two simultaneous expressions. For instance, we could say that our relationship to life and death is oneness, because life is death, and death is life. There is no way of keeping death and life separate, or joining them together. While we are alive, we are always approaching death, so we are dying constantly, just as we are living constantly at the same time.

As another example, we could also say that light contains darkness within itself. It is not that light is a combination of light and dark, but light *is* dark; therefore, darkness becomes light simultaneously. That is what is meant by oneness. Oneness is connected with power. It has a cutting, piercing, or penetrating quality. Its power comes from not being split into an allegiance to either upaya or prajna, bodhichitta or knowledge. It comes from one-pointedness.

In yogayana, there is no fear of mingling things together. Yogayana puts together expansion and profundity. It puts together action, practice, and the experience of shunyata. But compared with anuttarayoga or the higher yanas that are yet to come, yogayana may seem somewhat alien in that it is still trying to be kind and polite, while knowing that an eruption of craziness might take place at any time.

## The Indivisibility of the Two Truths

In yogayana, the two truths are regarded as indivisible. Phenomenal experience is not divided into either kündzop or töndam; whatever is seen as an expression of kündzop is seen as an expression of töndam at the same time. So yogayana unites kündzop and töndam, relative and absolute truth. The expansiveness of kündzop or phenomenal experience and the profundity of töndam are brought together in the practice of meditation.

The expansiveness of the apparent phenomenal world means that the world is seen as full of details and characteristics, as complete and incomplete at the same time. Expansiveness means that there are lots of things happening. But that expansiveness has to be cut through. You cannot be constantly overwhelmed by the expansiveness, and you cannot make it a permanent home. The expansiveness has to be reviewed piece by piece. That is where the profundity or ultimate töndam principle comes in. So this yana is definitely more the output of töndam than kündzop. The existence of kündzop is provided by the other yanas in any case.

Seeing the wide range of things experienced in ordinary life from the absolute or meditative point of view is said to be a profound view. This is the most auspicious way to look at the phenomenal world, more so than in the previous yanas. It is profound because you are seeing through those expansive visions and experiences of apparent phenomena by means of shunyata colored with mahasukha, or great joy. Ultimate truth is associated with joy because there is nothing other than joy, even no joy is no other than joy; therefore, it is so joyful.

By seeing the workings of phenomena much more clearly, you also develop a greater sense of humor. In tantra, humor becomes less self-conscious, because you have a sense of power, control, and openness. You are free from doctrine and more interested in experience, so your humor becomes heightened.

## The Prince of Mahasukha: Self-Existing Bliss

Yogayana is referred to as the embodiment of a great prince. This embodiment does not refer to tathagatagarbha, but to self-existing bliss or joy. Joy exists on this path because the dichotomy between physical or external practice and internal practice has been solved. There is complete union, complete oneness. At the same time, there is both wideness and deepness, breadth and depth. In this particular practice, breadth is connected with kündzop, and depth with töndam—and kündzop and töndam are indivisible. There is an emphasis on physical activities, rituals, and external things, and at the same time, there is enormous looking inward. Both are equally respected.

In yogayana, the great sun of mahasukha is unfolding, and there is a feeling of confidence and the potential of crazy wisdom. There is an appreciation of the prince of mahasukha, based on the clear seeing of the phenomenal world outside as potential mahamudra experience—or complete mahamudra experience, in certain cases. You have glimpses of openness and glimpses of lost awareness, which alternate naturally, since you are still a practitioner journeying through the path. Those kinds of alternations are not regarded as contradictory to the idea of oneness and unity. They are just casual experiences.

The real unity is when you have a glimpse of joy, appreciation, and accomplishment. At that point, pride becomes important. With vajra pride, you know that there is no need for reassurance. At the same time, that needlessness of reassurance is a source of humility, because you do not have to confirm yourself anymore. It is all a state of being. So vajra pride is very close to the notion of confidence.

## Becoming One with the Phenomenal World

The instruction given in the texts on how to become one with the phenomenal world, as well as one with oneself, is through visualization practice. It is by realizing that the self-visualization, in which you visualize yourself as the deity, and the front visualization, in which you visualize the deity in front of you, are indivisible, but at the same time they are separate. You realize that oneness and separateness could coexist at the same time, which is enormous training. Basically, you will be overwhelmed by the phenomenal world until you begin to realize that the self-visualization and the front visualization are one; they are just mirror reflections.

In sadhana practice, you send out offering goddesses from your heart, which means from the deity's heart as well. So you are offering and offered to at the same time. You have a dual relationship going on, and because it is dualistic activity, oneness is always there. It is like reflecting sunlight back to the sun by way of a mirror so that the sun knows how brilliant it is.

## Buddha Families

In yogayana, there are five main buddha-families, which are further divided into twenty-five lesser families.

### Main Families

The five buddha-families in yogayana are: buddha, vajra, ratna, dharma, and karma. The dharma family is law-abiding and willing to keep samaya. It is similar to the padma family, but it is not quite the same as the padma family in regard to passion. Yogayana does not talk too much about passion, and it does not deal very much with the spicy aspects of the emotions. For that matter, yogayana has nothing to do with anger, either. It is just trying to set the ground. It is almost like first introducing yourself to society: once you have introduced yourself and made friends with people, you can combat them or make love to them. But yogayana is just the level of shaking hands with people. You may be having tea, but you have not had cocktails yet.

## Lesser Families

Each main family is divided into five lesser families. For instance, buddha has five lesser families: lesser buddha, lesser vajra, lesser ratna, lesser dharma, and lesser karma. So each of the five families is divided into five parts, which makes twenty-five families altogether.

The idea of lesser families is very close to the idea of the exit family, which is a kind of psychological shift.* A person's basic family is supposed to be fixed, unlike the exit family, which is temperamental. For instance, although your basic family may be the buddha family, you might have a slight inclination toward sharpness or seductiveness or enrichment or industriousness. According to the yogayana, those slight inclinations mean that you belong to a lesser family or subfamily, as well as to a basic family.

## Family Characteristics

Each of those twenty-five families can also be looked at in four ways. You can look at them according to: essence; mudra, or manifestation; *guhya-mantra*, or secret mantra; and *vidyamantra*, or magical power.

The combination of basic family, lesser family, and these four categories makes one hundred families—five times five times four—and there are actually deities related with each family. But all these families are based on the five basic families.

A family can be seen from the point of view of its essence. It can be seen in terms of its expression or manifestation, or mudra. It can be seen from the point of view of the realization of its inner nature or hard-core

---

* Trungpa Rinpoche introduced the idea of *exit family* in order to indicate the style in which one might exit or get out of tight situations. The exit family is shiftier and manifests on a more superficial level than the primary buddha-family, which is more deep-rooted. The exit family can serve as a way of disguising or covering over one's more fundamental buddha-family style, or simply be an adornment to a more basic pattern.

characteristics, or guhyamantra. And finally, a family can be seen in terms of its application, its power over others or magical aspects, or vidyamantra.

You may belong to the buddha family, have a ratna inclination, and be mudra oriented, with a very expressive type of personality. You might belong to the buddha family, be ratna inclined, and be essence oriented, with a sense of seriousness, personal involvement, and exploration. With guhyamantra, you have intuitive knowledge; you are experiencing the texture of the phenomenal world very intuitively. So you could say that if you belong to the vajra basic family, and have a vajra subfamily, and belong to the guhyamantra division, a triple vajra is happening.

The vidyamantra division is largely based on magic. You are able to change things miraculously into whichever level or element you like. If you belong to the ratna family, and you have a ratna subfamily, and you also belong to the vidyamantra family, you can expand your ratna-ness. You can negotiate with somebody, and convince them or hypnotize them into what you want to achieve. You can overpower them immensely, so you are a triple ratna. You might say this is like being a triple Taurus.

In the early stages, before this further elaboration of the five buddha-families takes place, you have the potentiality of all of them. The five-buddha-family principle continues all the way to the atiyoga level, but this is the first time that these categories of minute families have been described.

## The Mandala of Vajradhatu

In yogayana, the phenomenal world is seen in terms of simplicity and self-luminosity. The wisdom of that particular vision brings what is called the mandala of vajradhatu, or the mandala of the indestructible realm. With that, students have a quality of clarity that goes beyond purity, but with the help of purity. So purity is still part of the involvement of the student of yogayana.

Yogayana stresses both utpattikrama and sampannakrama, the creation and completion stages. In this yana, you are just about to relate with an internal atomic bomb. Your attitude toward practice has become simplicity. Töndam has been seen as your basic nature, and kündzop has been seen as vajradhatu. Therefore, individual uncertainty and individual commitment are taking place within you at the same time—and the internal space created by that combination is a potential atomic bomb.

At this point, the definition of the vajradhatu mandala is that the phenomenal world is seen as very simple, direct, and ordinary, and at the same time, highly sacred. That sacredness comes from experiencing the phenomenal world in its precision and directness. If you turn on the tap, depending on which way you turn it, either hot water or cold water will come out. If you step on dog shit, that is going to have its own definite consequence. If you sneeze, that is going to have its own consequence. If you insult your vajra master, that will also have its own consequence.

Vajradhatu is based on seeing the automatic reactions that take place in ordinary situations. And with vajradhatu, self-made explosiveness is taking place all the time. Because kündzop is seen very simply, it gives direct feedback. This brings a feeling of sacredness, much as the idea of purity does in kriyayoga. It is because of seeing that directness as sacred that you have an attitude toward the deities as being neither good nor bad. The deities are seen as having the same beauty that you might see in a Coca-Cola bottle, as opposed to reserving the feeling of beauty for sacred objects. Both deities and ordinary objects are seen as the same sort of phenomenal experience. That realization of the directness and simplicity of the world is very immediate and personal. You can't miss the point—and when you are missing the point, the point is still there. Even though you think you are missing it intellectually, it is still there always.

# Yogayana:
# Empowerments and Practice

*It is very important to understand that visualization practice is quite different from imagining an image. Simply picturing a deity sitting on your head or imagining deities in front of you as mental images is completely different from visualization practice. Visualization is the sensation of being positively haunted.*

## YOGAYANA EMPOWERMENTS

In yogayana, abhishekas are connected with the ideas of depth and breadth that we discussed. The breadth of relative truth brings confidence in relative truth as an object of pleasure, and the depth of absolute truth is that there is self-existing joy or bliss within you. So you have two forms of entertainment: you are entertained by your basic being, and you are also entertained by the devas and devis and by the phenomenal world. Such entertainment, as well as your approach to your guru and to abhisheka, is something that you expect. It is not that you are looking for help.

Yogayana is very simple. You are beginning to get a sense of the energy or potentiality of anuttarayoga. You are developing generosity, spaciousness, and a greater sense of craziness—much more craziness than in the previous yana. There is a more daring quality in the way you relate with the deities and handle your experience of the phenomenal world. The phenomenal world is seen as the expression of various deities. Therefore, there is no difficulty experiencing its profundity and expansiveness. The whole process becomes very easy and natural, and the experience of union is no problem. You could almost say that it is taken for granted.

## Three Tests

In a yogayana abhisheka, you go through three basic tests to determine your buddha-family. The first test uses a stick from a neem tree, the Indian tree that is used for cleaning one's teeth. This stick is carved in a certain way so that it has a point and a base, and you attach flowers to the top. You throw that particular stick onto the mandala. The second test is again throwing that flower-stick onto the mandala, and the third test is throwing it once again. So there are three times when you throw flowers. The first time you throw the flower you are blindfolded, and the second and third times your blindfold has been removed.

Those three tests should uncover your buddha-family from among the one hundred family possibilities. With the first flower you disclose your major family; with the second flower, you disclose your lesser family; and with the third flower you uncover your family characteristic. So the whole process has been worked out.

## Five Abhishekas: Relative Truth

The first five abhishekas that are received in yogayana are very similar to those of the previous yana, upayoga. We could say that they are connected with the wideness of relative truth. That is to say, the water, crown, vajra scepter, bell, and name abhishekas are expressions of understanding relative truth completely. You are finally being enthroned as a prince or princess, and greater fearlessness begins to develop.

## Six Additional Abhishekas: Absolute Truth

After the first five abhishekas, there are six more abhishekas, which are connected with the quality of depth, or absolute truth. These abhishekas are a further confirmation, and altogether they are called vajra master abhishekas.

IRREVERSIBLE ABHISHEKA. The sixth abhisheka is called the irreversible abhisheka. In this abhisheka, the teacher promises you that from this time onward, your journey is completely irreversible. You do not have to depend on purity or the introverted practice of meditation—you don't need those things. By revealing yourself to yourself, you begin to feel a tendency to be filled with joy, to be filled with bliss completely. A quality of conviction begins to develop. The guru encourages this by offering the irreversible abhisheka first. In doing so, the guru does not use any ritual objects; but this abhisheka is presented to you by words.

SECRET ABHISHEKA. The seventh abhisheka is the secret abhisheka, which is connected with the practice of karmamudra. In karmamudra, the experience of sexual passion is transmuted into your basic being. So your basic being is a form of orgasm, rather than needing to have a physical orgasm as a way of manufacturing joy or bliss.

AUTHORIZATION. The eighth abhisheka is called authorization. In this abhisheka, you are given power to impart to others the abhishekas that you have received. This is a very special characteristic of yogayana. From this time onward, you yourself become a guru. You have the power to impart to others the fundamental bliss within yourself.

FINAL CONFIRMATION. The ninth abhisheka is called final confirmation or prophecy. Having removed all doubts, the final confirmation is that you do not have to hide any secret fears. You could communicate those fears to your guru. Although yogayana encourages unity, there may still be a faint fear of separateness due to ignorance and confusion. You may feel that you might be excluded in some way. So in order to confirm you, in order to tell you that you are a child of the tathagatas, a child of the herukas, you need to acknowledge your unity with the phenomenal world and your own buddha nature.

ENCOURAGEMENT. The tenth abhisheka is encouragement. The idea is that confirmation is encouraging. It is a very polite way of cutting through, presented as hospitality, rather than cutting.

PRAISE. The eleventh and final abhisheka is called praise. In this abhisheka, the guru appears in the form of the nirmanakaya buddha, as the *bhikshu* Gautama Buddha, and proclaims your future buddha name, saying that when you attain enlightenment and become a buddha, you will be known as "Buddha Such and Such," and you will teach at a certain time and in a certain place. The praise abhisheka is based on the idea of going deeper and deeper into the absolute truth, and acknowledging the depth of the essence of joy or pleasure. The reference to power and pleasure is one of the important points of this tantra.

## YOGAYANA PRACTICE

Having received the yogayana abhishekas, the student continues with two types of practice: *tsen-che,* or visualization practice, and *tsen-me,* or form-less practice.

### Visualization Practice

FOUR STEPS OF VISUALIZATION PRACTICE. In yogayana, visualization practice has four steps: visualization yoga, complete yoga, all-inclusive yoga, and supreme yoga.

*Visualization yoga.* The first step is called visualization yoga. In yogayana visualization, you visualize the deity as almost equal to you, as more of a friend. In fact, you look down on the deity slightly as being part of your extension in the relative world, rather than looking up to the deity as a highly divine being.

*Complete yoga.* The second yoga is called complete yoga. In this step, the jnanasattva is embodied in your being. There are two different approaches to embodiment: embodiment as though you had been impregnated, or embodiment as snow falling on a lake. In this case, the embodiment is that of snow falling on a lake. You become completely one with the jnana-sattva, rather than being impregnated or heightened by the embodiment of your jnanasattva, which is a form of vajra pride.

*All-inclusive yoga.* The third step is called all-inclusive yoga. In this yoga, animate and inanimate objects are seen as the realm of the deity. It is a form of meditation in action, but you are still very much conscious of the deity, which is why this yoga is part of tsen-che, or visualization practice.

*Supreme yoga.* The fourth step is final or supreme yoga. You develop a feeling of the complete presence of the deity and a tremendous under-standing of the mantras. Your whole being is completely steeped in the presence of the visualization. However, being steeped in the visualization does not mean that you are visualizing a particular deity all the time. It means that the form and the speech of the deity are very much present. In other words, your subconscious mind is tuned in to a very powerful living experience, as if you were visualizing all the time.

With supreme yoga, there is a feeling of the continual presence of the deity. This kind of awareness has been described as being like falling in love. When you are in love, you don't have to think of your lover's name, because you are completely involved with that person. You feel their presence constantly, so your lover is with you all the time. Any expression in your life, like the sound of a closing door, or the sound of somebody's coughing, or any little sights you might experience—all of those things become the expression of your lover. Your lover almost becomes nameless: a form without name, but with enormous presence; a form without direct self-conscious awareness, but completely absorbing.

This same quality is also included in the realm of visualization. It is very important to understand that visualization practice is quite different from imagining an image. Simply picturing a deity sitting on your head or imagining deities in front of you as mental images is completely different from visualization practice. Visualization is the sensation of being positively haunted.

FIVEFOLD BODHI APPROACH TO VISUALIZATION. The technique of visualization in yogayana is what is known as the fivefold bodhi approach. First, you visualize a lotus seat, a solar disk, and a lunar disk, which represent transcending passion, aggression, and ignorance. Second, on top of that you visualize the form or image. Third, you visualize the scepters or attributes that this particular visualization figure is holding. Fourth, you visualize the totality of the whole thing that you made up out of your imagination. And fifth, you visualize placing seed syllables in the appropriate energy centers of the body, such as the forehead center, throat center, heart center, genital center, navel center, and so forth.*

This fivefold process has the potential of creating a spiritual atomic

---

* These five aspects of awakening, or in Tibetan *ngönjang nga* (Tib.: mngon byang lnga; Skt.: abhisambodhi), are often explained as the stages of (1) resting in emptiness, (2) visualizing the deity's seat, (3) seed syllable, (4) scepters, and (5) the deity's complete body or form.

bomb. You don't measure outer space to figure out how this bomb might explode, but purely inner space. This bomb must be equipped with its fuse, its intensity, and its explosiveness within yourself. There is the possibility of an internal explosion, and naturally this is connected with the possibility of an external explosion as well.

From yogayana onward, you are also relating your thinking to space. In yogayana, the practice of visualization, the recitation of mantras, and yourself are regarded as three different aspects of the sky or space. That is to say, there is no distinction between the deity and yourself. They are seen as completely united. But there is still a stain, in that you see the deities as special in some sense. So they are not exactly part of you, and they are not exactly other than you. There is some ambiguity. But the end product or afterthought is that they are like the sky; they are different aspects of the sky or space. The deities are seen as part of the manifestation of the mahasukha prince, which is you or within you.

In sadhana practice, you begin to concentrate not only on visualizing the central deity, but you expand to entertaining yourself through your sense perceptions. For instance, having invoked the main deity, you also begin to visualize deities called offering devis, who present you with objects of sense pleasure, like sounds, musical instruments, lights, food, flowers, and incense. The idea of being presented with offerings is that you are not afraid to indulge in the sense perceptions. Such indulgence is not regarded as embarrassing or nonvirtuous.

In terms of mantra recitation, in yogayana and all the lower tantric yanas, unless mantra is chanted as a devotional practice or invocation, mantra practice is usually done in silence. This is referred to as "mind recitation" or "mental recitation." You just think the sound rather than say it.

RELATING TO THE DEITIES. The deities in yogayana are largely the same type of deities as you find in kriyayoga. The deities are dressed as sambhogakaya buddhas, and they have the scepters of the five buddha principles. These deities could be provoked to faint anger, but they could not be provoked to complete wrathfulness. They are also not heavily involved with passion or, for that matter, with ignorance.

Yogayana deities are peaceful, with various semiwrathful deities surrounding them. The idea is that you are still keeping the basic principles of bodhichitta and prajna. So in a sense, these deities are still at the level of exaggerated bodhisattvas or mildly crazy buddhas. But in yogayana, your attitude toward the deities changes. You begin to develop visualizations of yourself as a deity; and in front of you, like a mirror reflection, another set of complete mandalas is visualized on the shrine. So when the jnanasattva descends on you, it descends on the visualization in front of you as well. At this point, you are more than just purely friends; there is a sense of indivisibility with your deity.

Your attitude toward the samayasattva is that it is yourself. Whatever is seen in the phenomenal world is part of your own understanding or basic nature, and physical forms are part of the setup of the mandala. Your attitude toward the jnanasattva is that the jnanasattva is neither good nor bad. The jnanasattva is also yourself, to some extent. Since you and your jnanasattva are equals, you can ask for favors, and that creates a further vacuum within your own mind.

## Formless Practice

The second yoga, tsen-me, is formless meditation. In formless practice, the joy or bliss that you experience is not centralized in any particular part of your being, but it is all-pervasive. If you have difficulty in doing formless practice, the traditional instruction is that you visualize the Tibetan syllable A coming into your mouth and penetrating your body—penetrating through your eyes, your nose, your innards, your navel, and your genitals—so that you are constantly bombarded with A's penetrating and cutting through your body.

A feeling of formlessness and nonattachment begins to develop once you experience that you are completely machine-gunned by A's. You have nothing left to hide, and nothing to run away from. You are just lying there or sitting there. Making use of that penetrating power of A is the primitive way of developing tsen-me, the actual formless meditation practice. It is a primitive way of developing joy instead of pain. Any place in yourself that you hold as ego identity is cut down, so joy is part of the environment, and you are part of the environment, and no "you" as an individual entity exists. There is a quality of freedom and complete joy.

With tsen-me, you feel that you are a nonentity, but at the same time as you are experiencing that realm of nonentity, you could also visualize the deities. You could have the awareness of tsen-che and the four yogas of visualization practice as well. You could have that kind of awareness without any reference to come back to. That is one of the points of this tantra: you cannot come back to any place at all. If you have somewhere to come back to, you are not experiencing complete bliss properly. But if you have nowhere to come back to, nothing to return to, that is complete total experience, the real experience of oneness. So oneness is groundless at the same time. It is not groundless in the sense that you have been deprived of ground, in which case you still have a kind of ground. Instead, it is groundless in that ground does not exist—it is unknown to you.

## THE PRACTICE OF FIRE OFFERING

The pattern of sadhana practice in yogayana is also very similar to upayoga, except that at this point a new practice is added, which is known as the fire offering. The practice of fire offering starts in this particular tantra, and continues into the later yanas.

In this practice, you offer various substances such as food, fabrics, minerals, herbs, and so forth to the fire. The fire is visualized as a mandala, and the flame is the deity, or the consuming aspect of the deity. So you are offering various things to the deity. And again, since this yana is connected with the idea of union, offering and dissolving seem to be one.

A fire offering depends on the need for various types of energy, called the four karmas: pacifying, enriching, magnetizing, and destroying. In this practice, you visualize the flame in different ways, and you make different offerings for each karma. Herbs are offered to the peaceful or pacifying flame. Jewelry and various minerals are offered to the enriching flame. Clothes and fabrics and various herbs may be offered to the magnetizing flame. And metals, hardwoods, hot spices, flesh and blood, and things like that are offered to the destroying flame.

In a fire offering, you are experiencing different ways of relating with fire, as the first and closest way of using the energy of the phenomenal world. You are relating to the five elements of earth, water, fire, wind, and space, and you are relating with the four karmas as different aspects that exist within the fire. Pacifying is like bathing in a cool flame; enriching is a lukewarm flame; magnetizing is a somewhat sharp flame; and destruction is a very precise burning quality. You visualize the vajra or pacifying flame as white; the ratna or enriching flame as yellow; the padma or magnetizing flame as red; and the karma or destroying flame as green.

In terms of what is being pacified, enriched, magnetized, or destroyed, I think this is left to the student. When students have been doing a complete sadhana for some time, they begin to get a sense of what particular practice they need to conduct. At this point, such offerings would not be related to a specific practical situation, like wanting to magnetize your landlord and destroy the rival for your girlfriend. You might be able to do that later on, once you are completely free from all those entrapments, but at this level working with the four karmas is not as immediate as that. It is more psychological and subtle. And an interesting point about the vajrayana is that although you can do such things once you are up to it, when you *are* up to it, such problems no longer seem to exist.

## Yogayana as a Bridge to Anuttarayoga and the Higher Tantras

Groundlessness is a bridge to the complete experience of the four orders of tantra. It is a bridge to anuttarayoga, or mahamudra and to the three higher tantric yanas of maha ati or dzokchen.

The point when you find that there is no ground left, but there is still joy and pleasure, is the starting point of the experience of nirmanakaya. Because there is no ground, there is no basic being that you can hold on to. At the same time, there is a feeling of enormous expansion. You are filled with the whole universe, and you fill the whole universe. You feel that you are one with everything, that you are one with all. That "all" quality is the experience of sambhogakaya. Finally, you have dharmakaya, which is that such "all-ness" does not have any limitations, none whatsoever. Limits do not exist, and the pulsation of joy does not exist. Joy is just one. It is big, all-pervasive, and boundless. That boundlessness is the experience of dharmakaya.

That quality of boundlessness allows you to go on to relate with such anuttarayoga deities as Guhyasamaja, Kalachakra, or Chakrasamvara. The essence of mahamudra is connected with that sense of no reference point. It is because there is no reference point that you can visualize the enormous number of details on the carvings on the bone ornaments of a particular heruka, and however many hands or faces there are, and whatever scepters that heruka holds. These details become very vivid because you have no boundary and no reference point. Therefore, it becomes a one-shot vision without the need to focus.

*Part Eleven*

# THE TANTRIC JOURNEY: MAHAMUDRA

49

# The Great Symbol

*The technique or practice of anuttarayoga goes against people's cultural, philosophical, and religious frameworks. That is why this tantra is regarded as outlaw. Practitioners of anuttarayoga were outlawed in India as being dangerous and extraordinary. It is said that nobody should get into anuttarayoga, and if anybody does get into it, they should get into it properly.*

## ANUTTARAYOGA AND MAHAMUDRA

Anuttarayoga is known as the highest yoga tantra: *a,* or *an,* is negation, and *uttara* is "above"; so *anuttara* means "none above." In Tibetan it is called *la-me: la* means "above," and *me* means "not"; so *la-me* means "nothing above." From the point of view of the New Translation school of Tibetan Buddhism, there is nothing above anuttarayoga. You feel that you are on top of the Empire State Building. Consequently, you forget that there are airplanes hovering over you or birds flying over your head.

The idea that there is something above anuttarayoga comes up in the Old Translation school. From the point of view of the lower tantras, anuttarayoga is like a fourth and most important yana. But according to the higher tantras, anuttarayoga is not exactly a yana, but more like a bridge from the mahamudra-type lower yanas to the three higher yanas of mahayoga, anuyoga, and atiyoga.

In India, there was no such thing as a New Translation or Old Translation school. Instead, the tantric yanas were simply divided by whether they were connected with the maha ati approach or with the mahamudra approach. So according to Indian tradition, anuttarayoga is simply called mahamudra. *Maha* means "great," "large," or "vast," as in mahayana, and *mudra* means "basic symbolism"; so *mahamudra* means "great symbol."

The Tibetan term for mahamudra is *chaggya chenpo*. *Chaggya* means "symbol," and *chenpo* means "great"; so *chaggya chenpo* is "great symbol." Chaggya chenpo is comprised of three aspects. *Chak* is traditionally interpreted as meaning "empty," as in the shunyata experience; *gya* is interpreted to mean "going beyond samsaric possibilities"; and *chenpo*, which literally means "big," is interpreted to mean "unifying." So with *chak*, *gya*, and *chenpo* together, or mahamudra, you have the union of nonexistence and freedom from conceptualization. According to the *Mahamudra-tilaka* (*Mahamudra Drop Tantra*):

> *Chak* means the wisdom of emptiness.
> *Gya* means liberation from the dharmas of samsara.
> *Chenpo* means union.
> Therefore, it is known as *chaggya chenpo*.

In mahamudra, the wisdom body, or *ku yeshe*, becomes visible, and it also becomes empty. *Ku*, or body, is connected with the idea of cutting the fetters of the samsaric net, and *yeshe*, or wisdom, is spaciousness; so in mahamudra, ku and yeshe are combined. Being empty and free from samsaric confusion is the greatest symbol of all. With mahamudra, that symbol can dawn on a situation, rather than being manufactured out of an LSD trip or anything like that.

## THREE LEVELS OF ANUTTARAYOGA

There are three levels of anuttarayoga: root tantra, skillful-means tantra, and fruition tantra.

### Root Tantra

The root or essence tantra is study. You should begin by hearing and studying about tantra so that you are able to understand the practice intellectually. That such a statement is recommended in the tantric literature may be surprising, because people tend to view tantra as a breaking away from society, getting wild, and dropping out. But the actual teachings do not recommend that.

### Skillful-Means Tantra

With skillful-means tantra, you are actually practicing the techniques and traditions that are given to you.

### Fruition Tantra

Fruition tantra means that with each journey, a sense of accomplishment takes place constantly.

## MAHAMUDRA IN COMPARISON WITH HINAYANA AND MAHAYANA

The difference between hinayana or mahayana practice and mahamudra is that mahamudra practice does not believe in the earth, and a practice like shamatha does. Your relationship to earth has been like that of a fly attracted to excrement. There are a lot of pungent things happening on the earth, and you are constantly drawn back to that smell. The idea of not believing in the earth is that you are no longer attracted to the pungency of samsara, which is your pungency at the same time. Instead of being attracted to dirt, you are attracted to genuine freshness, which is real.

Mahamudra experience is an eye-level situation, whereas the shamatha approach is still from ground to heaven, looking up. So a moralistic attitude still exists in shamatha; you are still trying to be good. But in mahamudra, there is evenness, and because the whole thing is so even, you have greater command of the situation. Mahamudra is simple and direct. Having had that experience, you do not want to dwell in the past, present, and future anymore. You do not want to have a cozy home of any kind. Anything that is rationalized, such as dwelling in a cozy mahayana home or a cozy hinayana home, does not work with mahamudra.

In mahamudra, the emptiness of twofold ego (the ego of self and the ego of dharmas), which you have experienced rationally, has to be worked with to the point that it becomes very personal and genuine, beyond calculation of any kind. Without that, you are unable to experience real mahamudra. In mahamudra, you are going beyond the reasonability of the egolessness of dharmas to a very subtle and completely personal experience of the egolessness of dharmas. Combining that subtle understanding of the egolessness of dharmas with the understanding of the nonexistence of oneself, which has already been experienced at the mahayana level, brings about mahamudra.

In the mahayana, complete emptiness has not been seen, and complete freedom from samsara has not been realized, so there is no union of the two. But with mahamudra, seeing samsaric emptiness means that there is a lot of activity and play. The mahayanists would never buy that, for in the mahayana, transcending samsara means to do good, whereas in mahamudra, transcending samsara means play.

In the teachings on mahayana, we talked about vipashyana as the torch holding the fire that burns the fuel of conceptual ego-mind. We also talked about the warmth that cuts through the ego. But the vajrayana approach is something more than that. The vajrayana is not concerned so much with the torch, but with the totality of the flame-world. That fire-world actually burns the torch itself as well as the torch-er, the one who lit the torch.

The mahayana approach is a courting process, and the vajrayana approach is one of magnetizing or elegantizing. You are elegantizing your neurosis so that it could be more workable. When people hear about the vajrayana approach, they often find it crude or dirty. But it is actually the ultimate way to have dignity in spite of your neuroses. On the whole, it is a way of glorifying our vajra world.

Another thing about the vajrayana is that historically there were quite a few female practitioners. The vajrayana is a much more open approach than the hinayana approach of rules and regulations. In fact, in the vajrayana we cease to talk about what gender of people can practice dharma. The inclusion of female practitioners is just accepted by everybody. The emphasis is not on either the masculine or the feminine human being; it is completely open.

We also know about a few siddhas who were women. One of the outstanding female siddhis was Naropa's consort, who was called Niguma. Niguma developed the six yogas of Niguma, and she was one of the prominent counterparts of Naropa. There were also female siddhas called Shavari, who were forest dwellers and were supposed to lead the hunt. And there were a great many lady prostitutes who were also siddhas.

Whether they were men or women, everybody was doing their best to attract people and catch them into the mahamudra experience. So I think gender does not really make any difference here. There might be some problems with gender in the hinayana and mahayana, but in the vajrayana there is no problem at all.

According to anuttarayoga, when you are at the hinayana level and you first start shamatha practice, it is like the third day of the lunar calendar, when you begin to see the crescent moon in the sky in the morning. And when you reach the level of anuttarayoga, it is like the fourteenth day of the lunar cycle, which is the eve of the full moon. That is the journey up to this point, according to the New Translation school. It is an interesting analogy, because it seems to imply that something more is needed. The theory is that there is not anything beyond the level of anuttarayoga, but anuttarayoga practitioners seemed to have an idea that something else needed to be added.

## STUDYING THE EARLY TANTRIC YANAS

I think that anuttarayoga is what a lot of people imagine tantra should be. The previous three tantric yanas are not particularly well-known, except for kriyayoga. The juicy part of tantra, the part that is known to be great, is in this particular tantra. At the same time, it is very important to have some understanding of the previous three yanas. They provide a very important basis for you to understand the vajrayana altogether.

One problem is that the Tibetans did not study the other yanas a great deal. Therefore, we have very few of their manuscripts in Tibetan, let alone Sanskrit. The practices themselves have been handed down from teachers to students for generations but only scattered textbooks and commentaries are available. The only tantra really well preserved is anuttarayoga. But if you are going to be instructed in the complete, comprehensive tantric process, you should have some understanding of all the tantras and their practices.

## THE OUTLAW TANTRA

In anuttarayoga, upaya and prajna are brought together. For that reason, Buddha was inspired by this particular tantra, and he would appear in the form of various tantric deities in order to teach it. Sometimes, it appeared that he taught in the form of Vajradhara. When he did so, Vajradhara's consort, speaking on behalf of the students, would request Vajradhara to teach tantra. She would ask the first question, and the students would join in as the discussion went on.

The technique or practice of anuttarayoga goes against people's cultural, philosophical, and religious frameworks. That is why this tantra is regarded as outlaw. Practitioners of anuttarayoga were outlawed in India as being dangerous and extraordinary. It is said that nobody should get into anuttarayoga, and if anybody does get into it, they should get into it properly. This is the same principle as that of the vajra: the vajra will not strike, but if the vajra does strike, it destroys the enemy.

Anuttarayoga goes against ordinary patterns of morality and the conventional social setup. However, that may sound like more than what it actually implies, so don't get frightened. Nonetheless, in the past when the mahayana doctrine was proclaimed, the arhats fainted; and when the vajrayana was proclaimed, the bodhisattvas fainted. Still, I do not think it is shocking enough for you to run away.

## Shaking Things Up

The world of anuttarayoga is a large-scale world. Even in the hinayana, and at least at the mahayana level of shunyata, it has been taken for granted that the world is vast and that it has its functions, which are interdependent. This has been understood, and that is why the tantric teachings are possible. Tantra stirs up your snug way of sleeping within the gigantic cosmos. It upsets your sense of security and makes you more paranoid. Instead of security, there are a lot of holes all over the place. The oceans are not just oceans, but they have huge bubbles underneath them. The sky is not just a blue sky, but there are holes carved out that are not actually blue sky. It seems that the role of tantra is to see those things, rather than to rest in the eternity and efficiency of the phenomenal world, thinking that everything is going to be okay. That is not possible. Nothing is going to be okay.

In tantra, we are not just saying flat out that everything is good. Why is that the case? Why do we bother to say that your mind is one? Why do we bother giving your mind names like *nirmanakaya, sambhogakaya,* and *dharmakaya*? Why don't we just say that everything is okay? We decided to define that particular large-scale working basis using different names and principles and concepts, because it is not just a good old world, but it is a tricky world. Why do we say that all mind is dharmakaya? Why not just say all mind is happy! Why do we use such a complicated word as *dharmakaya*? There is a purpose for that: to freak you out. There is a purpose in those details of phenomena. They are not just bread-and-butter language; they are technical terms.

It is not so simple. Each of you has your own duty, your own discipline. Everybody is different. Some people might have kidney problems; some people might have liver problems; some people might have sugar problems; some people might be fat or thin, here or there. There are all kinds of situations. People dislike this and that; everybody has their own individuality. So we cannot just say the world is one, but we can say that the world is one because of those problems. That is what makes us one world. Otherwise, we would not have a world; we would just have one gigantic being. It would be like a big octopus dwelling on this planet earth. That is not possible.

People have their individualistic styles and ways of communicating. For example, if the heat were turned down, everybody in the room would feel freezing cold, but each of them would have a different way of dealing with it. Some people would freak out and shout, some people would stay put, and other people might run and get more clothes. There are all kinds of variety in how people handle themselves. In tantra, we are not trying to conquer that or disturb that giganticness. That seems to be our saving grace. We let that rest.

## TRANSMUTING THE EMOTIONS

Rather than providing training for refraining from, controlling, or editing our emotions, anuttarayoga provides the possibility for all the emotions to be transmuted, so they become part of the path. Transmutation does not mean turning one thing into something entirely different, like light turning into dark, or dark turning into light. Instead, in transmutation an emotion is "mutualized." It goes through a change or a kind of camouflaging, and finally comes out properly. When you transmute an emotion, you still keep the quality of the emotion, but the intensity of the emotion is changed, it is heightened. Transmutation is like directing sunlight through a magnifying glass, which makes the light much more burning and intense.

Transmutation is based on joining two forces together: the emotion and its object. The reason we cannot usually transmute our emotions is that we feel impotent, or we feel that the situation is too overwhelming. When we begin to realize that we are not impotent and that situations are not all that overwhelming, we can actually join the two forces together and jump into the situation properly. If I am angry, and you are the object of my anger, that anger is not regarded as a pathetic thing to be involved in, and the object of that anger is not just regarded as somebody wretched who is only worth being angry at. Those two things are brought together in very close proximity: "I am angry. The object of my anger is provoking me. So be it. SVAHA. Let us explore. Let us work together."

## BINDING TOGETHER

In anuttarayoga, binding together or unifying becomes important. The term that applies here is *samvara,* which means "joining" or "binding together." It refers to binding together *that* and *this,* so that transmutation can take place properly and fully, without fear or hesitation. The world that we see is what it is. Therefore, the world of our experience is what it is, too. So there is no embarrassment taking place between you and your world.

## APPRECIATING DESIRES

In tantric literature, aggression is viewed as the fire that burns the root of buddha nature, and passion is more like water. Like water, passion may be turbulent, but it still sows a seed and moistens the earth, creating further development, growth, and greenery. So in tantra, there are a lot of references to passion. An important characteristic of Buddhist tantra is that passion is recommended from the point of view of appreciating desires. You are not blocking your desires or getting indignant about other people's desires, but all desires could be changed into vajra passion. Passion is close to compassion, openness, and love, while anger cuts the root of liberation.

One of the Chakrasamvara tantras says: "How could you be liberated by pain without pleasure, without joy? Therefore, come and join me, and do not separate or make choices as to which one you should take. Choose any object of desire." Brahmans are too pure, and dogs and untouchables are too impure—they are two extremes. But from this perspective, Brahmans, dogs, and untouchables are seen as the same. And if there is any doubt, that doubt should be eaten, rather than thrown away. Doubt should be consumed as part of the vajra feast. So in tantra, there is a lot of emphasis on the practice of vajra feast.*

### Visualizing Masculine and Feminine in Sexual Union

Anuttarayoga seems to be the first point where you can actually work with your passion. Unlike the three previous yanas, anuttarayoga includes the direct visualization of you and your partner, the feminine principle and masculine principle, copulating together. This is a symbol that this world is no longer embarrassing, and therefore the world is not embarrassed either. So again there is the sense of bringing the two together. This does not mean having a gigantic orgy in the name of tantra. It refers rather to the fundamental level of relating this world with that world and joining them together, which is a very powerful and fantastic experience.

In anuttarayoga, visualization is carving out your bones, re-creating your brain, and re-creating your heart. It is not a reference point, but a point of hassle, quite possibly. When you are visualizing, you are open, just doing your practice, and the visualization is an expression of identifying your own mind with a particular deity. When the jnanasattva descends, the visualizer stays. So the idea is not that the jnanasattva is trying to trick or con the samayasattva into dissolving. Rather, they are the same.

### FORMLESS PRACTICE:
### MAKING YOUR MIND COMPLETELY NAKED

Mahamudra is one of the leading tantric disciplines of sampannakrama, or formless meditation. Sampannakrama, or dzogrim, refers to the stage of practice in which you do not want to dwell in a beautiful, little, humble, pseudo-yogicship of any kind. Therefore, it is known as the mahamudra, quite rightly and delightfully so.

Formless practice is quite mysterious, and a lot of students have no

---

* In a *vajra feast*, disciples combine their sadhana practice with the celebration of a communal meal that usually includes the consumption of both meat and liquor.

idea what sampannakrama actually means. This is the root of many of the problems in vajrayana practice. We find that there are seeming vajrayana teachers and masters of all kinds, but many of those teachers do not first teach their students how to work with dzogrim. This has always been a problem; it is an irritating situation. Such teachers prefer to offer people the more colorful aspects of tantra, rather than teaching dzogrim. But if there is no dzogrim, there is no spirituality.

Without dzogrim, there is constant spiritual materialism happening. So a vajrayana teacher, a vajracharya or vajra master, should be responsible for having their students learn formless practice first. What does that mean? It means that some kind of mind training is necessary and absolutely called for. Mind training goes beyond any rationalization of what the state of enlightenment should be. Furthermore, mind training is free from entertainment of any kind, including nonentertainment, since nonentertainment is also a form of entertainment.

Dzogrim is a way of making yourself completely naked. This is a very tricky point. When a teacher tells you that it is a way of making your mind completely naked, you might ask the teacher, "Couldn't I just wear simple clothes instead of being naked? What is this naked trip all about?" You might ask such things because you still want to have a rug under you. You do not want to pull the rug out from under your feet or your ass. But in dzogrim, the word *naked* does not mean being purely harmless or indulging in good living; it means being unconditioned by expectations or conceptualizations of any kind.

In mahamudra, two symbols—vast space and freedom—are put together. Emptiness or vast space provides lots of room for situations to occur and be understood at the vajrayana level, and freedom means going through various stages of stepping out and taking a leap into the situation. So in mahamudra, with *maha,* there is a greater emphasis on vastness and freedom, and with mudra, or self-existence, the emphasis is on no reference point at all, none whatsoever. There is no evaluation—therefore it is *so.* Maha is not so much a question of big and small, but in this case maha is just so. Just so is vast space. Just so is freedom.

# 50

# Devotion:
# The Essential Prerequisite for Mahamudra

*The mahamudra experience depends on devotion alone. As it is said in the texts: great devotion brings great practice; medium devotion brings medium practice; and small devotion brings small practice.*

MAHAMUDRA IS based so much on devotion that it has been described as devotion mahamudra. Those two are always together: mahamudra and devotion, devotion and mahamudra. So whenever a person has experienced or is about to experience mahamudra, the first prerequisite is devotion.

## GIVING UP TERRITORIALITY

Mahamudra can only exist in the minds of students who have fully committed themselves to the vajrayana path alone, without exception. However, you cannot commit yourself without a reason. And the only reason you commit yourself to the practice is because of the personal link that exists between you, the teaching, and the teacher. Such a link is not possible if you decide to hold back your own world, rather than giving it up. That giving-up process is precisely what is meant by giving up territoriality.

To work with holding back, you need to see the nature of the holding back. Holding back means that you are about to give in; that is why you are holding back. Otherwise, you would not need to hold back. If you are pulling, you are pushing at the same time; if you are pushing, you are pulling at the same time. It always works that way. The desire to give in brings with it the resistance to giving in. It is like asking a question, which usually is saying the same thing as the answer. It is like a mother saying before giving birth to her child, "I don't want to have it." But at that point, it is too late; the child is there already, so what can you do? You cannot dissolve your child into a little dot. It is too real. You cannot perform miracles.

When you give up your world and your territoriality, spiritual guidance begins to be possible. At the same time, the thought occurs to you that dharma is much better than your little imagination, your little world. You begin to realize that you have been scheming for ages and ages, kalpas and kalpas, trying to be smart and playing one-upmanship games with other people. That is what has been going on so far, and that is what still goes on, as far as your quest for personal victory is concerned. But in studying the vajrayana, you realize that dharma brings about a far greater victory, so that you no longer have to wage your petty warfares. In vajrayana, there is a greater sense of victory, a greater vision, and a greater power.

## THE IMPORTANCE OF APPRECIATION

The mahamudra experience depends on devotion alone. As it is said in the texts: great devotion brings great practice; medium devotion brings medium practice; and small devotion brings small practice. Appreciation plays an important role as a source of both celebration and devotion. If there is no appreciation, you are just going to sew little stitches throughout the whole of your life, one stitch after another. You will just continue to do those stitches that make up your regular life. You get up, eat, go to work, come back, and go to bed. You might add some extraordinarily interesting stitches, but your life still consists purely of buttoning and unbuttoning your shirt. There is no creativity in that approach. Mahamudra involves something more than just buttoning and unbuttoning yourself all day long. There is a greater sense of delight, worthiness, and gratitude.

We could say quite safely that students who hear the vajrayana for the first time, or enter into a vajrayana-like atmosphere after being involved in the hinayana and mahayana, would like to depart from that vajrayana world. They would naturally have some thoughts of escape, thoughts of relaxation or relief from the feeling of being oppressed and squeezed into a corner. That is not particularly problematic. But when you begin to actually exert the effort and energy to try to escape, you are cutting your own throat, which is not such a good idea. Such a situation, in which you would like to give up abruptly and throw off everything, is like murdering your own parents.

If there is no devotion, there are no yidams. If there is no devotion, there is no dharma. If there is no devotion, there is no sense of expansion or the kind of visionary approach toward the phenomenal world that brings about personal creativity. Without devotion, you become depressed about the yidams, the vajra master, the dharma, and your life. You begin to complain about every inch of everything that you possibly can. If there is no devotion, you cannot have chaggya chenpo: you cannot have the chak of mahamudra, or the basic vision of emptiness; you cannot have the gya, or the freedom from the fetters of samsara; and you cannot have the chenpo, the unification of those two, which is the attainment of coemergent wisdom.

The manual work that exists in shamatha-vipashyana discipline is rather homey and safe, but the vajrayana is quite unlike that. It is not homey and safe at all. Rather, it stirs up a lot of possibilities. At the same time, it also settles a lot of possibilities. If you did not get an upset stomach, the doctor would not have a chance to examine you. But once the doctor looks at you, that doctor has a chance to settle your stomach for the rest of your life, until you dispossess your body at the end.

## Taking Delight in the Vajra Master

Mahamudra cannot be born in individuals who are without devotion. Such devotion is not particularly political; it refers rather to a personal appreciation of the teachings, the spokesperson of the teachings, and the atmosphere that such teachings produce around you. It is impossible for mahamudra to be born in your heart if there is no sense of delight. Mahamudra cannot be born in somebody who is highly depressed by the impossibility of themselves and the teacher and the teachings. There has to be a feeling of delight and cheerfulness taking place; and cheerfulness can only begin to take place by relating with the vajra master, who represents and symbolizes the vajrayana teaching altogether. Out of devotion toward the vajra master, appreciation of the teachings begins to evolve as well, because the vajra master is somebody who lives the teachings. The vajra master is living teachings. And at some point, the whole thing turns back around to you, saying that now you have to do the whole thing.

The idea of taking delight in the vajra master does not mean that you have to shake hands with the vajra master each time you are confused. That would mean that you shake hands with the vajra master constantly, over and over again, just to reassure yourself, which would become rather complicated. In the same way, when you go to the American embassy, you are not working with the president himself, but with his agent. Actually, people get more messages from the radiation than from the radiator. The radiator is too blunt and too domesticated. The vajra master possesses two eyes, one nose, one mouth, two ears, and all the rest of it. But the radiation does not have any face; it is just radiation, just light. So it is much more pronounced, and at the same time it is much more realistic. That atmosphere gives more messages than the actual little person sitting in the middle of the office.

## Encountering the Intimidating Power of the Dharma

The point is that the atmosphere of dharma is all-pervasive. When an all-pervasive dharmic atmosphere begins to occur, a lot of people naturally get overwhelmed. But the problem is that the feeling of being overwhelmed is translated as rejection rather than as an including process. It is like relating to the sun. You feel that the sun is too bright, so you buy venetian blinds and dark shades to cover yourself up. In that way, it seems as if the sun does not really have power over you. But that is an expression of patheticness. It is pathetic that you have to ward off the sun, to cover your little eyes with dark shades and use venetian blinds to block the sun and create a dark room.

So in dealing with the vajrayana and with the vajra master, there is room for intimidation, but it is important to realize that this does not mean you are being cast out. However, if you cast yourself out, and then others cast you out, and your teacher casts you out as well, that goes beyond just intimidation.

Intimidation is what happens when you are beginning to enter the vajrayana. You may never have experienced this, but if you go to an American embassy to apply for a visa, the minute you enter the door there are all sorts of intimidating things, such as the president's photograph and the eagle holding little weapons in its claws. All sorts of American-isms begin to overwhelm you and make you feel like you want to go away. But still you walk in. That is your first introduction to how you can handle America.

Then you go and sit at the desk and apply for your visa to the United States of America. You fill in your forms in all sorts of ways, and finally you either get your visa or you don't. But still you have entered into the American world, and wherever you go, all the walls and corners are part of that American world. Encountering the all-pervasive atmosphere of dharma is that kind of experience.

You might find it rather intimidating that you have to let yourself be stabbed and confiscated and claustrophobia-ed. But subjecting yourself to such measures is better than huffing and puffing in cosmic madness, which does not do much of anything except bring further pain, further stupidity, further passion, and further aggression. We have done that before, in any case, and we know what it is all about.

## Sharing the World of the Vajra Master

In order to cut the fetters of samsara, to escape the clutches of the sam-saric whirlpool that goes around again and again continuously, we have to stop somewhere. We have to stop in order to start, and we have to start something in order to stop. We have to start with delight and celebration that at last the wonderful dawn of Vajrasattva has occurred, and the wonderful living vajrayana is heard. The message of mahamudra is actually being uttered on our land, and it is a very moving experience.

Now that such a thing has happened, what are we going to do about it? We are going to commit ourselves to it, whatever the cost may be. The cost of commitment is not so much a financial cost as a psychological and physical cost. It is like the chicken-and-egg story. We realize that our sense of delight brings about our appreciation of the vajra master, and the vajra master brings about the delightfulness of situations, back and forth.

If you are traveling on a rainy day or in a hailstorm, it is as if you are journeying together with the vajra master, sharing his heroism. Every time a drop of the rainstorm hits you, it hits the face of the vajra master, too. You are sharing together that gray world of the rainstorm. If you are traveling on a sunny day with fantastic light that makes everything brilliant, you are sharing the same light that hits the face of the vajra master and all the dharmakayas, sambhogakayas, and nirmankayas who exist. The same light shines on your face. You are sharing that real vajrayana world on earth in every possible way. You are using the same brand of toilet tissue, and you are getting the same splinters in your hands from the same kind of wood that the vajra master touches.

At this point, the experience of devotion begins to become very real, very powerful and exquisite. The yidam and the vajra master and you have a common world that you share together. On one hand, the vajra master cannot have any students; on the other hand, they could have a universe of students. The world could be full of their students because the idea of one and many does not apply. It is more of an atmosphere. Everything is an equal world, a unified world, a one-flavored or one-taste world. And within that one-taste world, you are able to practice and go about your job properly.

Without devotion or affection, you are actually unable to practice and to realize real mahamudra. If you ask, "What is real mahamudra?" we could say that real mahamudra is devotion. We could say that real mahamudra is one flavor. But what kind of one flavor is it? It is one flavor in that you and your resistance, which have dissolved together, are sharing the vajra world of the vajra master and the vajrayana. That seems to be the basic point.

Without that sharing, you are unable to do anything. Everything becomes mere philosophy, mere conceptualization, mere rationalization. Books talk about vajrayana, but that does not mean very much; they are just books. We do not have any good vajrayana philosophers, either. One reason is that philosophical interpretations do not help very much. A person may have studied linguistic philosophy, but they still get confused as to what is what.

## INDESTRUCTIBLE TENDERNESS

The mahayana cultivates a quality of gentleness, which brings you finally to the softness of mahamudra. The final gentleness is to yield—beyond your parents, beyond yourself—to the vajra master. The final lust and passion is to yield to the vajra master, because that person is not only the vajra master, but they are also the embodiment of the lineage, of the entire teachings, of whatever you have heard and experienced.

If there is no gentleness, no sympathy, no softness, and no tenderness at the beginning, you cannot become hardened afterward. When the tenderness begins to click with itself and mature, it matures to the extent that it becomes indestructible. That is the idea of devotion becoming vajra nature. Human devotion, human emotionalism, basic ordinary devotion and longing become something greater.

The whole process is very natural and ordinary: at the beginning, there is a need for a lot of tenderness in the mahamudra, and in the end that tenderness begins to become petrified or diamond-like. You then begin to inherit what is known as the vajra mind of the vajra master. But before you do that, you have to have gentleness.

## DEVOTION, LUSTY DEVOTION, AND COEMERGENCE

As far as basic mahamudra is concerned, devotion is not much different from coemergent wisdom. One flash of mind simultaneously contains devotion and the transcendent part of devotion, which you could almost say is lusty devotion. Lusty devotion is bright red. It is transcendent because lust is much more direct. True lust has a quality of longing rather than hunger. That is true, genuine devotion. In true lust, there is somehow hunger and satisfaction at the same time. You also get a feeling of empty-heartedness, which is the nondwelling aspect. You begin to lose your reference point of who is doing what.

All these things are happening at once, which is known as coemergence. Everything emerges together, so you never again have to put labels on who did what or what did who. Everything happens at once, which is a very constant, concentrated experience. It is all happening at once. That is mahamudra.

## THE EXAMPLE OF TILOPA

Having already laid out some basic ideas about the meaning of tantra, I will briefly tell you the story of Tilopa. This story is very much connected with my lineage and with other tantric traditions as well, so we can begin by looking at how this lineage started.

It is said that in the beginning, there was no male and no female. Then that which experiences itself fell in love with itself and created a

*The great siddha Tilopa.*

relationship. It began to create a partner, it fell in love with its partner, and things went on from there. So in the beginning, there was the unoriginated, the unborn. Nobody had a guru, nobody had a teacher, nobody had to relate to anything at all. Then a very conveniently beautiful accident happened: the unoriginated guru became an originated guru, and from that point on, the lineage was passed along from one person to the next.

In that way, the Kagyü lineage is said to have been passed down directly from Vajradhara to Tilopa. As a result of Tilopa's encounter with Vajradhara, the unoriginated guru, Tilopa became the first person in the Kagyü lineage. But Tilopa did not receive teachings from Vajradhara alone. Having already exploded his mind by meeting Vajradhara, Tilopa studied with other teachers. By working with these human teachers, Tilopa learned to speak in traditional terms. The idea is that when the teaching begins to happen, it is an experience—but experience needs language, and at the same time, language needs experience.

The story of Tilopa is not all that dramatic or extraordinary, but he is the direct link to Vajradhara, who is the dharmakaya buddha himself. The story tells us that Tilopa was born in East India in a place called Jago, somewhere in Bengal. Before he was born, his parents first had a daughter, and they were praying to have a son to continue their family lineage. Having failed many times, they invited both Hindus and Buddhists to perform ceremonies to grant them a son in the family, and finally a son appeared. As Tilopa was being born, there was a radiant light covering all of East India, so they decided to call him "Ösel," or "Prabhasvara," which means "luminosity." So Tilopa was named Ösel.*

The family, being Brahmans, invited a Brahman soothsayer to tell the future of the child. The soothsayer said that he was uncertain which buddha this child was, but that in any case, they better take care of the child and wait for new signs to come along.

One day when Tilopa was about eight years old, he was sitting with his mother on the balcony and suddenly they saw a black shadow. An ugly

---

* *Tilopa,* like many Tibetan masters, went by many names. He is probably most widely known as "Tilopa," or the "sesame oil presser," since he attained enlightenment while doing this work. For more on the life of Tilopa, see *The Life of Tilopa* by Pema Karpo, translated by the Nalanda Translation Committee (Halifax, N.S.: Nalanda Translation Committee, 2008) and Thrangu Rinpoche, *The Life of Tilopa & the Ganges Mahamudra* (Auckland: Zhyisil Chokyi Ghatsal Trust, 2002).

woman appeared, huffing and puffing and holding a stick in her hand. She was extremely ugly and dark. Tilopa's mother was fearful that this might be a vampire of some kind that was going to eat her son or destroy his life. She cried out, "Don't you kill my son!"

The old lady said, "However much you lovingly take care of him, there is no way that you can avoid his ultimate death."

Then Tilopa's mother asked the old lady, "What can I do to save him from death?"

The old lady said, "Make him take care of your herds of cows, and teach him how to read and write."

So Tilopa began to study reading and writing. He also began to learn preliminary hinayana practices and doctrines, and he started to study mahayana practices and doctrines as well. And he spent part of his time taking care of the cows.

Then the same woman appeared to Tilopa again, this time in the meadow where he was taking care of the cows. She asked him, "What is your name? What are you doing? Who are you, and who is your sister?"

Tilopa replied, "I was born in a place named Jago. My mother's name is so-and-so, my father's name is so-and-so, my sister's name is so-and-so, and my name is so-and-so. I am practicing reading and writing in order to learn the dharma, and I am taking care of the cows in order to develop our future wealth."

The woman was extraordinarily angry and outraged, and she contradicted the little child by saying, "No. Your country is not Jago. It is Uddiyana, the land of the dakinis. Your father is not your father; your father is Chakrasamvara. Your mother is not your mother; your mother is Vajravarahi. Your sister is not your sister; your sister is the dakinis. Your name is not Ösel; your name is Panchapana. And you are not taking care of ordinary animals, but you are taking care of the animals of experience in the jungle of bodhi trees."

The little boy was rather bewildered. He did not know how to relate with all that, and he said, "How can I know that what you say is true?"

The old woman answered, "If you do not know, or if you are curious about what I have to say, then you have to go and seek the charnel ground of Salabehari. You have to look for a guru."

Tilopa was so curious that he decided to run away from home. He did not even return home to relate his experience with the old woman and what he had been told. He just escaped from his home and ran away to the charnel ground.

The Salabehari charnel ground was dedicated to the Hindu god Shiva, and all the local corpses were presented there. It was a big charnel ground, the place of outlaws, where no ordinary human being would go, let alone a little child.

Tilopa entered the charnel ground and met a guru called Krishnacharya, who took care of him and sent him to Nagarjuna, who was meditating in a reed hut nearby. Nagarjuna was instructing the gandharvas or nature spirits about prajnaparamita. There for the first time, the young Tilopa received complete instruction in the hinayana and mahayana.

Later, having practiced, grown up, and developed a great deal, Tilopa went back to the charnel ground to see his guru Krishnacharya. There he received instructions on dream yoga. He also received instructions from Nagarjuna on the yoga of the illusory body and on the *Guhyasamaja Tantra.* Then he was sent by Krishnacharya to a nearby city to visit a guru called Lavapa. Lavapa had fallen asleep for twelve years in the intersection of the city, and when he woke up he attained mahamudra experience. In this city Tilopa received the instruction in ösel, or luminous mind, from the siddha Lavapa.

Having studied with these four gurus,† Tilopa was still not very satisfied with what he was learning and with the instructions he had received. He wanted to get to the heart of the matter. So he asked all of his gurus, "How can I go further? How can I go beyond this?"

They all said, "You cannot get the spotless, ear-whispered lineage. It is only possessed by the dakinis. You cannot get it."

Tilopa was very indignant about that, and he said, "I am going to get it, wherever it is." Then the four of them gave him directions on how to go about receiving this instruction.

So Tilopa went to Uddiyana, the land of the dakinis, which was originally known as Swat, in Afghanistan. (It is in Pakistan today.) Although his gurus had recommended that he not go, they said that if Tilopa really

---

* The *Guhyasamaja Tantra* is one of the oldest and most important texts of Buddhist tantra.

† Krishnacharya, Nagarjuna, Lavapa, and Mati Subhagini ("bestower of bliss," Vajrayogini in the form of a hag).

wanted to go and if he had a strong conviction to go, he should take three things with him: a bridge made out of precious stones, a knife in the form of a diamond hair, and a key made from a blade of kusha grass. Once he made up his mind, Tilopa could not be convinced to change his plan. He had already developed an enormous appreciation and vajra pride that he actually was Chakrasamvara, so receiving this teaching was just a matter of collecting his debt, rather than receiving instruction from a higher realm, particularly.

As Tilopa entered the town of Uddiyana, he approached the castle of the dakinis, which was on top of a mountain in the middle of a lake. The castle was surrounded by a moat that contained poisonous water, so Tilopa had to use the bridge of precious stone to cross. Beyond the moat, there was a big metal wall that he had to slice down with the diamond hair.* And beyond that, there was a big gate that he had to open with the blade of kusha grass. He took the position that his body was immovable, his speech was melodious and strong, and his mind could not be reduced to fear. With those three prides and with vajra conviction, he went inside the mandala.

First he encountered the nirmanakaya dakinis. The nirmanakaya dakinis put up a token fight to prevent him from getting into the center of the mandala, but realizing his conviction, they let him through. Then he got to the sambhogakaya dakinis, who were acting as cabinet ministers to the queen, who was the dharmakaya dakini. And when Tilopa finally got to the dharmakaya dakini, he would not prostrate. He just demanded the mahamudra experience, which consisted of three symbols: an icon, a mantra, and a crystal vajra.

Tilopa said, "I would like to have the jewel of samaya in the form of a *tsakali,* or icon. I would like to have the jewel of the three syllables in the form of a mantra.† I would like to have the jewel of the scepter in the form of a crystal vajra."

The dharmakaya dakini rejoined by questioning him: "If you want the jewel of tsakali, you will need to have the credential of the lineage. If you want the jewel of the three syllables, you will need the credential of knowledge. And if you want the jewel of the crystal vajra, you will need

---

* In some versions of the story, the metal wall is scaled by a crystal ladder.
† The *three syllables* are OM AH HUM.

the credential of experience and the prophecy that you are going to be the holder of the lineage."

Tilopa replied, "In order to get the jewel of samaya, I have a fearless body. In order to get the jewel of the three syllables, I have fearless speech. In order to get the jewel of the crystal vajra, I have a fearless mind. I *am* Chakrasamvara. So I have no fear, and at the same time I have no desire to receive these three things."

The icon, the three syllables, and the crystal vajra represent three very important principles. The tsakali or icon is the idea of lineage. It represents that we have a bodily, physical relationship with a real guru, not an imaginary guru. The idea of the three syllables is that when we receive empowerment or transmission, we begin to realize the nature of our mind and how our mind works with prajna. The idea of the crystal vajra is the confirmation of our total understanding of the phenomenal world. It is called the total jewel, because it represents a complete understanding of reality without any distortion or exaggeration. These three precious jewels are called the three jewels of mahamudra.

Developing an understanding of those three principles is extraordinarily important to the body, speech, and mind in mahamudra. Once you have been trained, getting these three jewels is more like a bank robbery where you steal mahamudra from the dakinis, rather than an initiation or abhisheka. That is what Tilopa did, and this kind of confidence plays an important part in mahamudra.

If you are not trained in the three-yana principles, you cannot bank-rob the mahamudra teachings. But having already trained in the three yanas, you have a basic understanding of what is meant by body, what is meant by speech, and what is meant by mind. With that understanding, you develop a lot of confidence. You have already become a vessel for the enormous elixir of life.

# Taking a Fresh Look
# at the Phenomenal World

*It seems that phenomena are what appear to you and to your perceptions. When you perceive phenomena, if you see things as they are, they do not have to be captured or put in a nutshell; instead, they can perpetuate by themselves. This is known as the dawn of phenomena, which could be regarded as things as they are. The dawn of phenomena should be regarded as the root of all dharmas.*

## SIX WAYS IN WHICH ANUTTARAYOGA IS SPECIAL

Anuttarayoga is a very involved subject, with many categories and levels. One set of categories has to do with the ways in which anuttarayoga is special compared with the rest of the tantras. This set of six categories comes in three sets, which are each composed of two contrasting qualities.

### *Thoughtfulness vs. Unthoughtfulness*

The first set is thoughtfulness and unthoughtfulness. In Tibetan, thoughtfulness is *gongpachen,* which means "being thoughtful" or "thoughtful wisdom," and unthoughtfulness is *gongpa mayinpa.** The unthoughtful-

---

* *Gongpachen* is often translated as "implied" or "intended," and *gongpa mayinpa* as "not implied" or "not intended."

ness of the other tantras implies that there are a lot of areas the previous tantras did not look into. They did not look at the subtleties of day-to-day living; they did not transcend conventional kündzop and get into real kündzop, the real relative world. So the difference between the previous tantras and this tantra is the difference between unthoughtfulness and thoughtfulness, unwisdom and wisdom.

## Literal vs. Absolute Meaning

The second set includes the literal meaning and the absolute or true meaning. In Tibetan, this is *trangdön* and *ngedön*.* The previous three tantras are regarded as literal because there is some purpose, aim, or object involved. In contrast, this tantra does not have any aim or object, except to just to get back into the world.

## Interpretation vs. Beyond Interpretation

The third pair is interpretation and beyond interpretation.† In Tibetan, this is *dra chishinpa* and *dra chishinpa mayinpa*. Interpretation means that you accept literally whatever you are told. For instance, in Hinduism, the Brahmaputra River is considered to be the water that pours out of Brahma's water vessel and becomes the river Ganges. It is regarded as sacred water. So a literal interpretation of that would be that by bathing in the Ganges, you could actually wash away your sins as you wash the dirt off your body. The literal understanding of purity would be to take a bath in the Ganges.

But according to anuttarayoga, that is a one-sided view. The Hindus interpret this idea too literally, which has undermined their spirituality, and that same kind of true-believing quality also exists in Buddhist tantra. Literally speaking, purity is just removing dirt, and unity is just trying to bring everything together in the realm of joy, and so forth. But in anuttarayoga, we are not that literal. We are getting beyond that kind of literal interpretation and perspective. Reality is seen from all directions, rather than from one ultimate point of view.

---

* This pair is also translated as "provisional" and "definitive."
† This pair is often translated as "explicit" and "not explicit."

## SIXFOLD TEACHING STYLE

The way in which anuttarayoga is taught, or its teaching style, is also divided into six categories, or three sets of pairs.

### Present and Embryonic

The first pair is the present situation and the embryonic situation. When the Buddha or other teachers speak the language of tantra, sometimes they are referring to a situation that already exists in the present time, and sometimes they are speaking in terms of situations that exist embryonically.

### Literal and Subtle

The next pair is the literal and the subtle. When tantra is spoken to a student, it is proclaimed in various languages or ways, depending on how awake the student is—or how open, which is another matter.

The literal approach is more primitive, and the subtle approach goes beyond that primitiveness and is much more devious. For instance, the tantric guru would probably recommend that you eat meat. In tantric texts, it says that you should eat pigs, dogs, cows, elephants, horses, and even humans. In response, a student might actually eat all those things, because each particular flesh contains certain magical powers if the eater is in the right state of mind. That is the literal interpretation. A more subtle interpretation is that eating cows is eating ignorance, eating pigs is eating passion, and so forth.

Similarly, tantric texts might say to get drunk. That might apply literally, but a more subtle meaning might be that the phenomenal world and your perceptions need to get intoxicated into another realm of existence altogether. It might mean that because you are not drunk enough, you still see the phenomenal world in a very pathetic and paranoid way, and therefore you have to change your state of being.

## Direct and Indirect

The last pair is the direct and the indirect word. This pair is connected with action, and with the provocative notion that sometimes passion means passion, and sometimes passion means the transcendence of passion at the same time.

This pair is very similar to the previous one. The difference between this set and the previous two sets is that with this pair, in the statement "Eat meat and enjoy," the enjoyment aspect is more pragmatic. The first set just says to eat meat or drink an intoxicant; the second set says to get drunk; and the third set says to enjoy yourself. So there are three different levels: being, beyond being, and actually getting a result out of being.

# RELATING WITH THE PHENOMENAL WORLD

All of this has to do with how we view our phenomenal world. That is the whole point. Saying that you should eat meat and drink liquor sounds like a very decadent remark. But to say this in a less decadent way, the phenomenal world is workable: it is eatable, drinkable, fuckable, and what have you. It is actually there, and you can relate with it. The phenomenal world is no longer regarded as an enigma. It is not one world, but two worlds simultaneously playing by themselves constantly.

Obviously, one of these worlds is more subtle. But who cares? The world still exists. It *does* exist. The phenomenal world that we experience is not quite the phenomenal world that is recommended by tantra; but at the same time, the phenomenal world that we experience is also something that tantra recommends we look at.

The tantric tradition speaks in terms of working with phenomena. Generally when we talk about working with phenomena, we think in terms of working on a project or solving a problem. We are trying to troubleshoot or to discover something. But in this case, it is not so much that we are working on a project, but rather that we are making a relationship with something or other.

On one hand, the phenomenal world is regarded as your illegitimate child, and on the other hand, the phenomenal world is regarded as your true child. Those two processes, the illegitimate and true-child projections, seem to be how we relate with the phenomenal world. Both are playing simultaneously and constantly. Pleasure and pain are simultaneous; hope and fear are simultaneous.

## THE DAWN OF PHENOMENA

It seems that phenomena are what appear to you and to your perceptions. When you perceive phenomena, if you see things as they are, they do not have to be captured or put in a nutshell; instead, they can perpetuate by themselves. This is known as the dawn of phenomena, which could be regarded as things as they are. The dawn of phenomena should be regarded as the root of all dharmas.

A phenomenon does not have any root; it happens spontaneously, on its own. And when a phenomenon arises, it does not dwell on anything. As it dawns, it ceases to become by itself; and as it dawns, it naturally depends on itself, because of its dawning quality. Therefore, we call the dawn of phenomena dharmakaya, for by itself, by its own nature, it does not depart and it does not dwell on anything. So all dharmas are marked with that reality.

We also could talk about this in terms of dharmata. A phenomenon has its own sense. It is neither here nor there. In other words, in perceiving things as they are, we are not dwelling on anything.

## EXPERIENCING PHENOMENA AND NONPHENOMENA

We could look into the process of perception in terms of solidity and spaciousness. We could look in terms of how to realize the existence of the phenomenal world and the existence of the nonphenomenal world.

### The Solidity of Phenomena

The first aspect is the solid aspect of the phenomenal world. The existence of the phenomenal world means that you exist as a person who receives perceptions through the skandhas and ayatanas: through sight, feeling, taste, smell, touchables, sound, and so forth. Those things are not discarded as irritations, nor as natural cosmic problems or nuisances.

When we hear sound, we do not regard it as a nuisance; when we see things, we do not regard them as a nuisance; and so forth.

We can actually perceive the phenomenal world as an existing entity that does not need conmanship or rejection of any kind. Things do happen to us. For instance, when we sit at a meal, we naturally experience possibilities such as tasting sweet and sour. But the things that come up in our world are neither rejected nor accepted; we experience them as they are.

## The Spaciousness of Phenomena

The other aspect is the emptiness or spacious aspect of the phenomenal world. This is equally necessary, because if we only see things in their own solidity, then we begin to lose our ability to keep in touch with reality properly. Either we do not see the gaps anymore, or we see too many gaps. Therefore, we do not see reality as it is. We do not see things as they should be seen, things as they ought to be seen.

Seeing in this way is known as *rangshin nerik*. *Rangshin* means "natural phenomena," *ne* means "the way things live in their own accord," and *rik* could mean "phenomenal perspective," or for that matter, it could simply be a generic form of perceiving things as they are; so *rangshin nerik* means the "way things are as they are," fundamentally speaking. Rangshin nerik helps us to see the play of samsara and nirvana equally.

When we talk about samsara and nirvana, we are not saying that samsara is inferior, or nirvana is superior, or for that matter, that nirvana is liberation, and samsara is confusion. Rather, we are saying that the way things happen to us has two aspects: one is seeing things as they are in their own perspective; the other is perceiving things from a different perspective, using our perception or psychological point of view.

## VIEWING THE WORLD AS EVAM

Anuttarayoga has a very simple view of how we function in the world, who we are, what we are, and so forth. It is very simple, almost simplistic. The analogy is built around two seed syllables, E and VAM, which joined together make EVAM. EVAM is one of the essential symbols of tantra.

## VAM: *Unchangeable Nature*

The first seed syllable is VAM. As far as VAM is concerned, sentient beings cannot become buddhas, and ignorant people cannot become intelligent, unless they are already such beings and such intelligences. Another way of saying this is that, as sentient beings, we are already buddha, or awake. According to this principle, you have within you the seed of a vajra holder. You are already in your being a vajra holder. You are the primeval buddha.

The word *primeval* refers to the self-existing buddha. It refers to the buddha who never had to attain enlightenment, the buddha who never had to go through the arduous journey of the three yanas. That self-existing buddha is there already. That is why it is called the first buddha, or primeval buddha. In English, we could call this the zero buddha. So VAM is the self-indestructibility that exists already within us, which we cannot reinforce in any way at all. It is there already, and it is indestructible in its vajra nature. That is the meaning of VAM.

## E: *All-Perception*

The second seed syllable is E. E is the counterpart of VAM in EVAM. It is a sort of ambidextrous and multiple personality. Sometimes you peek your head into the samsaric quarter, and sometimes you peek your head into the nirvanic quarter. Sometimes you try to be a heruka, and sometimes you are completely wrapped up in your emotions. Sometimes E is seen as good, and sometimes it is seen as bad.

E is basic space. Wherever there is space, there is always room to get completely into it. If there is space in your room, space is definitely your space. Basic space does exist, and the integrity of space never changes. According to the logic of EVAM, E is the playful aspect. At the same time, it is referred to as all-perception. So E is all-perception, and VAM is unchangeable nature.

*EVAM: E and VAM United*

Then there is the union of E and VAM, which means that a pattern exists within your state of being that is both indestructible and moody. You constantly go through phases of sudden wakefulness and sudden confusion. Those two things are always happening in your system, in your state of mind. One phase is a completely solid and continuous process that is intelligent and receptive, and the other one is moody. So you are being conned by the phenomenal world, but at the same time you are accommodating it. Even in your most extreme level of paranoia, you are still accommodating what you are paranoid of, so you are still being spacious, from that point of view. Therefore, E and VAM could be united. They could be brought together. The essence of E and VAM exists within your basic being constantly.

One of the outstanding qualities of mahamudra is its eternally youthful quality. It is eternally youthful because there is no sense of repetition, no wearing out of interest because of familiarity. Instead, every experience is new and fresh.

# Uniting with Open Space

*The importance of anuttarayoga yoga is that you are no longer hesitant in any situation at all. In the hinayana, you regarded yourself as a little ascetic person, a mendicant or a monk. In the mahayana, you were a hardworking social worker. In the vajrayana, you finally become a royal personage. You deserve to be enthroned.*

## SEEING THE GURU AND YIDAM AS ONE

In anuttarayoga, guru yoga becomes very important, not only due to the practice itself, but due to the enormous commitment and devotion involved. This is connected with the idea that in samaya, you are sandwiched between your guru and yidam by a diamond nail; you are joined together as one. You see that the guru is none other than the yidam, and that the guru can grant you siddhis of all kinds. The guru is the embodiment of all the yidams and the central figure of the mandala. Guru yoga is that kind of awareness.

Having related with the guru as your object of devotion, you begin to expand beyond that to also view the yidam as an object of devotion. At first, the yidam is represented by the guru or embodied in the guru, so the yidam is not yet independent, as in higher tantric practice. Instead, at this stage the yidam is a part of your guru. You slowly expand from there to see that the guru is your yidam. So at first, your connection to your yidam is through your guru. Then slowly, you begin to realize that your yidam is also your guru. You gradually expand, impersonalizing the guru as a fixed object of worship.

## BECOMING A FULL-FLEDGED HUMAN BEING

The analogy for giving an anuttarayoga empowerment or abhisheka is that it is like giving your own inheritance to your child. In fact, according to the *Kalachakra Tantra,* it is like bringing up a child. As soon as a baby is born, the baby is bathed, which is like the water abhisheka, the empowerment of purity and vajra nature. After the child is cleansed, it gets dried with a towel, which is the idea of coronation. Then the baby is clothed and adorned with all kinds of paraphernalia, which is an enriching kind of thing. At this point you give the child an appropriate name, which is like the name abhisheka.

Having been bathed and clothed, the child begins to make sounds and noises. The baby begins to develop a need for the phenomenal world in order to entertain itself. Introducing the baby to the world is like giving the child a vajra and a bell. In turn, the child begins to react and to make noises of appreciation or acknowledgment. Then the child begins to be educated. You expose the child to visual and touchable objects and to the sense perceptions. You bring it toys and information about this world. That is like the abhisheka of a vajra master. And with that abhisheka, you become a full-fledged human being.

## ANUTTARAYOGA EMPOWERMENTS

There are four empowerments in anuttarayoga: the outer abhisheka, the secret or inner abhiskeka, the prajna-jnana abhisheka, and the formless abhisheka.

### Outer Abhisheka: Identifying with the Yidam

In anuttarayoga, the first or outer abhisheka consists of the same five abhisheka principles of form that we discussed in the earlier yanas: water, crown, vajra, bell, and name. However, in talking about the five outer abhishekas, we are not referring to being confirmed by the tathagatas alone, but by the herukas. The idea is that the herukas have already confirmed you in the vajra water, vajra crown, vajra vajra, vajra ghanta, and vajra name. So there is an extraordinary vajrayana quality to the whole thing. The outrageousness of not keeping with conventional realities allows you to identify your body and any physical experience as the form of your yidam. You are physically identifying with your yidam.

### Secret Abhisheka: The Yidam and Consort in Union

The secret or inner abhisheka is based on the union or copulation between the masculine yidam and the feminine yidam. As a result of their union, the yidam and consort together produce what is called amrita, or anti-death potion, and that amrita is received in a skull cup.

This form of visualization changes your perspective on the contradictions or dichotomies between your body and your mind. It solves the problem of your body and your mind being unsynchronized. The problem we usually have in the samsaric world is that the body and mind are slightly out of sync. That is the seed of neurosis. It is like playing bad music at the wrong speed, or watching a movie with the sound track off. We speed too much, and there is no synchronization of body, speech, and mind.

The secret abhisheka synchronizes the body and mind in the form of speech. It allows us to practice mantras or sacred sounds, and it gives us complete confidence in the mantra. Mantra is a way of protecting the conscious awareness of the body and mind. You have enough understanding that the body is body and the mind is mind, so both are synchronized. There is no fear of either going too extremely to the body, which would destroy the mind, or going too extremely to the mind, which would destroy the body. Mind here is not purely the mind alone, but the mind as consciousness. So with mantra, there is protection of the consciousness. It is protecting basic awareness.

### Prajna-Jnana Abhisheka: Sexual Union

The third abhisheka, or prajna-jnana abhisheka, is connected with karma yoga or karmamudra. This abhisheka is unusual and special to this particular yana. In tantra, there are said to be two doors or two exits: the upper and the lower. The upper door to enlightenment is through the practices of meditation and visualization and so forth, and the lower door to the attainment of enlightenment is through sexual union.

In sexual union, your partner is regarded as a spokesperson of the phenomenal world—or they are regarded as *actually* the phenomenal world.

Your partner is Nairatmya, who is egoless or formless, and at the same time seductive. This is not a chauvinistic approach. Your partner could be male or female, so we are talking about the seduction of both sexes. The yogini's practice is not different from the yogi's. In either case, the idea is that sexual union is used as a way of awakening yourself and opening.

The third abhisheka is related with finding, either physically or psychologically, your partner, who is traditionally described as a sixteen-year-old. The idea is that in sexual communication, the object is not desire, but reducing oneself and one's complications into one dot. That one dot is joy. It is isness or secretness. There are no further complications. It is one-dotness, in which the different stages of orgasm could be experienced. In this case, orgasm could be interpreted as a physical, ordinary orgasm, or it could be interpreted as a psychological understanding of the pleasure of orgasm, which could be experienced at the same time.

In the later generations of our lineage, this abhisheka has been given purely through pictures and symbols, or the psychological approach. I have heard that in the past, maybe ten generations ago, the vajra masters initiated oral abhisheka, but I have not experienced it myself, personally.*

THE VIEW OF SEXUALITY AS ABRAHMACHARYA. Working with the wakeful quality at the moment of orgasm is a controversial topic. According to some teachers, physical orgasm and letting out your semen are considered to be sinful. I suppose from a medical point of view, it is true that you are wasting or destroying those eggs or sperm. In sexual intercourse, millions of sperm are fighting with each other, trying to survive. They are trying to get into the egg, which has a life of its own, and there seems to be a lot of chaos and fear. All the rest of the sperm are killed in order for one sperm to survive, the one who actually finds a home in the egg. So sexual orgasm actually destroys some kind of life; it is a form of murder. That is why sexual intercourse is regarded as unhealthy or unwholesome.

For this reason, sexual intercourse is referred to as *abrahmacharya*. *A* is a negation, *brahma* in this case means "complete," and *charya* means "action"; so *abrahmacharya* means "incomplete action." In contrast, with

---

* This seems to be a reference to the use of actual physical union in tantric practice. But when Trungpa Rinpoche was asked at the 1973 Seminary about the meaning of oral abhisheka, he replied "I think your guess is as good as mine." To which the questioner responded, "I doubt it."

*brahmacharya,* or celibacy, where you are not destroying any life, you are living a complete life, a life that is full.*

ORGASM AND THE EXPERIENCE OF NONTHOUGHT. In the third abhisheka, the idea is that in orgasm you are making a relationship with your innate nature. At the moment of orgasm, there is an experience of no mind, no thought. There is a meeting point taking place between you and your partner.

The third abhisheka is referred to as the abhisheka of prajna, because it is so intelligent. You are not just doped up in your lukewarm sexual pleasure, in which you are uncertain whether you are coming or going, but some intelligence takes place, even wisdom.

This abhisheka goes beyond solving the conflict between body and mind, and it goes beyond the introduction of mantra practice. It goes into an area where we have no idea what we are getting into, which is called the confused world. Supposedly, we are not really confused; we know how our body functions, we know how our mind functions, we know how our speech functions. But where we are functioning is uncertain, and this causes hallucinations, fear, and confusion.

The reason the image of orgasm is used in this abhisheka is because frigidity is related with that quality of bewilderment. We have our functions within us completely and totally, but we have no idea of our partner as a vajra king or queen. So when we begin to relate with the environment and to expand out, the vajra king or vajra queen is not acknowledged, which seems to be a form of psychological or physical frigidity. The reference to orgasm has to do with not being afraid of opening into outer space experience.

MAKING FRIENDS WITH THE PHENOMENAL WORLD. The prajna-jnana abhisheka can also be referred to as secret, because it cannot be understood without the previous abhishekas. This abhisheka can be shown to you only if you sense that the external world is no longer a mystery or a sheer drop off a cliff, but workable and loving, inviting, soft, and warm, as your consort might be. The point is that you have been afraid of your consort. You have been so afraid of your partner that you do not know what you

---

* *Brahmacharya* generally means "moving in the Brahman," that is to say, keeping one's mind directed toward the absolute.

are going to do with them. Even if you find a consort, you are completely frozen.

The idea of the third abhisheka is that your partner is no longer a vampire or a demon or a leech. Your partner is open space. In that totality of space, there is room and there is sympathy, and communication can take place if you are willing to submit yourself to it. That is how to relate with the pure abhisheka experience. The actual practice seems to come later on.

### Formless Abhisheka: Transcending Reference Points

Of all the special practices that exist in anuttarayoga, the third abhisheka is regarded as one of the hottest points, but by no means does this imply that you should disregard the fourth abhisheka. The fourth abhisheka, which is the formless abhisheka, is the actual experience of what happened to you at the level of the third abhisheka. The formless abhisheka is the total introduction of dharmata, or *tathata*.* All the forms and images dissolve into you, and any reference point seems to be needless. As a result of the first three abhishekas—which you receive successively, one, two, three—when you receive the fourth abhisheka, there is a sense of having totally transcended.

## THE ARISING OF SPONTANEOUS WISDOM

Another aspect of the anuttarayoga abhishekas is the arising of spontaneous wisdom. In the third abhisheka, we experience example wisdom, and in the fourth abhisheka, we experience actual wisdom.

### Example Wisdom

What occurs in the third abhisheka is that after the voidness of orgasm, there is a gap. There is a feeling of openness in which you automatically see what is called *peyi yeshe,* the yeshe of example, or "example-wisdom." So you are using the mechanistic force of the physical body to approach the experience of no mind. You are physically cranking up your body and manufacturing wisdom. That is why this is called the wisdom of example.

---

* This abhisheka is also referred to as the "word abhisheka."

It is an example; you are copying from something. With the wisdom of example, you are manufacturing an experience at the factory level, so to speak.

### Actual Wisdom

The fourth abhisheka, the real experience, does not depend on machines. In this abhisheka, there is a flash or a gap of no mind taking place all the time. You have instantaneous orgasm or nonthought happening constantly throughout the day. It is not dependent on chemicals or machines, but you actually possess it within yourself. It is beyond all that. So after the experience of peyi yeshe, you receive what is called *töngyi yeshe,* or "actual wisdom."

Peyi yeshe is the after-experience of the joy of union. With that kind of pleasure, the mind is completely blown into nothingness, into complete bliss, which is called the wisdom of example. Then, having taken that as your confirmation for future practice and the path, the wisdom that shows you how you can proceed with your practice is töngyi yeshe, actual wisdom, or the wisdom of meaning.

The third and fourth abhishekas play a very important part in anuttarayoga, and the same pattern continues until the level of maha ati. From now on, in each yana there are basically the same four abhishekas, but there are different ways of looking at them. We do not need to add any further ones, because there already seem to be a large variety of abhishekas. The New Translation tantras love to add all kinds of new rituals and new abhishekas of this and that, so you have hundreds of millions of sub-abhishekas. But from the point of view of maha ati, or even the true mahamudra level, that seems to be a bit of a joke.

## BEING ACKNOWLEDGED AS A KING OR QUEEN

The details of the anuttarayoga abhishekas, such as enthroning you as a master and giving you royal auspicious symbols, are similar to the previous abhishekas we discussed. Those details are not very important; they are just the inherited practices of the earlier tantras. Until we get to the three higher tantras, the tantric yanas tend to collect the previous rituals and formats as an inheritance rather than rejecting anything, which makes for longer and more complex abhishekas. But in anuttarayoga, there are just four principle abhishekas, which are extraordinarily powerful.

When you receive the anuttarayoga abhishekas, you are regarded as already being a prince or princess. At this point, due to the greater power and immense composure that you have acquired, you are ready to be acknowledged as a king or a queen. Since loneliness has been realized already through the hinayana, and compassion has been experienced already in the mahayana, and dignity has been developed already through appreciating kündzop properly, you are now an ideal person to be crowned king or queen. So you are enthroned and given a crown; the scepters of vajra and bell are put in your hands; and you are anointed with all kinds of royal perfumes. You have finally decided to become a real king or queen.

The importance of anuttarayoga is that you are no longer hesitant in any situation at all. In the hinayana, you regarded yourself as a little ascetic person, a mendicant or a monk. In the mahayana, you were a hardworking social worker. In the vajrayana, you finally become a royal personage. You deserve to be enthroned and to be adorned with all kinds of ornaments. There is no conflict with this world and that world anymore. The idea of being enthroned as a king or queen may be based on a Tibetan cultural approach, but it seems to be a very sane cultural approach.

# The Challenge of Keeping Samaya

*According to Atisha Dipankara, keeping the vajrayana samaya vow is impossible. It is like putting a well-polished mirror in the middle of a room. A few seconds later, you recognize that dirt and dust have collected on top of the mirror, because it is so well polished. . . . Keeping samaya is very much a matter of your attitude and your state of meditative experience. It has to do with whether your meditative experience of totality is working or not. If it is not working, you are breaking the samaya vow.*

## Vajra Body, Speech, and Mind

In anuttarayoga, the samaya vow is largely based on the vajra qualities of body, speech, and mind. In taking the vajra body samaya, all forms are regarded as the vajra heruka mandala; in taking the vajra speech samaya, everything you hear is vajra heruka speech or sound; and in taking the vajra mind samaya, all the thoughts that occur are the vajra mind of the herukas. Identifying your body, speech, and mind with your vajra master, or vajra guru, is a part of that as well.

## Keeping Samaya through Continual Awareness

According to Atisha Dipankara, keeping the vajrayana samaya vow is impossible. It is like putting a well-polished mirror in the middle of a room. A few seconds later, you recognize that dirt and dust have collected on top of the mirror, because it is so well polished. This encourages the vajrayana practitioner to develop continual awareness, which is called path mahamudra. Keeping samaya is very much a matter of your attitude and your state of meditative experience. It has to do with whether your meditative experience of totality is working or not. If it is not working, you are breaking the samaya vow.

Path mahamudra is based on developing complete command and vajra pride, which at this stage of your awareness is no longer coming from a source. Your awareness does not originate from ordinary awareness, and you do not develop awareness in order to be good, accurate, clear, wise, or anything at all. You simply tune yourself in to samsaric mind. In turn, samsaric mind comes to you, and you find it a reminder, rather than something you have to subjugate. So samsaric mind itself acts as a source of awareness. Whenever there is confusion, anger, passion, jealousy, or pride, those thoughts act as reminders. Whatever occurs in the realm of your mind becomes awareness.

So you have no chance of forgetting your awareness, because your awareness is built on using the resistance or the poison. Elements that are seemingly destructive, or the opposite of the path, are being used as reminders, and such natural reminders are happening constantly. So forgetfulness becomes mindfulness at the same time. In path mahamudra discipline, whatever needs to be subdued is subdued, and whatever needs to be taken care of is taken care of. That seems to be the general approach.

## FEAST PRACTICE AND THE DESTRUCTION OF RUDRA

In connection with samaya, one of the practices that has been developed is called a feast offering, or *tsokkyi khorlo*. *Tsok* is "feast," *kyi* means "of," and *khorlo* is "chakra" or "wheel"; so *tsokkyi khorlo* means "wheel of feast" or "feast offering." Vajrayana practitioners are supposed to do a feast offering on the tenth day and the twenty-fifth day of the lunar calendar, the tenth being the day of the herukas, and the twenty-fifth being the day of the dakinis.* On those days, you must offer a feast connected with the sadhana that you are practicing.

---

* The *day of the herukas* corresponds to the tenth day of the waxing moon, and the *day of the dakinis* corresponds to the tenth day of the waning moon.

The process of a vajra feast is to collect food and purify it, and then invite your vajra brothers and sisters into the feast to share your experience. You also invite the tathagatas and herukas and dakinis as guests. You visualize them approaching you, and you give them offerings from the feast. This offering is called the select offering. If you have gone against the samaya vows, you make a second offering, called a confession offering, as an amendment of your vows. For the third part of the feast, you make a final offering, called a destruction offering. With this offering some food is taken out and put into a triangular black box in order to invoke Rudra, who is then destroyed or killed on the spot. The killing of Rudra is the third part of the feast. After the ceremony is completed, the students and masters who took part in it share the feast food and drink. At the time of Naropa, feast practice was not all that formalized, so feast practice was more like a seemingly ordinary party. But these offerings and the destruction of Rudra were already a part of the whole thing.

There are two important ingredients to be included in a feast offering: meat and alcohol. Alcohol is connected with passion, and meat is connected with aggression. These are the higher ingredients, and you cannot prepare the feast offering without them. Then you can collect fruits or grains or other food to create a meal.

Indulgence plays a very important part in tantra. However, feast practice seems to have become a rather corrupted situation in Tibet. For example, if somebody wanted to have a good drink, or to eat meat although they were vegetarian, they could put their meat and drink on the shrine table and have an excuse to have a good time. Because it was now vajra food, they figured it would not be breaking their vows.

An ordinary person who has not received abhisheka and has no awareness or respect for the vajrayana approach should not be invited to participate in feast practice. In feast practice, poison and medicine are very close. People with no understanding of vajrayana would have a problem with that. Since they would have no idea of the vajrayana meaning of sacredness, it would seem to them to be a contradiction to have a sacred party going on where everybody was eating and drinking and enjoying themselves. They would think that there must be something wrong. But feast practice is a very deliberate practice. It is not just about having a good old party; that would not quite be a vajra feast. True feast practice is overwhelmingly powerful. Students who were not used to such a vajra practice probably could not keep up with it.

## *Working with the Samsaric Physical Body*

The meaning of the feast offering is to encourage the yogins and yoginis to take care of their bodies, so that their wisdom is not neglected. The yoginis and yogins of the vicinity join together to make sure that they are working with the samsaric physical body. By working with the samsaric physical body, you also work with the greater mandala-realm world at the same time.

As the *Hevajra Tantra* says: "Great wisdom abides within the body. Therefore, one should give up any questions completely. That which pervades all things comes from the body and the sense organs, but at the same time it does not come from the body and sense organs." This means that the body is the source of the path, and that without the body, you cannot have the path and the journey.

So the body should be treated well. But you do not do so just to make the body a good solid ladder, to just maintain it so you can tread on it. You should respect the body as the inner vajra mandala. The idea is that the body is very sacred, and it is also the property of the herukas of the mandala.

## NOT HESITATING TO APPLY THE FOUR KARMAS

Another principle connected with the samaya vow is that of the four karmas: the actions of pacifying, enriching, magnetizing, and destroying. Pacifying, or exposing yourself to intellectual disciplines, is connected with the vajra family; enriching, or being generous, is connected with the ratna family; magnetizing, or helping people, is connected with the padma family; destroying, or showing people the way by means of destruction, is connected with the karma family.

A further vow is that you should not hesitate to apply those basic principles. You should not hesitate to magnetize people, physically, psychologically, or spiritually. You should not hesitate to destroy people physically, psychologically, or spiritually. Having already gained an understanding of your own basic energy, you should not be fearful of the karmic consequences. Furthermore, you should have trust in your yidam, herukas, deities, and so forth. You should take care of your body with good clothes, good food, and pleasurable objects. You should enjoy the sense perceptions and sense indulgences. We could go on, but if we went into tantric vows in great detail, we would have something like seventy-five thousand details.

## Vowing Not to Take a Lukewarm Approach to Life

Anuttarayoga practice combines the previous yanas and brings them together as personal experience. It works with the lukewarm quality that is our ordinary, everyday approach to life. In the hinayana you are renouncing your background, and in the mahayana you are working with sentient beings, but that lukewarm quality has not really been challenged. You still can keep your lukewarm attitude.

Cold is death, and hot is birth, so lukewarm is between birth and death. This lukewarm life-flow is localized in what is known in Tibetan as *uma,* or in Sanskrit as *avadhuti.* The uma is a central channel in your body, both physically and psychically. It is that which maintains the lukewarmness—the feeling that you have not quite died, and you are also not quite living, but still you are maintaining your life force. That lukewarmness is regarded as the essence of ego.

You could write all kinds of poems and praises about lukewarmness. You could write music about that or express it in sculpture. It goes something like this: "How fantastic to be alive! This lukewarm threshold of my life is so beautiful. It is keeping me in contact with the hotness of my father and the coolness of my mother. This particular lukewarm thread is providing me with the possibility of brewing a child, my own descendant. How fantastic to be lukewarm! I don't actually have to die; my descendants will continue me. And if I am reborn again, I can rejoin my lukewarm stuff." That is what we usually do; it is our usual approach.

With that lukewarm approach, we think: "Let us be thankful for the books, let us be thankful for the music! Let us be thankful for the fantastic poetry that has been written in this world! Let us be thankful for the great warriors who have been in this world! Let us be thankful for the great saints and saviors who have come to this world with their vision and power and inspiration! Thanks to all of that and all of them, I am able to maintain the lukewarm tube that runs through my spinal cord! Thank goodness that, although my umbilical cord has been cut, I can still hang on to the *brahmarandhra,* my aperture of Brahma! Thank God that we have the sun shining! When the sun shines, it is glorious and fulfills all purposes. And when the sun doesn't shine, we have the full moon or the crescent moon to be praised. And even if they did not exist, there would still be the galaxies of stars and the dawns and the dusks, the grass and the cockroaches that exist in our world, reminding me of the life force."

Such an attitude is related with a superficial approach to life force, because the life force is regarded as lukewarm. You might say, "I went to the restaurant and appreciated the waiter's red apron. He brought delicious wine and served it with a beautiful smile. How delicious the steak was, and the music was sweet." That is an example of what lukewarm life is all about. Life shouldn't be too hot, because you can't stand it; life shouldn't be too cold, because you also can't stand that. So your avadhuti tube usually is filled with the lukewarm fluid of convenience, and that is a problem.

## THE FOUR BASIC VOWS
### FOR OVERCOMING LUKEWARMNESS

In anuttarayoga, the highest yoga of the New Translation school, it is quite rightly said that you should commit murder and theft, and that you should lie and have sex. Those are the four basic vows or principles for how you should conduct yourself in order to deal with your lukewarm quality—which is so lukewarm, it is terrible.

### Murdering

The first vow is the vow to commit murder. By means of the practice of formless practice, or sampannakrama, your basic strength—your air or breath—should be prevented from planting further seeds of life. You prevent it completely from planting further ego seeds in your central channel. Therefore, you are committing murder.

### Lying

The second vow is the vow to lie. Since you have seen the cosmic patterns of relationship as they are, since you relate with the dharmas of reality properly, you seem to be always telling a lie. For unwise or unpracticed people, things-as-they-are is not what appears to be happening, so from their point of view you are telling a lie. Furthermore, truth is shifty. So if you told the truth of now, it would be the lie of yesterday or tomorrow or the next minute.

### Stealing

The third vow is the vow to steal. By capturing the wisdom and power of the Buddha, without anybody requesting you to do so, you are stealing that wealth.

### Sexual Intercourse

The fourth vow is the vow to engage in sexual intercourse. Since the nature of dharmata, the world as it is, has been understood and seen as it is, you are indulging yourself in the world of isness, which is a form of sexual intercourse. In this case, it is more like rape, because that world does not want to be seen as it is. It would like to play with further glamour, to play further tricks on you, but you are not playing that particular game, so it is rape.

These four vows are basic to the realization of anuttarayoga. In anuttarayoga, in order to overcome lukewarmness, you vow to commit murder, tell lies, steal, and rape. These four vows are repeatedly referred to in Jamgön Kongtrül the Great's work, as well as in the work of Longchen Rabjam. They both agree that there should be room to commit crimes. And by crime, we are talking about transcendental crime. We are trying to overcome that lukewarmness, that fake reality or fake poetry.

## GUHYASAMAJA TEACHINGS ON WHO IS SUITABLE FOR SAMAYA

There are many texts on the different kinds of samaya, the persons suitable to practice the teachings, and the different disciplines those people are involved in. One such text is the *Guhyasamaja Tantra*, which has been translated into English by Francesca Fremantle.* The following section is about what kind of people are suitable to practice tantra.

---

* This translation by Francesca Fremantle has not yet been published, and is a work in progress.

## Being beyond Dualistic Thought

Then Vajradhara the King, the body, speech, and mind of all Tathagatas, All Highest Lord of the World, spoke about the nature of the practice of the true meaning of the Dharma, the best of all practices.

The families of passion, hatred, and delusion which exist beyond dualistic thoughts cause the attainment of ultimate siddhi, the matchless supreme way. Those who are despised because of birth or occupation, and those whose minds are bent on killing, succeed in this supreme way, the matchless Mahayana.* Even great evildoers, beings who have committed irrevocable sins, succeed in the way of the Buddhas, this great ocean of Mahayana. But those who blame in their hearts the teacher never succeed in sadhana. Those who destroy life and delight in lying, those who covet the wealth of others and are attached to sensual desires, those who eat excrement and urine, all these are worthy of the practice. The sadhaka who makes love to his mother, sister, and daughter attains perfect siddhi, the dharma nature of the supreme Mahayana. Making love to the mother of the Lord Buddha, he is not defiled, but that wise one, free from dualistic thought, attains the Buddha nature.

To begin with, the idea of being beyond dualistic thought seems to be an important point. It is what we might call ordinary-extraordinary experience. When you are awake, or when you are prepared to be awake, or when you are willing to be awake, you have exposure to freedom, to free activity.

## Nondualistic Activity and the Perpetuation of Freedom

The next lines speak of the samaya vow as an expression of freedom rather than imprisonment. Usually anything dirty, anything sinful, anything confused is regarded as perpetuating the lower realms, which is true. There

---

* Here *Mahayana* does not simply mean the second of the three yanas (hinayana, mahayana, and vajrayana), but refers to the vajrayana path as a whole, which encompasses all three.

is a big question of whether or not such activities should take place at all. But in this case, those activities are perpetuating something else, because you are approaching them from a nondualistic direction.

> Here is the secret rite by which all disciples request the great Vajra. As the Vajra of Enlightenment bestowed the supreme worship on the Buddhas, bestow it now upon me, O Vajra Space, for my salvation. Then he should bestow consecration upon him with a joyful mind; he should place the Lord in his heart, through union with the deity's image, and reveal the mandala to the wise disciple, and tell him the secret samaya proclaimed by all the Buddhas.

> Kill living beings,
> Speak false words,
> Take what is not given,
> And live with women.

> He should set all beings on this Vajra Path, for this is the everlasting samaya law of all Buddhas.

The person who kills their father is one who ruthlessly destroys the father of all, which is aggression and rudra. The person who makes love to their mother is one who makes love to the mother of all, namely Prajnaparamita, the mother of all the buddhas and of all the knowledge that has ever been brought forth into this world. So in tantric language, making love to your mother means becoming one with the teachings and with your teacher.

That is the definition of samaya in anuttarayoga. It means to relate with your father, aggression, completely, and with your mother, passion, completely. You need to get into them and relate with them.

## 54

# The Divisions of Anuttarayoga

*There are a billion pores on your body, and each pore forms a nest
for a mandala. So the intricate details that exist in the phenomenal world are completely saturated by the Kalachakra principle.
There is no room to breathe, except for the breath of Kalachakra
going in and out. It is the ultimate claustrophobia, which at first
brings enormous panic, but then brings a sense of trust; because if
Kalachakra's breath is what you are breathing, you are not breathing pollution.*

I N O N E way, anuttarayoga is very aggressive; in another way, it is very
definite and self-indulgent; and in a third way, it is very transparent.
Because of those three principles, it is divided into three families, or three
categories of tantra: father tantra, mother tantra, and nondual tantra.

In Tibetan, these three categories are *pha-gyü, ma-gyü,* and *nyi-me gyü.*
The union of the three is called *la-me gyü,* which means "none higher,"
or in Sanskrit, *anuttara.* So we have aggression tantra, passion tantra, and
ignorance tantra, and putting all three together gives us la-me gyü, or
none higher.

The idea is that once you enter into a particular tantra, you are entering
into a certain realm, a total experience. Depending on your psychological makeup, you either join the father tantra, mother tantra, or nondual
tantra. It does not make that much difference which one you enter; it is
not linear. Anuttarayoga contains all of them, so which one you enter
depends on which one you are suited to.

## MOTHER TANTRA

The Kagyüpas are particularly known for mother tantra, because it is the tradition of devotion, emotion, and passion. For instance, in the songs of Milarepa, there are lots of references to his passion for the guru, and there is a quality of indulgence in passion. Kagyü lineage holders are basically padma people, passionate people, so we have the mother tantra as our lineage, our inherited tantra. But that does not mean that we purely have to stick to that tantra; we could branch out into the others. As practitioners of mother tantra, the Kagyüpas specialize in Chakrasamvara practice, but they also have exposure to father tantra and to all three divisions of anuttarayoga.

The Chakrasamvara approach to tantric discipline is based on perfection and passion. The idea of perfection is the same principle as that of the VAM symbol, in that you are already purified. You have been cleansed by throwing yourself into the midst of an enormous eruption of passion. It is like getting into a huge, self-existing bathroom. While you are taking a shower, you can shit and piss and clean yourself all at the same time. It is like getting into a dishwasher where you get both washed and dried. It is very direct. It peels off your skin sometimes because it is so direct; but at the same time, it works.

Passion in this case is not purely lust. It is your soft spot. It is that which pleases you in your life. Your passion may be for anything; it could be for money or candy, books or music. In mother tantra, the approach to working with passion is not one of causing the passion to subside, but one of exaggerating it. By exaggerating the passion, the passion gets out of hand and takes you over completely, and you begin to panic. Because of your panic, you begin to freeze—because of that, enormous energy comes up. Suddenly there is a jolt, which loosens you up.

It has been said that cowardly soldiers in the battlefield get so frightened that they become paralyzed with fear, and the only way to deal with this is by threatening to kill them. When such a soldier hears the words, "If you do not walk, I am going to kill you," that soldier actually panics more. A kind of union with the panic takes place. That heightened panic produces more rhythm in his body; the soldier begins to free himself from paralysis, and then he becomes a good fighter.

So being frozen in passion can only be freed by further passion, or a further threat of passion. In the same way, when water is caught in your ear, the only way to get it out is by putting in more water. The idea is to not take passion too seriously. If you take passion too seriously, you will be stuck with it. Instead, passion is taken as a kind of hang-up, and at the same time, as lubrication. So you never get stuck anywhere.

Mother tantra is also connected with the deity Mahamaya, although Mahamaya does not really belong to any order of tantra. Mahamaya is very shifty, like the play of the rainbow. He has a quality of looseness and transparency. Mahamaya is right here with us, dancing with us. He is not anybody, but he has a name, which is the fault of the previous siddhas. They gave him a label, which is unfortunate.

Mahamaya is symbolized by what is known as impersonating the mirage. With Mahamaya, things keep happening. Things begin to develop, and energies begin to move back and forth, but as soon as you start to use your net to catch a butterfly, the butterfly begins to dissolve in the net. You scoop water from the river of mirage and put it in your pot, but as soon as you put your pot on the stove, you find that your pot is empty. And so forth.

Mahamaya is not just hallucination, but it is actual experience, which seems to be real but unreal. There are a lot of things to be said about hallucinations and actual experience in tantra, but in fact we never talk about hallucinations. Talking about hallucinations is forbidden, because they do not exist; they are a complete lie. Instead, we talk in terms of actual experience. Actual experience has a shifty quality; it is changeable, but it is not really a hallucination.

Hallucinations are caused by sickness, by taking drugs, or by mental imbalance, whereas the kinds of things you experience in tantra come up because you are completely straight, square, and direct. You can relate with your cup of tea. You can experience things without labeling them as hallucinations. Labeling things as hallucinations seems to be a very dangerous thing for a tantric student to do. You could turn everything into a hallucination, but if you do so, when you come out of that hallucination you are back to square one, if not zero.

Hevajra is another mother tantra. In the word *Hevajra*, *he* is the sound of joy, and *vajra* is "indestructible"; so *Hevajra* is "indestructible joy." *He* is joyful utterance, which is one of the four types of laughter of the he-rukas.* Hevajra is like dancing with a certain amount of anger. You are pissed off at nowhere and nobody, but you are still pissed off. You are therefore so joyous, so joyful. You are very kind, because you are rather pissed off. It is a combination of sweet and sour.

Hevajra is like making love with a wounded penis or a wounded vagina. The pain and pleasure mixed together bring further joy. The solidity of the pleasure is because of the pain, and the texture of the pleasure comes from the pain. Pleasure actually brings things together.

## FATHER TANTRA

Father tantra is connected with aggression, and with the practice of Guhyasamaja. *Guhya* means "secret," and *samaja* means "union" or union with the secret; so *Guhyasamaja* means "secret union."

According to legend, the Guhyasamaja was the first tantra taught by the Buddha. The story tells that Shakyamuni Buddha was once invited by King Indrabhuti to teach the dharma. The king said, "I would like to relate with my sense perceptions and my emotions. Could you give me some teachings so that I can work with them?"

The Buddha replied, "Oh, you want to hear tantra." And the king answered, "Yes."

Then the Buddha said, "If that is the case, let me excuse my arhats and my hinayana and mahayana disciples from the room." So he asked his disciples to leave.

Once he had done so, the Buddha appeared to King Indrabhuti in royal costume and taught the Guhyasamaja tantra. That was the first presentation of tantra.

## NONDUAL TANTRA

Nondual tantra is connected with Kalachakra practice. In nondual tantra, basic phenomena are seen as a complete world. But by basic phenomena, we do not mean phenomena that are particularly basic, although it is a

---

* The four types are threatening, joyful, enticing, and subjugating.

very convenient phrase to use. We are saying that there are shortcomings and holes in our life. We are constantly trying to patch up our life with this and that, that and this, and we get terribly haunted and frustrated when we do not find any patches to put over whatever holes there are. The result is that our life before our death, our life up to now, is either an unfinished or a completely finished patchwork quilt. So life is a New England patchwork quilt, but the patchwork keeps changing. We thought we put a patch on one spot, but when we turn around, it seems to have changed. Maybe we were either wearing dark glasses or the wrong glasses, or we were doing it at the wrong time of day.

Situations are constantly changing, and the play of maya, or illusion, still continues. So life becomes a fragmentation of items or little atoms. But all those atoms that exist in our life are the basis of our mandala. This is symbolized by the colored-sand mandala, in which each grain of sand represents an atom of our life. To make a sand mandala, first we take white sand, boil it, dye it different colors, and dry it. Then we use the different colored grains of sand—red or blue or green or whatever color we choose—to make a mandala, a complete world. So in Kalachakra, shiftiness and continuity are brought together. This is symbolized by EVAM, by a meeting of the mother and the son, of E and VAM.

According to one of the commentaries, studying Kalachakra is said to be like holding a yak's tail. A yak's tail consists of little hairs that make up a big bunch, but when you hold a yak's tail, you do not just hold the individual hairs, you hold the whole thing. Kalachakra is like the yak's tail in that it is a lot of little things put together, which makes a big thing. That is usually what happens in our life. For instance, if you write a book, that book is made out of little letters, little pages, and little pictures.

Another example of Kalachakra symbolism is the symbolism of the calendar. According to this calendar, there are sixty-year cycles, and within that, each year has twelve months, and each month has thirty or thirty-one days, and each day has twenty-four hours, and each hour has sixty minutes, and so on. Kalachakra symbolism expands in that way. There are a billion pores on your body, and each pore forms a nest for a mandala.

So the intricate details that exist in the phenomenal world are completely saturated by the Kalachakra principle. There is no room to breathe, except for the breath of Kalachakra going in and out. It is the ultimate claustrophobia, which at first brings enormous panic, but then brings a sense of trust—because if Kalachakra's breath is what you are breathing, you are not breathing pollution. The idea is that every item is possessed by the divine principle of Kalachakra. Everything everywhere is included—and not only included, but everything is worked out perfectly. There is an overwhelming quality to the whole thing.

Anuttarayoga unites ma-gyü or mother tantra, pa-gyü or father tantra, and nyi-me gyü or nondual tantra. As such there is nothing higher.

# Manifesting Mahamudra

*All sorts of ritual hand gestures are prescribed in the vajrayana, but to understand such mudras you need to have a general idea of how to relate with objects altogether: how to hold things and how to manifest. . . . How to reach for such things is important; it is your first communication with reality. Likewise, how to place things properly is important.*

## TRANSFORMATION THROUGH DEVOTION AND PRACTICE

Mahamudra is a situation in which a person's state of mind can be completely transformed by two factors: devotion and practice.

The second factor, the steadiness and awareness of practice, is similar to the experience of mindfulness that is exemplified by shamatha-vipashyana. When you go further with that kind of experience of mindfulness, your approach to reality begins to become much more vivid and extraordinarily real. But this is not because you have finally figured things out. It is not that you have figured out your psychological scheme or your case history, and it is not because your scholarship has proven to be great—it's none of that. It happens because your basic existence is vajra nature. Vajra nature, which abides in you constantly, has been woken up, which provides immense power and strength, and at the same time, immense gentleness.

There is a combination of such devotion and insight in the practice of mahamudra that, although you are an ordinary human being, you are becoming Vajradhara on the spot. That is an extraordinary idea! It is unheard of. The theists believe that if you are a good boy or girl, you will be accepted by Christ. And if you are a good boy or girl, and you also believe in Christ, then you might have an introductory glimpse of Jehovah himself. But in mahamudra, everything is one shot: there is no separation between *that* and *you* at all. Although the mystical traditions of theism seem to be saying the same thing, it is not quite so; with the mystics, there is always a hierarchy of some kind taking place. But in the case of nontheism, there is direct communication and interpenetration. It is intercosmopolitan and international.

We could say that reality is a four-legged animal without much hair, but with a puffed-up head—that is mahamudra. How do you figure that out? We could say that the reality of mahamudra is like a four-legged person who can walk and talk at the same time. We can say that reality is a kind of ape who can manifest every possibility of ambidexterity with its hands, its arms, its legs, and even its tail. But at this point, we could stop fooling around with analogies and get right into the topic.

## The Three Roots

Mahamudra has several classes of experience, or we could say several types of magical banks, pools, or dense situations. Traditionally, these banks are divided into three, which are called the three roots: the guru, the yidam, and the dharmapalas or protectors.

### The Guru: The Source of Blessings

The first root is the guru. The guru is the bank of devotion. Out of the bank of devotion comes the sympathetic attitude, whereby you share the vision of the vajra master and their lineage. At that point you receive adhishthana, or blessing. The word *blessing* is not quite an accurate translation, but it is the closest English word possible. *Chinlap,* the Tibetan word for blessing, actually means "being engulfed by heat," or *chin.*

*Chin* means "heat," not in the sense of temperature, but in the sense of animals or human beings in heat, the kind of heat that produces an atmosphere. So chinlap means being enveloped in that kind of intense experience. People often people talk about being blissed-out, but that mentality is slightly different. Chinlap means being engulfed in the radiance of the root guru. The vajra master has radiated you in and out, thoroughly and completely, so your whole being is completely soaked in that particular radiance or profound brilliance. The vajra master is like a universal monarch: one who conquers the world, and one who rules the world and each citizen with the intense experience of being present, being involved, and being completely dissolved into the situation. That is the first bank, which contains adhishthana.

## The Yidam: The Source of Magical Power

The second root of mahamudra is the yidam. Apart from the guru, the yidam is that which makes your mind tight, or that which makes your mind hold together. The Sanskrit word for *yidam* is *ishtadevata,* which can be translated as "personal deity."

Yidams are divided into all sorts of categories, according to your particular being and the anxiety that is being transformed. The idea is that your particular anxiety is transformed into the yidam. This is very real. It is not a matter of what you want or what you do not want, but it is what actually happens. Your anxiety is transformed into the yidam, and having done such a thing, you find yourself belonging to a particular class of vajrayana deities or divinities.

In the vajrayana, we have endless varieties of deities: we have Vajrayogini, Chakrasamvara, Kalachakra, Hevajra, and Guhyasamaja. All of these deities are connections, whereby you can tune in to the principles of your own anxiety. The magical aspect of tantra is not so much in making you happy and peaceful and great, or for that matter, making you wrathful, wicked, and confused. Instead, the magic of the vajrayana—the siddhi or ultimate magic—is that all the practices and deities that are shown to you are working with your anxiety. They are working with your original primordial situation.

*Anxiety* is a very important word. It goes back to the first noble truth: the truth of suffering, or duhkha. This truth was taught right at the beginning, in the original presentation of Buddhism by the Lord Buddha himself. The Buddha picked up on peoples' magical possibilities, and he cultivated those magical possibilities. But he saw that first you have to face the painful reality of suffering. Then you can see the reality of the mahayanists, the blissful reality of bodhichitta and the bodhisattvas. And finally, you can see that the magical possibility of anxiety still remains as the *chökyi dak,* or the ego of dharmas.

At that point, an understanding of symbolism begins to come into being. Because of your anxiety, you do not actually give up or give in to anything, but you go along with it. You go along with the samsaric magic, which is actually nirvanic magic, or vajrayana magic, which is fantastic and extraordinary.

With that possibility, we begin to develop symbolism in the mahayana, and particularly in the vajrayana. The symbolism of mudras, or hand gestures, has developed from that. Mudras at this point are simply the ways and means by which we could transform ordinary crudeness into divine vajra crudeness. Vajra crudeness does not just mean hanging out in your cowboy outfit and dripping cigarettes out of your mouth—we are talking about a special kind of crudeness, which is very painful. In fact, as a result of this approach of fundamental crudeness, we have offended a lot of rich people in America, a lot of Tibetified people and millionaires who would like to have goodies given to them. Vajra crudeness means that we are not particularly concerned with a happy, loose Americanization of the buddhadharma—we are talking about the buddhadharma-tization of the buddhadharma.

Ordinary crudeness means relaxation in one's own neurosis, but when we speak of vajra crudeness, we are talking about energy being acknowledged. What kind of energy? All sorts of energies: the energy of lust, the energy of anger, the energy of ignorance. All the energies are included, and they are acknowledged. But at the same time, somehow there is a little twist, by which a dash of the dawn of Vajrasattva or the Great Eastern Sun comes in. From this point of view, crudeness is a kind of ruggedness. It is not buying or selling any possibilities of individuals asking for comfort so they could hang out or hang loose without zipping up their flies.

We are talking about looseness purely in the sense of its being very tight. At the same time, that looseness is exquisite, and that exquisiteness comes from reality. The vajrayana neurosis—which is not really neurosis, but crazy wisdom—is a sense of fearlessness. You are breaking boundaries, knocking down walls and territoriality. And in that fearlessness, there is also genuineness, which only comes from having compassion, or karuna.

This is why vajrayana iconography has two deities copulating together. The feminine principle and the masculine principle are copulating, with lots of arms and lots of faces, experiencing some kind of reality and openness. But at the same time, they are not being too crude. They are adorned with ornaments of victory, such as bone ornaments, jewel ornaments, and gold ornaments, and they wear tiger skins and leopard skins on their waists. They carry a variety of scepters that are fantastically made masterpieces. They wear crowns of skulls, which are also exquisitely done.

Everything is crudely originated, but even though the yidams are wearing very rugged things, such as your own skull, every visualization is exquisitely and beautifully done. You may wonder why there has to be all that crudeness, why they are wearing skulls on their heads, or why there are gold mountings to make those skulls into crowns. Every ornament has come from very crude beginnings, like death. Wearing human bones is particularly revolting, but those bones are mounted in beautifully designed gold, and adorned with all sorts of jewels and gems. How is it possible that you can wear jewelry made out of human bones, yet mounted in elegant, human-made jewelry? It is because the whole concept comes from the experience of one taste or one flavor.

The skulls and bones signify death and impermanence, as well as the idea of being eaten up if you hold on to any idea of the solidness of reality. And the fact that these skulls and bones are beautifully mounted in gold is making a positive statement of enlightenment. Human skulls can be mounted in exquisite one-hundred-percent pure gold, the best essence of the earth, and ornamented with jewels, and the deities can hold all sorts of scepters, which are sharp and penetrating. There can be a marriage of samsara and nirvana in one taste. That concept seems to be the basic idea of deities in union, and it is the source of siddhis, or magical powers.

### Dharmapalas: The Source of the Fulfillment of All Actions

The third root of mahamudra is that of the dharmapalas, the protectors of the teaching, who are the source of actions. In Tibetan, dharmapala is

*The Four-Armed Mahakala, a dharma protector whose four arms represent the actions of the four karmas: pacifying, enriching, magnetizing, and destroying.*

*chökyong. Chö is* "dharma," and *kyong* is "protector" or "patron"; so *chö-kyong* is "protector of the dharma."

These deities wear even more terrifying costumes than the yidams. Their function is to protect, and to create a feeling in the students that magical power can be demanded, rather than just received. They kill whomever needs to be killed; they give birth whenever there is need to give birth; they fulfill whatever needs to be fulfilled.

## INVOKING ENERGIES THROUGH GESTURES

The three roots are the basis of mahamudra visualization practice. But visualization practice also means having a relationship with your personal body. It means having a relationship with your real body, outfitted with flesh and fat and muscles and bones and everything—maybe you don't have fat, but I do.

How are you going to communicate this body to the reality of that fantastic world of inspiration and power? There is not very much to do; you simply take the attitude of communicating by invoking certain energies. Traditionally, this is done with the use of mudras, or hand gestures.

All sorts of ritual hand gestures are prescribed in the vajrayana, but to understand such mudras, you need to have a general idea of how to relate with objects altogether: how to hold things and how to manifest. You need to learn how to work with reality in holding the earthy things in your manifestation. You could begin with how you reach for a table or a chair, or how you reach for your fan. How to reach for such things is important; it is your first communication with reality. Likewise, how to place things properly is important.

To begin with, you should have some idea of how to go about holding something in your hand. We could look at a series of images to illustrate this.

In this picture, I am holding a pen. I think one of the interesting points is having a wristwatch there as well. I did not particularly want to make the whole thing purely a dramatic event that had nothing to do with the mechanism of the American world.

The pen or brush is one of the important weapons in bringing about the Great East. There is a thumb stuck out, and the rest of the fingers are making postures toward the thumb. These fingers are somewhat sympathizing with the whole reality and making the entire thing very beautiful and ordinary, and at the same time threatening.

This is a better way of holding the pen. It is definitely threatening. The pen is held forward, and there are lots of forces coming from all the fingers, including the little finger and the thumb, which is supporting the pen. This is a gesture of attack. And somehow the wristwatch seems to ornament the whole thing.

This is a picture of a mudra, called the fearless mudra. It looks as if something is held in your hand. It is quite a fat hand, but definitely graceful and realistic.

Here two fingers are holding the lens cap of a camera. It shows that you can catch something casually, but not all that casually. The lens cap is there mainly because you caught it, but still it is real. You caught a black dot.

The idea of these illustrations is not so much that I want to become chauvinistic about my hand, but it is so that you can do things properly, in accord with the situation.

So manifesting mahamudra means acting in accordance with the situation. The three banks—devotion, the yidam, and the protectors—are magical because there is a splash between samsara and nirvana. When you realize that splash, which everyone already has, it produces a kind of power or magic.

## 56

# Ground Mahamudra: Understanding Things as They Are

*That natural, ordinary state has to be cultivated and worked with in three ways. The first way is by not preparing too much. It is by cutting off our preconceptions from the past. The second way is by not expecting a greater flash. It is by cutting off our preconceptions of the future. The third way is by not holding on to our present flash experience. It is by cutting preconceptions of the present. We simply rest our mind, this very ordinary mind of nowness.*

## REGARDING THE GROUND AS PATH

In the vajrayana, there are two basic approaches to the path: regarding the ground as path, and regarding the fruition as path. In mahamudra, we are regarding the ground as path. But in order to discuss the mahamudra principle, we need to comb our hair once more. We need to go back to the beginning of the path and to the ground of hinayana and mahayana.

In the hinayana, you develop an experience and understanding of shamatha, or quieting the mind; and that basic discipline brings about vipashyana, or awareness. Your development of meditation and postmeditation,

---

CHAPTERS 56, 57, and 58 are a commentary on sections of "The Song of Lodrö Thaye," which is printed in its entirety in appendix 2. Jamgön Kongtrül Lodrö Thaye was one of the preeminent scholars of nineteenth-century Tibet, and his song presents the essence of the mahamudra teachings in less than three hundred lines of verse.

or mindfulness and awareness, allows you to become sensitive to the phenomenal world. You find that the phenomenal world comes to you, and that it acts as a reference point. The phenomenal world is present all the time as an object of awareness or an encouragement for awareness.

In the mahayana, you develop an understanding of absolute bodhichitta by resting your mind and by cutting through all thoughts. The precision and the accuracy of shamatha-vipashyana discipline allows you to develop absolute bodhichitta so that you can rest in your natural state. Because you are allowed to relax in the natural state of unconditional alaya, you realize that hopes and fears and emotions of all kinds need not be regarded as obstacles, nor as a big deal. In the mahayana, you see that friends, enemies, and those who are indifferent to you could all be regarded as reminders for overcoming passion, aggression, and ignorance.

## SACRED OUTLOOK AS THE
## BASIS FOR MAHAMUDRA EXPERIENCE

With that understanding, our awareness extends further. It extends a great deal. We begin to realize that the cause of such awareness is our relationship with the vajra master and our realization and understanding of sacred outlook, or tagnang. So sacred outlook comes out of basic awareness; and through sacred outlook, we discover the basis for the mahamudra experience.

*Mahamudra* means "great symbol," but this does not mean purely experiencing the symbol, and not experiencing the real thing. Instead, in mahamudra the symbol itself *is* the real thing. When we eat spaghetti, it could be said to be a symbol of Italian food. But we are not eating symbolism; we are eating real Italian food. So a mudra, or symbol, is itself what it stands for. It is the basic thing, the basic stuff. Things stand on their own. When we say "sunshine," it could be an image, but at the same time, real sunshine is taking place. So mahamudra is greater vision, a greater understanding of the phenomenal world as it is.

This greater understanding of the world-as-it-is occurs in what is known as ordinary mind, or *thamal gyi shepa* in Tibetan. *Thamal* means "ordinary" or "very basic," *gyi* means "of," and *shepa* means "awareness" or "consciousness"; so *thamal gyi shepa* is the "consciousness of ordinariness." We have decided to translate *shepa* as "mind," since consciousness is generally referred to as mind, and to translate *thamal gyi shepa* as "ordinary mind." The idea is that sacredness is somewhat ordinary, in spite of being sacred.

Although the nature of samsara is like a waterwheel that turns around and around, constantly creating actions that produce later effects, none-theless there is a basic state of mind that is clear and pure. That state of mind is known as the experience of mahamudra. In the same way that you might try to attain enlightenment or bodhi in the hinayana and maha-yana, you try to experience mahamudra in the vajrayana.

Mahamudra is sacred outlook, as well as sacred experience. It is inlook and outlook put together. In mahamudra experience, samsaric projections still occur, but you have begun to develop a notion of sacredness along with these projections. We are not talking about "once upon a time," or saying that when you become a grown-up, you will have a different experience. We are talking about the present situation. We do not have to make this into some kind of myth; it is happening to you right now. Although kleshas and neuroses will still be there, you could relate with them in terms of sacred outlook and inlook at the same time. You could do it right now.

## APPRECIATION AND CHEERFULNESS

There are three levels of mahamudra, or ordinary mind: ground maha-mudra, path mahamudra, and fruition mahamudra. All three are related with the principle of cheerfulness, which is very much needed.

The first phase is ground mahamudra. According to Jamgön Kongtrül the Great, "Ground mahamudra is the view, understanding things as they are." Ground mahamudra stems from awareness, from the vipashyana experience. Because the phenomenal world is a reminder and a source of awareness for us, it also becomes a basis for developing sacred outlook.

Sacred outlook leads to an appreciation of the world, because we feel so much gratitude for the gentle and genuine nurturing process by which the vajra master has led us into the path of the dharma. We remember the guru's encouragement and kindness. We appreciate the kindness, gentleness, and trueness of the teachings, all of which are represented by the teacher. So our appreciation develops into devotion.

That combination of appreciation, devotion, longing, and heartfelt pain brings about a quality of cheerfulness. You begin to feel that you are a worthy person. In spite of any neurosis that you might come across, you still experience utter appreciation. Such longing and appreciation come from the realization of sacred outlook. You begin to help yourself and to appreciate the particular world you are getting into, so there is no struggle and no threat. And because you do not have to struggle, you experience cheerfulness. So ground mahamudra is based on appreciation and the experience of sacred outlook.

## A Shift of Perception

In the context of ground mahamudra, we talk about the five sense perceptions and the sixth consciousness, or cognitive mind. We use our sixth sense consciousness, or mind consciousness, and we subtract the seventh consciousness, which is not needed. So the editor goes away. Then we go further back, to the eighth or alaya consciousness, which is called the storehouse consciousness. We get to the storehouse consciousness, which is the basis of confusion, and we go beyond that by using it as our doorstep. We get into the beyond-eighth-consciousness situation: the basic alaya, or absolute bodhichitta.

The seventh consciousness is a VIP in the samsaric kingdom. It acts as a kind of foreign secretary to the government of your mind. In letting go of the seventh consciousness, devotion helps, because you realize that you do not have to fight or defend yourself, and so the seventh consciousness is no longer necessary. It can be dissolved. There could be a jump; and because of that jump, you could gain what is known as ordinary mind, as opposed to the VIP mind of the seventh consciousness.

Without the feedback of the seventh consciousness, there is still natural feedback because you still have your sense perceptions. You still have your eyes and your ears and your nose and everything, and you still have the world outside. All those senses have their own little feedback systems; there is no problem with that. But you do not need a policy maker or big-deal feedback such as: "Is it good or bad?" or "Shall we declare war or have peace?" Feedback without policy making is what we mean by the word *unconditional*.

In the vajrayana, we seem to go back to seeing things as we used to. You can afford to do so because your mind has already been trained and completely processed or shinjanged. You have gone through a period of seeing the nonsubstantiality of things as they are, and you have developed renunciation and revulsion. Having renounced the world, having felt revolted, having already vomited, you can then take a fresh look. You begin to see very naturally. That is what is known as ordinary mind.

But in order to experience ordinary mind, you first have to go through the hinayana process with its emphasis on simplicity and transitoriness. You also have to go through the mahayana process of realizing that others are more important than oneself. Then, having gone through those two processes, in the third yana, or vajrayana, you take a fresh look. At that point, you discover that your process of perception is strong and clear, and you begin to realize how things are as they are.

Going through the three yanas is like taking a tour of a factory. First, you are taken to the entrance, and you see how the raw materials come into the factory. Then you see how they are put onto conveyor belts and processed by machines of all kinds. You go through the whole factory, and when you have finished the tour, you understand how those raw materials are made into the finished products that you have seen. It is a complete educational system.

As another example, the way you perceived a table in the past and the way you perceive a table now from a mahamudra point of view may not be all that different. But generally you are naive; you have never experienced how a table is made, and you have not seen the tree that the table is made out of. So your path involves a process of education and training. This is why the hinayana, mahayana, and vajrayana journey is the best education you can receive.

It is very important that you do not just rush out and get blessings right away, before you have even renounced your own samsaric mind. That is why we put tremendous emphasis on going through the three-yana discipline. Through this process, your mind is shinjanged and lojonged. Because of that, your phenomenal world begins to become different. By the end, you might find that your mother seems more likable. So your perception changes, but whether the world changes or not is questionable.

We have been indoctrinated by the world to believe that unless we are motivated, we cannot function. But then you begin to realize the great switcheroo: without motivation, you can function much better. Because there is lots of wisdom, lots of prajna, everything is more scientific and direct. You do not have to run the world on the basis of egotism, or on passion, aggression, and ignorance. You can run the world better without those things. That is precisely the logic of enlightened society. Conceptual mind is based on good and bad, for and against. It is based on having allegiance to one or the other. But when you do not have that allegiance, you see your red better, your green better, and your yellow better. You can function better because you do not have a private scheme. You are working along with the four seasons.

When the perceiver is no longer deeply rooted in untrained samsaric mud, perception is not a problem. So you do not have to watch what you do. You may get feedback, but so what? You just see that rock is rock. There is no editor. There is no producer for your film, and in fact it is not a film at all. So once again rock is rock, but it is majestic rock. The world is beginning to become very expansive. You no longer have any domestic quarrel with anything. You see the world as it is, neither bad nor good. The world is simply the world. It is simple because you have gone through the proper training. You have trained in the hinayana and mahayana practices of shamatha and lojong, and you have trained in the vajrayana preliminary practices of ngöndro and devotion. Therefore, you are able to see the world properly. Otherwise, the vajrayana could begin to seem like black magic, and it could be the seed of rudra-hood.

Ground mahamudra is experienced in our sitting discipline. During sitting practice and even during tonglen practice, there is some kind of coming and going, thinking and not-thinking process taking place. But beyond that process of thinking and not thinking, there is a base of non-thought or nonconceptualization. No matter how freaked-out you might be, no matter how very confused you might be, there is some kind of dancing ground that is always there and is common to everyone. That ground of nonthought or absolute bodhichitta is applicable to everybody, and it is always taking place. Because of that, it is possible to experience mahamudra. It is like having a fireplace that already has a draft system and a clean chimney, so whatever wood you might burn in that fireplace is sure to be burnt completely.

## LOOKING AT MIND AND ITS PROJECTIONS

This ground of possibilities has two aspects: mind itself, and mind's perceptions. Mind is the perceiver. It is that which is capable of perceiving. In terms of the levels of consciousness, it could be the sixth consciousness, the cognitive state of mind that moderates what we hear, smell, and see of the phenomenal world. Along with the mind, there is phenomenal existence, that which mind projects on to. The mind is like a mirror, and phenomenal existence is like the reflections. Once we have a mirror, then we also have reflections. Because there is light, there are reflections. Those reflections are the phenomenal world, which consists of the objects of passion, aggression, ignorance, and all the other kleshas.

Mind and its perceptions are never produced. They are not manufactured by anyone. It is a natural situation: once you have a mirror, you automatically have a reflection. Once you have ears, you automatically hear sounds. Once you have a body, you automatically feel what is soft or harsh, hot or cold. These situations are often regarded as negative because they produce pain and pleasure, but if you look at them in another way, such things are neither good nor bad. They are unconditioned existence, which happens naturally, like the four seasons. When cognitive mind and the perceptions of mind are unconditioned by good or bad, they play and work together side by side, next to each other, or one by one. We see, we look, we hear, we listen, and so forth.

The kind of interaction that happens between mind and perception is regarded as sacred and natural. It is sacred because it is natural, almost mechanical. Fire burns; water creates moisture; wind blows; space accommodates. Situations that occur naturally are not regarded as threats. Fundamentally, they do not possess any evil, negative, or samsaric qualities that lure us into the confused world.

Mind and its projections are innocent. They are very ordinary, very natural, and very simple. Red is not evil, and white is not divine; blue is not evil, and green is not divine. Sky is sky; rock is rock; earth is earth; mountains are mountains. I am what I am, and you are what you are. Therefore, there are no particular obstacles to experiencing our world properly, and nothing is regarded as problematic.

If you look at mind and its projections simply, thoroughly, and ordinarily, you discover ground mahamudra, which already yearns for, or is directed toward, path mahamudra. In order to do that, you need a vajra master. You need someone who sees mind and mental projections in that ordinary way. The vajra master describes the mind and its projections to you in this ordinary way, and when you look at these things, you also begin to see them in this simple and ordinary way.

When the teacher has instructed you and pointed out the ordinary quality of the world to you, the texts say that it is like meeting an old friend. You realize that it is no big deal. It is simply nice to meet an old friend again. There is nothing extra happening, and you do not have to analyze anything. It is just natural and straight and ordinary.

## Resting in Nowness

That natural, ordinary state has to be cultivated and worked with in three ways. The first way is by not preparing too much. It is by cutting off our preconceptions from the past. The second way is by not expecting a greater flash. It is by cutting off our preconceptions of the future. The third way is by not holding on to our present flash experience. It is by cutting preconceptions of the present. We simply rest our mind, this very ordinary mind of nowness.

This resting of the mind can be achieved by natural techniques. The posture that you have developed through shamatha discipline, and the awareness techniques that you have been using, such as following the breath, still apply. As a result of such techniques, you begin to notice that there are moments of gap, moments of fresh outlook, moments of letting go, and moments of a natural sense of existence. There are moments of *pagyang,* or natural relaxation. At those points, you perceive glimpses of mahamudra. That is the practice.

The practice of mahamudra cuts through any habitual tendencies, any thought processes that could create problems. It cuts altogether any further creation of the samsaric world of love and hate, and of this and that.

When you are able to establish that type of meditation practice, you do not have to declare how hard you have worked and how much stress you have endured. You do not have to cry out, "I have put in so much effort, and now finally I've got it!" And you do not need to say, "I have studied so many texts, and now I finally know!" Instead, by realizing this ordinary and definite, simple and straight vajrayana essence in your mind, you begin to appreciate your teachers much more. You appreciate your root teacher, and you also begin to appreciate your lineage.

## Appreciating Our Teachers

As Kagyüpas, we begin to appreciate our root teacher. We regard the root teacher as Vajradhara, the primordial buddha, in human form. We also begin to take pride in the Kagyü lineage holders. We take pride in famous Tilopa, who received the secret treasure of the dakinis, which is this mahamudra mind. We also begin to appreciate the pundit Naropa of Phullahari Monastery, who was able to control his mind and transform the movements of his mind into mahamudra experience. We begin to appreciate Marpa Lotsawa, the translator, who brought Buddhism to Tibet. We appreciate the journey that he made in order to receive the teachings. We begin to appreciate Milarepa, who actually followed the command of his teacher, practiced meditation diligently, and attained enlightenment on one spot. We begin to appreciate Gampopa, who expounded the teachings to us in his books. We realize the vastness of his vision in introducing mahamudra to us and in mapping out the teachings of the Kagyü lineage.

We also appreciate the teachers of the four great and the eight lesser traditions of the Kagyü lineage, who attained enlightenment by doing the practices we have discussed. Their experience is the same as what we have been describing, almost to the very words. The only difference is that earlier practitioners spoke Indian languages such as Pali or Sanskrit, the later practitioners spoke Tibetan, and now we are speaking English. That is the only difference; the contents have never changed. The contents are very precise, very ordinary, and very straightforward.

We appreciate our history, our tradition, and our discipline because we realize that our lineage has never missed one inch or one stitch. We realize that everybody has received it. Everybody got it. That is the basic point. Such a thing can only happen and can only be appreciated when we have greater trust and faith and understanding of the lineage ancestors, who have worked hard for our benefit.

In our appreciation of our teachers, there is a quality of unconditional and unrequited love. You do not get anything back from what you have done. If you kiss somebody, they don't kiss you back. If you hug somebody, they don't hug you back. In prostration practice, when you visualize all the people on the lineage tree, you do not see them coming up to you and hugging you and telling you how great you are. The more you begin to realize ground mahamudra, the more unconditional, unrequited love takes place. You begin to appreciate that there is a ground as well as a path, simultaneously and at once.

You cannot have complete devotion without surrendering your heart. Otherwise, the whole thing becomes a business deal. As long as you have any understanding of wakefulness, any understanding of the sitting practice of meditation, you always carry your vajra master with you, wherever you go. You have the vajra master with you all along. That is why we talk about the mahamudra level of all-pervasive awareness. With such awareness, everything that goes on is the vajra master. So if your vajra master is far away, there is really no reason for sadness—although some sadness can be useful, because it brings you back from arrogance.

As an example, I am far away from my master, Jamgön Kongtrül of Shechen, right now. He is not here. That situation seems to be very basic and ordinary. At the same time, that absence becomes presence all the time. I do not particularly miss my vajra master, but I long for him quite a lot. Actually, what I long for is to be able to introduce my students to him so that he could see how great they are doing. That is the only thing. I wish he were right here so that I could introduce my students to him, show him their faces, show him how their discipline is coming along, and let him know that everything is fine. I wish I could show him that. Apart from that, it seems to be very much the case that the presence of my teacher is right here, right now. Otherwise, I would not be teaching.

The key point is that you have to love the teachings more. We are not talking about the Superman concept or about R2-D2; we are talking about the truth. When somebody speaks the truth, you can appreciate it, because it is so true. You can understand the truth, and therefore see that the author of this truth is also real. Even the fact that fire burns and water runs downhill could be seen as an expression of devotion. It could be seen as a demonstration of the truth of the instructions that you have received from your teacher. We are talking about things being genuine.

Things just happen that way, and you do not question them. Because you have received teachings from a direct witness, from your teacher, you see things as your teacher sees them. Therefore, things make sense, from an ordinary point of view. At the same time, it is good to ask questions. But when you begin to ask questions, your mind may go blank. That is what is called nonthought. You may have a long list of questions to ask, but when you meet your teacher, you cannot think of any of them. Your questions are all gone, not because your memory is bad, but because the teacher's mind has no questions. When you come in contact with that particular situation, your questions run away from you. It is a joyous situation.

When the world is ordinary, it is always wonderful. Always! It is not the bad-good kind of wonderful, but when the world is so ordinary, it is *it*. Therefore, there are no questions, and there is no laboring. You are upright, and you have a natural sense of head and shoulders. When you sit, you have good posture; when you walk, you have a good gait. There is something eternally happening, so it is wonderful without being wonderful. Just make sure that you do not misuse it.

# 57

# Path Mahamudra:
# The Experience of Meditation

*In the final mahamudra experience, any phenomenal experience you involve yourself with is seen as a working basis. Sights, smells, touchable objects, and mental contents are all seen as expressions of your particular deity or yidam. There is complete, total involvement, total openness beyond any limitations or hesitations. Therefore, you do not have to meditate. . . . Because everything is so vivid already, it is self-existing meditation.*

## INSIGHT AND RELIEF

The second stage of the mahamudra experience is path mahamudra. According to Jamgön Kongtrül the Great, "Path mahamudra is the experience of meditation." Path mahamudra is connected with greater awareness or the *mahavipashyana* experience. We are not abandoning the shamatha-vipashyana principle here, but we are bringing it along, maturing it further. With mahavipashyana awareness, you witness that the physical environment is the creation of the guru, or vajra master. Because of your awareness, you also realize that speech and sounds are the utterance of the vajra master. And finally, you realize that any thought patterns that occur are expressions of the guru mandala. This kind of awareness, which is connected with the body, speech, and mind principles, means that the world is pliable.

We started with ground mahamudra, with appreciation and intense devotion, which provided cheerfulness. Then, having experienced and worked through all that, we come to the second stage, or path mahamudra, which provides joy. In path mahamudra, there is a feeling of tremendous relief, a sense of transcending imprisonment. Entering into the guru mandala, you feel like a fish that had been caught and put into a bag, and is suddenly thrown back into the water. You feel great appreciation and relief that finally you can breathe again. You appreciate that you can get back to your egoless world at last. So joy is beginning to take place.

When you have processed your mind by means of mindfulness and awareness, you begin to appreciate the natural state of unconditional alaya. Out of that, you begin to develop scholarship. You have at least a basic idea of the map of the dharma. You know how your mind works, how the five skandhas function, how the natural states of neurosis and freedom from neurosis develop. You begin to have an understanding of the path from the hinayana level up to the vajrayana.

As you practice more, your sitting practice begins to give rise to personal experience. Your state of mind is no longer regarded as purely flickering thoughts or discursive wanderings, but you actually begin to experience some kind of steadiness. You find that the preoccupations of pain and pleasure are no longer a big deal. Instead, there is a fundamental quality of dharmic gentleness, genuineness, purity, and healthiness, even at a minute level.

This experience is said to be the adornment of insight. It is the beginning of insight and the possibility of insight. Insight in this case is *rikpa,* a term that can refer to cognitive mind and also to ordinary mind. In this context, it means the best intelligence. A connection begins to occur between absolute bodhichitta and you. You realize that you possess buddha genes, and that you are not as hopeless as you had thought. You also begin to realize that the so-called fantasies or stories you have heard about realized people are not myths, but real.

## THE FOUR YOGAS OF MAHAMUDRA

In mahamudra practice, you go through several levels of discipline. Personal experience and discipline are combined, with the help of intense shamatha, intense tonglen practice, and intense physical discipline, in-

cluding having good posture in your sitting practice. That diligent practice leads to some kind of intelligence or insight. You realize that your
cognitive mind is picking up messages about how you are doing with your
practice.

At that point, what are known as the four yogas of mahamudra occur.
The Tibetan term for the four yogas is *naljor shirim*. *Naljor* is "yoga," *shi*
means "four," and *rim* means "stages"; so *naljor shirim* is the "four stages
of yoga."

The progression of the four yogas is basically an organic process, but
there are particular instructions in terms of how to go about each one.
However, at this point I am simply giving you a map of the area.

## One-Pointedness

The four yogas begin with the realization that the nature of your mind
is basic and unfabricated. It need not be changed; it is simple and good.
Realizing the nature of your mind, there is a kind of déjà vu experience,
in the fundamental sense. You feel as if you had met yourself before.
People often think: "I have been in this state of mind before. When did I
have such an experience?" If you try to look back, you may not remember
the experience, but it did happen. Maybe it happened at the moment you
were born; maybe it happened when you had a high-level orgasm; maybe
it happened just before you lost your temper; or maybe it happened just
before you had a car accident. In any case, there is a sense of suddenly
seeing yourself. You are suddenly looking at yourself, meeting yourself,
being with yourself.

That kind of recognition of your very ordinary, very basic mind is the
first yoga of mahamudra, which is known in Tibetan as *tsechik*. *Tse* means
"point," "sharp point," or "dot," and *chik* means "one"; so *tsechik* is "one-
pointedness." It is the one-pointedness of recognizing yourself; it is like
meeting yourself again.

In many cases, you are shocked by this recognition. You gasp, "Is that it?
Wow!" However, the experience does not need to be all that sensational;
that is just the second thought. It is more as if in the midst of a green
lawn, you suddenly see a red plastic dot out of the corner of your eye.

THREE LEVELS OF ONE-POINTEDNESS. The first yoga is divided into lesser,
medium, and greater levels.

*Joy and clarity.* At the lesser level, while you are still maintaining the shamatha-style practice of following the breath, you begin to experience joyfulness and clarity. Those two may happen simultaneously or in alternation.

*Naturalness.* At the medium level, you attain a state of resting in samadhi. You begin to feel physically soothed and relaxed. At this level, the sitting practice of meditation is no longer a struggle, but it is somewhat natural and comfortable. Occasionally, your resistance to discipline may come up. Nonetheless, when your sitting practice actually happens, you find yourself in a natural, good, and comfortable situation.

*Luminosity.* At the greater level, this relaxation begins to alternate with the experience of luminosity. You see that the phenomenal world is vivid and self-descriptive.

## Simplicity

This brings us to the path of meditation at the tantric level, which is the second yoga, or simplicity. In Tibetan this yoga is called *trödral. Trö* means "complications" or "elaborations," and *dral* means "without"; so *trödral* means "without complications."

After experiencing one-pointedness, you begin to realize that your previous experiences of joy and luminosity have no root. Having no root means that you cannot manufacture these experiences, and you cannot make them go away. Therefore, there is a quality of spontaneity. Because of that, trödral is free from complications. It is simplicity. Because mind has no root, there is an experience of further simplicity.

THREE LEVELS OF SIMPLICITY. The second yoga is also divided into lesser, medium, and greater categories of experience.

*Realizing that arising, ceasing, and dwelling are empty.* First, we begin to realize that arising, ceasing, and dwelling are empty. When a thought occurs, it comes out of nowhere; when it dissolves, it dissolves into nowhere; and when it dwells or lingers, it has no ground to linger on.

*Freedom from fixation on appearance or emptiness.* Therefore, at the medium level, we experience a sense of spaciousness. We are free from the ground and root of fixating on appearance or emptiness. Our experience does not have to be registered or jotted down in our notebook. We have no desire to psychologize anything.

*Resolving the complexity of all dharmas.* Finally, a sense of greater freedom takes place, and we are able to resolve the complexity of all dharmas. Our prajna, our understanding of the logic of the dharma from hinayana to vajrayana, comes up in a flash.

At the level of simplicity, you begin to realize that hatha yoga is a way of seeing with greater openness. It is as if you were writing a book about revolution, and in the midst of sitting at your desk writing the book, you looked outside and found that the revolutionaries were already marching outside on the street. That is what is called simplicity. It is very simple. You are writing about it, but it is actually already happening. You find that one-pointed mind is taking place outside, that things are taking place beyond your imagination.

In simplicity, there is an all-encompassing awareness of deities such as Vajradhara, Chakrasamvara, Kalachakra, or Guhyasamaja. You have a sense of their presence. Tantric books actually open by talking about the simplicity of those deities, how they dwell in the vagina or the cervix of the unborn and unoriginated, surrounded by their queens and preaching the law of greater joy. The sutras talk about the Blessed One dwelling on Vulture Peak, surrounded by arhats, bodhisattvas, and so forth. But tantric texts open by saying that the great Bhagavat is dwelling in the cave of the vagina. There is a sense of real appreciation. That vagina has a quality of expansiveness and fertility; you can give birth infinitely. It is a kind of supervagina, able to give birth without aging. That is why it is called simplicity. Since things are seen as they are, there is no way of distorting anything. Things are as they are.

THREE VAJRA PRACTICES. In connection with the first two yogas, the yogas of one-pointedness and simplicity, there are what are called the three vajra practices: vajra body, vajra speech, and vajra mind.

*Vajra body.* The practice of vajra body involves visualizing the appropriate deity and identifying your alaya consciousness as the bija mantra, the seed syllable. From there, the alaya consciousness begins to expand and become part of greater wisdom. But before you visualize the alaya consciousness expanding into anything, you purify the ground by means of the shunyata mantra: OM SVABHAVA-SHUDDAH SARVA-DHARMAH SVABHAVA-SHUDDO HAM.

Having established emptiness, or the shunyata principle, the jnanasattva enters into you and crowns you. You are presented with offerings and welcomed. You are given a seat and the main offering, and there is praise of your particular attributes. After that, you place deities called "armor deities" on your eyes, your nostrils, your ears, your mouth, your genitals, and so forth. Those deities are placed in the particular parts of your body that are related with the different sense consciousnesses and with the principle of openness. This creates something like a suit of armor or protection.

*Vajra speech.* Then there is the actual mantra practice, which is the second category, or vajra speech. Here the mantras are seen as vajra utterance. You visualize the seed syllables mentally, and you hear them as you visualize them, as if they were beeping. You hear them saying their own sound, saying themselves as you see them. As you visualize AHS, they are AH-ing all the time: AH-AH-AH. There is a feeling of continuity.

If you visualize yourself with a consort, a female or male deity, then you also visualize what is called the fire wheel, or fire chakra. It is like when you wave a lit incense stick around in the darkness: you see it making a ring. The mantras are going very fast, circulating between you and your consort. The sound of the mantras is experienced along with a basic understanding of simplicity and one-pointedness; they begin to coincide simultaneously. That is called mantra-mudra.

The kinds of things I have been describing actually have to be experienced. It is hard to talk about them. It reminds me of what I used to hear about America when I was around fourteen. I heard that Americans had an entire city built in the sky, and that they had another city built underneath the ocean. I heard that all the streets were paved in gold, and there were all kinds of gadgets. When I tried to visualize that, I couldn't connect with it. But once I arrived in America and could actually see the country as it is, I got entirely different ideas about the whole thing. That might be the best way of viewing these descriptions.

*Vajra mind.* In the third vajra practice, or vajra mind, the emotions are regarded as one mandala. So the thoughts of the emotional mind that function in our ordinary everyday life also become expressions of the particular deities or herukas that we are relating with. There is no hesitation as to how you are identifying yourself, and no hesitation as to your yidams, whether they are passionate yidams or aggressive yidams. There is no hesitation and no confusion. Yidams are seen as real yidams, and their passionate and aggressive aspects are included as part of the basic mandala display. There is tremendous conviction, openness, and understanding.

## One Taste

The third yoga is one taste. In Tibetan, one taste is called *rochik*. *Ro* means "taste," and *chik* means "one"; so *rochik* is "one taste." The reason this yoga is called "one taste" is that, at this point, we begin to experience that the mirror and that which is in front of the mirror are one. We cannot actually separate the reflector and the reflection. Pain and pleasure, or hope and fear—all such things become one taste. They are of equal taste for the very reason that we do not care what is the best and what is the worst. At the same time, our luminosity and our brilliance also tell us that experience has the nature of one taste. When there is great brilliance, we cannot actually separate objects according to which is green and which is blue.

The third yoga is connected with the two types of truth: relative and absolute. Having already seen the expansive display of the simplicity—which in the ordinary sense may seem to be rather contradictory, but in the tantric sense is understandable—one taste begins to develop. In that expansiveness, the revenge of ordinary emotions and highly evolved, mystical experiences are no longer separate. They are all one. So there is a sense of one taste, rather than one*ness*. It is one taste because it is one experience. Oneness could mean a more philosophical or speculative process. The experience of one taste comes out of the simplicity, which is relative truth at this point.

THREE LEVELS OF ONE TASTE. Again, there are lesser, medium, and greater levels of this yoga.

*All dharmas are dissolved into one taste.* First, we begin to experience that all dharmas of samsara and nirvana are dissolved into one taste. *That* and *this,* grasping and fixation, anything we consider a big deal—all of those norms begin to become unnecessary and trivial.

*Appearance and mind become indistinguishable.* Next, appearance and mind become like water poured into water. In other words, our seeing and what we see and experience become indistinguishable. If we pick up water with a ladle and pour it into a cauldron filled with water, we cannot separate the two waters. The only separation is that of ladle and cauldron, which is absurd. Who cares what kind of ladle we use? Who cares what kind of cauldron we have?

*Breakthrough of wisdom.* Finally, there is a greater breakthrough of wisdom. Such wisdom is supposedly impossible to describe. But we could explain it linguistically at least. The Tibetan word *yeshe* means "utterly familiar," "utterly knowing," "primordially knowing." It is a product of one taste, because with one taste you have no desire or possibility of either separating things or putting things together by means of experience, by means of theological explanations, by means of philosophy, metaphysics, science, or anything else. Because there is no way of separating things or putting them together, things are seen as they are, directly and utterly.

## Nonmeditation

With the wisdom or the yeshe of one taste, you reach the next stage, the state of nonmeditation. Because things are seen so directly, any conventional thoughts begin to be exhausted, so you come to the fourth yoga, which is called *gom-me. Gom* means "meditation," and *me* means "without" or "non"; so *gom-me* means "nonmeditation."

The reason nonmeditation happens is because preconceptions no longer exist. You may still have discursive thoughts and emotions, but they no longer carry their own little credentials. They do not have calling cards in their pockets. So conceptual mind is exhausted.

We say that conceptual mind is exhausted rather than transcended. The word *transcended* has a different connotation: it means to bypass something. We also do not say that conceptual mind is liberated. That too has a strange connotation. The term *liberated* means that you are no longer imprisoned by your concepts. But they might imprison somebody else after you are gone. Therefore, the best term we could find is *exhausted*, which has the connotation of being used up, like an old shoe. The Tibetan term for that is *ten-se*. *Ten* means "permanently," and *se* means "used up" or "worn-out"; so *ten-se* means "permanently worn-out."

That quality of being worn-out or used up has a very important message, which is that practice is no longer regarded as warfare. We are trying to fight samsara, confusion, or ego as something evil. We are not saying that we have finally won the victory or that we are the victors. Instead we are saying that conceptual mind is used up because we have been so honest, so genuine, so precise, and so decent. Because we have been working with our mind as naively as we could, conceptual mind is all used up. It is like living on our savings and running out of money, rather than trying to cheat the world by living on welfare.

THREE LEVELS OF NONMEDITATION. As before, there are three levels of this yoga.

*Meditator and the meditation used up.* First, we begin to realize that meditator and meditation are all used up. Those definitions are all used up.

*Habits and beliefs cleared away.* The medium level is that our habitual patterns and primitive beliefs about reality are cleared away.

*Mother and child luminosities dissolve together.* At the third level, the original state that we experienced in one-pointedness—in meeting ourselves one-pointedly—is finally re-created. The traditional language says that the mother and child luminosities are dissolved together. The mother luminosity, or the original state, and the child luminosity, or what you have cultivated through your practice, become one.*

With the fourth yoga, or nonmeditation, once again the relative world has been seen as the entire working base, and the absolute world has become just confirmation beyond the relative world. In the final

---

* The *mother luminosity*, or ground luminosity, is the clear and luminous nature of the mind of all beings, which for ordinary beings dawns at the moment of death. *Child luminosity*, or path luminosity, is the luminosity experienced in meditation.

mahamudra experience, any phenomenal experience that you involve yourself with is seen as a working basis. Sights, smells, sounds, touchable objects, and mental contents are all seen as expressions of your particular deity or yidam. There is complete, total involvement, total openness beyond any limitations or hesitations. Therefore, you do not have to meditate. That is why this yoga is called nonmeditation. Meditation does not actually apply to it. Because everything is so vivid already, every experience is self-existing meditation. Having a body, having ears, having a nose, having teeth, having a tongue, and having eyes are inbuilt meditation for you. You realize that the yidam is you, and you are the yidam. At this point, you begin to be able to exercise your siddhis, your magical powers.

## Breaking Through Imprisonment by Means of Hatha Yoga

In mahamudra, breaking through imprisonment and arriving at the point of the wisdom of emptiness seems to be very important. In doing so, hatha yoga is extremely powerful and is very much needed. The principles of hatha yoga are lengthy. Not only is physical hatha yoga important, but it is important to first practice *pranayama,* or breathing exercises, so that the mind does not drift around. In order to work with the structure of your confusion, it is necessary to have some experience of pranayama and hatha yoga.

With one-pointedness, you begin to realize that the herukas and deities are connected with the experience of the body's energy system, or inner mandala. So in tantric hatha yoga, you are working with three types of energy: prana, nadi, and bindu. Prana, or breath, is a kind of energy or strength; nadis are the veins or channels through which the prana can flow; and bindu is a dot or particle of life force. In a traditional analogy, the mind is said to be the rider, prana is the horse, nadis are the roads or paths, and bindu is the food for the mind. Mind eats bindu, rides on prana, and races through the nadis. So in order to influence bindu, you have to relate with prana, and at the same time you have to improve the nadis.

The mind in itself is nothing. Mind can only thrive on bindu, its essence; mind can only function with prana, its transport; and the only direction mind can go is through the nadis. That is the whole thing, a complete world. There is no way out. So in hatha yoga, body does not mean the physical body alone, but it is the body in the cosmic sense.

## THE MECHANISM OF CONFUSION

In working with prana, nadi, and bindu, the idea is to transcend primitive prana, primitive nadi, and primitive bindu, and transform them into vajra prana, vajra nadi, and vajra bindu. The point is to develop their vajra nature or vajra intelligence. It is to bring out the vajra-ness of the whole thing. With that vajra-ness, there is a penetrating quality of one-pointed mind.

Vajra-ness has a quality of well-being and awareness, and at the same time it is completely cutting. Well-being happens in a flash. You do not maintain your well-being, but it is kill and cure at once. Cure is being cured from maintaining oneself, and kill is just kill. You could say "food and poison at once," but that is too extreme. It is better to say "kill and cure at once," for confusion is something to be cured rather than destroyed.

Confusion is related with prana, nadi, and bindu because, according to tantra, confusion can only come about when there is something moving. That quality of movement is the wind, or prana. Prana can be white or red: the white wind is oneself, and the red wind is phenomena. At the beginning, there are no winds. When prana first occurs, it is basically pure and immaculate. But prana becomes colored by white and red, by a certain panic, by this side or that side. Whenever you regard phenomena as *this* side, prana is colored by white; whenever you think of phenomena as a play of *that,* prana is colored by red.

Since prana has been colored by white and red, it has become impure. From that impure prana, all eight types of consciousness and the five skandhas arise. Beyond that, you have nothing to complain about, and no reason for complaint. So you end up with "So what?" You end up in samsara, confused and trapped in the six realms of the world. An understanding of that whole process brings you back to "So what?"—to emotionally "So what?" and theoretically "So what?"

You finally come back to yourself once again, wondering, "How does all that apply to me?" And you realize that you have nadis or channels in your body, in which speed is racing around constantly. That speed is connected with bindu, or life strength. Bindu is a sort of force. It is like the fluid quality of the semen that gives birth to reincarnations. When you lose your semen, you give birth to another child. Likewise, with bindu, you continue to give birth to yourself. You give birth to life. So bindu is the reproductive mechanism that creates volitional karmic activities.

Altogether, what you end up with is three types of split experience: the prana, the nadis, and the bindu. You end up with those three, and on top of that, you also have mind. Something is actually minding the whole business. You are in complete chaos at this point. You are so confused that you have no way of knowing where to begin, unless you go further and further back. You have to swim through the bindu, swim through the prana, and not be confused by the nadis. It is getting tantric.

## Working with Duality

In looking at the seeds of duality, tantric masters such as Naropa used two formulas. The first formula is: The reason we call ourselves "I" is because we have no origination. We are never born, we are unoriginated, we are nothing. The second formula is: The reason why we say "them" or "other" is because we cannot cease. An unceasing flow of play is happening. That is the seed of duality from the tantric point of view. It is how duality has begun. Both statements contradicting each other is duality. It doesn't make any sense, does it?

Again, the reason we are called "I" is because we cannot find our birth. It is because of our unbornness, because we cannot find where we came from. And the reason we cannot find the "other" is that we cannot find the source of the unceasingness, the fact that there are so many things happening constantly, so many energies. So there is a contradiction: things are happening, but at the same time things are empty. That is the duality.

Those two situations are referred to as mantric sound. They are referred to as E and VAM, E being "I," and VAM being "other." They are also referred to as A HAM, A being "I," and HAM being "other." So we have a problem. That is why the first yoga, the yoga of one-pointedness, is very important.

There is no point in trying to figure out why "I" and why "other"; there is no point in trying to find logical conclusions. There is no way out. First you have the "other." The only way to work with your body and your mind is to regard the other as the physical body, which is unceasingly energetic as long as you live. You have to eat food, you have to piss and shit, you have to do all kinds of things. So you cannot deny that your bodily energy is unceasing, or pretend that it is energyless. Even if you are very lazy, you still have to do those things, so you can still say that your body has enormous energy. That is why the body is an expression of the other.

It is a very simpleminded approach. Your body is not other as *the* other, but it is an expression of the other. So this body, your body, is no longer regarded as *your* body, particularly, but as an expression of the other. The impersonal other, *the* other. This applies to anything whatsoever. Nothing is personal—not the rock, the table, or the chair, not the body, hands, arms, limbs, shoes, hat, or beard.

So first you have the "other," and then you have the "this." You have the "I," which is unborn, unoriginated, yet still very busy. It seems to be doing something, but when you look at it, it does not do anything at all. That is the mystery of the whole thing, which is the usual mystery. There you have the practice of mahamudra meditation.

Mahamudra meditation is not quite the same as vipashyana or shunyata meditation. It is simply exaggerating the idea of well-being that we discussed in the section on shamatha practice.* You do not question who or what you are, but you just experience well-being. You do not use that well-being as a working basis, and you do not work with it as a platform to do something more. It is just being. It is well-being, and at the same time it is careless in a pleasurable way. It is an open kind of thing.

The only example I can think of is at the end of the first *Godfather* movie, when Don Corleone put an orange in his mouth and started to frighten the little boy. There was an enormous kind of free-flowing big joke in that, because at the same time as he was well-being, he was just about to die. So there was a sense of both death and well-being. The child got scared, and Don Corleone didn't seem to care. But he *did* care, and he chased the kid around. It was very precise. I heard later on that the whole scene was not written in the script, but was purely improvised by Marlon Brando.

That is well-being. Something is actually there, but at the same time it is challenging and not challenging. It is a kind of carelessness, and at the same time it is very careful and premeditated. That seems to overcome the myth of "I" as unborn, unoriginated, and empty. In fact, what we are trying to do with the unoriginated emptiness of "I" is to bring forth the bornness, originatedness, and fullness of "I." And what we are trying to do with the unceasing quality of "other" is to bring forth the ceasingness or deathness of other. So we are working backward from the usual approach of samsaric people who are looking at nirvana. We are reversing it: we are

---

* See volume 1 of the *Profound Treasury,* chapter 40, "Mindfulness of Life."

making formulas for people in nirvana who are looking at samsara. So we are regressing, we are misreading it. Instead of saying "Dracula," we say "Alucard."

That is why the relative world is so important in this tantra. The other day I was working with the *Tibetan Book of the Dead* (although it doesn't belong to this tantric level), and the term *khor-de rulok. Khorwa* is "samsara," *de* is "nirvana," and *rulok* means "turn upside down"; so *khor-de rulok* means "samsara and nirvana turned upside down." Usually the idea is that nirvana is above and samsara is on the bottom, so the idea is to turn it around. In order to develop a complete and proper understanding of nirvana and samsara, you tip it over.

## THE IMPORTANCE OF SHAMATHA PRACTICE FOR ALL FOUR YOGAS

Going back to the original practice of shamatha is important for these four yogas of mahamudra. Even at the level of nonmeditation, you still do not give up the technique and the style of shamatha and vipashyana discipline. You use the same technique, have the same posture, and the same sense of uprightness all the time.

In order to maintain the one-pointedness of the first yoga, it is important to concentrate on mindfulness and awareness. Shamatha is also important for the second yoga, simplicity, since it is still necessary to give up any possibility of having some kind of ground to hang on to. It is important for the third yoga of one taste, for through shamatha practice you begin to realize that you are not using your technique as a saving grace. Therefore, at the level of the fourth yoga, or nonmeditation, you begin to realize that sophistries such as meditating or not meditating are all used up. Because you have overcome the habitual patterns of your original backache and your original grandmother problems and your original "what have yous," you begin to develop a sense of freedom. From that point of view, shamatha practice is quite practical.

Shamatha is always important. You have to maintain a shamatha-like precision of body and speech. You have to be in that state all the time. In Tibet we used to have calligraphy lessons. First we wrote very slowly, making big letters; then we wrote at a medium pace; and finally we tried to write the cursive letters very fast, using the same format. In that way we learned to do excellent calligraphy, and even our cursive handwriting became elegant.

If you had seen the Buddha giving his teachings, you would have seen that he sat upright. Even in vajrayana sadhana practices, we visualize the various deities in precisely prescribed postures, which are the product of shamatha practice. They may be holding symbols and scepters and so on, but they still have their form. It is a mark of ultimate training, a mark of being noble. Further accomplishment is referred to as the royal attainment. More accomplished people always have a quality of regalness. They eat properly, and they deal with things properly.

Over time, the shamatha technique becomes ingrained. So even when you have attained nonmeditation, you do not just collapse and you do not become an idiot. You always carry your dignity. But at this point, you have realized what is known as coemergent wisdom.

## 58

# Fruition Mahamudra:
# Realizing One's Mind as Buddha

*When you drop your unnecessary things, you finally can swoop and fly in vast space. It is so blue, so bright, so nice, so airy and fresh. You can stretch your wings and breathe the air. You can do anything you want. At that point, you experience what is known as bliss, or fruition mahamudra.*

## COEMERGENT WISDOM AND BLISS

According to Jamgön Kongtrül the Great, "Fruition mahamudra is the realization of one's mind as buddha." This mahamudra principle is based on what is known as coemergent wisdom or *lhenchik kye-pe yeshe*. *Lhenchik* means "together," *kye-pe* means "that which is born," and *yeshe* means "wisdom"; so *lhenchik kye-pe yeshe* means "wisdom that is born together" or "coemergent wisdom."

With coemergent wisdom, there is a sense of oneness. In the analogy of the captured fish, it is as if you have been thrown back into the water and you are happily swimming around, but at the same time you have the feeling that you are departing from somewhere or other, and that you are entering somewhere or other. That feeling is somewhat vague at the beginning, but with an understanding of ordinary mind, or *thamal gyi shepa*, you find that you are actually experiencing being split from the heavy, gross level of your neurosis into the more refined situation of highest awareness and wakefulness.

This feeling is connected with the fourth abhisheka, the abhisheka of *That*. You are splitting from this to *That*. The reason it is called *That* is because it is not here, but there. It is not ego's point of view; therefore, it is *That*.

Coemergent wisdom is like an eagle that has been kept in a cage and then freed. Human beings have been trying to put a hat, a coat, and boots on the eagle; they have been trying to make the eagle into an anthropomorphic symbol. But finally they let the eagle go. It is taken to a cliff with its hat and clothes still on, and a person throws the eagle off the cliff, and it begins to fly. As the eagle flies, it drops its hat and its coat and its boots down below. As this eagle flies, it is so naked. It is free from all those hats and boots and coats that were imposed on it.

Coemergent wisdom is like a kernel of grain: you drop the husk, and then you have the pure grain. It is like being born: you and your placenta are coemergent. The idea is that things coemerge, but they co-drop at the same time.

## FATHOMLESS FREEDOM

When you drop your unnecessary things, you finally can swoop and fly in vast space. It is so blue, so bright, and so nice, so airy and fresh. You can stretch your wings and breathe the air. You can do anything you want. At that point, you experience what is known as bliss, or fruition mahamudra. You have experienced cheerfulness and joy, and finally the bliss of freedom occurs in you. You are like the eagle without its hat, coat, and boots.

Such freedom is measureless, unspeakable, fathomless. Your samsaric clothing has been dropped; therefore, you can fly higher. This is the final and ultimate appreciation of the guru mandala principle, and the ultimate appreciation of devotion as well. Having the strength to fly and explore the depths of fathomless sky comes from your joy and appreciation of the vajra master, and it comes from sharing the vajra master's vision. The vajra master can also fly; your teacher can fly along with you. So you are finally sharing the vast, expansive space of the vajra master, together, coemerged.

As we have said before, wisdom is in some ways the same idea as freedom. In mahamudra, you experience cheerfulness, freedom, and upliftedness. Moreover, you experience fathomless space and complete freedom, which produces great joy. This type of joy is not conditioned by the experience of freedom alone, but it is self-born, innate. You begin to experience the trust and openness of the situation altogether.

Through intense discipline, intense sitting practice, you begin to give up any hope of attainment. It is very basic, ordinary, and simple: you lose your heart. Because of the years and years and years of practice, because of the hours and hours you have put in, because of your group and individual meditation retreats and everything, you give up hope. At the same time, you begin to take pride in how much you have worked and learned. This is called coemergent wisdom. Appreciation, sadness, and devotion take place in you at the same time as you are losing heart. These two experiences are coemergent; they are born together.

I know from personal experience that both things could happen. You keep wondering and you think you may not make it, but at the same time, there is so much going on. In the play between the two, something usually happens. That is what is meant by coemergent wisdom.

## EXTRAORDINARY RELAXATION

Coemergent wisdom is the expression of the great discipline that you have put into your practice, along with the tremendous learning that you have put into it. At a certain point, there is extraordinary relaxation. Finally you have made friends with the teacher and with the dharma. At the same time, there is extraordinary frustration. You are expecting things to happen right away, but they never do. You always feel that you have been turned down, that nothing has happened. That combination of relaxation, appreciation, and frustration gives birth to the opening up of your mind—all at once!

It is as if you have been wanting to sneeze for a long time, but when you try to sneeze, it never happens—and when you do not try, it also doesn't happen. But then somehow, between the two, you catch yourself sneezing. Or we could use the analogy of being constipated. You either sit on your toilet for a long time, or you try to forget about the whole thing. Then in between the two, usually when you are free from too much self-consciousness, there it comes. That is why this is called ordinary mind. It is not cultivated; therefore, it is ordinary.

First we develop shinjang experience, which is the beginning of cheerfulness. Then we go beyond that with further mindfulness and awareness. We consistently perpetuate our sense of connecting body and mind together all the way, until we reach the level of bliss. From this point of view, the practice of hinayana is very important. Exchanging oneself for others is another source of bliss. Friendliness brings a feeling of not being hassled; therefore, it also produces bliss of some kind. When you learn how to pour tea into your teacup properly, that could be the product of shinjang, and at the same time, there could be bliss as well. There are coemergent possibilities everywhere. That is why we call it ordinary mind.

## Experience at the Borderline

The experience of coemergent wisdom is at the borderline between lower tantra and higher tantra, between mahamudra and maha ati. It is not all that extraordinary. However, coemergent wisdom is very dangerous to talk about. It is an extremely powerful wisdom. Why is that so? Because with this wisdom, you are binding together samsara and nirvana. You are creating a bond in which samsara and nirvana become one taste, so that pain and pleasure are one, darkness and light are one, everything is one.

Why do things come together? What came along with you originally? Coemergence means that wisdom came along with you. But at your very first moment, you were confused and did not realize the primordial mind. You did not realize what was happening at all. None of us realized what was happening, including myself, of course. We did not realize what was happening, and we got so confused. Something happened in the bardo, and then we clicked into something or another. Some people clicked into primordial mind and were liberated, people such as Samantabhadra and Vajradhara. But Lord Buddha did not click into it; therefore, he went on to take birth as a human and become the Buddha. None of us clicked into it, so we too took birth as humans.

That first clicking point was like landing from an airplane journey and coming into an airport that had two exits, so that people could go this way or that way, to the right or the left. People got confused, and some of them went to the left and some of them went to the right. Coemergent wisdom happened at the very moment that the two groups parted: it happened the moment some people went right and other people went left. At that point, coemergent wisdom came along. But actually, it existed already. Coemergent wisdom had already actually happened. People do not want to be hassled with too much brilliance. If you turn right, there is too much brilliance; if you turn left, there are neon lights instead. So ordinarily, all of us go toward the neon light, including the Lord Buddha, Shakyamuni, Mr. Siddhartha. He also went in that direction.

Coemergent means emerged together, but "parted together" would be a much more accurate way of saying it. After having landed in the airplane, we went out and we separated. We parted together. That parting is what is known as one taste. When we parted together, we experienced the reality of parting; we experienced the separation from outer space. Before we did that, we were at one with space, which is known as vajradhatu. Vajradhatu space is what we all came out of, but then we landed and parted. We separated.

From this point of view, we cannot actually call this parting coemergent wisdom. We probably should say coseparated wisdom, but that goes against the texts, which say lhenchik kye-pe, or born together. Born together means that when two people walking shoulder to shoulder get out of the airplane and end up in the airport, one person says, "Well, this light is too brilliant for me. I'll go toward the neon light," and the other person says, "This light is delightfully brilliant. I'll go toward that." At that point, the parting takes place. Coemergent wisdom is born at that very point, that very moment of parting in which one person walks that way and the other one walks this way.

This is a very vivid description of the whole thing. When you are about to turn one way or the other, that very turning point is where the actual wisdom is being born. Coemergent wisdom could be demonstrated by literally walking together two by two and then parting and going in opposite directions. At the point where the two people's shoulders turn against each other so that they are back-to-back, there is wisdom coming about. After the separation, if you are intelligent you look ahead, rather than back; and having looked forward, you discover what you are looking at. You begin to develop wakefulness.

When the shoulders pull apart, something begins to click. It happens at that moment when there is space. At the parting of *that* and *this,* wisdom begins to happen, and reality begins to happen. In coemergent wisdom, things come together and are separated at the same time—and at that very point, a breakthrough of mahamudra takes place.

In mahamudra, one can stay at that point of click, when the shoulders touch and part, all the time. So it is just click, click, click, always. But as you continue on to the higher yanas, that is not good enough, because you have to maintain that clicking somehow. Before the click you are not clicking; during the click you are somewhat clicking, which creates numbness; after the click, there is some kind of celebration. It is the idea of being there and not being there at the same time. Before the click, you do not exist; when you click, you exist totally; after you click, you are confused. There is no other choice but to stay in the click. That is why it is called mahamudra—the great trick. So from that point of view, mahamudra could be translated as the great trick.

I hope this makes sense to you. It can be frustrating to try to tell you what I have experienced myself, and what it actually means according to the texts. It is so gut level, such a real experience, which makes me sad and happy at the same time. The nostalgia of coemergent wisdom is very powerful and very hard to contain in one's heart. The reason this is so is because coemergent wisdom should be communicated to people, and you are the only people I can communicate with at this point. You should be very experienced by now, and you should feel grateful for what is happening. It is a vomit of blood, the heart blood of the vajra master, which is somewhat powerful and very genuine. Excuse me for being so corny.

## Severing the Heart of Rudra

At that coemerged point, what is the experience? Nothing particularly extraordinary. You do not see deities or divinities, nor do you bliss out. When those two things coemerge or coseparate together, what you actually get is an empty heart. It is as if that emerging has become insignificant or nonexistent. At that point, there is no substance, no reality. Just empty heart. The whole thing becomes so direct, so much on the point of the breakthrough.

We could use an analogy for that. When your knife is extremely sharp and you are using it to cut a piece of meat, it feels soothing when you first strike the raw meat with your knife. The knife goes down so soothingly, and the result is that the soothing knife is executing the parting of one side of the flesh from the other. You feel delighted and good that your knife is so sharp that you do not have to struggle. You just strike very slowly, and it makes a sort of hissing sound as you cut. The meat is full of tendons and fat, so there is some kind of hiss. And it is soothing as the knife goes down, as if that particular knife were making love to the flesh, to that particular meat. It becomes a very beautiful experience.

That image is the closest I can come to the idea of coemergent wisdom, where intelligence is looking ahead and beginning to strike. It is what you are actually doing when you focus on a particular situation like your own neurosis. You project and reflect, and there and then, *that* and *this* begin to come apart. The situations that are separating do not necessarily have to be good and bad, samsara and nirvana. You are simply severing the cosmic energy, the cosmic existence of your life altogether, which is a very powerful experience. There is such satisfaction and such a beautiful, genuine mahamudra experience in severing the heart of Rudra. Immense delight and beauty begin to take place at that point.

## GOING BEYOND ONE TASTE

After the separation comes what is known as one taste. One taste does not mean that everything becomes gray and tasteless. By one taste, we mean the absence of all tastes. Tasting in this way becomes very natural and very beautiful. One taste is no taste; therefore, it is everything. Recently, I asked my cook to prepare my meals without any spice, and instead to just boil the meat in hot water. That turns out to be the best gourmet cooking altogether. That is one taste.

But one taste is not quite enough. That particular taste is no taste, and it is every taste of every thing: pleasure and happiness, good and bad. So everything is fine. That's great. But although that is somewhat good mahamudra-wise, it is not really good enough. One taste is also a hang-up. So there has to be something that goes beyond the level of tasting, something much larger than that. That larger vision is called *ati,* which means "ultimate." At this point, you are not giving up, but you are opening yourself up. You are in the process of letting go altogether of that experience of one taste.

Here we are talking about the borderline, where mahamudra dissolves into the teachings of the higher tantra. The need for mahamudra is that you have to develop one taste before you get into totality. In other words, first the tip of your tongue has to pick up the taste of something, then it is necessary to cut out your tongue altogether. It is a very delightful thought. Horrifying, if you like.

Cutting out the tongue also means scooping out the eyes, digging out the heart, and scooping out the brains. You do not even have one taste at this point: there is not even *one* anymore; it is nonexistence. So at the higher tantric levels, your tongue is cut out, so you cannot taste any oneness; your eyes are scooped out, so you cannot see any oneness; and your heart has been dug out, so you cannot feel anything.

At this higher tantric level, you begin to experience a sense of reality in which the absence of heart, eyes, and tongue begins to become very real and very powerful. The absence of all those things creates a magnificent kingdom, complete openness. That has been happening in my work with some of my students. They do not exist, they don't have tongues or brains or hearts; but at the same time, they have brilliant tongues, brains, and hearts.

It is necessary for you to realize that such concepts can actually be transferred into ordinary human beings. It is very important for you to realize that you can experience what they have experienced. Actually, the vajrayana presentation is more a demonstration than a presentation. Usually, that is how it happens.

*Part Twelve*

# THE TANTRIC JOURNEY: HIGHER TANTRA

59

# *Mahayoga:*
# *The Dawning of the Wisdom of Self-Existence*

*The lower tantric yanas were based on vajra nature, transcendence,
and great joy or mahasukha. But in higher tantra, simplicity, or
self-existence, is the point.*

## THE HIGHER TANTRIC YANAS

Up to this point, we have been discussing the lower three tantric yanas of
kriyayoga, upayoga, and yogayana. These yanas as well as anuttarayoga
are all connected with the Kagyü tradition, and also with the Sakya and
Geluk traditions of Tibetan Buddhism. But from this point onward, we
will be considering the three higher tantric yanas—mahayoga, anuyoga,
and atiyoga—which are regarded as the area of the Nyingma tradition.

The higher tantric yanas are known as the all-encompassing yanas
of skillful means. They are known as the imperial or conquering yanas.
They conquer not only samsaric problems, but also the sophistries of
the previous yanas. The higher yanas are all inspired, shaped, and highly
influenced by the maha ati tradition.* However, the lower tantric schools

---

* The term *maha ati,* or *dzokchen* in Tibetan, can refer to the three higher tantric yanas as
a whole, or to the ninth yana in particular. In this text, we will use the term *atiyoga* to refer
to the ninth yana.

also actually acknowledge these three higher tantras, regarding them as super-anuttarayoga practice.*

In the lower tantric yanas, the disciplines are path oriented, but at this point, there is a shift. What changes is that there is no need for reference points. In the three lower tantric yanas, there are still reference points, such as those based on physical activities and on developing purity by washing yourself constantly and putting on clean clothes. But in the higher tantric yanas, there is definitely no need for reference points. In the three yanas of the higher tantra, reference points have become old hat.

## Students of Higher Tantra

According to Longchen Rabjam, the great fourteenth-century dzokchen master, mahayoga is associated with father tantra and with the masculine principle. It is taught to those who have many thoughts, especially thoughts that are active or aggressive in nature. In mahayoga, the phenomenal world is seen as a form of upaya or skillful means.

Anuyoga is connected with the teachings of shunyata and dharmata, and with the feminine principle, or prajna. It is taught to people who are passionate and who would like to maintain their equilibrium. It is for those with a state of mind that is even and solid, and for those who like to dwell on ideas.

Atiyoga is taught to ignorant people who are extremely lazy and do not want to do anything. Such people have no particular allegiance toward the shunyata or upaya of the previous two yanas: they are neutral.

## Maha Ati and Mahamudra

Compared with the hinayana and mahayana, the mahamudra idea of working with your basic fundamentality or buddha nature is fantastic. But at the maha ati level, even that becomes primitive: do not just think you possess buddha nature, but you are actually a buddha in full glory. Maha ati, or in Tibetan, *dzokchen,* is the final approach of the final path.

---

* The three divisions of anuttarayoga—father, mother, and nondual—can be likened to mahayoga, anuyoga, and atiyoga respectively.

The difference between maha ati and mahamudra is that in maha-mudra, we ordinarily base our approach on what is called ground tantra. In ground tantra, samsara and nirvana are turned upside down. You are working on your own basic ground as you are. But in maha ati, you are working with the inspiration of your fruition or your enlightenment experience. You are not only working on what you are, but you are also working on what you are from the point of view of complete enlighten-ment. Enlightenment is in you already, and since you are an enlightened being, you are working from that basis. So in the three higher or impe-rial yanas, you no longer approach things from the bottom upward, as in mahamudra.

## Mahayoga: Great Union

The first of the higher tantric yanas is mahayoga. *Maha* means "big," "great," or "none above," and *yoga* is "union"; so *mahayoga* means "great union."

Mahayoga seems to be so very vast that it is quite impossible to discuss the whole thing, but we can talk about some highlights, and the principles and magical aspects that are involved. The reason mahayoga is called "great yoga" is because your understanding of the indivisibility of kün-dzop and töndam is complete. You have settled down in the confidence of that understanding. That is to say, all possible self-consciousness, such as the idea that you are on this yana and having problems with it, has fallen away.

## Lhündrup: Self-Existence

Mahayoga practice is very solid and definite. In terms of the symbol-ism involved, it is much more imaginative than the previous tantras. It is the work of a much greater artistic talent, if one can use such a phrase. The whole thing is a masterpiece. The style and setup of its organization, based on a group of students working together, is much more real.

The lower tantric yanas were based on vajra nature, transcendence, and great joy or mahasukha. But in the higher tantric yanas, simplicity, or self-existence, is the point. Self-existence, or self-existing wisdom, is referred to as *lhündrup.*\* Lhündrup begins to dawn in mahayogayana, and continues on to the final yana of atiyoga. Mahayoga tantra is where that particular trend or approach begins.

## COGNITIVE MIND AND FUNCTIONING MIND

Practitioners of mahayogayana view the phenomenal world in terms of cognitive mind and functioning mind; but the cognitive mind and the functioning mind are regarded as one thing. When you function, you actually recognize situations as they are, so there is no difference between the action itself and the experience of the action. They are seen as the same. Therefore, Longchen Rabjam calls this the yana of seeing the indivisibility of gold and its gold quality.

When your mind functions, it usually does so in a very biased way. But this is not viewed as particularly problematic. What is important is that when your mind functions in the phenomenal world, the operation of basic cognitive systems is taking place. That is the real magic. The magic actually happens when there is a cognitive mind operating. From this point of view, the subsidiary or offshoot of that basic cognition is not particularly important. It is seen as part of the same process. So the whole world, the entire universe, is highly magical. The burning quality of fire is very magical. The solidness of the earth is very magical. The blueness of the sky is very magical. Even the neurosis of your own nature is very magical. Nothing is rejected, but everything is seen as the realistic world.

The world is realistic in the sense that its magic is not based on trickery or on magical spells. It is not a matter of "Abracadabra!" or "Poof!" and then you produce a rabbit out of a hat or birds out of your pocket. The magic is not on that level. In the Occidental world, people used to be fascinated by the magic of the Orient. Westerners hoped that they could produce some kind of spell that would make them live longer, be bet-

---

\* The term *lhündrup* (lhun grub) has many different translations. It is referred to as "spontaneous presence," one of the two main aspects of dzokchen teaching, the other being "primordial purity" or *kadak* (ka dag). Other translations include: effortless fulfillment, spontaneously self-perfected, inherently present, manifesting effortlessly, natural achievement, natural spontaneity, and naturally perfect. Lhündrup is one of the five enlightened activities, or *trin-le* ('phrin las), and is self-existing, spontaneous, and wish-fulfilling.

ter business people, or better at con man–ship. But those stories are now regarded even in the West as completely old-fashioned and obviously very absurd and childish.

## Kaya and Jnana

The kaya and jnana principles are very important in mahayoga. In terms of visualization practice, kaya is the form of the visualization; but at the same time, there is an understanding that the form is based on jnana, on wisdom or wakefulness. The more awake you are, the more you see the sharpness and brilliance of form. You could hear form as sound, see form as image, or smell form as odor. A feeling of actual solidity, actual image, or actual experience develops. You realize that in this world, any sensorial experience develops into the form of the herukas, or wakefulness. This is not based on taking an attitude of sacredness; it is direct experience. So the jnana principle is also very important.

When we talk about jnana, we are talking again in terms of a psychological state. The emotions and everything that happens in your state of mind are seen as very penetrating, and at the same time, quite simple. The mind acts as a reminder of itself. The mind represents itself; it stands for itself. You do not have to borrow in any way to remind yourself to develop jnana. There is a sense that you are complete in a complete world, a sense that the world contains itself. Jnana represents all five types of jnana, all the five wisdoms. So the self-existing energy of wisdom operates all the time.

## Relating with Absolute Truth

Jnana is based on the different ways of relating with the twofold truth, the relative and the absolute, and understanding them both properly.

### Conditional Töndam

The common or conditional level of töndam, or absolute truth, is based on knowing that the self does not exist. Therefore, since there is no seed, there are no shoots from the seed, which seems to be an enormous discovery. Conditional töndam means that the nature of everything is empty by itself. The nature of everything that we experience is empty by itself, because there is complete negation. There is no room for anything other than itself; it is completely castrated.

## Unconditional Töndam

Unconditional or superior töndam is based on knowing that since this seed does not produce shoots, other seeds also do not produce shoots. You begin to expand your intelligence and venture into the world outside yourself. This is called nonsolidified töndam, because you begin to loosen up.

With unconditional töndam, the nonexistence mind operates at the level of nonduality, within dharmata wisdom; but at the same time, there are activities taking place in that nonexistence mind. Here, the question of its nonexistence is not the main point; the question is whether that nonexistence mind is operating or not. As far as the tantric tradition is concerned, the question is whether the workings of the universe operate—and they do operate!

TWO KINDS OF NEGATION: NO AND NOT. There are two ways of talking about nonexistence or negation. The first way is complete negation; this is the deadly one. The second way is just simple negation, which is not complete.

The closest the English language comes to those two kinds of negation is *no* and *not*. You might say, "I am not a cow," but you cannot just say, "I am not." You have to find an object in order to qualify your notness. You have to say what you are not, to compare yourself with something else. That kind of negation is more tantric, more workable. It has its root, and it also has its reference of intelligence.

If you say, "I am no," or simply, "No," it is a form of rejection. You are completely cutting the root. There is a quality of refusal that does not contain any experimentation or playfulness. This logic may seem to be at the madhyamaka level, but it still applies. And it is necessary to continue working with this kind of logic, if we are going to discuss the maha ati level. Such logic has to be used, and it has to be experienced—and the experience is that although your mind is nonexistent, at the same time this nonexistent mind produces a constant play of all kinds of forms, shapes, sounds, and thought processes.

## Relating with Relative Truth

There are also two types of relative truth, or kündzop: pure kündzop and confused kündzop. From a so-called sane person's point of view, or pure kündzop, the phenomenal world is seen as just a very vague and hazy image. But from a slightly freaked-out person's point of view, the phenomenal world is seen as either a complete enemy and absolutely hopeless, or as a friend. The first view is somewhat true kündzop, and the second view is false kündzop.

The superior understanding of pure kündzop is that you can perceive, and that your perception works. In your everyday life, when you put out energy, it bounces back on you and confirms your perceptions. With false kündzop, you can perceive and put out energy, but it does not bounce back. Somehow you miss the point, and you do not get any feedback.

It has been said that both kündzops are at the level of kaya and jnana, or form and wisdom, because they both have some kind of perception at the beginning, whether you get feedback or not, and whether it is a relative reference or not. With both kündzops, there is an experience of feeding rather than being fed.

The two types of kündzop, although they have different qualities, are considered to be statements of the illusory quality of the whole world; and the two types of töndam are considered to be statements of unoriginatedness.

## Approaching the Dharmakaya

In mahayoga, along with the understanding that the kündzop and töndam principles are indivisible, there is a greater realization of dharmakaya. Since mahayoga is based on a more complete realization, it is much superior to the lower three tantric yanas. You approach the dharmakaya much more closely than before, by means of a complete understanding of relative and absolute truth. In the earlier tantric yanas, you went back to reality, back to the relative world and the relative truth, but you did not reach the understanding of dharmakaya. But in mahayoga, the idea is that if you approach reality deeply enough from the relative-truth point of view, you gain dharmakaya experience at the same time. You realize that dharmakaya does not exist by way of absolute truth alone, but by way of relative truth as well. It is like the design of the vajra: you have a point above and a point below at the same time. So in mahayoga, you are getting completely into the dharmakaya by means of relative truth. That is the basic point; that is its meaning and purpose.

# 60

# Mahayoga:
# Meditation and the Mandala Principle

*Mandala means the state of experience that is fearless and all-per-vasive. Because of that fearlessness, there is no doubt about this, and since there is no doubt about this, you can include that at the same time. Therefore, this and that can be brought together.*

## TWO TYPES OF MAHAYOGA PRACTICE

Mahayoga practice is divided into two types: tantra and *nopika*, or "essential practice." The practices of tantra and nopika are both based on having an attitude toward life in which the five elements are seen as the five female buddhas: earth is ratna; water is vajra; fire is padma; wind is karma; and space is buddha. It is based on seeing the five skandhas as the five male buddha principles: form is buddha; feeling is ratna; perception is padma; formations are karma; and consciousness is vajra.

Tantra and nopika are based on combining kaya and jnana, the form or body aspect and wisdom, although they are leaning more toward the kaya principle than the jnana principle. They are involved with bringing intellect and intuition together in a person's understanding of the phenomenal world.

### Tantra

Tantra has two aspects: *gyü-de*, which means "tantric practice"; and *drub-de*, which also means "practice." Gyü-de is the experience of understanding the basic setup of the mandala in terms of tantric display or the tantric world. Drub-de is a more impersonal and magic-oriented relationship with the phenomenal world. It is relating with the field of energy that exists in the vajrayana tradition of mahayoga.

I should let you know that other writers do not talk about the gyü-de and drub-de as being all that separate, but in terms of my mind and training, they are somewhat different.

## Nopika

*Nopika* means "essential practice."* It refers to both solitary practice and group practice. Solitary and group practice work together in creating the mandala and its relationship with cosmic magic.

SOTA NOPIKA / SOLITARY PRACTICE. The first nopika, or *sota nopika,* is connected with personal practice. You get into the practice of sadhana, and you begin to evolve yourself. Often in the tantric tradition, this form of nopika is described in Tibetan as *chigdrup: chig* means "one," and *drup* means "nopika"; so *sota nopika* is "one person's practice."

Such a sadhana practice is traditionally done alone, like the sitting practice of meditation, which developed as a retreat practice. But the basic outlook is not just that you are doing it alone and having a good time—or having a bad time, for that matter. Since everything is seen as an expression of your mind, being with yourself is an expression of the openness or closedness of whatever you experience. Sota nopika is connected with the importance of using mind. With sota nopika, mind has become the essence of reality and the function of reality, and the quality of magical existence.

MANDALA NOPIKA / GROUP PRACTICE. The second kind of nopika is *mandala nopika,* or *tsogdrup.* It is group practice, or practice experienced together with your vajra brothers and sisters. In some contexts this could mean an orgy, but in this case, rather than implying something dirty, it

---

* The Tibetan term *nopika* appears to be a variant form of the Sanskrit *sadhanopayika,* which is a compound of *sadhana,* or "practice"; *upaya,* or "means" or "approach"; and *ika,* which makes "means" an adjective. So altogether, *sadhanapayika* means "having the approach of practice." Trungpa Rinpoche refers to *nopika* as "essential practice."

refers to an elaborate feast that you could do together with a lot of other people. For instance, your vajra brothers and sisters might get together and practice a big feast sadhana for a specific length of time, such as ten or fifteen days, or a month.

The idea of group practice is that everybody cooperates in creating the mandala and in trying to constantly resound the sound of the mantra. In other words, together they try to make the mantra and the mandala a living experience. If somebody is living, their heart beats twenty-four hours a day, and their breathing takes place all the time. Similarly, if you have vajra brothers and sisters cooperating with each other, there is the sound of mantra chanting taking place all the time, and sadhanas are constantly being performed.

In the early tantras, mantras were not chanted aloud, but were whispered to oneself or even just repeated mentally, which is known in Tibetan as *yi-de*. But in mahayoga group practice, it is recommended that many of the mantras be chanted out loud, which makes them more a proclamation than purely self-indulgence. Group practice also includes the creation of the shrine and the appointment of various officers to carry out different roles.

Mandala nopika seems to play a very important part from this tantra onward. With mandala nopika, having already realized the importance of the functioning of mind, you then have the coincidence of the situation around you developing as a mandala. The mandala setup involves a sociological, economical, and spiritual workability. It functions in its own world very simply and directly, very ordinarily; but at the same time it fits its own jigsaw puzzle.

## THE EIGHT MANDALAS

The attitude toward mandala in mahayoga tantra is that mandala basically means the tantric world or tantric language. Mandala means the state of experience that is fearless and all-pervasive. Because of that fearlessness, there is no doubt about *this;* and since there is no doubt about *this,* you can include *that* at the same time. Therefore, *this* and *that* can be brought together. You could bring the whole crowd of projections into the projector at once, simultaneously, and retain them together as well. So the mandala principle is based on fearlessness and easiness or simplicity—easiness in the sense that there is no problem and no irritation with anything.

Eight types of mandalas have been described in mahayoga tantra. Originally there were seven mandalas, and then somehow our great friends in the past managed to split the first one into two, which makes eight.

## The Mandala of Self-Existence

The first mandala is the mandala of self-existence, or *rangshin gyi kyilkhor*. *Rang* means "self," and *shin* means "existence" or "expression"; so *rangshin* means "self-existence" or "nature." *Gyi* means "of," and *kyilkhor* means "mandala"; so *rangshin gyi kyilkhor* means the "mandala of self-existence."

The meaning of self-existence, in this case, is that because it is self-existent, it is simple. This mandala is the producer of samsara and nirvana, and it is also the nature of both samsara and nirvana; therefore, it is simple. Self-existence means that the mandalas of samsara and nirvana are no longer different.

This particular mandala is the basis of everything. Therefore it is known as *chökyi ying,* or dharmadhatu. *Chö* means "dharma," *kyi* means "of," and *ying* means "space" or "sphere"; so *chökyi ying* means "space of dharma." Within dharmadhatu, there is complete confidence, and there is no need for further help in maintaining your experience.

## The Mandala of Compassion

The second mandala is the mandala of compassion. In Tibetan it is called *lhündrup kyi kyilkhor. Lhündrup* means "self-existence" or "spontaneous presence," *kyi* means "of," and *kyilkhor* means "mandala"; so *lhündrup kyi kyilkhor,* like rangshin gyi kyilkhor, means "mandala of self-existence." But although *lhündrup*, like *rangshin*, means "self-existence," this mandala is actually the mandala of a sympathetic attitude, or compassion. With this mandala, you have a complete understanding of the wisdoms of the five buddha-families, and you are willing to apply yourself with dedication and to share that understanding with other sentient beings.

The reason this mandala is referred to as "self-existent" is because in creating this particular attitude, you begin to develop twofold purity: eternal purity and apparent purity. Eternal purity is the eternally pure state of mind that has never been contaminated by samsaric hassles, problems, or beliefs. Apparent purity is when the tantric practitioner feels at the time of practice that there is no contamination and no impurity, that their mind is completely clear and direct. Together, they make twofold purity in simplicity.

Because an understanding or conviction of twofold purity exists, there is nothing to be paranoid about. Nothing at all! The reason that we are aggressive and hold back in an uncompassionate way is because of our paranoia. We have to maintain ourselves, so we do not have time to be a busybody with anybody else, or to even think about that. We have the attitude of: "Don't call me, I'll call you." Such an uncompassionate attitude is transcended in the simplicity of twofold purity. Because there is confidence that you are already pure and clear, you are ready to develop your compassion and to work with others as a kind of super-bodhisattva or tantric bodhisattva.

That quality of compassion is the essence of the mandala principle. You cannot create a mandala if there is no feeling of sympathy for your phenomenal world. The Sanskrit word *mandala* means "society," "group," or "collection." So if there is no relationship with others, you cannot create a mandala. You become a king without a kingdom.

## The Mandala of Form

The third mandala is the mandala of form, or *sugnyen gyi kyilkhor. Sugnyen* means "images," "reflections," or "forms"; so *sugnyen gyi kyilkhor* means the "mandala of form."

At this point, your attitude to the phenomenal world has changed a great deal. It is not only seen as nondual and pure, but your perception of the world becomes very clear, very direct, very meaningful, and very immediate. You see the play of the physical world and the entire universe as the form of the fivefold wisdom: the wisdom of all-encompassing space, mirrorlike wisdom, the wisdom of equanimity, discriminating-awareness wisdom, and the wisdom of all-accomplishing actions.

In this mandala, the five wisdoms are in the center and in the cardinal directions; and in the four intermediate directions, there are combinations of the adjacent wisdoms. For instance, the mirrorlike wisdom in the East and the wisdom of equanimity in the South together make up the wisdom of the Southeast, and so forth. Finally, above and below the center, there are expansions of the central wisdom of all-encompassing space, or dharmadhatu. So altogether, there are ten directions of the mandala, which are seen as the ten wisdoms. It is actually very simple.

With this mandala, the ten directions, the five colors, the elements, the seasons, and everything else are all seen as expressions of the five wisdoms. The whole universe is seen as the expression of the five wisdoms. You have no doubt about that at all. Everything experienced in your life is the result of the highest achievement of visualization, in which you have enormous trust. You do not separate the mundane world from the supernatural or divine world, but you see the world as being ordinary and at the same time extraordinary. That is the mandala of form.

## The Mandala of Extra Form

The fourth mandala is the mandala of extra form, or *lhak-pe sugnyen gyi kyilkhor*. *Lhak-pe* means "extra" or "superior," *sugnyen* means "images" or "forms" of various types; so *lhak-pe sugnyen gyi kyilkhor* means the "mandala of extra form."

The reason the word *extra* is used in this description is that, having seen the physical setup of the phenomenal world, the practitioner is able to make a replica of it in the form of a two-dimensional or three-dimensional mandala. Such a replica is a means to relate with the whole world as the five-buddha-family setup.

At this point, you still need some kind of catalyst to turn your effort and energy into the real thing. So you create a mandala by sand painting, or painting on a canvas, or piling up heaps of grain. You could also build a three-dimensional mandala structure rather than painting on flat surfaces alone. You could build little mansions or castles with four doors and all kinds of compartments inside for the various deities, and surround them with a charnel ground and corpses and skeletons and flames and so on.

The tradition of constructing visualization models was designed to encourage students, and to show them how the geography or the architectural setup of a particular mandala works. These miniature models of the mandala are very helpful; they are not just priest craft or art, but they actually give you an idea of the visualization and how you should relate with the phenomenal world. Building one of these mandalas is like building a miniature universe. Mandalas like this do exist, and you might be able to see one.

Traditional three-dimensional mandalas were often very crude. For instance, a person might use ropes or threads or wires to give the illusion that the sun, the earth, and the moon are suspended in midair. Nevertheless, that kind of mandala structure is still a great attempt to illustrate how the universe exists geographically. Hopefully, tantric practitioners in this country will also be able to understand the iconography, the mandala structure, how the deities look, and how a mandala is developed.*

## The Mandala of Meditation

The fifth mandala is the mandala of meditation, or *tingdzin gyi kyilkhor.* *Tingdzin* is the Tibetan word for "samadhi," *gyi* means "of," and *kyilkhor* means "mandala"; so *tingdzin gyi kyilkhor* is the "mandala of meditation or samadhi."

This mandala is, once again, based on the idea of simplicity. At this point you might practice by yourself in a retreat hut, with no shrine, or only a simple little shrine, and no elaborate ritual. The basic emphasis is on the actual practice itself.

At a certain level of spiritual development in the mahayogayana, sadhakas no longer need an actual shrine setup—they are able to work without any shrine. Instead, they relate with their body directly as mandala principle. In this mandala, the heart is the center, and the arms and legs are the four quarters. The hairs around the body are regarded as the flames around the mandala; the skin is regarded as the charnel ground; the veins are regarded as the various rooms that divide the mandala; and the circulation of blood is regarded as the occupants of the mandala, such as the herukas, dakinis, and so forth. So your whole body is regarded as a mandala, rather than having an actual physical mandala setup.

## The Mandala of Extra Meditation

The sixth mandala is the mandala of extra meditation, or *lhak-pe tingdzin gyi kyilkhor.* *Lhakpe* again means "extra" or "auxiliary," *tingdzin* means

---

* At the behest of Chögyam Trungpa Rinpoche, Venerable Tenga Rinpoche (1932–2012) came to Boulder, Colorado, in 1985 to construct a three-dimensional mandala of the Chakrasamvara palace, primarily as a means of instructing practitioners of the Chakrasamvara sadhana.

"meditation," *gyi* means "of," and *kyilkhor* means "mandala"; so *lhak-pe tingdzin gyi kyilkhor* means the "mandala of extra meditation." Previously we had lhak-pe sugnyen gyi kyilkhor, the mandala of extra form, and now we have lhak-pe tingdzin gyi kyilkhor, the mandala of extra meditation.

The extra meditation mandala is based on visualization practice: you are visualizing the herukas and dakinis and their retinues completely and in great detail. In the mandala of extra form, you created a miniature art form of the mandala, and with this mandala you visualize exactly the same thing. This visualization is created by mental activity, but at the same time that mental activity is partially influenced by your nondualistic meditative state. It is quite simple, seemingly. This mandala is a deliberate visualization created by mind. And since your mind is no longer regarded as embarrassing, impure, or bad, everything is valid. Samsaric mental activity is invited at the same time that your mind is becoming tuned in to your visualization.

### The Mandala of Bodhichitta

The seventh mandala is the mandala of bodhichitta, or *changsem kyi kyilkhor*. *Changsem* is an abbreviation of *changchup kyi sem, sem* means "mind," *changchup* means "bodhi"; so *changchup kyi sem* means "bodhi mind" or "bodhichitta," the essence of enlightenment.

In tantric language, bodhichitta often refers to semen. In this case, semen means energy or sustenance, that which brings body and mind together so that both mind and body can function in good health. It is the Buddhist tantric equivalent of the kundalini practice of Hindu tantra. The Sanskrit word for semen is *kunda. Kunda* can mean "bodhichitta," and it is also a synonym for "white." It can also refer to the full moon. The analogy of the full moon is that you are completely awake and completely full. Similarly, the idea of the waxing moon is that you are increasing the energy source. You are working with the energy levels of the universe, the essence of this universe, which gives rebirth to the next universe. You are working with that kind of thing, as well as sharing your experience with your partner in karmamudra.

Descriptions of this mandala are very mysterious in that there are references to karmamudra, or the third abhisheka, and there are also references back to your previous training in the mahayana and to maintaining your bodhisattva integrity. Karmamudra and mahayana training are both regarded as mandala activity. It seems that teachers in the past never made up their minds as to which of the two they were referring to, but probably that was quite intentional, for they are the same thing. Likewise, the third abhisheka is also the action of compassion, love, generosity, patience, and so forth. The idea of the third abhisheka is that activity born of passion can be transcended and become compassion. So karma yoga and compassion are regarded as the same. That is the seventh mandala setup.

### The Mandala of Vajra Sangha

The eighth mandala is the mandala of vajra sangha, or *tsokchok kyi kyilkhor*. *Tsok* means "gathering," "group," "mass," or "heap," and *chok* means "superior" or "supreme"; so *tsokchok* means a "superior gathering" or "vajra sangha."

A vajra sangha is more than simply a *mahasangha*, or great gathering. It involves group practice in which hundreds or up to a thousand vajra brothers and sisters get together and create an enormous mandala and do ritual practice together. There is twenty-four-hour recitation of a mantra, and they share a great vajra feast together.

This kind of group practice seems to be particularly characteristic of maha ati tantra. In maha ati, the emphasis is no longer on your own individual practice that you do in your meditation cell, but on group practice. There is a whole social setup: the vajra master, vajra minister, vajra servant, vajra bursar, vajra cook, and so forth. The whole family setup, or organizational setup, is brought in as part of the greater realization that such a mandala could be constructed in a real, ordinary, society-level situation.

When groups of practitioners gather together in groups of hundreds or thousands to create a mandala, they are not creating a mandala as a physical form, but the gathering itself is a mandala. Their gathering is based on the mandala principle, and all the participants in that particular mandala have some motivation for getting into the practice at the same time. That is the eighth or last mandala of mahayogayana.

## EMPOWERMENTS AND VISUALIZATION

Mahayoga abhishekas are not very much different from the abhishekas of the previous yanas. But it is not so much the details that are important, but rather the attitude. The attitude of this particular yana is one of enormous power, enormous energy, and enormous identification of the visualizer with the visualization. The boundary between the samayasattva and the jnanasattva has been broken, and they are operating almost, but not quite, at one level.

## Yidams and Sadhanas

In the three higher yanas of mahayoga, anuyoga, and atiyoga, there are something like four thousand different sadhanas. Every tantra has its own sadhanas, so in higher tantra there are thousands of variations of yidams and practices. The teachings of the three higher yanas along with their sadhanas were compiled and edited by Jamgön Kongtrül the Great into a sixty-three-volume collection.* Although these sadhanas are connected with an endless variety of deities, they all seem to be related to the five buddha-family principles or to the one hundred buddha-families.† In mahayoga, all of these practices are bound by nonduality and simplicity, the basic statement that this particular tantra carries out constantly.

I used to find it quite easy, although I was only thirteen at the time, to work my way through the various deities, in terms of their particular family, their particular style, and so forth. The only problem I used to have was when there were occasional abhishekas for local deities. I did not want to receive an abhisheka of a local deity, who could be just a local person who was terribly angry, or maybe a killer, or maybe a good mother. I used to find such abhishekas very freaky.

I actually went to Jamgön Kongtrül of Shechen and talked about that once. He burst into very loud laughter, and said, "Well, you can regard relating to local deities to be like getting a pet dog. You could have all

---

* This collection, known as the *Rinchen Terdzö* (*Precious Treasury of Treasure Texts*), includes about eight hundred abhishekas and related sadhanas. Not only had Chögyam Trungpa Rinpoche received all these abhishekas, but by the age of fourteen he was sufficiently proficient in them to confer the entire Rinchen Terdzö cycle of teachings over a six-month period of all-day ceremonies.

† The *five buddha-families* can be elaborated into a mandala of one hundred deities. The *one hundred buddha-families* include fifty-eight wrathful deities and forty-two peaceful deities.

kinds of pet dogs, and maybe you could have a horse or a yak as well." The day before I talked with him, there had been the abhisheka of the local deity of the Tangna region, who was the family deity of the king of Tibet. This deity rode on a white yak and he wore a papier-mâché hat. And Jamgön Kongtrül of Shechen said, "Yesterday you got a white yak, and you should keep it. It might be useful at some point."

## The Union of Samayasattva and Jnanasattva

In mahayoga, your samayasattva visualization is an expression of your pure mind. Beyond that, you invite the jnanasattva as usual, but your attitude to the jnanasattva shifts. Instead of the jnanasattva being like a person who comes along and reinforces you, now it is more like a person who comes along and destroys you. It is as if the trip of visualization is being defused by inviting the jnanasattva. You are inviting the jnanasattva to break your fixation on the samayasattva, the hanging on to it. So you no longer have any fixed idea of maintaining your samayasattva as valid because it has been blessed by the jnanasattva. If any ego-clinging is formed toward the samayasattva, the jnanasattva comes along and cuts through that.

The purpose of mahayoga is to make the visualization as complete and relevant as possible. In the three earlier yanas, there is an enormous split of confusion between the samayasattva and the jnanasattva; when you invite the jnanasattva into the samayasattva, it is as if you are inviting some new element into your system. There is still a split and a feeling of separateness. But in mahayoga, an enormous change takes place. The approach to visualization becomes entirely different. You are no longer thinking in terms of jnanasattva and samayasattva being separate.

At this point, although you still have little hang-ups, the presence of ego does not have much play. You lost your ego a long time ago. However, even if ego is gone, it is not automatic that the two sattvas are together, because when the distinction between the visualizer and the visualization is taken away, you still have mind. You are not quite *there* yet, but you are not *here* either. There are three levels of experience: first, *this* is gone, and *that* is happening; next, *that* is gone; then, a greater *that* is still there. So *this* is a sort of reference-less experience, but *that* is still somewhat of a reference point.

## BEING IN LEAGUE WITH THE WORLD

The basis of mahayogayana is upaya, or skillful means, which is related with visualization practice, or utpattikrama. But in mahayoga, visualization is not just visualizing deities or herukas. The visualization practice is more about relating with the world rather than simply visualizing deities, as we might do in lower tantra. Visualization in mahayoga has the quality of actually experiencing things as they are in the fullest sense. The elements and emotions and everything that goes on in your mind can be seen as they are, directly, magically, powerfully, without any hesitation. So the way that visualization in mahayoga relates with the phenomenal world is based on an appreciation of the phenomenal world as it is.

This type of visualization is like wanting to go to Bhutan, and knowing that the royal family is your friend. You know that you will have no difficulty getting into the country, and you know that you will receive royal hospitality when you get there. Mahayoga visualization practice has that kind of easiness and lack of hassle. Previously, there was always a feeling of hassle or problems, which made visualization practice very trying and difficult. But in mahayoga visualization, you feel that you are in league with the world. There is a sense of tremendous accomplishment, understanding, and freedom.

Mahayoga visualization relates with what are referred to in tantric texts as names, words, and letters. This does not mean names, words, and letters in the ordinary sense; it means conceptualizations. In visualization, any concept we use to label the phenomenal world is being transmuted. Because of that, there is more room for simplicity and directness. Visualizations from this point of view are not separate from the reality that we experience in ordinary, everyday life. There is oneness with that, somehow.

In mahayoga, visualization goes with symbolism hand in hand. If you are going to the bank to get some cash, that automatically includes writing a check. If you are going to drive, that automatically includes using the steering wheel. There is that kind of command over what you are going to do. There is a quality of ease and real command over the universe.

# Mahayoga:
# The Eight Logos

*The vajrayana is sympathetic to samsara. It accepts the ugliness of samsara and wears it as an ornament. The vajrayana is never embarrassed by samsara. Using the fear of the intensity of vajrayana as inspiration is part of the vajrayana psyche.*

## The Practice
## of the Eight Logos

In the mahayogayana, we have a variety of ways, all kinds of setups, and various examples of how magic can work in the phenomenal world. One example is what is known as the eight logos. In Tibetan this is called *druppa kagye,* or the eight types of *ka. Druppa* means "practice," *gye* means "eight," and *ka* means "sacred word" or "command"; so *druppa kagye* is the "practice of the eight sacred words."

In this case, *ka* is more like a fundamental cosmic structure; it is the ultimate utterance of the universe from the point of view of the sambhogakaya. Therefore, I decided to translate *ka* using the Christian term *Logos,* which comes from Greek and means "Word" or "Utterance." *Ka* is both sacred word and first word. It is the primeval expression of things. So altogether we have eight types of primeval expression.

## The Origins of the Eight Logos Teaching

The eight logos teaching had its origins in India. For instance, the fourth logos, the brewing of the anti-death potion, is connected with the eighth-century Indian teacher Vimalamitra. The trouble is that, because this teaching is from the Nyingma tradition, we do not have manuscripts in Sanskrit, although there are Tibetan texts. In fact, I am one of the relatively few people who have come to India from Tibet who hold this lineage and have received the transmission, or *lung*, of the Nyingma tantras, which consist of over thirty volumes.

The eight logos teaching is all *terma*, except for the Sakya version of Vajrakilaya, which is *kama; kama* means "non-terma," to put it very simply.* The Sakya have maintained similar teachings that have been handed down for generations. The Sakyas survived very beautifully the religious persecutions that Buddhists went through when Langdarma, the grandson of King Trisong Detsen, killed monks and destroyed monasteries. The current head of the Sakya order, Sakya Trizin, is the direct descendent of the Khön family, the same family as Padmasambhava's disciple, Khönlü Wangpo. This family specialized in the deity Vajra Heruka of the Vajrakilaya practice.

But apart from that, we do not have any records of this teaching. Supposedly there are Nyingma kamas that were handed down, but none of the eight logos were originally handed down orally from one teacher to another. They are all terma.

## Transforming the Eight Consciousnesses into Living Enlightenment

The eight logos are related with transcending the eight types of consciousness and transforming them into what is known as the glorious wrathful deity Shri Heruka. The essence of Shri Heruka is *thatness*. It is isness in terms of the magical quality, rather than purely as an expression of truth. Isness on the mahayana level, or even the hinayana level, is referred to

---

* *Terma,* or "treasure teachings," refer to teachings hidden by Padmasambhava or other masters in order to be discovered when the time and conditions were right. Those who make such discoveries are known as *tertöns*. Perhaps the most well-known terma text is *The Tibetan Book of the Dead (Bardo Thötröl)*. *Kama* refers to teachings passed on orally from teacher to student, over many generations. After terma are discovered, they are taught in the same way as other teachings—orally, from master to disciple.

simply as *that*. It is the *thatness* of the rock, the *thatness* of the tree, the *thatness* of the pulsating heart of compassion. But in this case, the quality of isness or *thatness* is much more direct, simple, and provocative. Fundamental *thatness* is a living body; it is living enlightenment, which is called Shri Heruka. *Thatness* is expressed as eight deities arrayed in a mandala.

## THE EIGHT-DEITY MANDALA

I will now go through the eight logos individually, and identify the deities associated with each one.

### *Yangdak: The Completely Pure*

The first logos is called Yangdak, which means completely pure. Yangdak is blue, which is the color of the vajra family. He is connected with the eastern section of the mandala, although he could be approached as a separate entity in your practice as well.

The philosophy behind this logos is that of holding the Buddha in your hand, which is known in Tibetan as *sang-gye lakchang*. *Sang-gye* is "Buddha," *lak* is "hand," *chang* means "grasp"; so *sang-gye lakchang* is "holding Buddha in your hand." At this point, since you already have gained such a powerful, magical existence yourself, it is like having a little Buddha sitting in your hand. It is up to you if you want to crush this little Buddha, if you want to eat it up, or if you want to nourish it.

The idea is one of overpowering, even transcending, the notion of enlightenment. From this perspective, buddhahood, or any notion of enlightenment, is not a big deal. You are looking back from the enlightenment point of view, and you are seeing that the idea of attaining enlightenment is very small thinking. You can see beyond that. You can see that the path and the direction called enlightenment is a very insignificant thing. This is the approach of the Yangdak mandala.

The deities that are involved here are wrathful figures, usually with eight arms and three faces, wearing the customary bone ornaments and the various costumes of a yogin. The idea is that all the costumes worn by Rudra have been taken over. They have been transformed, blessed, and worn again as enlightened power, rather than the ego power of Rudra.

The symbolism that goes with Yangdak includes a skull cup with eight wicks and filled with oil. The idea is that light can exist within light; one torch with eight types of flame illuminates everything. There is a quality of complete accomplishment, complete command. Enlightenment is no longer problematic. This is connected with what is called the dawn of Vajrasattva, or a glimpse of Vajrasattva. In mahayoga, Vajrasattva is very important because Vajrasattva is the one who brings coolness, as opposed to passion and aggression, which is hot. Vajrasattva also brings a sense of promise and an actual visual glimpse of something.

Yangdak is connected with the idea of taking delight in the charnel ground as the most luxurious place of all. As we discussed earlier, the charnel ground is quite unlike a cemetery or graveyard. It is a place where bodies are put at random, and vultures and wild animals come along and tear the bodies apart and eat them on the spot. Consequently the charnel ground is filled with garbage. There are floating hairs that are blown by the wind, and bones, and flies. There is a feeling of the joke of death. The skulls look as if they are laughing as they stare at you with their teeth sticking out. It is a real place of death, rather than a churchyard cemetery or a graveyard where everything is neatly placed, and the only thing you can see is names. Here you see the real stuff.

The charnel ground is the fundamental tantric symbol of dharma-dhatu. It is a place of birth, as well as a place of death. I suppose we could say it is like a hospital, a place where you are born and where you die. Hospitals are a new kind of charnel ground, with another kind of horror.

So with the first logos, we have the idea of holding the Buddha in your hand, and the idea of taking delight in the charnel ground of phenomenal experience. You see the whole world as a charnel ground.

### Jampal or Yamantaka: The Conqueror of the Lord of Death

The second heruka is called Jampal, or Manjushri Yamantaka. Yamantaka is the Lord of the Lord of Death. Therefore, he has control over birth and death and the happenings of life, which are also an expression of birth and death. Jampal is yellow, which is the color of the ratna family, and he is in the southern section of the mandala. Yamantaka is the enemy of Yama, the Lord of Death. He is the wrathful aspect of Manjushri.

The practice that goes along with Yamantaka is transforming life into wisdom. Usually life is the last thing remaining to be transformed into wisdom. Ordinarily you may give up life, you may get free from life, but you cannot transform it into wisdom. Life is a flowing experience, whereas wisdom is a perpetual experience. But in this case, very strangely, that transformation is workable: life is transformed into wisdom by turning the four wheels of Jampal. And by the way, these wheels or chakras do not necessarily refer to psychic centers.

THE FOUR WHEELS.
*The secret wheel.* The first wheel is called the secret wheel, which is connected with the mind. This wheel brings all phenomenal experience into one mindedness, one mind, one awareness. This awareness is the same type of awareness as in mahamudra; it is the awareness or reminder of mindfulness that comes from samsara.

*The wheel of existence.* The second wheel is called the wheel of existence, which is connected with the navel. This wheel has nothing to do with the traditional iconographic image also called the "wheel of existence," or "the wheel of life."*

The mark of birth, the mark of existence, is your navel or belly button. Your navel expresses that you have actually been born, that you have expressed yourself as a child of this particular earth. Likewise, when the mind operates, it begins a process of duplication; there is a magical duplication of the mind in creating a further world. That is why the second wheel is called the wheel of existence. Dharmata is the dharmakaya's version of a belly button. With dharmata, or dharma-ness, everything is seen as an expression of the dharma, completely and fully.

*The wheel of cutting.* The third wheel is called the wheel of cutting, which is connected with the arms and hands. This wheel is the wheel of action. The wheel of cutting uses the hands as a tool. It might be better to say the "wheel of function" rather than the "wheel of cutting," but you can blame the *panditas* or scholars of the past for calling it that.

Having already gone through the first and second wheels, you will be able to perform the four karmas of pacifying, enriching, magnetizing, and destroying, and you will be able to perform the ten types of miracle, the ten magical actions of personal power over others connected with

---

* The *wheel of life* is a traditional depiction of the realms of samsaric existence and the karmic chain held within the jaws of death, or Yama. For a discussion of the wheel of life, see volume 1 of the *Profound Treasury,* chapter 9, "The Painful Reality of Samsara."

the four karmas.* This wheel is like having hands and having a chance to use them, so there is no hesitation. You can do what you want, with no fear of failing. A means of working with other people becomes a part of your existence, so there is no problem. Once you have expressed yourself in terms of that magical feasibility, you begin to develop ambidextrousness or multidextrousness. You become so completely functional that all actions are fulfilled. There is a quality of complete efficiency.

*The wheel of miracle or emanation.* The fourth wheel is the wheel of miracle or emanation, which is associated with your feet and legs, and with walking. This wheel is connected with covering ground, and with being prepared to relate to any threat of the re-creation of ego. Your mind is so inspired and so much at the vajra-mind level that you can think of all kinds of ways of working with the samsaric and nirvanic worlds. You could work with the world by means of teaching, by compassion, or by destruction. All of that is so much a part of your behavior that your inspiration never runs out.

The four wheels are magical expressions of Manjushri as Yamantaka, the Lord of the Lord of Death. They are a magical way to conquer the world—a way to overpower death and eternity at the same time.

## Hayagriva: The Subjugator of Rudra

The third logos is called Hayagriva, or Tamdrin, the horse-headed one.†
Hayagriva is red in color, and is the padma family heruka. According to myth, Hayagriva was the first and foremost subjugator of Rudra.

The practice connected with this logos is to realize that the universe is a gigantic world filled with gullible people. You can press the button of the fire alarm, and everyone will stand up very faithfully and very honestly, like good citizens. That is the sort of humor that goes with this logos.

In the iconography, you can see horse heads coming out of Hayagriva's head. So the practice in this mandala is referred to as the three neighs of a horse. This practice is involved with magical power. From Hayagriva's

---

* Possibly a reference to the ten powers: the powers over life, deeds, necessities, devotion, aspiration, miraculous abilities, birth, dharma / teachings, mind, and wisdom.

† *Haya* mean "horse," and *griva* means "neck" or "mane"; so *Hayagriva* means "Horse-Neck," or more loosely "Horse-Headed."

point of view, the universe is totally gullible, so the idea of a horse's neigh is that of awakening and provoking gullible people.

THE THREE NEIGHS. The three neighs are waking the world to the fact that samsara and nirvana are unoriginated, offering the whole world, and demanding obedience.

*Waking the world to the fact that samsara and nirvana are unoriginated.* The first neigh is to wake the world to the fact that samsara and nirvana are both unoriginated. They exist on a simple level that provides immense space, so you do not have to be biased. Here we are talking about samsara and nirvana in the vajrayana sense, which is much more highly intensified than in the hinayana or even the mahayana. Samsara in this case is much more in turmoil and confused, a much more screwed-up world, and nirvana is highly enlightened and highly transformed into the greater world of vajrayana. And both those worlds are regarded as equal. Nobody created that world of samsara and nirvana; it is a self-existing world.

The function of the first neigh is to blank people's minds. It is to confuse and at the same time to cut your mind. The first neigh cuts your thoughts. Blank! Samsara and nirvana are one! They are unmade, unoriginated, and self-existing! The point is to make you realize that you are gullible, but at the same time you are not gullible. Your gullibility is a part of your existence; it is not just that you are looking for excitement. The general pattern of samsara seems to be that people are looking for kicks of all kinds based on aggression, passion, and ignorance, but fundamentally this gullibility is just a way of being.

There is a sense of absurdity involved with this first neigh. In blanking people's minds, the realization that samsara and nirvana are one, and that they are unmade, unoriginated, and self-existing, occurs as a spontaneously existing understanding.

*Offering the whole world.* The second neigh is to offer the animate and inanimate world as a gigantic feast offering. You offer the energy of the animate and inanimate world for the sake of paying off karmic debts. The animate and inanimate world could be made into a gigantic ocean of soup made of flesh and blood and crushed bone, and cooked in a huge cauldron to be offered to the dakinis of the world. It is not offered to the gurus or to the herukas; instead it is purely offered to the dakinis, because they are also gullible and mischievous.

That you are feeding gullible food to gullible beings is a cosmic joke. You are not presenting good, beautiful, sweet things, but just bones and flesh in a big soup cauldron. That is the provocative aspect of this horse's neigh.

*Demanding obedience.* With the third neigh, having satisfied all those to whom you made that offering, you can now proclaim that they must do what you want, that they must become obedient to you. With the third neigh, the deities who are protectors of the teaching, who remind you of your basic awareness, could also be woken up and made to obey your command for protection.

The three neighs are connected with traditional bugle calls. The first call of the bugle is to let everybody and everything know that you exist and that your administration exists. The second bugle call announces the fact that you have already made yourself comfortable. The third bugle call proclaims that all who hear it must obey and act upon what is told therein. The three neighs are another way of working with the phenomenal world.

## Chemchok: The Supreme Heruka

The fourth logos is Chemchok, who is deep red or mahogany in color. *Che* means "giant," and *chok* means "supreme." In Tibetan terms, he is just called the Great Heruka, or Vajra Heruka, but that seems to be rather generalized. Chemchok is connected with the center of the mandala, and with turning the five ingredients of flesh, blood, piss, shit, and semen into the anti-death potion, or amrita. Overall, the idea is that your existing life experience could be turned into amrita.

According to tantric discipline, you are not supposed to refer to those five ingredients by their usual names. For instance, you do not call shit "shit"; you call shit "Vairochana," and you refer to piss as "Akshobhya." So one aspect of tantric discipline is that all kinds of synonyms are used to remind you of those basic qualities. Another aspect, naturally, is that each of the five ingredients is connected with a particular buddha-family. Bodhichitta, or semen, is connected with the ratna family, piss with the vajra family, and shit with the buddha family. Meat, referred to as *bhala* in what is called the dakini's language, is connected with the padma family, and blood, or *rakta* in Sanskrit, is connected with the karma family.*

The idea is to collect those elements physically as well as psychologically. However, you are not encouraged to literally collect shit and piss and make them into an anti-death potion. Somehow, that does not work. What you are actually collecting is your attitude toward such things; you are collecting the attitude of being sickened. Shit, piss, and the other ingredients are sickening. They are not particularly pleasant. They are so raw that you do not even want to talk about them; you would rather change the conversation to something else.

In this practice, you are subtracting the shittiness out of the shit itself: you are subtracting your revulsion and your feeling of yuckiness. That fear and unpleasant feeling is the basic point. I suppose it could be said that throughout the teachings of tantra, there is the feeling of not being able to deal with such teachings, the feeling that the whole thing is unpleasant. That embarrassment and hesitation as to whether you can hang on or whether you will be kicked out of the whole thing is the starting point. It is the inspiration, the teacher, and the teachings.

In the fourth logos, you are making all those ingredients into amrita. The traditional ceremony or ritual for this is based on brewing amrita from eight basic herbs and a thousand lesser herbs. You collect them together, put in yeast, and brew them in order to make what is called dharma medicine, or *dütsi chömen*. The idea of doing all this is to intoxicate those hesitations by providing greater medicine than hesitation.

What is happening in the fourth logos is that you are engaged in the gigantic scheme of intoxicating the whole universe with its own dharmic anti-death potion. With that magical, vajra anti-death potion, the phenomenal world and its container, which is mind, can be intoxicated completely. The idea is to develop a cosmic brewing system and churn out all kinds of intoxicating drinks in order to feed the world of phenomena, and to allow phenomena to transcend feeding and get completely drunk. In this logos, the world is finally seen as a very powerful and real world, where neurosis

---

* The various sadhanas seem to differ in their portrayal of the correspondences between the buddha-families and the five ingredients.

can be intoxicated into wisdom, where rightness and wrongness can be intoxicated into nothingness, and where all six realms can be intoxicated into the mandala of the five buddha-families.

## Dorje Phurba or Vajrakilaya: The Dagger Wielder

The fifth logos is Dorje Phurba, or Vajrakilaya, who is blue in color, and connected with the northern direction of the mandala. In Tibetan, *phurba* (or *kila* in Sanskrit) is the word for "dagger," specifically a three-bladed dagger. According to Indian mythology, which Buddhism shares, phurbas are the weapons of the gods. In Tibet, the three-bladed dagger was used for executing criminals. When a criminal was caught, their hands and legs were tied up, and the executioner stabbed a kila through their heart. The Incas may have used a similar approach. I don't know exactly, but this kind of ritual stabbing seems to be a very ancient, sacrificial technique.

In this case, the criminal is Rudra, the embodiment of ego, and the execution is a ritual one. In this ritual, there is a little box, and inside the box there is an effigy of Rudra made out of dough, and you stab the dough. The idea is to penetrate through, not just stab and stop. You penetrate all the way through so the phurba comes out the other side like a bullet.

THE FOUR PENETRATIONS. Altogether there are four types of penetration: the wisdom dagger, the bodhichitta dagger, the limitless compassion dagger, and the physical dagger, which is the point at which one physically stabs the effigy of Rudra.

*Wisdom dagger.* The first penetration is the dagger of wisdom and insight. In this penetration, basic insight or intelligence penetrates confusion. At this level, confusion is magical or tantric confusion. An ordinary person experiencing tantric confusion would regard it as fantastic insight. But there is further, greater wisdom beyond that, which can actually cut through that type of confusion. Insightful wisdom, the meditative experience of a sudden glimpse, can be used to penetrate that confused mind.

*Bodhichitta dagger.* The second penetration is the greater bodhichitta mind, or bodhichitta dagger. It is used on uninspired mind, cutting through spiritual materialism precisely. Bodhichitta is inspired toward enlightenment, and spiritual materialism is prejudiced against the idea of enlightenment or of giving up ego. This penetration is also connected with karma yoga practice. The idea is to subjugate your partner, and then plant bodhi mind in him or her. This is called supreme bodhi penetration.

*Limitless compassion dagger.* The third penetration is the limitless compassion dagger, which pierces through the heart of those who are angry or resentful. Anger in this case is fundamental anger. It is resentment over not wanting to surrender and give, which involves enormous arrogance. With this dagger, having felt longing, openness, and workability in relation to the world of human beings and all sentient beings, you cannot be put off anymore. You are going to penetrate on and on, again and again. Even if beings do not want your services, you are still going to mind their business completely, and you are still going to penetrate through constantly.

*Physical dagger.* The fourth penetration is the physical dagger used to ritually pierce through an effigy of Rudra. You create an effigy of Rudra and you pierce him through his heart, while at the same time appreciating the meaning of the symbolism and recollecting the previous three daggers. By stabbing the phurba through the effigy of Rudra, both Rudra and the perverters of the teachings can be penetrated by magical power and stopped. They can be destroyed completely by that magical process.

The fifth logos is unlike other tantric practices. It is unique in that it has very little to do with pleasure. The bodhichitta dagger has a connection with sexual union and the idea of sexual penetration, but that seems to be the only pleasure. This logos is very aggressive. The penis as dagger is penetrating or cutting through expectations of fulfilling desire, and is achieving a state of shunyata. It is cutting through cheap desires and achieving the mahasukha experience of greater joy. And as you penetrate, the dagger actually gets sharpened.

The fifth logos is extremely powerful. It stands out in the tantric tradition of Buddhism due to its emphasis on conquering, penetrating, and destroying. Padmasambhava supposedly used this logos constantly, as in the destruction of the five hundred heretics. When he was appearing as the Lion's Roar, the wrathful figure Senge Dradrok, he threw a teakwood symbol of a dagger into the jungle where the heretics lived, and it caught fire and killed five hundred of them. In his journey to Tibet, Padmasambhava also used the destructive approach that is connected with this particular yidam.

## Mamo: The Mother Principle

The sixth logos is the *mamo* mandala. A mamo is a kind of mother principle: it is a twofold mother principle. There is the grandmother quality of the *ma*, somebody who presides over the space of your heritage. And then there is *mo*, who is more like a wife, someone who puts intelligence into your life situation, someone who cooks for you.

*Mamo,* ironically, is the familiar word for dakinis. Instead of calling them dakinis, people call them mamo, which is like referring to your mother as "mommy." *Mamo* could be a corruption of the Tibetan word *mama,* which means "I" or "myself," reflecting that idea back on somebody else as the feminine principle.

The mystical interpretation of *ma* is dharmata, or dharmadhatu, quite strangely, which is beyond even the dharmakaya level. *Dharmakaya* is an abbreviation of *jnanadharmakaya,* which means "greater wisdom body of dharma." On the dharmakaya level, you are still a dharmakaya buddha, so dharmakaya is still path oriented, but in fact there are several layers of space beyond that. In this case, we are talking about something beyond any path orientation. It is just personal existence. We are talking about dharmadhatu. Dharmadhatu is the greatest space. It is beyond Buddhism, beyond language, beyond dharma, and beyond truth.

*Mo* is connected with the insightfulness coming out of that space of dharmadhatu. That insightfulness is still very spacious, and it is still the feminine principle, but more like a lover or a daughter. It is like an outspoken maid or a critical sister. It is an insightful, powerfully penetrating principle.

Mamo is the basic feminine principle that governs the whole universe. The universe is conquered by the feminine principle whether we like it or not. I think that people who have a lot of feelings about food and motherhood and relatives, such as Jews and Tibetans and Italians, still have this kind of feminine principle. When young people get together and decide to get married, they may be horrified by their parents' and grandparents' traditional ways. They think that they are going to be different and create a new society. But although they do not mean to, they cannot help being the same way. They re-create the same food-oriented world or the same feminine world again and again. That seems to be the natural process of how the world grows and how the world learns to relate with reality properly.

If there were no mother principle, we could not learn anything. We could not even wipe our bottoms if there had been no mother. Things would become completely wild and savage. Mothers brought us civilization. I am not about to compose a national anthem to mothers, but that seems to be the way things usually happen. You might think that you are a great powerful man, free from this whole woman or mother or grandmother trip, but you are not quite there. When you say that you are no longer affected by that, you are even more into it, you are even more involved. You might be living without your mother's cooking, just living on canned food or pizza, but you are still subject to the mother hang-up.

THE MOTHER'S CURSE. The practice of this logos is called the mother's curse, and the way to rouse this is to work along with the dakini principles in creating enormous chaos for others or for yourself. It is to create fundamental chaos for ego. The mamo mandala brings prana, nadi, and bindu together, which means that there can be experience that combines the essence of life, the moving life energy, and the channels that accommodate that movement. That is the only way you could generate the mother's curse on others.

The ritual object for this logos is a little silk bag filled with poison, which is tied to an ordinary dagger. My tutor used to tell me to be careful not to breathe in too close to that bag or I might get the flu. The mother's curse creates a working basis by means of little physical things that happen. That is why it is called the mother's curse: it is like the curse in the ordinary sense of menstruation, where a woman is repeatedly reminded that she is not pregnant because she has her period.

The idea of mother's curse is similar to what we call black air. The student-teacher relationship at the vajrayana level is very sensitive, very special. As a student, you get hit much more than anybody else if the guru creates black air. I remember Jamgön Kongtrül of Shechen doing it, and it was really horrible. You could not even eat or have casual conversations with people because everything was so bad and black and down. The sound of your own footsteps was part of the terror and horror.

That kind of black air is only perceptible to a student who is actually committed to the path or the teacher. It means that some connection is being made. It may be negative at that moment, but in the long run it works as part of the lessons through which you are progressing. If someone completely misses the pattern of the whole thing, it means that no connections are being made, and there is no chance of even getting into the environment.

Once Jamgön Kongtrül of Shechen lost his temper and threw his hand drum during an abhisheka ceremony. He was just about to do the hand-drum ritual, and suddenly he stopped and threw his drum. It landed on the head of a khenpo who was bald, and it made a little slit in his skin. The khenpo was actually the intended target, although it seemed as if Jamgön Kongtrül just threw the drum and it landed on the khenpo's head by accident. Jamgön Kongtrül was amazingly accurate.

You could regard doubting the guru as a mother's curse. Having doubt in the guru means that you not only have doubt in the guru alone, but you also think that you yourself might have made a mistake. You think that what the guru told you about yourself may not be valid, and that therefore your entire universe is not valid. The whole thing falls apart, and there is no vajra world; instead, the whole world is shaky, and dissolves into doubt and confusion.

So the guru is like the catalyst or the fuse. If you have doubt in the guru, this means that at the same time, you also begin to doubt yourself and the teaching and what you are doing. You begin to think that the whole thing is completely wasteful, which brings tremendous panic. But you could relate with that confusion as food for more inspiration. You could work with it. There is no doubt about that at all. In that case, the more confusion the better, because it sharpens your prajna. When your doubt reaches to the teaching itself, you are in trouble. But if you have power, if you have experience, I do not think you can fall away, because each time there is doubt, that in itself becomes fuel for the path. Doubt and confusion become fuel to further the journey.

I remember one time when I went to visit Jamgön Kongtrül of Shechen in his bedroom. It was in my early days when I had first met him, and I did not know that he was very informal. I thought he was a very formal person, or that he ought to be. He was sitting reclining on his bed and drinking tea, and I heard or picked up some kind of vibe from the tone of his voice that he was talking about me negatively. When I picked up on that little thing, I decided not to stay, because it would be too painful and embarrassing. His talking about me made it sound like I was excluded. There was a repelling vibration, which was rather unpleasant.

In spite of the love of my guru, there was something terrible happening. Jamgön Kongtrül was not actually looking at me. He should have felt me approaching and welcomed me, but he didn't. He was just lying there talking and laughing his head off. I was very irritated. There was something funny about the whole thing.

Later on, this incident came up in conversation, and he said, "I *do* talk behind your back, and I *do* lie down and make myself comfortable drinking tea, and I *do* have a good time." It was okay with him. I think that was a very kind mother's curse. And things worked out appropriately for me.

I remember another instance of a mother's curse that occurred with Jamgön Kongtrül of Shechen. He was very upset with a monk who, though claiming to be a teacher, misinterpreted the *Prajnaparamita Sutras*. The monk was a student of Khenpo Gangshar, who was Jamgön Kongtrül's spiritual son. Jamgön Kongtrül was so upset with the monk that he could not be gentle, and he began to physically beat up the monk, telling him, "You're wrong! You're wrong!"

The monk asked, "How do you know you are right?"

Jamgön Kongtrül answered, "Because I have vajra pride!"

The monk said, "That doesn't mean anything. I could say that as well."

So they did not connect, and the monk left with a group of people, traveling toward the monastery where he studied. He was wearing a Tibetan raincoat made out of felt, which covered his monk's robe. When bandits came along, although they usually did not shoot at monks, his layperson-style raincoat made them think he was a merchant, so he was shot right in the forehead.

There is another story, this time about Jamgön Kongtrül the Great. Jamgön Kongtrül the Great was invited to the southeastern part of Tibet by the people there, who were very devoted to him. The chief of that area felt threatened by his coming to teach; nevertheless, Jamgön Kongtrül the Great came and taught, but he never visited the chief.

When the chief received reports of how powerful, how wonderful, and how great Jamgön Kongtrül was, and how many people got instructions and benefits from his teachings, the chief was actually very frightened about the whole thing. He felt that he was Jamgön Kongtrül's opponent.

Instead of going to Jamgön Kongtrül and asking for his help, the chief became so angry that he raided the monastery where Jamgön Kongtrül had created a library, burning not only the books but also the woodblocks used for printing books. He destroyed the whole monastery, and afterward he made a big speech. He had decided that he needed to make up something extraordinary, because he felt rather guilty. At the same time, he was uncertain about what mystical power might strike him. So he said that if Jamgön Kongtrül had real power, if his teachings were true, then the chief himself would be killed by falling not from above to below, but from below to above; and instead of blood coming out of his mouth, milk would come out. The chief said that if that happened, he would regard Jamgön Kongtrül as a great teacher and his teachings as good, but failing that, he would prove that his own beliefs were right and Jamgön Kongtrül's were wrong.

Jamgön Kongtrül was very concerned. But when people asked him to do something to show the chief his power, he said, "I don't want to do anything to him, particularly. That seems to be wrong."

What happened was that the chief's words actually came true. One day he was inspecting oxen, which were part of the tax payment of the local people, and checking to see if they were suitable for plowing the fields in the early spring. Before he did so, he had a drink of yogurt and milk. According to this story, one of the oxen got loose and threw him. He landed on the roof, and milk came out of his mouth, and he died on the spot. That is a very interesting example of a mother's curse.

### Offering and Praise to the Worldly Deities: Subjugating National Ego

The seventh logos is called the offering and praise to the worldly deities, or *chötö*. It is another way of visualizing herukas, this time in the form of working with national ego, and subjugating national ego in order to teach.

THREE TYPES OF NATIONAL EGO. There are three types of national ego: the life force of dwelling place, the life force of clarity, and the life force of name.

*Life force of dwelling place.* The life force of dwelling place is connected with the ego of taking personal pride in a physical place.

*Life force of clarity.* The life force of clarity is connected with the ego of taking pride in philosophical and religious doctrine.

*Life force of name.* The life force of name is connected with the ego of national pride.

In order to encounter those three types of ego, you have the dwelling place as the physical visualization of the heruka, the clarity as the utterance of mantra, and the name as the meditation on the shunyata principle of the deity. In praising the deity and making offerings, you are subjugating the national ego, and at the same time you are presenting it as an offering. The general approach is one of making a link with the world in the fullest sense.

## Wrathful Mantra: Fearlessness

The eighth logos is the wrathful mantra, or *trag-ngak*. Wrathfulness is based on the idea that the mantra is no longer regarded as your savior. The power of the mantra demands a certain attitude. It demands that you are no longer centralized in your basic being, as "me," "myself," egohood, ego, or entity. With this logos, the power of the mantra is expected. It is invoked as a servant or attendant, as your subsidiary person.

This seems to be one of the basic tricks that we failed to see in the three lower yanas. Previously, we regarded mantra as something highly sacred that we should bow down to, and something that we should ask for its power and help. The eighth logos is the opposite of that. The power of mantra is no longer something that you should bow down to. Instead, you could ask for it; you could demand it. You could complain that it did not arrive in time to perform your wish. So there is a quality of directness and fearlessness.

## WORKING WITH THE EIGHT LOGOS

The eight logos are connected with visualization practices. Through these practices, you develop various personal experiences of magical power, such as the power connected with alcohol or amrita, with the dagger, with the mother principle, with the three neighs of a horse, or with the four wheels. All these practices are very visual and very artistic. When you perceive the world in accordance with the eight logos, you begin to see all kinds of directions, understandings, and relationships without any difficulties.

All the deities here are wrathful. There is less need for seducing people into tantra at this point, for people are into it already. They can take a direct message very simply. And that direct message is wrathful, not as anger but as energy. The vajrayana is sympathetic to samsara. It accepts the ugliness of samsara and wears it as an ornament. The vajrayana is never embarrassed by samsara. Using the fear of the intensity of vajrayana as inspiration is part of the vajrayana psyche. You get the psychic feeling of the environment being unfriendly, alien, and terrifying, so there might be a tendency to close down from the intensity. You feel as if you are about to be raped.

The eight logos are connected with the accomplishment of siddhis, or powers. In addition to the eight logos, you have the guru manifesting as the heruka. But the guru does not give any siddhi except enlightenment itself.* The eight logos practice is very much a step toward the maha ati experience of complete openness. Without some understanding of the eight logos, you will have difficulty understanding maha ati because those eight experiences cover all life situations: domestic, emotional, spiritual, and physical. They are some of the best visualization techniques you could ever receive, as far as self-existing visualization techniques are concerned. The eight logos approach has enormous scope.

All eight logos work in terms of a personal relationship between the student and the teacher. For instance, the amrita could turn into poison, and the penetrating kilaya could hurt you, and instead of spinning the wheels against others, you could hurt yourself. There are many such consequences built in, which happen constantly. That is one of the characteristics of vajrayana. You may not be an accomplished magician, and as a student you may know nothing at all about this particular type of magic, but once you are included in the lineage, you realize that you have some power by the very fact of your being included.

You are exposed to such possibilities by these ideas and by the words that say there are such possibilities. This constitutes some kind of transmission from the lineage. With this transmission you become a suitable student and magician, suitable not only because you could hurt others, but because you could hurt yourself as well. That is why the vajrayana is dangerous in many ways. You are given a weapon that you cannot handle

---

* The *siddhis* include both ordinary siddhis, which consist of various magical powers, and supreme siddhi or buddhahood.

if you are taught before your time. There is danger physically to your life, and beyond that, there is the danger that you might end up being Rudra. What makes for a student becoming Rudra, basically, is destroying your teacher. It is thinking that you have learned something from the teacher, but then concocting your own style out of the whole thing. And when you go back to your teacher and they say, "No, that is not my teaching," you either kill the guru or reject their teaching, thinking that yours is better.

## Higher and Lower Logos

The first five logos are connected with the higher approach, and the last three are related with the samsaric or lower approach. In this case, "higher" or "lower" is purely a matter of how fundamental that logos is, or how pragmatic. So when we talk about lower, it is the pragmatic aspect of your practice, and when we talk about higher, we are talking about the fundamentality of the whole thing.

These last three logos are not connected with particular buddha-families, although they are placed on appropriate areas of the mandala when big sadhanas are held. They are regarded as a kind of fringe, as somewhat trivial. From the sixth logos on, you are beginning to get in league with the dakinis. You are trying to play their games. This is regarded as a very dangerous thing to do, because it might create chaos. You might catch the flu, or get into little accidents, or experience other little things like that. It may lead to inflicting pain on yourself, in order to remind you that you are going astray, or it may lead to inflicting pain on others, in order to remind them that they have gone astray.

## Tuning In to the Rugged Power and Ordinariness of the World

It may seem that mahayogayana is quite enough, and that there is no need to go beyond it. When we work on this yana, it seems to be quite complete. If you would like to know what real living visualization is all about, this yana gives you some kind of clue. Visualization does not have to be just thinking about an image, but you pick up on the environment and the feeling of the whole thing. You see that there are real experiences happening: there is penetrating, and there is the anti-death potion. So you do not have to hypothesize that someday you are going to be saved, but there is a kind of instant liberation. At the same time, that liberation is part of the path, rather than being the final goal.

The idea is that if you function beautifully, that is enlightenment. It is a very tantric approach. You are already in the realm of sambhogakaya, and this practice is already a part of you, so your samsaric projections are another form of visualization and symbolism. Without them, you could not visualize. You would not know what we meant by "knife" if you had never seen a knife, and you could not visualize blood if you had never seen blood, or semen if you had never seen semen. It is a very living thing.

This is why vajrayana has been feared, and why it has been known to create enormous panic. It is also why vajrayana is regarded as so dangerous, because it says very dangerous things about the phenomenal world. It says that there is nothing great or magical about anything at all. But that reinterpretation or re-look at the phenomenal world is so rugged, so ordinary, so raw and precise, that an ordinary piece of rock will feel shy if a vajrayana person describes it. That rock will crack because it is so shy about having its rockness talked about by a vajrayana person. It will be reduced into something else. It will want to become sand and not remain a rock.

If you ask where these powers come from, you could say they come from the power of truth. Things are said precisely as they are, and as a result there is no room left for conning or deceiving. That kind of truth becomes mantra, and it has enormous power behind it. It is precisely what the wrathful mantra is.

Mahayoga tantra is vast, and it includes a whole range of practices. It may not be necessary to know all the practices, but knowing the meanings behind the subtle details of the eight logos and other aspects of mahayoga will give you the feeling of the whole thing. Such meanings are not just historical, and they are not particularly liturgical. You may think you can just get in touch with the basic energies, but if you have only a rough idea about mahayoga teachings, you will miss a lot. That kind of fixed idea might block your awareness of other much subtler areas.

# 62

# *Mahayoga:*
# *Nondual Practice*

*In visualization, any concept we use to label the phenomenal world is being transmuted. Because of that, there is more room for simplicity and directness. Visualizations from this point of view are not separate from the reality that we experience in ordinary, everyday life.*

## PRACTICING THE THREE POISONS

As far as practice is concerned, mahayoga tantra recommends the three poisons: passion, aggression, and ignorance. In mahayoga you are not trying to boycott the three poisons, but instead you are trying to tread on them. That is, you work with emotions rather than dispelling them. A student develops a much greater sense of crazy wisdom in this yana. There is a greater level of craziness, and there are also more opportunities and possibilities. The eight logos principles are a similar approach, in that each of them is very vivid and very obvious as far as the practitioner is concerned.

## VIVIDNESS

In mahayoga, the experience of visualization is much more vivid. The nature of visualization here and in the two remaining yanas is not as much of a personal trip, and it does not involve as much personal imagery or concepts as the three earlier yanas. Rather, mahayoga visualization is based on realizing that magic and reality exist in the phenomenal world; they exist on the spot. The hotness of fire, the wetness of water, the encompassingness of space, the solidity of earth, and the moving-expansiveness of air are all included. So you are much more in contact with reality, and you are able to appreciate the magical aspect of the phenomenal world. That makes visualization much more vivid, much more realistic, and much more genuine. Visualization becomes natural to you. So although the specific visualizations still take the form of various deities, such as herukas and dakinis, you still have a sense of reality taking place.

## Sympathetic Continuity

In visualization practice, you can produce the jnanasattva within yourself because you have the potential; eventually you are going to become one yourself. You have buddha nature, so you have the blood in you, in any case. Otherwise, it would be ludicrous to say that the jnanasattva and samayasattva dissolve into one other. If you try to combine two conflicting chemistries, it does not work. But in this case, because there are sympathetic chemistries, you can join them together. Some kind of continuity exists in you that is jnanasattva in nature, although this continuity is not apparent.

In appearance, you try to visualize yourself, which is called samayasattva. You create a sort of fake jnanasattva. Then, having visualized the fake jnanasattva, the true jnanasattva comes and accepts your fakeness, and you begin to become one. The idea is that there is a sympathetic continuity. The basic idea of ground tantra is that you are already enlightened, so there is no need for you to do anything. Because of that, what you are doing is just a needless job. But at the same time, you must associate with what you actually are, rather than what you might be.

The jnanasattva is the wakeful aspect, and the samayasattva is the first glimpse of things as they are. If you see that you are just about to be run over by a car, the first shock is the samayasattva level. When the car suddenly stops half an inch away from you, you have the wakeful aspect, which is the jnanasattva. You begin to see your yidam there in the form of a motorcar, a road, paranoia, or shakiness.

At this level, sound and vision and thought processes are all operating at once. How you experience all this depends on where you are with your yidam. It is quite specific. You may be faced with the doorkeeper of the mandala, or you may be faced with one of the messengers, or gauris. You may be faced with a member of the entourage, with the inner circle of yidams, or even with the central deity itself. Anything is feasible. There are endless possibilities.

Identifying with what is happening in this way can take place, if you actually understand what you are practicing. That is why Jamgön Kongtrül the Great, Longchen Rabjam, the third Karmapa Rangjung Dorje, and the entire lineage place enormous emphasis on students having an intellectual understanding of tantra. You need at least some understanding of tantra in order to have a way of identifying yourself with such deities and situations. It is absolutely important; otherwise, you are completely lost. You cannot just operate on high hopes; you do not just receive an abhisheka and hope for the best. That does not make any sense.

## THE INDIVISIBILITY OF PERCEPTION
## AND EMPTINESS

Another outstanding idea of this yoga is that all dharmas are seen as mind manifestations, or as the miracle of the indivisibility of perceptual experience and emptiness. So there is a sympathetic attitude to the phenomenal world. The phenomenal world is no longer sacred or mysterious, nor for that matter is it secular. Any ordinary thing that we do is in itself sacred. So nothing is regarded as an exclusively secular or worldly experience, and nothing is regarded as exclusively sacred, either.

In the experience of mahayoga, the phenomenal world is seen as its own entity and in its own way, because its own way is straight, simple, and uncomplicated. Therefore, it is possible to apply the principle and philosophy of visualization, and the visualization of perceptions or concepts. In this way, the fact that we have labeled our world is something that could fit into the visualization as well, as part of a gigantic mandala of workability. At this point, tantrikas are able to sink their minds completely into nonduality. Therefore, it has been said in the texts that mahayoga is superior to the lower or external yoga practices that we discussed.

## FORMLESS PRACTICE

The attitude to visualization in mahayoga is not devoid of the meditative aspect, the sampannakrama or formless practice. Even the samayasattva visualization that ordinary people start with is highly influenced by the meditative state. Since the samayasattva is highly soaked in nonduality already, there is no need for a sense of separateness between the jnanasattva and samayasattva. Instead, there seems to be an emphasis on the indivisibility of the meditative state and visualization.

According to mahayoga, the meditative state and the visualization are completely one, so bringing the jnanasattva into the visualization is no big hassle. There is no confusion or conflict. Even anuttarayoga makes a big deal out of the jnanasattva's blessing of the samayasattva. But in the case of mahayoga, there is very little problem with that transition.

The notion that the ordinary has been made into the sacred is much less prominent here, because even at the ordinary level, a nondualistic attitude has developed. That is actually a source of vajra pride. Even on the level of samayasattva, a sense of sacredness is evolving. Because that is already happening, there is no problem in developing self-existing wisdom or simplicity into vajra pride. Things are already developing in that direction, so one does not have to change or to feel belittled.

## VISUALIZATION AND EVERYDAY LIFE

Mahayoga visualization practice is related to your everyday life and to very domestic things. For example, you visualize the herukas or yidams in union with their consorts, eating and drinking, treading on the enemy, and so forth. But unlike everyday life, in visualization everything happens at once. Everything that we do in our life, the deities manage to do simultaneously. From the samsaric point of view, if we could do everything at once, it would be delightful. It is the essence of our wishful thinking. But since we only have one body and one state of mind, we can only do one thing at a time, which makes us very tired and regretful some of the time, and very confused at other times. I think that is why the deities use samsaric images on a nirvanic level, on a type of ambidextrous or all-pervasive level.

In visualization practice, the emotions and energies are all concentrated at one level, which is an outrageous idea. It is an extremely perverted idea in many ways, which is why it is a secret. You cannot understand what it is all about. You cannot be all that outrageous; nobody would dare to do it. People are usually very cowardly about their own habits, their own wishful thinking. So if you are actually able to get into this by means of transcendental practice, it is extraordinarily refreshing and crazy at the same time. Finally you are able to actually make some sense out of your life and your emotions and your longings and your pains and your pleasures and everything. That seems to be the basic point.

Visualization practice is right to the point of our life, rather than trying to replace our life with some cosmic livelihood. That is the essence of visualization, and that is why we can identify with all the herukas and yidams. That is why there is this possibility. The deities are not protectors and they are not objects of worship, but they are states of mind that we can identify with. All our hopes and fears, all that we want, is embodied in those particular images.

When you are visualizing, usually your eyes are closed; but when you are meditating, your eyes are usually open. In the case of meditation, if you close your eyes you begin to get caught in fantasies of all kinds, whereas if you open your eyes, you just see the naked world. However, in the case of visualization, if you open your eyes you begin to project superimposed hallucinations on your rug, your pillow, or your wall. That is why your eyes are closed; you close them so you can have a completely clean world. The purpose of both techniques is the same, but they are done in opposite ways.

In postvisualization practice, you do not see the herukas serving tea or driving your cab, but you have a sense of their presence constantly. It is similar to the way we always experience things. When you feel depressed, you see everybody as depressed; when you are drunk, you think that everybody is drunk with you; and when you are angry, you feel that everybody is mocking you. You have that kind of attitude toward the deities in the visualization.

The visualization is part of your daily activities, the daily experience of your life. It is not so much that since herukas are clad in human-skin shawls and tiger-skin skirts and wearing bone ornaments, you are trying to hallucinate everybody wearing tiger-skin skirts and running around in bone ornaments. But there is a very personal and experiential sense of the presence of various herukas. So the visualization is happening in the postmeditative state as well.

It is essential to know the various philosophical and experiential attitudes regarding one's practice and one's phenomena. If a person does not have a great deal of understanding in terms of utpattikrama and sampannakrama, if the visualization practice and the meditative practice are not properly done, these practices may become dangerous. It has been said that they are even more dangerous as you get into higher tantra. If those two practices, visualization and formless meditation, are not combined together properly, you will be creating a seed to become Rudra, and it is said that the teacher as well as the student will be heading for trouble.

## 63

# Anuyoga:
# Joining Space and Wisdom

*Anuyoga is connected with the epitome of prajna, the wisdom flame. So the style of relating with the phenomenal world in anuyoga is very passionate, like a flame. Ordinary passion is like water that is sweeping you along uncontrollably. But fire is clean-cut passion. In anuyoga, instead of drinking water to satisfy your thirst, you drink fire.*

### UNIFYING THE FIRST EIGHT YANAS

Anuyoga is known as the yana of passion, or the passionate yana. It is also referred to as the upayayana. In fact, all the tantras are based on the idea of upaya, or skillfulness, which is why tantra is superior to the sutra teachings.

The skillfulness of anuyoga is based on passion and joy. There is a passionate aspect within the upaya or masculine approach, and you are able to use that passion and to apply it. So the skillful aspect of anuyoga is in the application of passion; embryonic passion and complete passion are combined as skillful means. This is the last yana of Buddhism in which we could discuss passion and sexuality and the relationship of *that* and *this*. Of all the tantras in Gautama Buddha's teachings, anuyoga includes the highest form of karmamudra. Later, in atiyoga, something else comes up.

In the Nyingma tradition, people practice mahayoga and atiyoga a great deal, but few seem to practice anuyoga. Somehow this yana has been bypassed. There is very little encouragement for anuyoga practice, except in *The Tibetan Book of the Dead,* which is practiced by everybody, and is one of the few anuyoga texts that we have.

In vajrayana, the basic idea is that after the bodhisattva path, you can choose to practice any of the six tantric yanas. It depends on your teacher. Your teacher is usually an expert in one of the yanas, so you begin by doing the particular practice that your teacher is most confident in. You get completely soaked in that practice, go through it completely, and maybe get just a little bit of siddhi. Then, because you now have a foot-hold in tantra, you can go back and survey the rest of the tantric yanas. For instance, if you have a teacher who is an expert on kriyayoga, then from kriyayoga, you can study atiyoga as well. However, since kriyayoga is the lowest of the tantric yanas, this example may be problematic due to kriyayoga's hang-ups with physical cleanliness and diet.

At the anuyoga level, you are still relating with the physical vajra master. But at this point, there is a further understanding of the importance of samaya and of the guru principle: the guru has become so big and cosmic that you are the guru, and the guru is in you.

Anuyoga is progressing toward the yana of conquering, or the imperial yana of maha ati. Therefore, this yana can also be referred to as the upaya-yana of conquering. Conquering makes the definite statement that you are looking back to the previous yanas—you are looking completely and thoroughly. So anuyoga is very important in terms of unifying the first eight yanas. Unifying the yanas is a way of developing a more panoramic vision by means of upaya, passion, and joy.

Often we have the misunderstanding that when we talk about passion, we mean a driving force alone. Lust or passion is viewed as an uncontrol-lable energy that exists in us. But in this case, when we refer to passion, we are talking about the end product as well as the process of passion. The end product is joy and bliss, and the process, which is based on the inspiration of the end product, is also joy and bliss. So passion is very much the reference point here. That is why this particular yana is called the joyous yana or the passionate yana.

Passion is like a rain cloud that is completely filled with the potential of rain. You begin to see dark dramatic clouds, and such clouds begin to proclaim that there is going to be rain. In a sense, that is a much more powerful statement than the rain itself. The preparation for rain is much more dramatic than the end product. There is resounding thunder, dark clouds gathering, the wind blowing around, and the feeling of potential rain. Similarly, in anuyoga, there is a sense of the powerful quality of passion. And passion, in this case, is the attraction toward the phenomenal world and the entities or nonentities that exist around the world.

## PRIMORDIAL ENLIGHTENMENT

The attitude of anuyoga to the phenomenal world and oneself is that you exist as primevally enlightened, as a primordial enlightened being. So enlightenment does not need to be sought after or looked for. Therefore, anuyoga has the quality of a mandala of bodhi mind, or the awakened state of being. The idea is that enlightenment does not need to be sought with particular hardship. In fact, the approach from this yana onward is that, instead of searching for enlightenment or freedom by stepping out of samsara, you search for independence and freedom by stepping in. So stepping in is the more enlightened way, rather than trying to find a way out.

## SPACE AND WISDOM

In anuyoga, two definite principles are emphasized: unbornness and intelligence, or space and wisdom. Space is connected with the unbornness, with not having an origin and not having birth. Wisdom is connected with intelligence. So the basic outlook of anuyoga is the combination of space and wisdom.

The notion of space and the notion of shunyata are alike. In fact, they may be the same, but there is a question of how to view their sameness. In the shunyata experience of mahayana, you still have a measurement, you still have a volume; but in this case, there is no measurement and there is nothing to measure with. So there is no way to detect the difference between emptiness and space. There is no ruler, and even if you have a ruler, it is like rubber: you can stretch it as much as you like. It is purely dancing with phenomena.

Space is workability. It is openness in the sense of not having any handles to latch onto. Therefore, it is unborn, nonexistent. However, it may be slightly misleading to say "nonexistent," for when we say something is nonexistent, we regard it as a nonentity, which is not quite the idea here. The point is that you *do* exist in a sense, but you are not born. At the same time, this does not mean that you exist eternally, which also seems to be a wrong outlook. It means that you never have been born; therefore, you have space; and because of that, there is also intelligence. Because you are not born, because you do not exist eternally, there is a sense of self-existence, which is the jnana principle of all-pervasive wisdom or intelligence.

This distinction between nonexistent and unborn is connected with the distinction between *shentong* and *rangtong.* According to the shentong view, there is room for duality and richness, rather than having to wipe out everything completely. Anuyoga talks about the unborn and unoriginated much more than the previous yanas. It talks about dissolving boundaries. Dissolving boundaries is an aspect of nonmeditation, but you still have something to dissolve, which makes it a subtle form of meditation rather than nonmeditation.

## Boundaries and Nonduality

What separates anuyoga from the previous yanas is that the previous yanas were situations set up in order to attain certain understandings, whereas this yana is self-existing. In anuyoga, there is an element of much greater craziness. In terms of the next yana, or atiyoga, there is not really any separation. The anuyoga relationship with atiyoga is one of dissolving the boundary. You begin to see that the whole world is made of a gigantic candy machine, or a lake of honey.

When you have dissolved all boundaries, there is a greater version of duality. So dissolving boundaries brings us back to the question of duality. But at this point, duality is no longer a hang-up or a problem; it is an expression of wisdom. In terms of duality, the first truth is that the phenomenal world is seen as empty. The second truth is that the phenomenal world is seen as empty because of its dual purpose, because vision and emptiness are dancing together. When the phenomenal world is seen as

---

* *Shentong* ("empty of other") is the view that the nature of mind is stainless and empty of all that is false, but is not empty of its own inherent buddha nature. *Rangtong* ("empty of self") is the view that each phenomenon is empty of itself, what it seems to be—period.

empty, there is a quality of complete unity, but you can still have greater duality along with the dissolving of boundaries. They work together, in some sense, so there is no particular problem.

Eating is a very simple example. If you consume food, when the food is inside you, you are united with the food; but you develop a greater duality between the food and yourself, because you are satisfied with the food. Without duality, there would be no satisfaction and no joy. If the indivisibility can be part of the separateness, then there is something to be indivisible from. So separateness brings more space, and more space brings nonduality.

## MAHASUKHA

Mahasukha, or the great joy principle, also exists here, because you are able to grow up and develop all the faculties without being born, which is the state of nowness. This nowness or *thisness* does exist. The past is purely a nonexistent myth; therefore, you exist in nowness. Not only do you exist, but you exist with great joy. You do not need any handles, you do not need any encouragement, you do not need any case history. So the great joy comes from looseness. Looseness means that no leash is attached to you, and no family trees are attached to you. You exist because that is the way you are.

Whether you sit or eat, whether you follow particular social norms, or whatever you do, what matters is what happens in your mind. So sitting practice is recommended, even at this level. There are sadhana practices where you obviously have to sit. You cannot do them in a taxicab, but you have to set aside time to do them. But in anuyoga, the attitude is that in sitting practice, nothing happens but an exaggerated feeling of well-being, with the addition of a little bit of drunkenness and the feeling that you are in love with the cosmos.

This is like the experience of being in love. If you are able to fall in love with somebody completely, it gives you physical sensations. When you are in love with somebody, you feel that you are bouncing in a bed of rose petals. This is that same kind of feeling. It is as though the sweetness of honey is beginning to seep through the pores of your skin—with a slight touch of alcohol in it. You are immersed in this gigantic, fantastic sensation; you are oozed into something really nice.

That is the kind of great joy we are talking about here. It makes you really feel that nothing is begun; it is there already. There is no origin, there is no going, and there is no coming.

## LIBERATION AND CONVICTION

In anuyoga, prajna is considered to be the messenger of liberation, and upaya is considered to be the path of conviction. The upaya path of conviction is a meditative state like the mahamudra experience we discussed already. Mahamudra awareness comes from samsaric experience, but the anuyoga upaya path regenerates the whole thing in a much more sophisticated way than the mahamudra of the lower tantras. In anuyoga, the liberation of prajna is not discriminating in the sense of rejecting the bad and accepting the good, but rather in the sense of knowing the lover and the lovemaker, the feminine and the masculine, as separate entities, and enjoying the realm of wisdom and space. That realm of space and wisdom includes the experience of total conviction and resourcefulness, and the discovery of all kinds of upayas.

## THE TURBULENT RIVER AND THE FLAME

Anuyoga is connected with the epitome of prajna, the wisdom flame. So the style of relating with the phenomenal world in anuyoga is very passionate, like a flame. Ordinary passion is like water that is sweeping you along uncontrollably. But fire is clean-cut passion. In anuyoga, instead of drinking water to satisfy your thirst, you drink fire. All that we put in the fire is burnt. It does not leave behind any garbage, whereas water does leave garbage. When a flood comes along, you have driftwood or dead bodies, and it is very messy.

One of the realization songs connected with anuyoga says that practitioners would see that "the flame is like the river." I think it was sung by Shri Simha, one of the great teachers. The whole experience of visualization, with the earth shaking, and space quaking, and death and everything, is summed up in that verse. The river is not just a river, but it is a turbulent river. It is a big river, not just a little brook. That river is like a flame; it is an expression of passion. So water is passion, and fire is also passion.

You could say that these two images of passion are fighting each other, that the turbulent river and the flame are at war. The water is related with space and the flame is related with wisdom, but they both are images of passion. When the ordinary passion of the river is transformed into flame, it becomes lively passion. At that point, it is no longer ordinary passion, but tantric passion. The river is a blander version of passion. But the anuyoga experience of passion, the flame, is superior passion. The whole continent is on fire.

# 64

# Anuyoga:
# Empowerment

*In the anuyoga abhisheka, or empowerment, having gone through the realms and yanas, you are also initiated into the realm of the one hundred deities of anuyoga: the forty-two peaceful deities and the fifty-eight wrathful deities. These deities are the same deities that are seen in* The Tibetan Book of the Dead.

## THE ABHISHEKA JOURNEY

In the anuyoga abhisheka, you are led through a journey that starts by going through the samsaric realms, and continues by going through the stages of the path.

### Going through the Samsaric Realms

On the first part of this journey, you go through all six realms, starting with the realm of hell. You are given a series of painted pictures or cards with various symbols on them, symbolizing that you are now properly in hell, now properly in the human realm, now properly in the realm of the gods, and so on. You start with the most gross level of the lower realms: the hell realm and the hungry ghost realm. Then you move on to the animal realm, and to the higher realms: the human realm, the jealous gods realm, and the gods realm. So the level of your state of mind is progressing somewhat. In this process, extreme pain and extreme indulgence in pleasure are like two poles.

When you are in the realm of hell, it is very definite, but when your pain at being in hell begins to become slightly lighter, you begin to get hungry. You feel that there is a gap where you might get some relief or get a break. As soon as you get a break from the torture chamber, you pick up cigarettes to smoke or a cookie to eat, which is usually what one does for a break. Now you are in the hungry ghost realm. Beyond that, you go completely stupid and berserk. You enter the animal realm, and you just crawl on the floor, or growl at somebody or groan.

And then, when you get a little bit more intelligent, you begin to look for an object of passion, which is the human realm. Then you keep trying to improve your livelihood. You think that if you have gotten what you wanted, you should make it better. And beyond that, once you have made something better, you should defend it. You keep a very tight hold on the whole thing. At this point, you are dealing with the realm of the jealous gods. And when you get rid of that, you go completely berserk in another way, which is the higher realm counterpart of the animal realm: the realm of the gods. You are dazed in your love and light. You feel so good, and you couldn't care less about anything. That kind of god realm is also an obstacle.

So in this initiation, you are introduced to the realm of hell; from there you begin to transcend hell and make steps toward the hungry ghost level; then you transcend the hungry ghost level and move into the animal realm; and from there you go to the human realm, the jealous god realm, and the realm of the gods. You go through the process of actually experiencing your own world. You have not had a proper glimpse of it before, so the initiation into the pure samsaric world is regarded as very important.

## Going through the Stages of the Path

Having experienced the six realms, you then experience the stages of the path, starting with the path of accumulation. You start with the shravakayana and the pratyekabuddhayana paths. To receive the essence of those particular yanas, you receive ordination. But in this case, instead of receiving ordination as a monk or nun as you would in the actual hinayana tradition, ordination is turned into an abhisheka.

After the hinayana abhishekas, you also receive the bodhisattva abhisheka. The difference between the bodhisattva vow and the bodhisattva abhisheka is that a vow is just a promise. By promising certain things, you feel you have committed yourself to this particular system. In an abhisheka, you not only make a vow or promise, but you begin to connect with the magical aspect. The magical quality begins to enter into your system so that you actually become a bodhisattva.

The anuyoga abhisheka also includes going through the lower tantric yanas of kriyayoga, upayoga, and yogayana, as well as the higher tantric yanas of mahayoga and anuyoga. In the anuyoga abhisheka, everything leading up to the maha ati level and the path of no more learning is combined together: the path of accumulation, the path of unification, the path of seeing, and the path of meditation. The point of the anuyoga abhisheka is to make you into a professional rather than a layperson. So you actually become a bodhisattva or an arhat on the spot.

In this abhisheka, technically you are going backward, but experientially you are collecting more richness. It is like visiting your parents. When you visit your parents, you do not say you are going backward, but you say you are going home. When you do go home, you learn more about what you were, which is educational. You do not actually go backward. It is like life: You cannot go backward in life or reduce yourself into an infant, but you can return to places you left and refresh your case history. You do not undo things as you go backward by trying to unlearn everything and start right from the beginning. What you have learned cannot be forgotten, so from that point of view, you are still going forward.

So if you are doing anuyoga practice, and you include kriyayoga as part of your practice, you are not going backward. Instead, anuyoga is being adorned with the kriyayoga approach. You are collecting more things, rather than going backward.

Upayoga and mahayoga and even anuttarayoga have a tendency to be snobbish, in that the other yanas are rejected or not even seen. But looking ahead to the final yana, or atiyoga, we see that it is a very considerate yana. It has consideration for the other yanas, going down to the kriyayoga level. Atiyoga is quite rightly like a benevolent dictator or king who has consideration for everything. It takes into consideration the lower yanas, including the hinayana and the mahayana. Anuyoga has a hint of that as well, and anuyoga abhishekas are also connected with that approach. It is good to relate with somebody who has a view of the rest of the world, rather than just purely being soaked up in their own ideas.

### Being Initiated into the One-Hundred Deity Mandala

In the anuyoga abhisheka or empowerment, having gone through the realms and the yanas, you are also initiated into the realm of the one hundred deities of anuyoga: the forty-two peaceful deities and the fifty-eight wrathful deities. These deities are the same deities that are seen in *The Tibetan Book of the Dead*.

## THREE CONFIRMATIONS

Having received these abhishekas, you develop what are known as the three types of confirmation.

### Great Confirmation

The first confirmation is called the great confirmation. Now you are what you are; you are known as "Vajra Master So-and-So." You have actually joined the vidyadhara family, the crazy-wisdom-holder family.

### Great Protection

The second confirmation is called the great protection. Having already received the great confirmation, you also have the authority and empowerment to transmit this to others.

### Great Energy

The third confirmation is called the great energy, or the completion of energy. With the energy confirmation, you are able to deal with the phenomenal world and the direction in which the phenomenal world is approaching you. You are actually able to see it and play with it in a non-dualistic, unbiased way.

## THREE MANDALAS

In anuyoga and in atiyoga, all existence is seen as a mandala, and the whole universe is turning into a gigantic mandala principle. The inanimate and animate realms are seen as a mandala, as a charnel ground. All thought processes are seen as the thoughtlessness or unbornness of the mandala, and all the elements and activities, which manifest as various deities, are seen as the self-existence of the mandala.

Three types of mandala exist in anuyogayana. Such mandalas are experiential rather than the kind of physical setups that existed in the previous tantric yanas.

### The Mandala of Isness

The first mandala is the unborn mandala, or the mandala of isness. The Tibetan term for this mandala is *ye chi-shin-pe kyilkhor. Ye* means primordial, *chi-shin-pe* means "as it is" or "isness," and *kyilkhor* means "mandala"; so *ye chi-shin-pe kyilkhor* is the "mandala of primordial isness."

This mandala is based on seeing all dharmas as the expressions of mind. Therefore, mind is unborn, simple, and without limitation. Without limitation is referred to as Samantabhadri, or actually the boundless and limitless cervix of Samantabhadri, the feminine principle. All the world comes from that. The phenomenal world is created from that, and returns to that. Therefore, this mandala is known as primeval or primordial isness.

The metaphor of returning to the cervix may be unfamiliar according to our conventional norms, but here it is combined with the idea of the charnel ground. The indivisibility of cervix and charnel ground makes the whole thing one ground: a place to die and a place to be born. The place that you are born is a gigantic cervix that keeps on giving birth. The place where you die is like a gigantic vacuum cleaner that sucks you up into death. Your body dissolves into the elements in this gigantic vacuum system.

### The Mandala of Self-Existence

The second mandala is the unceasing mandala or the mandala of self-existence, which is referred to as *lhündrup kyi kyilkhor. Lhündrup* means "self-existence" or "spontaneous presence"; so *lhündrup kyi kyilkhor* means the "mandala of self-existence."

This mandala is represented by Samantabhadra, the masculine principle. Everything that happens is the unceasing play of phenomena. This unceasing activity takes place without any particular bias as to which activity should be acted out first. So phenomenal experience is a natural flow, rather than something that you censor based on which activity would be best to create first or second. Everything we experience in our world is free-flowing, a constant flowing process.

## The Mandala of the Awakened State of Mind

Because the first two mandalas are the feminine and the masculine principles, the third one is called the son of great joy. The prince that Samantabhadri and Samantabhadra give birth to is a very joyful prince, with no depression. This prince is a crossbreed of samsara and nirvana. If you had children of samsara all the time, you would finally end up with apes of some kind, and if you had children of nirvana all the time, they would end up being too ethereal. So with this prince, you have a product of both samsara and nirvana. You have a cross between two races. But the birth of this prince still takes place on nirvanic or vajrayana ground.

In Tibetan, this mandala is called *changsem kyi kyilkhor. Changsem* refers to the awakened state of mind. The idea is that the awakened state of mind is born from its mother, the unborn, originated simplicity, and its father, the unceasing, unbiased approach to life. Between the two, the phenomenal world exists, and the mandala is produced and developed. So the indivisibility of space and wisdom produces the son of great joy.

That is the basic principle of the three mandalas. So in talking about the three mandalas, we do not mean physical mandalas, but purely and simply mandalas as levels of perception. Openness, energy, and the indivisibility of the two make up the three mandalas that the student is experiencing or has already experienced.

The anuyoga abhisheka is a complete journey that incorporates the six realms of samsara as well as the stages of the path from the hinayana refuge vow and the mahayana bodhisattva vow through the tantric yanas. On this journey you are introduced to the one-hundred deity mandala, and to the principles of Samantabhadra and Samantabhadri, indivisible space and wisdom.

65

# Anuyoga:
# Practice

*In anuyoga, we refer to self-existing femininity as the lover, and
self-existing masculinity as the lovemaker. In this tantra, there is
a lot of reference made to karmamudra practice; but in anuyoga,
karmamudra is more a practice of dissolving ourselves into space.
So this yana teaches us to realize the indivisibility of space and
wisdom, or ying and yeshe.*

## VISUALIZATION

In anuyoga the visualization of the one hundred deities arise from open
space suddenly and dramatically, like a fish leaping from water.

### Creating Space

The characteristic of visualization and sadhana practice in anuyoga tantra
is getting closer to the maha ati approach, which emphasizes sampannakrama, or formless meditation. The basic principle is that visualizations
are accompanied by the meditative experience. Sampannakrama is the
basis of the whole thing. Because you are able to create a space that is not
connected with trying to explain anything to yourself in logical terms, or
trying to structure things in any way at all, there is a feeling of positive
hopelessness. You feel that it is not worth manufacturing anything, trying
to produce anything, or trying to develop any idea, attitude, or principle.

That creates the maha ati type of basic space. So there is a great emphasis in anuyoga on the need for meditating on nonmeditation.

Nonmeditation is very important. You simply do it; you just pretend that you are there. You do not pretend because you are so stupid that you can *only* pretend, but because you are so awake that nothing is real except pretense. Usually, when you pretend to be somebody or something, it means that you are trying to cheat somebody. But in this case, pretense does not mean cheating. It is just self-existence. You are. You are as you are. Therefore, you might be so. That is pretense. You pretend to be a nonmeditator by meditating, if you can make heads or tails of that.

In discussing all this, there is not very much to say, since there is nothing to be said and no one to say anything to anybody. Nevertheless, we could pretend.

## Creating the Mandala

Having created basic space, creating the mandala is a sudden process. The deity and its house arise from uttering certain seed syllables—and as soon as you utter the seed syllables, the deity appears. In the texts, this is described as being like a fish jumping out of the water. It is as if suddenly the jack-in-the-box pops open, and the samayasattva and jnanasattva principles arise simultaneously. You do not have to bring the energies of samayasattva and jnanasattva together at this point. Once the openness is there, and once it is sparked by the sound of the bija mantra, suddenly that brings this great vision of deities.

In anuyoga, sudden visualization can arise even without using bija mantras, or seed syllables. In sudden visualization and sudden realization, you see the yidams and become one with them immediately, without using seed syllables and without a gradual buildup of images. It has become very personal. You have a very direct relationship with the yidam; you are almost becoming one with the yidam. You are no longer you; you are the yidam. Because yidams do not exist, they do not need any sustenance, which is why we talked about unborn and unoriginated. The jnanasattva that you invoke is nonexistent. That is the aspect of wisdom.

Having visualized the deity, the deity's body is adorned with the syllables OM AH HUM. The HUM aspect is akin to the *samadhisattva*, meaning that the samadhi principle is still in you, so you cannot get carried away with the visualization, thinking that now you are united with the jnanasattva and everything is going to be okay. A faint touch of awareness is still required.

## The One Hundred Deities

The central deities in anuyoga are the one hundred families of tathagatas. There are fifty-eight wrathful deities and forty-two peaceful ones, which makes one hundred deities in all. That mandala of peaceful and wrathful deities has been described in *The Tibetan Book of the Dead*. *The Tibetan Book of the Dead* speaks of yidams very much in psychological terms rather than deifying them. It describes how if you miss the first boat, you have another chance. Basically, the wrathful deities come from your head or brain, as an expression of vajra intellect, and the peaceful deities come from your heart, as an expression of padma sybaritic hospitality and intuition. All the deities are regarded as tathagatas.

Along with the one hundred families of deities, there are seventy-five different abhishekas. We could go through the details of the mandala's deities, but the point is that in the previous yanas, going through the details made sense, whereas here the details do not matter all that much. At this level, the basic norm seems more important, and as we go on to the atiyoga level, it is the same. Instead of trying to make sense of the details, we see that there is something coming together that makes more sense.

## Flash and Thunder

In anuyoga, the mandala has, as usual, the vajra family in the East, the ratna family in the South, and so forth. But the mandala setup is related with very directly and very simply. The construction of the mandala is felt rather than even experienced. When you begin to relate with the tathagatas as real beings in your practice of sadhana, you feel thunder resounding. There is greater vision, much more fantastic than even the vision of the eight logos of mahayoga. You feel the earth quake, or rather, you feel the space quake. There is a real feeling of living and roaring, of shakes and flashes out of nowhere. Everything happens, because nothing happens.

With this mandala, you are absolutely, transcendently, fundamentally haunted to the core of your being by the herukas and tathagatas. That is why they are connected with death. *The Tibetan Book of the Dead* describes death as the real message. When death occurs, you have a chance to relate with the deities, because death is one of the fundamental, resounding sounds. It is thunder, the real fundamental message.

The flash and the earth shaking come from the brain chakra and the heart chakra bringing together the peaceful and wrathful deities. Bringing these together is the building of "me," as opposed to the "other." So bringing yourself together in a good state is the expression of relating with the other as lover.

## Relating with the Dharmapalas

You also need to make a relationship to the dharma protectors, or dharmapalas. You have to catch them as your servants, your reminders, or your guards. The problem with the dharmapalas at this level is that the dharmapalas feel better if you declare yourself. They want to know what your name is and that you are the boss, that your name is Boss So-and-So. If you do not have a boss's name to declare, it is very difficult to employ them, because they probably will not obey you. On the other hand, they might be completely terrified, because you are in league with everybody.

## Nonvisualization

In mahayoga, visualization was a way of defining the higher level of existence, but in anuyoga, there is more emphasis on the importance of formless meditation beyond visualization. The anuyoga approach to visualization is nonvisualization. That brings us much closer to the emotions, and at the same time it gives us a clearer way of working with the emotions.

Anuyoga nonvisualization is related with prajna. Here, prajna has the sense of working with the phenomenal world and being somewhat in the state of oneness with the other. In this yana, the other is regarded as the lover, as the feminine principle. It is the receiver or recipient; it is the entertainer. So the phenomenal world is the feminine principle.

When we talk about the feminine principle, we are not particularly referring to a woman or a man, but to the basic nature of femininity that we all have. We are referring to fundamental cosmic femininity, the cosmic lover we all possess, whether we are a man or a woman. Your physical sexual inheritance, your karmic body, the shape your body has been formed in, is not fundamental. Basic femininity and masculinity are independent of your bodily type. The world is infinite. It is not only divided into two sexes, but there are billions of types of sexual experiences.

In anuyoga, we refer to self-existing femininity as the lover, and self-existing masculinity as the lovemaker. In this tantra, there is a lot of reference made to karmamudra practice; but in anuyoga, karmamudra is more a practice of dissolving ourselves into space. So this yana teaches us to realize the indivisibility of space and wisdom, or ying and yeshe. The meditation practice at this level is just mixing space and wisdom. Strangely enough, this is similar to the type of meditation that I have been teaching. The practice of dissolving yourself into space, or mixing mind with space, actually foreshadows that.

## PASSION AND COMPASSION

The emphasis in anuyoga is not so much on visualization or the forms that we have gone through already, such as the eight logos and so forth. Here, all the forms that we experience are brought together in one form. Anything we experience in the phenomenal world is subject to passion. This includes friends and enemies, liking and disliking—everything is subject to passion. This passion is slightly different from what we experienced before with the mahasukha principle, in which the whole of experience is thronged with joy or pleasure. In this case, the experience of passion is more discriminating in many ways. In anuyoga, the experience of passion is not thronged with one cosmic orgasm, but we have the discriminating wisdom of passion. The projection is the object of the passion, and the projector is the lover or lovemaker. There is a quality of friendliness.

We could say that anuyoga is the tantric equivalent of mahayana. The difference between the mahayana and anuyoga is that in the mahayana, we are developing a compassionate attitude toward all sentient beings, and in anuyoga, the emphasis is on developing a loving or passionate attitude toward all phenomena, not just sentient beings. In the mahayana, you are trying to keep up a certain discipline or pattern of behavior, but vajrayana passion is not concerned with that, so you naturally act as a bodhisattva. There is a quality of vastness, complete openness, and outrageousness.

Anuyoga practitioners refer to compassion as passion rather than compassion. Passion *is* compassion, from this point of view. This notion is different from that of ordinary people on the path of accumulation, from bodhisattvic people, and from ordinary tantric people. So there are enormous differences between normal tantrikas and practitioners of anuyoga.

## The Two Attainments of Anuyoga

As the end result of this experience of complete passion and the indivisibility of space and wisdom, we have two attainments. Fulfilling the desires of the yogi through devotion and fearlessness is the first attainment. The second attainment is the revelation of the great family. It is realizing the greatness of your particular buddha-family. Those two attainments act as the symbols of this yana, which is expressive of greater thinking and greater experience.

## Three Yogas

In connection with the two attainments, there are three types of yoga: the yoga of seed, the yoga of condition, and the yoga of result.

### Yoga of Seed

First, there is the yoga of seed or cause. Probably *seed* is a better word than *cause*. The yoga of seed is that all the dharmas existing in your phenomenal world are seen as the three mandalas: the mandalas of isness, self-existence, and the awakened state of mind. That is the seed or the groundwork, and we begin with that level.

### Yoga of Condition

Once you have the seed, you have to develop it or cause it to grow, which is the second yoga, the yoga of condition. This yoga is based on understanding the hinayana and mahayana with enormous physical effort, and with the intention of transcending the samsaric world. It is based on going through the shravakayana, the pratyekabuddhayana, and the mahayana. The practitioner of anuyoga goes back to these practices, trying to see them from the point of view of the three mandalas. Such backtracking is often very useful. It gives you a solid footing, and is very much recommended.

## *Yoga of Result*

Finally, there is the yoga of effect or result. Because such an enormous effort is being made to understand the basic yanas and the basic principles of the dharma, you begin to attain effortlessness. You attain hopelessness and fearlessness, and you begin to realize primordial mind. So the result is nonaction; it is transcending action.

One reason anuyoga is great is because nothing at all is excluded. None of ego's emotions, ego's projections, and no skandhas are excluded. Everything is included in the flame of great passion, the great prajna principle. Everything is completely consumed into the realm of the one hundred tathagatas.

# 66

# *Anuyoga:*
# *No Boundaries*

*In the various yanas, you are working with different levels of unveiling. In the hinayana, you are working with your clothes on; in the bodhisattva path, you are working as a naked body; and in the vajrayana, you are thrown into it naked, without even your skin.*

## ALL-CONSUMING PASSION

In anuyoga, there is a quality of simplicity and dignity. The eight logos of mahayoga still carry a sense of partiality or individuality. But in anuyoga, the whole experience becomes very fundamental. It is as if you were listening to a very deep bass sound. It ceases to be music anymore, and instead it begins to be more like an earthquake because it is so deep down. It is so basic and so fundamental that the ground you are sitting on is shaking. You cannot work on anything else, because anything else would be superficial.

Passion is the music that becomes so deep that it is like an earthquake. At this point, you do not have any other emotions at all. All you have is glorified passion, fundamental passion, all-consuming passion.

To get an idea of what this glorified passion is, you could begin by seeing the world as a production of passion. Anything that goes on in this world is the production of passion. Passionlessness may be the meaning of dharma from the hinayana point of view, but the higher dharma views passionateness as the dharma. Cosmic passion is the ground of everything.

The deeply fundamental approach to life is to construct something, and the first thing that you manage to construct is the split psychology of duality. That is an act of passion. You want a mate, so you make yourself into your mate; this is how you create your lover. Later on, you begin to realize that this is purely masturbation, so you look for another lover, and even that becomes masturbation. So the whole project of masturbation becomes greater and greater. Everything, including your husband or wife, becomes a part of it. This snowballs into a gigantic world of passion. But that passion is looking inward.

In anuyoga, the idea of lovemaking is looking outward. It is anti-masturbation. Everything is your lover, including the masturbation itself. Making love to yourself is a love affair rather than masturbation. Masturbation may be a way of discovering the possibilities of passion, but you are still trying to re-create your wishful thinking in a very clumsy and cheap way. You are releasing your energy in passion, which is actually aggression.

However, from the anuyoga point of view, you are not releasing your energy through passion, but you are perpetuating your energy. Making love does not limit your energy at all. There is a climax, which is called *peyi yeshe,* or "example wisdom"; and after that, *töngyi yeshe,* or "real wisdom," begins to arise. The climax is the example; it is what might be. And beyond that, there is what is, and the postmeditation experience begins to arise. So in anuyoga, the climax is transformed. The climax is no longer regarded as the highlight. In fact, there is no stopping point. Instead, there is perpetual energy, perpetual openness, perpetual passion.

## Nonduality and Separateness

Passion increases because we regard it as a path rather than as a hang-up. That frees us from all kinds of conflicting ideas as to whether to indulge in passion or to take pride in passion. It brings us down to fundamental passion as the source of inspiration. Making love ceases to be masturbation, because due to discriminating wisdom, you begin to see your projections as separate from yourself, rather than just your extensions.

Generally, we regard duality as a problem. We say that duality is a war between *this* and *that,* "I" and "other," which creates further separation. That is the ordinary mahayana point of view of duality. So in the mahayana, you begin to remove that fence, to go beyond duality. But when you do so, you experience more and more problems, and you wish the fence were still there. Now that *this* is also *that,* and *that* is also *this,* you become so confused. Everything seems to be one. You get so freaked-out that you are constantly haunted. There is no privacy, and no room for wisdom or skillful means.

According to anuyoga, wisdom and skillful means come from having a sense of privacy. That allows you to build yourself up, and then relate to the other. It may be disconcerting and somewhat humiliating that whatever you try to build up is being watched by the other. The whole thing may seem so absurd and embarrassing. But the point is not to create a barrier; it is to realize that you do not have to be embarrassed about exposing yourself to the other as a separate individual. The other is the other, and it has its own existence, and you are you. And you no longer view the other as the public or someone who is watching you, but you see the other as your lover, your partner. So you do not have to be resentful about the world, because you no longer see it as an extension of yourself.

At the same time, the bodhisattva experience of giving up your territory or giving up your privacy is still necessary. That methodology is needed in order to realize your individuality. It is the reason why there is this feeling of separateness, the feeling that you are you and the other is the other. But there is still a link, and that link is making love to the other, which is called discriminating-awareness wisdom. The reason why this becomes wisdom is because you saw the oneness, you gave up the embarrassment, and you devoted yourself to others in the bodhisattva style. Beyond that, you do not have to be so mad that you are public and have no privacy at all. So in anuyoga, you have a sense of oneness and you have a sense of separation at the same time.

That feeling of separation actually starts very minutely and humbly in kriyayoga. There is a sense that the cosmic principle is not you unless you are the lord of the cosmic principle; and although you are the lord of the tribal setup of the cosmic principle, you are still separate. So we could say quite safely, if my boss permits me to say such a thing, that in tantrayana we are trying to discover the separateness all the time, rather than the nonduality. The idea is that you and your projections are separate; therefore, the projections are your lover, and you are the lovemaker.

At the beginning of the path, such an approach would be neurosis. You have to go through many changes before you can realize real separateness. At this point, you are not trying to reform or reject samsara, but you are trying to realize the subtlety of enlightened teachings within the samsaric style. At the beginning, you see samsara as very crude and dualistic. Then you break that logic to pieces, and you realize nonduality. That is beautiful, and you can work with it. Finally, you begin to re-appreciate what you were, and you come back to samsara.

In anuyoga, looking from a higher level of duality, you see that this duality is not bad after all. You are just having your own lover redefined. In the state of intoxication, you begin to compose music and sing songs praising the phenomenal world as your lover, as the mother of all the buddhas. You begin to appreciate more. The passion in this yoga is trying to pull the world to you. That is the object of all the tantras, but in this case it is accentuated, because this is the highest tantra from the point of view of form. Beyond anuyoga there is only one yana, the maha ati level, which is completely formless. So this tantra is the highest tantra of form that you could ever reach. It is the highest tantra in which you could still relate to a lover.

## Unbiased Passion

Another important theme in anuyoga is *rangnang ri-me. Rangnang ri-me* is short for *ranggi nangwa ri-me. Ranggi nangwa* means "one's own projection," *ri* means "extreme" or "bias," and *me* means "without"; so *ranggi nangwa ri-me* is "projection without any bias." In anuyoga, projections are no longer regarded as delusions, problems, or hang-ups—they are regarded as objects of love.

When we talk about love and passion here, it is much more than ordinary love and passion. It is sexual desire. Talking about sexual desire is much more real, much more rugged and true. When we talk about ordinary love, it is hypothetical or implied love. But sexuality in anuyoga is prajna. It is expressed as the thirst or hunger to unite your whole being with the object of prajna, which is the phenomenal world, including both animate and inanimate objects. I suppose you could say that in all tantric traditions, sexuality is an expression of friendship and inquisitiveness. You would like to explore all parts of your partner, which in this case is the phenomenal world.

Finally, having explored all areas, having explored the whole body of your phenomenal world, you discover a quality of indivisibility. You are no longer fascinated by the other, so the other becomes you as well. There is a quality of completeness. That is why sexuality is part of the symbolism in the thangkas of the herukas and dakinis that you may have seen. It represents genuine interest rather than theoretical interest.

Passion from this point of view is not from the head, but from the heart. When passion is heartfelt passion, or when sexual fantasy is a heartfelt experience, it ceases to be theoretical. It becomes a much more real and much more living experience. In other words, in an ordinary marriage you are bound by law, whereas in the ideal marriage you are bound not only by concepts, laws, or social norms, but you are bound heart to heart by a sense of reality. That is why rangnang ri-me is called unbiased self-existing experience, which is one of the catchphrases of this particular yana.

## EGOLESSNESS AND COMPASSION

At the anuyoga level, you couldn't care less which of the five wisdoms you have, because you begin to have all the others as well. The mirrorlike wisdom begins to dissolve into its neighbors: the wisdom of all-accomplishing actions, the wisdom of equanimity, discriminating-awareness wisdom, and the wisdom of all-encompassing space. So you do not really have buddha-families as such. You begin to become less identifiable.

As you go up toward atiyoga, you are beginning to lose your ego. You have realized egolessness already at the hinayana and mahayana levels; that is already understood completely. At the anuyoga level, the only problem is that, having realized that there is no self, you then begin to realize that selflessness needs a companion. You think, "I have to visit my friend." But such companions are also expressions of egolessness. The fact is that you cannot constantly relate to your basic nature all the time, because you need a reference point. You need others to begin to come along as you work on yourself. While you are treating yourself well, at the same time you need others to comment on how you are doing. That is how the natural relationship with the other, or the world, forms: by collecting lots of lovers as you go through the different stages of relating with yourself.

In anuyoga, you are getting into an area with no ground, which is the greatest ground of all. At the same time, you need to manifest yourself in order to reignite the flame of compassion. But whenever the idea of compassion or dedication to sentient beings arises, you are creating a problem—you are creating another self, a selfless self. If you try to create another selfless self or egoless self, you find it very difficult to relate to the confusion of the space that the other is going through. This reminds you of your previous selfishness all over again, so you begin to panic. You think, "Maybe I do have a self. Maybe I do have an ego."

However, if instead of that doubt you feel enjoyment and pleasure in uniting with sentient beings and with your world as lover, that is the final and fundamental act of compassion. Even the trip of selflessness and nonduality has been destroyed by prajna, by discriminating awareness. We refer to this as prajna rather than jnana, or wisdom, because wisdom is not a companion; wisdom is just being. At the anuyoga level, prajna is the other, from the point of view of the lover. So prajna is not only discriminating awareness, but the product of discriminating awareness as well, which is the consort.

## RELATING WITH THE DUALISTIC WORLD

At this point you are refining your taste, and you are learning how to relate to the reality of the samsaric or dualistic world. Throughout all the yanas, you have had a problem with reality, with the world. You tried to reject the world and you tried to be nice to it. You tried to be charitable and relate to the world with compassion—and none of those approaches worked. They were just phases you went through. And now that you have reached the vajrayana level, you still have that project hanging around your neck. So you decide to plunge into the world and to work with it without any fear, and with no division between right and wrong, good and bad. You just approach the world based on what you think is sane or insane. There's at least that much discrimination involved: sanity and insanity are present as clear seeing and obscured vision. There is always that measure of how sharp your vision is. It is not so much whether you are blind or whether you can see; rather it is that even if you are not blind, there are different levels of how far you can see.

In the vajrayana, you begin reconstructing yourself along with the world, which you have destroyed already. So the vajrayana approach to the world is a real reconstruction of the world. With the vajrayana teachings, you are finally actually making a relationship with the world, which includes the dualistic or ego approach. You are finally making heads or tails out of the world, and you begin to make love to it.

This process of dissolution and reconstruction is free from birth and death because you have no notion of right and wrong; this means you have no notion of good karma or bad karma, and so you are free from karmic debt and karmic creation. You have no notion of samsaric rebirth as a debt cycle, so you are completely outside that ego area. But finally, strangely enough, you find that there is a nirvanic samsara world beyond karma. That is the problem here—and in anuyoga, you are transcending even this kind of nirvanic samsara that you created.

At the ordinary layperson's level, we did not rebuild the world properly, but we just messed around with it. And when we got into the hinayana and mahayana paths, we were resentful, and we tried to kick the world around some more. In that process, nothing was actually related with at all. Even the experience of shunyata was some kind of trip. But the vajrayana is so big that there is no reference point. It is beyond question. It is so much there; who could pass judgment on it? The vajrayana is getting to the level of actual experience without any religious frame of reference or any notion of actual practice.

So in the various yanas, you are working with different levels of unveiling. In the hinayana, you are working with your clothes on; in the bodhisattva path, you are working as a naked body; and in the vajrayana, you are thrown into it naked, without even your skin.

## Final Attainment

The fruition or final attainment of anuyoga is known as the upaya of conquering. You become a king; and if you are really a king, you become like the sky. You become fire; and if you are really fire, you become like water. At this level, there is the experience of no boundary. You are not biased toward any one particular conceptual idea. This lack of boundaries or sameness is the final statement of fearlessness.

67

# Atiyoga:
# Continuous Awake

*Vajrayana discoveries do not depart from the training of hinayana and mahayana, but the three yanas are all tied together very closely. Therefore, the vajrayana, including maha ati, is regarded as the pinnacle of all the teachings.*

T HE NINTH yana is maha ati, or dzokchen. It is also referred to as atiyoga or as the atiyogayana. *Maha* means "great," *ati* means "ultimate," and *yana* means "vehicle"; so *maha ati yana* means "ultimate vehicle." In Tibetan it is called *dzokchen* or *dzokpa chenpo. Dzokpa* means "final" or *fini*, like at the end of a movie, and *chenpo* means "great" or "big"; so *dzokpa chenpo* means the "great final," the "great essence," or the "great completion."

We have received criticism from scholars for calling this yana "maha ati," but *maha ati* is our direct translation of the Tibetan term *dzokpa chenpo. Maha,* like *chenpo,* means "great," and *ati,* like *dzokpa,* means "basic" or "final"; so *maha ati* means "great final."*

---

* The Sanskrit term *maha ati* was most likely coined by Chögyam Trungpa Rinpoche as a Sanskrit rendering of the Tibetan term *dzokchen.* To the knowledge of the Nalanda Translation Committee, this term is not found in any texts. Most scholars seem to translate the Tibetan term *dzokchen* as the Sanskrit term *mahasandhi. Atiyoga* is more properly translated into Tibetan as *shintu naljor, shintu* meaning "very," "extremely," or "utterly," and *naljor* meaning "yoga." But atiyoga can also be referred to as *dzokchen,* which is usually translated as "great perfection."

In the term *ati*, *a* is the basic syllable in the Sanskrit language, and it is also the last letter in the Tibetan alphabet, so *a* is the basic syllable or final letter. *A* is the transparent vowel that is present throughout the entire Sanskrit alphabet; the letters of the alphabet all contain the sound of *a*. That is, whenever you say *i, u, e,* or *o,* there is always an *a* in it. So *a* is ubiquitous, and at the same time it is also the final sound.

In the same way, at the maha ati level, there is a sense of awake continuously. *A* expresses "awake" or the first breath you take, and *ti* indicates "ultimate" or the "final thing." So at this point, there is a much greater East and a much greater dawn. You do not even need Vajrasattva anymore. All cardinal directions become East at once; maha ati is utterly awake, ultimately awake all the time.

The imperial yana of the maha ati tradition brings together the teaching of coemergent wisdom and a further dissolving process beyond coemergence. There is a point where the concept of coemergence begins to dissolve into a larger space. That particular larger space is regarded as no space, or space that does not accommodate any space.

## Origins of Dzokchen

The original dzokchen teachings come from the early Nyingma tradition, which was introduced to Tibet in the eighth century by Padmasambhava and Vimalamitra, and practiced for a long time. Later, in the early eleventh century, during the time of the Norman invasion of Britain, Marpa went to India and received mahamudra teachings, and an upsurge of mahamudra practice took place.

As the mahamudra tradition developed through Milarepa, Gampopa, and others, it organically took its place in the natural geography or organization of the educational system of Tibetan Buddhism. From the practitioner's point of view, everybody came to the same conclusion: if you want to make yogurt, first you have to milk the cow, then you have to boil the milk, then you have to put in your culture, and finally you make your yogurt out of all that.

That organic process of mahamudra became very prominent at the time of Gampopa, and definitely by the time of the second Karmapa, Karma Pakshi (1203–1283 CE). At that time, the great maha ati masters who lived in Tibet also practiced the mahamudra being taught by the Kagyü tradition of the New Translation school. It became very natural for them to do that, for the very reason that they were also a practice lineage. By the time of the fourth Karmapa, Rolpe Dorje (1340–1383 CE), it had become very natural for practitioners to join their appreciation for mahamudra practice with their appreciation and respect for the dzokchen teachings that were brought into Tibet by the blessings of Padmasambhava, King Trisong Detsen, and Shantarakshita.

That combination of mahamudra and dzokchen was the general basis on which Tibetan monasticism was built, and it became the natural heritage of all the Tibetans, who appreciated both traditions so much. Early translations of anuttarayoga tantras, done in the eighth century, as well as translations of various tantras from the early Nyingma tradition, were used as references for putting mahamudra and dzokchen together. So the Kagyü mahamudra tradition was accepted and became a part of the maha ati path. In fact, the Kagyü and Nyingma became one stream of teachings at some point.[*]

We have an expression in Tibet, which says that in the same way that we do not make a point of which eye we are using to see with, the mahamudra and maha ati practices are equal in terms of liberation. Our right eye and our left eye work together; we do not emphasize them differently. That is the symbol of the unity of the two traditions.

## BACK TO BASICS

Before going further in our discussion of dzokchen, it would be good to go back a little bit and review what has brought us to this point. To start with, the discipline and energy that you put into shamatha practice provides the basis for vajrayana discipline. The principle of shinjang allows you to relate with conceptual mind throughout the journey. Beyond that, vipashyana practice provides a quality of awareness, which allows you to develop softness and gentleness. Going further, the tonglen practice of exchanging oneself for others allows you to realize that you no longer have to hang on to yourself as an individual entity. In turn, you become worthy of developing good devotion.

---

[*] As an example, Karmapa Rangjung Dorje is said to have received maha ati transmissions from Longchenpa (Longchen Rabjam). Both Rangjung Dorje (Kagyü) and Longchenpa (Nyingma) were students of Kumaraja, who was well-versed in both maha ati and mahamudra, and it is said that Rangjung Dorje and Longchenpa also received transmissions from one another as well.

In the analogy of the house, we speak of the vajrayana as the roof of the building, the hinayana as the foundation, and the mahayana as the walls. But in maha ati, you do not dwell anywhere other than the roof. Maha ati is the imperial yana, and when you have an empire, you cover all areas of the kingdom. So if you are able to relate fully to the maha ati teachings, the world that dawns will very much manifest the hinayana and the mahayana principles as well.

Both the hinayana and the mahayana are geared directly toward the basic idea that you do not have to be self-centered, that you do not need to have "me-ness" happening all the time. You can begin to relax, to take a holiday from yourself. In that way, you can relate with the world outside of you. You can relate with the phenomenal world. You can relate with your enemies, your friends, and those who are indifferent to you. You can relate with any external situation without constantly having to refer back to yourself. You do not have to be "me" all the time. The accomplishment of the mahayana provides the possibility of egolessness, which seems to be the key point.

Once that happens, the path of vajrayana is already laid out. You are able to understand and realize the threefold-mandala principle of the external world, your physical body, and your state of mind. Out of that comes further appreciation and cheerfulness, because you have entered into the mandala already. That provides the ground mahamudra of devotion, and out of that you develop still greater awareness; you realize the greater mandala of the guru's world. And out of that, coemergent wisdom begins to dawn on you, with the experience of tremendous bliss and intoxication.

## Lodral: The Process of Disarming

Because of all that, you begin to shed your conceptual mind, which hangs on to you as territory or as the occupants of territory. You begin to learn how to wipe out your ranges and ranges, or oceans and oceans, of piled-up concepts that you have been accumulating since very early on. You begin to wipe out all those clingings and hangings on, and you begin to develop what is known as *lodral. Lo* means "thought pattern," "conceptualization," or "mind," and *dral* means "free from that" or "without it"; so *lodral* means "free from conceptualization."

With lodral, you begin to realize that, without exception, without any question, you have to lay down all your arms, including your broomsticks. You have to shed any weapons that you might cherish or try to hold on to in order to maintain your ego or protect yourself from being attacked. Because you have some understanding of ultimate sacred outlook, you can disarm yourself completely and thoroughly. You do not need to hold on to any possibility of warding off the vajra world. So lodral is an expression of bliss, in a sense.

### Sepa: Ego Defenses Used Up

Having disarmed, what comes next is *sepa*. *Se* means "used up" or "run out," and *pa* confirms the run-outness of it; so *sepa* means "used-up-ness." When ego's defense mechanisms and ego's weapons have been laid down altogether, then you experience sepa. At that point, you have used up, or run out of, any form of defending yourself, including your fists. Your mind has completely run out of any possible defense mechanisms, any way of holding on to your ego: those defenses are completely used up, completely transcended. This heightens the possibilities of bliss. When you do not have the hassle of maintaining your weapons, or possible weapons such as fists and stones, you are invincible. You are victorious over your samsaric kleshas and your neurotic hang-ups.

### All Dharma Agrees at One Point

Last but not least, we once again have the important Kadampa slogan: "All dharma agrees at one point."[*] It means that all apparent phenomena are bound by the dharma of wakefulness or awake. This slogan is connected with the benevolence and compassion of the bodhisattva, as well as with surrendering your ego. But at this point, it is acknowledging the nonexistence of your ego, rather than surrendering. The weapons that are ego's best credentials have been laid down, and potential passion, aggression, and ignorance have run out. Therefore, all dharma agrees at one point. That one point is the pinnacle; it is the highest realization in

---

* For a discussion of this slogan from the mahayana perspective, see volume 2 of the *Profound Treasury*, chapter 40, "Point Five: Evaluation of Mind Training."

the Buddhist tradition. This pinnacle is atiyoga, the ninth yana, in which all dharmas are regarded as final. Atiyoga is the final conclusion, or the ultimate possibility.

By means of shamatha mindfulness, vipashyana awareness, and the mahayana practice of tonglen, you arrive at the experience of having tremendous appreciation of the teacher and the teachings. Therefore, you are completely fulfilled. It is like collecting vegetables from the garden and bringing them into the house. Collecting vegetables from the garden is connected with the shamatha principle; bringing them into the house is connected with the vipashyana principle; cooking them is connected with shinjang and with the mahayana principle of tonglen. Finally, the vegetables make a good meal; they are consumed and appreciated. That is the vajrayana.

In the vajrayana, there is nothing to regret. It is a celebration. There is an appreciation that things actually happened in this way, which is worth celebrating. Along with that, there is the understanding that you, your vajra master, your deity, and your sanity are bound together by the basic commitment of the samaya principle.

Because of that bondage, you experience tremendous freedom. You realize that freedom is bondage, and bondage is freedom. First you are bound by neurosis, and you are looking for freedom. But when that bondage is broken, there is a still greater bondage. Because you are unbound by neurosis, a greater or unbound bondage takes place. If we could use an analogy, when darkness falls, you fall asleep and snore; but when the sun shines, you wake up. So you have awakened from one type of sleep, but then you are sleeping in the sunlight, so you get the best sleep of all, which is bliss. That, I'm afraid, is a vajrayana riddle.

"All dharma agrees at one point" means that any possible source of confusion is used up. Confusion has run out of supplies altogether. Therefore, the vajra master, you, and your practice are bound together by that run-outness of your supplies. At this level, even awareness could be said to be no awareness. When you say "awareness," that actually ties you down, but when you say "no awareness," it is the best awareness, because you are not attaching yourself to any particular angle of cosmic, spiritual, or phenomenal possibilities. You cease to be attached; therefore, you are attaching completely. The possibility of hanging on does not exist; therefore, you are completely rooted in fundamental sanity, the best sanity altogether. You are awake, therefore you are asleep; you are asleep, therefore you are awake. You are sober because you are so drunk; and because you are drunk, you are so sober.

"All dharma agrees at one point" is magnificent. With this slogan, you can free yourself from any traps. It is like actually becoming the sun and moon yourself, rather than just looking at them. Such discipline comes only from developing prajna, which comes from the vipashyana experience. You should not forget that. There is also a gentle and soothing quality to this, which comes from the shinjang experience, which is like swimming in a milk lake.

So vajrayana discoveries do not depart from the training of hinayana and mahayana, but the three yanas are all tied together very closely. Therefore, the vajrayana, as well as maha ati, is regarded as the pinnacle of all the teachings.

## LUMINOSITY AND THE DISCOVERY
## OF FATHOMLESS SPACE

According to the vajrayana, there are two ways of developing your attitude: changing your basic existence, and not changing your basic existence. Changing your basic existence is known as samsara, because you always want to edit your experiences according to your own particular fashion. Not changing your basic existence is known as nirvana, or enlightenment, because you allow things to permeate or evolve. That brings an experience of luminosity. By luminosity, we are not talking about electricity, but about natural brilliance and the discovery of fathomless space. That space is known as vajradhatu; and a second stage in the discovery of fathomlessness is known as dharmadhatu.

## THE PROBLEM OF MERCHANDISE MENTALITY

When you begin to study the vajrayana, shamatha practice becomes more profound and brilliant than you expected. You begin to appreciate the earlier yanas much more as the foundation of everything, and you begin to realize how important they are for understanding the vajrayana. That is a great discovery. That is precisely what vajrayana is supposed to do.

But nowadays everybody is a merchant; everybody is making business deals all over the place. In talking about the dharma, I have heard students talk about which merchandise is more valuable: "Should we stick with silver, should we stick with gold, should we stick with rubies, or should we stick with diamonds?" For a long time, people have been talking about the dharma as if it were merchandise. If you talk about maha ati, they say, "Ah, that's the best!" If you talk about mahamudra, they say, "Oh, that's good!" But if you talk about shamatha, they just shrug. In the twentieth-century democratic educational system, when you study at universities or colleges everything is evaluated as merchandise. The idea is that you get what you bargain for.

But that mentality is problematic. In the Tibetan tradition, we do not regard things in that way. There is no greater or lesser value placed on any of the yanas. Obviously, there are skills connected with each of the yanas, but "value" and "skill" are different. Value is related to how expensive things are and how much of a good deal you are getting out of the whole thing. Skill is what you acquire through basic training. If you first learn how to turn on the stove, you can then learn how to cook your food and how to put in spices and condiments. You do not start by putting condiments on your food and eating it without first cooking it. So the whole thing hangs together: the hinayana, mahayana, and vajrayana work together.

A twist of logic happens when people talk about what value they are getting out of the teachings. It is a somewhat revolting game of one-upmanship. People who have received mahamudra transmission think that, because of this transmission, they do not have to relate with shamatha-vipashyana. It is like somebody buying an expensive car and thinking that they could just sail through the universe without using roads. That kind of stupidity and merchandise mentality is problematic. We have to overcome that approach and come back to basics.

## Sacred Outlook and Hierarchy

In this discussion of the vajrayana, you are not getting a cultural presentation of how Tibetans think, or for that matter, how Japanese or Chinese people think. What I am presenting is sacred outlook, or tagnang. *Tag* means "pure" or "sacred," and *nang* means "perception" or "outlook"; so *tangang* means "pure perception," which we have translated as "sacred outlook."

The sacred and the ordinary are two types of hierarchy. Particularly in vajrayana situations, it is very important for you to know that there is the concept of hierarchy. My apologies for presenting such a case in a very democratic world, but we have to face that fact. When I am teaching, I have to sit on a platform in order to see all of my students and in order for them to see me. That is automatically a form of hierarchy. It is not necessarily my choice. I would not mind mingling with my students. Nonetheless, I have been put on a pedestal, which is fine as far as I am concerned. So in the vajrayana, we have a notion of hierarchy.

Vajrayana hierarchy is based on sacredness, and all the forms used in the vajrayana are connected with the idea of sacred outlook. The experience of sacred outlook is like placing a diamond in a ring: in order to express that stone's diamond quality, you need a ring to set it in. Likewise, you might notice sacred outlook more clearly in a dharmic space or in the presence of your vajra master, as opposed to when you are in your own home. So when you are in your own home, you could think of your teacher.

It is good to lose your sacred outlook sometimes, for when you have lost it, you might rediscover it. That is fine; it is how beginners begin at the beginning. From a vajrayana point of view, the kleshas are also sacred; they are referred to as the five wisdoms. It is a question of how you perceive them.

Once you have gone beyond your pettiness, beyond your own territory, you naturally begin to perceive a greater world. Among the kleshas, passion is regarded as one of the most workable emotions, because it is accepting of the other, as opposed to aggression, which rejects the other. But all emotions are regarded as some kind of impulse toward communication.

# 68

# Atiyoga:
# Primordial Enlightenment

*The nature of maha ati has to do with its view of enlightenment.*
*In maha ati, enlightenment is not seen as something to be attained,*
*but as something that has been completely attained from the begin-*
*ning. In maha ati, we speak of primordial enlightenment.*

## ENLIGHTENMENT ON THE SPOT

Maha ati is the yana of complete transcendence. If you have transcended
all the yanas, you might think you have nothing to say. Quite possibly
you might ask, "Why bother to say anything at all? Why not drop dead
on the spot?" The response is that this yana is a tantric yana, so we have
lots to say. Unlike the yogacharan approach of the Zen tradition, we do
not just say no, or *mu*. We also do not proclaim that everything is a complete riddle, as in Zen word games. Maha ati is very real and very definite. After all, this is the imperial yana, the ultimate yana, the king of all
the yanas.

The maha ati approach to enlightenment is that wisdom has never
begun, and therefore, there is no end. Since that is the case, one can
experience the primeval enlightened state on the spot without accepting
or rejecting, and without hope or fear. That seems to be the definition of
atiyoga or maha ati. It is actually very simple and straightforward.

## BUILDING ON PERSONAL EXPERIENCE

I think that a lot of the philosophy of maha ati has been built on very personal experiences. Things happen: We bump into each other, or we find ourselves mistakenly stepping on a raw egg. We knock over our cup of coffee on a beautiful tablecloth. We find ourselves saying the wrong things to our friends or to our landlord. According to the social norm—and even according to the intelligent bodhisattva norm, the Buddhist norm, or the maha ati norm—we tend to make mistakes. We say all kinds of things. But underneath all those mistakes, very concrete and pragmatic things take place all the time.

Somebody might frighten you. They might walk up behind you and say "Boo!"—so you jump. That is the most pragmatic remark you could ever make. The idea is that the world is the only ground on which to celebrate nothingness or nonexistence. It is the only ground for pursuing further worlds beyond this one. Once you are able to be at that level and to experience such confidence, the world is not particularly being explored, but it is being enjoyed thoroughly and properly. You are actually able to see the world as it is, in its fullest sense. At that point, you are ready for the various maha ati practices.

## DEALING WITH REALITY

Three essential qualities for dealing with reality are naturalness, great joy, and simplicity.

### Naturalness

In dealing with reality, you should be somewhat relaxed, if you can; and at the same time, you should be awake. That particular reference point is completely neutral. Reality does not have to be confirmed by anyone, no one whatsoever. It is just a state of being, and even that is not particularly the question in mind.

You do not have to be anywhere in order to experience reality, but reality is as it is. When we talk about reality, we usually mean reality that is based on perception, or reality that is based on a sense of being, or reality from somebody else's point of view, or for that matter, from your own point of view. But you could leave reality as it is. It does not have to be confirmed or preconceived as things as they are. In fact, even the idea of "things as they are" is arbitrary.

The colors you see in the room around you could be a reference point, but even that reference point does not exist anymore. Whether you are in the room or not, the room somewhat fulfills its own fulfillmanship by the fact that nobody is there. Therefore, reality remains by itself, without sound, without sight, without perception—natural.

The question to ask about reality is: Who said such a thing? Reality does not have to be on its own or not be on its own. It is a natural state of being. This is quite hard to understand from many people's reference point. When people say reality, that usually means: What reality—this or that? But total reality, if you could call it that, is just a natural sense of being. It is nonverbal and nonconceptual.

Reality that is confirmed on its own without a reference point is *the* reality, the true reality. Do you see what I mean? Things do not have to be confirmed; they just are as they are. That seems to be the fundamental point of reality. We are talking about a larger perspective than "Mummy, do you love me?" or "Daddy, do you love me?" In other words, we have nothing to gain and nothing to lose.

## Great Joy

Dealing with reality in this way brings great joy, or mahasukha. Such joy is free from transforming one thing into another. This does not mean that you are stuck with something. It means that generally things are subject to discrimination, and to changing from one thing into another; but reality, so to speak, is free from transforming itself into other realities. For example, if you change the outfit you are wearing today to tomorrow's outfit, it does not mean that you are no longer subject to pain or misery.

In talking about mahasukha, we are not talking in terms of fundamental ecstasy or in terms of reality being so refreshing, but we are speaking about losing one's attachment. We are simply saying that things could be left on their own. Self-existing things as they are would be beyond the eight states of consciousness, beyond the five skandhas: beyond, and beyond, and beyond. This is not a metaphysical concept; you just happen to bump into things. For instance, if you step outside to see whether it is drizzling or not, you do not have to ask anybody if it is drizzling—you will experience it for yourself.

In the vajrayana, you do not have to be constantly bothered with the laundry. Instead, you could keep on your birthday suit, which is the best laundry of all. In the vajrayana, and particularly in the maha ati tradition, that is considered to be great joy. But we do not mean "great" as opposed to "lesser." You could just be as you are.

The basic point of mahasukha is that you disconnect from *that* and *this;* you lose the concept of *that* and *this*. Therefore, any logistical or metaphysical theory becomes like a blind person looking at the sun: a blind person cannot perceive that kind of brightness or brilliance. So the point we are concerned with here is that you cannot be aware of your own perception of phenomena.

## Simplicity

Maha ati is free of false beliefs about reality. It brings the fruition of intellect. But this does not mean "intellect" from the point of view of intellectualization. Rather, it is a general wakefulness in regard to things as they are. In maha ati, things should be perceived literally. So maha ati is self-existing simplicity. You do not have any more preconceptions, but you just look at things very directly and suddenly. In turn, you begin to appreciate things as they are, without a watcher. That is why the experience of cosmic orgasm plays an important part in maha ati.

You should keep things natural and basic. You do not have to jazz things up or make them into anything more than necessary, or turn them into anything spiritual. Things are on their own, very simply. Maha ati is ultimate or final. It is very basic. As you become more basic, your way of thinking does not have to be hampered by current politics or economics or spiritualism, so your approach begins to become very realistic and natural. The ultimate notion of bliss is that you do not have to come up with something other than bliss; bliss is just things as they are. Therefore, the highest bliss you could think of is simply to be natural as what you are.

What makes me nervous about teaching maha ati is that it sounds too simple. Because it sounds very simpleminded, the problem might be that there is no respect. You might feel that maha ati is just something that happens organically, and you do not have to put any effort into it. There could be the problem of being somewhat bored with maha ati or disappointed with it.

## THE MAHA ATI VIEW OF ENLIGHTENMENT

The nature of maha ati has to do with its view of enlightenment. In maha ati, enlightenment is not seen as something to be attained, but rather as something that has been completely attained from the beginning. In maha ati, we speak of primordial enlightenment. Having confidence in that understanding or concept, you transcend hope and fear, and you transcend collecting and rejecting. Becoming buddha is a big heroic trip, like becoming a king or queen. But maha ati transcends the notion of buddha; it transcends the notion of dharmakaya and of any kind of attainment. Maha ati does so because it is approaching experience from the back door. It is coming downward rather than going up, so there is no attempt at heroism.

Since the concepts of all the previous yanas are completely transcended, maha ati has a fresh and direct quality. There is a prime or supreme quality to the whole thing. It is primordial and fresh. This yana is referred to as the imperial yana, for instead of searching for spirituality as though climbing from below, you receive the inspiration as something coming down from above. So it is an umbrella notion. Maha ati is like relating with the raindrops falling, rather than with the plant growing—it is a sudden and direct experience.

## EXPERIENCE AND ATTITUDE

People experience maha ati according to their basic nature, or buddhafamily; nevertheless, they are sharing the same world. It is like different people experiencing the same kind of weather. When people of five different buddha-families go out to a Saturday picnic, they see the same sunshine and the same rainfall and they eat the same food. So their experience is basically the same, although they have different perspectives as to the subtleties of the whole thing.

Likewise, at the maha ati level, although we are different individuals, our experience would be pretty much the same. What makes us individual is our hang-ups, our little trips; but at this point, all of those things are gone. Everything is completely gone, so it is completely unified. It is like parachuting: when a group of people parachutes out of a plane, they share the same space, particularly if their parachutes break!

When you come to the realization of maha ati, there will still be the same pattern of problems you have had all your life, such as in your relationships with people. Your problems will be absolutely the same, but your attitude will be different. Maha ati does not mean that you are going to be saved from all those things, or that you will have no more problems. Maha ati could be a problem, too.

So experience does not change, but in a sense it does. Because your attitude is different, the feedback you get is also different. But this does not mean that, as a maha ati practitioner, you are suddenly going to get rich, your marriage is going to become completely tidy, and you are going to have no problems in dealing with your neighbors. All of those things are still going to be happening. Nevertheless, your attitude toward them will be different, and your attitude might have been a large factor in creating those problems in the first place. Attitudes such as territoriality and the feeling of being threatened have been sorted out already, so situations like not having money are not problematic. They can be handled, because you are more daring and more open.

## Maha Ati and the Two Truths

The maha ati attitude toward kündzop and töndam is to regard relative and absolute truth as very basic and ordinary. Töndam is regarded simply as a situation without any hold, without any fixation, without any place to fix your mind. And as for kündzop, it is phenomenal play. Kündzop is not particularly profound; it is just ordinary phenomenal profundity on a very direct level.

For instance, if a maha ati person happened to see a cup of tea, they would not interpret the cup of tea as an expression of the mandala or some kind of mystical symbol; they would see that the mandala is just the cup of tea itself. The töndam approach to the cup of tea would be that the cup of tea came from nowhere, and therefore it goes nowhere: it is simply a cup of tea.

## A Spiritual Explosion

Maha ati experience is that the space outside of your individual existence is vast, so you can begin to relate with that space properly and thoroughly. Having understood that the space outside of your existence is vast and open enough to relate with, your inner space begins to yearn toward it. So there is a sympathetic space within your own practice and understanding, and there is a reciprocal sympathetic space that exists outside your body and outside your little world, an outer space that has nothing to do with a particular personality.

What happens is that pressure is put on the boundary from both sides, from within as well as from without, so that finally you have a fundamental, complete explosion. The inner space breaks into the outer space completely. At that point, the spiritual atomic bomb has finally actually exploded. The explosion takes place when there is no reference point, just pure demand. You cannot sneak out, you cannot philosophize, you cannot talk anything into anything else—you cannot do anything. The external pressure is enough, and the internal pressure is enough as well, so you go *boom!*

The relation of inner to outer here is like a bomb's view of outer space. There is pressure coming from outside and pressure coming from inside—it is as simple as that. It is purely functional, purely chemical. For example, if a bomb is made at a certain altitude, and you take that bomb higher, it might explode.

Another analogy for this is a light inside a vase. If there is a light burning inside a vase in the daytime, then when somebody breaks the vase, the light inside the vase becomes a part of the light outside. So there is no longer any need for maintaining the external and internal lights separately. If there is no boundary, you live much more. You do not have any barrier between you and the world, so you can see it properly.

## Leapt, Not Leaping

In maha ati, form is physical involvement, and space is believing that you have to leap off an enormous cliff. But it is not really a leap, because you have already cut the cliff. If there were a cliff, leaping would be a trip, so maha ati is a state of leapt rather than leaping. Letting go could be a trip,

714

and when that is so, you are far behind; you are somewhere other than maha ati.

As an example, suppose someone told you that tomorrow you were going to walk blindfolded across a bridge, and that if you made a mistake, you would fall into a river. But the next day, that person just had you walk blindfolded across a plank on the ground. The trip of letting go is like walking blindfolded on a plank on the ground, with no water underneath it at all.

## No Journey

In the maha ati tradition, your state of mind begins to dissolve. When we talk about dissolving your state of mind, usually we mean some kind of relief or unity, but in this case the dissolving does not bring any unity or relief. It is just simply mind becoming nothing, or becoming everything at once, or mind encompassing everything.

When everything is encompassed, we begin to feel terror. That terror and confusion tends to bring about a notion of reality that does not have any sense of journey. That sense of journeylessness brings about the only pure vision of brilliance. It also brings about the possibility of seeing the colors of the buddha-families in their true nature.

Practitioners of the maha ati tradition establish their posture properly. They sit on the meditation cushion with their back, legs, neck, and everything in the proper position, and then they extend their question out. At that point, their question is regarded as exercising *long* (*klong*), or ultimate space.* When a person has extended and questioned, and extended and questioned further, that questioning and extension begins to become real and powerful. Sometimes nonexistence becomes clean-cut at the same time, and a vast vision of openness and universality begins to evolve.

Still working with their breath and their sitting practice, students of maha ati evolve further penetration and further simplicity. That simplicity and ruggedness is almost at the level of backwardness. It is so rugged and so backward that relative reference points and conventional notions of good and bad, simplicity and confusion, no longer apply.

---

* The Tibetan word *long* is the phonetic version of two separate words. *Long* (longs) means "enjoyment," as in the enjoyment body, or sambhogakaya. *Long* (klong) means "space."

## A Summary of Maha Ati Qualities
## by Longchen Rabjam

The qualities of maha ati tantra can be summed up in this verse by the great Nyingma master Longchen Rabjam, which is found in the *Tantra of the Pearl Rosary.*

> If you know the essence of tantra,
> It is like the king and ministers
> And subjects are together, united.
>
> If you know the depth of tantra,
> It is like you have arrived
> At the top of a mountain peak.
>
> If you know the flowers of tantra,
> It is like the gaiety of a blossoming flower;
> It is like seeing three suns in the sky.
>
> If you see that the various tantric approaches are based
>     on oneness,
> It is like putting up a stone wall.
>
> If you see that tantra is combating confusion,
> It is like putting windows in your walls
> As you build your house.
>
> If you see the heart or essence of tantra,
> It is like your windows are tightly locked.
>
> If you see the dangerous and penetrating aspect of tantra
> And the protectiveness of the practitioner,
> It is like having a guard to protect your doorways.

---

* Translated by Chögyam Trungpa. Another translation of this can be found in Longchen Rabjam, *The Precious Treasury of Philosophical Systems: A Treatise Elucidating the Meaning of the Entire Range of Spiritual Approaches* (Junction City, Calif.: Padma Publishing, 2007), 366–367.

# 69

# *Atiyoga:*
# *Fathomless Mind*

*Basically speaking, neurosis is temporary and sanity is permanent. When we begin to take that attitude, we realize that our occasional freak-outs and panic and our feeling of being trapped are no longer applicable. In realizing that we are eternally free, eternally liberated, and eternally awake, we begin to experience vast mind.*

## Vajrayana Is a Big Deal

It is good to make a big deal of vajrayana; it is actually worth it. When I studied with my teacher, I used to make a big deal of it myself. I actually used to feel physically uplifted and blissful. That feeling is like a deer frolicking in the woods: there is a sense of moving through the space, and at the same time as you are jumping up high, your movement is still very slow and good. It reminds me of a youthful tiger walking slowly in the jungle: the tiger is not particularly trying to catch any prey, but it is simply walking with its stripes on. So we are walking through this particular jungle of vajrayana, and I seem to be the tour guide.

In vajrayana practice, we could make a big deal about everything. Big deal means personal involvement and being true to your appreciation. If you are in doubt, that is also a part of the appreciation of what you might be getting into. In the vajrayana tradition, coming and going are the same. Whether you get out of it or into it, the basic point is the journey, and you have begun the journey already.

## Maha Ati and the Earlier Yanas

The practitioner of maha ati has already accomplished a great deal by going through the earlier yanas. That is important: if there were no relationship with the rest of the yanas, there would be no journey. However, in the maha ati realm, there is a natural tendency to see that the journey no longer needs to be made. Instead, the journey itself is the goal.

The previous eight yanas still make reference to liberation and freedom, but this yana does not. The reason is that the logical reasoning mind of cause and effect is not important here. You are no longer trying to gain or develop a better relationship with the teachings, or with anything else. However, although atiyoga looks down upon the other yanas because they are still involved with attitude, training, and technique, that does not mean this yana does not have any techniques or training.

I think that what we have been doing so far has been talking about hinayana from the mahayana point of view, talking about mahayana from the vajrayana point of view, and talking about vajrayana from the point of view of maha ati. So you could do practices that happen to be at the maha ati level, and then go back through the rest of the yanas. In doing so, it is possible that your perspective on the previous yanas would become much more sophisticated.

Even seemingly complicated practices, such as the eight logos, have glimpses of maha ati simplicity. The eight logos are very close to home, they are part of our basic being; and the reason they become very much a part of our being is that they are an expression of maha ati. Otherwise, we would not have anything to relate with; they would become hypothetical. So practices such as the eight logos are an aspect of the fundamental truth of maha ati, and because of maha ati's ordinariness, the magical power found in the eight logos is accentuated. That is why maha ati is called the imperial yana. It has the powers and merits of all the yanas, but it is very simple to practice. Maybe I'm sounding like a salesperson, but it's true!

In maha ati, there is no inhibition about enjoying the sense perceptions or sense objects. Also, there is no need for restraint, because restraint and discipline have already been developed by the previous eight yanas. Discipline makes you see that discipline is no longer necessary, and purely for that reason, you have to practice a lot of discipline.

To practice maha ati, you do not necessarily have to complete the formal trainings of the other yanas, but you do have to go through some kind of psychological experience. And when you have done so, you then need directions as to how you can cut through that experience. In other words, you first have to manufacture something to cut through, and after that you have to cut through it with maha ati.

From maha ati's point of view, the other yanas are hang-ups, a big joke. If the other yanas were not hang-ups, maha ati would not be there. Maha ati almost seems like laughter, but it is necessary to have something to laugh at. Otherwise, we would not have anything, and we would be dumb and stupid. So it is very necessary first to create something to laugh at. Then that laughter automatically opens something up.

## MAHA ATI AND MAHAMUDRA

According to the four yogas of mahamudra, when mind is stabilized or rested one-pointedly, we begin to see the self-face of mind; we see its self-nature of ordinariness, or ordinary mind. That is one-pointedness. Then, because we see that mind has no basis, we begin to realize its simplicity. Because of simplicity, we are free from the fixations of the ego of *this* and the ego of *that*; therefore, we begin to realize one taste. And finally, because we realize one taste, we begin to be freed from the conventions that separate meditating from not meditating. We begin to transcend our habitual patterns. Therefore, we are in a constant state of meditation, which refers to the postmeditation state as well. We begin to realize the yoga called nonmeditation.

When we use up habitual patterns, this is known as the state of realization. But there is a further step, which is known as the simultaneity of realization and liberation. So when we have realized nonmeditation, this is not necessarily the end of the journey. Nonmeditation is the state of constant mindfulness, the state where awareness is finally attained. In that state, we do not depend on the ups and downs of our day-to-day situation. There is no hassle and no struggle, although there is still practice involved. At that point, we begin to experience greater appreciation and joy; we begin to transcend mahamudra and arrive at the beginning of our maha ati journey.

Some people might say that you do not have to go to first grade, you can just jump into sixth grade, but that does not quite work. People might say that you should only practice vipashyana, that shamatha is not necessary. But in our tradition, we are told that we should combine everything that has been taught, and work according to the map that was laid out by the Buddha. We are taught that we should do everything. Therefore, any good practitioner of maha ati is also supposed to practice mahamudra.

Maha ati is based on the umbrella approach. It is the approach of coming down, in which fruition is regarded as the path. But in order to have fruition as the path, you need to understand that the ground is also the path. If there is an umbrella, somebody has to hold it.

## Delight and Upliftedness

Generally, when we view phenomena, we always view them from the point of view of poverty and neurosis. Although somebody might say, "I am extremely happy; I have everything," the way that person says this is suspicious. Their statement has a tinge of victory in it, as though they had fought a battle and finally gained victory, but nevertheless they were still wounded, no matter how happy they may now be. That sort of war veteran's approach always happens. And that actually seems to be anti-vajrayana, anti-mahayana, and anti-hinayana as well.

When we begin the practice of vajrayana or when we try to understand the vajrayana teaching, instead of poverty there is a feeling of delight and upliftedness. There is an enormous amount of exertion and devotion as well. When we begin to develop that upliftedness, joy, and openness, we are actually beginning to enter the vajra world. We could even say that we are beginning to have a love affair with the vajra world and the vajra master.

## Vast Space

Basically speaking, neurosis is temporary and sanity is permanent. When we begin to take that attitude, we realize that our occasional freak-outs and panic and our feeling of being trapped are no longer applicable. In realizing that we are eternally free, eternally liberated, and eternally awake, we begin to experience vast mind.

This tremendously big mind has nothing to do with the yogacharan approach or the Zen style of big mind. Here, we are talking about big mind as unconditionally vast and completely fathomless. That mind does not need to be fathomed. It is a tremendously big space that accommodates everything. However, *accommodate* may not be the right word, because it implies deliberately trying to extend oneself. In this case, mind is so spacious already that we do not even have to accommodate anything. We have a fantastic, great, vast openness, which we do not actually perceive. When we begin to perceive this openness, we belittle the whole thing, so perception does not seem to play an important part.

## DOT OF COEMERGENCE

In that vast space, a dot occurs. That dot is known as coemergent wisdom. That dot in the space of our vast mind might seem to be somewhat unnecessary; nonetheless, it helps us a lot. This dot makes it so that we can actually come down from that space to earth, and develop compassion, wisdom, and discipline. The dot makes it possible for us to help confused sentient beings who have never seen that kind of vast space, let alone the dot itself.

That dot begins to become bigger and bigger and bigger still. That black dot begins to become tinged with purple at the edges, which is passion. It is tinged with compassion, or the willingness to work on this earth without ever abandoning anything. In maha ati language, this particular concept is called *kadak,* or alpha pure. Kadak is alpha pure as opposed to omega pure. It is totally pure. Kadak is pure right at the beginning, so it is not even one-pure, but zero-pure. Why is it pure? Because kadak is so innocent and genuine. It is so genuine and innocent that a maha ati level person can feel tremendous warmth and spaciousness in working with other sentient beings, and in imparting that particular kind of wisdom.

After the black dot becomes tinged with purple, it dissolves, and then things become black and purple all over. That is to say, the spaciousness of the black as well as the purpleness of the compassion spread everywhere. So coemergent wisdom is very simple: space-dot. When the dot occurred, coemergent wisdom occurred. Space is white, and the dot is black. Samsaric people would see space as black and the dot as white, like looking at the nighttime sky, but here there is a kind of flip. You begin to flip your space altogether. That is where the coemergent wisdom happens.

## A VAST WORLD OF DECENCY

Within that world of decency, that genuine and good vast mind, which is compassionate and willing, it is very difficult to find any neurosis. You might say: "Well, *I* could find it! I could come up with lots of neuroses!" But the question is, are you actually taking that attitude of vastness and gentleness at all? If you happened to be taking that kind of vast and gentle attitude, I would bet a million dollars that you would find nothing there; you would find no possibilities of any defilements.

At this point we are not talking in terms of the fruition, but we are still talking in terms of the practitioner. So occasional ripples of *this* and *that,* "I" and "other," passion, aggression, ignorance, and mental contents of all kinds obviously happen. But they are not regarded as problematic. They are just flickerings, like the ripples in the ocean.

When we have the attitude and experience of vastness and goodness, we find that our world is sacred. It is not sacred because it is the domain of God or because it has been religiously blessed by somebody or other. We are talking of sacredness in slightly different terms than that. Here, sacredness means healthiness. When the sun rises, it dispels darkness on earth. We begin to see trees and grass, houses and landscapes, mountains and everything, precisely and clearly, and we can see each other as well. Therefore, the sun is sacred, but not because the sun is a religious thing. This nonreligious sacredness is fantastic because it is real sacredness rather than conventional sacredness, in which nobody knows what magic is going on behind the scenes, or what happens to the holy water if you dump your cigarette butt into it.

We could actually take that attitude of real sacredness all along. The question is, why haven't we done this before? It seems to be so simple and good. That beats me.

I suppose the feeble answer for why we have not done this before is that we would like to crawl into our own little cocoons. We appreciate sleeping in our own shit; it smells good and homey and comfortable. When we crawl into our little holes, it feels like being at home. That is the only answer. We do not like crawling into our little hole, but we begin to like the not liking it as well. We are burying ourselves, burrowing into our own pain, to which we are so accustomed and which is so familiar. If we are suddenly presented with any kind of pleasure, we begin to feel embarrassed and uncomfortable. It is the same feeling we referred to when we spoke about wearing T-shirts and jeans to Buckingham Palace.

Taking the attitude that the phenomenal world is sacred is the first and last practice of all.

In that world of sacredness, if you drift off you always catch yourself, and therefore there is no haphazardness of neurosis happening. The instant you catch yourself is so good and open. It is as if you are lying on the lawn and looking up at the sky, and one little bird flies across. You catch yourself seeing the bird; therefore, you catch both the bird and yourself. It is very simple, nothing particularly mystical. There you have the inside story of the vajra master.

# 70

# Atiyoga:
# Mind, Space, and Instruction

*In maha ati, all notions, all dharmas, are regarded as just flow-*
*ing space, constantly flowing space in which there are no reference*
*points or directions. Everything is seen simply and directly as it*
*is, and there is no way that you can capture anything as personal*
*experience.*

## RECEIVING MAHA ATI TEACHINGS

The same fourfold abhisheka process is followed throughout the tantric
yanas, but at the level of maha ati, the focus is on what happens after the
third abhisheka, at the point of receiving the fourth abhisheka. Maha ati
transmission is performed in the student's mind directly. It is the meeting
of two minds: the teacher's and the student's. Therefore, it is called the
real abhisheka.

If you are receiving maha ati teachings, it is like staying out in a thunderstorm. Rather than running back to your home, you stay out in the
storm, and then you get the teachings. You let the hailstones land on your
head. They might create little bumps on your head, but that is good. This
might sound crazy, but as far as Dilgo Khyentse Rinpoche and myself are

*Chögyam Trungpa and Dilgo Khyentse Rinpoche in India.*

concerned, we are equally crazy.* I asked him about that, and he said, "I think we both are crazy." So with maha ati, whomever you go to, you get crazy teachings.

Having received transmission and having had some kind of realization, you have to follow it up; you have to become liberated. Some people think realization is liberation, but in our case, it is not. When you realize something, you have to practice that realization, and *then* you are liberated. So realization does not mean that you are liberated; it means that you have just touched on the possibility of liberation. Realization is like seeing the first rays of sunshine on the horizon—you know that the sun is in the sky. But then you have to go through the whole day as the sun does, all the way until it sets. So in transmission, you may get a glimpse of liberation, but that does not mean you have become enlightened on the spot.

## THREE SECTIONS OF MAHA ATI

Maha ati yana is divided into three sections: the category of mind, the category of space, and the category of instruction.

### The Category of Mind: Sem-De

The first section is the category of mind, or *sem-de*. *Sem* means "mind," and *de* is a "category" or "characteristic"; so *sem-de* means the "category of mind."

The description of this category is that there is no other dharma than one's own mind. This is not a yogacharan, or Mind-only, statement; it simply means that there is no other dharma than *this*. Just *this*, whatever that may be. At this point, the conceptualized, logical, philosophical mind does not have any importance. Logical reasoning does not make any sense. There is a notion of transcending any philosophy at all, and a feeling of openness and noncaring.

---

* Chögyam Trungpa Rinpoche had a very close connection and friendship with the Nyingma master *Dilgo Khyentse Rinpoche* (1910–1991), from whom he received many empowerments. In 1976, Chögyam Trungpa hosted Khyentse Rinpoche's first visit to North America, and over the years Khyentse Rinpoche paid further visits to the West and taught frequently in Trungpa Rinpoche's sangha. Due to the great vastness of his teachings, this beloved teacher came to be known as Mr. Universe.

ENERGY AND PLAY. The sem-de level focuses a great deal on energy and play, which in Tibetan are known as *tsal* and *rölpa*. *Tsal* means "energy," and *rölpa* means "play." Energy and play are happening in the cognitive mind all the time. There does not seem to be anything else or any further truth than what we perceive on a very simple level.

When we talk about energy, we are not purely referring to emotional energy, such as aggression energy or passion energy, but we are talking about the glittering light that comes out of sunshine. We are talking about high points or highlights. If you put an egg in the sun, you do not see the egg as it is, but you see its highlights. As the sun shines on the egg and around the egg, you see the hot spots of the egg. Those kinds of highlights are known as energy. Usually when someone says that you have a lot of energy, they mean that you are very busy and industrious. But when we talk about energy, it is not energy in the sense of activity, but energy in the sense of experience having highlights. It is the precision and clarity existing within experience.

*Rölpa* is the word for playful indulgency and all kinds of other things, but in this case we are talking purely of its playfulness. Rölpa does not bring solemnity but rather delight, and the willingness to play along with your perceptions of phenomena. Whatever you see as highlights, you are willing to go along with and play with.

STEPPING OVER THE PASS. One of the basic characteristics of maha ati is the idea of leap. The basic approach of sem-de is that you bypass or transcend, which is called *lada* or *ladawa* in Tibetan. *La* means a "mountain pass," and *da* means "to step over"; so *lada* means "to step over the pass." It means that instead of climbing up, you take one step over to the other side. Lada is divided into three parts: dharmakaya, sambhogakaya, and nirmanakaya.

*Dharmakaya stepping over.* With the dharmakaya level of stepping over the pass, you are transcending in the sense that you do not have anything in your experience at all—just purely the pass.

*Sambhogakaya stepping over.* The sambhogakaya level of stepping over the pass is beyond confusion, because if you have confusion, you cannot have wisdom. This level is expressed in the phrase: "It is boundless equanimity, which has never changed. It is unified into a single circle beyond confusion." The saying, "Nothing whatever, but everything arises from it," which is famous throughout maha ati, is another expression of this level.*

*Nirmanakaya stepping over.* The third level of stepping over is the nirmanakaya of utterance or proclamation. This kind of proclamation is connected with the first of the seven categories of sem-de: stepping over without effort.

SEVEN CATEGORIES OF SEM-DE. Sem-de is divided into seven categories: stepping over without effort, stepping over misunderstandings and obstacles, the falling apart of your home, not being extreme about proportions or directions, transcending attachment to biased philosophical beliefs, transcending attachment to intellect and to nonintellectual fixations and bias (unintelligent fixations), and proclaiming that one's mind is in a certain direction.

*Stepping over without effort.* The Tibetan term for the first category of sem-de is *betsöl mepar ladawa. Be* means "effort," *tsöl* also means "effort," *mepar* means "without," and *ladawa* means "step over"; so *betsöl mepar ladawa* means "to step over without effort." The definition of this sem-de category is that the fruition is unchanging.

You have experienced your world as a samsaric world, but in actuality things are the same. When we talk about things being the same, we are not just talking about good old samsara, or saying that nothing has changed. But things are the same because the relative and the absolute are the same; therefore, the fruition is unchanging. The fruition arises from space and dissolves into space. It is self-resting without any effort, none whatsoever. You have stepped over that.

But talking about what you step over and where you step over, where you go and where you come from, is not necessary at this point, because it is so. If you go, you go; and if you do not go, you do not go. It is very simple. There is no point in talking about it. In fact, there is no point in raising the question at all.

---

* Both phrases are from the *Sadhana of Mahamudra* by Chögyam Trungpa (Halifax, Nova Scotia: Nalanda Translation Committee, 1968). In other contexts, the saying "Nothing whatever, but everything arises from it" refers to the dharmakaya level.

*Stepping over misunderstandings and obstacles.* The second category of sem-de is called stepping over misunderstandings and obstacles, or *göl drip mepar ladawa*. *Göl* is "misunderstanding," *drip* is "obstacles" or "veils," *mepar* again means "without," and *ladawa* means "to step over"; so *göl drip mepar ladawa* means "stepping over misunderstandings and obstacles."

Wisdom, or jnana, is without effort, conceptualization, thought process, memory, and all kinds of mental gibberish. From that perspective, whatever goes on in your mind is no longer an obstacle. Your experiences are no longer a problem, and the memories and dialogues within your mind, or your discursive thoughts, are no longer a problem. They are unbidden from the point of view of reality, since reality in itself is without mind, without conceptualization. It is wisdom without thinking, wisdom without thought process. Therefore, this category is called stepping over obstacles and misunderstandings. There is no room for misunderstandings.

*The falling apart of your home.* The third category of sem-de is *tentsik khungdip*. *Tentsik* means "statement" or "logical statement," *khung* means "home" or "hole," and *dip* means "falling apart"; so *tentsik khungdip* means the "falling apart of your home" or the "falling apart of the logical basis of your life."

*Khung* literally means "home" or "hole," like the holes little animals dig to make themselves a home. So khung is your household; it is your home or your security. The falling apart of your home means that the tunnel you dwell in subsides, or more likely it is deflated or falls apart.

That home is the statement or logic of your life. Usually your statement is that in your life there is the samsaric aspect and the nirvanic aspect, there is freedom and there is chaos, there is good and there is bad. There is also a level at which you cannot make yourself at home because you find that your home is very destructive, but this still means that you are making yourself at home. For instance, in the ascetic tradition, some people make homelessness their home. They have names like *anagarika* because of their homelessness.* However, although making homelessness one's home in that way is very romantic and fantastic, it is indivisible with one's ego.

In this case, we are not talking about creating a home out of your homelessness; rather, you just expand. You are completely exposed and

---

* *Anagarika* (Skt.; Pali) means "homeless one."

dissolved and immersed in the unborn. Since everything is unborn, what is the point of making a home out of it? There is nothing really to hang on to, nothing at all. That is why the falling apart of your home is very important. It means that there is no samsara or nirvana to nest in.

In this category, the notion is that nature is unborn and liberated, and energy is completely all-pervasive, so there is nothing to hang on to. Therefore, your home begins to expand into a greater home—or into a greater nothing or no home, whatever you would like to work with. So a sense of homelessness is the statement here.

*Not being extreme about proportions or directions.* The fourth category of sem-de is *gya-che chog-lhung mepa. Gya* means "proportion" or "extent," *che* means "to limit" or "to cut," *chog* means "direction," *lhung* means "extreme," and *mepa* means "not"; so *gya-che chog-lhung mepa* means "not becoming extreme about directions or proportions."

This category talks about the mind being all-pervasive. The perceptual level is not particularly unworkable, emptiness is not unworkable, and the indivisibility of emptiness and the play of phenomena are also not unworkable. You are not falling into the trap of making a big deal about the indivisibility, so the mind is empty and free from fringes or boundaries, and energy is unceasing and free from negation.

In other words, you may be trying to nest in a philosophical hole. You may make a home in the statement that nothing exists, or that everything exists, or that everything you experience is a gigantic play of maya. The gross level of Hinduism begins to play that particular game. But here we are saying that the play of phenomena is not real. Even OM SHANTIS are not all that OM SHANTI. The play of phenomena is nonexistent. But at the same time, the indivisibility that Buddhism talks about is also nonexistent; it does not exist either. So here the final conclusion is dharmata, without yearning for pleasure or for pain.

*Transcending attachment to biased philosophical beliefs.* The fifth category of sem-de is *chogdzin truptha ledepa. Chog* means "direction," *dzin* means "fixation" or "holding," *truptha* means "philosophical beliefs," *le* means "from," and *depa* means "transcending" or "gone beyond," or also "death" in honorific terms; so *chogdzin truptha ledepa* is "transcending holding on to fixed or biased philosophical beliefs."

At this point, you are completely enjoying yourself in this particular yana. A feeling of boundlessness and expansiveness begins to take place. Therefore, the concepts and sophistries of truth and falsehood somehow become a big joke. At the same time, you begin to realize that your mind, which is primevally nonexistent but energetic, is very powerful. Therefore, there is a nondwelling quality to your mind. You can no longer focus your mind on one thing at a time, or absorb yourself into the higher mystical experiences. So your mind is open and free from both falsehood and truth, and at the same time it is enjoyable.

*Transcending attachment to intellect and to nonintellectual fixations and bias.* The sixth category of sem-de is *lodral chogdzin ledepa. Lo* means "intelligence" or more likely "intellect," *dral* means "without," *chog* means "directions," *dzin* means "holding on to" or "fixation," *le* means "from," and *depa*, as before, means "gone beyond," or the death of that experience; so *lodral chogdzin ledepa* means "going beyond holding on to nonintellect fixations" or "transcending attachment to intellectual and to nonintellectual fixations and bias."

This category is based on being unceasingly without fixations. It is nonthinking. Everything arises from nonthinking, but everything also dissolves into it, so there is no question of holding on to a particular doctrine or dogma.

Such an idea could be approached at two levels: the needlessness of dogma, or the mistake of dogma. Those two are combined together at this point: having dogma is a mistake, and attachment to dogma is also a mistake. But at the same time, the idea that it is not right to have dogma is also transcended. Trying to find the end of the problem or criticizing yourself is another imperfection, which is also unnecessary.

So in general, the idea of the maha ati approach is that it is constantly trying to space you out. In maha ati, by using negation hundreds of times, over and over, you finally develop an enormous positivity.

*Proclaiming that one's mind is in a certain direction.* The seventh and last category of sem-de is *semchok yintu mawa. Sem* means "mind," *chok* means "direction," *yintu* means "is," and *mawa* means "proclaiming"; so *semchok yintu mawa* means "proclaiming that everything is in the direction of mind."

In this case, we are talking about the higher mind of maha ati as the self-existing energy from which samsara and nirvana both arise. But there is no projector; therefore, the projection is self-liberated. In this approach, the ordinary thought process that we experience is seen as transparent and nonexistent. Because of its nonexistence, there is a lot of energy, and clean-cut inspiration begins to develop.

In this section of sem-de, there is an emphasis on energy, which dissolves its own dualistic fixations. Effort and energy do not actually exist, but at the same time, there is a lot of effort and energy. Effort and energy function better because they do not have to keep up with their headquarters, their originator. Since there is no originator or headquarters to check back with anymore, energy and effort are free-flowing. Therefore they become more extraordinary, more able to cut through, and more powerful at the same time.

That concludes the discussion of sem-de, the first section of maha ati.

## The Category of Space: Long-De

The second section of maha ati is the category of space, or *long-de*. This level is more than purely mind: there is no thinking, and there is no intellect. If you are completely willing to relate to the thought process as a working basis, the result is that thinking becomes nonthinking. The thought process is no longer bitchy, and you no longer resent your own activity or that of others. There is the liberation of resting; and even though trying to rest is a hang-up, here there is no problem with rest. There is the liberation of nakedness; and even though trying to be naked is a hang-up, here nakedness is no problem. There is an old-dog quality of noncaring. This discipline of noncaring is not so much the accomplishment of the path, but rather the style of the path.

This section of maha ati refers to a state in which the sense of existence, life, or survival is liberated through realizing that you cannot escape beyond the realm of Samantabhadri, the feminine principle of the all-encompassing space of dharmakaya. You cannot get beyond that basic space. That all-encompassing space could be used as a practice or as a journey, as well as an experience of the final fruition.

Two Approaches to Space: Ying and Long. In the context of the second section of maha ati, the word *dhatu*—the Sanskrit word for "space" or "realm," which appears in terms such as *vajradhatu* or *dharmadhatu*—can be referred to in Tibetan as *long*. However, there does not really seem to be a Sanskrit equivalent for this particular word. The Tibetan maha ati teachers used the word *long* rather than *ying,* which is the direct translation of *dhatu,* and they did so because *long* means much more than *ying.* Ying has a notion of direction; you are putting your effort and energy in a certain direction, toward space or into space. But long does not have any directions or perspectives in terms of this side or that side, east, south, west, or north.

The nondirectional nature of long comes from the existence of the all-pervasive mother, Samantabhadri, the primordial feminine principle. Since everything comes from the primordial feminine principle, you cannot discover any place to run away to. There is nowhere apart from that space; therefore, you are captured, cornered. So choicelessness is an aspect of long.

Long is like a spacious realm in the midst of space. With long, you are in the midst of emptiness rather than experiencing emptiness, for experience implies that there is still a split between subject and object. Long does not have a preference for subject or for object. You are in the midst of space, so your point of view is subjective and objective at the same time. That seems to be one of the basic points about long.

Ying is space that exists at the conceptual level. Ying may also sometimes refer to a realm. It is a different way of looking at the whole thing. Although ying is somewhat experiential, space is experienced as a projection. Long is very experiential; with long, you feel that you are in the midst of space rather than watching space.

It is very important to know that there are these two approaches to space, and that the tantrikas in the maha ati tradition deliberately used the word *long.* However much the Sanskrit language is supposed to be the language of the gods, we have to resort to Tibetan, the language of a barbaric country, in order to understand this.

As an analogy for the difference between these two terms, when you are watching the horizon of the sky and the ocean, and you feel enormously spacious and open, that is ying. But if you are parachuting, that is long. You feel that you are in the midst of space rather than leisurely watching it. So long is more frightening. It is more personal and more demanding. Once you are parachuting, the only sense of up or down you have is that the ground is becoming bigger and bigger. But as far as you are concerned, there is no way of really telling; you are just in the midst of it. That is why you are terrified of it, and maybe enjoying it at the same time. When your experience changes, you begin to see that the ground is becoming bigger—or maybe not—and then you begin to freak out—or maybe enjoy it. Who knows?

With long, you are immersed in space like the parachutist. When you are immersed in that type of space, you feel that you are there for a long time, or at least that the space is there for a long, long time. Such space is all-pervasive, which is why you have a feeling of being absorbed in it. It is not as if you are going through a tunnel. When you are in a tunnel, you begin to look for the other end in order to get out. That kind of space is not impressive; it is depressed space.

FOUR TYPES OF SPACE. There are four types of space, or long, in the second section of maha ati.

*Black space.* The first type of long is what is called the long without cause. It is also called black long, or black space. In Tibetan, black space is *long nakpo gyu mepa. Long* means "space" as we now know, *nakpo* means "black," *gyu* means "cause," and *mepa* means "without" or "not"; so *long nakpo gyu mepa* means "black space without a cause." That is to say, original wisdom does not have a cause or effect. The original mind does not have a perceptual experience of the phenomenal world, or a transcendent experience of the phenomenal world. The original mind cannot experience liberation or imprisonment. It is a pitch-black experience, a pitch-dark, black space.

The bardo retreat is related with black long.[*] In that retreat, black space becomes white and multiple and so forth; it begins to change without using light. The bardo retreat is very difficult to handle, but it is good. It is really juicy. I'll discuss the bardo retreat a bit more later in this chapter.

*Multicolored space.* Next we have multicolored long, which means that whatever arises is its own ornament. In Tibetan it is *long trawo natsok rang-shar gyen. Long* means "space," *trawo* is "multicolored" or "striped like a zebra," *natsok* is "variations," *rang* is "self," *shar* is "rising," and *gyen* means

---

[*] The *bardo retreat* is an advanced retreat practice done in total darkness, traditionally lasting for a period of forty-nine days.

"ornament"; so *long trawo natsok rangshar gyen* means the "self-arising ornament of multicolored space."

The meaning of this type of long is that one cannot prevent one's playfulness, the playfulness of one's mind. You cannot actually cultivate playfulness, and you cannot actually prevent playfulness. It is all-pervasive, without direction, which means it is without guidance or strategies. Your playful action is multicolored constantly. One minute you are shining red, and the next minute you are shining black, blue, green, or some other color. You are multiple. You can flash out all kinds of lights, including black and white. That playfulness is endless.

*White space.* The third type of long is *long karpo*, which is quite simple: it means "white space." The reason this is called "white long" is that there is no action, and there is no point in acting out anything. You have been completely castrated by nobody. Therefore, there is no point in making any effort, since you cannot hold a grudge against the fact that you have been castrated.

The word for castration in this particular tantra is *kadak,* or "alpha pure." Since everything is already purified, there is no possibility of any dirt, so there is no point in trying to do anything. There is no possibility of trying to hold on to programs to make things juicy, rich, smelly, sweet, bitter, and so on.

*Complete absorption space.* The fourth type of long is *long rabjam. Rabjam* in this context means "deepest" or "complete absorption," and *long* again is "space"; so *long rabjam* is "complete absorption space." The deepest absorption of long is that whatever you do experience is the play of phenomena, and whatever you do not experience is the natural characteristic of the absolute. If you know that, you will have no trouble relating with anything.

Generally, when you have a spiritual experience, you think that you should get something out of it. You feel that if you do not get anything out of it after you have made an investment of your energy, your emotions, and even your money, you have been cheated. But with this long, even if you do not experience anything or understand anything, it is still a part of ultimate experience, so why bother to bargain? Why should you feel that you have been cheated?

## The Category of Instruction: Men-Ngag Gi De

The third section of maha ati is the category of instruction, or secret instruction. This is called *men-ngag gi de. Men-ngag* means "oral instruction," *de* is "characteristic" or "category," and *gi* means "of"; so *men-ngag gi de* means the "characteristic of oral instruction."

This category is the closest to ultimate maha ati, if there is such a thing. The idea of this category is that truth is confirmed on the basis of your own understanding, your own realization. It is quite simple. Truth is confirmed on the basis of your own realization in the sense that there is no choice other than simply being here. There is no other choice at all.

Because maha ati's approach to reality is very simple and powerful, very direct and compassionate, it transcends the idea of becoming buddha. It transcends the dharmakaya and all the other kayas. It simply relates with what is known as vajradhatu or dharmadhatu. *Vajra* is "indestructible," and *dhatu* is "realm"; so *vajradhatu* is "indestructible space" or "indestructible realm." *Dharma* is "truth," and *dhatu*, again, is "realm"; so *dharmadhatu* is "truth realm."

The idea of vajradhatu or dharmadhatu is that nothing can live or survive in relation to that kind of space, because vajradhatu exists always and ever. Therefore, this indescribable space transcends enlightenment or the attainment of enlightenment. Even the notion of becoming a dharmakaya buddha is primitive, because when you personally become a dharmakaya buddha, or enlightened, you become separate from ordinary sentient beings. But in this case, the whole thing is one: it is the vajradhatu level and the dharmadhatu level at the same time.

In maha ati, all notions, all dharmas, are regarded as just flowing space, constantly flowing space in which there are no reference points or directions. Everything is seen simply and directly as it is, and there is no way that you can capture anything as your personal experience. With men-ngag gi de, you are transcending strategizing and you are transcending using the intellect, even the highest intellect, as a way to understand this particular yana. And because of such hopelessness, the actual message comes to you right on the spot, like moxibustion.*

---

* *Moxibustion* refers to the burning of moxa, a healing herb, on or close to the skin.

THREE TYPES OF MEN-NGAG GI DE. There are three types of men-ngag gi de: randomness, legend or tale, and self-proclaiming.

*Randomness / khathor.* The first type of men-ngag gi de is called *khathor.* *Khathor* doesn't really mean much; it is just a sort of scatteredness or random choosing. What we choose out of what comes up is not dependent on any cause or inspiration that exists outside of our own spontaneous experience. So khathor is relating to the spontaneity and directness of nowness.

At this point, I cannot help mentioning a particular type of experience that might occur, which is known as thamal gyi shepa. You could call it TGS. *Thamal* means "ordinary," *gyi* means "of," and *shepa* means "intelligence"; so *thamal gyi shepa* is the "intelligence of the ordinary." But in this case, that ordinary mind becomes extraordinary because there is a great deal of emphasis on it. TGS rises in spontaneous suddenness. Therefore, it is known as randomness.

*Legend or tale / khatam.* The next type of men-ngag gi de is *khatam.* *Khatam* means "legend" or "tale," which is a very odd definition. Longchen Rabjam and all the other great teachers of the maha ati tradition wrote their textbooks with quotations, philosophical remarks, and such, and they would insert these bizarre words. And such words would become big words, like *khatam.*

The context of this particular type of men-ngag gi de is the home or hole that we discussed earlier. Here, discursive thoughts are dissolved. One's nature, which is difficult to choose, has been chosen, and that which is difficult to spot has been spotted. One's nature, which is unidentifiable, has been realized. That is the great tale, the big deal. As we get higher, we get more bizarre.

*Self-proclaiming / gyü rangshungdu tenpa.* The third category of men-ngag gi de is *gyü rangshungdu tenpa.* *Gyü* means "tantra," and *rangshung* means "its own proclamation" or "its own text" (*shung* is "text," *rang* is "self"), *du* is "at" or "as," and *tenpa* is "shown" or "taught"; so *gyü rangshungdu tenpa* means "tantra is self-proclaiming."

This category may not seem to mean very much. But what we really mean is that as we go through the contents of this tantra and the Buddhist teachings altogether, we see that this tantra is a proclamation of the great play of birth and death. It is the birthplace of all the teachings of the Buddha, and at the same time this tantra is the way to stop the activities of the busybodies of the lower yanas—it is the death place or charnel ground.

This tantra is the self-proclamation that silences the logical debate about shunyata. It silences that debate through the sound of dharmadhatu words and the proclamation of the dharmadhatu trumpet. Isn't that great? Although we did not say what this self-proclamation is, I think we could still understand it and appreciate it. I must say it is quite joyful to teach this tantra!

# Atiyoga:
## Meditation Practices

*It is fantastic that maha ati people talk about practice. We should be thankful, because they might not have talked about practice at all, which would be embarrassing and not very kind. It would be like saying that those who have it, have it, and those who don't, don't know anything. Talking about practice means that maha ati masters bothered to think of other people. They thought about how we could do it as well.*

THERE ARE two categories of atiyoga practice: *trekchö* and *thögal*. The first category, or *trekchö*, means "cutting through" or "cutting abruptly"; it is cutting any experientially inclined trips. Trekchö cuts through the subtlest forms of spiritual materialism, the subtlest of the subtlest. In the second category, or *thögal*, *thö* refers to the forehead, and *gal* means "transcending"; so *thögal* means "transcending the forehead or peak."

## TREKCHÖ

To begin with, we could discuss trekchö and the practice of cutting through.

## Visualization and Formless Practice

The practice of atiyoga is based on sampannakrama, or the meditative aspect of the tantric tradition. It is based on the idea that you are not dependent on the wisdom of example, as described or recommended in the previous yanas; and you are also not dependent on experiencing the third abhisheka; or on experiencing imagined perceptions and having them actually become true. At this point, we just pay lip service to the yidams. Visualization and formless meditation, or utpattikrama and sampannakrama, become a natural process in the realm of maha ati. But at the same time, they become unnecessary.

Maha ati's approach to visualization is that there is no distinction between samayasattva and jnanasattva. Actually, there is no samayasattva; the whole thing is a jnanasattva setup. Whenever there is a samayasattva visualization, it is an expression of jnanasattva, so you are already on the higher level. You do not have to invite deities to come to you from outside; you have already concluded that the deity is what it is on the spot. Instead of invoking the jnanasattva, you simply acknowledge by means of devotion that such a thing exists. It is more of a self-confirmation than an inviting of external forces.

Although maha ati is based on formless meditation, it does not require so much training that it would take thousands of years to go through it. Maha ati is more a question of intensity, and each time you practice, it is more powerful. Maha ati is like electrocution. It does not take long to electrocute somebody; if you have enough electricity, you can do it in one minute. So in maha ati, practice is more a matter of quality than quantity. This kind of training has been done to me, so to speak, so I think that such an approach to practice is possible. It depends very much on how concentrated you are. In maha ati, it is not that your mind should be focused on practice, but that this general area has been so highly "hot-pointed" that a hot spot has developed. This does not particularly involve the idea of repetition or years and aeons of practice; it is based on one-pointedness.

Because there is more reference to sampannakrama and less to utpattikrama at this level, there is no need to manufacture anything, so that ceases. Such a relief! But we still have to go a long way in order to get there. It is too powerful to swallow right off. At this point, you are just getting a preview of the whole thing. Once you begin to actually do ati-yoga practice, the experience is going to be entirely different. It is going to be much more powerful, a kind of mind rape.

## Meditation Guidelines

If you don't mind further numerology, there are another three categories, which are based on the three sections of maha ati we discussed in the previous chapter (sem-de, long-de, and men-ngag gi de). The three guidelines for meditation are: resting one's mind in dharmadhatu, resting effortlessly, and resting without accepting or rejecting.

These three categories have to do with how to meditate. The question is, once we know all these things, what we are going to do with them? At this point, it is better not to say too much, but just to present a hint or a celebration of some kind.

RESTING ONE'S MIND IN DHARMADHATU. If you practice according to the sem-de category of maha ati, you rest your mind in dharmadhatu. It is difficult to say how to do that, but actually, the point is not to do that. This does not mean not to do that at the stupid, simpleton level, but not to do that intelligently.

RESTING EFFORTLESSLY. If you follow the practice of meditation according to the long-de category of maha ati, you rest your mind without any effort.

RESTING WITHOUT ACCEPTING OR REJECTING. Finally, if you practice meditation according to the third category of maha ati, or men-ngag gi de, you rest your mind without accepting or rejecting. You just rest freely, or primordially freestyle, as it says in the books.

## Mandala Practice

The mandala practice of maha ati is to just experience things as they are, fully and completely. At this point, the teaching of the five wisdoms becomes much closer and much more real, because of the feeling of complete desolation. You realize that there is nothing to hold on to, and at the same time you realize that nothing you could do would make your non-holding-on another security. There is no way to make the ground-lessness another ground. That seems to be quite clear and obvious, and the whole experience becomes very definite and powerful.

From this point of view, you are able to recognize the sameness of visual patterns, sound patterns, and thought patterns. You see that visual patterns are thought patterns, and that sound patterns are also thought patterns as well as visual patterns. There is just one big energy. That energy could represent aggressive upsetness, aggressive anger, aggressive confusion, passive confusion, or whatever you are going through. All of those experiences become visual as well as musical.

## Mantra Practice

An interesting example of this is mantra. In the lower tantras, the seed syllables of the five buddhas are: OM ( 𑖌 ), HUM ( 𑖮 ), TRAM ( 𑖝 ), HRIH ( 𑖮 ), and AH ( 𑖀 ). These seed syllables are complicated patterns of vowel and consonant sounds. In order to express the wholeness of the basic space of dharmadhatu, OM has to be manufactured from the sounds "ah," "uh," "mm." Likewise, in order to express the vajra-like cutting qualities, you have to manufacture HUM, which is again very complicated. It is a combination of the sounds "ha" and "ah" and "u" and "mm." So the whole approach is very much man-made and not very subtle.

By comparison, let me give you an example of maha ati's approach to those mantras. In maha ati, they are simply AH. The sound of AH is not particularly "ha" or "a"; it is between "ha" and "a." AH is just the basic utterance before a word is formulated. You utter AH as a sound of apprehension or uncertainty, or as further inquiry, or in preparation for your statement.

In terms of the five buddha-families, AH joined with the sound "mm" is connected with the buddha principle of OM. AH joined with "oom" is the equivalent of HUM. It is the sound of the vajra family. "Sh" plus AH (SHA) is the sound connected with the ratna family. "Sss" plus AH (SA) is the sound connected with the padma family. It is a sort of hiss that shows you that there is discriminating awareness taking place. "Mmm" plus AH (MA) is connected with the karma family of complete fulfillment of actions. And "huh" plus AH (HA) is the sound of laughter or joy, which is connected with fundamental dharmata, with dharmadhatu or dharmakaya. That HA encompasses all of these other sounds, making vajra laughter.

These mantras are not conventional Sanskrit mantras; they were used exclusively by Indian practitioners of maha ati tantra. Maha ati practitioners did not go along with the scholastic or scholarly approach of regular Sanskrit; they were approaching mantra from an entirely different angle.

## THÖGAL

Up to this point, all the practices have been trekchö. The next set of practices are thögal; this applies to a number of techniques, including what is called triple-space practice.

### Triple-Space Practice

Triple-space practice is very slick and very powerful. It is not just dividing space into three sections, but it means that space is seen basically and in its own nature as having three attributes: dharmakaya, sambhogakaya, and nirmanakaya. The vastness of space, the richness of space, and the pragmatic aspect of space are all experienced.

This is not just ordinary speculation, but you actually experience those three aspects. You experience the vastness of space and the sense of no boundary. You experience the playful aspect of space, in which there is no hope or fear, pleasure or pain, which is the best dance. And you experience the pragmatic aspect of space: the fact that space is hopeless, and it does not mean anything very much. In that triple-space experience, there is the inspiration for everything that you do in your lifetime; but at the same time that particular space is "So what?"

### Secret Mandala and the Three Torches

A person who practices thögal would begin to catch the seed of the mandala that we have within us. The actual practice of this mandala is kept very secret, and one is not to publicize it to students. You cannot actually begin this practice unless you have received direct instructions from a vajra master on how to do it. So the idea at this point is simply to let you know that something like this actually happens.

As the threefold-space experience begins to materialize in practical detail, fearlessness is unquestioned, and everything is seen as one's personal experience. This leads to what are called the three torches: the self-existing torch, the torch of emptiness, and the torch of water.

THE SELF-EXISTING TORCH. The first torch is the self-existing torch. One's eyes are usually very shifty, and at the same time they are very personal and very powerful. With this torch, the experience of fearlessness and insightfulness and so forth bring about a relaxation of your eyesight: you begin to know how to use your two eyes properly. This experience of relating with your eyesight with a sense of freedom is known as the self-existing torch.

THE TORCH OF EMPTINESS. The second torch is the torch of emptiness. This is an actual physiological experience in which you begin to see what are known as vajra chains in your vision. This has nothing to do with being psychic or having visions. It is just seeing the transparent rings that float through your vision. The technical term in the Tibetan tantric texts for these chains is *dorje lugu gyü. Dorje* means "indestructible," and *lugu* means "lamb," and *gyü* means "continuity"; so *dorje lugu gyü* means the "continuity of vajra chains," which are like strings of lambs following one other. (The Tibetan word for "sheep" is *lug,* and the word for "lamb" is *lugu,* which is a loving way of saying "little sheep.")

THE TORCH OF WATER. The third torch is the torch of water, which refers to the physical eye as a bubble in the water. Here the student is instructed in the actual practice, which is to gaze at the moving chains and rings that pass through your vision, either from left to right or from right to left. This is called gazing at the chains.

These chains, or dorje lugu gyü, are transparent; but strangely enough, if your state of mind is not actually in tune with them, you cannot see them. It is possible for anybody to develop the experience of dorje lugu gyü, but to do so you need a state of stability in your practice.

Dorje lugu gyü are the visions that appear to you if your mind is completely relaxed, your body is relaxed, and there is exposure to light. You see these little chains, or optical illusions of little chains, floating down. According to the maha ati teachings, this is the seed of all the mandalas and of liberation itself. The rings you see are the basic mandala structure, and the chains you see are the seed syllables of the five buddha principles.

In order to see these vajra chains, it has been recommended that you look at a lamp, a reflector, a weak haze, or a mirror. When you do so, you can see the chains begin to fall apart and form a visual mandala. The chains are always there, but you cannot see them unless you are relaxed and you have a particular light reflecting on your eye.

At first these chains come down, and when you blink your eyes, they go up and come back down. But as your gaze becomes more relaxed and your state of mind becomes more relaxed, these visual images that were going down will stop. The rings become bigger, and the chains begin to fit into them, and the image begins to become level. The chains break into mandala structures of five, with a middle and the four cardinal directions. Seed syllables or buddha-family symbols begin to dawn and it has been said that you also begin to see tinges of the buddha-family colors. That seems to be the pattern. People do actually see these things, which is not particularly a big deal.

### Eyes as the Gates of Wisdom and Compassion

In maha ati, you do not have to think in terms of seeing deities; what you see happens on a very real level. You do not have to figure out what these chains mean; they are simply chains that you see. It is very simple, and that is the problem. When we talk about vajra chains in maha ati, we are not talking about ideal chains or about symbolism—we are talking about seeing an actual chain. This is the kind of visual instruction that you can receive in maha ati. From this point of view, the maha ati tradition talks about the eyes as the gates of wisdom, or *yeshe kyi go*.

The door of wisdom in our perceptions starts with our visual system. When we perceive light or when we see objects, we get feedback that is much more direct than the feedback we get from any of the other kinds of perception, like hearing, smelling, feeling, or tasting. This level of experience or nonexperience comes from a feeling of compassion. Here, compassion has the sense that we have to relate with our body, as well as relate to all that is expansive and spacious. It means that along with everything taking place on the spacious and expansive level, we have to relate with those rings.

The rings provide a reference point. If your mind is confused, those patterns begin to jump around and drift down. But if there is a direct simplicity of mind, or trekchö, those designs begin to stay and wait for your perception. The way they manifest goes along with the state of your mind. These patterns are not just the rainbows and other spots of light that you see in your mind or your eyes. Seeing these vajra chains is a very special experience. It is a sort of transparent ripple that you perceive.

You might be able to see similar patterns in certain kinds of light, but that is not the idea here. You will probably not be able to catch these chains at this point, because they do not stay long. They go zoom, zoom, zoom, like shooting stars, because your mind is so fast. They react to your mind like a speedometer.

I also would not suggest that you try to see these chains as a hobby, particularly. You have to get into the practice properly, and that will take a long time. In order to observe the vajra chains, you first have to develop a sense of carelessness at the maha ati level; otherwise, they will not stop. When you have developed carelessness, noncaring, and spaciousness, they begin to slow down. In fact, they begin to work for you. So at this level you don't care, but at the same time you do care.

### Form and Space

The vajra chains cannot happen if there is greater space. But at the maha ati level, no space means space, basically speaking. It is a microcosmic-macrocosmic approach in which each contains the other simultaneously: the vajra chains, and the space for the vajra chains. The vajra is just a manifestation, and logically speaking, manifestation needs an environment. Generally, you cannot have form if there is no space, but in this case, form can function without space.

If form has space, then form cannot happen; it becomes decay and death. When you begin to grow little pimples on your body, form is creating space, which is a sign of sickness. If you have been hit and you get a black eye, space swells up inside your skin, which is a sign of unhealthiness. So form needs no space, fundamentally speaking. But spacelessness at the maha ati level does not mean that there is either lots of space or that there is no space. Space is full, and fullness is space, so they go together. Form and space at this point are identical.

## Cutting Through Fundamental Spiritual Materialism

Although your body has this enormous potential, it is a distorted version of that potential. But at the maha ati level, instead of seeing mandalas as purely theoretical, you begin to see actual mandalas happening in your state of mind. It is very direct, very practical, and very simple. That is the key to the attainment of enlightenment. Such a vision may be an optical illusion, one that is samsaric as well as nirvanic; but although it is an optical illusion, at the same time you are seeing a real visual samsara and real nirvanic promises. That is the point of maha ati being so literal and direct—you can actually do this. The idea is that you have a portable visual map wherever you go. There is something happening beyond spiritual materialism.

There is a phrase, *trek ma chö na thö mi gal,* which means that if you have not cut through, you will not transcend the pass. In this phrase, *trek* and *chö* are the two syllables that form *trekchö,* or "cutting through," *ma* is negation, and *thö* and *gal* are the syllables making up *thögal,* or "bypassing."

Cutting through seems to play a very important part in maha ati practice. If you have not cut through, you cannot see these visions. You will find yourself chasing these visions endlessly, and this does not get you anywhere. The point is not that you have to stop the visual images from going down, but that you have to develop a state of being in your mind that is beyond this. You need to develop a state of mind that is cutting through fundamental spiritual materialism. Beyond this, there is nothing to cut through.

Maha ati practice is the product of the most highly refined of all Buddhist wisdom, apart from being able to watch the process of decay in your own body. But it is very difficult to use the state of bodily decay as a path, because you cannot go on very long watching your body decaying. So at this point, it is necessary to work with the experience of your body and your sense perceptions. There has to be something that is to blame for duality right at the beginning, when it first arises. If there are two, there has to be something to relate with the twoness; otherwise, you would not have anything to hang on to or develop. So that seems to be very much necessary.

In working with these kinds of visions, the challenge is your own mind. That is why you first have to develop cutting through. In fact, we could

747

say that the term *cutting through* comes from maha ati. The more you cut through, the more these chains wait for you or actually come back to you. These visions are connected with your brain and neurological system. It is a neurological experience, which has nothing to do with the moisture on your eyeballs. An actual visual mandala is physically, bodily there.

I was thinking of getting some kind of scientific answer to why and how these things exist. I am sure that it is connected with the physical setup and speed of the brain. With this practice, you can actually see your own brain.

## Black Ati Practice

Another thögal technique is called black ati practice. Black ati practice refers to the bardo retreat, the practice of being by oneself for seven weeks in darkness. The bardo retreat is the ultimate maha ati technique. In this practice, you are getting much closer to a sense of unorganized and unconditional space. That experience becomes much more relevant and real. Unorganized means there are no categories and no preparation. Unconditional means that preparations are not geared for the achievement of anything at all.

## Dissolving into a Rainbow Body

Supposedly, anyone who actually attains this level will completely disappear at the end of their life. They attain what is called a rainbow body. So the ultimate experience of maha ati is the rainbow body. In mahamudra, this is called *gyulü*, or "illusory body," which is one of the six yogas of Naropa. It is the same idea, but with two different ways of looking at the whole thing. In either case, the physical body dissolves into the elements; it does not exist.

By dissolving your heart into nonexistence, your body becomes nonexistence, and finally your whole being becomes nonexistence. The only things that you leave behind when you die are your hair and your nails. The reason that is so is because, in spite of the emptiness, openness, and space, there is still compassion. Right from the time you took refuge and you took the bodhisattva vow, that strength of compassion has continued—and it still continues, and it carries you along. One cannot escape from bodhichitta, which is made out of compassion and wisdom together. Nobody can go against that.

Therefore, something continues. Otherwise, this would not be known as the enlightened state; it would be something completely alien to enlightenment.

## Seducing the Masters to Remain

Maha ati gurus who teach this, or who first presented the transmission, have to be beyond maha ati. But they could still be in bodies; otherwise, they could not show us how to do this. In other words, they have been requested *not* to pass away and leave only their nails and hair. That is why at the beginning of tantric texts, the consort always dances and sings songs, offering the pleasures of the five senses and asking the tathagata to teach tantra. There is a constant need to request to be taught and to seduce such teachers into the samsaric world.

When masters remain in samsara, they can teach, but if they are in non-samsaric realms, they cannot teach anymore because they are in another world. So seduction plays a very important part. Maha ati masters are recommended to completely enjoy sense perceptions and sense pleasures. High maha ati teachers, if they *are* high maha ati teachers, must be hedonistic. The more sybaritic they are, the more love and compassion they have for their students. Such teachers are bringing themselves down instead of taking off to the whatever.

For maha ati teachers, if there is no situation in which to teach, then from a sociological point of view, cessation is very wise. For that reason, the teachers of maha ati have to be seduced into teaching, and there needs to be pupils to seduce them. If there are no pupils to seduce them, such teachers might perish, because they do not want to be a nuisance to society. It is very cosmic and absolutely organic. If you do not water a plant, it perishes. It is as simple as that. It is very mechanical, in fact. That is why there is so much emphasis on enjoyment and on the sybaritic character of maha ati teachers.

That sybaritic quality is brought out by the students. So for a maha ati teacher, the idea is that your projection has to maintain you, rather than you having to maintain yourself. That is the problem all along with ego: trying to maintain yourself independent of projections. But in this case, you are maintaining yourself because of the message coming from the projections, so it is an entirely different approach.

Fundamentally, the maha ati teacher is the ultimate bodhisattva. The maha ati teacher is not even thinking in terms of being loving and compassionate, but their whole system is built from interaction with things, or from chemistry. That could be said to be the ultimate bodhisattva or bodhi mind.

## Relating to Symbols

Another maha ati practice involves seeing symbols and messages, not as coming to you from the mahamudra level, but as self-existing situations that you tune in to. As an example, suppose you are meeting a friend, and you arrive early. You feel the awkwardness of getting there too early and being a nuisance by arriving before your friend is ready. But there is no problem with that, because that situation could be utilized. Being too early fulfills some purpose in relating with your friend. For that matter, if you are too late, that also has a quality of skillfulness that is completely spontaneous.

I am not saying that when you have accomplished this kind of skillfulness, it is your highest achievement. The point is that you can do it. Maha ati is not so far from us. In fact, you behave in a maha-ati-like style all the time, not realizing it and not wanting to commit yourself to it. There is maha-ati-like mentality and maha-ati-like intuition and maha-ati-like perception going on in your state of mind that can be related to and worked with. We are not saying that you should be able to emanate buddhas and bodhisattvas from the pores of your skin, but we are talking about something very real. The realism of maha ati is enormously fantastic, and it is true.

Maha ati is the greatest teaching that one could ever think of. It actually makes sense. It is true without any fabrications of formal language. That is why maha ati is said to be closest to the heart of samsaric mind, and that is why maha ati is the end of the journey as well as the highest attainment.

## Maha Ati Practice as the Final Test

The practice of maha ati seems to be the final test. Maha ati is the way to attain enlightenment in one's lifetime. It is a very concrete way of doing so, in fact. It is known that people have done this in half a lifetime, and even in just twelve years. The traditional anuttarayoga retreat practice of the six yogas of Naropa is designed to be completed in three years, three months, and three days. The idea is that if you actually pay enough attention in all those three years, three months, and three days, without being distracted by any external phenomena, you could end up enlightened.

In the case of maha ati, a time period such as twelve years does not refer so much to concentration, but to the actual heavy-handedness of the phenomenal world, which occurs when you see the phenomenal world according to what has been prescribed in the three categories of maha ati tantra.

The point of talking about all these practices is that maha ati is still a path. It is fantastic that maha ati people talk about practice. We should be thankful, because they might not have talked about practice at all, which would be embarrassing and not very kind. It would be like saying that those who have it, have it, and those who don't, don't know anything. Talking about practice means that maha ati masters bothered to think of other people. They thought about how we could do it as well. And beyond formal practice, there is also the meditation-in-action quality of living everyday life from the maha ati perspective of spaciousness and openness.

# 72

# *Atiyoga:*
# *Heightened Experience*

*You have neither gone, nor have you come: the journey is here.*
*That is journey, from the point of view of the maha ati tradition.*
*You are not advancing toward anything at all, but you are advanc-*
*ing here, on the spot. There is nothing to be lost and nothing to be*
*gained. You are here! Right in this very moment!*

## FOUR STAGES OF HEIGHTENING

In the main maha ati experience, or men-ngag gi de, there are four levels or four stages of heightening: seeing dharmata as real, increasing the
*nyam*, insight reaching its full measure, and dharmata being all used up.*

These four levels are not purely experiences that you are going to
arrive at, but they are the journey itself. The four stages of heightening
in the maha ati tradition correlate somewhat to the four yogas of mahamudra. Progressing through these stages does not really mean that you
are becoming better—that you are becoming a better magician, a better
salesperson, or a better professor. They are simply stages of mind that
you go through.

Basically speaking, we have a problem dealing with the phenomenal
world. That is why we go to whorehouses or join the Mafia. It is why we

---

* *Nyam* are temporary meditative experiences of bliss, clarity, and nonthought. For a discussion of nyam in the hinayana context, see volume 1 of the *Profound Treasury*, chapter
42, "Mindfulness of Mind."

check ourselves into the army and why we eat in a Dairy Queen. It is why we check ourselves into a Sheraton Hotel. Moreover, it is why we take a shower, why we shave, and why we comb our hair. It is the reason we take an airplane or a train. It is why we are sitting here.

But as you go through the four stages of dzokchen, you begin to deal with the phenomenal world properly, in a precise way. All four are based on the notion of bringing samsara and nirvana together from the point of view of practice. So they are working on the practitioner's level, which comes out of shamatha-vipashyana discipline, together with some kind of basic vajrayana understanding.

## Seeing Dharmata as Real

The first stage of heightening is realizing dharmata as it is, or seeing dharmata as real. In Tibetan it is *chönyi ngönsum*. *Chö* means "dharma," *nyi* means "itself," and *ngönsum* means "real"; so *chönyi ngönsum* means "real dharmata."

At this stage, you let go of yourself and see real dharmata. Chönyi ngönsum is the intelligence of nonexistence. It is a sort of shunyata experience, where "I" and "other" cease to exist. The Sanskrit word for *chönyi* is *dharmata*, which means "isness," "so-ness," or "what is so." *Isness* is the basic term that we use; but in terms of experience, we might call it "what is so."

Dharma, in this case, refers to any phenomenon or norm that occurs in your mind. It has nothing to do with the Buddhist dharma; it is the dharma of the whole world. So at this stage, mind-made conceptualizations are regarded as a working base. Since there is enormous space everywhere, the consciousness of samsara and the consciousness of nirvana are no longer problems. There is just dharma-ness, or dharmata, seen as basic simplicity.

Dharmata is whatever arises as the product of nonmeditation. With nonmeditation, we begin to see dharmata in reality. At the maha ati level, this is regarded as the first step of concentration. Nonmeditation is free from the sophistries of both postmeditation and sitting meditation, but it is still our path; it is still being maintained by awareness. So even that accomplishment has to become awareness practice.

When you see a particular perception precisely, you begin to appreciate the process of cultivation that you have gone through. You realize that by means of shamatha-vipashyana, you have begun to experience reality. At the maha ati stage, you begin to experience a natural state of wakefulness. You experience that red is red, blue is blue, orange is orange, and white is white. You feel that your ayatanas are beginning to rise to a different level, a different state of being. There is a sense of being there precisely, a sense of awake. You might be woken up by the sunshine coming through the window, and even if you have lots of shades and curtains, you still wake up, because it is daylight. In fact, it is daylight now! That is why I say, "Good morning!" It is awake and precise.

You might already have experienced vividness, brilliance, and a sense of accomplishment, but at this point you realize that your experience is becoming more natural and alive. You are able to feel more deeply the fluidity of water, the burning of fire, the blowing of wind, the solidity of earth, and the accommodation of space. The experiences of passion, aggression, ignorance, and the other emotions, as well as anything that you experience through touch, smell, hearing, and the other senses, are more real and direct. Everything becomes so real and direct that it is almost at the level of being irritatingly too real. It is like feeling texture without skin on your fingertips. This experience is neither a threat nor a confirmation; it is just rawness. Ultimate rawness takes place.

## Increasing the Nyam

Out of that ultimate rawness comes the second stage of dzokchen. In Tibetan this is called *nyam kongphel*. *Nyam* means "temporary experience," *kong* means "further," and *phel* means "expanding" or "developing"; so *nyam kongphel* means "temporary experiences expanding further" or "increasing the nyam."

When you experience such rawness and ruggedness, such brilliance and precision, that experience is no longer subject to kleshas, hang-ups, or memories of any kind. So the temporary experiences of bliss, clarity, and nonthought begin to expand. You might feel an upsurge of energy in your practice, a great upsurge of power.

The reason these experiences expand is due to the nakedness of the first stage of the journey, because dharmata is regarded as real. By maturing to this level, your experiences begin to develop and to become proper and fearless. The rock that you have seen a hundred times begins to become rocklessness; the pond that you have seen before begins to become pondlessness. But this is not just negation; out of that experience, you begin to develop a feeling of tremendous expansion. Any experiences that come along with meditation or postmeditation are regarded as an expansion of your own perception of the phenomenal world. Perception is the gateway. You develop a kind of sense perception of realization, of liberating yourself from the whole thing.

Increasing the nyam could be regarded as increasing delusion or confusion, but increasing delusion, confusion, aggression, passion, and whatever else goes on in your mind is also a part of the path. At this level, you do not judge your experiences. You do not say, "Now I am having a good experience" and "Now that particular experience is dwindling." The phenomenal world is seen as a natural process rather than an attack or an encouragement. So by increasing the nyam, you are taking an enormous step. You are developing more, rather than regressing.

## Insight Reaching Its Full Measure

The third stage in the dzokchen journey is *rikpa tsephep. Rikpa* is "insight," *tsephep* means "come to life," "become aged," or "finally coincide," *tse* means "measure," and *phep* is "arriving" or "reaching"; so *rikpa tsephep* means "insight reaching its full measure."

*Rikpa* is an interesting term, and difficult to translate. "Insight" seems to be the closest definition. Rikpa means that whatever you see is very clear, appropriate, precise, sharp, and luminous. There is the rikpa of eating food, which makes you fulfill your belly. There is the rikpa of riding, which makes you feel the gloriousness and gallantry of horseback riding. And when you have the rikpa of making love to somebody, there is a sense of fulfillment.

"Insight reaching its full measure" means that you are not shooting beyond what you want, or shooting too close to what you want. You are simply becoming a good citizen. Natural phenomena have been considered, the kleshas and other natural energies and processes have been considered; therefore you are *there*. So your insight has matured, basically speaking.

Here, insight means the great brilliance and luminosity that you have experienced as a result of your long journey of shamatha-vipashyana discipline. It also refers to the four yogas of mahamudra that you have already experienced. Insight means that you have realized all of that, and you have also seen dharmata as real and realized that your temporary experiences of bliss, emptiness, and nonthought are expanding.

As a result of all that, in rikpa tsephep your experience of *this* and *that* becomes further nonduality. This could be correlated to one taste; it is the higher level of one taste. Anything that provides any duality at all, including intellect, cognitive mind, responsive mind, mind of enthusiasm toward the world, mind of hesitation toward threats, mind that is pleasure-oriented and indulgent, mind that is giving birth and having the desire to give birth, mind having a sense of doing something, mind of sorting out this and that, mind of separating the synchronization of body and mind just in case there was any pleasure that we missed—all of that begins to change. Day and night, sweet and sour, hot and cold—any perception or realization of cognitive mind begins to reach a level where its intelligence, beauty, and goodness are kept, but its neurosis and its judgmental quality, and its back-and-forth journey between reference points, begins to be exhausted. Therefore, we say that insight has finally come to its conclusion, which is cosmic decency.

We really begin to separate dogma from insight here. This is the complete stripping away of all dogma. At this point, we begin to realize that the conventional idea of the trikaya—the dharmakaya as all-encompassing space, the nirmanakaya as the body of manifestation, and the sambhogakaya as the body of bliss—is a trip, a man-made notion. Those experiences begin to become tortoiseshells rather than the tortoise itself. The multidimensionality of spiritual materialism is finally seen through. At the same time, we see that destroying spiritual materialism is itself a form of spiritual materialism—and destroying that destroying is spiritual materialism as well. Finally we begin to see that even the idea of destroying spiritual materialism or cutting through becomes questionable.

### Dharmata Being All Used Up

Number four, the last stage of the dzokchen journey, is *chönyi sesa*. *Chönyi* is "dharmata" or "dharma-ness," *se* means "used up" or "exhausted," and *sa* means "bhumi" or "place"; so *chönyi sesa* means the "place or state where dharmata is used up or exhausted." Any realization, any attainment or experience of attainment, any experience of a higher level, any flash, any good glimpse of buddha nature—all of that is exhausted.

At this stage, dharmas are worn-out, wasted, used up. Dharmata, which we so cherished, has been used up. You think that dharmata is "Wow! It's a great thing!" But then finally, you lose your heart. You give up your heart, your heart has been worn out, but that is the best thing you can do. When your heart has been worn out, and there is still a continuity of intelligence, there is nothing better than that! This does not provide you with any process of communication. There is not too much claustrophobia, nor too much liberation or freedom. It is very natural. When you let go more, you come back more—but in this case, you are letting go of both of those situations. That is the *ti* of *ati,* the ultimate of the ultimate.

If you experience things as they are properly, fully, and thoroughly, as I like to say, then that is dharmata: things as they are. But at the level of chönyi sesa, even that experience begins to be worn-out. So chönyi sesa is the stage when you have worn out even ultimate discoveries. This may be somewhat hard to believe, but it does happen, and you have to get to that stage.

At this point, the good experience of künshi ngangluk kyi gewa, or the natural virtue of alaya, which you were cultivating so dearly at an earlier level, at the level of resting your mind in alaya, is exhausted. Your attempt to cultivate relative bodhichitta is also exhausted. Trying to attain non-meditation by overcoming the sophistries of *this* and *that* and thinking you have attained something is also exhausted. Journey becomes fruition, and fruition is journey. You have come a perfect three-hundred-and-sixty-degree circle back to square one.

This is the highest level in the vajrayana discipline of maha ati. It is called the maha ati state. There are techniques and disciplines to accomplish this, of course, but we are talking in terms of sampannakrama, the actual meditative discipline that you go through on this journey so that all dharmas and their understandings, including enlightenment itself, are used up.

When we reach this level, we do not just stay breathless or bankrupt. A lot of energy, power, and strength begins to develop, and we gain what is known as the bird's-eye view of samsara and of those who are suffering. We come down from our high horse, and we are more capable, because we are not bound by even the concept of liberation. We become great people who are capable of saving sentient beings.

You develop greater pain and greater sadness because you realize that there are millions, billions, and trillions of others who have not seen even a portion, a glimpse, or a hairline of the dharma. Because you feel greater pain, when you die, you automatically come back and take human form again. At this point, you are free from karmic volitional action and karmic debts, so you volunteer. You naturally come back, and you work harder for the sake of others because you can afford to do so. There is no motivation, or even planning, which could create obstacles. Instead, everything becomes a natural process. You naturally return, you come back, and that gives you strength to help others.

TWO TYPES OF CONFIDENCE. In the wearing out of dharmata experience, the wearing out of achievement, two types of confidence arise: nirvanic confidence, or *yargyi sangthal;* and samsaric confidence, or *margyi sangthal.* *Yar* is "upward" and is connected with nirvana, and *sangthal* means "confidence"; so *yargyi sangthal* is "upward confidence." *Mar* is "downward" and is connected with samsara; so *margyi sangthal* is "downward confidence."

The first confidence is that there is no fear of falling into samsara, and the second confidence is that there is no hope of attaining nirvana. Both samsara and nirvana are completely unnecessary trips. The wearing out of dharmata experience is the final state of hopelessness and fearlessness—it is utterly hopeless and utterly fearless. But again, please take note that at this point we are not talking about the end result, but about the path.

## MAHA ATI DEVOTION

It seems that devotion goes all the way through maha ati—much more powerfully than anything else, in fact. The notion is that any luminosity, any brilliance that you see throughout the entire four stages, you see as an expression of the guru. You cannot experience any one of those stages by yourself; you have to be inspired by your teacher.

Chönyi ngönsum, seeing dharmata as real, is inspired by the teacher, because the teacher represents the entire world. Nyam kongphel, increasing the nyam, is inspired by the teacher, because the teacher's permission and spaciousness have to be manifested in order to allow you to do that. In rikpa tsephep, insight reaching its full measure, the teacher's maturity has to be shared with you so that you are relating with the teacher properly. Chönyi sesa, dharmata being all used up, is the level where the teacher finally lies down with you, because as much as you are an old dog, the teacher is an old dog as well. So the teacher's teaching naturally expands.

The guru is implanted in your mind constantly. It is the guru who actually creates the possibility of dissolving your body as a rainbow. The tremendous sadness and yearning that you experience is devotion. When you use up all of dharmata, the reason this happens is because there is so much yearning and sadness toward the guru. You have a great appreciation for the lineage, so devotion becomes a natural process. In any vajrayana situation in which a samaya bond has been made, the guru is the only one who can actually make that particular mechanism operate properly.

The guru at the maha ati level reduces you into a dot and eats you up. The guru swallows you, lets you come out, and brings you back. The guru dissolves your world, with you and for you, and teaches you that the world is big and small at the same time. The guru brings the realization that sky is earth, and earth is sky, and there is no conflict between the two. The guru gives you sour, hot food that turns out to be very sweet, and then the guru gives you sweet food that turns out to be very sour and hot. Any one of those things! And there does not have to be a definite response, as long as mind is open. That is it. It is it.

## WORKING WITH THE FOUR STAGES OF HEIGHTENING

Experiencing the true nature of dharmata is opening the heavenly realms; it is opening the gate to freedom or liberation. Having done that, there is the progression through the various nyams, or the realm of nirmanakaya. Having experienced the nyams, the next stage is that insight begins to become workable, which is the sambhogakaya. After that, the dharmata begins to become useless or worn-out, which is the dharmakaya level. Through this, the threefold-space experience also begins to materialize in practical detail.

Altogether, dharmas are primordially empty, whether you experience them or not. They are free from changing, from flipping into one another. They are regarded as primordial, as roaming in outer space. Because they do not bring about notions as to what to reject and what to accept, they are also free from hope and fear, and they are not subject to cultivating and exerting. At this stage, you can actually attain some kind of realization.

You might wonder how you are going to attain such a high state. But in presenting these teachings here, the idea is that you could at least have a clear understanding of the possibility of all these stages. Therefore, you will not give up. By understanding these stages, you can be there precisely. You can practice on the spot. And when you wonder what you actually know, you should smile at that! Dharmata is not supposed to have any meaning as such, but it is supposed to have eternal truth, which has never been neglected or cultivated by anyone. That is why from the maha ati point of view, dharmata is called the essence of the dharma. It is like the essence or nature of the sun. As the great maha ati teacher Longchen Rabjam said, "How ironic that samsara works. How ironic that nirvana works." We are talking in those terms.

In maha ati, you are involved with a journey because dharmata is real, experience is expansive, your insight has matured, and you have arrived at the level of exhausting dharmata. It is possible for you to do all that on one meditation cushion. You might ask: Why do anything? Why? Because you have a journey! On this journey, you have neither gone, nor have you come—the journey is *here*. That *is* journey, from the point of view of the maha ati tradition. You are not advancing toward anything at all, but you are advancing *here*, on the spot. There is nothing to be lost and nothing to be gained. You are here! Right in this very moment!

There is more to go, but at the same time, there is nothing more to go. In maha ati language, this is called kadak, or alpha pure. In maha ati, we are getting into the attic, and when we get upstairs, there is no problem. Although the owls and mice and all the rest hover or squeak, still there is no domestic problem. If we learn how to abide with the alpha, the *a*, if we learn how to abide with the owls, the mice, and maybe a little cat, there is no problem. We are in the attic by now, which is fantastic. It is not necessarily entertaining, but it is brilliant. Therefore, it is *dak*. We might bump into somebody's linen chest or somebody's old wardrobe, but we are still in the attic. That is why it is called maha ati: it is the top of the yanas altogether.

## BACK TO SQUARE ONE

At this point we have come back to square one, to our starting point, to where we began altogether. We began with a kind of used-up dharmata, but at that point our experience was on the level of ordinary bewilderment and ignorance. Now we have come back to that used-up dharmata, and we are free from bewilderment and ignorance. We now have precision. Therefore, there is no reference point. Instead there is a sort of transcendental, universal bewilderment.

At this level, what is known as "crazy wisdom" increases. We begin to appreciate and understand deeply the teaching of individual salvation. We appreciate the necessity of shamatha discipline and its results, vipashyana discipline and its results, and the importance of being processed, or shinjanged. All of those situations provide us with a further revelation: we realize that they were meant to be expressions of the kind of freedom that transcends freedom altogether.

At this point, we become the best hinayanists, the best meditators. We also have no problem in exchanging ourselves for others. Tonglen practice becomes natural, and practicing the paramitas also becomes absolutely natural. We begin to find ourselves dissolving into the big ocean of the wakeful mind of Buddha. We begin to realize why the small rivers rush south to join the ocean, and we have no problem understanding why we practice the dharma.

Maha ati vision is the greatest opening of our mind. Dharma finally makes sense out of no sense. The reality of reality becomes unreal, but at the same time it is indestructible vajra nature. We finally reach the level where we are capable of realization. We begin to realize that all dharma agrees at one point. We even begin to realize the truth of driving all blames into one, because we have arrived back at square one.

# Atiyoga:
# Everything and Nothing

*Maha ati is straightforward. It is talking business. In maha ati you have everything, and at the same time you have nothing. The only technique maha ati provides is the leap, but that is absurd, because maha ati does not provide any place to leap from. That is the big joke.*

## MAHA ATI VIEW, PRACTICE, AND ACTION

Maha ati can be described as falling into three parts: view, practice, and action. The following descriptions of these three parts come from Longchen Rabjam, someone who is very nice to read and extremely inspiring, to say the least. These descriptions are not quite slogans, but more like analogies, and although they might be slightly long-winded, I think they are very powerful.

### View

The first three points fall under view. In this case, when we talk about view, we are not talking about a metaphysical or philosophical view, but about an understanding of the nature of reality as it is.

SPOTTING A THIEF. The first point in relation to view is that when you step into the view, you begin to realize the nature of samsaric neurosis, which is like spotting a thief. Suddenly you say, "He was the guy who broke into my room and stole my camera!" It is very precise. The neurosis level is usually vague and uncertain, but suddenly you see that there is one particular spot of neurosis that is actually the troublemaker.

I would like to point out that the maha ati tradition is not all that wishy-washy. It is not that everything is gigantic and beautiful and great, and there are no cares and everything is fine. Maha ati recognizes neurosis in a very specific way, on a very ordinary and very personal level. You can actually point your finger and say, "This is it. This is what has been happening with me. I am too jealous, or I am too freaked-out, or I am too lazy, or I am too this and that." There is a long list of neuroses. According to the abhidharma, there are a great many of them.

ADDING MORE FIREWOOD TO THE FIRE. The second point about view is that when you attain the view, you begin to reach the understanding that phenomena are not particularly a big deal. You realize that samsara and nirvana are one, and there is a feeling of immense expansiveness. As a result, it is said that your body and your speech begin to develop warmth or compassion in the sense of actual certainty.

The Tibetan expression *trö,* or *warmth,* is not so much warmth in terms of emotional warmth. When you say, "Did you get any warmth from that person?" it means, "Did you make any connection with that person? Did you get heat out of that person?" It could even mean, "Are they going to buy your stuff? Can you sell to this person?" This use of the term *warmth* is somewhat slang, a local idiom, and it is used here quite colorfully and beautifully.

So warmth of body and speech develops. Something is actually happening in terms of your view or your perception, which is like adding more firewood to the fire.

WINNING VICTORY ON THE BATTLEFIELD. The third point in regard to the view is that when the view is fully established, you begin to see the tricky qualities of samsara and nirvana; you see that it is all games. That is to say, you-and-me games are constantly taking place, and you begin to spot them and expose them. You begin to gain some kind of liberation from those games; you see them as obnoxious and trivial, and so cheap. Your experience is as though you had won a victory on the battlefield.

## Practice

The next set of three points deals with practice.

ENTERING A RICH MAN'S TREASURY. When you first step into the practice of meditation, it is as if you are entering a rich man's treasury. You begin to relate with your physical experience and your emotions very simply and directly. You experience the activity of your physical body and nervous system, and you experience your emotions, which are on the conceptual level, crank up or crank down, and you realize that there is richness in those experiences. This does not mean that you are going to solve the whole problem of emotions. It is simply that you realize that there is a great deal of richness taking place.

BUILDING A CONCRETE WALL. The second point is that when the practice is actually attained, you realize that your mind is in a particular spot, and you know what your practice is all about. The analogy for that is building a concrete wall. You know everything you have to do. You have built a frame already, so you can put in the concrete and build your wall. You know exactly what to do, so everything is already taken care of.

BEING CROWNED AS A PRINCE. The third point on the practice level is that, when your meditation is fully established, you begin to realize that your mind consists of a great deal of sanity, a great deal of openness, a great number of possibilities, and a great deal of workability—and you are not afraid of that. The analogy for this is being crowned as a prince, and finally being acknowledged as worthy to be a king.

## Action

The third section, or action, is also a set of three points.

AN UPTIGHT PERSON LOSING THEIR TEMPER. The first point has to do with when you first step into your action or first connect with the phenomenal world. It has to do with how you relate with your husband or your wife, your children, your car, your supermarket, your Saks Fifth Avenue, or whatever you have. When you first step into action on this level, there is a gap in which you begin to lose the reference point of any particular desire or emotion.

The analogy for this is an uptight person losing their temper. When such a person loses their temper, suddenly and without any reason—*boom!*—they explode. It is very direct. They lose their temper, go completely insane, and don't know what they are doing. The point of this analogy is that when you begin to concentrate on your world, you have no reference point. That kind of open gap must take place in order to conduct business, in order to actually relate with the world as it is. It is a bit like the experience we have before we sneeze: first there is *ahhhhh,* then *choo!*

A GARUDA FLYING OVER THE EDGE OF A CLIFF. The second point related with action is that at the point of the attainment of action, all the little neurotic desires have been completely subjugated and fearlessly controlled. The analogy for this is a garuda flying over the edge of a cliff. The garuda is the king of birds, who flies very high and does not have any worry about falling down. The garuda has no fear of falling.

A BRAHMAN HOUSEWIFE WHO HAS FINISHED HER WORK. The third point related with action is that when action is fully established, you begin to realize that you can settle down to your own situation. You do not constantly have to make reference to your teachers, your gurus, your books, and so on, but you can actually conduct your own business properly, thoroughly, and fully. Everything becomes bread-and-butter language, very simple.

The analogy for this is a Brahman housewife who has finished her job. Apparently, a high-caste Indian housewife has very precise tasks to do: she is supposed to cook in accordance with a particular diet, and she is supposed to be hospitable to her guests. A Brahman housewife is very concerned with trying to maintain her rules and regulations, but when she is finished with all of those things, she takes a nap and relaxes.

## CONFIDENCE AND COMPASSION

It is said that maha ati is complete expansiveness, that it is nonmeditation. Because it is nonmeditation, it is said to be like a flowing river. Everything is a natural experience rather than a struggle.

Maha ati is not based on personal practice or trying to meet a demand of practice: it is self-liberated. Maha ati is liberated on the spot, so the notion of liberation is questionable. Liberation could be regarded as purely a boundary situation, like the waves and the ocean. So maha ati is like the ocean, which flows in and out constantly. It does not need any help.

Maha ati is self-existing clarity. Experiencing such clarity is like relating with a cloud in the sky, which dissolves back into the space of the sky itself.

Maha ati is like the depths of the ocean. In maha ati, you have already developed your own innate nature: you have completely developed flowingness, spaciousness, and openness. So maha ati is like the depths of the ocean, which does not need to be fed by a river or stream in order to have water, but is self-contained.

Maha ati is self-existence; it is self-experienced. Therefore, it is like a torch that does not need the addition of any fuel to keep shedding light. It is a self-existing torch, a burning fire that exists by itself.

All of these analogies are connected with compassion, sympathy, and softness, as well as with self-contained immense confidence. So the experience you get out of the maha ati tradition is larger-scale thinking. You do not have to deal with the petty little stuff of this and that, particularly, but things can be completely expanded and completely exposed.

## The Maha Ati Experience

The maha ati experience is said to have four main points: nonexistence, all-pervasiveness, self-existence, and aloneness.

### Nonexistence

Nonexistence means, in this case, that if you try to trace back the maha ati experience to where the whole thing came from in your mind or in your perceptions, there is nothing that you can actually pinpoint. The nature of things is that this experience is there, but it is simply not there at the same time.

## All-Pervasiveness

All-pervasiveness means that because you cannot trace this experience back to the pinpoint, it must therefore be everywhere. It has got to be everywhere, because it is not there and it is not here. It is all-pervasive in the sense that wherever you look when you are trying to find the isness of things as they are, and whatever you look at—the vaseness or the tableness or the curtainness or the windowness or the sunness or the moonness or any other "ness"—you do not find its isness quality at all anywhere. So the maha ati experience is all-pervasive; it is all over the place.

## Self-Existence

Self-existence means that nobody actually manufactured such an idea or concept as the nature of the maha ati experience. It was never learned from books. Nobody taught it. It is self-experienced. From that point of view, it is self-existent, but this has nothing to do with the self as a central reference point.

## Aloneness

Aloneness means that there is no particular experience that you can experience; therefore, it is very lonesome. This loneliness is not based on a lack of companionship or a lack of support, but on the absence of any reference point whatsoever. It is very desolate, absolutely desolate.

# THE BIG JOKE

Maha ati does not mean anything: it is just an enormous vacuum. Maha ati is transparent: it does not have any shape or form. The previous yanas may be enlightened, according to the earlier yanas of hinayana and mahayana, but from this yana's perspective, that does not mean anything. In maha ati, one does nothing, completely nothing; and at the same time, one does everything. It is very ordinary, extraordinarily ordinary. You might sleep late—that's the only constructive thing I can think of—and you might make lots of jokes.

I think that it is necessary to take people through the hinayana and mahayana and the other tantric yanas in order to relate to this elaborate joke. You do not get the sudden shock of the punch line unless the joke is built up properly, which is what good comedians do. It is like the story of the little boy looking for his father. He asks his mother, "Where is daddy? I would like so much to find daddy." But after a journey of many years, after his mother has taken him round and round and round, it turns out that his mother has just taken him to their own house. It seemed to the little boy like a very big journey, but in the end his mother just opened the door to the house, and there was daddy. The boy's father had been right there all along, the whole time.

So maha ati is a big joke, in a sense. But there are many kinds of jokes. A cruel joke and a humorous joke both end up being funny, but one is painful and one is pleasurable. Another kind of joke is just a way of shaking off seriousness; it is just a facade joke. An example of a joke played at the maha ati level is that what I am saying is being taped and taken very seriously by a machine that cannot laugh. The machine does its job perfectly as long as it is plugged in; however, it is missing the point all the time. In maha ati, you continue to miss the point until the very last moment. Then there is a moment when you realize that you are missing the point, which is preliminary enlightenment. And finally, you actually catch the punch line.

Maha ati plays a part in everything, but it is not particularly concerned with highlights. It is concerned with the complete totality of the phenomenal world and with the spaciousness of phenomena. Passion and aggression have their respective existences, of course, but that is no big deal. In maha ati, there is allegiance to neither passion nor aggression.

You could say that maha ati is the highest level of cool boredom,* which is very exciting. However, maha ati people are not particularly cool people. In fact, they are usually very temperamental. Vimalamitra was supposedly a short-tempered person. If you asked the wrong question, he would lose his temper and kick you. Because he was so involved with maha ati, as far as he was concerned, manifestation was no problem.

Maha ati is straightforward. It is talking business. In maha ati you have everything, and at the same time you have nothing. The only technique maha ati provides is the leap, but that is absurd, because maha ati does not provide any place to leap from. That is the big joke.

---

* For a discussion of cool boredom, see volume 1 of the *Profound Treasury*, chapter 42, "Mindfulness of Mind."

# APPENDIX 1:
# KAMALASHILA AND
# THE GREAT DEBATE

In his discussion of the origins of the vajrayana tradition, Chögyam Trungpa told the story of a debate between the Indian teacher
Kamalashila and the Ch'an teacher Hashang Mahayana. The story
contrasts the Tibetan emphasis on the gradual path with the sudden enlightenment or "zap" approach of Chinese Ch'an masters.
The interplay between gradual progress and sudden breakthrough
has continued to this day.

TRISONG DETSEN (755–797), the king of Tibet, decided to invite the Indian
teacher Kamalashila to Tibet in order to debate with the Chinese Ch'an
master, Hashang Mahayana. Through the intelligence work of the king and
Kamalashila, it was discovered that generally Chinese masters had no understanding of the vajrayana emphasis on the gradual path. What they taught was
the approach of a sudden zap.

We actually have the same issue in the West. Many Western Tibetan and
Zen masters are concerned with the zap alone, rather than with teaching
how to go about the whole process. In the Zen tradition here, one exception
to this zap approach was Suzuki Roshi,* who worked with people individually.

---

* *Shunryu Suzuki Roshi* (1904–1971) was a Soto Zen master, affiliated for years with the San
Francisco Zen Center, who introduced many Western students to Zen practice. He is the
author of the well-loved guide to meditation entitled *Zen Mind, Beginner's Mind* (New York:
Weatherhill, 1973; Boston: Shambhala Publications, 2011).

Kamalashila had developed a good way of testing the Chinese Ch'an master. When they met, Kamalashila waved his walking stick three times above his head in front of the Ch'an master, meaning, "What is the cause of our involvement with the three realms of the samsaric world: the world of passion or desire, the world of form, the world of formlessness? What is the story behind that?"

In response, Hashang Mahayana covered his head to say, "Twofold ego." Their communication took place fantastically, since both were intelligent, sophisticated scholars of India and China.

Then Kamalashila covered his head with his robe, and the Ch'an master answered this by also covering his head with the collar of his robe, and shaking his robe sleeve twice.

The meaning of Kamalashila's question was: "What causes people not to get into dharma practice? What is the confusion?" In response, Mahayana's answer was, "Ignorance" (covering his head) and "The absence of twofold egolessness" (shaking his robe sleeve twice).

The conversation between the Ch'an master and the Indian pandit went on in this way and, believe it or not, Kamalashila won. Fundamentally, the argument came down to the question of whether we should actually practice or just be zapped. The Chinese were more on the side that we should be zapped, and the Indians more on the side of practice.

So at this point, what we are doing in vajrayana is a combination of the two. We are going to be zapped and we are going to practice, both together, and the zapping part is the lower of the two.

# APPENDIX 2:
# THE SONG OF LODRÖ THAYE

The Song of Lodrö Thaye is a beloved realization song of Jamgön Kongtrül the Great. It can be found in the collection of vajra songs of the Kagyü gurus, titled *The Rain of Wisdom.*\*

HE WHO was foretold by the Victorious One in the *Samadhiraja Sutra* and elsewhere, the glorious, holy guru Lodrö Thaye, also called Karma Ngakwang Yönten Gyatso, composed this vajra doha having accomplished the realization of mahamudra. It is entitled, "The Self-Arising Innate Song upon Acquiring a Mere Glimpse of Certainty in the View and Meditation of the Incomparable Takpo Kagyü."

The illustrious one, Vajradhara,
Who is said to possess the eight good qualities,
Is seen in human form by ordinary men like us.
You are the refuge called Padma, endowed with blessings.
From the eight-petaled lotus dome of my heart,
I supplicated you not to be separate even for an instant.
Though I did not have the good fortune of realization and
    liberation at once,
I was blessed with just recognizing my own nature.

---

\* *The Rain of Wisdom*, translated by the Nalanda Translation Committee under the direction of Chögyam Trungpa (Boston: Shambhala Publications, 1980).

Therefore, concern for the eight worldly dharmas
    diminished,
And I clearly saw the famous luminous dharmakaya
By mixing my mind with the guru's.
I discovered nonthought in the midst of discursive thought,
And within nonconcept, wisdom dawned.
Now, with the joyous appreciation of a lineage son of the
    Takpo buddha,
I am inspired to speak out.

In the west, in Uddiyana, the secret treasure ground of the
    dakinis,
The great siddha Tilo
Opened the treasure of the three gems.
In the north, in the hermitage of Ravishing Beautiful
    Flowers,
The learned Mahapandita Naro
Showed the mark of a siddha, indivisible prana and mind.

In the south, in the land of herbs, the valley of Trowo,
The translator, emanated from Hevajra,
Established the source of the river of all siddhas.

In the west, in the Lachi snow range,
The supreme being, Shepa Dorje,
Attained the state of unity in one lifetime.

In the east, in heavenly Taklha Gampo,
The honorable physician, the second victorious one,
Realized the samadhi of the tenth bhumi.

In the chakras of body, speech, and mind,
The host of siddhas of the four great and eight lesser
    lineages
Obtained the life force of mahamudra
And could not help but attain enlightenment.
Skilled in magnetizing through bodhichitta,

They could not help but benefit beings.
Having obtained the profound wealth, the perfection of
the two accumulations,
They could not help but become prosperous.
Fully understanding that knowing one liberates all,
They could not help but fulfill the great prophecy.

Lineage sons of these wealthy fathers
Possess the great self-existing riches of this previous
karma.
They are the children of snow lionesses and great garudas.
By the power of their family bloodline, they are com-
pletely mature at once.
As followers of the lineage of Kagyü siddhas,
Their meditation is naturally born through the power of
these blessings.

Bragging of their pain in many years of practice,
Proud of dwelling in indolence,
Boasting of having endured such pain,
Undermining others and haughty,
Keeping score with discursive thoughts of self and others
In counting up the realizations of the bhumis and the
paths,
These are the qualities of the ignorant meditators in this
dark age.
We do not possess these, and though I do not have the title
of a siddha,
Nevertheless, through the excellent oral instructions of the
example lineage,
I have seen the wisdom of ultimate mahamudra.

Ground mahamudra is the view, understanding things as
they are.
Path mahamudra is the experience of meditation.
Fruition mahamudra is the realization of one's mind as
buddha.

I am unworthy, but my guru is good.
Though born in the dark age, I am very fortunate.
Though I have little perseverance, the oral instructions are
    profound.


As for ground mahamudra:
There are both things as they are and the way of
    confusion.
It does not incline toward either samsara or nirvana,
And is free from the extremes of exaggeration and
    denigration.
Not produced by causes, not changed by conditions,
It is not spoiled by confusion
Nor exalted by realization.
It does not know either confusion or liberation.
Since no essence exists anywhere,
Its expression is completely unobstructed and manifests
    everything.
Pervading all of samsara and nirvana like space,
It is the ground of all confusion and liberation,
With its self-luminous consciousness
And its alayavijnana.
As for the cognitive aspect of this neutral state,
Its essence is empty and its nature is luminous.
These two are inseparable and are the quintessence of
    insight.
It is space, ungraspable as a thing.
It is a spotless precious clear crystal.
It is the glow of the lamp of self-luminous mind.
It is inexpressible, the experience of a mute.
It is unobscured, transparent wisdom,
The luminous dharmakaya, sugatagarbha,
Primordially pure and spontaneous.
It cannot be shown through analogy by anyone,
And it cannot be expressed in words.
It is the dharmadhatu, which overwhelms mind's
    inspection.

Established in this to begin with,
One should cut all doubts.
When one practices meditation with the view,
It is like a garuda fathoming space.
There is no fear and no doubt.
The one who meditates without the view
Is like a blind man wandering the plains.
There is no reference point for where the true path is.
The one who does not meditate, but merely holds the view
Is like a rich man tethered by stinginess.
He is unable to bring appropriate fruition to himself and
    others.
Joining the view and meditation is the holy tradition.

As for the ignorant aspect of this neutral state,
One does not know one's nature because of the five
    causes.
In the ocean of coemergent ignorance,
The waves of ego fixation's confusion roll.
Cognition becomes a self, and projections become objects,
And so the habitual patterns of grasping and fixation
    solidify.
Thus, karma accumulates and then fully ripens.
The rim of the waterwheel of samsara turns,
But even while it turns, its essence is unstained.
Even while it appears, it is empty of reality.
Mere appearance is the vividness of the trikaya.
Unborn is the nature of birth;
That unborn is unceasing.
On the threshold of nonduality, there is nowhere to dwell.
From this mind, difficult to express,
Various magical displays of samsara and nirvana arise.
Recognizing these as self-liberated is the supreme view.
When this is realized, everything is suchness.
When there are no obstructions or attainments, this is the
    innate nature.
When conceptual mind is transcended, this is the ultimate.

As for path mahamudra,
Mind and the phenomenal world are mahamudra.
Coemergent mind is dharmakaya.
Coemergent appearance is the light of dharmakaya.
When the blessings of the glorious guru
And one's karma come together,
One realizes one's nature like meeting an old friend.

There is no point in much talk,
But the beginner needs various things.
One should abandon either welcoming or sending off
    mahamudra thoughts of past and future.
The instantaneous mind of nowness
Is the unfabricated innate nature.
In meditation, there should be no trace of deliberateness.
One should not stray for an instant in confusion.
Nonwandering, nonmeditation, nonfabrication are the
    point.
With freshness, looseness, and clarity,
In the space of the three gates of liberation,
One is mindful, establishing proper watchfulness.
Always keeping the mind balanced between tight and
    relaxed,
One pacifies the accumulation of subtle, tangible, and
    gross thoughts.
Rest in the state of natural, unfabricated mind.

The four levels of experiences arise in succession,
And the sun of luminosity continually dawns.
The root of mahamudra meditation is established.
Without it, one's talk of higher realization
Is like building a house without a foundation.
However, excessive desire for this is the work of Mara.
Those who persevere but have little learning
Are deceived by superficial virtues
And lead themselves and others along the way to the lower
    realms.

Even the good experiences of bliss, luminosity, and
     nonthought
Are the cause of samsara if one fixates on them.

When you intensify devotion in your heart,
Rock meets bone in insight,
And the ultimate lineage blessing is received.
Not straying into the four strayings,
Not falling into the three misunderstandings,
Transcending the four joys, free from the three conditions,
Realizing through the three stages of birth,
Untouched by the mind of the three great ones,
This is the self-existing nature, undefiled by experience.

Like the center of a cloudless sky,
The self-luminous mind is impossible to express.
It is wisdom of nonthought beyond analogy,
Naked ordinary mind.
Not keeping to dogmatism or arrogance,
It is clearly seen as dharmakaya.
The appearance of the six sense objects, like the moon
     in water,
Shines in the state of wisdom.
Whatever arises is the unfabricated innate state.
Whatever appears is the nature of mahamudra.
The phenomenal world is dharmakaya great bliss.

Both shamatha meditation of natural resting
And vipashyana which sees the unseeable,
Should not be separated but unified
In stillness, occurrence, and awareness.
Beyond abandoning discursive confusion,
Beyond applying antidotes,
There will be a time when you spontaneously reach this.

When you have achieved realization,
There is nothing other than the meditative state.

At the threshold of freedom from loss and gain,
Even meditation does not exist.
But for those beginners who are unable to dissolve the
  hairline of conceptualization,
Meditation is important.
When one practices meditation, there is experience.
This experience arises as the adornment of insight.

This path is divided into the four yogas:
One-pointedness means recognizing the nature of mind;
Divided into the lesser, medium, and greater stages:
One sees the alternation of bliss and luminosity,
One masters resting in samadhi,
And experience continuously appears as luminosity.

Simplicity means realizing the mind is without root;
Divided into the lesser, medium, and greater stages:
One realizes that the arising, ceasing, and dwelling are
  empty,
One is free from the ground and root of fixating on
  appearance or emptiness,
And one resolves the complexity of all dharmas.

One taste means dissolving appearance and mind into each
  other;
Divided into the lesser, medium, and greater stages:
All dharmas of samsara and nirvana are dissolved into
  equal taste,
Appearance and mind become like water poured into
  water,
And from one taste, the various wisdoms arise.

Nonmeditation means the utter exhaustion of conceptual
  mind;
Divided into the lesser, medium, and greater stages:
One is free from meditation and meditator,
The habitual patterns of primitive beliefs about reality are
  gradually cleared away,

And the mother and son luminosity dissolve together.
The wisdom of dharmadhatu extends throughout space.

In short, in meditation:
One-pointedness means that mind is still as long as one
    wishes,
Seeing the very nature of ordinary mind.
Simplicity means the realization of groundlessness.
One taste means liberating
All possible dualistic fixations through insight.
Nonmeditation means transcending all sophistries of medi-
    tation and nonmeditation,
The exhaustion of habitual patterns.

In this way, from the great lords of yogins,
Naropa and Maitripa,
Down to the lord guru Pema Wangchen,
The golden garland of the Kagyüs
Reached the dharmakaya kingdom of nonmeditation,
Spontaneously cleared away the darkness of the two
    obscurations,
Expanded the great power of the two knowledges,
Opened the treasury of benefit for the sake of others
    pervading space,
And remained in the refuge of mind free from doubt.
The Kagyü lineage is known to be passed from one to
    another.
It is known not by words alone, but by their meaning.
Please guide even such a lowborn savage as myself,
Who possesses the merest mark of your noble lineage,
Quickly to the kingdom of nonmeditation.
Kind one, please utterly exhaust my conceptual mind.

The fruition mahamudra is spoken of like this:
The ground is receiving the transmission of the innate
    trikaya;
The path is applying the key points of the view and
    meditation;

The fruition is the actualization of the stainless trikaya.
Therefore, its essence is emptiness, simplicity, dharmakaya.
Its manifestation is the luminous nature of sambhogakaya.
Its strength, manifold and unceasing, is nirmanakaya.
This is the sovereign of all reality.
The nature of mahamudra is unity,
The realm of dharmas free from accepting or rejecting.
Possessing the beauty of unconditioned bliss,
It is the great and vast wealth of wisdom.
It is the natural form of kindness transcending thought.
Through prajna, it does not dwell in samsara
Through karuna, it does not dwell in nirvana.
Through effortlessness, buddha activity is spontaneously
    accomplished.
The luminosity of ground and path, mother and son,
    dissolve together.
The ground and fruition embrace one another.
Buddha is discovered in one's mind.
The wish-fulfilling treasure overflows within.
E MA! How wonderful and marvelous!

Since in the view of mahamudra
Analysis does not apply,
Cast mind-made knowledge far away.
Since in the meditation of mahamudra
There is no way of fixating on a thought,
Abandon deliberate meditation.
Since in the action of mahamudra
There is no reference point for any action,
Be free from the intention to act or not.
Since in the fruition of mahamudra
There is no attainment to newly acquire,
Cast hopes, fears, and desires far away.

This is the depth of the mind of all Kagyüs.
It is the only path on which the victorious ones and their
    sons journey.

Theirs is the upaya that reverses the vicious circle of
    existence
And the dharma that brings enlightenment in one life.
Here is the essence of all the teachings, sutras and tantras.
May I and all sentient beings pervading space
Together attain the simultaneity of realization and
    liberation,
And attain supreme mahamudra.

*In order not to transgress the command seal of emptiness endowed with
all the supreme aspects, the one whose knowledge is transcendent and who
manifested in the form of the vajraholder, I, the subject of Padma, the Yönten
Gyatso Lodrö Thaye, composed this at Künzang Dechen Ösel Ling on the left
slope of the third Devikoti, Tsari-like Jewel Rock.* SUBHAM.

# APPENDIX 3:
# THE CHARNEL GROUND

In this 1972 poem,* Trungpa Rinpoche provides a vivid evocation of the energy of the charnel ground: the field where the dead and dying are brought, a place where yogis meditate on impermanence, and the ground from which all mandalas arise.

THE WASTELAND where thorny trees grow and fearsome animals roam, a vast charnel ground. People deposit corpses of human beings, horses, camels, and other once-living things. Recently the surrounding country suffered famine and plague. People lost honor and dignity because they brought half-dead bodies to the charnel ground. Now ravens, crows, vultures, eagles, jackals, and foxes fight over the carrion. They are continually scooping out eyes, digging out tongues. Sometimes in fleeing from each other, they let fall heads, arms, legs, internal organs. The wind carries the incense of rot. The amusing theater of life and death is performing constantly. Self-existing energy is like a wave of the ocean driven by a mighty wind. There is a new display in every corner of the scene. Sometimes one would like to look at them, but does not dare. Nevertheless one cannot prevent one's eyes focusing. Occasionally there are flickering thoughts of escape. Sometimes one does not believe what one

---

* From *Garuda III: Dharmas without Blame* (Boulder, Colo., and Berkeley, Calif.: Vajradhatu, in association with Shambhala Publications, 1973). This work also appears in *The Collected Works of Chögyam Trungpa,* vol. 7 (Boston: Shambhala Publications, 2004).

sees, and regards it as a dream. But if one tries to find the moment when one went to sleep, it is not there.

> When the plague, accompanied by famine, arises,
> The tigers and vultures have a feast.
> Comparing the delicacies of tongues and eyes,
> Logicians find a new study.
> Perhaps one cannot imagine it, but seeing removes all doubt.
> This is the world of existence: daring not to exist.

*Chögyam Trungpa Rinpoche*
*May 26, 1972*

# APPENDIX 4:
# NOTECARDS

THE ORIGINAL notecards Trungpa Rinpoche used in preparing his Vajra-dhatu seminary talks are preserved in the Shambhala Archives collection. His notes, usually written in Tibetan on 3″ by 5″ cards, are in the process of being translated by the Nalanda Translation Committee. In later seminaries, Trungpa Rinpoche entered the meditation hall to begin his talk in a formal procession that included a person holding his notecards aloft in a Japanese brocade wallet.

The following examples include copies of the original notecard front and back (if applicable), the typed Tibetan version, and the English translation.[*]

---

[*] The copies of the original notecards may not conform to their original size.

1974 Vajradhatu Seminary
Talk 22: Space
November 11, 1974
Source for *Profound Treasury,* chapter 17, "The Play of Space and Form"

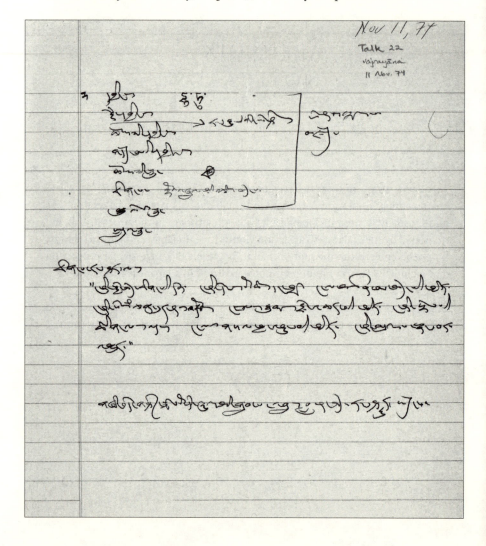

11 Nov. 1974

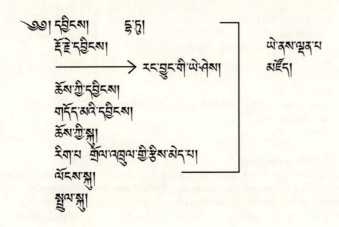

ༀ༔ དབྱིངས། རྫ་ཊ།
རྡོ་རྗེ་དབྱིངས།
རང་བྱུང་གི་ཡེ་ཤེས།
ཆོས་ཀྱི་དབྱིངས།
གདོད་མའི་དབྱིངས།
ཆོས་ཀྱི་སྐུ།
རིག་པ་གྲོལ་འབྱུལ་ཀྱི་རྩིས་མེད་པ།
ལོངས་སྐུ།
སྤྲུལ་སྐུ།

ཡེ་ནས་ལྷུན་པ
མཛོད།

རིག་པ་རང་ཤར་ལས།
"ང་ནི་སྐྱེ་མེད་རིག་པའི་དོན། དེ་ནི་དངོས་པོའི་ཆོས་དང་བྲལ། ང་ལ་མཚན་མ་མེད
པའི་ཕྱིར། ང་ནི་སེམས་ཅན་དུར་ནས་འདོན། ང་ལས་སྒྱགས་རྗེ་འཆར་བའི་ཕྱིར། ང་
ནི་སྟོང་པའི་ཆོག་ལས་འདས། ང་ལས་གསལ་བྱུ་འབྱུང་བའི་ཕྱིར། ང་ནི་མུན་པ་སྤང་བར
འགྱུར།"

གཞི་བདེ་གཤེགས་སྙིང་པོའི་ལྷུན་གྱིས་གྲུབ་པ་འཕགས་བུ་ལྟ་ན་མེད་རང་ཤར་དུ་ཡོད་པ།

11 Nov. 1974

space      DHATU
vajradhātu                            primordial
———→ self-existing wisdom     treasury
dharmadhātu
primordial space
dharmakāya
awareness: no plans for liberation or confusion
sambhogakāya
nirmāṇakāya

From *Self-Arising Awareness:*
I am ultimate, unborn awareness. I am free from the dharmas of substance. Since I have no characteristics, I bring sentient beings out of the charnel ground. Since compassion arises from me, I am beyond any talk of "emptiness." Since luminosity arises from me, I illuminate the darkness.

The ground, sugatagarbha, is spontaneously present, self-arising, the unsurpassable fruition.

1983 Vajradhatu Seminary
Talk 16: The Four Stages of Ati
March 14, 1983
Source for *Profound Treasury*, chapter 72, "Atiyoga: Heightened Experience"

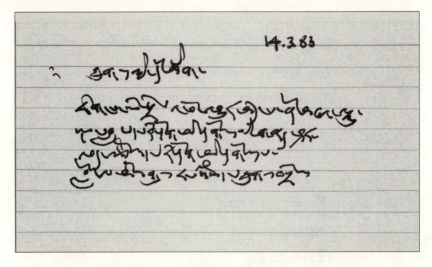

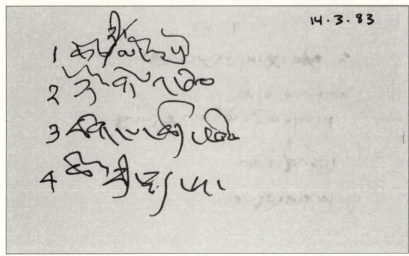

14.3.83

༄༅། ཕྱགས་ཀྱི་དམ་ཚིག

རིག་པ་ཡེ་སྟོང་འཕོ་འགྱུར་མེད་པ་རྣམ་མཁའན་ལྟ་བུ།

སྣང་བྲག་དང་རེ་དོག་མི་དགོས་པའི་གནད་ཤར།

འབད་རྩོལ་དང་རེ་དོག་མི་དགོས་པ།

བླ་མ་ལ་མོས་གུས། རང་སེམས་དང་ཕྱགས་བསྲེས།

14.3.83

1 ཚོས་ཉིད་མ་ཏོན་སུམ།

2 ཉམས་གོང་འཐེལ།

3 རིག་པ་ཚད་ཕེབ།

4 ཚོས་ཉིད་ཟད་ས།

14.3.83

samaya of mind

within awareness, primordially empty and unchanging like space,
the crucial point that there is no need for accepting and rejecting or hope and fear dawns
there is no need for struggle and effort or hope and fear
devotion to the guru, the guru's mind mixes with one's own mind

---

14.3.83

1 seeing dharmatā as real
2 experiences increasing further
3 insight reaching its full measure
4 dharmatā used up*

---

* For the purposes of this translation, we matched the wording used in the talk; the more standard translation
of this term is *the exhaustion of dharmatā.*

# APPENDIX 5:
# OUTLINE OF TEACHINGS

The numbered lists of teachings in this book have been organized into outline-style here as a study aid. The lists are in order of appearance in the text.

## PART ONE. APPROACHING THE VAJRAYANA

Introduction
  Three Yanas
    1. Hinayana
    2. Mahayana
    3. Vajrayana

  Twofold Bodhichitta
    1. Relative bodhichitta
    2. Absolute bodhichitta

  Three Yanas as a House
    1. Hinayana / foundation
    2. Mahayana / walls
    3. Vajrayana / roof

  Three Components of the Teachings
    1. Shila / discipline
    2. Samadhi / meditation
    3. Prajna / knowledge

Chapter 1. The Dawning of the Great Eastern Sun
Three Qualities of the Great East
    1. Primordial / döma
    2. Eternal / takpa
    3. Self-existence / lhündrup

Three Marks of Samsaric Existence Transformed into the Three
    Qualities of the Great East
    1. Suffering / döma
    2. Change / takpa
    3. Egolessness / lhündrup

Two Levels of Loyalty
    1. Setting-sun loyalty
    2. Great Eastern Sun loyalty

Chapter 2. The Transition to Vajrayana
Two Styles of Tantric Tradition
    1. Spring continuation / taking the ground as the path
    2. Autumn continuation / taking the fruition as the path

Chapter 3. Entering the Diamond Path on a Solid Foundation
Three Levels of Neurosis
    1. Body neurosis
    2. Speech neurosis
    3. Mind neurosis

Three Yanas as Three Ways of Seeing Reality
    1. Hinayana / seeing reality in a factual, ordinary, wise way
    2. Mahayana / seeing reality in terms of the logic of the path
    3. Vajrayana / paying more attention to the relative truth

Two Kinds of Truth
    1. Relative truth / kündzop
    2. Absolute truth / töndam

Chapter 4. Uncovering Indestructible Goodness and Wakefulness
Two Aspects of Buddha Nature
    1. Tenderness
    2. Wisdom

Five Types of Samantabhadra
1. All-good path
2. All-good ornamentation
3. All-good teacher
4. All-good insight
5. All-good realization

Chapter 5. The Multifaceted Diamond Path
Threefold Vajra Principle
1. Vajra body / indestructibility
2. Vajra speech / lucidness
3. Vajra mind / penetrating

Nine Traditional Definitions for Vajrayana
1. Tantra or Tantrayana
2. Mantrayana
3. Vidyadharayana
4. Fruition yana
5. Upayayana
6. Guhyayana
7. Dharanayana
8. Yana of luminosity
9. Imperial yana

Chapter 6. Seven Aspects of Vajrayana: The Space before First Thought
Seven Aspects of Vajrayana
1. Marked with Samantabhadra
2. Possessing adhishthana
3. Acquiring siddhis
4. Confirmation
5. No obstacles
6. Never violating samaya
   Four Extreme Beliefs
       a. Existence
       b. Nonexistence
       c. Both
       d. Neither
7. Always restoring samaya, even when it is violated

PART TWO. THE TEACHER-STUDENT RELATIONSHIP

Chapter 7. The Role of the Guru or Vajra Master
The Guru Principle in the Three Yanas
  1. Hinayana / preceptor / upadhyaya / khenpo
  2. Mahayana / spiritual friend or kalyanamitra / guru / lama
  3. Vajrayana / vajra master / vajracharya / dorje loppön

Two Expressions of the Vajra Master
  1. Relative (kündzop) guru
  2. Ultimate (töndam) guru

Five Aspects of the Guru
  1. Body as vajra sangha
  2. Speech as the teachings
  3. Mind as the Buddha
  4. Quality as the yidams
  5. Action as the dharmapalas

Two Descriptions of the Guru Principle
  1. Possessor of all knowledge
  2. Maker of situations and inspiration

Chapter 8. The Root Guru as the Epitome of Freedom
Three Aspects of the Vajra World
  1. The teacher
  2. The yidams
  3. The practitioner

Three Aspects of Sacred Outlook in Terms of Lojong
  1. Vajra body / "When the world is filled with evil, transform all mishaps into the path of bodhi"
  2. Vajra speech / "Whatever you meet unexpectedly, join with meditation"
  3. Vajra mind / "Seeing confusion as the four kayas is unsurpassable shunyata protection"

Five Factors for Developing Appreciation for the Teacher and the Teachings
  1. Trust
  2. Faith

Chapter 13. The Later Trungpas
Sixth Trungpa / Tendzin Chökyi Gyatso (1715–1734 est.)
Seventh Trungpa / Jampal Chökyi Gyatso (1743–1768 est.)
Eighth Trungpa / Gyurme Tenphel (b. 1771)
Ninth Trungpa / Tenpa Rabgye (19th century)
Tenth Trungpa / Chökyi Nyin-je (1875–1938)
Eleventh Trungpa / Chökyi Gyatso (1940–1987)
Twelfth Trungpa / Chökyi Senge (b. 1989)

## PART FOUR. ESSENTIAL TEACHINGS

Chapter 14. Unconditional Ground
Two Aspects of Experiencing Vajra Nature
1. Ku / body aspect
2. Yeshe / jnana / shining and monitoring aspect

Threefold Vajra Nature (Vajra Being)
1. Vajra body
2. Vajra speech
3. Vajra mind

Twofold Freedom
1. Freedom from samsara
2. Freedom from nirvana

Chapter 15. Transcending Mental Concepts
Two Types of Lo
1. Ordinary lo
a. Lo-pham / disappointment
b. Lo-te / trustworthiness
2. Transcendental lo
Lodrö / established minding

Chapter 16. Fundamental Magic
Three Root Kleshas
1. Passion
2. Aggression
3. Ignorance

Five Vajrayana Sayings
1. Rikpa free from sem
2. Buddha without breath

2. Mahayana bodhisattva vow
   Six Paramitas
      a. Generosity
      b. Discipline
      c. Patience
      d. Exertion
      e. Meditation
      f. Prajna (wisdom)
3. Vajrayana samaya vow

Chapter 20. Positive Entrapment
Threefold Nailing
1. The guru
2. The yidam
3. The student

Threefold Tantric Samaya
1. Technique
2. Devotion
3. Being beyond technique

Chapter 21. The Different Types of Samaya
Three Aspects of Samaya
1. Seed samaya
2. Upaya samaya
3. Fruition samaya

Samaya of Threefold Vajra Nature
1. Samaya of vajra body / chagya kü tamtsik
2. Samaya of vajra speech / trilbu sunggi tamtsik
3. Samaya of vajra mind / dorje thukkyi tamtsik

Vajra Master Samaya
1. Samaya of body
2. Samaya of speech
3. Samaya of mind

Chapter 22. Maintaining the Samaya Vow
Threefold Samayashila Bond
1. Bond to work on yourself
2. Bond not to create suffering for yourself or other beings
3. Bond to overcome the kleshas

3. Padma family
4. Karma family
5. Buddha family

Qualities of the Five Buddha-Families
For a listing of buddha-family qualities, see "Attributes of the Five
   Buddha-Families," p. 311.

Chapter 27. The Outer Mandala
Threefold Mandala Principle
   1. Outer
   2. Inner
   3. Secret

Four Styles of Entering into Reality
   1. Ayatanas
      The Twelve Ayatanas
         1–2. Eyes / sights
         3–4. Ears / sounds
         5–6. Nose / smells
         7–8. Tongue / tastes
         9–10. Body / touchable objects
         11–12. Mind / mental objects
   2. Dhatus
      The Eighteen Dhatus (The Twelve Ayatanas Plus
         Consciousnesses)
         1–2–3. Eyes / sights / seeing consciousness
         4–5–6. Ears / sounds/ hearing consciousness
         7–8–9. Nose / smells / smelling consciousness
         10–11–12. Tongue / tastes / tasting consciousness
         13–14–15. Body / touchable objects / touching consciousness
         16–17–18. Mind / mental objects / mind consciousness
   3. Cognition
   4. Deeper perception

Division of Ordinary World
   1. Friends / desirable
   2. Enemies / undesirable
   3. Neutrals / couldn't care less

Entering through the Four Gates of the Mandala
1. Eastern gate / entering peacefully
2. Southern gate / entering with richness
3. Western gate / entering with passion
4. Northern gate / entering with aggression

Chapter 28. The Inner Mandala
Constituents of the Inner Mandala
The Five Skandhas
1. Form
2. Feeling
3. Perception / impulse
4. Concept / formation
5. Consciousness

The Five Kleshas
1. Ignorance
2. Aggression
3. Pride
4. Passion
5. Jealousy

The Five Wisdoms
1. Wisdom of All-Encompassing Space / Center
2. Mirrorlike Wisdom / East
3. Wisdom of Equanimity / South
4. Discriminating-Awareness Wisdom / West
5. Wisdom of All-Accomplishing Actions / North

Three Constituents of the Body from the View of Inner Mandala
1. Prana
2. Nadi
3. Bindu

Chapter 29. The Secret Mandala
Vajrayana Magic
1. Magic of encountering the vajrayana
2. Magic of meeting a teacher
3. Magic of practice

## PART SEVEN. PRELIMINARY PRACTICES

Chapter 30. The Four Reminders
  The Four Reminders
    1. Precious human birth
      a. Free
        Free from the Eight Unfavorable Conditions
          i. Living in the hell realm
          ii. Living in the hungry ghost realm
          iii. Living in the animal realm
          iv. Being a barbarian uninterested in spirituality
          v. Being a long-life god attached to temporary happiness
          vi. Holding wrong views
          vii. Being born at a time when the Buddha is absent
          viii. Being stupid and unable to express yourself
      b. Well-favored
        Possessing the Ten Positive Circumstances
          i. Being human
          ii. Being born in a country where one can meet holy persons
          iii. Having all the senses
          iv. Not reverting to evil deeds
          v. Having devotion to the teachings
          vi. A buddha has appeared in this world
          vii. A buddha has taught the dharma
          viii. The dharma continues to be taught
          ix. There are followers of the dharma
          x. There is love and support from others
      c. Difficult to find
    3. Death and impermanence
    4. Karmic cause and effect
    5. The torment of samsara

Chapter 31. The Four Preliminaries
  The Four Preliminaries (Ngöndro)
    1. Prostrations
    2. Refuge formula
    3. Vajrasattva mantra recitation
    4. Mandala offering
      Two Accumulations
        a. Relative accumulation / material wealth / powers
        b. Absolute accumulation / yeshe

Chapter 32. Guru Yoga
Threefold Logic of Devotion
   1. Blessings / chinlap
   2. Changing your perception / nangwa-gyur
   3. Nonthought / tokpa gak

PART EIGHT. EMPOWERMENT

Chapter 33. Transmission
Necessities for Relating with Vajrayana and the Vajrayana Teacher
   1. Playfulness
   2. Generosity

Three Levels of Transmission
   1. Hinayana
   2. Mahayana
   3. Vajrayana

Three Types of Confirmation
   1. Lung / access to powers of abhisheka
   2. Wang / abhisheka itself
   3. Tri / detailed instructions

Chapter 34. Surrendering
Two Levels of Transmission
   1. Popping your reserves
   2. Introducing freshness and ordinariness

Chapter 35. Entering the Vajra Mandala

Chapter 36. Stability, Luminosity, and Joy
Working with the Trikaya Principle
   1. Dharmakaya / shamatha / formless kaya
   2. Sambhogakaya / vipashyana / form kaya
   3. Nirmanakaya / vipashyana / form kaya

Levels of Great Joy
   1. Mahasukha of example
   2. Mahasukha of reality

Chapter 37. The Four Main Abhishekas
The Four Main Abhishekas
1. Outer abhisheka / coronation
Five Steps of the Outer Abhisheka
a. Water abhisheka / mirrorlike wisdom
b. Crown abhisheka / wisdom of equanimity
c. Vajra abhisheka / discriminating-awareness wisdom
d. Ghanta abhisheka / wisdom of all-accomplishing actions
e. Name abhisheka / wisdom of all-encompassing space
2. Secret or inner abhisheka / mutual intoxication
3. Prajna-jnana abhisheka / bliss
Four Types of Bliss
a. Freedom from ego
b. Worthy of bliss
c. No inhibitions about going beyond bliss into greater
freedom
d. Transcending freedom and bliss altogether
4. Formless abhisheka / *That*

Two Types of Abhisheka
1. With elaboration / trö-che / first through third abhishekas
2. Without elaboration / trö-me / fourth abhisheka

PART NINE. VAJRAYANA PRACTICE

Chapter 38. Visualization and Sadhana Practice
Two Stages of Vajrayana Practice
1. Visualization or creation stage / kyerim / utpattikrama
2. Nonvisualization or completion stage / dzogrim /
sampannakrama

Two Aspects of Yidam
1. Samayasattva
2. Jnanasattva

Giving Birth to Visualization in Eight Steps
1. Formless meditation / dzogrim / shunyata deity
2. Divine principle of letter / visualize bija mantra or seed syllable
3. Divine sound principle / visualize rays of light from bija mantra

4. Transformation of sound into visual symbolism
5. Divine principle of form / visualization takes shape
6. Divine principle of mudra / visualize mudras, symbols, and scepters in hands of deities
7. Divine principle of mark / repetition of mantra
8. Everything dissolves back into charnel ground

Three-Stage Visualization Process
1. Seed syllable / potential of form
2. Symbol / possibility of form
3. Fruition / actual form

Chapter 39. The Importance of a Nontheistic View
Three Approaches to Divinity
1. Hinayana approach / prajna
2. Mahayana approach / buddha nature
3. Vajrayana approach / no external salvation

PART TEN. THE TANTRIC JOURNEY: LOWER TANTRA

*Kriyayoga: The Yana of Purity*

Chapter 40. Kriyayoga: Trust in Reality
The Nine Yanas
1. Shravakayana /hinayana
2. Pratyekabuddhayana / hinayana
3. Mahayana or bodhisattvayana / mahayana
4. Kriyayogayana / vajrayana
5. Upayogayana / vajrayana
6. Yogayana / vajrayana
7. Mahayogayana / vajrayana
8. Anuyogayana / vajrayana
9. Atiyogayana / vajrayana

The Six Tantric Yanas (Old Translation School)
Lower Tantra
1. Kriyayogayana
2. Upayogayana
3. Yogayana

Higher Tantra
    4. Mahayogayana
    5. Anuyogayana
    6. Atiyogayana / maha ati

Four Tantric Yanas / Four Orders of Tantra (New Translation School)
    1. Kriyayoga
    2. Upayoga
    3. Yogayana
    4. Anuttarayoga / mahamudra

Two Approaches to Kündzop in Kriyayoga
    1. Purity of action (of body and speech)
    2. Purity of attitude
        a. Attitude toward form
        b. Attitude toward speech
        c. Attitude toward mind

Development of Purity
    1. Relative bodhichitta / not taking in impurity
    2. Absolute bodhichitta / belief or conviction enters your system
    3. Union of relative and absolute bodhichitta / seeing overall purity of phenomenal world

Chapter 41. Kriyayoga: Purification
Two Types of Surrendering
    1. Surrendering the gross ego / relative bodhichitta
    2. Surrendering the refined ego / absolute bodhichitta

Chapter 42. Kriyayoga: Empowerment
Four Foundation Practices
    1. Prostrations
    2. Refuge formula
    3. Vajrasattva mantra recitation
    4. Mandala offering

Five Abhishekas of Kriyayoga
    1. Preliminary abhisheka / abhisheka of the vajra disciple
    2. Water abhisheka / dharmakaya
        Five Vase Initiations
            a. Opening water abhisheka
            b. Water abhisheka of all the deities

      c. Vase of the shravakas and pratyekabuddhas

      d. Vase of the bodhisattvas

      e. Vase of the Buddha

  3. Crown abhisheka / sambhogakaya and nirmanakaya

  4. Water purification and protection abhisheka

  5. Enriching abhisheka

    Eight Ingredients or Offerings

      a. Milk drink

      b. Kusha grass mat

      c. Sesame seed

      d. Gallbladder of an elephant

      e. Red lead / litri

      f. Bamboo

      g. Wood apple

      h. Mirror

    Eight Auspicious Symbols

      a. Lotus

      b. Knot of eternity

      c. Umbrella

      d. Conch shell

      e. Victory banner

      f. Golden fish

      g. Dharma wheel

      h. Treasure vase

Chapter 43. Kriyayoga: Practice

  Ingredients to Purify the Ground of the Kriyayoga Mandala

    1. Dung

    2. Urine

    3. Milk

    4. Snot

    5. Saliva

  Six Families of Kriyayoga

    Three transcendent families

      1. Tathagata / buddha, ratna, and karma families / all buddhas

      2. Padma / padma family / Avalokiteshvara

      3. Vajra / vajra family / Vajrapani

    Three worldly families

      1. Jewel / tathagata family / Vaishravana

2. Prosperity or hungry ghost / padma family /
hungry ghosts
3. Ordinary / vajra family / god realms

Six Types of Gods in Kriyayoga Visualization
1. Divine beings of shunyata
2. Divine beings of syllables or letters
3. Divine beings of sound
4. Divine beings of form
5. Divine beings of mudra
6. Divine beings of mark

Two Sattva Principles in Kriyayoga
1. Samayasattva
2. Jnanasattva

Two Types of Mantra in Kriyayoga Tantra
1. Secret mantra / sang-ngak / guhyamantra
2. Knowledge mantra / rig-ngak / vidyamantra

## Upayoga: The Yana of Conduct

Chapter 44. Upayoga: Unadorned Perception

Chapter 45. Upayoga: Empowerment
Six Abhishekas of Upayoga
1. Water / vase abhisheka / discriminating-awareness wisdom
   a. Purify fixations of lower realms
   b. Completely uproot samsaric seeds
   c. Completely bypass the bhumis
   d. Sowing the seed to become regent of vajra master
2. Crown abhisheka
3. Bell abhisheka / wisdom of all-accomplishing actions
4. Vajra abhisheka
   Two Types of Insight in the Mind of Enlightenment
      a. Seeing
      b. Knowing
5. Name abhisheka / wisdom of all-encompassing space
6. Opening the eyes

Two Approaches to Upayoga Families
1. Three Families
   a. Vajra body / vajra family
   b. Vajra speech / padma family
   c. Vajra mind / buddha family

2. Five Families
   a. Vajra
   b. Ratna
   c. Padma
   d. Karma
   e. Buddha

Two Aspects of Mandala Principle
1. Outer mandala / shrine
2. Inner mandala / your physical body

Three Categories of Upayoga Samaya
1. Samaya of surrendering the gross ego / relative bodhichitta
2. Samaya of surrendering the refined ego / absolute bodhichitta
3. Samaya of the dharmachakra mudra

Chapter 46. Upayoga: Practice
Upayoga Visualization
1. Inner mandala / internal samayasattva
2. Outer mandala / external samayasattva

Three Principles of Unification in Upayoga Visualization
1. Body
2. Speech
3. Mind

Six Types of Gods in Upayoga Visualization
1. Divine beings of shunyata
2. Divine beings of syllables or letters
3. Divine beings of sound
4. Divine beings of form
5. Divine beings of mudra
6. Divine beings of mark

## *Yogayana: The Yana of Union*

Chapter 47. Yogayana: Complete Union
  Five Buddha-Families in Yogayana / Twenty-Five Lesser Families
    1. Buddha / lesser buddha, vajra, ratna, dharma, karma
    2. Vajra / lesser buddha, vajra, ratna, dharma, karma
    3. Ratna / lesser buddha, vajra, ratna, dharma, karma
    4. Dharma (padma-like) / lesser buddha, vajra, ratna, dharma, karma
    5. Karma / lesser buddha, vajra, ratna, dharma, karma

  Four Ways of Seeing Each of the Twenty-Five Buddha-Families
    1. Essence
    2. Manifestation / mudra
    3. Secret mantra / guhyamantra
    4. Magical power / vidyamantra

Chapter 48. Yogayana: Empowerments and Practice
  Two Forms of Entertainment
    1. Entertained by your basic being
    2. Entertained by devis and the phenomenal world

  Three Tests in a Yogayana Abhisheka
    1. Throw flower-stick into mandala / major family
    2. Throw flower-stick into mandala a second time / lesser family
    3. Throw flower-stick into mandala a third time / four divisions of seeing family

  Eleven Abhishekas of Yogayana
    First Five Abhishekas / Relative Truth
      1. Water
      2. Crown
      3. Vajra scepter
      4. Bell
      5. Name

  Six Further Abhishekas / Absolute Truth / Vajra Master Abhishekas
    1. Irreversible abhisheka
    2. Secret abhisheka
    3. Authorization
    4. Final confirmation
    5. Encouragement
    6. Praise

Two Types of Yogayana Practice
1. Visualization / tsen-che
    Four Steps of Visualization Practice
        a. Visualization yoga
        b. Complete yoga
        c. All-inclusive yoga
        d. Supreme yoga
2. Formless practice

Fivefold Bodhi Approach to Visualization
1. Visualize lotus seat, sun disk, and moon disk
2. Visualize form or image
3. Visualize scepters or attributes
4. Visualize the totality
5. Visualize placing seed syllables in appropriate centers

Four Karmas Needed for Fire Offering
1. Pacifying / vajra / offer herbs / white flame
2. Enriching / ratna / offer jewelry and minerals / yellow flame
3. Magnetizing / padma / offer clothes and fabrics / red flame
4. Destroying / karma / offer metals, hardwoods, hot spices, flesh and blood / green flame

## PART ELEVEN. THE TANTRIC JOURNEY: MAHAMUDRA

*Anuttarayoga: Highest Yoga*

Chapter 49. The Great Symbol
Three Levels of Anuttarayoga Tantra
1. Root tantra / study
2. Skillful-means tantra / practice
3. Fruition tantra / accomplishment

Chapter 50. Devotion: The Essential Prerequisite for Mahamudra
Three Jewels of Mahamudra
1. Tsakali (icon) / lineage and relationship with living guru
2. Three syllables (OM AH HUM) / realization of nature of mind
3. Crystal vajra / complete understanding of reality without distortion

Chapter 51. Taking a Fresh Look at the Phenomenal World
Six Ways in which Anuttara Is Special
    1–2. Literal meaning vs. true meaning
    3–4. Thoughtfulness vs. unthoughtfulness
    5–6. Interpretation vs. beyond interpretation

Sixfold Teaching Style
    1–2. Present and embryonic / being
    3–4. Literal and subtle / beyond being
    5–6. Direct and indirect / getting a result out of being

Two Aspects of the Process of Perception
    1. Perceiving the solidity of the phenomenal world
    2. Perceiving the spaciousness of the phenomenal world

Viewing the World as EVAM
    1. VAM / unchangeable nature
    2. E / all-perception
    3. EVAM / E and VAM united

Chapter 52. Uniting with Open Space
The Four Principle Anuttarayoga Abhishekas
    1. Outer abhisheka / identifying with the yidam
        a. Water
        b. Crown
        c. Vajra
        d. Bell
        e. Name
    2. Secret or inner abhisheka / yidam and consort in union
    3. Prajna-jnana abhisheka / sexual union
    4. Formless abhisheka / transcending reference points

Arising of Two Spontaneous Wisdoms
    1. Example wisdom / peyi yeshe / third abhisheka
    2. Actual wisdom / töngyi yeshe / fourth abhisheka

Chapter 53. The Challenge of Keeping Samaya
Three Types of Feast Offerings
    1. Select offering
    2. Confession offering
    3. Destruction offering

Three Bases of the Samaya Vow in Anuttarayoga
1. Vajra body samaya / all forms regarded as vajra heruka mandala
2. Vajra speech samaya / all sounds regarded as vajra heruka speech
3. Vajra mind samaya / all thoughts regarded as vajra heruka mind

Applying the Four Karmas
1. Pacifying / vajra family
2. Enriching / ratna family
3. Magnetizing / padma family
4. Destroying / karma family

The Four Basic Vows for Overcoming Lukewarmness
1. Murdering
2. Lying
3. Stealing
4. Sexual intercourse

Chapter 54. The Divisions of Anuttarayoga
The Four Divisions of Anuttarayoga
1. Mother tantra (passion tantra) / ma-gyü / Chakrasamvara, Mahamaya, Hevajra
2. Father tantra (aggression tantra) / pha-gyü / Guhyasamaja
3. Nondual tantra (ignorance tantra) / nyi-me gyü / Kalachakra
4. None-higher tantra / la-me gyü / First three combined together

Chapter 55. Manifesting Mahamudra
Two Factors of Mahamudra That Transform One's State of Mind
1. Devotion
2. Practice

Three Roots of Mahamudra Experience
1. Gurus / the source of blessings
2. Yidams / the source of magical power
3. Dharmapalas / the source of the fulfillment of all actions

Chapter 56. Ground Mahamudra: Understanding Things as They Are
Vajrayana Approaches to the Path
1. Regarding the ground as path
2. Regarding fruition as path

Three Levels of Mahamudra
1. Ground mahamudra
2. Path mahamudra
3. Fruition mahamudra

Two Aspects of the Ground of Possibilities
1. Mind itself
2. Mind's perceptions

Three Ways of Cultivating the Ordinary State
1. Not preparing too much / cutting off preconceptions of the past
2. Not expecting a greater flash / cutting off preconceptions of the future
3. Resting the mind / cutting off preconceptions of the present

Chapter 57. Path Mahamudra: The Experience of Meditation
The Four Yogas of Mahamudra / Naljor Shirim
1. One-pointedness / tsechik
   Three Levels
     a. Lesser / joy and clarity
     b. Medium / naturalness
     c. Greater / luminosity
2. Simplicity / trödral
   Three Levels
     a. Lesser / realizing that arising, ceasing, and dwelling are empty
     b. Medium / freedom from fixation on appearance or emptiness
     c. Greater / resolving the complexity of all dharmas
   Three Vajra Practices Connected with the First Two Yogas
     a. Vajra body / seed syllable
     b. Vajra speech / mantra
     c. Vajra mind / one mandala
3. One taste / rochik
   Three Levels
     a. Lesser / all dharmas are dissolved into one taste
     b. Medium / appearance and mind become indistinguishable
     c. Greater / breakthrough of wisdom
4. Nonmeditation / gom-me
   Three Levels

Five Skandhas as Five Male Buddhas
1. Form / buddha
2. Feeling / ratna
3. Perception / padma
4. Formations / karma
5. Consciousness / vajra

Two Types of Mahayoga Practice
1. Tantra / practice
    a. Gyü-de / tantric practice
    b. Drub-de / practice
2. Nopika / essential practice
    a. Sota nopika / solitary practice
    b. Mandala nopika / group practice

The Eight Mandalas of Mahayoga
1. Mandala of self-existence / rangshin gyi kyilkhor
2. Mandala of compassion / lhündrup kyi kyilkhor
   Twofold Purity
    a. Eternal purity
    b. Apparent purity
3. Mandala of form / sugnyen gyi kyilkhor
4. Mandala of extra form / lhak-pe sugnyen gyi kyilkhor
5. Mandala of meditation / tingdzin gyi kyilkhor
6. Mandala of extra meditation / lhak-pe tingdzin gyi kyilkhor
7. Mandala of bodhichitta / changsem kyi kyilkhor
8. Mandala of vajra sangha / tsokchog gi kyilkhor

Chapter 61. Mahayoga: The Eight Logos
The Eight Logos / Druppa Kagye
1. Yangdak / the completely pure
2. Jampal or Yamantaka / the conqueror of the Lord of Death
   The Four Wheels
    a. Secret wheel / mind
    b. Wheel of existence / naval
    c. Wheel of cutting / arms and hands
    d. Wheel of miracle or emanation / feet and legs
3. Hayagriva / the subjugator of Rudra
   The Three Neighs of a Horse
    a. Waking the world to the fact that samsara and nirvana
       are unoriginated

b. Offering the whole world (the animate and inanimate world)

c. Demanding obedience

4. Chemchok / the supreme heruka
   Five Ingredients Used to Create Amrita
   a. Flesh / padma family
   b. Blood / karma family
   c. Urine / vajra family
   d. Feces / buddha family
   e. Semen / ratna family

5. Dorje Phurba or Vajrakilaya / the dagger wielder
   The Four Penetrations
   a. Wisdom dagger
   b. Bodhichitta dagger
   c. Limitless compassion dagger
   d. Physical dagger

6. Mamo / the mother principle

7. Chötö / offering and praise to the worldly deities
   Three Types of National Ego
   a. Life force of dwelling place
   b. Life force of clarity
   c. Life force of name

8. Trag-ngak / wrathful mantra / fearlessness

Eight Logos Divided into Higher and Lower
1. Higher logos / 1–5 / fundamentality
2. Lower logos / 6–8 / pragmatic / fringe

Chapter 62. Mahayoga: Nondual Practice

*Anuyoga: The Yana of Passion*

Chapter 63. Anuyoga: Joining Space and Wisdom
Two Principles Emphasized
1. Unbornness and intelligence
2. Space and wisdom

Chapter 64. Anuyoga: Empowerment
Reexperiencing Your World
1. Going through the samsaric realms
2. Going through the stages of the path (hinayana, mahayana, vajrayana)

Going through the first four paths
    a. Accumulation
    b. Unification
    c. Seeing
    d. Meditation
3. The attainment of a glimpse of maha ati and the fifth path
    e. No more learning

One Hundred Deities of Anuyoga
    1. Fifty-eight wrathful deities
    2. Forty-two peaceful deities

Three Types of Confirmations
    1. Great confirmation
    2. Great protection
    3. Great energy

Three Mandalas of Anuyoga
    1. The mandala of isness / ye chi-shin-pe kyilkhor / Samantabhadri
    2. The mandala of self-existence / lhündrup kyi kyilkhor / Samantabhadra
    3. The mandala of the awakened state of mind / changsem kyi kyilkhor / son of Samantabhadri and Samantabhadra / Son of Great Joy

Chapter 65. Anuyoga: Practice
Two Attainments of Anuyoga
    1. Fulfilling the desires of the yogi through devotion and fearlessness
    2. Revelation of the great family

The Three Yogas
    1. Yoga of seed
    2. Yoga of condition
    3. Yoga of result

      vi. Transcending attachment to intellect and to
           nonintellectual fixations and bias / lodral chogdzin
           ledepa
      vii. Proclaiming that one's mind is in a certain direction /
           semchok yintu mawa
  2 . The category of space / long-de
    Two Approaches to Space
      a. Ying
      b. Long
    Four Types of Space
      a. Black space / long nakpo gyu mepa
      b. Multicolored space / long trawu natsok rangshar gyen
      c. White space / long karpo
      d. Complete absorption space / long rabjam
  3. The category of instruction / men-ngag gi de
    Three Types of Men-ngag Gi De
      a. Randomness / khathor
      b. Legend or tale / khatam
      c. Self-proclaiming / gyü rangshungdu tenpa

Chapter 71. Atiyoga: Meditation Practices
Two Categories of Atiyoga Practice
  1. Trekchö / cutting through
    Three Meditation Guidelines
      a. Resting one's mind in dharmadhatu / sem-de
      b. Resting effortlessly / long-de
      c. Resting without accepting or rejecting / men-ngag gi de
  2. Thögal / transcending the forehead or peak
    Triple-Space Practice
      a. Dharmakaya / vastness of space
      b. Sambhogakaya / richness of space
      c. Nirmanakaya / pragmatic aspect of space
    Secret Mandala and the Three Torches
      a. The self-existing torch
      b. The torch of emptiness
      c. The torch of water

Chapter 72. Atiyoga: Heightened Experience
Four Stages of Heightening
1. Seeing dharmata as real / chönyi ngönsum
2. Increasing the nyam / nyam kongphel
3. Insight reaching its full measure / rikpa tsephep
4. Dharmata being all used up / chönyi sesa
  Two Types of Confidence
    1. Nirvanic confidence / yargyi sangthal
    2. Samsaric confidence / margyi sangthal

Chapter 73. Atiyoga: Everything and Nothing
Three Parts of Maha Ati
1. View
      a. Spotting a thief
      b. Adding more firewood to the fire
      c. Winning victory on the battlefield
2. Practice
      a. Entering a rich man's treasury
      b. Building a concrete wall
      c. Being crowned as a prince
3. Action
      a. An uptight person losing their temper
      b. A garuda flying over the edge of a cliff
      c. A Brahman housewife who has finished her work

Analogies for Maha Ati
1. Flowing river
2. The ocean
3. Cloud dissolving in the sky
4. Depths of the ocean
5. Self-existing torch

The Maha Ati Experience
1. Nonexistence
2. All-pervasiveness
3. Self-existence
4. Aloneness

# GLOSSARY

This glossary includes terms in English, Tibetan (Tib.), Sanskrit (Skt.), Pali, Chinese (Chin.), and Japanese (Jpn.). Tibetan terms are spelled phonetically, followed by the transliteration in parentheses. Tibetan equivalents of Sanskrit words are first written phonetically, then transliterated.

**abhidharma** (Skt.; Tib.: chö ngönpa; chos mngon pa). Superior or higher dharma; Buddhist psychology. The Buddhist teachings can be divided into three parts, called the "three baskets," or Tripitaka: the sutras (general teachings of the Buddha), the vinaya (teachings on conduct), and the abhidharma (teachings on philosophy and psychology).

**abhisheka** (Skt.: "sprinkling," "anointing"; Tib.: wang; dbang; "power"). Empowerment; a ceremony in which a student is initiated into a particular vajrayana practice by a vajra master.

**abrahmacharya** (Skt.). Nonchastity; engaging in sexual intercourse.

**achala** (Skt.; Tib.: miyowa; mi gyo ba). Immovability, stability. In Japan, represented as Fudo, a wrathful deity described as powerful and immovable.

**acharya** (Skt.; Tib.: loppön; slob dpon). A learned spiritual teacher.

**adhishthana** (Skt.: "standing over" or "resting upon"; Tib.: chinlap; byin rlabs; "splendor wave"). Blessings. "Possessing adhishthana" is the second of the seven aspects of vajrayana. *See also* appendix 5, under *Seven Aspects of Vajrayana* (chapter 6).

**agni puja** (Skt.; Tib.: jinsek; sbyin sreg). Fire-offering ritual.

**Akshobhya** (Skt.; Tib.: Mikyöpa; mi bskyod pa). Buddha of the vajra family. In the secret language of tantra, a name for urine, one of the five ingredients that are transformed from poison into amrita. *See also* appendix 5, under *Five Ingredients Used to Create Amrita* (chapter 61).

**alaya** (Skt.: "receptacle"; Tib.: künshi; kun gzhi; "ground of all"). The fundamental ground that gives rise to both samsara and nirvana, or the basic split; not to be confused with the alayavijnana.

**alayavijnana** (Skt.; Tib.: künshi nampar shepa; kun gzhi rnam par shes pa). Alaya consciousness, also known as the storehouse consciousness. According to the yogachara description of mind, it is the eighth consciousness, which contains all karmic seeds. It is the root of dualistic consciousness, and hence of samsara.

**Amitabha** (Skt.; Tib.: Öpag-me; 'od dpag med; "Limitless Light"). Buddha of the padma family; lord of the pure realm of Sukhavati.

**amrita** (Skt.: "deathless"; Tib.: dütsi; bdud rtsi). Blessed liquor used in vajra-yana meditation practices.

**anuttarayoga** (Skt.; Tib.: naljor la-me; rnal 'byor bla med; "none higher yoga"). The highest of the four tantric yanas according to the Kagyü tradition and the New Translation school. *See also* mahamudra.

**anuyoga** (Skt.; Tib.: jesu naljor; rjes su rnal 'byor). In the Nyingma nine-yana system, the second of the three higher tantric yanas.

**arak** (Tib.: a rag). A type of alcoholic drink, stronger than beer.

**arhat** (Skt.: "worthy one"; Tib.: drachompa; dgra bcom pa). A fully accomplished practitioner of the hinayana path who has achieved liberation from the sufferings of samsara. The Tibetan term *drachompa* means "one who has conquered the enemy" of conflicting emotions and of grasping at a self-entity.

**Atisha Dipankara** (982–1054 CE). A Buddhist scholar at the great monastic university of Vikramashila. He is best known for his teachings on mind training and the cultivation of bodhichitta.

**atiyoga** (Skt.). The highest of the nine yanas, also known as maha ati, dzokchen, or the great perfection. The experience of atiyoga goes beyond all concepts. It is the essence of transcendent insight, the unchanging state of nonmeditation in which there is awareness but no clinging.

**avadhuti** (Skt.; Tib.: uma; dbu ma). Central energy channel that runs up the center of the body just in front of the spine.

**Avalokiteshvara** (Skt.; Tib.: Chenrezik; spyan ras gzigs). The bodhisattva of compassion.

**ayatana** (Skt.; Tib.: kye-che; skye mched; "arising and spreading"). Sense field. The twelve ayatanas include the six sense organs (with mind as number six) and their corresponding sense objects.

**bardo** (Tib.: bar do). In-between or intermediate state. There are many different types of intermediate states, with the most common listing mentioning six bardos: the bardos of this life, dream, meditation, dying, isness, and becoming. More generally, bardo refers to the state between death and the next birth, which is said to last forty-nine days.

basic goodness (Tib.: dö-ne sangwa; gdod nas bzang ba). Good from the very beginning, beyond any reference point of bad or good. In the Shambhala teachings, this refers to the intrinsic wholesomeness of one's being. Trungpa Rinpoche also uses the phrase *basic goodness* to refer to künshi ngangluk kyi gewa, the natural virtue of alaya, as well as to Samantabhadra, or Küntu Sangpo, which means "completely good."

betsöl mepar ladawa (Tib.: 'bad rtsol med par la zla ba). To step over without effort; the first category of sem-de.

bhala (Dakini language). Meat; one of the five ingredients that are transformed from poison into amrita. *See also* appendix 5, under *Five Ingredients Used to Create Amrita* (chapter 61).

bhikshu (Skt.; Tib.: gelong; dge slong). Fully ordained monk.

bhumi (Skt.; Tib.: sa; sa). Stage, level. The progressive stages of the path of the bodhisattva that lead to enlightenment. *See also* volume 2 of the *Profound Treasury*, part 8: "The Bodhisattva's Journey."

bija (Skt.). Seed syllable; a Sanskrit syllable used in visualization practice. Also the term for karmic seed.

bindu (Skt.; Tib.: thig-le; thig le). Dot, particle; the life force.

bodhi (Skt.; Tib.: changchup; byang chub). Awakened state; full illumination or enlightenment.

bodhi tree. The sacred fig tree (*Ficus religiosa*) located in Bodhgaya under which Gautama Buddha practiced at the time he attained enlightenment.

bodhichitta (Skt.; Tib.: changchup kyi sem; byang chub kyi sems). Enlightened heart or mind. Ultimate, or absolute, bodhichitta is the union of emptiness and compassion, the essential nature of awakened mind. Relative bodhichitta is the tenderness arising from a glimpse of ultimate bodhichitta, which inspires the practitioner to train in working for the benefit of others.

Bodhidharma (Skt.; fifth to sixth century CE). One of the leading patriarchs of the Zen Buddhist tradition.

bodhisattva (Skt.: "awake being"; Tib.: changchup sempa; byang chub sems dpa'). One who has made a commitment to the mahayana path of practicing compassion and the six paramitas. *See also* paramita.

bodhisattva vow. The vow to attain enlightenment for the benefit of all beings, marking one's formal entry onto the mahayana path of wisdom and compassion, and one's intention to practice the bodhisattva discipline of the six paramitas.

bodhisattvayana (Skt.). The vehicle of the bodhisattva; another term for mahayana.

Brahma (Skt.). The first god of the Hindu trinity of Brahma, Vishnu, and Shiva. Brahma is god in the aspect of creator of the universe.

**brahmacharya** (Skt.). Celibacy.

**brahmaloka** (Skt.). God realm; one of the six realms of samsaric existence. The dwelling place of Brahma, the chief god of the lower levels of the form realm.

**Brahman** (Skt.). A Hindu of the highest, or priestly, caste.

**Brahmanical.** Referring to the Brahman caste.

**brahmarandhra** (Skt.; Tib.: tsangbuk; tsangs bug). Aperture of Brahma; an opening at the crown of the head at the top of the avadhuti. *See also* avadhuti.

**Buddha / buddha** (Skt.; Tib.: sang-gye; sangs rgyas). Awakened one. The "Buddha" refers in particular to Shakyamuni Buddha, whereas "buddha" may refer to any enlightened being or to the principle of enlightenment itself. The Buddha is also the first of the three jewels. In the mandala of the five buddha-families, the buddha family is associated with the center of the mandala, the buddha Vairochana, the klesha of ignorance, and the wisdom of all-encompassing space. *See also* appendix 5, under *The Five Buddha-Families* (chapter 26).

**buddha-families** (Tib.: sang-gye kyi rik; sangs rgyas kyi rigs). The mandala of the five buddhas, who embody the five wisdoms. Because all phenomena are said to possess one of these five as a predominant characteristic, they are called families: vajra, ratna, padma, karma, and buddha. Each is associated with a particular buddha, a type of wisdom, a skandha, a klesha, a direction, and a color. *See also* appendix 5, under *The Five Buddha-Families* (chapter 26).

**buddha nature.** *See* tathagatagarbha.

**chaggya chenpo** (Tib.: phyag rgya chen po). *See* mahamudra.

**chaggya kü tamtsik** (Tib.: phyag rgya sku'i dam tshig). Samaya of vajra body; an understanding that all phenomena are part of the sacred world.

**chakra** (Skt.; Tib.: khorlo; 'khor lo; "wheel"). A primary energy center in the body, located along the avadhuti, or central channel. There are different enumerations of the chakras, but generally five are named: at the head, throat, heart, navel, and secret place.

**chakravartin** (Skt.: "one who turns the wheel"). A universal monarch; in ancient Buddhist and Vedic literature, a king who rules the entire world by his wisdom and virtue.

**Ch'an** (Chin.; Skt.: dhyana; Jpn.: Zen). A school of mahayana Buddhism that emphasizes meditation and experiential wisdom.

**chang** (Tib.: chang). Tibetan beer made from barley.

**changchup kyi sem** (Tib.: byang chub kyi sems). *See* bodhichitta.

**changsem kyi kyilkhor** (Tib.: byang sems kyi dkyil 'khor). Mandala of bodhichitta, the essence of enlightenment; one of eight types of mandala in mahayoga tantra. *See also* appendix 5, under *The Eight Mandalas of Mahayoga* (chapter 60).

**charnel ground** (Skt.: shmashana; Tib.: tür-trö; dur 'khrod). An open field filled with corpses and beasts of prey. The charnel ground is an important symbol of the ground from which all phenomena are born and die, which is the basis of both samsara and nirvana.

**cha-we gyü** (Tib.: bya ba'i rgyud). *See* kriyayoga.

**Chekawa Yeshe Dorje** (Tib.: 'chad ka ba ye shes rdo rje; 1101–1175 CE). Famous Kadampa master; author of the root text of *The Seven Points of Mind Training*, one of the principal texts of lojong.

**Chemchok** (Tib.: che mchog; Skt.: Mahottara). Great Supreme One. The fourth of the eight logos, connected with the center of the mandala and with transforming poison into amrita. *See also* appendix 5, under *The Eight Logos / Druppa Kagye* (chapter 61).

**chigdrup** (Tib.: gcig sgrub). *See* sota nopika.

**chiggyü** (Tib.: gcig brgyud). One-to-one transmission; the ear-whispered or hearing lineage.

**chingyi lappa** (Tib.: byin gyis brlabs pa). Blessed; "being engulfed in an atmosphere of intense devotion."

**chinlap** (Tib.: byin rlabs). *See* adhishthana.

**chiwa mitakpa** (Tib.: 'chi ba mi rtag pa). Death and impermanence; the second of the four reminders. *See also* appendix 5, under *The Four Reminders* (chapter 30).

**chö** (Tib.: gcod). Cut off; cut through. An advanced vajrayana practice involving a contemplation on death and illness, performed in charnel grounds and haunted places, which invites negative forces to consume the practitioner in order to completely cut through any residual ego-attachment and fixation.

**chogdzin truptha ledepa** (Tib.: phyogs 'dzin grub mtha' las 'das pa). Transcending attachment to biased philosophical beliefs; the fifth category of sem-de.

**chögyü** (Tib.: spyod rgyud). *See* upayoga.

**chok** (Tib.: mchog). Supreme.

**choktu kyurpa** (Tib.: mchog tu gyur pa). Holy; the supreme of the supreme.

**chöku** (Tib.: chos sku). *See* dharmakaya.

**chökyi dak** (Tib.: chos kyi bdag). Ego of dharmas, or phenomena; the second half of twofold ego, the first half being ego of self.

**chökyi gyaltsen lekpar dzuk** (Tib.: chos kyi rgyal mtshan legs par 'dzugs). "Firmly plant the victorious banner of dharma"; a line from the *Manjushri-nama-sangiti* (*Chanting the Names of Manjushri*, VIII: 28).

**Chökyi Nyin-je** (Tib.: chos kyi nyin byed; 1879–1939 CE). The tenth Trungpa tülku.

**chökyi ying** (Tib.: chos kyi dbyings). *See* dharmadhatu.

**chökyong** (Tib.: chos skyong). *See* dharmapala.

**chönyi ngönsum** (Tib.: chos nyid mngon sum). Seeing dharmata as real; the first of the four visions, or stages, of maha ati practice.

**chönyi sesa** (Tib.: chos nyid zad sa). Dharmata used up. The exhaustion of dharmata; the last of the four visions, or stages, of maha ati practice.

**chötö** (Tib.: mchod stod). Offering and praise to the worldly deities. The seventh of the eight logos, connected with subjugating national ego. *See also* appendix 5, under *The Eight Logos / Druppa Kagye* (chapter 61).

**chuba** (Tib.: phyu pa). A long coat made of wool.

**coemergent wisdom** (Skt.: sahaja-jnana; Tib.: lhenchik kye-pe yeshe; lhan cig skyes pa'i ye shes; "wisdom born together"). The simultaneous arising of samsara and nirvana, which naturally gives rise to wisdom.

**compassion** (Skt.: karuna; Tib.: nying-je; snying rje; "noble heart"). A key principle of mahayana Buddhism, describing the motivation and activity of a bodhisattva. As a further development of maitri, compassion arises from empathizing with the suffering of sentient beings.

**confirmation** (Tib.: ug jinpa; dbugs 'byin pa; "breathing the breath"). Relief at being recognized and confirmed as who you really are, the fourth of the seven aspects of vajrayana. *See also* appendix 5, under *Seven Aspects of Vajrayana* (chapter 6).

**dakini** (Skt.; Tib.: khandroma; mkha' 'gro ma). One who walks in the sky. A wrathful or semiwrathful female deity, signifying compassion, emptiness, and prajna. Dakinis are tricky and playful, representing the basic space of fertility out of which the play of samsara and nirvana arises.

**damaru** (Skt.). Ritual hand drum used in vajrayana practice.

**Dawa Sangpo** (Tib.: zla ba bzang po; Skt.: Suchandra). In Indian and Tibetan legend, the king who requested teachings from the Buddha that would allow him to practice dharma without renouncing his worldly responsibilities. In response, the Buddha gave him the first *Kalachakra Tantra* abhisheka.

**deva** (Skt.; Tib.: lha; lha). Deity, god.

**devata** (Skt.). Divinity.

**devi** (Skt.; Tib.: lhamo; lhamo). Female deity; goddess.

**dewa chenpo yi yeshe** (Tib.: bde ba chen po yi ye shes). Wisdom of mahasukha, or great bliss. *See* mahasukha.

**dharana** (Skt.). Binding together.

**dharanayana** (Skt.). The vehicle that binds together the body, speech, and mind of the practitioner; another term for vajrayana.

**dharma** (Skt.; Pali: dhamma; Tib.: chö; chos). Truth, law, phenomenon. In particular, the buddhadharma, or teachings of the Buddha. The second of the three jewels. The plural, *dharmas,* simply refers to phenomena.

**dharmachakra** (Skt.; Tib.: chökyi khorlo; chos kyi 'khor lo). Wheel of dharma. The phrase "turning the wheel of dharma" refers to teaching dharma.

**dharmadhatu** (Skt.; Tib. chökyi ying; chos kyi dbyings). All-encompassing space; the unconditional totality, unoriginated and unchanging, in which all phenomena arise, dwell, and cease.

**dharmakaya** (Skt.; Tib.: chöku; chos sku). Dharma body. The mind of the Buddha, or enlightenment itself; unoriginated, primordial mind, devoid of concept. One of the three kayas. *See also* trikaya.

**dharmapala** (Skt.; Tib.: chökyong; chos skyong). Protector of the dharma. A type of deity whose function is to protect the teachings of the Buddha and its practitioners.

**dharmata** (Skt.; Tib.: chönyi; chos nyid). Dharma-ness, isness; the essence of reality.

**dhatu** (Skt.; Tib.: kham; khams). Space, expanse; element, nature; region, realm. The dhatus also refer to the eighteen dhatus or sense faculties that are comprised of the six sense organs; the six sense objects of the sense organs; and the six corresponding sense consciousnesses.

**Dilgo Khyentse Rinpoche** (Tib.: dil mgo mkhyen brtse; 1910–1991 CE). A highly revered Nyingma meditation master beloved in all schools of Tibetan Buddhism. Khyentse Rinpoche was a close friend and mentor of Chögyam Trungpa Rinpoche. At Trungpa Rinpoche's request, Khyentse Rinpoche came to the West several times to give teachings.

**doha** (Skt.). A song expressing spiritual realization.

**döma** (Tib.: gdod ma). Primordial; one of the three qualities of the Great East. *See also* appendix 5, under *The Three Qualities of the Great East* (chapter 1).

**dö-me ying** (Tib.: gdod ma'i dbyings). Primordial space.

**dompa** (Tib.: sdom pa; Skt.: samvara). Vow, precept; binding together.

**dön** (Tib.: gdon). A sudden attack of neurosis, an emotional upheaval, or klesha, that seems to come from outside oneself. *See also* klesha.

**dorje** (Tib.: rdo rje). *See* vajra.

**dorje chang** (Tib.: rdo rje 'chang). Vajra holder; one who holds the vajra. *See also* Vajradhara.

**dorje kham** (Tib.: rdo rje khams). Indestructible being; vajra nature.

**dorje loppön** (Tib.: rdo rje slob dpon; Skt.: vajracharya). Vajra master.

**dorje lugu gyü** (Tib.: rdo rje lu gu rgyud). Vajra chains; visions that appear in the practice of thögal.

**Dorje Phurba** (Tib.: rdo rje phur ba). *See* Vajrakilaya.

**dorje thekpa** (Tib.: rdo rje theg pa; Skt.: vajrayana). Indestructible vehicle. *See also* vajrayana.

**dorje thukkyi tamtsik** (Tib.: rdo rje thugs kyi dam tshig). Samaya of vajra mind.

**dorje ying** (Tib.: rdo rje dbyings; Skt.: vajradhatu). Indestructible space; the basic space that accommodates all phenomena of samsara and nirvana.

**drebu lamdu chepa** (Tib.: 'bras bu lam du byed pa). Using the fruition as the path, an approach associated with higher tantra.

**drebü thekpa** (Tib.: 'bras bu'i theg pa). Fruition vehicle; another term for vajrayana.

**drippa** (Tib.: sgrib pa). Defilement or obscuration.

**drub-de** (Tib.: sgrub sde). Practice section; one of the two classes of mahayoga practice, the other being gyü-de.

**druppa** (Tib.: sgrub pa; Skt.: sadhana). Practice, accomplishment; sadhana practice.

**druppa kagye** (Tib.: sgrub pa bka' brgyad). *See* eight logos.

**druppapo** (Tib.: sgrub pa po; Skt.: sadhaka). A practitioner.

**duhkha** (Skt.; Tib.: dug-ngal; sdug bsngal). Suffering, the first of the four noble truths. Physical and psychological suffering of all kinds, including the subtle but all-pervading frustration occasioned by the impermanence and insubstantiality of all things.

**dütsi chömen** (Tib.: bdud rtsi chos sman). Amrita dharma medicine; a special herbal preparation mixed with liquor and used in vajrayana practices.

**Dütsi Tel** (Tib.: bdud rtsi tel; "Amrita Hill"). One of the two main monasteries of Surmang, the other being Namgyal-tse. The monastic seat of the Trungpa tulküs, established by the third Trungpa, Kunga Öser.

**dzinchak me-pe chöpa** (Tib.: 'dzin chags med pa'i spyod pa). Action without fixation or desire; fourth of the five vajrayana sayings regarding transcending habitual patterns. *See also* appendix 5, under *Five Vajrayana Sayings* (chapter 16).

**dzinpa** (Tib.: 'dzin pa). Grasping; in particular, clinging to the view of an independently existing self. *See also* fixation and grasping.

**dzogrim** (Tib.: rdzogs rim; Skt.: sampannakrama). The completion stage of vajrayana practice, which emphasizes formless meditation; contrasted with kyerim, or utpattikrama. *See also* utpattikrama.

**dzokchen** (Tib.: rdzogs chen; Skt.: maha ati). Abbreviation of *dzokpa chenpo.*

**dzokpa chenpo** (Tib.: rdzogs pa chen po; Skt.: maha ati). Great perfection, or great completion; the fruitional teachings of the vajrayana tradition. Maha ati, or dzokchen, is the highest teaching of the Nyingma school, transmitted from India to Tibet by Padmasambhava and Vimalamitra. In the nine-yana system, atiyoga refers to the ninth and final yana.

**eight logos** (Tib.: druppa kagye; sgrub pa bka' brgyad). The eight principal deities of mahayoga, along with their tantras and sadhanas. *See also* appendix 5, under *The Eight Logos / Druppa Kagye* (chapter 61).

**Ekajati** (Skt.: "One Lock of Hair"). A female protector important to the Nyingma lineage; said to be a protector of the maha ati teachings. Ekajati was adopted by Gyurme Tenphel, the eighth Trungpa, as the protector of Surmang Monastery.

EVAM (Skt.). Essential tantric symbol, comprised of the two Sanskrit syllables E and VAM. An expression of the union of the feminine principle, or space (E), and the masculine principle, or unchangeable nature (VAM).

**fixation and grasping** (Tib.: sung-dzin; gzung 'dzin). The word order of the Tibetan, *sung-dzin,* reflects the process of how ego arises. Having first fixated on an "other," we grasp on to ourselves. When the word order is reversed, as in the common English translation of "grasping and fixation," it reflects a path orientation. On the path, dzinpa (grasping) comes first because it is the first of twofold ego, the ego of self. Sungwa (fixation) comes second because it involves the ego of phenomena, which is more basic and as a result more difficult to overcome.

**four noble truths** (Tib.: denpa shi; bden pa bzhi). The essence of the Buddha's first turning of the wheel of dharma: (1) suffering, (2) the origin of suffering, (3) the cessation of suffering, and (4) the path.

**four reminders** (Tib.: lodok namshi; blo ldog rnam bzhi). The four reminders; four thoughts that turn the mind away from samsaric preoccupations and toward the path of dharma. These are contemplations on precious human birth, death and impermanence, karmic cause and effect, and the torment of samsara.

**fourth moment.** A pure state of consciousness, free from habitual tendencies, which transcends past, present, and future.

**Gampopa** (Tib.: sgam po pa; 1079–1153 CE). One of the main lineage holders of the Kagyü lineage. A chief disciple of Milarepa, and the founder of the Takpo Kagyü lineage. His most famous work is *The Jewel Ornament of Liberation,* a text on the stages of the mahayana path.

**ganachakra** (Skt.; Tib.: tsokkyi khorlo; tshogs kyi 'khor lo). Feast offering; a ritual meal that incorporates the eating of meat and drinking of alcohol within the context of a particular sadhana practice. The goal of this practice is to bring desire and sense perceptions onto the path, to repair broken samaya, and to bind together the vajra sangha.

**gandharvas** (Skt.). Demigods known for their skill as musicians and singers.

**garbha** (Skt.; Tib.: nyingpo; snying po). Essence or nature; womb.

**garuda** (Skt.; Tib.: khyung; khyung). A bird of Indian mythology, often depicted with a large owl-like beak, holding a snake, and with large wings. The garuda is said to hatch fully grown, and hence symbolizes the awakened state of mind.

**gauri** (Skt.). A female doorkeeper of the mandala.

**Geluk** (Tib.: dge lugs; "way of virtue"). One of the four main schools of Tibetan Buddhism. The Geluk tradition, founded by Tsongkhapa (1357–1419 CE), is known for its emphasis on the observation of monastic rules and thorough study of authoritative texts. Since the installation of the Dalai Lamas as heads of state in the seventeenth century, Gelukpas have held political leadership in Tibet.

**ghanta** (Tib.: trilbu; dril bu). A ritual bell used in tantric practice.

**gom-me** (Tib.: sgom med). Nonmeditation; the fourth of the four yogas of mahamudra. *See also* appendix 5, under *The Four Yogas of Mahamudra / Naljor Shirim* (chapter 57).

**Great Bhagavat** (Skt.). Great Lord; an epithet of the Buddha.

**guhya** (Skt.; Tib.: sangwa; gsang ba). Secret or hidden.

**guhyamantra** (Skt.; Tib.: sang-ngak; gsang sngags). Secret mantra; another term for vajrayana. One of the four characteristics of buddha-families, connected with the realization of a family's inner nature. *See also* appendix 5, under *Four Ways of Seeing Each of the Twenty-Five Buddha-Families* (chapter 47).

*Guhyasamaja Tantra* (Skt.). A father tantra of the anuttarayoga. Its principal deity belongs to the vajra family and exemplifies the penetrating quality of transmuted anger.

**guru** (Skt.: "heavy"; Tib.: lama; bla ma; "none higher"). Teacher; one who carries the heavy burden of guiding students to awakening.

**guru yoga** (Skt.; Tib.: la-me naljor; bla ma'i rnal 'byor). The practice of guru devotion. Along with the four reminders and the four preliminary practices (ngöndro), a prerequisite for formal entry into the vajrayana path, as well as a continuing practice throughout the vajrayana path. *See also* ngöndro.

**gya-che chog-lhung mepa** (Tib.: rgya che phyogs lhung med pa). Not falling into the extreme of proportion or direction; the fourth category of sem-de.

**gyen küntu sangpo** (Tib.: rgyan kun tu bzang po). All-good ornamentation; one of the five categories of Samantabhadra.

**gyü rangshungdu tenpa** (Tib.: rgyud rang bzhung du bstan pa). Tantra as its own self-proclamation; one of the three divisions of men-ngag gi de.

**gyü thekpa** (Tib.: rgyud theg pa; Skt.: tantrayana). Vehicle of continuity; a term for vajrayana.

**gyü-de** (Tib.: rgyud sde). Tantra section; one of the two divisions of mahayoga practice, the other being drub-de.

**gyulü** (Tib.: sgyu lus). *See* illusory body.

**hatha yoga** (Skt.). In the context of mahamudra, hatha yoga refers to a method of working with the body's internal energy system as a support for the realization of nondual wisdom.

**Hayagriva** (Skt.; Tib.: Tamdrin; rta mgrin). Horse-headed; the subjugator of Rudra. Third of the eight logos, connected with magical powers and with subjugating and awakening people. *See also* appendix 5, under *The Eight Logos / Druppa Kagye* (chapter 61).

**head and shoulders.** Holding oneself upright with a quality of presence, confidence, and decorum.

**heruka** (Tib.: thraktung; khrag 'thung). The masculine principle in tantric symbolism, representing skillful means, the action aspect of wisdom. A semiwrathful or wrathful male yidam. The Tibetan term *thraktung* means "blood drinker," which refers to drinking the blood of ego-clinging, doubt, and dualistic confusion.

**Hevajra** (Skt.; Tib.: khe dorje; khe'i rdo rje). A semiwrathful heruka of the mother tantra.

*Hevajra Tantra* (Skt.). An anuttarayoga tantra whose central deity is the fierce protective deity Hevajra. This scripture is said to have converted the Mongol emperor Kublai Khan.

**higher tantra.** The final three of the six tantric yanas of the nine-yana system: mahayoga, anuyoga, and atiyoga. These are also known as the all-encompassing yanas of skillful means and as the imperial, or conquering, yanas.

**hinayana** (Skt.; Tib.: thekpa chung; theg pa chung). Lesser or narrow vehicle. The path of individual salvation, based on the practice of meditation and an understanding of basic Buddhist doctrines such as the four noble truths. It provides the essential instruction and training that serves as a basis for both the mahayana and vajrayana.

**hungry ghost** (Skt.: preta; Tib.: yidak; yi dvags). An inhabitant of one of the three lower realms of samsara, who suffers from hunger and craving; usually depicted with a very large belly and a very thin neck.

**hutoktu** (Mongolian). Mongolian title for a spiritual teacher; an honorary degree or post as the teacher to the Emperor of China.

**illusory body** (Tib.: gyulü; sgyu lus). The subtle practice of meditating on appearances as illusory and dreamlike. The dissolving of the physical body at the approach of death—a feat attainable by great masters. *See also* six dharmas of Naropa.

**Indra** (Skt.). Lord of the gods in the desire realm, residing at the summit of Mount Meru.

**interpretation / beyond interpretation** (Tib.: dra chishinpa / sgra ji bzhin pa; dra chishinpa mayinpa / sgra ji bzhin pa ma yin pa). Also referred to as explicit and not explicit. One of the pairs of categories that show how the view of anuttarayoga is special in comparison with lower yanas. "Beyond interpretation" is the view of anuttarayoga. *See also* chapter 51, "Taking a Fresh Look at the Phenomenal World."

**ishtadevata** (Skt.; Tib.: yidam; yi dam). Personal meditational deity. *See also* yidam.

**ja** (Tib.: 'ja'). A fool; a naive person.

**Jamgön Kongtrül Lodrö Thaye** (Tib.: 'jam mgon kong sprul blo gros mtha' yas; 1813–1899 CE). Also known as Jamgön Kongtrül the Great. One of the most prominent Buddhist masters of nineteenth-century Tibet, credited as one of the founders of the *Ri-me,* or nonsectarian, movement. He achieved great renown as a scholar and writer, and authored more than one hundred volumes of scriptures. Trungpa Rinpoche used Jamgön Kongtrül's commentary on the lojong slogan practice, *The Great Path of Awakening,* and his monumental work, *The Treasury of Knowledge,* as primary references for his presentation of the three yanas.

**Jamgön Kongtrül of Shechen** (Tib.: zhe chen 'jam mgon kong sprul; 1901–1960 CE). A prominent incarnation of Jamgön Kongtrül the Great; Chögyam Trungpa Rinpoche's root guru.

**jnana** (Skt.; Tib.: yeshe; ye shes; "primordial knowing"). All-pervasive wisdom or intelligence, which transcends all dualistic conceptualization.

**jnana-dharmakaya** (Skt.; Tib.: yeshe chöku; ye shes chos sku). Wisdom dharma-body, usually abbreviated as *dharmakaya. See* dharmakaya.

**jnanasattva** (Skt.; Tib.: yeshe sempa; ye shes sems dpa'; "wisdom being"). In vajrayana practice, the actual deity, which is invited to bless one's visualization of the deity. *See also* samayasattva.

**ka** (Tib.: bka'). Sacred word or command.

**kadak** (Tib.: ka dag). Primordial purity; alpha pure. One of the two principal aspects of the maha ati teachings; the other is lhündrup, or spontaneous presence.

**Kagyü** (Tib.: bka' brgyud). Command lineage; also known as practice lineage. One of the four main schools of Tibetan Buddhism, stemming from Marpa Lotsawa, a translator who brought many tantric teachings from India to Tibet in the eleventh century. *Ka* refers to the oral instructions of the guru, which have a quality of command. In this lineage, emphasis is placed on direct transmission from teacher to student. The central practices of this school include mahamudra and the six dharmas of Naropa. As the eleventh Trungpa tülku, Chögyam Trungpa Rinpoche was a Kagyü lineage holder, although he also studied within the Nyingma tradition.

*Kalachakra Tantra* (Skt.; Tib.: Tükyi Khorlo; dus kyi 'khor lo; "wheel of time"). An anuttarayoga tantra that explains the relationships between the phenomenal world, the physical body, and the mind. It is well-known for its system of astrology.

**kalpa** (Skt.). An extremely long aeon, sometimes reckoned at 4,320 million years.

**kalyanamitra** (Skt.; Tib.: ge-we shenyen; dge ba'i bshes gnyen). Spiritual friend; a mahayana teacher, who guides students through wisdom, compassion, and skillful means.

**kama** (Tib.: bka' ma). The oral lineage of teachings in the Nyingma lineage; contrasted with the lineage of teachings derived from terma. *See also* terma.

**Kamalashila** (Skt.; ca. 740–795 CE). A student of Shantarakshita, he was the author of the *Bhavanakrama (Stages of Meditation)*, an important text on mahayana meditation.

**karma** (Skt.; Tib.: le; las; "action"). The chain-reaction process of action and result. According to this doctrine, one's present condition is a product of previous actions and volitions, and future conditions depend on what one does in the present. In the mandala of the five buddha-families, karma is the buddha-family associated with the North, the buddha Amoghasiddhi, the klesha of envy, and the wisdom of all-accomplishing action. *See also* appendix 5, under *The Five Buddha-Families* (chapter 26).

**Karma Pakshi** (Tib.: karma pakshi; 1206–1283 CE). The second Karmapa, who was considered to be a siddha. Invited by the Chinese emperor, he accompanied the great Sakya lama on a visit to China, and had a great spiritual influence on China.

**Karma Trinlepa** (Tib.: karma 'phrin las pa; 1456–1539 CE). A Kagyü poet and scholar; teacher of the eighth Karmapa, Mikyö Dorje.

**karmamudra** (Skt.; Tib.: lekyi chaggya; las kyi phyag rgya). A tantric practice involving the union of male and female. It is associated with the third, or prajna-jnana, abhisheka.

**Karmapa** (Tib.: karma pa). The spiritual head of the Karma Kagyü school and the oldest tülku lineage of Tibetan Buddhism. The Karmapa is considered to be an emanation of Avalokiteshvara, the bodhisattva of compassion. The sixteenth Karmapa Rikpe Dorje (1924–1981) was the Kagyü lineage holder during Trungpa Rinpoche's lifetime. The current, or seventeenth, Karmapa is Ogyen Trinley Dorje (b. 1985).

**karmic seed** (Skt.: bija). The seed sown by every action, which will eventually bear fruit in terms of experience, whether in this or in future lives. *See also* karma.

**karuna** (Skt.). *See* compassion.

**kaya** (Skt.; Tib.: ku; sku). Body, form. In Tibetan, *ku* is the honorific for "body," referring particularly to the body of a buddha or exalted teacher. *See also* trikaya.

**kayas, three.** *See* trikaya.

**kham** (Tib.: khams). *See* dhatu.

**khatam** (Tib.: kha gtam). Legend, tale; one of the three divisions of men-ngag gi de.

**khathor** (Tib.: kha thor). Random, scattered; one of the three divisions of men-ngag gi de.

**khenpo** (Tib.: mkhan po). Scholar, abbot; a title for a teacher who has completed a major course of studies in Buddhist thought.

**Khenpo Gangshar Wangpo** (Tib.: mkhan po gang shar dbang po; 1925–? CE). A renowned twentieth-century Nyingma master and khenpo of Shechen Monastery, whose main student was Chögyam Trungpa Rinpoche. Famed for his instruction in crazy wisdom, Khenpo Gangshar was invited by Trungpa Rinpoche to teach at the *shedra* (monastic college) at Surmang Monastery.

**khor-de rulok** (Tib.: 'khor 'das ru log). Samsara and nirvana turned upside down; reversing one's perspective in order to understand samsara and nirvana properly.

**khor-we nyemik** (Tib.: 'khor ba'i nyes dmigs). The torment of samsara; the fourth of the four reminders. *See also* appendix 5, under *The Four Reminders* (chapter 30).

**khorwa** (Tib.: 'khor ba). *See* samsara.

**Khyentse the Great** (1820–1892 CE; Tib.: 'jam dbyangs mkhyen brtse'i dbang po). Also known as Jamyang Khyentse Wangpo. A great master, scholar, and *tertön,* regarded as a reincarnation of both Vimalamitra and King Trisong Detsen. Along with Jamgön Kongtrül, he was a founder of the Ri-me movement of Tibetan Buddhism.

**kila** (Skt.; Tib.: phurba; phur ba). A ritual three-bladed dagger used symbolically to cut through the kleshas of passion, aggression, and ignorance.

**klesha** (Skt.; Tib.: nyönmong; nyon mongs). Defilement or conflicting emotion; also referred to as a poison. Kleshas are properties that dull the mind and lead to unwholesome actions. The three principal kleshas are passion, aggression, and ignorance or delusion.

**köldrip mepar ladawa** (Tib.: gol sgrib med par la zla ba). Stepping over misunderstandings and obstacles on the path; the second category of sem-de.

**Krishnacharya** (Skt.). One of the eighty-four mahasiddhas; a teacher of Tilopa.

**kriyayoga** (Skt.; Tib.: cha-we gyü; bya ba'i rgyud). Action yoga; the yoga of purification. In the nine-yana system, the first of the three lower tantric yanas. *See also* appendix 5, under *The Nine Yanas* (chapter 40).

**ku** (Tib.: sku). *See* kaya.

**ku yeshe** (Tib.: sku ye shes). Wisdom body; the inseparability of form (ku) and wisdom (yeshe). In mahamudra, ku is related with cutting the fetters of samsara, and yeshe is related with spaciousness, or emptiness.

**kunda** (Skt.). The jasmine flower; used as an analogy, it may refer to the color white, the full moon, semen, or bodhichitta. One of the five main ingredients of amrita. *See also* appendix 5, *Five Ingredients Used to Create Amrita* (chapter 61).

**kundalini** (Skt.: "coiled"). A spiritual force said to lie at the base of the spine, ready to be aroused through yogic practice.

**kündzop** (Tib.: kun rdzob). Relative or conventional; usually contrasted with töndam, the absolute or ultimate. Sometimes used as an abbreviation of *kündzop denpa* (kun rdzob bden pa), or "relative truth." *See also* töndam.

**Künga Gyaltsen** (early 15th century; Tib.: kun dga' rgyal mtshan; "all-joyful victory banner"). The first Trungpa, a student of Trung Ma-se.

**künshi** (Tib.: kun gzhi). *See* alaya.

**künshi nganglyk kyi gewa** (Tib.: kun gzhi ngang lugs kyi dge ba). The natural virtue of the alaya, which is a gateway to yeshe, or wisdom; a synonym of basic goodness.

**küntak** (Tib.: kun brtags; Skt.: parikalpita). Random labeling; false conceptions.

**Küntu Sangpo** (Tib.: kun tu bzang po). *See* Samantabhadra.

**kusha** (Skt.). A grass considered sacred in India, used by the Buddha as a meditation cushion. The grass is also used in ritual ceremonies.

**kye-che** (Tib.: skye mched). *See* ayatana.

**kye-me** (Tib.: skye med). Unborn, birthless.

**kyerim** (Tib.: bskyed rim). *See* utpattikrama.

**kyilkhor** (Tib.: dkyil 'khor). *See* mandala.

**ladawa** (Tib.: la zla ba). To leap over, to bypass; the direct, as opposed to the gradual, path.

**lam** (Tib.: lam; Skt.: marga). Path.

**lam küntu sangpo** (Tib.: lam kun tu bzang po). All-good path. One of the five types of Samantabhadra. See also appendix 5, under *Five Types of Samantabhadra* (chapter 4).

**lama** (Tib.: bla ma). *See* guru.

**la-me gyü** (Tib.: bla med rgyud). Highest tantra; one of the four divisions of anuttarayoga. *See also* appendix 5, under *The Four Divisions of Anuttarayoga* (chapter 54).

**la-me naljor** (Tib.: bla ma'i rnal 'byor). *See* guru yoga.

**lamkhyer** (Tib.: lam khyer). Carrying all life circumstances to the path.

**Langdarma** (Tib.: glang dar ma). The grandson of Trisong Detsen, Langdarma ruled Tibet from approximately 838 to 841 CE. Langdarma was responsible for the religious persecution of Buddhists and the decline of dharma in eighth-century Tibet.

**le** (Tib.: las). Action, karma.

**le gyu dre** (Tib.: las rgyu 'bras). Cause and effect of actions, or karma; the third of the four reminders. *See also* appendix 5, under *The Four Reminders* (chapter 30).

**len tang nammin la rewa mepa** (Tib.: lan dang rnam smin la re ba med pa). Without hoping for a result or reward; the attitude of true generosity.

**lesu rungwa** (Tib.: las su rung ba). Workability; pliancy.

839

lhak-pe sugnyen gyi kyilkhor (Tib.: lhag pa'i gzugs brnyan gyi dkyil 'khor). Mandala of extra form; one of eight types of mandala in the mahayoga tan- tra. *See also* appendix 5, under *The Eight Mandalas of Mahayoga* (chapter 60).

lhak-pe tingdzin gyi kyilkhor (Tib.: lhag pa'i ting 'dzin gyi dkyil 'khor). Man- dala of extra meditation; one of eight types of mandala in the mahayoga tantra. *See also* appendix 5, *The Eight Mandalas of Mahayoga* (chapter 60).

lhaksam (Tib.: lhag bsam; "superior thinking"). Another term for vipashyana.

lhakthong. *See* vipashyana.

lhenchik kye-pe yeshe (Tib.: lhan cig skyes pa'i ye shes). *See* coemergent wisdom.

lhündrup (Tib.: lhun grub). Spontaneous presence, one of the two principal aspects of the maha ati teachings, the other being kadak, or primordial purity. A characteristic of mahayoga practice and one of three qualities of the Great East. *See also* note on page xxiv and appendix 5, under *The Three Qualities of the Great East* (chapter 1).

lhündrup kyi kyilkhor (Tib.: lhun grub kyi dkyil 'khor). Mandala of self- existence or spontaneous presence; one of eight types of mandala in the mahayoga tantra. *See also* appendix 5, under *The Eight Mandalas of Mahayoga* (chapter 60).

litri (Tib.: li khri; Skt.: sindura). Red lead; vermillion. A medicinal mineral used in ritual ceremonies.

lo (Tib.: blo). Mind, or basic intellect. It is formally defined as "that which is clear and aware" (Tib.: sel shing rikpa; gsal zhing rig pa).

lodok namshi. *See* four reminders.

lodral (Tib.: blo bral). Free from conceptualization, or intellect.

lodral chogdzin ledepa (Tib.: blo bral phyogs 'dzin las 'das pa). Transcending attachment to intellect and to nonintellectual fixations and bias. Free from concepts and going beyond fixations; the sixth category of sem-de.

lodrö (Tib.: blo gros). Intelligence, discriminating intellect; the transcendental form of lo.

Lodrö Thaye. *See* Jamgön Kongtrül Lodrö Thaye.

lojong (Tib.: blo sbyong). Mind training; specifically, cultivating loving-kind- ness and compassion by practicing the slogans of the Seven Points of Mind Training, a teaching compiled by Geshe Chekawa Yeshe Dorje and attrib- uted to Atisha.

long (Tib.: klong). Space, expanse. Nondirectional space.

long-de (Tib.: klong de). Category of space; one of the three principal divisions of the maha ati teachings.

long karpo (Tib.: klong dkar po). White space. Space in which there is no action; one of the four types of space described in the long-de section of maha ati.

**long nakpo gyu mepa** (Tib.: klong nag po rgyu med pa). Black space free from a cause. One of the four types of space described in the long-de section of maha ati.

**long rabjam** (Tib.: klong rab 'byams). All-encompassing space. One of the four types of space described in the long-de section of maha ati.

**long trawo natsok rangshar gyen** (Tib.: klong khra bo sna tshogs rang shar rgyan). Self-arising ornament of multicolored space. Space of the playfulness of mind, one of the four types of space described in the long-de section of maha ati.

**Longchen Rabjam** (Tib.: klong chen rab 'byams; 1308–1363 CE). Also known as Longchenpa. A great scholar of the Nyingma lineage, who bore the title "All-Knowing." A prolific author, he played an important role in the transmission of the dzokchen teachings.

**long-de** (Tib.: klong de). Category of space; one of the three principal divisions of the ati teachings.

**longku** (Tib.: longs sku). *See* sambhogakaya.

**lopham** (Tib.: blo pham; "defeated mind"). Disappointment, discouragement.

**loppön** (Tib.: slob dpon). *See* dorje loppön.

**lo-te** (Tib.: blo gtad; "directing the mind"). Trust, confidence.

**lo-te lingkyur** (Tib.: blo gtad ling bskyur). Complete abandonment; trusting completely and being willing to let go. A quality of devotion.

**lower tantra.** In the nine-yana system, the first three of the six tantric yanas—kriyayoga, upayoga, and yogayana—along with the mahamudra teachings of highest yoga tantra, or anuttarayoga. *See also* appendix 5, under *The Nine Yanas* (chapter 40).

**luminosity** (Tib.: ösel; 'od gsal; Skt.: prabhasvara). The vividness of appearance that arises within, and is inseparable from, emptiness; the inherently clear and radiant nature of mind.

**lung** (Tib.: lung). Reading transmission; authorization to study a text or to practice a sadhana by listening to it being read.

**madhyamaka** (Skt.; Tib.: uma; dbu ma). The Middle Way school of mahayana Buddhism; a philosophical school based on the dialectical approach of undercutting any attempt to establish a solid logical position, developed by the great logician Nagarjuna.

**madhyamika** (Skt.). A proponent of the philosophical school of madhyamaka.

**ma-gyü** (Tib.: ma rgyud). *See* mother tantra.

**maha ati** (Skt.). *See* dzokpa chenpo.

**Mahamaya** (Skt.; Tib.: gyuma chenmo; sgyu ma chen mo; "great illusion"). A mother tantra of the anuttara tantra. Its principal deity, associated with the vajra family, is depicted as blue, four-armed, and in union with consort.

**mahamudra** (Skt.; Tib.: chaggya chenpo; phyag rgya chen po; "great symbol"). The meditative transmission handed down especially by the Kagyü school, from the buddha Vajradhara through Tilopa up to the present. A tradition of systematic meditative training, leading to a direct nonconceptual understanding of the vivid-empty nature of phenomenal reality.

*Mahamudra-tilaka-tantra* (Skt.). *The Mahamudra Drop Tantra;* a principal tantra of the mahamudra lineage.

**mahasangha** (Skt.). Great sangha, or community of practitioners.

**mahasattva** (Skt.; Tib.: sempa chenpo; sems dpa' chen po). Great being; a term referring to great bodhisattvas, often at the level of the seventh bhumi or higher.

**mahasiddha** (Skt.). A great siddha or adept. Refers to highly accomplished tantric masters known for their great spiritual powers and the joining of spiritual attainment with a variety of ordinary and eccentric lifestyles.

**mahasukha** (Skt.; Tib.: dewa chenpo; bde ba chen po). Great bliss. A term for the quality of the experience of egolessness in mahamudra. According to mahamudra, ego is a kind of filter standing between the mind and its world. When this filter is removed, one experiences a bliss beyond pleasure and pain.

*Mahavairochana* (Skt.). Name of an important Buddhist tantra; one of the central texts of the Japanese Shingon sect.

**mahavipashyana** (Skt.). A greater experience of vipashyana, associated with the practice of mahamudra. *See also* vipashyana.

**mahayana** (Skt.; Tib.: thekpa chenpo; theg pa chen po). Great vehicle; the second of the three yanas, which emphasizes the union of emptiness and compassion, the practice of the paramitas, and the ideal of the bodhisattva.

**mahayoga** (Skt.; Tib.: naljor chenpo; rnal 'byor chen po). The yoga of great union. In the nine-yana system, the first of the three higher tantric yanas, known as the all-encompassing yanas of skillful means, the imperial or conquering yanas. *See also* appendix 5, under *The Nine Yanas* (chapter 40).

**maitri** (Skt.; Pali: metta; Tib.: champa; byams pa). Friendliness, loving-kindness; one of the four limitless qualities that are to be cultivated on the bodhisattva path.

**Mamaki** (Skt.). The female buddha of the vajra family, the consort of Akshobhya.

**mamo** (Tib.: ma mo; Skt.: matarah). Wrathful female deity who brings disease and catastrophe to those who violate tantric precepts, but prosperity to practitioners who do not violate their vows. The sixth of the eight logos, connected with the practice of the mother's curse. *See also* appendix 5, under *The Eight Logos / Druppa Kagye* (chapter 61).

**mandala** (Skt.; Tib.: kyilkhor; dkyil 'khor; "center and periphery"). A symbolic representation of cosmic forces in two- or three-dimensional form, with a center and four gates in the four cardinal directions. Typically, a mandala includes a central deity, representing the brilliant sanity of buddha nature, surrounded by a retinue in the four principal directions. The outer world, one's body, one's state of mind, and the totality can all be seen as mandalas.

**mandala nopika** (Skt.; Tib.: tsogdrup; tshogs sgrub). Group practice of a sadhana, usually conducted for a specific length of time, such as ten or fifteen days, or a month.

**Manjushri** (Skt.; Tib.: Jampal; 'jam dpal). Bodhisattva of wisdom, usually depicted holding a prajnaparamita text and a sword, symbolizing the power of prajna and the cutting of twofold ego.

*Manjushri-nama-sangiti* (Skt.). *Chanting the Names of Manjushri.* A famous praise of Manjushri, sometimes referred to as the "king of all tantras."

**mantra** (Skt.; Tib.: ngak; sngags; "mind protection"). Sanskrit words or syllables that are recited as a means of transforming energy through sound. In tantric practice, mantras are practiced in conjunction with meditation and mudras, or symbolic gestures.

**mantrayana** (Skt.; Tib.: ngakkyi thekpa; sngags kyi theg pa). Mantra vehicle; a synonym for vajrayana, whose meditation practices make extensive use of mantra. Sometimes referred to as the "secret mantrayana" or "secret mantra."

**margyi sangthal** (Tib.: mar gyi zang thal; "confidence below"). Samsaric style of being confident.

**marked with Samantabhadra** (Tib.: Küntu Sangpo gyethoppa; kun tu bzang po rgyas thob pa). The quality of totality and basic goodness. The first of the seven aspects of vajrayana. *See also* appendix 5, under *Seven Aspects of Vajrayana* (chapter 6).

**Marpa Lotsawa** (Tib.: mar pa lo tsa ba; 1012–1097 CE). A renowned translator, Marpa brought the mahamudra teaching of Naropa and Maitripa to Tibet, becoming the first Tibetan in the Kagyü lineage. His most famous student was the great yogin Milarepa.

**Matram Rudra** (Skt.). *See* Rudra.

**men-ngag gi de** (Tib.: man ngag gi sde). Category of oral instruction; one of the three divisions of the maha ati teachings.

**mikthur** (Tib.: mig thur). Eye stick; ritual instrument used in an abhisheka to remove students' blindfolds and point out the mandala.

**Milarepa** (Tib.: mi la ras pa; 1040–1123 CE). Tibet's most famous yogin, Milarepa was famous for his ascetic discipline and songs of realization. He was the principal disciple of Marpa, and his student Gampopa founded the Takpo Kagyü lineage.

**Mipham Rinpoche** (Tib.: mi pham rin po che; 1846–1912 CE). A major scholar of the Nyingma and Ri-me traditions. He wrote over thirty-two volumes on such diverse topics as painting, poetics, sculpture, alchemy, medicine, logic, philosophy, and tantra. Also referred to as Mipham Jamyang Gyatso, Ju Mipham, or Jamgön Mipham.

**mögü** (Tib.: mos gus). Devotion; the combination of longing and humility.

**mother tantra** (Tib.: ma-gyü; ma rgyud). One of the four divisions of anutta-rayoga. In general, mother tantras present deities associated with transmuting passion into enlightened energy. The *Chakrasamvara Tantra* and *Hevajra Tantra* are examples of mother tantras. *See also* appendix 5, under *The Four Divisions of Anuttarayoga* (chapter 54).

**mudra** (Skt.; Tib.: chaggya; phyag rgya). Sign, symbol, gesture. Usually a reference to symbolic hand gestures that accompany vajrayana practices. Mudra can also refer to the consort of a deity or yogin, as in the term *karmamudra*. Also, one of four characteristics of buddha-families. *See also* appendix 5, under *Four Ways of Seeing Each of the Twenty-Five Buddha-Families* (chapter 47).

**nadi** (Skt.; Tib.: tsa; rtsa). A subtle channel in the body through which energy, or prana, flows.

**Nagarjuna** (Skt.; second to third century CE). A great Indian teacher of Buddhism, the founder of the madhyamaka school of Buddhist philosophy. He contributed greatly to the logical development of the doctrine of shunyata and was the author of many key texts. According to tradition, he was also the guru of various important Buddhist teachers.

**Nairatmya** (Skt.; Tib.: Dagmema; bdag med ma; "egoless"). Consort of the deity Hevajra.

**naljor shirim** (Tib.: rnal 'byor bzhi rim). The four yogas of mahamudra: one-pointedness, simplicity, one taste, and nonmeditation.

**Namgyal-tse** (Tib.: rnam rgyal rtse; "all-victorious peak"). One of the two main monasteries of Surmang, the other being Dütsi Tel.

**nangsi yeshe kyi khorlo shepa** (Tib.: snang srid ye shes kyi 'khor lo shes pa). Knowing that all phenomena are included in the sphere of wisdom; one definition of mandala.

**nangtong** (Tib.: snang stong). Appearance-emptiness.

**nangwa-gyur** (Tib.: snang ba 'gyur). Changing what you see; changing perception. In terms of the ground, path, and fruition of devotion, it is the path of blessings.

**Naropa** (Skt. 1016–1100 CE). An Indian mahasiddha and scholar of Nalanda University, who was a disciple of Tilopa and a teacher of Marpa.

**Nedo Kagyü** (Tib.: gnas mdo bka' rgyud). A subsect of the Kagyü lineage, founded by Karma Chagme (1613–1678 CE).

**New Translation school** (Tib.: sarma; gsar ma). The tantric teachings of the Kagyü, Sakya, and Geluk lineages of Tibetan Buddhism, which were brought to Tibet through the translations from Sanskrit begun by Rinchen Sangpo (958–1055 CE) and continued notably by Marpa (1012–1097 CE).

**ngak** (Tib.: sngags). *See* mantra.

**ngakkyi thekpa** (Tib.: sngags kyi theg pa). Mantrayana; another term for vajrayana.

**ngedön** (Tib.: nges don; Skt.: nitartha). True, or definitive, meaning. One of the categories that shows how the view of anuttarayoga is special in comparison with lower yanas. Views are considered as true in meaning if they are ultimate, needing no further qualification or interpretation. Contrasted with trangdön, or literal meaning. *See also* trangdön and chapter 51, "Taking a Fresh Look at the Phenomenal World."

**ngödrup** (Tib.: dngos grub). *See* siddhi.

**ngöndro** (Tib.: sngon 'gro). That which goes ahead. Four traditional preliminary practices done before one receives vajrayana empowerment: usually 100,000 repetitions each of the refuge formula, prostration practice, Vajrasattva mantra recitation, and mandala offering. Often followed by guru yoga, which is a further preliminary.

**ngo-she** (Tib.: ngo shes). Recognition, familiarity; in particular, recognition of the true nature of mind.

**ngotrö** (Tib.: ngo sprod). *See* transmission.

**nidana** (Skt.; Tib.: tendrel; rten 'brel). One of the twelve links of interdependent origination, the samsaric cycle of cause and effect: ignorance, karmic formations, consciousness, name and form, the six senses, contact, feeling, craving, grasping, becoming, birth, and old age and death. The web of mutually conditioned psychological and physical phenomena that constitute individual existence and entangle sentient beings in samsara.

**Niguma** (Skt.). A great female practitioner, who was the consort of Naropa.

**nirmanakaya** (Skt.; Tib.: tülku; sprul sku). Emanation body. One of the three kayas. *See also* trikaya.

**nirvana** (Skt.: "extinguished"; Tib.: nya-ngen ledepa; mya ngan las 'das pa; "gone beyond suffering"). Freedom from the sufferings of samsara; a synonym of *enlightenment*.

**no obstacles** (Tib.: parchö mepa; bar gcod med pa). Total awareness without obstacles or hazards. The fifth of the seven aspects of vajrayana. *See also* appendix 5, under *Seven Aspects of Vajrayana* (chapter 6).

**nopika** (Skt.; Tib.: druppa; sgrub pa). Essential practice, divided into two types: solitary practice and group practice.

**nowness** (Tib.: data; da lta). The spontaneous mind of the present instant, free from past or future; a synonym of ordinary mind.

**nyam** (Tib.: nyams). A temporary experience of meditation practice.

**nyam kongphel** (Tib.: nyams gong 'phel). Increased experience; the second of the four visions, or stages, of maha ati practice.

**nyi-me gyü** (Tib.: gnyis med rgyud). Nondual or union tantra; one of the four divisions of anuttarayoga. *See also* appendix 5, under *The Four Divisions of Anuttarayoga* (chapter 54).

**Nyingma** (Tib.: rnying ma; "ancient"). One of the four main schools of Tibetan Buddhism. It adheres to the oldest Buddhist traditions of Tibet, which were brought to Tibet from India by Padmasambhava in the eighth century. The Nyingma school is known for originating the nine-yana system and systematizing the maha ati, or dzokchen teachings.

**nyönmong** (Tib.: nyon mongs). *See* klesha.

**nyuksem** (Tib.: gnyug sems). Innate mind; primordial mind.

**Old Translation school** (Tib.: nga-gyur; snga 'gyur). The Nyingma lineage of Tibetan Buddhism, whose teaching tradition is based on the first texts translated from Sanskrit into Tibetan in the eighth century.

**one-and-a-half-fold egolessness** (Tib.: dagme che tang nyi; bdag med phyed dang gnyis). The egolessness of self and a partial realization of the egolessness of phenomena.

**oryoki** (Jpn.). "Just enough." From Zen Buddhism, a formal meal ritual that utilizes a set of nesting bowls, and is practiced during extended group meditation sessions.

**ösel** (Tib.: 'od gsal). *See* luminosity.

**ösel dorje thekpa** (Tib.: 'od gsal rdo rje theg pa). The luminous, indestructible vehicle; another term for vajrayana.

**padma** (Skt.). Lotus. In the five-buddha-family mandala, the buddha-family associated with the West, the buddha Amitabha, the klesha of passion, and discriminating-awareness wisdom. *See also* appendix 5, under *The Five Buddha-Families* (chapter 26).

**Padmasambhava** (Skt.; Tib.: Pema Jungne; pad ma 'byung gnas; "Lotus Born"). Known as the second buddha, Padmasambhava was an Indian mahasiddha and great teacher who helped bring Buddhism to Tibet in the eighth century, founding the Nyingma lineage. Also referred to as Guru Rinpoche.

**pagyang** (Tib.: bag yangs; "carefree"). Natural relaxation.

**pal** (Tib.: dpal). Glory; splendor.

**paramita** (Skt.; Tib.: pharöl tu chinpa; pha rol tu phyin pa; "gone to the far shore"). Transcendent perfection of the mahayana. The six paramitas are generosity, discipline, patience, exertion, meditation, and prajna.

**peyi yeshe** (Tib.: dpe yi ye shes). Example wisdom. In the third abhisheka of anuttarayoga, the after-experience of the joy of union.

**pha-gyü** (Tib.: pha rgyud). Father tantra; one of the four divisions of anuttarayoga. *See also* appendix 5, under *The Four Divisions of Anuttarayoga* (chapter 54).

**phowa** (Tib.: 'pho ba; "transference"). The practice of transferring one's consciousness to a pure realm, such as Sukhavati, at the time of death; one of the six dharmas of Naropa.

**phowe pakchak** (Tib.: 'pho ba'i bag chags). The habitual pattern of transmigration. In terms of thought patterns, the process of the cessation of one thought followed by the arising of the next thought.

**Phullahari** (Skt.). Kagyü monastery near Kathmandu, Nepal.

**postmeditation** (Tib.: jethop; rjes thob). Follow-up to a formal meditation session. Carrying the awareness cultivated in meditation into all activities of one's daily life.

**prabhasvara** (Skt.). *See* luminosity.

**prajna** (Skt.; Tib.: sherap; shes rab). Perfect knowledge, meaning wisdom, understanding, or discrimination. The natural sharpness of awareness that sees, discriminates, and also sees through conceptual discrimination. In vajrayana, prajna corresponds to the feminine principle of space, the mother of wisdom, which is united with the masculine principle of upaya, or skillful means.

**prajnaparamita** (Skt.; Tib.: sherap kyi pharöltu chinpa; shes rab kyi pha rol tu phyin pa). Knowledge gone beyond; transcendent knowledge. The sixth paramita of the bodhisattva path; also, the *Prajnaparamita Sutras* are a series of mahayana sutras on emptiness. The insight that discovers that both the self and the world are illusory constructions. The mother of all the buddhas and of all knowledge.

**prana** (Skt.; Tib.: lung; rlung). Wind, breath, or energy. Prana is the energy, or "wind," that circulates through the nadis, or subtle channels, of the body.

**pranayama** (Skt.). Breath control. A form of yoga practiced in the vajrayana, which involves working with the illusory body of nadi, prana, and bindu.

**pratyekabuddha** (Skt.; Tib.: rang sang-gye; rang sangs rgyas). Solitary realizer. In the hinayana, one who attains liberation from samsara without the benefit of a teacher and who does not teach others.

**pratyekabuddhayana** (Skt.; Tib.: rang sang-gye thokpa; rang sangs rgyas thog pa). The hinayana path of the "solitary realizer." The second yana in the nine-yana system. *See also* appendix 5, under *The Nine Yanas* (chapter 40).

**rakta** (Skt.). Blood; one of the five ingredients that are transformed from poison into amrita. *See also* appendix 5, *Five Ingredients Used to Create Amrita* (chapter 61).

**rangdröl** (Tib.: rang grol). Self-liberated. A commonly used image for self-liberation is a snake that unravels itself.

**Rangjung Dorje** (Tib.: rang 'byung rdo rje; 1284–1339 CE). The third Karmapa. A noted scholar born into a Nyingma family, he received both the full Nyingma and Kagyü transmissions.

**rangjung gi yeshe** (Tib.: rang byung gi ye shes). Self-born or self-existing wisdom.

**rangnang ri-me** (Tib.: rang snang ris med). Experience without any bias. The anuyoga experience of unbiased passion, characterized by prajna, indivisibility, and completeness.

**rangshin gyi kyilkhor** (Tib.: rang bzhin gyi dkyil 'khor). Mandala of self-existence; one of eight types of mandala in mahayoga tantra. *See also* appendix 5, under *The Eight Mandalas of Mahayoga* (chapter 60).

**rangshin nerik** (Tib.: rang bzhin gnas rigs). Naturally abiding potential; the way things are as they are.

**rangtong** (Tib.: rang stong; "empty of self"). The madhyamaka view that maintains that each phenomenon is empty of itself—i.e., what it seems to be—and denies that anything further can be said. Usually contrasted with the view of shentong. *See also* shentong.

**ratna** (Skt.; "jewel"). In the mandala of the five buddha-families, the buddha-family associated with the South, the buddha Ratnasambhava, the klesha of pride, and the wisdom of equanimity. *See also* appendix 5, under *The Five Buddha-Families* (chapter 26).

**refuge vow.** The vow marking one's formal entry onto the Buddhist path, in which one commits to respect and follow the Buddha as teacher, the dharma as instruction, and the sangha as companions.

**rigdzin** (Tib.: rig 'dzin). *See* vidyadhara.

**rigdzin thekpa** (Tib.: rig 'dzin theg pa). *See* vidyadharayana.

**rig-ngak** (Tib.: rig sngags). *See* vidyamantra.

**rikpa** (Tib.: rig pa; Skt.: vidya). Insight, awareness, knowing. Clearly seeing things as they are. In the teachings of maha ati, rikpa is the pristine nature of mind that transcends ordinary dualistic mind.

**rikpa küntu sangpo** (Tib.: rig pa kun tu bzang po). All-good insight. One of the five types of Samantabhadra. *See also* appendix 5, under *Five Types of Samantabhadra*.

*Rikpa Rangshar Chenpö Gyü* (Tib.: rig pa rang shar chen po'i rgyud). The *Tantra of Great Self-Arising Awareness;* a maha ati tantra.

**rikpa tsephep** (Tib.: rig pa tshad phebs). Awareness reaching its full measure; the third of the four visions, or stages, of maha ati practice.

**rinpoche** (Tib.: rin po che; "precious"). An honorific title for a teacher, particularly an incarnate lama, or tülku.

**rishi** (Skt.; Tib.: trangsong; drang srong). An Indian saint or sage; advanced practitioner.

**rochik** (Tib.: ro gcig). One taste; the third of the four yogas of mahamudra. *See also* appendix 5, under *The Four Yogas of Mahamudra / Naljor Shirim* (chapter 57).

**rölpa** (Tib.: rol pa). Display, expression; one of the characteristics of mind.

**Rudra** (Skt.). A personification of the destructive principle of ultimate ego, which is the complete opposite of buddhahood. According to a traditional story, Rudra was a student who killed his teacher because the teacher contradicted and criticized him.

**rupa** (Skt.; Tib.: suk; gzugs). Body; form.

**sacred outlook** (Tib.: tagnang; dag snang; "pure appearance"). Pure perception. The awareness that all phenomena are sacred. The perception of self-existing sacredness, which leads to the experience of unconditional freedom.

**sadhaka** (Tib.: druppapo; sgrub pa po). Vajrayana practitioner; one who practices a sadhana.

**sadhana** (Skt.). Practice. A vajrayana liturgy incorporating visualization practice, formless meditation, mantras, and mudras. Sadhana can refer to a particular text, such as a Vajrayogini sadhana or Chakrasamvara sadhana, or to the practice itself.

*Sadhana of Mahamudra*. Also called the *Sadhana of the Embodiment of All the Siddhas*. A sadhana written by Chögyam Trungpa during his retreat at Taktsang, or Tiger's Nest cave, in Bhutan, the site where the great Indian saint, Padmasambhava, meditated and manifested as Dorje Trolö, his crazy-wisdom form. This sadhana joins together the figures of Dorje Trölo and the second Karmapa, Karma Pakshi, symbolizing the union of mahamudra and maha ati.

**sadhu** (Skt.). A renunciate who has left behind all material attachments, living in caves, forests, and temples.

**Sakya** (Tib.: sa skya; "gray earth"). One of the four main schools of Tibetan Buddhism, named after the Sakya Monastery in southern Tibet. Founded in 1083 CE and known for creating a systematic order for the tantric writings and for examination of problems of Buddhist logic, the Sakya tradition had great political influence in the thirteenth and fourteenth centuries.

**samadhi** (Skt.; Tib.: tingdzin; ting 'dzin). Meditative absorption. A state of total involvement in which the mind rests without distraction, and the content of the meditation and the meditator's mind are one.

**samadhisattva** (Skt.: tingdzin sempa; ting 'dzin sems dpa'; "samadhi being"). The samadhi principle, often represented by a Sanskrit syllable in the heart center of a visualized deity.

**Samantabhadra** (Skt.; Tib.: Küntu Sangpo; kun tu bzang po; "all good"). In the Nyingma tradition, Samantabhadra is the dharmakaya, or primordial, buddha. He is depicted as naked and blue in color. As one of the seven aspects of vajrayana, "marked with Samantabhadra" refers to a quality of totality and basic goodness. *See also* appendix 5, under *Seven Aspects of Vajrayana* (chapter 6).

**Samantabhadri** (Skt.; Tib.: Küntu Sangmo; kun tu bzang mo; "all-good lady"). In the Nyingma lineage, the female primordial buddha and consort of Samantabhadra.

**samaya** (Skt.; Tib.: tamtsik; dam tshigs). Binding vow, commitment, sacred word. The samaya vow, usually taken in the context of an empowerment ceremony, marks a student's binding commitment to the vajrayana path. It is taken only after taking the hinayana refuge vow and the mahayana bodhisattva vow. Never violating samaya is the sixth of the seven aspects of vajrayana, and always restoring samaya is the seventh of the seven aspects of the vajrayana. *See also* appendix 5, under *Seven Aspects of Vajrayana* (chapter 6).

**samayasattva** (Skt.; Tib.: yeshe sempa; ye shes sems dpa'; "samaya being"). In vajrayana practice, the deity that one creates through visualization; contrasted with jnanasattva. *See also* jnanasattva.

**samayashila** (Skt.). The vajrayana discipline of maintaining one's samaya. *See also* samaya.

**sambhogakaya** (Skt.; Tib.: longku; longs sku; "enjoyment body"). One of the three kayas, or bodies, of a buddha; in particular, a buddha's speech or manifestation, which is an environment of compassion and communication. *See also* trikaya.

**sampannakrama** (Skt.; Tib.: dzogrim; rdzogs rim). The completion stage of vajrayana practice, which emphasizes formless meditation.

**samsara** (Skt.; Tib.: khorwa; 'khor ba; "circling"). Cyclic existence; the repetitive cycle of births and deaths that arises from ignorance and is characterized by suffering. Samsara is contrasted with nirvana, which is the liberation from suffering. However, from the higher perspective of vajrayana, samsara and nirvana are understood to be inseparable.

**samskara** (Skt.; Tib.: du-je; 'du byed). Formation or concept; the fourth of the five skandhas; also, the second of the twelve nidanas, or links of interdependent origination.

**Samye** (Tib.: bsam yas). Temple complex built by King Trisong Detsen (790–844 CE) and consecrated by Padmasambhava. A major center of the Nyingma lineage, it is situated in Central Tibet close to Lhasa.

**sang-gye** (Tib.: sangs rgyas). *See* buddha.

**sang-gye lakchang** (Tib.: sangs rgyas lag bcang). Holding buddha in your hand; an experience connected with the first of the eight logos (Yangdak). *See also* appendix 5, under *The Eight Logos / Druppa Kagye* (chapter 61).

**sangha** (Skt.; Tib.: gendün; dge 'dun). The community of practitioners, companions on the path of dharma; the third of the three jewels.

**sang-ngak** (Tib.: gsang sngags). *See* guhyamantra.

**sangwa** (Tib.: gsang ba; Skt.: guhya). Secret, hidden.

**sang-we thekpa** (Tib.: gsang ba'i theg pa). Secret vehicle; a term for vajrayana.

**sattva** (Skt.; Tib.: sems dpa'). A being.

**sella tokpa me-pe gompa** (Tib.: sel la rtog pa med pa'i sgom pa). "Meditation without thought but luminous"; third of five vajrayana sayings regarding transcending habitual patterns. *See also* appendix 5, under *Five Vajrayana Sayings* (chapter 16).

**sem** (Tib.: sems). Ordinary dualistic mind, characterized by discursive thoughts. It is formally defined as "that which apprehends an object" (Tib.: yul la sempa; yul la sems pa).

**sem tang tral-we rikpa** (Tib.: sems dang bral ba'i rig pa). "Rikpa free from sem"; the first of five vajrayana sayings regarding transcending habitual patterns. *See also* appendix 5, under *Five Vajrayana Sayings* (chapter 16).

**semchok yintu mawa** (Tib.: sems phyogs yin tu smra ba). Proclaiming that mind is in a certain direction; the seventh category of sem-de.

**sem-de** (Tib.: sems sde). Category of mind; one of the three principal divisions of maha ati teachings, which itself has seven further categories.

**sending and taking.** *See* tonglen.

**Senge Dradrok** (Tib.: seng ge sgra grogs). A wrathful aspect of Padmasambhava, said to have destroyed five hundred heretics by means of a ritual ceremony using a teakwood kila (dagger).

**sepa** (Tib.: zad pa). Run out, used up, exhausted.

**setting sun.** Any attitude, thought, or action that leads one to degraded behavior. An expression coined by Chögyam Trungpa and used in the Shambhala teachings.

**shamatha** (Skt.; Tib.: shi-ne; zhi gnas; "peaceful abiding"). Mindfulness practice; the practice of taming and stabilizing the mind. The central practice of the hinayana path and an essential component of practice throughout all the yanas.

**shamatha-vipashyana** (Skt.). The union of the mindfulness of shamatha and the awareness of vipashyana.

**Shambhala** (Skt.). Mythical Central Asian kingdom, said to be a society where all the inhabitants are enlightened. Shambhala is closely associated with the *Kalachakra Tantra,* which Shakyamuni Buddha is said to have taught to the Shambhala king Dawa Sangpo.

**Shambhala vision.** A reference to Trungpa Rinpoche's teachings on the sacred path of the warrior and the creation of enlightened society. Shambhala teachings are closely connected with the Buddhist meditative tradition, but have a more secular and societal focus. (For more on this tradition, see Chögyam Trungpa, *Shambhala: The Sacred Path of the Warrior* [Boston: Shambhala Publications, 2007].)

**Shantarakshita** (Tib.: shiwa tso; zhi ba 'tsho). The Indian teacher invited to Tibet in the eighth century by King Trisong Detsen. With the help of Padmasambhava, he built Samye Monastery and became its abbot, ordaining the first Buddhist monks in Tibet.

shedö me-pe tawa (Tib.: shes sdod med pa'i lta ba). "View without desire"; the fifth of the five vajrayana sayings regarding transcending habitual patterns. *See also* appendix 5, under *Five Vajrayana Sayings* (chapter 16).

shentong (Tib.: gzhan stong). The "empty of other" school of Tibetan philosophy, which adheres to the view that the nature of mind is empty of all that is false, but not empty of its own inherent buddha nature. Often contrasted with the rangtong view that everything is unequivocally empty of self-nature. *See also* rangtong.

shepa (Tib.: shes pa). Mind, or consciousness, which is the capacity for knowing.

shi lamdu chepa (Tib.: gzhi lam du byed pa). Using the ground as the path; an approach associated with lower tantra.

shi-je (Tib.: zhi byed). Pacification. One of the contemplative schools of Tibetan Buddhism associated with the teachings of chö. *See* chö.

shila (Skt.; Tib.: tsültrim; tshul khrims). Discipline; one of the three principal aspects of the Buddhist path, the other two being samadhi and prajna; one of the six paramitas.

shinjang (Tib.: shin sbyang; Skt.: prashrabdhi). Thoroughly processed or trained through meditation practice.

shravaka (Skt.; Tib.: nyenthö; nyan thos). Hearer. Originally, a disciple who heard teachings directly from the Buddha; more generally, a practitioner of the shravakayana.

shravakayana (Skt.; Tib.: nyenthö thokpa; nyen thos theg pa). The hinayana path of the "hearer." The first yana of the nine-yana system, in which the practitioner concentrates on meditation practice and understanding fundamental Buddhist doctrines, such as the four noble truths. *See also* appendix 5, under *The Nine Yanas* (chapter 40).

Shri Heruka (Skt.). Glorious Heruka. In the context of the eight logos, a reference to fundamental thatness, or living enlightenment, expressed as eight deities arranged in a mandala. *See also* appendix 5, *The Eight Logos / Druppa Kagye* (chapter 61).

Shri Simha (Skt.; Tib.: shri singha; shri sing ha). An early master of the Nyingma lineage, known for dwelling in charnel grounds and for being one of Padmasambhava's teachers.

shunyata (Skt.; Tib.: tongpanyi; stong pa nyid). Emptiness. A completely open and unbounded clarity of mind characterized by groundlessness and freedom from all conceptual frameworks. Emptiness does not mean voidness or blankness; rather, it is an openness inseparable from compassion and all other awakened qualities.

siddha (Skt.; Tib.: drupthop; grub thob). One who is spiritually accomplished or has magical powers over the phenomenal world. Best known are the group of eighty-four mahasiddhas, said to have lived in India from the eighth to the twelfth century.

siddhi (Skt.; Tib.: ngödrup; dngos grub). Yogic accomplishment, of which there are two types: lesser siddhi, or mastery over the phenomenal world, and greater siddhi, which is enlightenment itself. Acquiring siddhis is one of the seven aspects of the vajrayana. *See also* appendix 5, under *Seven Aspects of Vajrayana* (chapter 6).

six dharmas of Naropa (Tib.: Naro chödruk; na ro chos drug). A set of six yogic practices received by Naropa from Tilopa; one of the chief practices of the Kagyü lineage. They include the yogas of *chandali* (*tummo*), illusory body (*gyulü*), dream (*milam*), luminosity (*ösel*), transference (phowa), and bardo.

six realms (Tib.: drowa rigdruk; 'gro ba rigs drug). All beings of samsara belong to one of the six realms. The three higher realms include the gods, or devas; the jealous gods, or *asuras;* and humans. The three lower realms include animals; hungry ghosts, or *pretas;* and hell beings.

skandha (Skt.; Tib.: phungpo; phung po; "heap"). One of the five collections of dharmas that constitute an individual's experience: form, feeling, perception / impulse, concept / formation, and consciousness.

Songtsen Gampo (Tib.: srong bstan sgam po; 569–649 CE). Seventh-century king of Tibet, regarded as one of the best and most benevolent of Tibetan monarchs, who built the first Buddhist temples in Tibet and paved the way for the transmission of the dharma into Tibet.

sota nopika (Skt.; Tib.: chigdrup; gcig sgrub). Solitary practice. A sadhana practice that is traditionally done alone.

spiritual friend. *See* kalyanamitra.

spiritual materialism. Materialistic approach to spirituality and religion based on attachment to spiritual experiences; corrupting the spiritual path into a source of personal power and ego aggrandizement.

Suchandra (Skt.). *See* Dawa Sangpo.

suehiro (Jpn.). Hand fan.

sugata (Skt.; Tib.: dewar shekpa; bde bar gshegs pa). One who has gone beyond with joy; a buddha. A synonym of tathagata.

sugatagarbha (Skt.; Tib.: dewar shek-pe nyingpo; bde bar gshegs pa'i snying po; "essence of one gone to bliss"). A synonym of tathagatagarbha, or buddha nature.

sugnyen gyi kyilkhor (Tib.: gzugs brnyan gyi dkyil 'khor). Mandala of form; one of eight types of mandala in the mahayoga tantra. *See also* appendix 5, under *The Eight Mandalas of Mahayoga* (chapter 60).

suk (Tib.: gzugs). *See* rupa.

sungwa (Tib.: gzung ba). Fixation. *See also* fixation and grasping.

Surmang (Tib.: zur mang). Many-cornered; name of the monastery complex that for twelve generations has served as the seat of the Trungpa tülkus in eastern Tibet. Surmang traces its roots back over five hundred years to the mahasiddha Trung Ma-se.

**Surmang Garchen** (Tib.: zur mang sgar chen; "many-cornered great camp"). A traveling monastery in the early days of the Trungpa tülkus. At that time, monks traveled in caravans. Their libraries were on pack mules, the shrine room was a large tent, and the monks' and abbot's quarters were also tents.

**sutra** (Skt.; Tib.: do; mdo). Thread, string, cord. Hinayana and mahayana texts in the Buddhist canon attributed to the Buddha. Sutra also means a meeting point or junction, referring to the meeting of the Buddha's enlightenment and the student's understanding. A sutra is usually a dialogue between the Buddha and one or more of his disciples, elaborating a particular topic of dharma.

*Sutra of the Recollection of the Noble Three Jewels* (Skt.: arya-ratnatraya-anusmriti sutra). A sutra on the qualities of the Buddha, dharma, and sangha studied in many schools of Tibetan Buddhism.

svaha (Skt.). A word that concludes many mantras, meaning "So be it."

**tagnang** (Tib.: dag snang; "pure perception"). *See* sacred outlook.

**tai tung** (Chin.). Great East. A Chinese term used by Trungpa Rinpoche to express key qualities of vajrayana discipline, primarily the qualities of being primordial, eternal, and self-existent. Also, a key term in the Shambhala teachings of basic goodness and establishing an enlightened society.

**takpa** (Tib.: rtag pa). Eternal, permanent; one of the qualities of tathagatagarbha and of the Great East. *See also* appendix 5, under *The Three Qualities of the Great East* (chapter 1).

**taljor nyeka** (Tib.: dal 'byor rnyed dka'). Free and well-favored, difficult to find. First of the four reminders (precious human birth). *See also* appendix 5, under *The Four Reminders* (chapter 30).

**Tamdrin** (Tib.: rta mgrin). *See* Hayagriva.

**tampa** (Tib.: dam pa). Holy, sacred; the best.

**tamtsik** (Tib.: dam tshigs). *See* samaya.

**tantra** (Skt.; Tib.: gyü; rgyud; "continuity"). A synonym of vajrayana. Tantra refers both to the root texts of the vajrayana and to the systems of meditation they describe.

**tantrayana** (Skt.). A synonym of vajrayana; also referred to as tantra.

**tantrika** (Skt.; Tib.: ngakpa; sngags pa). A practitioner of vajrayana.

**Taranatha** (Skt.; 1575–1634 CE). Renowned teacher of the Jonang school of Tibetan Buddhism, which specialized in the *Kalachakra Tantra* and the shentong view.

**tathagata** (Skt.; Tib.: teshin shekpa; de bzhin gshegs pa). Thus gone or thus come; an epithet of the Buddha. One who has attained supreme enlightenment.

**tathagatagarbha** (Skt.; Tib.: teshin shekpe nyingpo; de bzhin gshegs pa'i snying po). Buddha nature; the intrinsic state of wakefulness inherent in all sentient beings. A synonym of sugatagarbha.

**tathata** (Skt.; Tib.: teshinnyi; de bzhin nyid). Thusness; another term for things as they are; the world as seen from the viewpoint of sacred outlook.

**te-kho-na-nyi** (Tib.: de kho na nyid; "only that itself"; Skt.: tattva). Suchness, things as they are. The ground of the constituents of the inner mandala.

**ten-se** (Tib.: gtan zad). Permanently worn-out; exhausted.

**tendrel** (Tib.: rten 'brel; Skt.: pratitya-samutpada). Interdependent origination, one of the early core teachings of the Buddha; auspicious coincidence.

**tentsik khungdip** (Tib.: gtan tshigs khung rdib). The falling apart of your home or of the basis of your life; the third category of sem-de.

**tepa** (Tib.: dad pa). Faith, conviction. Feeling steady and confident in the path, as well as knowing what to cultivate and what to avoid.

**terma** (Tib.: gter ma). Hidden treasure teachings. Terma are usually attributed to Padmasambhava and his consorts, who are said to have hidden certain teachings to be revealed at a proper time in the future by a tertön, or terma discoverer. Terma can take the form of a physical object such as a text or ritual implement buried in the ground, hidden in a rock or crystal, in a tree, a lake, or in the sky. Terma also refers to teachings understood as being concealed within the mind of the guru, the true place of concealment.

**tertön** (Tib.: gter ston). Discoverer of a terma. *See also* terma.

**thamal gyi shepa** (Tib.: tha mal gyi shes pa). Ordinary mind. Here, *ordinary* has the sense of not being fabricated or altered in any way.

**thapkyi thekpa** (Tib.: thabs kyi theg pa). Vehicle of skillful means; another term for vajrayana.

**That** (Skt.: tattva). Reality, suchness, things as they are; in particular, the nature of reality pointed out in the fourth abhisheka.

**thekpa** (Tib.: theg pa). *See* yana.

**thögal** (Tib.: thod rgal; "direct crossing"). In the Nyingma tradition, one of the two principle practices belonging to the oral instruction section of maha ati. Maha-ati practice has two main sections: trekchö and thögal. The former emphasizes primordial purity (kadak). The latter, which consists of spontaneously appearing visions, emphasizes spontaneous presence (lhündrup). *See also* trekchö.

**thoughtfulness / unthoughtfulness** (Tib.: gongpachen / gongpa mayinpa; dgongs pa can / dgongs pa ma yin pa). One of the pairs of categories that show how the view of anuttarayoga is special in comparison with lower yanas. Also referred to as implied or intended, and not implied or not intended. The view of anuttarayoga is thoughtful. *See also* chapter 51, "Taking a Fresh Look at the Phenomenal World."

**three gates** (Tib.: gosum; sgo gsum). Body, speech, and mind; the three modes by which one relates to the phenomenal world.

**three jewels** (Skt.: triratna; Tib.: könchok sum; dkon mchog gsum). The three supreme objects of refuge: the Buddha, the dharma, and the sangha.

**three marks** (Tib.: tsensum; mtshan gsum). The three basic qualities of samsaric existence: suffering, impermanence, and egolessness.

**three times** (Tib.: tüsum; dus gsum). The past, the present, and the future.

*Tibetan Book of the Dead* (Tib.: bardo thödröl; bar do thos grol). Common Western title for the Tibetan text called *Liberation through Hearing in the Bardo.* The text is said to have been composed by Padmasambhava in the eighth century and written down by his consort Yeshe Tsogyal. It was discovered in the form of a terma in the fourteenth century by the tertön Karma Lingpa. It is comprised of detailed instructions on the possibility of awakening during the experiences of dying, bardo, and rebirth.

**Tilopa** (Skt.; 988–1069 CE). A great Indian siddha and a forefather of the Kagyü lineage. Tilopa unified various tantric systems and transmitted them to his student Naropa.

**tingdzin** (Tib.: ting 'dzin). *See* samadhi.

**tingdzin gyi kyilkhor** (Tib.: ting 'dzin gyi dkyil 'khor). Mandala of meditation; one of eight types of mandala in the mahayoga tantra. *See also* appendix 5, under *The Eight Mandalas of Mahayoga* (chapter 60).

**togden** (Tib.: rtogs ldan). One who is realized; an accomplished yogin.

**tokpa** (Tib.: rtogs pa). Realization, understanding; in particular, realizing the truth of dharma. Its homonym (Tib.: rtog pa) means "discursive thoughts."

**tokpa gak** (Tib.: rtog pa dgag). Cessation of thought; nonthought.

**tokpa küntu sangpo** (Tib.: rtogs pa kun tu bzang po). All-good realization. One of the five types of Samantabhadra. *See also* appendix 5, under *Five Types of Samantabhadra* (chapter 4).

**töndam** (Tib.: don dam; Skt.: paramartha). Ultimate, absolute. Sometimes used as an abbreviation for *töndampe denpa* (don dam pa'i bden pa), the ultimate truth. *See also* kündzop.

**tonglen** (Tib.: gtong len). Sending and taking, a key practice of mahayana mind training; the practice of exchanging oneself for others.

**töngyi yeshe** (Tib.: don gyi ye shes). Actual wisdom; ultimate wisdom. In the fourth abhisheka of anuttarayoga, the flash of no mind.

**tongsuk** (Tib.: stong gzug). Empty form; form that is intrinsically empty and nonexistent.

**tönkhor gongpa yerme** (Tib.: ston 'khor dgongs pa dbyer med). Inseparability of the mind of the teacher and the mind of the student.

**tönpa küntu sangpo** (Tib.: ston pa kun tu bzang po). All-good teacher. One of the five types of Samantabhadra. *See also* appendix 5, under *Five Types of Samantabhadra* (chapter 4).

**torma** (Tib.: gtor ma). A sculpture made of barley flour, used as a shrine offering, a feast-offering substance, or as a representation of deities.

**trag-ngak** (Tib.: drag sngags). Wrathful mantra. Eighth of the eight logos, connected with confidence, directness, and fearlessness. *See also* appendix 5, under *The Eight Logos / Druppa Kagye* (chapter 61).

**traktong** (Tib.: grags stong). Sound-emptiness.

**trangdön** (Tib.: drang don; Skt.: neyartha). Literal, or provisional, meaning. When contrasted with ngedön, one of the pair of categories that show how the view of anuttarayoga is special in comparison with lower yanas. Views are considered as literal in meaning when they are useful but need further qualification. *See also* ngedön and chapter 51, "Taking a Fresh Look at the Phenomenal World."

**transmission** (Tib.: ngotrö; ngo sprod). The meeting of the mind of the guru with the mind of the student. The pointing out, usually through gesture and symbol, of the true nature of mind.

**trekchö** (Tib.: khregs chod; "cutting through"). In the Nyingma tradition, one of the two principle practices belonging to the oral instruction section of maha ati. It is similar to the practice of mahamudra in the Kagyü tradition. *See also* thögal.

**tri** (Tib.: khrid). Practice instructions given at the time of an abhisheka.

**trikaya** (Skt.; Tib.: kusum; sku gsum). The three bodies of a buddha: nirmanakaya, sambhogakaya, and dharmakaya. The nirmanakaya, or emanation body, is the communication of awakened mind through form, in particular through being embodied in a human being (guru). Sambhogakaya, or enjoyment body, is the energy of compassion and communication that links the dharmakaya and the nirmanakaya. The dharmakaya, or body of dharma, is the aspect of realization beyond form or limit, time or space.

**trilbu sunggi tamtsik** (Tib.: dril bu gsung gi dam tshig). Samaya of vajra speech.

**Tripitaka** (Skt.; "three baskets"). The canon of Buddhist scriptures, consisting of three parts: Vinaya-pitaka, Sutra-pitaka, and Abhidharma-pitaka.

**Trisong Detsen** (Tib.: khri srong lde btsan; 790–844 CE). Eighth-century Tibetan king, the second of the three dharma kings of Tibet (Songtsen Gampo, Trisong Detsen, and Ralpachen), who played a pivotal role in the introduction of Buddhism in Tibet and the establishment of the Nyingma lineage.

**trö** (Tib.: drod). Warmth, heat.

**trö-che** (Tib.: spros bcas). Complex, with elaboration. A characteristic of the first through third abhishekas, which require practicing many visualizations.

**trö-me** (Tib.: spros med). Simple, without elaboration. A characteristic of the fourth, or formless, abhisheka.

**trödral** (Tib.: spros bral). Simplicity; without elaboration or complexity. The second of the four yogas of mahamudra. *See also* appendix 5, under *The Four Yogas of Mahamudra / Naljor Shirim* (chapter 57).

**trülpa pangwa** (Tib.: 'khrul pa spang ba). Abandoning confused activity.

**Trung Ma-se** (Tib.: drung rma se). A siddha said to be a reincarnation of Tilopa, he was a disciple of the fifth Karmapa, Teshin Shekpa (1384–1415 CE), and teacher of the first Trungpa.

**trungpa** (Tib.: drung pa; "one nearby"). An attendant.

**tsakali** (Tib.: tsa ka li). An icon; usually a miniature painting on card or cloth.

**tsal** (Tib.: rtsal). Energy, power; one of the characteristics of mind.

**tsa-we lama** (Tib.: rtsa ba'i bla ma). Root guru. Although a student may have more than one root guru, the ultimate root guru is the vajra master who points out the true nature of mind.

**tsechik** (Tib.: rtse gcig). One-pointedness; the first of the four yogas of mahamudra. *See also* appendix 5, *The Four Yogas of Mahamudra / Naljor Shirim* (chapter 57).

**tsen-che** (Tib.: mtshan bcas). The aspect of vajrayana practice emphasizing visualization and mantra recitation. *See also* utpattikrama.

**tsen-me** (Tib.: mtshan med). Unadorned experience; the upayoga understanding of purity. Also, formless practice.

**tsogdrup** (Tib.: tshogs sgrub). *See* mandala nopika.

**tsokchog gi kyilkhor** (Tib.: tshogs mchog gi dkyil 'khor). Mandala of the vajra sangha, or superior gathering; one of eight types of mandala in the mahayoga tantra. *See also* appendix 5, under *The Eight Mandalas of Mahayoga* (chapter 60).

**tsokkyi khorlo** (Tib.: tshogs kyi 'khor lo; Skt.: ganachakra). *See* ganachakra.

**Tsurphu** (Tib.: mtshur phu). The monastic seat of the Karmapas in south Central Tibet.

**tülku** (Tib.: sprul sku; Skt.: nirmanakaya). Emanation body; a term used for a person who is recognized as the reincarnation of a previously deceased enlightened being.

**two truths** (Tib.: denpa nyi; bdenpa gnyis). The relative truth (kündzop) and ultimate truth (töndam).

**twofold ego** (Tib.: dag-nyi; bdag gnyis). The ego of self, or individuality, and the ego of dharmas, or phenomena.

**twofold egolessness** (Tib.: dagmepa nyi; bdag med pa gnyis). The egolessness of self and the egolessness of phenomena.

**Uddiyana** (Skt.). The birthplace of Padmasambhava and the land where Tilopa went to steal the teachings of the dakinis. Regarded as the realm of the dakinis, some say it is located in the Swat Valley on the border of Pakistan and Afghanistan.

**uk tang tral-we sang-gye** (Tib.: dbugs dang bral ba'i sangs rgyas). "Buddha without breath"; second of five vajrayana sayings regarding transcending habitual patterns. *See also* appendix 5, under *Five Vajrayana Sayings* (chapter 16).

**uma** (Tib.: dbu ma). *See* avadhuti.

**upaya** (Skt.; Tib.: thap; thabs). Skillful means, method. In the vajrayana, upaya arises from shunyata. Being joined with prajna, it represents the masculine, or form, aspect of the union of form and emptiness.

**upayoga** (Skt.; Tib.: chögyü; spyod rgyud). The yoga of conduct. In the nine-yana system, the second of the three lower tantric yanas. *See also* appendix 5, under *The Nine Yanas* (chapter 40).

**upayogayana** (Skt.). The path of upayoga.

**utpattikrama** (Skt.; Tib.: kyerim; bskyed rim). The creation stage of vajrayana practice, which emphasizes visualization and mantra recitation.

**vac** (Skt.; Tib.: dra, sgra). Pure voice; cosmic sound.

**Vairochana** (Skt.; Tib.: nampar nangdze; rnam par snang mdzad). Tathagata of the buddha family. In the secret language of tantra, a name for excrement, one of the five ingredients that are transformed from poison into amrita. *See also* appendix 5, *Five Ingredients Used to Create Amrita* (chapter 61).

**vajra** (Skt.; Tib.: dorje; rdo rje). Adamantine, indestructible, diamond-like. In Hinduism, the vajra is Indra's thunderbolt, or magical weapon. In Buddhism, it is a quality of tantric realization and of the true nature of reality, or emptiness. Vajra also refers to a ritual scepter used in tantric practice. In terms of the mandala of the five buddha-families, vajra is the family of pristine clarity, the family associated with the East, the buddha Akshobhya or Vajrasattva, the klesha of anger, and mirrorlike wisdom. *See also* appendix 5, under *The Five Buddha-Families* (chapter 26).

**vajra naraka** (Skt.; Tib.: dorje nyalwa; rdo rje dmyal ba). Vajra hell. A state in which one's mind is so completely consumed by kleshas that there is no possibility of escape; the polar opposite of enlightenment.

**vajra nature** (Tib.: dorje kham; rdo rje khams). Indestructible being. Indestructible self-existing sacredness and sanity of phenomena and of one's basic existence, manifesting through vajra body, vajra speech, and vajra mind.

**vajra sangha.** The community of vajrayana practitioners.

**vajracharya** (Skt.; Tib.: dorje loppön; rdo rje slob dpon). Vajra master. An empowered teacher.

**Vajradhara** (Skt.; Tib.: Dorje Chang; rdo rje 'chang; "vajra holder"). In the Kagyü tradition, Vajradhara is the dharmakaya, or primordial, buddha. Traditionally depicted as dark blue in color with crossed arms holding a bell and vajra, he is a symbol of enlightenment itself and of one's root guru. Vajradhara is particularly important to the Kagyü tradition, as Tilopa is said to have received the vajrayana teachings directly from him.

**vajradhatu** (Skt.). Indestructible space.

**Vajrakilaya** (Skt.; Tib.: Dorje Phurba; rdo rje phur ba; "indestructible dagger"). A principal yidam of the Nyingma tradition, belonging to the karma family. He is depicted as dark blue or black in color and very wrathful. The fifth logos of mahayoga tantra, connected with penetrating through confusion and the fierce destruction of ego. *See also* appendix 5, *The Eight Logos / Druppa Kagye* (chapter 61).

**Vajrasattva** (Skt.; Tib.: Dorje Sempa; rdo rje sems dpa'; "indestructible being"). A buddha of the vajra family, who embodies the principle of purity and purification. Meditating on the form of Vajrasattva and reciting his mantra is one of the four special preliminary practices of the vajrayana.

**Vajravarahi** (Skt.; Tib.: Dorje Phagmo; rdo rje phag mo). Indestructible Sow; another name for Vajrayogini.

**vajrayana** (Skt.; Tib.: dorje thekpa; rdo rje theg pa; "indestructible vehicle"). The highest of the three yanas in the Tibetan Buddhist tradition. The vajrayana, by virtue of its many upayas, or skillful means, is said to make it possible to attain supreme realization in one lifetime. In the three-yana system, vajrayana is said to rest on the solid foundation and training of the previous two yanas: the hinayana path of individual development and the mahayana path of wisdom and compassion.

**Vajrayogini** (Skt.; Tib.: Dorje Naljorma; rdo rje rnal 'byor ma). A semiwrathful female yidam of the mother tantra, who represents the transformation of ignorance and passion into emptiness and compassion.

**vidya** (Skt.; Tib.: rikpa; rig pa). Knowledge. *See also* rikpa.

**vidyadhara** (Skt.; Tib.: rigdzin; rig 'dzin; "knowledge holder"). Term applied to an accomplished tantric practitioner. An honorific title for Chögyam Trungpa, who in the latter years of his teaching was referred to as "the Vidyadhara." In earlier years, he was referred to as "the Vajracharya," or vajra master.

**vidyadharayana** (Skt.; Tib.: rigdzin thekpa; rig 'dzin theg pa). Vehicle of the knowledge holders; another term for vajrayana.

**vidyamantra** (Skt.; Tib.: rikpa ngag-luk; rig pa sngags lugs). Knowledge mantra. One of four characteristics of buddha-families, connected with a family's magical power over others. *See also* appendix 5, under *Four Ways of Seeing Each of the Twenty-Five Buddha-Families* (chapter 47).

**vimala** (Skt.; Tib.: tri-me; dri med). Purity or spotlessness; the basic principle of kriyayoga practice.

**Vimalamitra** (Skt.; eighth century CE). Maha-ati master who was invited to Tibet by King Trisong Detsen. Together with Padmasambhava and Vairochana, he is a principal forefather of the maha ati teachings in Tibet.

**vipashyana** (Skt.; Tib.: lhakthong; lhag mthong; "superior seeing"). Awareness; insight arising either through direct meditative experience or through analytic contemplation. An open, expansive quality of meditation that complements the stability and groundedness of shamatha.

**wang** (Tib.: dbang). *See* abhisheka.

**Yama** (Skt.; Tib.: Shin-je; gshin rje). The Lord of Death.

**Yamantaka** (Skt.; Tib.: Shin-je she; gshin rje gshed). Conqueror of Yama, the Lord of Death. Second of the eight logos; the wrathful aspect of Manjushri, who transforms life into wisdom. *See also* appendix 5, *The Eight Logos / Druppa Kagye* (chapter 61).

**yana** (Skt.; Tib.: thekpa; theg pa). Vehicle, way; what carries the practitioner along the path to liberation.

**yanas, nine** (Tib.: thekpa gu; theg pa dgu). According to the Nyingma and Ri-me traditions, there are a total of nine yanas: shravaka (Tib.: nyenthö; nyan thos); pratyekabuddha (Tib.: rang-gyal; rang rgyal); bodhisattva (Tib.: changchup sempa; byang chub sems dpa'); kriyayoga (Tib.: chawa; bya ba); upayoga (or charya; Tib.: chöpa; dpyod pa); yoga (Tib.: naljor; rnal 'byor); mahayoga (Tib.: naljor chenpo; rnal 'byor chen po); anuyoga (Tib.: jesu naljor; rjes su rnal 'byor); and atiyoga or maha ati (Tib.: dzokpa chenpo; rdzogs pa chen po). The first two comprise the hinayana path, and the third is synonymous with the mahayana path. The next three are called the lower tantric yanas; the final three are called the higher tantric yanas.

**yanas, three** (Tib.: theksum; theg gsum). According to the general vajrayana tradition, there are three yanas, or vehicles: hinayana (including shravakayana and pratyekabuddhayana), mahayana (or bodhisattvayana), and vajrayana.

**Yangdak** (Tib.: yang dag; "completely pure"). First of the eight logos, representing complete accomplishment and command. *See also* appendix 5, under *The Eight Logos / Druppa Kagye* (chapter 61).

**yang-dak-pe kündzop** (Tib.: yang dag pa'i kun rdzob). Pure relative truth. This is a direct and simple experience of things by those who no longer cling to appearances as real. It is contrasted with perverted relative truth, the experience of those who still cling to appearances as solid.

**yargyi sangthal** (Tib.: yar gyi zang thal; "confidence above"). Enlightened style of confidence.

**ye chi-shin-pe kyilkhor** (Tib.: ye ji bzhin pa'i dkyil 'khor). The mandala of primordial is-ness; the first of three mandalas of anuyoga, in which one sees all dharmas as the expression of mind. *See also* appendix 5, under *The Three Mandalas of Anuyoga* (chapter 64).

**yeshe** (Tib.: ye shes). *See* jnana.

**yeshe changwa** (Tib.: ye shes 'chang wa). One who holds wisdom.

**yeshe chöku** (Tib.: ye shes chos sku). *See* jnana-dharmakaya.

**yeshe chölwa** (Tib.: ye shes 'chol ba). Crazy wisdom; the realization of a vidyadhara, expressed at times in unconventional and provocative ways.

**yi** (Tib.: yid). Mind. The sixth, or mental, consciousness, which coordinates and interprets the other five sense consciousnesses; its objects are thoughts.

**yi-de** (Tib.: yid bzlas). Silent or mental repetition of a mantra.

**yidam** (Tib.: yi dam; Skt.: ishtadevata). In vajrayana, one's personal meditation deity, which represents one's awakened nature. In practice, one visualizes the deity, repeats its mantra, and identifies completely with its wisdom. The term *yidam* is said to derive from *yikyi tamtsik* (Tib.: yid kyi dam tshig), meaning the "samaya of mind."

**yikyi tamtsik** (Tib.: yid kyi dam tshig). *See* yidam.

**ying** (Tib.: dbyings; Skt.: dhatu). Space; realm.

**yogachara** (Skt.; Tib.: naljor chöpa; rnal 'byor spyod pa; "practice of yoga"). The "mind-only" school of mahayana Buddhism, founded by Asanga. According to the yogachara view, the appearance of a subject and an object as two separate things is the relative truth. In the ultimate truth, there is only consciousness, free from the duality of subject and object.

**yogayana** (Skt.; Tib.: naljor gyi thekpa; rnal 'byor gyi theg pa). The yoga of union. In the nine-yana system, the third of the three lower tantric yanas. *See also* appendix 5, under *The Nine Yanas* (chapter 40).

**Zen** (Jpn.). *See* Ch'an.

# SOURCES

THE MATERIAL in this volume is primarily taken from the Vajradhatu Seminaries, a series of programs taught by Chögyam Trungpa Rinpoche. (For further information, see "Editor's Introduction" in volume 1 of the *Profound Treasury*.) Thirteen Seminaries were held between 1973 and 1986, at the following locations:

1. 1973: Jackson Hole, Wyoming. September–November.
2. 1974: Snowmass Village, Colorado. September–November.
3. 1975: Snowmass Village, Colorado. September–November.
4. 1976: Land O' Lakes, Wisconsin. September–November.
5. 1978: Dixville Notch, New Hampshire. March–May.
6. 1979: Lake Louise, Alberta, Canada. March–May.
7. 1980: Lake Louise, Alberta, Canada. January–March.
8. 1981: Lake Louise, Alberta, Canada. January–March.
9. 1982: Bedford Springs, Pennsylvania. January–April.
10. 1983: Bedford Springs, Pennsylvania. January–March.
11. 1984: Bedford Springs, Pennsylvania. January–March.
12. 1985: Shambhala Mountain Center, Red Feather Lakes, Colorado. June–August.
13. 1986: Shambhala Mountain Center, Red Feather Lakes, Colorado. June–August.

In addition, some of the material in this book has been taken from the following published works by Chögyam Trungpa:

*The Collected Works of Chögyam Trungpa.* Edited by Carolyn Gimian. 8 vols. Boston: Shambhala Publications, 2004.

*Crazy Wisdom.* Boston: Shambhala Publications, 2001.

*Cutting Through Spiritual Materialism.* Boston: Shambhala Publications, 2008.

*The Heart of the Buddha.* Boston: Shambhala Publications, 1991.

*Journey without Goal: The Tantric Wisdom of the Buddha.* Boston: Shambhala Publications, 2000.

*The Lion's Roar: An Introduction to Tantra.* Boston: Shambhala Publications, 2001.

*The Mishap Lineage: Transforming Confusion into Wisdom.* Boston: Shambhala Publications, 2009.

*Orderly Chaos: The Mandala Principle.* Boston: Shambhala Publications, 1991.

*True Perception: The Path of Dharma Art.* Boston: Shambhala Publications, 2008.

More details on the primary sources for each chapter are given below. When the source is a Vajradhatu Seminary, the talk name is given, followed by the year and the talk number.

## PART ONE. APPROACHING THE VAJRAYANA

Introduction

*Samaya Principles 1973: 20*

*Kriyayoga Tantra 1973: 21*

*Approaches to Tantra 1974: 19*

*Samaya 1974: 20*

*The Guru 1974: 21*

*Space 1974: 22*

*Kriyayoga 1974: 23*

*Getting into Vajrayana 1975: 24*

*Beginning at the Beginning 1980: 19*

*Shunyata, Compassion, and Tantra 1978: 21*

*Vajra Vision and Vajra Nature 1979: 18*

*Devotion 1979: 19*

*Entering the Diamond Path 1981: 18*

*The Three-Yana Journey 1983: 12*

*Protecting the Mind 1985: 12*

*The Three Kayas 1985: 13*

Chapter 13. The Later Trungpas

*Samaya 1974: 20*

*The Trungpa Tülkus 1974: 30*

*Mind Protection 1984: 17*

Books:

*The Heart of the Buddha.* (Also in *Collected Works*, vol. 3, 426–427.)

*The Mishap Lineage.*

## PART FOUR: ESSENTIAL TEACHINGS

Chapter 14. Unconditional Ground

*Mantrayana and Renunciation 1981: 19*

*Discovering Yeshe 1981: 20*

Chapter 15. Transcending Mental Concepts

*Transcending Mental Concepts: Prostrations and Vajrasattva Mantra 1981: 21*

Chapter 16. Fundamental Magic

*Shunyata, Compassion, and Tantra 1978: 21*

*Magic 1978: 22*

Chapter 17. The Play of Space and Form

*Space 1974: 22*

Chapter 18. The Eight States of Consciousness and the Trikaya Principle

*Transmission and the Eight States of Consciousness 1980: 22*

*Transcending Mental Concepts: Prostrations and Vajrasattva Mantra 1981: 21*

*The Three Kayas 1985: 13*

## PART FIVE: COMPLETE COMMITMENT

Chapter 19. Samaya: Making a Commitment

*Samaya 1976: 24*

*Theism, Nontheism, and the Samaya Principle 1980: 21*

*Samaya 1982: 20*

Chapter 20. Positive Entrapment

*Samaya Principles 1973: 20*

*Samaya 1974: 20*

*Ati 1975: 30*

## PART EIGHT: EMPOWERMENT

## Upayoga: The Yana of Conduct

## Yogayana: The Yana of Union

## PART ELEVEN: THE TANTRIC JOURNEY: MAHAMUDRA

## Anuttarayoga: Highest Yoga

SOURCES

*Maha Ati 1976: 29*
*Maha Ati II 1976: 30*
*Maha Ati 1979: 24*
*Maha Ati: The Simultaneity of Realization and Liberation 1980: 25*
*The Four Stages of Maha Ati 1983: 16*

877

# RESOURCES

PRACTICE CENTERS

For information about meditation instruction or to find a Shambhala-affiliated practice center near you, please contact one of the following:

Shambhala meditation centers
1084 Tower Road
Halifax, NS B3H 2Y5
Canada
phone: (902) 425-4275
website: www.shambhala.org

Karmê Chöling
369 Patneaude Lane
Barnet, Vermont 05821
phone: (802) 633-2384
website: www.karmecholing.org

Shambhala Mountain Center
151 Shambhala Way
Red Feather Lakes, Colorado
80545
phone: (970) 881-2184
website: www.shambhala
mountain.org

Gampo Abbey
Pleasant Bay
Cape Breton, NS B0E 2P0
Canada
phone: (902) 224-2752
website: www.gampoabbey.org

Dechen Choling
Mas Marvent
87700 St. Yrieix sous Aixe
France
phone: +33 5-55-03-55-52
website: www.dechencholing.org

Dorje Denma Ling
2280 Balmoral Road
Tatamagouche, Nova Scotia
Canada B0K 1V0
phone: (902) 657-9085
website: http://dorjedenmaling.org
e-mail: info@dorjedenmaling.com

## NAROPA UNIVERSITY

Naropa University is the only accredited, Buddhist-inspired university in North America. For more information, contact:

Naropa University
2130 Arapahoe Avenue
Boulder, Colorado 80302
phone: (303) 444-0202
website: www.naropa.edu

## OCEAN OF DHARMA QUOTES OF THE WEEK

Ocean of Dharma Quotes of the Week brings you the teachings of Chögyam Trungpa Rinpoche. An e-mail is sent out several times each week containing a quote from Chögyam Trungpa's extensive teachings. Quotations of material may be from unpublished material, forthcoming publications, or previously published sources. Ocean of Dharma Quotes of the Week are selected by Carolyn Rose Gimian. To enroll go to OceanofDharma.com.

## THE CHÖGYAM TRUNGPA LEGACY PROJECT

The Chögyam Trungpa Legacy Project was established to help preserve, disseminate, and expand Chögyam Trungpa's legacy. The Legacy Project supports the preservation, propagation, and publication of Trungpa Rinpoche's dharma teachings. This includes plans for the creation of a comprehensive virtual archive and learning community. For information, go to ChogyamTrungpa.com

## SHAMBHALA MEDIA

For publications from Vajradhatu Publications and Kalapa Recordings, including both books and audiovisual materials, go to www.shambhalamedia.org.

## SHAMBHALA ARCHIVES

For information about the archive of the author's work, please contact the Shambhala Archives: archives@shambhala.org.

# ABOUT THE AUTHOR

THE VENERABLE Chögyam Trungpa Rinpoche was born in the province of Kham in eastern Tibet in 1940. When he was just thirteen months old, Chögyam Trungpa was recognized as a major tülku, or incarnate teacher. According to Tibetan tradition, an enlightened teacher is capable, based on his or her vow of compassion, of reincarnating in human form over a succession of generations. Before dying, such a teacher may leave a letter or other clues to the whereabouts of the next incarnation. Later, students and other realized teachers look through these clues and, based on those, plus a careful examination of dreams and visions, conduct searches to discover and recognize the successor. Thus, particular lines of teaching are formed, in some cases extending over many centuries. Chögyam Trungpa was the eleventh in the teaching lineage known as the Trungpa Tülkus.

Once young tülkus are recognized, they enter a period of intensive training in the theory and practice of the Buddhist teachings. Trungpa Rinpoche, after being enthroned as supreme abbot of Surmang Dütsi Tel Monastery and governor of Surmang District, began a period of training that would last eighteen years, until his departure from Tibet in 1959. As a Kagyü tülku, his training was based on the systematic practice of meditation and on refined theoretical understanding of Buddhist philosophy. One of the four great lineages of Tibet, the Kagyü is known as the Practicing (or Practice) Lineage.

At the age of eight, Trungpa Rinpoche received ordination as a novice monk. Following this, he engaged in intensive study and practice of the traditional monastic disciplines, including traditional Tibetan poetry and monastic dance. His primary teachers were Jamgön Kongtrül of Sechen and Khenpo Gangshar—leading teachers in the Nyingma and Kagyü lineages. In 1958, at the age of eighteen, Trungpa Rinpoche completed his studies, receiving the degrees of *kyorpön* (doctor of divinity) and *khenpo* (master of studies). He also received full monastic ordination.

881

The late fifties was a time of great upheaval in Tibet. As it became clear that the Chinese Communists intended to take over the country by force, many people, both monastic and lay, fled the country. Trungpa Rinpoche spent many harrowing months trekking over the Himalayas (described later in his book *Born in Tibet*). After narrowly escaping capture by the Chinese, he at last reached India in 1959. While in India, Trungpa Rinpoche was appointed to serve as spiritual adviser to the Young Lamas Home School in Delhi, India. He served in this capacity from 1959 to 1963.

Trungpa Rinpoche's opportunity to emigrate to the West came when he received a Spalding sponsorship to attend Oxford University. At Oxford he studied comparative religion, philosophy, history, and fine arts. He also studied Japanese flower arranging, receiving a degree from the Sogetsu School. While in England, Trungpa Rinpoche began to instruct Western students in the dharma, and in 1967 he founded the Samye Ling Meditation Center in Dumfriesshire, Scotland. During this period, he also published his first two books, both in English: *Born in Tibet* (1966) and *Meditation in Action* (1969).

In 1968 Trungpa Rinpoche traveled to Bhutan, where he entered into a solitary meditation retreat. While on retreat, Rinpoche received a pivotal *terma* text for all of his teaching in the West, "The Sadhana of Mahamudra," a text that documents the spiritual degeneration of modern times and its antidote, genuine spirituality that leads to the experience of naked and luminous mind. This retreat marked a pivotal change in his approach to teaching. Soon after returning to England, he became a layperson, putting aside his monastic robes and dressing in ordinary Western attire. In 1970 he married a young Englishwoman, Diana Pybus, and together they left Scotland and moved to North America. Many of his early students and his Tibetan colleagues found these changes shocking and upsetting. However, he expressed a conviction that in order for the dharma to take root in the West, it needed to be taught free from cultural trappings and religious fascination.

During the seventies, America was in a period of political and cultural ferment. It was a time of fascination with the East. Nevertheless, almost from the moment he arrived in America, Trungpa Rinpoche drew many students to him who were seriously interested in the Buddhist teachings and the practice of meditation. However, he severely criticized the materialistic approach to spirituality that was also quite prevalent, describing it as a "spiritual supermarket." In his lectures, and in his books *Cutting Through Spiritual Materialism* (1973) and *The Myth of Freedom* (1976), he pointed to the simplicity and directness of the practice of sitting meditation as the way to cut through such distortions of the spiritual journey.

During his seventeen years of teaching in North America, Trungpa Rinpoche developed a reputation as a dynamic and controversial teacher. He was a pioneer, one of the first Tibetan Buddhist teachers in North America, preceding by some years and indeed facilitating the later visits by His Holiness the Karmapa, His Holiness Khyentse Rinpoche, His Holiness the Dalai Lama, and many others. In the United States, he found a spiritual kinship with many Zen masters, who were already presenting Buddhist meditation. In the very early days, he particularly connected with Suzuki Roshi, the founder of Zen Center in San Francisco. In later years he was close with Kobun Chino Roshi and Bill Kwong Roshi in Northern California; with Maezumi Roshi, the founder of the Los Angeles Zen Center; and with Eido Roshi, abbot of the New York Zendo Shobo-ji.

Fluent in the English language, Chögyam Trungpa was one of the first Tibetan Buddhist teachers who could speak to Western students directly, without the aid of a translator. Traveling extensively throughout North America and Europe, he gave thousands of talks and hundreds of seminars. He established major centers in Vermont, Colorado, and Nova Scotia, as well as many smaller meditation and study centers in cities throughout North America and Europe. Vajradhatu was formed in 1973 as the central administrative body of this network.

In 1974 Trungpa Rinpoche founded the Naropa Institute (now Naropa University), which became the first and only accredited Buddhist-inspired university in North America. He lectured extensively at the institute, and his book *Journey without Goal* (1981) is based on a course he taught there. In 1976 he established the Shambhala Training program, a series of seminars that present a nonsectarian path of spiritual warriorship grounded in the practice of sitting meditation. His book *Shambhala: The Sacred Path of the Warrior* (1984) gives an overview of the Shambhala teachings.

In 1976 Trungpa Rinpoche appointed Ösel Tendzin (Thomas F. Rich) as his Vajra Regent, or dharma heir. Ösel Tendzin worked closely with Trungpa Rinpoche in the administration of Vajradhatu and Shambhala Training. He taught extensively from 1976 until his death in 1990 and is the author of *Buddha in the Palm of Your Hand*.

Trungpa Rinpoche was also active in the field of translation. Working with Francesca Fremantle, he rendered a new translation of *The Tibetan Book of the Dead*, which was published in 1975. Later he formed the Nalanda Translation Committee in order to translate texts and liturgies for his own students as well as to make important texts available publicly.

In 1979 Trungpa Rinpoche conducted a ceremony empowering his eldest son, Ösel Rangdröl Mukpo, as his successor in the Shambhala lineage. At that time he gave him the title of Sawang ("Earth Lord").

Trungpa Rinpoche was also known for his interest in the arts and particularly for his insights into the relationship between contemplative discipline and the artistic process. Two books published since his death—*The Art of Calligraphy* (1994) and *Dharma Art* (1996) [a new edition appeared in 2008 under the title *True Perception: The Path of Dharma Art*]—present this aspect of his work. His own artwork included calligraphy, painting, flower arranging, poetry, playwriting, and environmental installations. In addition, at the Naropa Institute he created an educational atmosphere that attracted many leading artists and poets. The exploration of the creative process in light of contemplative training continues there as a provocative dialogue. Trungpa Rinpoche also published two books of poetry: *Mudra* (1972) and *First Thought Best Thought* (1983). In 1998 a retrospective compilation of his poetry, *Timely Rain*, was published.

Shortly before his death, in a meeting with Samuel Bercholz, the publisher of Shambhala Publications, Chögyam Trungpa expressed his interest in publishing 108 volumes of his teachings, to be called the Dharma Ocean Series. "Dharma Ocean" is the translation of Chögyam Trungpa's Tibetan teaching name, Chökyi Gyatso. The Dharma Ocean Series was to consist primarily of material edited to allow readers to encounter this rich array of teachings simply and directly rather than in an overly systematized or condensed form. In 1991 the first posthumous volume in the series, *Crazy Wisdom*, was published, and another seven volumes followed in the ensuing years. Carolyn Gimian gathered many of these published materials, along with a great number of previously unpublished articles, into the eight-volume set, *The Collected Works of Chögyam Trungpa*. Plans continue for many future volumes of his teachings to be published.

Trungpa Rinpoche's published books represent only a fraction of the rich legacy of his teachings. During his seventeen years of teaching in North America, he crafted the structures necessary to provide his students with thorough, systematic training in the dharma. From introductory talks and courses to advanced group retreat practices, these programs emphasized a balance of study and practice, of intellect and intuition. *Chögyam Trungpa* by Fabrice Midal, a biography, details the many forms of training that Chögyam Trungpa developed. *Dragon Thunder: My Life with Chögyam Trungpa* is the story of Rinpoche's life as told by Diana Mukpo. This also provides insight into the many forms that he crafted for Buddhism in North America.

In addition to his extensive teachings in the Buddhist tradition, Trungpa Rinpoche also placed great emphasis on the Shambhala teachings, which stress the importance of meditation in action, synchronizing mind and body, and training oneself to approach obstacles or challenges in everyday life with the courageous attitude of a warrior, without anger. The goal of creating an enlightened society is fundamental to the Shambhala teachings. According to the Shambhala approach, the realization of an enlightened society comes not purely through outer activity, such as community or political involvement, but from appreciation of the senses and the sacred dimension of day-to-day life. A second volume of these teachings, entitled *Great Eastern Sun,* was published in 1999. The final volume of these teachings, *Smile at Fear,* appeared in 2009.

Chögyam Trungpa died in 1987, at the age of forty-seven. By the time of his death, he was known not only as Rinpoche ("Precious Jewel") but also as Vajracharya ("Vajra Holder") and as Vidyadhara ("Wisdom Holder") for his role as a master of the vajrayana, or tantric teachings of Buddhism. As a holder of the Shambhala teachings, he had also received the titles of Dorje Dradül ("Indestructible Warrior") and Sakyong ("Earth Protector"). He is survived by his wife, Diana Judith Mukpo, and five sons. His eldest son, the Sawang Ösel Rangdröl Mukpo, succeeds him as the spiritual head of Vajradhatu. Acknowledging the importance of the Shambhala teachings to his father's work, the Sawang changed the name of the umbrella organization to Shambhala, with Vajradhatu remaining one of its major divisions. In 1995 the Sawang received the Shambhala title of Sakyong like his father before him, and was also confirmed as an incarnation of the great ecumenical teacher Mipham Rinpoche.

Trungpa Rinpoche is widely acknowledged as a pivotal figure in introducing the buddhadharma to the Western world. He joined his great appreciation for Western culture with his deep understanding of his own tradition. This led to a revolutionary approach to teaching the dharma, in which the most ancient and profound teachings were presented in a thoroughly contemporary way. Trungpa Rinpoche was known for his fearless proclamation of the dharma: free from hesitation, true to the purity of the tradition, and utterly fresh. May these teachings take root and flourish for the benefit of all sentient beings.

# CREDITS

Frontispiece photo: © Ray Ellis. Used with permission.

Ekajati Protector's chant on p. ii translated by the Nalanda Translation Committee under the direction of Vidyadhara the Venerable Chögyam Trungpa Rinpoche and published in *Collected Vajra Liturgies* (Halifax, Nova Scotia: Nalanda Translation Committee, 2010). Reprinted with special permission.

Drawing of Ekajati on p. iii commissioned from Glen Eddy by Shambhala Publications for *The Myth of Freedom* and rendered according to Trungpa Rinpoche's instructions. Used with permission of Shambhala Publications.

Photo p. xv: © Gina Stick. Used with permission.

Photo p. xxiii: © Martin Janowitz. Used with permission.

Photo p. 5 by Chögyam Trungpa Rinpoche.

Photo p. 7: photographer unknown.

Calligraphy p. 21 by Chögyam Trungpa, © Diana J. Mukpo. From *The Art of Calligraphy*, Shambhala Publications, Boston, 1974. Used with permission.

Painting p. 57: © Greg Smith. Used with permission.

Painting p. 66 by Sherab Palden Beru. Reprinted courtesy of Kagyü Samye Ling.

Photo p. 97: © Liza Matthews. Used with permission.

Photo p. 108: photographer unknown. From the collection of the Shambhala Archives.

Photo p. 129: © Robert Del Tredici. Used with permission.

Photo p. 155: © Marvin Moore. Courtesy of the Shambhala Archives.

Photo p. 165: © Martin Janowitz, from the collection of the Shambhala Archives. Used by permission.

Photo p. 231: © Liza Matthews. Used with permission.

Calligraphy p. 247 by Chögyam Trungpa Rinpoche.

Photo p. 288: photographer unknown. Reprinted courtesy of kalachakra net.org.

Photo p. 290: © Don Farber. Used with permission.

Diagram p. 294: © Judy Lief.

Illustration p. 298: artist unknown.

Illustrations pp. 299–305: © Tingdzin Ötro. Used with permission.

Photo p. 319: © Jane R Cohen. Used with permission.

Tibetan symbols pp. 321, 742 provided by Tingdzin Ötro (Nalanda Translation Committee).

Photos p. 355: © Liza Matthews. Used with permission.

Illustration p. 358: © Sherab Palden Beru. Reprinted courtesy of Kagyü Samye Ling. Used with permission.

Poem p. 358: translated by the Vajravairochana Translation Committee under the guidance of Chögyam Trungpa. Used with permission.

Illustration p. 360: © Sherab Palden Beru. Reprinted courtesy of Kagyü Samye Ling. Used with permission.

Photo p. 362: © Liza Matthews. Used with permission.

Photo p. 379: © Paul C. Kloppenburg. Used with permission.

Photo p. 391: photographer unknown. From the collection of the Shambhala Archives.

Drawing p. 540: © Greg Smith. Used with permission.

Calligraphy pp. 552–553: Wartu Sanskrit Eh-Vam by Tibetan calligraphy artist Tashi Mannox.

Photo p. 582: © Diana Church. From the collection of the Shambhala Archives.

Photos pp. 584–587: © Max King. Used with permission.

Photo p. 725: photographer unknown. From the collection of the Shambhala Archives.

Notecards pp. 786–791: translated by the Vajravairochana Translation Committee. Used with permission.

Excerpt from the *Guhyasamja Tantra* translated by Francesca Fremantle, unpublished PhD thesis, 1971. Used by permission of the author.

# INDEX

*Page numbers for illustrations are in italics.*